THE FORGOTTEN
PRIME MINISTER

Praise for the first volume:

'The first volume leaves him on the brink of his first ministry; the second volume is eagerly awaited ... [a] fine work.'
A. W. Purdue, *THES*

'Hopefully readers will not have to wait long for the remainder of this impressive work.'
Terry Jenkins, *BBC History Magazine*

'This, the first full-length biography of Derby to be written with access to the archives, will be the only one needed this century ... The next volume is eagerly awaited.'
Andrew Roberts, *The Sunday Times*

'Almost a century and a half after [Derby's] death, Angus Hawkins sets out to rescue this clever, diffident politician from relative obscurity and give his life the full proper treatment it deserves. It is an impressive and serious piece of work that reminds us of the value of the scholarly monograph.'
George Osborne, *The Spectator*

'This is real history. Unlike so many political biographers, Hawkins has really mastered the archives. There is much in this book that is new, much that will permanently change interpretations of the period. It is about real politicians, not caricatures or faceless abstractions. Those who already have some acquaintance with the early years of the nineteenth century will find great pleasure in reading this book.'
Leslie Mitchell, *Literary Review*

THE FORGOTTEN PRIME MINISTER

The 14th Earl of Derby

VOLUME II
ACHIEVEMENT: 1851–1869

ANGUS HAWKINS

OXFORD
UNIVERSITY PRESS

OXFORD
UNIVERSITY PRESS

Great Clarendon Street, Oxford OX2 6DP

Oxford University Press is a department of the University of Oxford.
It furthers the University's objective of excellence in research, scholarship,
and education by publishing worldwide in

Oxford New York

Auckland Cape Town Dar es Salaam Hong Kong Karachi
Kuala Lumpur Madrid Melbourne Mexico City Nairobi
New Delhi Shanghai Taipei Toronto

With offices in

Argentina Austria Brazil Chile Czech Republic France Greece
Guatemala Hungary Italy Japan Poland Portugal Singapore
South Korea Switzerland Thailand Turkey Ukraine Vietnam

Oxford is a registered trade mark of Oxford University Press
in the UK and in certain other countries

Published in the United States
by Oxford University Press Inc., New York

British Library Cataloguing in Publication Data

Data available

Library of Congress Cataloging in Publication Data

Hawkins, Angus.
The forgotten prime minister: the 14th Earl of Derby / Angus Hawkins.
p. cm.
Includes bibliographical references and index.
ISBN 978–0–19–920440–3 (v. 1: alk. paper) 1. Derby, Edward George
Geoffrey Smith Stanley, Earl of, 1799–1869. 2. Prime ministers—Great
Britain—Biography. 3. Great Britain—Politics and government—1837–
1901. 4. Statesmen—Great Britain—Biography. I. Title.
DA565.D35H39 2007
941.081092—dc22
[B]
2007023084

Typeset by Laserwords Private Limited, Chennai, India
Printed in Great Britain
on acid-free paper by
Biddles Ltd, King's Lynn, Norfolk

ISBN 978–0–19–920441–0

1 3 5 7 9 10 8 6 4 2

To John Vincent
in gratitude for his inspiration,
encouragement, and support

Preface

Although thrice prime minister and Conservative leader for twenty-two years, the 14th Earl of Derby has hitherto lacked a full biography based upon his papers and correspondence. As a result, Derby has become the forgotten prime minister. Conventionally portrayed as a dull and politically uninterested aristocrat, his historical presence has been reduced to the role of remote Conservative caretaker, whose apathy suppressed the talents of Benjamin Disraeli as the frustrated genius of the mid-Victorian party. This orthodoxy is wrong and misleading in almost all respects. A substantial and influential politician in his own right, astute, resourceful, and intelligent, Derby emerges from posterity's disparagement as a key figure in the events of his time. An understanding of Derby is crucial to an appreciation of the successes and limitations of the mid-Victorian Conservative party. His Whig education, his moderate evangelical Anglicanism, his commitment to the authority of parliament, the rule of law, and the Church Establishment were essential elements in the dynamics of party politics during the 1850s and 1860s. Thus stable progress might be safeguarded and rising social interests brought within the political nation, while the supremacy of parliament and the status of the aristocracy were preserved.

Derby was the first British statesman to become prime minister three times and he remains the longest-serving party leader in modern British politics. Yet politics is not a one-man show. Even leading men rarely stand constantly in the full glare of the footlights. In reflecting the varying tempo of Derby's political activity I have examined periods of intense endeavour, such as 1866–7, closely. The thinning of the narrative at other times, such as the early 1860s, mirrors a slackening of Derby's political efforts, when ill health or private pursuits, such as Homeric translation, horse racing at Epsom and Ascot, or alleviating suffering and remedying industrial pollution in Lancashire occupied his time. This recovery of the view from Knowsley is a conscious corrective to those celebrated perspectives from Gladstone's Hawarden, Peel's Drayton, Russell's Pembroke Lodge, or Palmerston's Cambridge House, which have hitherto commanded the historical vista. From the standpoint of Knowsley, for example, Gladstone's personal journey from Peelite to popular Liberal tribune and Disraeli's apotheosis as an unlikely Conservative hero become less prominent features in the landscape of mid-Victorian politics, as alternative routes and different destinations open up before us.

As noted in volume I, I have incurred many debts in exploring the view from Knowsley. The present Lord Derby, who gave generous permission to reproduce portraits hanging at Knowsley, has helped and encouraged by his kind interest. The convivial conference at Knowsley, graciously hosted by Lord Derby in March 2004, bringing together those with an active historical interest in the earls of Derby, was an enjoyable and rewarding occasion. A huge debt is owed to John Vincent, hence the grateful dedication of this work. Andrew Jones and Alan Beattie guided my early thinking on Derby's career. The late Colin Matthew warmly encouraged the project, as have my Oxford colleagues Lawrence Goldman and Peter Ghosh. Jeremy Black, David Brown, Tom Buchanan, Joe Coohill, Richard Davis, David Grylls, Theo Hoppen, Tony Howe, Terry Jenkins, Bruce Kinzer, John Powell, John Prest, Philip Salmon, and Mark Smith have all given much-appreciated advice. Seaborne conversations with David Cannadine and Linda Colley brought illumination. Those young historians at the University of East Anglia who, under the guidance of John Charmley, are extending our knowledge of the Victorian Derbys in important ways, Geoff Hicks, Bendor Grosvenor, and Lloyd Mitchell, provided an enjoyable and beneficial stimulus. The comments of seminar groups at the universities of Oxford, Cambridge, London, Exeter, and East Anglia have helped to clarify my understanding of Derby. The suggestions of the two anonymous readers for Oxford University Press were invaluable. Peter Elvins performed a critical service as an interested and intelligent general reader. For any surviving errors I am solely responsible.

I am grateful to the National Trust, Disraeli Papers, the Trustees of the Broadlands Archives, and the Hampshire Record Office for permission to quote from papers for which they hold the copyright. I am also grateful to the staff of the National Register of Archives, both in London and in Edinburgh; the Clerk of the Records, the Record Office, the House of Lords; the Suffolk Record Office; Lambeth Palace Library; the British Library; the University of Nottingham Library; the Leeds District Archives; the Department of Palaeography and Diplomatic, the University of Durham; University College London; the Scottish Record Office; the National Library of Scotland; the Glamorgan Archive Service; the Somerset Record Office; the Hertfordshire Record Office; the Borthwick Institute of

Historical Research, York; the Kent Archives Office; and the National Archives, Kew. I am grateful to the University of Oxford for permission to reproduce the portrait of Lord Derby as Chancellor of the University. This image forms part of a research programme coordinated by the University of Oxford and is supplied under licence by Isis Innovation Ltd ©Isis Innovation Ltd 2006. I apologize for any inadvertent infringement of copyright.

I owe a great debt to the successive archivists of the Derby Papers at Liverpool Record Office, Naomi Evetts and Ruth Hobbins, and the professional guidance of their staff, as well as the Curator of Collections at Knowsley, Emma Tate. Alison Adam and Hazel Arrandale expertly prepared the typescript, while Christopher Wheeler, Matthew Cotton, and Laurien Berkeley have been supportive and patient editors. For longer than I care to remember, my family, Esther, Emma, and Kate, have lived with the 14th Earl of Derby; their tolerance and encouragement have been unstinting and beyond repayment.

Angus Hawkins
Oxford
February 2007

Contents

List of Plates

Plate 2 forms part of a research programme coordinated by the University of Oxford and has been supplied under licence by Isis Innovation Ltd. © Isis Innovation Ltd 2006. Plate 3, licence granted courtesy of The Rt Hon. The Earl of Derby 2007. Plates 4, 5, 6, 7, 8, 11, and 13, National Portrait Gallery , London.

The Stanley Family

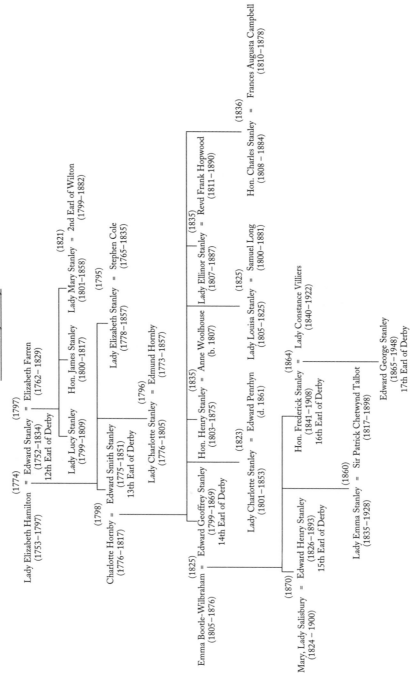

The Hornby-Stanley Family

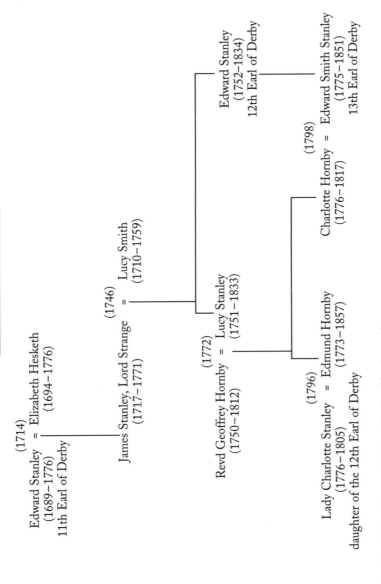

Edward Stanley = Elizabeth Hesketh (1714)
(1689–1776) (1694–1776)
11th Earl of Derby

James Stanley, Lord Strange = Lucy Smith (1746)
(1717–1771) (1710–1759)

Edward Stanley
(1752–1834)
12th Earl of Derby

Revd Geoffrey Hornby = Lucy Stanley (1772)
(1750–1812) (1751–1833)

Charlotte Hornby = Edward Smith Stanley (1798)
(1776–1817) (1775–1851)
13th Earl of Derby

Lady Charlotte Stanley = Edmund Hornby (1796)
(1776–1805) (1773–1857)
daughter of the 12th Earl of Derby

Note: Not all the children of the Revd Geoffrey Hornby are shown.

The Bootle-Wilbraham Family

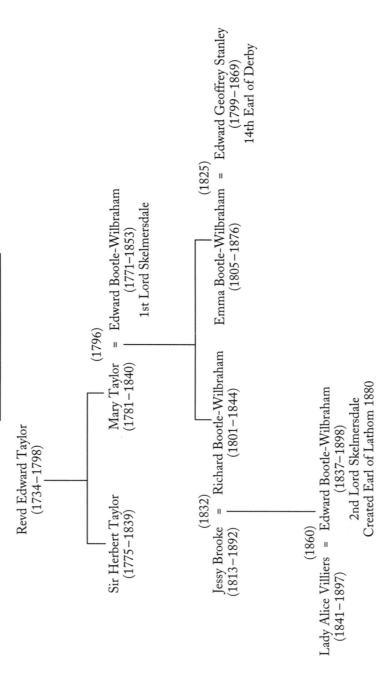

Revd Edward Taylor
(1734–1798)

(1796)

Mary Taylor   =   Edward Bootle-Wilbraham
(1781–1840)   (1771–1853)
                         1st Lord Skelmersdale

Sir Herbert Taylor
(1775–1839)

(1825)

Emma Bootle-Wilbraham   =   Edward Geoffrey Stanley
(1805–1876)   (1799–1869)
                                    14th Earl of Derby

(1832)

Jessy Brooke   =   Richard Bootle-Wilbraham
(1813–1892)   (1801–1844)

(1860)

Lady Alice Villiers   =   Edward Bootle-Wilbraham
(1841–1897)   (1837–1898)
                                 2nd Lord Skelmersdale
                                 Created Earl of Lathom 1880

Note: Not all the children of the 1st Lord Skelmersdale are shown.

CHAPTER I

Derby's First Premiership: 1852

I avow that we cannot command a parliamentary majority. I avow, my Lords, that, in the face of this conviction, I have felt it to be my duty not to decline the responsibility which has been thrown upon me. I know that in conducting the affairs of the country in such circumstances, Her Majesty's Government will have to appeal to the forbearance of its opponents, and in some cases to the patient indulgence of its friends; but my Lords, I have that confidence in the good sense and judgement of the House of Commons that they will not unnecessarily introduce subjects of a controversial and party character for the mere purpose of interrupting the course of sound and useful legislation, and of driving the Government out of that moderate and temperate course which the Government has prescribed itself.

(Derby, 27 February 1852, *Hansard Parliamentary Debates*, 3rd ser. (1830–91), cxix. 899–900)

O n Sunday 22 February 1852, five weeks short of his fifty-third birthday, Lord Derby became prime minister. This was the political summit upon which, nearly twenty years before, as a young man in his mid-thirties, he had set his sights. It was as an older middle-aged politician that he eventually completed the ascent. Yet, the assumption of office, without the possession of power, rendered the event less than a moment of triumphant fulfilment. He headed a party in a Commons minority. No rich vein of experience or talent compensated for lack of numbers. The incubus of Protectionism, despite popular endorsement in rural constituencies, provided ground upon which a hostile Commons majority was gathered. Paucity of talent, lack of official experience, and a defining policy condemning his party to minority status in Westminster proffered him the premiership on highly conditional terms.

As, during the last months of 1851, Derby scaled the final slopes to office an anxious foreboding, rather than celebratory elation, shrouded his sense of events. He saw the impregnability of Free Trade within Westminster as proof of the declining power of the landed aristocracy. Benjamin Disraeli shared his despondency. With neither of the aristocratic parties able to govern the country, Disraeli observed, urban radicalism threatened to deliver power to the likes of Richard Cobden. In his biography of Lord George Bentinck, the writing of which engrossed Disraeli during the recess of 1851, he observed: 'There are few positions less inspiriting than that of a discomfited party.'[1] All that could be done was to attempt to check urban self-interest and defend the landed aristocratic constitution whenever possible. This was a task which Lord John Russell, impeded by Peelite self-regard and vulnerable to radical pressure, seemed incapable of undertaking.

He thus with prudent words the chiefs address'd.

(Lord Derby, *The Iliad of Homer* (1864), i. 14)

As, in the damp fastness of Knowsley in late 1851, Derby succumbed to his seasonal illness, he looked to an imminent Conservative resumption of office. More than five chill years of opposition seemed to be thawing. Three issues encouraged this cautious expectation. First, he saw parliamentary Reform deepening divisions among non-Conservatives. Secondly, he recognized the quiet abandonment of Protection as necessary to the parliamentary recovery of Conservatism. Thirdly, he anticipated the sectarian excitement created by Russell's Durham Letter disrupting ministerial ranks, as popular anti-Catholicism clashed with principles of religious liberty. While dampening down Conservative anti-Catholicism, he was content to watch Russell's self-imposed difficulties in reconciling anti-popery with liberal religious reform.

During 1851 Derby carefully prepared the ground for the eventual abandonment of Protection, less because it was discredited economics than because it was a hopeless parliamentary cause. Agricultural distress during 1849 and 1850 had revived the rural demand, headed by Lords Richmond, Eglinton, and Granby, for a restoration of import duties. But Disraeli advocated fiscal reform as a substitute for the reimposition of tariffs. In February 1850 his call for a revision of local taxation was defeated, in a division which split the Peelites by a slim Commons majority of twenty-one votes. In February 1851 his proposal to alleviate agricultural distress by tax reform was defeated by just fourteen Commons votes. During the same period Peelites, Whigs, Liberals, and radicals affirmed their unanimous opposition to the reinstatement of import tariffs. Within Westminster, Free Trade commanded firm majority support as a central article of faith for non-Conservative MPs. In February 1851 Derby acknowledged that an accession of support from outside the Conservative party was impossible while Protection remained the party's defining policy. Privately, he accepted that fiscal reform must replace the call for import tariffs. But, as party leader, he also recognized that the abandonment of Protection required a careful and dignified retreat. To act precipitously would be to alienate the bulk of his Conservative Commons support. To this end he privately subdued Protectionist agitation in the constituencies, publicly supported fiscal reform as a response to agricultural distress, and openly recommended that Protection be dropped as party policy should the next general election pronounce in favour of Free Trade. So might the retreat from Protection be safeguarded, with the party kept intact, and the parliamentary liability of import tariffs cast off.

In September 1851 Granby resigned from the opposition front bench because of the vagueness of the leadership's commitment to Protection. At a meeting of the National Protection Association on 12 December dissatisfaction with the 'ambiguous, uncertain' and 'wavering policy' of the party leadership was expressed.[2] But Derby was undeterred. When, in November, Eglinton complained of a speech by Disraeli at Aylesbury 'seeming to abandon Protection', Derby calmly replied that 'Disraeli said nothing more than he said a dozen times before, and I had said myself, that to look for a restoration of Protection in this parliament was idle.'[3] To Disraeli himself Derby declared the Aylesbury speech, delivered to the Royal Buckinghamshire Agricultural Association, 'a judicious' statement, although he hesitated to endorse Disraeli's call, as reported in *The Times*, for the government to extend the principle of Free Trade by removing the restrictive tax on barley.[4] At Aylesbury, Disraeli urged farmers to fight, not for a return of Protective duties, but for social justice in the form of equal taxation and the removal of injurious restrictions. Following a visit to Knowsley, Lord Malmesbury delivered in late November a speech in Sussex intended to keep up the spirits of the agricultural interest, 'without raising them too high by expectations that the old Protective duties could ever return even if we come into office'.[5] Derby recommended Malmesbury's speech to Richmond.[6] But the difficulty of maintaining this delicate 'policy of finesse'[7] was shown, in January 1852, by Derby's intense irritation at Samuel Phillips's correspondence with Knox of the *Morning Herald*, suggesting the necessity of immediately relinquishing Protection. 'The time is very critical—the game is, I believe, in our hands,' Derby declared, 'but in order to be played with ultimate success, it must be played honestly and manfully and to take office with the purpose of throwing over, voluntarily, the main object of those who have raised us to it is to follow too closely an *exemplar vitiis imitabile*, to which I never can submit.'[8] He dismissed the course of taking office as a Protectionist, only to renounce at once the principle of Protection—a base emulation of Peel's gross crime. But an eventual electoral endorsement of Free Trade would finally absolve them from protracting a hopeless struggle.

Parliamentary Reform, however, occupied more of Derby's thoughts than Protection and fiscal reform. Russell was committed to introducing a parliamentary Reform Bill during the 1852 session. This enabled him to hold off Peter Locke King's motion for the extension of the county franchise. But the Whig prime minister was now, Derby observed to John Croker, 'in the condition of a man in one of the old stories, who, having sold himself to the devil, is anxious to cheat the devil, and get out of his bargain. But I am afraid the devil will be too much for him.'[9] Though Russell was clearly 'anxious to do as little mischief as possible, consistently with keeping himself and his friends in office, he will be driven, in spite of himself, into a larger measure than he wishes for'. In particular, Derby dreaded the swamping of county representation by the influence of the towns. Since 1832, 40s. freeholds, even when situated within an existing parliamentary borough, conferred county votes. Increasing numbers of urban voters in county constituencies, Derby feared, were accelerating the subversion of landed influence. Already, over 25 per cent of the voters within the county constituency of South Lancashire were residents of Manchester. As shown by a Home Office inquiry in 1852, nearly one-fifth of the county electorate in England were enfranchised by urban property. The penetration of urban voters into county constituencies became for Derby a major concern. Yet he wished to avoid resisting all change, despite denying its necessity. Change might be given a Conservative tendency. More importantly, 'an absolute and unflinching adherence to the present system ... would give the government an advantage which one can ill afford to give them when they start with the prestige of "enlargement of the franchise" in their favour'.[10] This had been the Duke of Wellington's great error in November 1830 and Derby remembered well the price paid for inflexible Tory obduracy.

Again, it was parliamentary considerations that shaped Derby's thinking. He feared that the court, in the person of Prince Albert, and Sir James Graham, for the Peelites, were prepared to throw their weight into the democratic scale and support a large Reform measure, despite there being no widespread demand in the country for extensive change.

Russell had 'put himself in a position in which he must upset himself or ruin the country'.[11] The Conservatives should, Derby believed, avoid opposing all change, while protesting in the strongest terms against any measure calculated to increase the democratic influence and extend the power of the towns over the counties. To Disraeli on 26 October he confirmed that, despite the feeling of their Tory supporters, the party should avoid pledging themselves to resist any and every Reform measure brought forward. At the same time, any extensive alteration should be deprecated as uncalled for by necessity or strong public feeling, apart from the desire 'to save a tottering administration by diverting public attention from its misgovernment to a subject of popular discussion and agitation'.[12] Any attempt to give additional power to large urban masses, or swamping the county representation resting on landed property, by assimilating the borough and county franchise, must be resisted. All else could await the precise form any government measure might assume. Meanwhile, Russell's predicament, caught between Whig and moderate Liberal caution and Peelite and radical enthusiasm, was evident in the fact that the government's measure was, as yet, 'immature'. In late November, Derby noted that the ministry were 'still at sixes and sevens about their Reform bill'.[13]

Over papal aggression Derby remained convinced that the Conservatives 'must avoid irritating language to the Roman Catholic *laity* and abuse of their religion', while attacking 'the political power of the priesthood'.[14] The issue had, by autumn 1851, become 'mixed up with the question of [Irish] Education, which it is quite clear the Priests mean to have, if possible, entirely in their own hands'.[15] He hoped to take different aspects of the subject up by moving for committees in both the Commons and the Lords. The Upper House could address 'the legal position of Roman Catholics with reference to the pretensions of Rome, their civil rights, the affairs of their church, and the condition of their schools, charities and religious establishments'. This would leave the Commons 'with the narrower question of the National Board of Education in Ireland'.[16] So militant anti-Catholicism within the Conservative Commons party might be contained. Derby urged Spencer Walpole to prevent Protestant feeling in the Commons from 'running into any violent excesses'.[17] While avoiding hurting the feelings of the Catholic laity, which would only unite them with their ultramontane priesthood, it was the growing political power of the Catholic Church, including the assumed authority of Cardinal Wiseman, that must be the subject of inquiry. On the eve of the session, in February 1852, Derby learned from Charles Newdegate that the

'Protestants' intended to bring forward a motion on the Catholic seminary at Maynooth in the Commons. He remained convinced, however, that a move in the Lords for a committee on the whole Roman Catholic question would be a safer and more 'useful safety valve'.[18]

The visit of the Queen and Prince Albert, accompanied by the 9-year-old Princess Alice and 7-year-old Prince Alfred, to Liverpool in early October 1851 drew Derby into the attendant public celebrations. Travelling by train, the royal party progressed from Balmoral to Lancashire, via Edinburgh and Carlisle, to a banquet hosted by the Earl of Sefton, as Lord Lieutenant, at Croxteth Park, neighbouring Knowsley. On Thursday 9 October, Lord and Lady Derby joined Lord Sefton's banquet for the royal party. The following day the Queen visited Liverpool town centre and the docks, which were decked with flags and banners, as well as an elaborate triumphal arch, for the occasion. But Derby's private mood of despondency contrasted with the exuberant public celebrations. Throughout the autumn he was dogged by gout. When Malmesbury visited him on 10 November he found his host looking very ill, although this did not prevent them from enjoying 'great *battue* shooting for the next three days'.[19] Despite his illness, Derby travelled to London for the wedding of Lady Augusta Gordon-Lennox, seventh child of the Duke of Richmond, on 27 November at St George's, Hanover Square, to Prince William of Saxe-Weimar-Eisenach. After the ceremony a fatigued Derby then visited Disraeli at Grosvenor Gate to discuss the approaching session.

Following their meeting Disraeli sought, through correspondents such as Lord Ponsonby, reliable information about the government's Reform Bill. But intelligence was hard to acquire. One barometer of opinion, *The Times*, printed a leader on 8 December decrying the corruption prevalent in certain small boroughs, which should, it urged, be disfranchised.[20] On 11 December, Derby, back at Knowsley, advised Disraeli that he believed the cabinet were still undecided on a Reform plan. He was certain they were much embarrassed by the necessity of bringing forward a measure. Yet ignorance of the ministry's intentions posed a strategic dilemma. If the Conservatives rejected the ministry's bill on the second reading, without proposing a measure of their own, success would only be secured if the radicals also repudiated the scheme. In this case, the Conservatives would be far less enthusiastic in throwing the government bill out. If, on the other hand, the Conservatives proposed an alternative scheme, then this, rather than the ministerial plan, would become the target of combined attack. Should the government secure the second reading of their measure, then only the details of the ministerial scheme would be open to modification.[21]

Derby nipped in the bud the proposal, which had come to Disraeli while on the train to Hatfield, of giving the colonies direct representation at Westminster by apportioning them seats vacated by disfranchised small boroughs. Russell and Lord Grey, during November 1849, had also given thought to creating a colonial franchise, but, like Disraeli's proposal, it was quickly dropped.

Of one thing, however, Derby was firmly convinced. Following their experience over the Irish Reform Bill and the failure to form a broad Conservative government the previous February, it was clear that 'any concert with the *disjecta membra* of the Peelite (or what used to be the Peelite) section is wholly out of the question and that the attempt would only lead to misunderstanding and disappointment'.[22] It is better to have '*a party* at my back', Malmesbury concurred, 'than one of those "*able*" halfpay officers called Peelites without a single soldier. ... They can never be anything as long as they go by the *name* of a Man and not of a principle. Englishmen don't care *out of the house* for any Man unless he is identified with a principle.'[23] Reform might secure realignment with far more reliable allies, namely Whigs and moderate Liberals alienated by radical demands for extensive change. Dramatic events across the English Channel, however, forestalled debate on Reform.

On 2 December 1851 Louis Napoleon mounted a *coup d'état* in France, proclaiming martial law in Paris, dissolving the French Assembly, and arresting suspected opponents. Without consulting his ministerial colleagues, on 3 December Lord Palmerston conveyed, through the French Ambassador, Count Walewski, his approval of the Emperor's actions. The cabinet, meanwhile, decided to adopt a position of strict neutrality, Palmerston remaining silent about his conversation with Walewski. This dissembling erupted into a public crisis. On 13 December, as news of Palmerston's conversation with Walewski leaked out, the Queen demanded an explanation from Russell of the government's inconsistency. Events moved swiftly. On 17 December, Russell promptly seized the opportunity to dismiss Palmerston from the Foreign Office. Palmerston ascribed his dismissal to Russell's long-standing jealousy of his popularity in the country. Certainly Russell's cold and reserved manner denied him the easy acclaim enjoyed by his affable former Foreign Secretary. The final disintegration of Russell's ministry quickly followed. Desperate attempts to bring the Duke of Newcastle and Graham into the cabinet failed. The court was delighted by Palmerston's departure, Prince Albert being gratified by Palmerston's having 'cut his throat himself'.[24] Russell's Whig confidants declared Palmerston 'too fond of popularity hunting to fit the Foreign Office'.[25] But the government supporter Joseph Parkes immediately recognized that Palmerston's going had put 'a shot in our hull'.[26] The cabinet, Disraeli advised Derby, was 'now very sick'.[27]

On hearing of Palmerston's forced resignation, Derby anticipated an attempted Whig–Peelite reconstruction. Nonetheless, he believed the government's prospects were 'gloomy'; 'whether any government can be formed, and stand, out of the heterogeneous materials to be dealt with, is a very different question'.[28] He had no doubt that both Palmerston and Lady Palmerston were furious at the turn of events and he warned Disraeli of 'a lively scene in your House on the first night of the session'.[29] He was pleased that Disraeli held back from contemplating an immediate coalition with Palmerston. For the moment he preferred the Conservatives to side with neither of the rival factions, leaving them to fight it out between themselves. But if Palmerston mounted a strenuous objection to Russell's Reform Bill then 'his opposition may very materially affect our tactics on that subject'. 'The feud between Palmerston and John Russell is of old standing,' Derby observed to Stanley.[30] Russellite ministers had much disliked the support they were obliged to give Palmerston over the 'Don Pacifico' affair and other aspects of foreign policy, 'on which Palmerston acted off his own bat, without previous concert with the prime minister'. The Grey camp, Earl Grey, Sir Charles Wood, and Sir George Grey, particularly objected to Palmerston's diplomacy. Moreover, Palmerston had become 'absolutely *odious* to the Queen and Prince Albert', the former Foreign Secretary treating 'their opinions with a contempt which they both felt'. It was also true, Derby noted, that Russell had left Palmerston 'in the dark' on other details of government policy. All this, he anticipated, would lead to 'a very piquant debate in the Commons at the beginning of the session'. Clearly, Derby observed to William Beresford, 'the cabinet is in a most rickety state; so much so that they may even fall to pieces without any external violence'.[31]

With regard to events in Paris, Derby believed it 'abundantly plain that France and Frenchmen are incapable of rational self-government and that sooner or later they will give themselves a master'.[32] Like most of his English contemporaries, whose youth had been overshadowed by the titanic conflict with Napoleon Bonaparte, Derby believed that the self-indulgent French nation lacked the moral qualities, public disinter-estedness, and sense of civic duty necessary to the blessings of British parliamentary government, rule of law, religious freedom, and liberty of the press. Rather, selfish individualism, love of luxury, fondness for military glory, and a weakness for abstract theory condemned France to a chronic constitutional instability, as republic, empire, and monarchy followed the convulsions of 1789, 1799, 1830, and 1848. Louis Napoleon's actions in December 1851 were just the latest attempt to preserve order in a country incapable, as he termed it, of 'rational self-government'. Britain, he maintained, should abstain from comment on the morality of events in France.

Derby's broad view of British foreign policy remained that of maintaining cordial relations with all the major European powers established by the Vienna Settlement, while following a cautious policy of non-intervention in continental struggles. British interests in Europe, he believed, were best served by not being drawn into Great Power rivalries, but by preserving friendly relations with Russia, Austria, and France, the conciliatory policy adopted by Lord Aberdeen between 1841 and 1846. While in exile in London in 1848 Louis Napoleon had served alongside Derby's elder son as a special constable during the Chartist demonstrations. Malmesbury enjoyed a long-standing friendship with Louis Napoleon. These personal relationships reinforced Derby's own conviction that the *entente cordiale* with France established by Aberdeen should be preserved. Louis Napoleon, he believed, had not violated the French constitution until its inherent weakness was clear and contending factions had brought the existing machinery of government to a deadlock. In these circumstances Louis Napoleon's prompt action had saved France from civil war. Moreover, Derby believed that Louis Napoleon's decisiveness had forestalled more general unrest in Europe, 'which would have followed upon the success of the Reds' in France.[33] If Louis Napoleon now applied himself to promoting the material prosperity of his country, while devoting his military power to controlling 'the turbulent spirits' infesting it, then, Derby anticipated, he would 'merit the title of a general benefactor'. But if, for the purpose of conciliating the army, Louis Napoleon adopted a warlike policy then, he warned, 'I should look upon him as the most dangerous neighbour we could have.' He acknowledged that nothing would be so popular with the bulk of the French population as a war with England, and 'the end of a war once kindled in Europe no man living can foresee'.[34] But unlike Russell, who he believed had panicked upon hearing of Louis Napoleon's action from fear of an imminent war with France, Derby, reassured by Malmesbury, trusted that Louis Napoleon had no wish to instigate hostilities with Britain. Through Croker, Derby's views were faithfully laid out in the *Quarterly Review*.

As the pulse of political events quickened, so Derby's health and spirits improved. Disraeli reported to his sister Sarah that 'affairs are very stirring' and, although it was difficult to foresee the precise turn of events, 'there ought, I think, to be a Conservative government'.[35] To his lawyer and confidant Philip Rose, Disraeli observed that 'Lord Derby will turn out a better general, than the world imagined, a few months ago.'[36] On Monday 26 January 1852 the Conservative leadership, including Derby, Lord Salisbury, Malmesbury, Disraeli, Granby, and John Herries, gathered at Burghley House. Thinner for his illness, but as a consequence looking ten years younger, Derby seemed in good heart. He expressed a clear determination to accept office if it should be offered to him. What course Palmerston would adopt upon meeting parliament and the nature of Russell's Reform measure would shape events. In characteristically melodramatic terms Disraeli anticipated 'tremendous troubles ahead, if not breakers, waves mountains high'.[37] Derby arrived in London on 29 January and, on Monday 2 February, hosted a grand dinner at St James's Square for the Conservative peerage, the dukes of Richmond, Beaufort, Montrose, Northumberland, and Cleveland, the earls of Eglinton, Cardigan, Lonsdale, Malmesbury, Wilton, Stradbroke, Glengall, and Hardwicke, as well as Lord Redesdale, being among those who attended. A magnificent gold centrepiece, presented to Derby's father by the Deputy Lieutenants of Lancashire, and three beautiful pieces of racing plate, won at Goodwood and Doncaster by Cazenou, set off the table, with a superb dessert service, purchased by Derby at the Great Exhibition, being used for the first time.[38] The following morning he hosted a large meeting of Conservative MPs at St James's Square. At the gathering it was decided not to oppose the introduction of the government's Reform Bill. Since coming to London, Derby had spent much time analysing and then discussing with Disraeli census and electoral statistics, the most reliable figures, he judged, being those drawn from the recent 1851 census.[39] As a result, he concluded that a £20 county franchise would be quite as good for the Conservatives as the £50 suffrage. But a £10 county franchise would be 'destruction'.[40] He now awaited the implosion of Russell's ministry.

To seize the spoils of war.

(Derby, *The Iliad of Homer*, i. 167)

When parliament assembled on Tuesday 3 February 1852 Derby delivered what Malmesbury judged a 'magnificent' speech on the Address intended to reassure the farmers.[41] It rallied support, put the Conservatives on notice that a Whig ministerial collapse was imminent, but deliberately stopped short of striking a lethal blow. Ministerial self-immolation suited Derby's purposes better. In the Commons a beleaguered Russell explained the circumstances of Palmerston's resignation and, on 9 February, introduced his Reform Bill. It proposed lowering the county franchise to £20 and the household borough franchise to £5. Originally Russell had wished to omit any redistribution of seats, so as to preserve the balance of representation established in 1832. But the notoriety of electoral corruption in certain small boroughs, notably St Albans, made it impossible to avoid any, even if limited, proposals for redistribution. Russell adopted the option of extending the boundaries of sixty-seven small boroughs so as to increase the electorate to over 500 votes in each. Under pressure from Sir George Grey and Charles Wood, he also proposed the limited transfer of a single seat from a number of small two-member boroughs. This avoided any total disfranchisement. Recognizing that the Conservatives were not strong enough to amend or throw it out without Peelite support, Derby rejected Disraeli and Malmesbury's suggestion of meeting the bill with a hostile resolution. He did approve, however, of Disraeli's alternative proposal that the Commons opposition attack Lord Grey's troubled policy in South Africa and he supported Lord Naas's motion criticizing the government's colonial policy. The military adventurism of the Governor of Cape Colony, Sir Harry Smith, had instigated a protracted war with the Xhosa and disrupted Grey's plan to introduce self-government. During January, Grey recalled Smith, and the Conservatives in both Houses denounced the Colonial Secretary's handling of affairs in the Cape. Privately Palmerston, and also William Gladstone, made their disapproval of Grey's policy known to Derby.[42]

On Friday 20 February, Derby left London for a weekend shooting party at Badminton, hosted by the Duke of Beaufort. That same evening Palmerston delivered his 'tit for tat' in the Commons, moving a hostile amendment to the ministry's Militia Bill. Russell introduced the measure in response to apprehension about Louis Napoleon's militaristic ambitions, following the coup of December. Since 1815 parliament had maintained a small regular British army, a large standing army raising concerns about threats to domestic liberties and augmented expense. Britain's national defence was viewed as primarily dependent upon a strong navy. Auxiliary forces, such as a local militia, offered an inexpensive supplement to a limited military establishment, although the raising of a local militia itself posed difficulties over the militarization of working men, its disruption of the labour force, and the potential political use of the militia against domestic civil disorder. These concerns were aired by radical and Irish Catholic opponents. Palmerston criticized the measure as inadequate and too responsive to radical anxieties. His hostile motion was carried by 136 to 125 votes.[43] Disraeli entered the division lobby alongside Palmerston, Gladstone, and Sidney Herbert.

With a difficult debate looming over their colonial policy in the Cape, the cabinet, Palmerston noted, 'were glad to make use of the militia question as a convenient parachute to avoid a ruder descent and a more dangerous one in Table Bay'.[44] Russell immediately announced his government's resignation, advising the Queen that Derby should be sent for, Palmerston having no party in the Commons. In response to an urgent note from Disraeli, Derby quickly returned, on Saturday 21 February, to London. Fearing a commotion over Protection, the Queen favoured calling on Aberdeen or Wellington to form a government, but both men declined the invitation. As a result, at Buckingham Palace on Sunday 22 February, Derby promptly accepted the Queen's commission to form a ministry. On this occasion there was no hesitation. A jubilant Disraeli subsequently exalted: 'Now we have got a *status*.'[45]

Derby readily acknowledged during his audience with the Queen that, being in a minority in the Commons, a Conservative cabinet would draw strength from Palmerston's debating skills. To exclude Palmerston would be a dangerous move. During November 1851, when the exiled Hungarian nationalist leader Louis Kossuth had visited England, to the delight of radicals, Palmerston had expressed his sympathy for the struggles of Hungarian nationalists for independence from Austria and Russia. Out of government, Derby feared, Palmerston would establish himself as head of a party demanding his restoration to the Foreign Office. But, by bringing Palmerston into a Conservative cabinet as, say, Chancellor of the Exchequer, Derby suggested, Palmerston might be safely harnessed and his pretensions to the Foreign Office waived. Merely making such an offer, Derby hoped, even if it was refused, would appease potentially hostile feeling in the Commons, his government undoubtedly having to face the enmity of leading Peelites and radicals.[46] Disraeli immediately indicated to Derby his willingness to serve under Palmerston in the Commons, if this secured Palmerston's presence in a Conservative cabinet. Palmerston, Disraeli observed, would not like to serve under a man he looked upon as 'a whippersnapper'.[47] Derby welcomed Disraeli's offer, suggesting that it 'must ultimately rebound to the credit and advantage of the man who makes it from public motives'. He also confirmed that he had 'already had other intimations that P. is not unwilling to join us'.[48] Beresford strongly advised recruiting Palmerston.[49] If the prospect of enlisting leading Peelites to a Derby cabinet now seemed unlikely, then the value of denouncing Palmerston's diplomacy, as a basis for bringing Conservatives and Peelites together, was much reduced. An isolated Palmerston's conservative views on domestic policy, meanwhile, enhanced his worth to a Derby cabinet, if he could be placed in a post other than the Foreign Office.

During his audience with the Queen on Sunday 22 February, Derby advised the monarch of his intention to invite Palmerston to join him. The Queen, seemingly distressed, bluntly warned that Palmerston 'will never rest till he is your master'.[50] Nevertheless, Derby straight away met Palmerston at Piccadilly Terrace. Disraeli, for one, was optimistic; Palmerston's 'position was very desolate. He had no party. Not a single man of work had followed him when he was ignominiously ejected from office.' Palmerston's intentions, however, remained 'a mystery'.[51] During their interview Derby impressed upon Palmerston that the offer of office in his cabinet was made with Disraeli's agreement, who would prove an able and loyal lieutenant. In response, Palmerston denied any objections to personnel, but stated that Protection could not be left in an ambiguous position as an open question. Though in 1846 he had favoured a moderate fixed duty on foreign corn it was, he pronounced, impossible to contemplate such an option in 1852. He could not, he concluded, be part of any ministry which might modify Free Trade. This unsatisfactorily ended the meeting. Clearly, for the moment, Palmerston intended to stand aside, possibly playing for higher stakes. As he observed to his brother, his deficiencies as a prime minister were 'not greater than those of Derby and John Russell, or of any other person who at present could be chosen for such a duty'.[52]

Immediately, Derby joined Disraeli at Grosvenor Gate. Any further overtures to Palmerston, Derby decided, would be a waste of time. Similarly, he declined to squander time sounding out the leading Peelites. The experience of twelve months earlier suggested such efforts would be futile. Putting aside Disraeli's lack of experience, he promptly offered Disraeli the Chancellorship of the Exchequer. 'You know as much as Mr Canning did. They give you the figures,' Derby declared.[53] Malmesbury was to be given the Foreign Office, though Malmesbury regretted that it would require him to remain in London all year.[54] Herries was placed at the Colonial Office, Joseph Henley at the Board of Trade, and Walpole at the Home Office. Derby then returned to St James's Square to draw up the appropriate letters, report in writing to the Queen, and prepare for the necessary succession of interviews.

On Monday 23 February, Derby gathered together the Conservative ministerial aspirants. Manners remembered waiting with his future colleagues, 'all looking nervous and miserable', at 8 St James's Square, prior to their individual summonses into Derby's library.[55] Aggrieved at not being given the Exchequer, the cantankerous Herries refused the Colonial Office. Upon Disraeli's recommendation, Derby subsequently gave Sir John Pakington the Colonies, Pakington's face during his interview with Derby betraying 'a remarkable mixture of astonishment and self-complacency'.[56] Something of a dandy, Pakington was to prove a fluent, but rather ineffective, speaker in the Commons, while his tendency to pomposity made him an easy target for Derby's cutting humour. At a subsequent dinner party Lady Clanricarde, baiting Derby about the obscurity of his appointees, asked across the table whether Pakington was a real man. With characteristic jocularity Derby replied that he believed so given that Pakington had been married three times.[57] Herries, as a consequence of Pakington's success, was given the Board of Control. On account of age and ill health the elderly Peelite Lord Lyndhurst declined the Lord Chancellorship. Similarly, the banker Thomas Baring refused to join a Derby government. The highly respected 71-year-old lawyer and prominent legal theorist Edward Sugden, who had served as Peel's Lord Chancellor of Ireland in 1834–5, was offered and accepted the Lord Chancellorship, following Lyndhurst's refusal, with the title of Lord St Leonards. It proved one of Derby's most successful appointments. Though arrogant in manner, St Leonards was intimate with the arcane details of English law, was very popular within the legal profession, and was committed to reforming judicial procedures.

Other cabinet appointments were swiftly dispensed, the Earl of Lonsdale becoming Lord President, the Marquess of Salisbury Lord Privy Seal, the Duke of Northumberland First Lord of the Admiralty, and the Earl of Hardwicke Postmaster-General. Derby looked to bring Lord Granby, despite his expressed reluctance, into the cabinet as a sop to the hardline Protectionists. But instead, upon Disraeli's insistence, Granby's younger brother, a surprised Lord John Manners, Disraeli's friend and Young England colleague, was appointed First Commissioner of Works. Six ministers sat in the Commons, with seven cabinet ministers drawn from the Lords. The wealthy noble heads of the Cecil, Percy, and Lowther families provided 'at least as good padding as is usual in ministries',[58] and ensured, Disraeli drolly observed, that 'never was a faction so feasted!'[59] But only three of the cabinet, Derby, Lonsdale, and Herries, had held office before. Disraeli, with no previous official experience at all, was Leader of the Commons. Little wonder that he 'felt just like a young girl going to her first ball'.[60] Derby's elder son Lord Stanley (abroad on a tour of India) was given, in his absence, the Foreign Office Under-Secretaryship under Malmesbury.

Derby's Irish appointments were notably moderate. The shrewd Earl of Eglinton assumed the office of Lord Lieutenant of Ireland and the able young Lord Naas became Chief Secretary. Eglinton's lavish entertaining at Dublin Castle, which compared favourably with the parsimony of his predecessor, Lord Clarendon, combined with carefully calculated patronage, immediately found favour in the Irish capital. Naas's appointment, as an Irishman, to a post formerly usually occupied by an Englishman assisted in the formation of the Central Conservative Society undertaking the monitoring of Irish electoral registers and the selection of parliamentary candidates. Nonetheless, Naas subsequently complained that his liberal views were blocked by the bigotry of Northern Irish Tory MPs. Minor government appointments, however, proved troublesome. The young peer Lord Ossulston refused the Treasuryship for fear of electoral expenses, while Charles Adderley declined a post at the Board of Control under Herries. Some former Peelites, nevertheless, were secured: Viscount Hardinge accepted the Master Generalship of the Ordnance, Henry Baillie took the Joint Secretaryship of the Board of Control, Sir Frederick Thesiger became Attorney General, and Lord Claud Hamilton Treasurer of the Royal Household. Thesiger had served briefly as Peel's Attorney General in 1845–6; his pleasant manner, fund of good stories, and scrupulous honesty made him a popular social figure, although his weakness for overlong speeches hampered his success in parliament. Initially, Prince Albert created difficulties about Derby's proposed appointments to the Royal Household. But by the end of February a mutually acceptable list of names was agreed. Because of doubts about Derby's commitment to Protection and the Protestant constitution, Newdegate declined the Vice-Presidency of the India Board of Control. Newdegate's exclusion from the ministry, alongside that of Granby, left an Ultra Tory knot of fervent Protectionists outside the constraint of ministerial responsibility.

The inexperience of Derby's new government was embarrassingly exhibited by the necessity for a mass swearing-in at Buckingham Palace, on Friday 27 February, of seventeen ministers as Privy Councillors. Disraeli drew on the extraordinary scene in his last published novel *Endymion*, where he graphically described a crowd of novice ministers, all on their knees in genuflection at the same moment, before a serene and imperturbable Queen. Victoria privately declared it 'a very sorry cabinet'.[61] Not recognizing many of the ministerial names, Aberdeen believed Derby's great talents and high character were being thrown away in a hopeless undertaking.[62] Most famously Wellington, in the stentorian tones of the deaf, kept interjecting 'Who? Who?' during the announcement of ministerial appointments in the Lords. *The Economist* dubbed Derby's ministry 'the Great Unknown'.[63] *The Guardian* believed the astonishment at Derby's appointments was only exceeded by the anxiety they created.[64] Clearly, the survival of the ministry was dependent, to an extraordinary degree, on Derby's own experience, capability, and success as prime minister. Disraeli's assiduous cultivation of John Delane, however, produced a markedly uncensorious comment on the new government from *The Times*. The nation should not begrudge 'twenty or thirty new hands a little taste of office', it concluded. Otherwise, 'a perpetual monopoly of power' would be conferred 'on a small clique consisting of a few noble families'.[65]

> The smooth-tongued chief, from whose persuasive lips,
> Sweeter than honey flow'd the stream of speech.
>
> (Derby, *The Iliad of Homer*, i. 14)

No other government position is shaped so much by the personality of the individual who holds it as the prime ministership. The job is largely defined by the character of the premier. Derby's self-confidence, intelligence, ability, and the inexperience of his colleagues ensured he was *primus inter impares*. He clearly commanded his ministry, as he mentored his apprentice ministers, guiding them through the unfamiliar demands of their new responsibilities. A strong influence on the governing style of all prime ministers, as distinct from differences over policy, is a determination to avoid the perceived failings of their immediate predecessor. Conciliatory premiers are followed by prime ministers resolved to assert strong leadership. Firm divisive premiers are succeeded by prime ministers anxious to establish ministerial consensus. For Derby, Russell's deficiencies were his failure to control his cabinet (both Palmerston and Grey proving dangerous ministerial loose cannons) and his vulnerability to his extreme supporters (radical demands often shaping his government's agenda). Derby, therefore, was determined to control his cabinet and restrain his Ultra Tory support. He oversaw all aspects of government policy, an ascendancy facilitated by the poverty of administrative experience and the absence of disruptive ambition among his cabinet. Only Disraeli at the Exchequer, in the terms with which he presented his budget to the Commons in April, broke away from Derby's direction. In turn, curbing the Ultra Tories complemented Derby's wish to restore the Conservatives as a moderate party of government. Within weeks of Derby assuming the premiership Queen Victoria noted that '*he* is the government. They do *nothing* without him. He has all the Departments to look after, and on being asked by somebody if he was not much tried, he said, "I am quite well with my babies!" '[66] He reported to Croker that 'my troops are taking well to their work, and will, I think, acquit themselves creditably'.[67] Following their first cabinet meeting, he brightly declared to Lady Malmesbury: 'I have been driving a team of young horses this morning; not one had ever been in harness before, and they went beautifully; not one kicked amongst them.'[68]

Under his firm rein Derby's novice ministry performed better than detractors predicted. In the face of a numerous and talented opposition, mere survival was no mean ambition. Russell smugly dubbed the new government 'Derby's militia'; 'called out for twenty days, and then ... sent home'.[69] The Duke of Argyll deemed Derby 'too rollicking, too apt to treat everything as a joke; the result was a government obviously provisional'.[70] While being the linchpin of the cabinet, Derby's difficulties in preserving Conservative unity in the Commons were significant. Disraeli remained unpopular. His shifting moods and reputation for unprincipled opportunism compounded suspicion. Moreover, Derby's peerage isolated him from the Commons where, it was clear, the fate of the government would be decided. When he became premier in February 1852 it was the first time in eleven years, since Lord Melbourne's resignation in 1841, that the prime minister was in the Upper House. Through Disraeli and Beresford he was kept informed of feeling in the Commons. Yet, at the same time, his nonchalant aloofness and remoteness in the Lords prevented him from fostering party unity through constant social attentions bestowed directly on the Commons rank and file. He well appreciated that his government's survival rested on the shifting foundation of Commons sentiment. He recognized that successful party leadership required shepherding back-bench opinion, rather than driving it in a desired direction. Repeatedly, he lectured Disraeli on the need to consult, rather than cajole, Commons support. Yet, his peerage, his sense of his own social position, and his bluff manner prevented him from courting MPs on a personal day-to-day basis himself. His political sensitivity was rarely translated into easy familiarity. Nonetheless, on 17 March, Lady Derby gave the first of a number of large receptions at Downing Street, attended by 700 guests, intended to consolidate party support. Though not a natural hostess, the physically frail Lady Derby did her best to support her husband in his position of pre-eminence. Derby chose to reside in St James's Square while premier, using 10 Downing Street solely for conducting business and official entertaining. During the session ministers took turns in hosting cabinet dinners each Wednesday evening, these social occasions reinforcing their sense of collective purpose.

Before a crowded Lords on Friday 27 February 1852 Derby delivered his first prime ministerial statement. A large number of MPs visited the Upper House to listen. He had, he confessed to Disraeli, 'ticklish ground to go over'.[71] When Lord Campbell, encountering Derby in the robing room, congratulated him on assuming office, Derby replied he was more to be pitied than congratulated.[72] In his speech Derby began by acknowledging Lord Lansdowne's gracious recent reference to him as 'a noble and much valued friend … though a political opponent'. These words Derby described as 'particularly gratifying to me in a public, and also in a private, capacity, as coming from one to whom, since my earliest boyhood, I have been accustomed to look up to with hereditary respect and deference'.[73] Political differences, he declared, had not impaired their private friendship. Moving on to review foreign affairs, Derby then characterized the diplomatic policy he intended to pursue, a policy laid out in his earlier denunciations of Palmerston's inveterate meddling. Towards all foreign powers, whether powerful or weak, he would undertake 'a calm, temperate, deliberate and conciliatory course of conduct'. Interference in the affairs of other nations would be avoided, the European status quo established by the Vienna Settlement respected, and due regard for international treaties maintained. European stability would allow British prosperity and commerce, founded on an empire safeguarded by British naval supremacy, to flourish. Protection, however, remained the immediate and most difficult issue confronting him. Corn, Derby declared to the Lords, should not be an exception to a general system of imposing duties on foreign imports. But, he acknowledged, no financial scheme of this kind could be introduced except by a government strong in the confidence of both parliament and the country. Thus he sought to maintain the commitment to opposing Free Trade while, at the same time, allaying opposition fears that Protection would be immediately reimposed. Similarly, over parliamentary Reform he affirmed his implacable resistance to democracy, which would throw the power and authority of government into the hands of the masses, led by demagogues and republicans, while being open to judicious amendments to the representative system responding to genuine grievances.

Campbell observed that Derby danced 'his hornpipe among the burning ploughshares with considerable dexterity and felicity'.[74] A dissolution, Derby declared, would have to await the settlement of prior necessary measures. He wished to avoid unnecessary party questions and hoped his ministry, even as a minority in the Commons, would prove neither useless nor dishonourable in their conduct of the public affairs of the country. The Conservative government would pursue non-interference in the domestic affairs of other nations, consolidate national defences, remove corrupt electoral practices, desist from any unnecessary Reform of parliament, and, while protecting the interests of the Established Church, support religious liberty. Despite possessing power on sufferance, he was committed to restoring the Conservatives as a credible party of government.

Derby's statement offered reassurance on two pressing issues, Protection and the prospects of a dissolution. His strategy was to avoid commitment on the former until a general election had affirmed Commons feeling. As he informed Disraeli at the beginning of the year, he was not prepared to maintain a hopeless struggle over Protection indefinitely. Yet, until the country pronounced its opinion, he would publicly continue to declare a reimposition of duties on imports, including corn, desirable.[75] When accused by Lord Grey in the Lords, on 27 February, of intending to introduce a duty on foreign corn, Derby firmly repeated his intention not to do so without the sanction of an election. When Grey persisted in pressing the point, Derby sharply snapped back that 'the noble earl misunderstood, and now upon that misunderstanding, so corrected, he is proceeding still to argue'.[76] On Monday 15 March, Disraeli also informed the Commons that they had no intention, during the life of the present parliament, of reimposing a duty on foreign corn. This left open, Disraeli noted, the question of alleviating agricultural distress by readjusting the tax system, 'a declaration received with universal favour on the government side'.[77] In the meantime, he announced, the government would introduce bills disfranchising the notoriously corrupt constituency of St Albans, reforming Chancery, and attending to the militia. Derby congratulated Disraeli on a '*magnificent* speech'; 'I have no fear that there should appear any divergence of opinion which could by possibility be laid hold of between us.'[78]

Derby wished a dissolution to be deferred for as long as possible. 'I should not', he advised Disraeli, 'deprecate a little *factious* delay to *our* necessary measures, which should *unavoidably* carry on parliament till June or July.'[79] The longer the Conservatives held power, with Protection held in abeyance, the better, he judged, the party's prospects became. Aberdeen privately promised Derby the Peelites' support in carrying out the necessary business of the session, on the understanding of a dissolution during the summer. If, Derby concluded, 'the Peelites act on their personal intentions and we are firm but temperate in tone, our game is won'.[80] During March he was called on by Newcastle and Minto in the Lords to declare when an election would be called. But he refused to make any commitment. This line had been confirmed at his first cabinet meeting on Saturday 6 March held at the Foreign Office. In the Lords on Monday 15 March, when pressed by Lord Beaumont on whether the ministry intended to bring back the Corn Laws after the coming election, the prime minister evasively replied that he would not announce his election platform until such time as the interests of the country required a dissolution of parliament. In his reply to Beaumont, Disraeli reported to his sister, 'Lord Derby did wonders.'[81]

During a dinner, given for the cabinet by the Lord President, Lord Lonsdale, at his residence in Carlton House Terrace on Wednesday 17 March, Derby urged upon Disraeli the supreme importance of maintaining exactly this same line in the Commons.[82] The next morning Derby was visited by Lord Hardinge at St James's Square, who conveyed word from Gladstone confirming that the Peelites intended to support his government on the understanding of a dissolution during the summer and a new parliament in November. On this basis the Peelites would not oppose a vote on supplies. Derby promptly summarized for Disraeli the position to be taken in the Commons: a pledge to dissolve with least delay once all necessary measures, including the Militia Bill, were secured; Protection to be finally settled in an autumn session, so as to start fair in 1853; income tax should be renewed for a year, so as to avoid the necessity of parliament meeting before 10 October; such pledges and provisions for parliament meeting in October enabling supplies to be voted for the next twelve months.[83] Firmness and moderation, he encouraged, would secure success.[84] As Derby hoped, in light of the government's pledge to dissolve parliament as soon as possible, on Monday 22 March Russell withdrew his opposition to the army and navy estimates.

Despite the highly regarded Lord St Leonards, as Lord Chancellor, spearheading the government's law reforms (streamlining common-law procedure and remodelling Chancery practice), and Malmesbury addressing foreign affairs, Derby immediately took upon himself the main burden of speaking to the government's policies in the Lords. In response to Lord

Clanricarde, on Tuesday 16 March, he supported the establishment of an inquiry into the system of combined national education in Ireland for Catholics and Protestants.[85] On Thursday 18 March he spoke against the proposal to form a volunteer rifle corps to supplement rural police forces in England. The same evening he parried Lord Shaftesbury's request for reform of the regulations regarding lunatic criminals[86] and responded to the motion brought forward by Newcastle, similar to that presented by Russell in the Commons, calling for clarification of the government's commercial policy. Once again, Derby declared that this contentious issue would be finally decided in the autumn, once the country had had an opportunity to pronounce on this critical question.[87] Aberdeen declared himself satisfied with the prime minister's response. The attempt by Graham to bring both Russell and Cobden behind a Free Trade initiative in the Commons was forestalled. In an audience with the Queen at Buckingham Palace on 21 March, Derby reported that 'the government had gained a good deal of ground during the last week, and that there was now a general disposition to let the necessary measures pass parliament'.[88] Fear of radical democracy might in due course, he anticipated, rally more MPs, including anxious Whigs, around the Conservative banner. In writing to his sister, Disraeli concurred: 'I think we have turned the corner. The public seems with us, and our raw recruits have not made a single mistake.'[89]

In close encounter stand ye firm!
(Derby, *The Iliad of Homer*, ii. 9)

With characteristic self-assurance Derby took the burdensome task of defending the government's policies in the Lords on himself. Colleagues were given little encouragement to speak. On Thursday 25 March he replied to Ellenborough's request for further information regarding the outbreak of hostilities in Burma. In response to the ill treatment of two British sea-captains in Rangoon, the Indian Governor General, Lord Dalhousie, had dispatched a small naval force, under Commodore Lambert, to negotiate an indemnity from the Burmese Governor of Rangoon. After being snubbed by the Governor, Lambert's frigate was fired upon by the Burmese. Although the reports received in London were incomplete, Derby informed the Lords that a clash of arms had occurred but no declaration of war had yet been issued.[90] The following evening, Friday 26 March, he responded to Lord Wicklow's enquiry as to whether or not the government planned to renew the Irish Encumbered Estates Court Act, due to expire during the coming year. While intending to extend the Act for a period, the prime minister advised the Lords that the Lord Chancellor would consider the current arrangement with a view to transferring the implementation of the Act to the Court of Chancery.[91] On Monday 29 March, Derby defended the decision of Lord Dalhousie and the directors of the East India Company to confiscate the territories of Ameer Ali Marad in Sindh.[92] And the following evening he responded to Minto and Newcastle's demand for a statement of the government's intentions as to when the present parliament would be dissolved. He wished to avoid an early dissolution, he pronounced, which would only bring on a short and hurried summer session. The present parliament would, in all likelihood, sit for a further three months, after which a general election would be called prior to an autumn session.[93]

Alongside championing the government in the Lords and guiding his ministerial novices in their departmental business, Derby also kept in close touch with Disraeli and Beresford in the Commons. It was in the Lower House that the fate of his government would be decided. The Militia question, which had occasioned Russell's departure from office, now stood as the immediate test of the government's capability. On Monday 29 March, Derby celebrated his fifty-third birthday. The same day Walpole, despite Beresford's reservations, introduced his Militia Bill, creating an additional permanent force of 80,000 men for national defence, financed by bounties of £3 or £4, the period of training and drilling to be twenty-one days. Control of the militia was transferred from the Home Office to the Secretary of War. Only opposed by the Manchester School radicals, Cobden wishing to challenge the ministry to instant combat, the measure was generally welcomed. Prince Albert, to Derby's relief, agreed to keep his criticisms of the bill confidential. But Walpole's idiosyncratic proposal, endorsed by Disraeli, to grant the parliamentary vote to all volunteers, ruffled Derby, who promptly ensured that this particular clause was dropped. The unexpected attempt on Friday 23 April by Russell, courted by Cobden, subsequently to scuttle the bill on its second reading was rapidly quashed by Palmerston's vigorous defence of the measure. The bill was easily passed by 355 to 165 votes.

Palmerston decried Russell's factiousness over a measure accepted in principle by both sides of the House. Herbert considered Russell's move 'disastrous'.[94] Charles Greville concluded that Russell had 'set up the government completely. Nothing could exceed the exultation of the ministerialists.'[95] Prince Albert thought that 'Lord John Russell has by his false move ... quite destroyed his position as leader of the liberal party. The Whigs are all furious with him and declare that they won't follow him any longer.'[96] As a result, the bill was finally carried, on 26 April, with a significant number of Whigs and Peelites supporting the government. To a man the Conservatives voted for the bill. In an impressive demonstration of unity 234 Conservative MPs supported the measure; none opposed it. With divisions within the opposition, in particular the bitter rivalry between Russell and Palmerston, securing a majority for the ministry, Palmerston's future intentions became the object of great interest. Considering Russell to have forced him into an independent position, Palmerston refused to acknowledge Russell as his leader and radiated a marked benevolence towards Derby's ministry. Aided by Wellington and his new Conservative whip in the Lords, the adroit Lord Colville, Derby quickly steered the Militia measure through the Upper House, despite the opposition of Lansdowne and Grey.

Derby's wearying exertions in the Lords, meanwhile, continued. On 2 April he proposed a Select Committee, in anticipation of the renewal of the East India Company's Charter, to inquire into the future government of the Asian subcontinent. His cabinet, he declared, would be guided by the opinion of parliament. Three days later he confirmed that war with Burma now existed. A military force under the command of General Godwin was being sent to Rangoon from India. The Indian government, he explained, had hoped to avoid war, but prompt measures by Lord Dalhousie meant there was a reasonable expectation of a short conflict leading to a decisive victory by British troops. The government had no wish to annex Burma. The compulsory annexation of the Burmese Empire would be 'a great misfortune'. Yet, Derby insisted, the dignity of British interests and the safety of their Indian Empire must be maintained.[97] The announcement of a motion by Lord Albemarle on 2 April on the Maynooth grant led to an awkward debate on Tuesday 20 April. Clanricarde pressed the government on their attitude to the 1845 Act, which made the grant permanent. Derby, who had as a member of Peel's cabinet strongly advocated the measure, repeated that his cabinet had no plans to alter the Act. Grey, Minto, and Clanricarde declared the prime minister's response unsatisfactory. Once again, Derby stated that the government had no immediate intention of altering the law, although he conceded that they might, at some time in the future, come to a different conclusion. For the present, however, he wished to avoid exciting religious feelings on the matter.[98]

Lord Shaftesbury's detailed Lords statement on the unsanitary conditions prevailing in the metropolis, on Thursday 29 April, brought on a major debate about the disease, high mortality, wretched housing, deficient water supply, fetid sewage, and noxious smoke pollution blighting London. In response, Derby acknowledged the great evils Shaftesbury vividly described, but regretted that Shaftesbury proposed no practical remedies. Nonetheless, the prime minister assured the Lords that Lord John Manners, as Head of the Board of Works, was considering what might be done. Derby identified four major causes of disease. First, there existed overcrowded burial grounds and cemeteries; secondly, there was a deficient supply of clean water; thirdly, there were inadequate means of disposing of sewage; and finally, these sources of pollution were exacerbated by the accumulation of waste and rubbish in the capital. He opposed bringing these problems under the provisions of the 1848 Board of Health Act. Although solutions sought through a single statutory authority, such as the General Board of Health, might appear desirable, he believed enforced obedience to new sanitary regulations would be difficult to secure and that voluntary compliance was preferable. To this end, he amended Shaftesbury's call for the government's interposition in these matters to the statement that they required the ministry's attention. The compulsory powers enjoyed by the General Board of Health, established in response to Edwin Chadwick's campaign for the centralized regulation of public health, were already generating a political reaction to state control of social issues. Derby promised further discretionary powers to enhance the authority of local bodies to deal with the sanitary afflictions of London, but he declined to pursue statutory state solutions.[99]

Derby's diligence brought immediate reward. On 1 May the *Illustrated London News* suggested a change in the popular perception of his government. 'It seems no longer to be a Ministry on sufferance or of necessity, in default of any and every other, but a Ministry on its own merits, with an obedient House of Commons to work on its behalf, and a prosperous career before it.'[100] Even more strikingly, Greville noted in his journal on 12 May that, 'while a short time ago everybody said a Derby government was impossible, it now appears to be the only government which is possible'.[101] The possession of office might yet deliver the reality of power.

The prospect of Disraeli's budget on 30 April inevitably raised the spectre of Protection. The court was initially alarmed at rumours of the cabinet reimposing duties on foreign imports. But, as Derby made clear to the sovereign, privately he regarded the immediate imposition of even a moderate duty on foreign corn as impracticable. A relieved Queen Victoria concluded that Derby was 'quite prepared to drop Protection'.[102] Both Walpole, from within the cabinet, and Lord Shaftesbury, from without the ministry, advised Derby publicly to renounce Protection. This, however, he was reluctant to do until the futility of the Protectionist cause was clearly affirmed. His cabinet colleagues, Lord Hardwicke, Manners, and Henley, fiercely maintained their opposition to Free Trade. Shortly before taking office Manners had declared 'that we cease to be a party if we drop the principle of Protection'.[103] Derby could not, he told Prince Albert, with honour or credit abandon Protection until the country had delivered its judgement against it.[104] The upcoming election, he anticipated, would return a Free Trade, though Conservative, majority. Only then could he honourably renounce his party's commitment to Protection. He proposed to Disraeli a 'provisional' budget with an extension for one year of the income tax. Disraeli, however, favoured an immediate renunciation of Protection. In the event of a dissolution, Disraeli believed, Protection would prove an electoral liability. To his friend the radical MP James Clay, Disraeli commented that Protection was not only as dead as Lazarus, but 'already stinketh'.[105] On 27 February *The Times* declared the established system of Free Trade to be 'as unassailable a part of our present constitution as the Catholic Relief Act or the Reform bill'.[106]

Derby and his Chancellor differed over the precise moment to surrender their commitment to Protection. While the prime minister wished publicly to maintain the commitment to Protection until after the next election, Disraeli looked to jettison the policy prior to facing the hustings. As a result, Disraeli's budget speech to a packed Commons on Friday 30 April proved, Derby protested fiercely, 'one of the strongest Free Trade speeches … ever heard'.[107] The scene reminded an incensed Derby of the biblical complaint 'I called thee to curse mine enemies, and lo thou hast blessed them altogether.' Disraeli, while extending the income tax for a year and proposing no further change of taxation, dwelt at length on the benefits to the nation produced by Wood's Free Trade budget of 1851. 'We saw with our own eyes', *The Times* approvingly commented, 'the last rag of Protection put into a red box, and when the lid was opened, a perfect Chancellor of the Exchequer appeared, who immediately opened his mouth and made a first rate financial statement.'[108]

Disraeli, Derby rightly suspected, hoped to force the premier's hand by bringing Derby's private opinion into alignment with his public statements. In a long, impassioned remonstrance to Disraeli, penned that evening, an irate Derby reported the description of the Chancellor's performance as a 'eulogy of Peel by Disraeli'.[109] Disraeli's speech, he feared, would result in the government being 'justly stigmatised as impostors who have obtained office under false pretences'. Despite the lucidity of the speech, he continued, 'I think the silence of our own friends, and the rapturous and triumphant cheers' of the opposite side of the House, were warnings of 'great discontent' among the government's supporters and future 'great embarrassment'. A premature abandonment of Protection, Derby believed, would be a strategic error. In the future Disraeli must, he insisted, 'take a more accurate measure of the feelings of the party with whom we act and *must act*'. Malmesbury thought the budget speech had 'produced a bad effect in the country, for the farmers, though reconciled to giving up Protection, expected relief in other ways ... I fear this will tell at the next election.'[110] Greville judged Disraeli's speech 'a great performance, very able, and ... received with great applause in the House', but 'extraordinary' for 'the frank, full, and glowing panegyric he passed on the effect of the Free Trade measures passed by Sir Robert Peel'.[111] Prince Albert observed that Disraeli's speech had 'caused the greatest sensation. All the newspapers particularly the liberal and radical ones are singing his praise ... The *protectionists* themselves (if one can call them any longer so ...) are a good deal startled and don't know what to make of the triumph of Peel which the very man gives him who mercilessly hunted him down.'[112]

A few days later, in a speech at a Mansion House banquet, Derby sought to repair the situation. Where Disraeli proposed a contentious clarity, he restored a conciliatory ambiguity. Derby was careful to praise his Chancellor, so as to avoid any public appearance of ministerial division. Disraeli's speech, he observed, showed how a man of high ability, vivid imagination, and great eloquence could master the driest financial topics. Yet, he continued, no government could lose sight of the interests of those large classes unconnected with commerce who were mainly producers. Reconciling competing interests required mutual concession. Thus, while avoiding any specific commitment, he sought to assuage the agricultural Protectionists. The soothing balm of mutual compromise, he hoped, might ease Conservative indignation. Despite Derby's efforts, Greville regarded the Mansion House speech, with its 'long and laboured exposition on the doctrine of compromise', as 'a snub to Disraeli'.[113] Yet Derby's hope of calming agricultural alarm succeeded. In the peroration of his Mansion House speech he declared that the government's aim was to show that they were not a set of reckless men. Conciliatory moderation was their watchword. When his elder son arrived back in England from India in late May, Lord Stanley noted that 'the farmers, and country gentlemen generally, appeared satisfied that nothing more could be done for them: at least no complaint was heard from them, nor did any unreasonable expectation seem to be excited'.[114] The most obstinate resistance came from Protectionists within the cabinet. The press drew from the episode the conclusion that old party distinctions were being eradicated. As well as Palmerston's repudiation of Russell's leadership, it was noted that Graham no longer sat with the Peelites in the Commons, but took a place alongside Russell. 'Common sense and arithmetic', the *Illustrated London News* declared on 8 May, 'have remodelled factions ... the old traditions have grown dim, the old watchwords have become obsolete'. Finance was 'more than ever the touchstone of political capacity; and face to face with that practical monster, the shadowy ghosts of Whig and Tory dwindle and fade away'.[115]

With the Commons preoccupied with finance, Derby continued to shoulder the burden of ministerial speaking in the Lords. On Monday 3 May he countered the Earl of Rosse's criticisms of the Board of Works' management of land drainage in Ireland. Irish landowners, Rosse complained, faced excessive expenditure for work undertaken without an open tender for contracts, projects often being left unfinished. Nor were the Board of Works' accounts available for proprietors to examine. Derby acceded to Rosse's request for a Committee of Inquiry, agreeing that, where extensive public power was exercised, the conduct of officials must be strictly monitored.[116] Later that evening he reassured Lord Granville that there was no plan to transfer the TransAtlantic Packet Station from Liverpool to western ports in Ireland.[117] Similarly, the following evening he sought to defuse debate over the fines imposed upon Sir David Salomons, elected as MP for Greenwich in June 1851, for refusing, as a practising Jew, to take the parliamentary oath. Derby declined to enter into a discussion of the general principles raised by the case, but indicated that the government would favour a conciliatory course with regard to Salomons personally. So might sectarian dispute be avoided.[118] In the same spirit, on 10 May, he supported the Bishop of London's announcement of a forthcoming bill giving the bishops greater influence in ecclesiastical cases brought before the Privy Council. In matters of false doctrine and heresy, Derby pronounced, the judgement of the bishops should be regarded as decisive. Thus might outcries over cases such as the Gorham judgement, with the Erastian views of Liberal Privy Councillors overriding ecclesiastical opinion, be avoided.[119] Consistently, during early 1852, he sought to soothe divisive passions.

Having survived the budget debate, on 10 May Disraeli moved for leave to introduce to the Commons a bill assigning the four seats disfranchised from the boroughs of St Albans and Sudbury to the West Riding of

Yorkshire and South Lancashire. The disfranchisement of St Albans had
proceeded quickly through parliament. Introduced by Sir George Grey
as Home Secretary, prior to Russell's resignation, on 16 February, the
bill was passed by the Commons during March. On 22 April, Derby
oversaw the second reading of the St Albans Disfranchisement Bill in
the Lords. As shown by the Committee of Inquiry, he observed, since
1832 and the creation of the £10 householder vote, the borough had
become even more venal than before the Reform Act. In St Albans direct
bribery had been practised over many elections. Between 1832 and 1852
some £24,000 was spent on corrupt practices. Even Lord Verulam, who
exercised the strongest influence in the borough from his neighbouring
estate at Gorhambury, felt incapable of defending the corrupt constituency
from disfranchisement. On 3 May the royal assent was given to the
Disfranchisement Bill and St Albans was stripped of its parliamentary
representation. As, during early May, Disraeli prepared to reassign these
seats, and the two seats disfranchised from Sudbury in Suffolk in 1844, to
West Yorkshire and South Lancashire, Derby supplied him with detailed
information about the two county divisions. By splitting each division
into two parts, along geographical boundaries recommended by Derby,
it was hoped to preserve at least two Conservative seats in each. The
prime minister also wrote privately to Gladstone on 9 May requesting
his support for the measure. But Gladstone replied the following day
that he regarded the bill as a violation of the government's agreement
not to introduce controversial legislation prior to the upcoming election.
Gladstone thought the proposed reassignment a reform too far. He would,
he warned Derby, have to oppose it.[120] In the Commons that evening
Gladstone attacked the proposal as unnecessary before the dissolution
and Disraeli's motion was rejected by 234 to 148 votes, despite Disraeli's
adept use of the statistics provided by the prime minister. But Derby did
not believe much harm was done by the defeat. It 'will not, I think', he
reassured Disraeli, 'hurt us in the country'.[121] Upon meeting Russell at the
Queen's Ball that evening, Derby affected a calm indifference, declaring
to Russell, 'what will you get by all this?'[122]

Derby, suffering from the onset of gout, was much more anxious about
the impending Commons debate on Maynooth, an issue he had already
defused in the Lords. This was particularly the case given Eglinton's reports
from Dublin Castle of the peace currently prevailing in Ireland, which, if
it continued, would soon lead, he commented, to the Irish forgetting how
to shoot each other.[123] On Tuesday 11 May, Richard Spooner delivered a
violently anti-Catholic speech in the Commons calling for a Committee

of Inquiry into Maynooth College, with a view to revoking the permanent grant established in 1845. Prolonged acrimonious debate followed during May, with Disraeli eventually securing the abandonment of Spooner's motion in mid-June. Thus Disraeli sought to calm 'the excited tone of the House'.[124] As always, Derby exerted his influence to dissipate impassioned sectarian feelings. Likewise, when Graham provoked bitter exchanges on Irish education, during Commons discussion of supplies on 3 June, the debate was swiftly curtailed. 'A studied ambiguity', Greville observed, cloaked the government's policy.[125] They were 'afraid in one case of affronting Protestant bigotry, and in the other of wanting to stimulate the zeal of the churchmen in their favour'.[126]

The government's tactic of anaesthetizing discussion was reinforced by Derby's ill health during early May. Gout kept him away from Westminster between 10 and 18 May and produced momentary, though acute, alarm in Disraeli; 'how things are to go on without him baffles my imagination', Disraeli confessed.[127] Derby's enforced absence from the Lords on 14 and 17 May threw the burden of ministerial speaking onto an anxious Malmesbury. Nonetheless, Derby rallied himself to attend Malmesbury's cabinet dinner on Wednesday 12 May and Lady Derby's large reception at Downing Street the following day, celebrating the Queen's birthday, to which nearly 800 guests came. By 11 p.m., the *Morning Post* reported, the guests had completely filled the rooms at No. 10 and blocked the staircase, the party continuing until 2 a.m.

By 18 May, Derby was again on his feet in the Lords and the following weeks brought an unrelenting stint of speaking on all aspects of government policy. His critical role as the mainstay of the ministry, underlined by his temporary absence, was apparent to all. His first task, supported by Ellenborough, was to defend General Godwin from accusations of delay in sailing for Burma.[128] On Friday 21 May, having earlier that day been visited at St James's Square by his elder son fresh off the boat from India, and after an audience with the Queen at Buckingham Palace, he was then drawn into another unwelcome debate on Maynooth, Lord Breadalbane presenting petitions calling for repeal of the permanent grant to the Catholic seminary. Derby rejected Breadalbane's argument that it was contrary to all principle to give assistance to the education of Roman Catholics. At the same time, he rejected Lord Beaumont's argument from the opposition benches that the education given at Maynooth was a matter of indifference to the government. If, he concluded, it was proved that the education of the Roman Catholic priesthood at Maynooth inculcated doctrines subversive of loyalty to the Crown and morality, he would consider amending the 1845 Act. But, until then, the government had no intention of altering the existing legislation.[129] On Monday 24 May, Derby initiated debate on the second reading of the Property Tax Continuance Bill. He avoided any statement on the general principles of the nation's financial affairs and dampened down any broader discussion. The bill extended the tax for one year as part of the status quo, prior to a wider-ranging debate in the next parliament. Extension of the property tax in the interim avoided a deficit of £250,000 in the current year and £500,000 in the coming year. After a long debate, during which he spoke twice, Derby secured approval of the second reading.[130]

Three days later, on Thursday 27 May, petitions presented by the Whig Lord Harrowby, calling for separate parliamentary representation to be given to the educated intelligence of the country, occasioned a debate on the current franchise. In the Commons debate, on the assignment of the seats disfranchised from St Albans and Sudbury on 10 May, Disraeli had considered the enfranchisement of professional bodies and unenfranchised universities, but dismissed the option as impractical, though perhaps desirable. In the Lords, on 27 May, Derby reaffirmed this view. He agreed with Harrowby that, since 1832, it had become increasingly difficult for men not known to the public, not possessing that readiness of speech, nor avowing those extreme opinions which recommended them to populous constituencies, to obtain seats in the Commons. He concurred that it was undesirable to reduce everything connected with representation of the nation's interests to mere numbers. Property and intelligence must also be weighed. But enfranchising intelligence was difficult. Enfranchising the Scottish universities on the same basis as Oxford, Cambridge, and Trinity College Dublin was problematic, because the Scottish universities were numerically small. Enfranchising Inns of Court would give further representation to lawyers, who found least difficulty in getting into parliament, while it was hard to differentiate between the numerous learned societies and to decide which might be enfranchised. Harrowby raised the issue of the decline in the representation of colonial interests in the Commons since 1832. Derby acknowledged this fact, but again found an acceptable solution difficult to formulate. He declared introducing greater representation of intelligence, education, science, and colonial expertise into the Commons to be an important subject worthy of serious consideration. This was particularly so if it helped to neutralize the prevailing tendency to throw all power, not into the hands of the most intelligent and most enlightened, but into the hands of the most numerous and most easily misguided. But the government could not see any practical immediate means of securing such a desirable end.[131]

Derby's unrelenting exertions in the Lords continued into June. He defended the government's handling of the construction of the Halifax to Quebec railway against Grey's criticisms.[132] An awkward debate was occasioned on 10 June by Lord Brougham's presenting petitions from West Indian proprietors complaining that the 1846 Sugar Duties Act had increased foreign traffic in slaves, diminished property values, and impoverished West Indian landowners. Grey vehemently attacked Brougham. In a deliberately neutral brief response, Derby regretted that, in the present state of the public mind, a remedy was impractical.[133] On 11 and 14 June, Lansdowne initiated a debate on education, pressing the government on whether it intended to alter the current administration of the parliamentary grant for educational purposes. Once again, in a deliberately neutral response, Derby espoused religious moderation and sought to avoid exciting extreme opinions. As Disraeli described it to the Queen, the government were opposed to 'both the violent parties in the Church, and in favour of a firm, though temperate, course ... which may conciliate a vast majority, and tend to terminate dissension'.[134] As in foreign affairs, so on religious issues, Derby looked to follow a calm, deliberate, and conciliatory course. Later in the evening of 14 June, Derby carried an amendment to the bill championed by Lansdowne establishing tribunals for the consideration of cases of electoral corruption, Derby's amendment excluding university and county seats from the provisions of the legislation. In addition, it was agreed that both the Lords and the Commons must concur in the appointment of an inquiry, so as to prevent the Commons from exercising such power arbitrarily. After a prolonged debate Derby finally secured the second reading of the government's Militia Bill on 15 June and, after attending a ball given by his aunt Lady Wilton the following evening at 7 Grosvenor Square, he rebuffed a hostile amendment from Lord Stradbroke in the committee stage on 17 June.

Meanwhile, Pakington, as Colonial Secretary, steered through the Commons legislation establishing a new constitution for New Zealand, the suspension of the 1846 constitution expiring in March 1853. Pakington's measure marked a further step towards colonial self-government. This was a move welcomed by the Governor George Grey and the constitutional associations formed by white settlers. The new constitution comprised a quasi-federal system with six provinces being represented in a bicameral General Assembly. The franchise was granted to adult males who owned or rented property, adult male Maori holding land according to English tenurial conditions also being enfranchised. The General Assembly controlled most internal matters, with external relations and Maori land purchase being reserved to the British government and the Governor. Initially one of the most criticized of Derby's cabinet appointments, Pakington established 'a very tolerable character in his office for industry and apprehension'.[135] Pakington saw his bill through committee in the Commons in early June and secured the third reading on 17 June. One week later Derby steered the bill through its committee stage in the Lords, seeing off a hostile amendment proposed by Newcastle. The constitutions of the colonies, he informed the Lords, must be based on British rather than American models, on the monarchical rather than the republican principle of government, which meant having property, not just population, duly represented.[136] Pakington's bill received the royal assent on 30 June.

As premier Derby exercised a particularly close oversight of foreign policy. Conservative foreign policy in 1852 was shaped by Derby, as much as being proposed by Malmesbury. On assuming office Derby reassured the Queen that he would carefully review all drafts coming from the Foreign Office, prior to them being sent on to the monarch.[137] The dangerous tendencies that Palmerston had shown for unilateral action under Russell would be avoided. Not that Malmesbury's views did not match Derby's own aims; each shared common diplomatic objectives. Amicable agreement characterized their close consultation. But Derby's close control of the Foreign Office, at one remove, reassured the Queen about Malmesbury's official inexperience and the influence of his long-standing friendship with Louis Napoleon. Over the following months Malmesbury proved Derby's diligent junior partner in pursuing a calm, temperate, deliberate, and conciliatory foreign policy, while Derby's conscientious annotations and careful redrafting of Malmesbury's dispatches maintained his tight control of his government's diplomacy. The wish to retain, as far as possible, cordial relations with all the major European powers, not to disturb the European status quo established by the Vienna Settlement, to avoid binding bilateral alliances, to refrain from interference in the internal affairs of other European nations, and to adhere faithfully to existing treaties, underpinned Derby and Malmesbury's cooperation. So might European stability be assured, limited British military resources managed, and the prosperity of Britain's maritime colonial relations undisturbed. Both agreed that the entente with France should be preserved, though not to the exclusion of continuing cordial relations with Austria, Prussia, and Russia. In this spirit Malmesbury, as closely advised by Derby, restored friendly relations with Vienna, which, following an assault by an Austrian army officer on a British subject, Erskine Mather, in Florence, had become dangerously acrimonious. While refusing to accept Austrian complaints about Britain sheltering political refugees, during March 1852 Derby and Malmesbury resolved what they regarded as a hazardous wrangle. By presenting compensation for the Mather incident as a matter best placed before the Tuscan government, Malmesbury removed it as a dangerous irritant in Anglo-Austrian relations.

During March improved diplomatic relations with Russia were established, the veteran Russian Chancellor Count Nesselrode conveying his satisfaction with the Conservative government's commitment to considered conciliation. This, in turn, allowed Derby and Malmesbury to encourage a concerted diplomatic response, including Austria and Russia, effectively countering fears of a French invasion of Belgium; hostile attacks on Louis Napoleon in the Belgian press were creating anxieties that France might occupy her vulnerable immediate neighbour, to whose independence Britain, under the terms of an 1839 treaty, was a guarantor. By March concerted diplomacy was appearing to defuse this dangerously destabilizing issue. Malmesbury also presided over the final discussions leading to the London Treaty in May 1852, temporarily resolving the dispute between Denmark and the German States over Schleswig-Holstein; a settlement of the succession to the Greek throne was secured; and the status of the Swiss canton of Neuchâtel was clarified.

Derby praised Malmesbury's efforts, his Foreign Secretary's instructions being '*excellent*—terse, clear and admirably expressed. If all my young soldiers show as well, we shall exhibit a formidable line of battle.'[138] Aberdeen privately expressed his 'very good opinion of Lord Derby's principles of foreign policy'.[139] As Malmesbury's Under-Secretary, Lord Stanley acquired a high regard for the Foreign Secretary. Malmesbury's judgement 'on indifferent matters' was 'sound' and his Tory opinions 'not beyond the limits of commonsense'. He 'goes at once to the point', Stanley noted; he 'has no illusions, no favourite theories: a good judge of character, agreeable in conversation, fond of anecdote ... no malice, good temper, considerable patience' and 'very industrious'. He 'gave up his whole time to labour while in power'. Malmesbury's deficiencies as a speaker, however, did not do justice to his merits. Therefore, 'his real claims [were] very far above his reputation'.[140]

Yet Derby's supervision and Aberdeen's endorsement did not prevent the opposition from eagerly criticizing the conscientious Malmesbury. His inexperience, laying him open to charges of naivety, ineptitude, and negligence, made him an easy target. In the Lords in mid-March

the Whig Lord Beaumont accused the Foreign Secretary of intending
to compromise British law in response to Austrian complaints over the
granting of asylum by Britain to political refugees, following the revolutions
of 1848. Malmesbury successfully saw off this attack by firmly repudiating
Beaumont's charge, while restating his belief in negotiation as essential
to preserving Britain's cordial diplomatic relations in Europe. Continuing
difficulties over the Mather incident offered both Beaumont and Granville
a further opportunity to declare that Malmesbury was insufficiently robust
in his defence of British interests. Privately, Malmesbury believed Mather
had behaved belligerently and that the cash reparation of £5,000 demanded
by Mather's family was exorbitant. But opposition accusations that an inept
Malmesbury had shown weakness in his defence of British interests proved
an unconvincing characterization of the Foreign Secretary's instinctive
wish for mutual compromise. In an extended Lords statement on 21 June,
Derby defended Malmesbury's handling of the issue. He advised the
Lords that the government's response had been as much his own as it was
Malmesbury's policy:

> for the whole course of these proceedings I avow myself as fully and entirely
> responsible as my noble Friend; for not one step did he take, not one
> direction did he give, without my previous knowledge and consent; and if
> he is to be censured, I am just as much and as entirely open to censure as he
> from whatever the quarter the censure my proceed.[141]

The prime minister repelled Beaumont and Granville's attacks, finally
forcing Beaumont to withdraw his motion criticizing Malmesbury's conduct. A similar motion moved by Russell in the Commons was also
defeated. Malmesbury believed 'the whole thing' was 'got up for the
coming elections'.[142]

While defending his Foreign Secretary, Derby also dutifully supported
his Lord Chancellor's law reforms, speaking in favour of the Suitors in
Chancery Relief Bill on 24 June and overseeing the third Lords reading of
the Irish Encumbered Estates Bill on Monday 28 June, designed to render
the sale of Irish estates more efficient and the work of the Irish encumbered estates commissioners easier. This legislation complemented Lord
St Leonards's other legal reforms streamlining common-law procedure, remodelling Chancery practice, and overhauling the system of equity. These
legal reforms, Derby believed, comprised an important substantiation of
his government's claim to be delivering careful improvement.

In shouldering the greater burden of Lords speaking on behalf of the
government himself, Derby's exertions embraced not just the sublime,

but also the mundane. In April, Viscount Torrington presented to the Lords the complaints of respectable London coffee traders about the practice engaged in by unscrupulous competitors of mixing chicory with ground coffee beans. This, they feared, was destroying the market and the consumption of coffee was diminishing. Accepting that it was the duty of the government to protect the public from fraud, Derby promised action.[143] On 24 June he outlined new regulations ensuring the purity of coffee sales. Immediately Lord Redesdale enquired if the same restrictions would apply to the use of the mangel-wurzel. Derby happily confirmed that all articles that might be mixed with coffee, whether mangel-wurzel, roasted corn, or roasted horse beans, would be prohibited by the regulations.[144]

Having held off a general election until the summer, in June Derby requested a dissolution of parliament. On Wednesday 30 June he delivered a review of his government's performance since March, prior to a dissolution on 1 July. He defended their legislative achievement, which was due, in some measure, he claimed, to the absence of party spirit which had characterized the session. Upon becoming prime minister he had identified certain measures as of paramount importance. The Militia Bill had been an imperative. Next in importance had been the legal reforms seen through by Lord St Leonards. Also, a modified New Zealand constitution had established representative institutions in the colony. Beyond this, sanitary reform for London had been recognized as desirable. Over the four months since March his government had abstained, as far as possible, from controversial or party topics. During 'this *interregnum* of parties', he concluded, we 'have had an opportunity of submitting to the calm and dispassionate consideration of both Houses of parliament measures absolutely and entirely stripped of all party character'.[145] In the next session, he continued, it would be the government's duty to bring forward a measure endeavouring to do justice to those classes of the community suffering under an inequality of pressure and injustice of taxation. Not just agriculture, but also the nation's colonial and shipping interests, Derby believed, had been harmed by Free Trade legislation since 1846. At the same time, the government would seek to reconcile, rather than aggravate, class animosity. Instead of supporting the interests of one class over the interests of others, their object would be to obtain the confidence of the country at large by doing justice to all the various interests of the country. Protection, he thereby implied, would not be reimposed. Derby's message was clear. The Conservatives could be trusted to provide safe, moderate government serving the interests of all sections of the community. The debate ended sourly, however, when both Grey and Beaumont accused

Derby of merely implementing measures prepared by his predecessors which, if he had been in opposition, he would have resisted. The following day parliament dissolved.

> Arose contention fierce, and discord dire,
> Their warring passions rous'd on either side.
>
> (Derby, *The Iliad of Homer*, ii. 301)

The 1852 general election heralded, *The Economist* pronounced, 'an era of transition and disruption; and such are the necessary and most pregnant preliminaries of eras of reorganisation and action'.[146] With characteristic underlining Queen Victoria also caught the mood: '*One* thing is pretty *certain*—that *out* of the *present state* of confusion and discordance, a *sound state* of *parties* will be obtained, and *two parties*, as of old, will again exist, without which it is *impossible* to have a *strong* Government. *How* these parties, will be formed it is impossible to say at present.'[147] An acute sense of flux prevailed. 'All', Greville confirmed, 'is confusion and uncertainty.'[148]

Early in June, prior to attending the Ascot races, Derby received a draft of Disraeli's election address to the voters of Buckinghamshire, which the prime minister carefully annotated. It was subsequently submitted to the cabinet and approved by all, except Herries and Henley. Derby advised Disraeli 'to let down the Agricultural body as easily as one can'.[149] But Disraeli's address offered little comfort. It presented a Conservative policy reconciled to Free Trade, securing the Protectionists' aims by alternative fiscal means. 'The spirit of the age', Disraeli pronounced, 'tends to free intercourse, and no statesman can disregard with impunity the genius of the epoch in which he lives.'[150] The revision of taxation offered 'the possibility of greatly relieving the burdens of the community by adjustment and reduction', while 'the principles of Conservative progress' could 'terminate for ever, by just and conciliatory measures ... the fatal jealousy that rankles between town and country'. 'Conservative progress', Disraeli proposed, embraced maintenance of the colonial empire, the investigation of electoral corruption, and the commitment to the Protestantism of the English Crown. Thus, the *Edinburgh Review* mocked, 'an abstract entity was formed, called *Derbyism*; and the persons who were initiated into the mysterious and hidden doctrines to it, were called *Derbyites*'.[151]

The Derbyites' 'malleable and uncertain creed', as opponents characterized it, brought little clarity to the hustings.[152] The government, *Fraser's*

Magazine observed, 'looks, like Janus, two ways at once, and never looks steadily either way'.[153] A hostile Greville judged that 'Derby himself has shuffled and prevaricated and involved himself in a studied and laboured ambiguity, which has exposed him to bitter taunts and reproaches,' while Disraeli was 'a perfect will-o'-the-wisp'.[154] But for Derby himself, studied ambiguity, enabling him to keep Conservatives united, while carefully weaning his backbenchers from Protection, was a shrewd strategy for a minority ministry looking to deliver moderate policies. A larger number of candidates, 952 in all, stood for election than in the previous general elections of 1841 and 1847. The number of uncontested seats was lower than in the two previous general elections: 170 constituencies were uncontested. In many rural areas Protectionism remained prominent in backbench Conservative candidates' speeches. In North Lincolnshire the Conservative Robert Christopher won his seat with an explicit commitment to Protection, an embarrassment to Stanley, who, in King's Lynn, with the consent of his father, expressly abandoned the Protective principle in finance. Herries, in his election for Stamford, Stanley noted, was 'very Christopherian in his language'.[155] Anti-Catholicism also permeated many contests. Near Knowsley, in Liverpool, the sitting Peelite, Edward Cardwell, was defeated and the second seat, formerly held by the Liberals, also gained by the Conservatives. In the wake of large-scale Irish emigration into the borough anti-Catholicism clearly played a part in the Conservative success, particularly in the election of the staunchly Protestant William Mackenzie. This was a result Lord Henry Lennox privately denounced as 'absurd and bigoted'.[156] Following a petition the election was declared void, but in July 1853 the Conservatives retained both seats. In July 1852 in North Lancashire the former Peelite John Wilson Patten was re-elected as a Conservative, while in Preston one of the two seats, formerly both held by Liberals, was won by the Conservative Townley Parker. Yet, while playing well in Lancashire, anti-Catholicism, Disraeli feared, only alienated moderate opinion elsewhere.

Derby hoped the Conservatives might gain ten to sixteen seats in Ireland: landlord support and available campaign funds promised well, with support for the Whigs estranged by the Ecclesiastical Titles Bill. Under the chairmanship of Lord Naas at the Irish Office, supported by Lord Glengall, a small committee encouraged party activists in the Irish constituencies and dispersed funds. But Walpole's bungling pronouncement on the illegality of Catholic processions and his defence of electoral violence, principally the killing of six Irishmen by troops at Six Mile Bridge in Co. Clare, scuttled such hopes. While Walpole's reputation as a zealous Protestant was enhanced, the attempt to appease Catholic voters was dashed. Walpole's blunder was all the more damaging because of Derby and Malmesbury's secret diplomatic approaches to the Vatican. Rapprochement with the Pope, Derby hoped, might dampen hostility among Catholic priests in Ireland. As a member of Peel's cabinet in 1844 Derby had advocated the conciliation of Irish Catholics, if it could be done without alienating the great body of Irish Protestants. In late May 1852 Derby and Malmesbury confidentially discussed how formal diplomatic relations with the Vatican might be established, with a view to Pope Pius IX using his authority to prevent Irish priests engaging in political agitation.[157] But Walpole's bungling compromised their plans. As a result, the Catholic clergy in Ireland directed their congregations to vote against Conservative candidates, aided in their exertions by the newly formed Tenant Right League. Eglinton declared to Derby that 'the whole misery of Ireland is owing to the thraldom of the priests'.[158] From Co. Cork, Lord Ponsonby complained of those he described as Jesuits dragging his tenants to vote against his wishes, while the *Morning Post*, on 6 August, reported 'fresh indications' of that 'sectarian spirit, and of that hatred of race' which 'so palpably obstructed the social progress of Ireland'.[159] It proved one of the most violent periods of Irish electioneering in living memory.

In England electoral intimidation and bribery were also prominent. Most notoriously, the hot-headed Conservative chief whip, Beresford, became implicated in paying off electors in Derby. To the prime minister the ill-tempered Beresford admitted to having written 'some indiscreet letters'.[160] This error was compounded by Beresford's shouting at the crowd attending his own election in North Essex, 'I despise you from my heart as the vilest rabble I ever saw.' With his elder son pleading that the Conservatives must 'lighten the ship of such Jonahs', Derby prepared to abandon Beresford to a subsequent parliamentary inquiry.[161] The prime minister judged 'it would be worse now to try to evade enquiry than upon enquiry to be censured'.[162] Beresford's official days were numbered.

As the elections proceeded during July, Derby remained hopeful of 330 Conservatives in the new parliament. Indirectly he also reopened negotiations with Palmerston. The moment for 'the attempt at a coalition' seemed propitious.[163] Protection, the barrier in their discussion of February, was now, with the government looking to fiscal reform rather than the reimposition of import duties, no longer an obstacle. Openings in the Canadian and Indian governments would allow room to be made in the cabinet for Palmerston, with the hapless Walpole being made Speaker and Pakington elevated to the Lords. If Palmerston joined the government, Disraeli anticipated that Gladstone and Herbert would follow. Stanley agreed that Disraeli might allow 'an old helmsman' to take a 'spell at the wheel ... I think the time is fully come when you may act in the Palmerston affair. Everybody is talking about the probability of his joining us; his friends, as well as ours ... and I can see no motives for delay.'[164] Through Lady Bulwer, Disraeli sounded out Palmerston. But, while a guest of the Duke of Richmond at the Goodwood races at the end of July, Derby received word that negotiation with Palmerston had come to nothing. Lady Palmerston conveyed her husband's opinion 'that in England change of principle was more easily forgiven than change of party'. Believing he had few followers, Palmerston had no intention 'to walk across the House alone',[165] although he wished Derby all success and would assist him to the best of his power. As a result, Derby prepared to 'meet parliament without reconstruction'.[166] Disraeli reluctantly accepted that immediate reconstruction was now 'out of the question'.[167]

The final election returns frustrated Derby's early optimism and fulfilled Malmesbury's gloomier prediction that they would not get more than 300 supporters in the new Commons. *The Economist* calculated 290 Conservatives in the new parliament, *The Globe* estimated 289 Conservative MPs, while *The Times* on 28 July gave the Conservatives a total of 284 MPs.[168] Calculating the precise strength of Conservative support awaited the meeting of the new Commons. 'He is a bold one', Disraeli observed, 'who, in this rapid age, will prophesy.'[169] Though gaining some seats in English counties, the Conservatives failed to gain a Commons majority. The commitment to Free Trade of a majority of MPs survived and Protectionism affirmed as a minority cause. Disraeli's judgement was blunt: 'We built an opposition on Protection and Protestantism. The first the country has positively pissed upon,' while their 'second great principle' seemed 'to have worked us harm'.[170] In Ireland the Conservatives did not achieve the major breakthrough they hoped for, gaining only four additional seats. During the following weeks Derby also became increasingly pessimistic about the prospects of their secret initiative, pursued through Sir Henry Bulwer as Envoy Extraordinary to Tuscany, to establish diplomatic relations with the Vatican. The wish to encourage Pope Pius IX to condemn 'the crusade instituted by the R.C. priesthood [in Ireland] against the temporalities of the Established Church' looked hopeless.[171] Moreover, when rumours of the initiative were picked up by the British press during September, the prospect of diplomatic dealings with the Vatican were loudly denounced. The collapse of Irish electoral support for the Whigs, however, allowed a 53-MP-strong

Irish Independent party to be returned, committed to Irish tenant law reform and parliamentary independence from both the Whigs and the Conservatives. Greville judged there was 'no strong current of public opinion in favour of or against any men or any measures'.[172] While at Goodwood in early August and again troubled by gout, Derby 'was not in his usual uproarious spirits, chaffing and laughing from morning to night, but cheerful enough, though more sedate than is his wont'. Maintaining that he was 'well satisfied' with the election results, Derby, 'half in joke and half in earnest', talked of his government being forced out in a year's time.[173] Malmesbury was more optimistic. 'The present or rather future fate of the government depends on our bringing forward grand and good measures. If we do this and expound them to the country, Lord Derby will be *in again* even if turned out by faction for a few months.'[174] Clarendon concurred: 'the country at large being conservative wishes to keep the government in for fear of worse things'.[175]

Following the election Russell appeared to be 'dying for a fight and for office'.[176] But Whig resentment of Lord John was encouraging malcontents at Brooks's to think of bringing the elderly Lansdowne forward as the head of a reunified opposition. The leading Peelites, meanwhile, appeared increasingly hostile to the government. The Lord Chancellor, Lord St Leonards, reported that 'nothing can equal the *venom* of the Peelites'.[177] The vehement anti-Catholicism of many Conservative candidates in England had ensured the Peelites' collective disgust. Graham, Derby learnt from Disraeli, was prepared to serve under Russell, with only Gladstone's intentions remaining obscure.[178] During August, Aberdeen agreed with Russell to a Free Trade assault upon the ministry when parliament reassembled. To be put in a minority in the first week of the new parliament, Disraeli warned Derby, 'would be like a paralytic stroke in youth'.[179]

During late August, Derby became increasingly despondent. As in previous years, illness and depression descended during the end of the summer, as irritability and gloom clouded his demeanour. If much remained opaque about the results of the general election, one fact was clear. Protection was now dead. Despite widespread rural distress, a commanding majority of MPs remained firmly committed to the gospel of Free Trade. As the joyless Croker affirmed: 'The House of Commons is King, as the first attempt of any opposition to his popular Majesty will show.'[180] Apprehension broke through in an ill-tempered interview Derby requested with the British Ambassador to Paris, Lord Cowley. Having accepted his post on the understanding that it was not a political appointment, Cowley was taken aback by Derby's seeking to have Cowley's proxy vote in the Lords placed in his hands. When Cowley declined, Derby was infuriated. The prime minister declared that 'he was placed in a very difficult situation, not even knowing that he had a majority in the House of Lords, and as he considered this the last chance of establishing a Conservative government in this country he felt bound to make every exertion to maintain himself in power'.[181] As a compromise Cowley agreed to place his proxy with Wellington. But Derby's anxious tone betrayed his growing apprehension. Was the corpse of his administration to be buried in the coffin of Protectionism? The 'paralytic stroke' feared by Disraeli now appeared to Derby a distinct possibility.

Staying during the summer at St Leonard's, the house near Windsor which he rented for his convenience when attending the Queen, Derby's spirits were partly lifted by visits from friends, including the 40-year-old artist Edward Lear. He took the opportunity to purchase some of Lear's Mediterranean landscape paintings. Lord and Lady Derby then visited the Duke of Rutland at Longshaw Lodge, Derbyshire, on 30 August, en route to Knowsley. Once back briefly at Knowsley, a weary Derby prepared for the approaching critical session, prior to travelling to Scotland to attend the Queen at Balmoral. Malmesbury was already in the company of the royal party, first at Holyrood and then at Balmoral, 'an old country house' he thought 'in bad repair'.[182] Meanwhile, at Hughenden, Disraeli was busy preparing a wide-ranging budget whose brilliance, the Chancellor hoped, would rescue the government's position. A Free Trade budget, incorporating a revision of direct taxation, might resurrect their prospects. 'We ought now', Disraeli informed Malmesbury, 'be for as complete Free Trade as we can obtain.'[183] In early August, Disraeli proposed reducing the malt tax and tea duty, the removal of light duties on shipping, and the relief of advertisement duty on newspapers. To meet these concessions the house tax would be increased and extended, income tax retained with modifications for all annual incomes above £100, and a fiscal distinction drawn between temporary and permanent income. This was a budget carefully designed to capture moderate Free Trade opinion and represented a formal elaboration of the fiscal strategy espoused by Disraeli since 1849. Supported by a majority of the Commons, such a budget, Disraeli confidently anticipated, 'would give the government of the country' to Derby 'for life'.[184] On learning from his father some of what Disraeli intended, Stanley excitedly wrote to the Chancellor of the Exchequer: 'Great will be your glory ... but it sounds too good to be true.'[185] At the same time Disraeli and Malmesbury, with Derby's approval, undertook confidential discussions with the French government over drawing up an Anglo-French commercial treaty proposing a mutual reduction in tariffs. This too, in a foreshadowing of the famous Cobden–Chevalier Treaty of 1860, it was hoped, would disrupt the parliamentary opposition unified in its advocacy of Free Trade.

But even before parliament had the opportunity to pass its verdict on Disraeli's bold financial scheme, events required budgetary modifications. Persistent fears of French military ambitions, in particular continuing rumours of an invasion of Belgium, prompted Derby to insist on increased military expenditure. Since assuming office, Derby, with the assistance of Malmesbury, had pursued diplomatic entente with France, while at the same time looking to enhance Britain's military and naval strength in order to discourage any aggressive moves by Louis Napoleon in Europe. The carrot of détente and the stick of increased defence expenditure, he believed, would keep Louis Napoleon on a peaceful course. But this additional expenditure dashed Disraeli's initial hope of abolishing the advertisement duty. Meanwhile, the continued campaign to suppress the Xhosa uprising in the Cape Colony, Disraeli complained, was 'a terrible running sore in our finances'.[186] In early September, Derby authorized further military preparations for the seizure of the lower province of Burma, a decision Disraeli deeply disliked as threatening Indian revenues. At the same time, cautious Treasury officials persuaded Disraeli to reduce his calculation of the budget surplus. Meanwhile, diehard Protectionists continued to snipe at the party leadership. On 12 August, Malmesbury warned Disraeli that 'the theatre of your glory and tomb of the present Government must be the H. of Commons' where 'a knot of men ... will be obstinate on Protection'. The Foreign Secretary cautioned: 'Ten crochets will do for us, so look to your children of the H. of C.'[187] But Disraeli refused 'to vex' himself 'about the Protectionist rock ahead'.[188] Only a Free Trade budget, he believed, could offer the Conservatives an escape from permanent minority status. The appointment of Granby, bitter at the leadership's apostasy, as Lord Lieutenant of Leicestershire, it was hoped, might help to sooth bruised Protectionist feeling.

Patronage decisions, commercial relations with France, and a fishing dispute with the United States occupied Derby's correspondence until, on Saturday 11 September, he travelled to Balmoral to join the Queen and Prince Albert in deer stalking on the estate, salmon fishing in the Dee, and games of billiards in the evening. He was pleased to find his relations with the Queen and Prince Albert greatly improved and earlier royal suspicions evaporating. In June the rumoured reluctance of the Queen and Prince

Albert to have him accompany the royal party to the Ascot races, for fear of the government's unpopularity, had been an embarrassing episode. But by September, Derby's relations with the monarch were repaired. Fear of Protectionism no longer clouded their dealings. Derby's loyal support for Albert's Great Exhibition further improved their relations. During the previous months Derby had promoted Albert's proposal to establish a National Gallery and to use the profits from the Great Exhibition to purchase land in South Kensington as sites for museums and colleges dedicated to science, technology, natural history, and music. 'The Queen and Prince are both friendly and communicative,' he reported to Disraeli from Balmoral. 'We must keep *him* with us, which I think may be managed. His influence is boundless.'[189] But Derby was not impressed by either the spartan accommodation or the dull routine at Balmoral. The Queen had just bought the small whitewashed granite castle with its numerous small turrets and the surrounding 17,400-acre estate. The house, Derby confided to his wife, was wretched, the deer shooting poor, and he felt obliged to let Prince Albert win at billiards in the evening. His accommodation was a small servant's room up a back staircase and he came away from the Presbyterian service at nearby Crathie church thinking fondly of the beauties of the Anglican liturgy.

Then, on 15 September, Derby received the news that the nation's great military hero and former prime minister the Duke of Wellington had died the previous day, aged 84, at Walmer Castle. Derby undertook the melancholy duty of confirming to his sovereign that the initial rumours were accurate. Victoria's grief at the loss of her 'most *devoted* and *loyal* subject' was great. The Duke had been, the Queen immediately wrote to her uncle the King of Belgium, 'a true kind friend and most valuable adviser'.[190] Much of Derby's early political career had been devoted to opposing Wellington, particularly over parliamentary Reform. But since 1846 Wellington had dutifully supported him. Derby came to appreciate the Duke's self-reliance, truthfulness, dislike of dissembling, and abiding sense of duty, despite Wellington's well-known prejudices, particularly his aversion to the reform of military administration, becoming more marked during his solitary last days. As a supporter of the Conservative party in its duty to the monarch, the victor of Waterloo had offered Derby an unquestioning loyalty during the difficult years following the Conservative schism over Corn Law repeal. Wellington's prestige had helped to buttress Derby's authority.

While at Balmoral, Derby discussed with Prince Albert who should succeed Wellington as Commander-in-Chief of the Army. To Derby's

relief Albert confirmed that he had no wish to assume the post himself.
Lord Hardinge was chosen as 'the only man fit to command the Army'.[191]
Lord Fitzroy Somerset, raised to the peerage as Lord Raglan, was appointed
to the Ordnance. The Wardenship of the Cinque Ports was given to Lord
Dalhousie (Derby refusing the appointment for himself), and royal assent
given to Lord Londonderry's receiving the Order of the Garter. The
prime minister proposed a public funeral for Britain's greatest general
and, unprecedentedly for a subject not a member of the royal family,
a lying-in-state in Westminster Hall was granted. Widespread national
mourning followed. The Queen and Prince Albert also agreed to Derby's
proposal that a public subscription be raised to establish a school for the
orphan sons of army officers—what became Wellington College, located
near the Royal Military Academy at Sandhurst.

Having travelled south through a heavy snowfall on 21 September
and after resting at Knowsley, Derby arrived in London on Tuesday
12 October. A cabinet meeting was called for Saturday 16 October, at
which it was decided to hold Wellington's funeral on 18 November,
with parliament meeting briefly to dispose of preliminary business on
4 November, primarily the re-election of Charles Shaw-Lefevre as Speaker
of the Commons. But continuing anxieties about a French occupation of
Belgium and the expectation that Louis Napoleon was about to trade in
his title of Prince President for Emperor heightened European diplomatic
tensions. Reports had been circulating since April that Louis Napoleon
intended to proclaim himself Emperor. During October sharp criticism of
Louis Napoleon increased in the English opposition press. But, consistent
with his principle of not interfering in the internal affairs of other
European nations, Derby did not regard such an act, provided Louis
Napoleon maintained his professions of peaceful intention, as requiring a
hostile British response. French disruption of the status quo by a move
on Belgium, however, would be a reckless act directly involving British
interests. Though it appeared by October that the announcement of an
empire in France was fast approaching, Derby remained hopeful that
Louis Napoleon would refrain from invasion.[192] Malmesbury agreed that
it was 'out the question' that Louis Napoleon should sacrifice his relations
with other European powers for Belgian annexation.[193] On the basis of
his long-standing friendship, Malmesbury discounted any personal wish
by Louis Napoleon to incite war. Both Derby and Malmesbury noted
approvingly that, in a speech at Bordeaux on 11 October, Louis Napoleon
expressed a strong wish for European peace. Popular fears of French
aggrandizement, however, created a feverish backdrop to mourning over

Wellington's death, the great hero who had vanquished earlier Napoleonic ambitions in Europe. On Monday 25 October the cabinet agreed to increased naval expenditure, as pressed by the Duke of Northumberland. Although the 59-year-old Duke had last seen active service as a naval officer aged 23 in 1815, he remained a zealous promoter of the Navy's interests and his forceful advocacy secured an increase of £800,000 in the Admiralty estimates. The Queen also continued to urge Derby to ensure that national defences were adequate to respond to any European crisis. On 4 November the French Senate announced that a plebiscite would be held proposing the establishment of the Second Empire and bestowing on the Prince President the title of Napoleon III. Correctly, all foreign observers assumed that the democratic formality of a plebiscite would endorse the establishment of a new imperial regime.

In a characteristic tour de force, on 8 November, Derby drew up the memorandum outlining his government's response himself, writing it straight off, without a single erasure, in copperplate hand. 'Adding and Mellish, the oldest and ablest *redactors* at the Foreign Office, said that neither Canning nor Palmerston could have done the like.' Malmesbury thought it 'one of the best papers I ever read'.[194] It clearly laid out Derby's thinking and was a striking example of his ability to consider a complex issue and immediately arrange a cogent view. While allowing that the change of regime and Louis Napoleon's assumption of the title of Emperor were matters legitimately left to the French nation itself, Derby argued for a concerted diplomatic response from the other European powers and expressed objections to any implication that the title of Napoleon III rested upon hereditary right. Such an inference, he pointed out, would be a repudiation of the Vienna Settlement and the Bourbon monarchy established under the terms of that treaty. Summoned to Windsor by an anxious Queen the following day, Derby reassured Victoria that he did not contemplate a defensive alliance against France, merely the preservation of the Vienna Settlement as the basis for continued European stability. On 11 November, Louis Napoleon assured the British government that he did not regard his prospective imperial title as a hereditary right, as shown by the need for a plebiscite as an endorsement for the constitutional change. This explanation Derby and Malmesbury immediately accepted as a satisfactory answer to their concerns. Formal British recognition of Napoleon's imperial title followed.

The British government's response to the establishment of the French Second Empire was a striking illustration of Derby's administrative capability. Far from being an aristocratic dilettante, it showed him to be a resourceful executive politician. In one concentrated sitting he drew up the detailed statement of his government's policy, deeply impressing even old Foreign Office hands. It affirmed that it was Derby who was firmly guiding Malmesbury's diplomacy. It revealed the basis upon which he exercised an unchallenged authority within his cabinet. Further recognition of Derby's personal standing was expressed by a deputation from Oxford University, which the prime minister met in Downing Street on Thursday 21 October. Wellington's death having vacated the Chancellorship of the University, the deputation informed Derby of Oxford's wish to appoint him as their new Chancellor. Receiving the deputation with a widely admired Latin speech, he delightedly accepted the honour. The appointment gave him immense personal pleasure. It was an honour he felt all the more keenly following the impressive scenes of mourning accompanying Wellington's funeral four weeks later.

As, on the dreary wet morning of Monday 18 November, huge silent crowds reverently watched Wellington's cortège process along the Mall, Constitution Hill, Piccadilly, and on to St Paul's, a solemn and unbroken order prevailed. As Derby described it in the Lords the following day, every house, every window, every rooftop along the route was loaded with people anxious to pay their last respects to the memory of the nation's greatest son. Yet their Lordships might look with 'pride and gratification' on 'the admirable temper, patience, forbearance, and good conduct which was manifested by the whole of those incredible crowds'.[195] Inside St Paul's, Derby joined the official congregation, who, to the majestic sonorities of Handel anthems sung by a choir of 2,000 and guns fired in salute from different parts of London, solemnly watched Wellington's coffin being lowered into the vault of the cathedral. With unusual candour and sentiment Derby subsequently informed the guests at a Lord Mayor's dinner that 'he was proud to be the countryman of those masses who ... had shown such an example of good conduct and self-restraint, and that when he saw them he had asked himself with a feeling of self-humiliation "what have I done to hold so high a place among such a people?"'[196]

The fatal strike provok'd.

(Derby, *The Iliad of Homer*, i. 1)

Yet impressive public mourning did not subdue political asperities. Ill-tempered cabinet meetings chaired by Derby during October and early

November left Disraeli in low spirits as increased expenditure on national defence forced further compromises to his bold budgetary plan. Derby continued to press Disraeli 'on the subject of *immediate* Naval preparation, about which the Queen is very urgent'.[197] The Chancellor reluctantly agreed to finance an additional 5,000 seamen and 2,000 artillerymen. Further pressure from Derby ensured that Prince Albert's particular request for additional Marines was also incorporated into the government's finances. At the same time Derby explained to the Queen that, with regard to diplomatic communications with Paris, it was 'the more desirable to hold conciliatory language, and to make it evident that the measures which are in progress are measures of precaution, and not of hostility'.[198]

The Royal Address agreed by the ministry and delivered to parliament by the Queen on Thursday 11 November, while acknowledging the generally improved condition of the country, especially of the industrial classes, declared that this happy result had inflicted unavoidable injury on the nation's agriculture. Parliament must consider dispassionately how far it was practical equitably to mitigate that injury. The passage was inserted on Derby's insistence and against Disraeli's wishes, in part because of the pressure exerted in cabinet by Lord Hardwicke, Walpole, and Manners on behalf of the diehard Protectionists. The Address also announced that diplomatic negotiations were being conducted with the United States over their infractions of the Fishery Convention of 1818 which threatened the livelihood of Canadian fishermen in the Bay of Fundy; that a special mission had been sent to Argentina with a view to opening up commerce with the region; that an Ecclesiastical Commission was to be established; and that further law reforms would bring into harmony the Testamentary Jurisdiction of different courts.

In closing the Lords debate on the Address, Derby concentrated on the financial condition of the country. He acknowledged the general prosperity prevailing, especially among the labouring classes, owing to the advantage of cheap and abundant food. The injurious effects of Free Trade had been neutralized by the discovery of extensive gold deposits in different parts of the world, particularly in California, and by a great deal of emigration. This had prevented falling prices from leading to lower wages. Derby accepted that the electoral judgement of the country had now been decisively given in favour of Free Trade:

> this system is now established, and working more advantageously for the labouring classes than we had anticipated ... On the part then of myself and my colleagues, I bow to the decision of the country ... we shall endeavour

as honestly to carry the policy to which we have hitherto objected as if we ourselves had been the authors of that policy.[199]

Nonetheless, he hoped that, without interfering in the general policy which for shortness was called Free Trade, the government might confer advantages on those sectors which had suffered from its adoption, such as agriculture, colonial trade, and British shipping. In doing so, he wished parliament to display that good sense and moderation which did not sacrifice the great interests of the nation for the purpose of indulging in personal recrimination or personal charges. But Derby's pronouncement was received with an ominous silence from both sides of the House. Compliant acquiescence appeared a poor substitute for sincere belief.

The prime minister's statement also failed to appease the opposition in the Commons, meeting in Sir Charles Barry's newly completed chamber. While Gladstone spoke out against the reference in the Address to injuries to the agricultural interest, Charles Villiers, Lord Clarendon's brother and a prominent Anti-Corn Law campaigner, gave notice of a provocative resolution declaring Corn Law repeal to have been a wise, just, and beneficial measure. At a subsequent Conservative party meeting

> Derby informed his followers that he must reserve to himself entire liberty of dealing with Villiers's resolution as he thought best, but if he contested it, and was beaten, he would not resign. He then requested that if anyone had any objection to make, or remarks to offer, on his proposed course, they would make them then and there and not find fault afterwards.

All present, however, 'cheered, and nobody said a word'.[200] But when, on 17 November, Derby read the precise wording of Villiers's motion, to be proposed in the Commons on 23 November, he immediately informed Disraeli that it must be opposed. Indeed, upon hearing of the unified Conservative support shown for Derby, Villiers, Russell, and Graham had introduced more stringent language into their original resolution. Disraeli feared Villiers's motion was not intended to break up the government, but rather to keep them in 'a humiliating tenure'.[201]

During the afternoon of Friday 19 November, Derby agreed that Disraeli should move an amendment to Villiers's motion, affirming the government's commitment to unrestricted competition as the principle of the nation's commercial policy. The success of this amendment, Disraeli believed, would expose the factious intentions of their opponents. It would be 'a bold move' against the opposition which, Disraeli hoped, 'may turn their flank'.[202] But following Disraeli's announcement of his amendment, Palmerston, on Monday 22 November, privately proposed to

Disraeli a middle course, both saving the honour of the government and clearly affirming their acceptance of the policy of Free Trade. Palmerston submitted the draft of a motion, to be moved by himself, similar to Disraeli's own, but omitting any description of the 1846 legislation as wise and just. It is possible that Gladstone and Herbert assisted Palmerston in drafting his motion. Derby and Disraeli willingly accepted Palmerston's offer. Derby now entertained a hope that, following Palmerston's aid in defeating Villiers's motion and Disraeli's scoring a success with his budget, a reconstruction of his government, bringing about a junction with Palmerston, might be realized over the Christmas recess.

During the evening of Wednesday 24 November, Disraeli had a private meeting with Palmerston and sounded him out about joining the Conservative cabinet. Palmerston declined, not wishing to join by himself and reporting that the Peelites, with whom he was acting, felt no disposition to join Derby's ministry. Nonetheless, Palmerston affirmed his wish to defeat Villiers's motion. Thus, after debate on Villiers's motion began and after Disraeli, in an elaborate and audacious speech, had spoken, Palmerston brought forward his compromise motion. Adopting a deliberately judicious tone, Palmerston spoke of 'fair play', 'English gentlemen', and 'not establishing a political inquisition', all of which was gratefully cheered by the Conservative benches.[203] During subsequent debate Herbert, Graham, Russell, and Gladstone sought to disengage themselves from Villiers's resolution. Following the second night of Commons debate, on Friday 26 November, Villiers's motion was defeated by 336 to 256 votes and Palmerston's amendment overwhelmingly passed by 468 to 53 votes, a majority of 415. Thirty-three Liberals joined the Conservatives in support of Palmerston's motion. Palmerston's benevolence towards the government corroborated Greville's judgement, following conversations with Palmerston, Lady Palmerston, and Lord Shaftesbury, that there existed a strong conviction in favour of eventually joining Derby. Lady Palmerston evidently wished it very much,[204] although Sir George Cornewall Lewis predicted that, should Palmerston enter Derby's cabinet, the prime minister would acquire 'a master who made him feel his servitude every day—and rode him with a sharp bit and hard hand'.[205]

Derby was 'much pleased' at the result of the Villiers debate, but 'a good deal galled' by the tone of some speakers.[206] In particular, he was stung by Herbert's vitriolic barb that 'if people wish for *humiliation* let them look at the benches opposite'. Yet, he believed Herbert had not meant to be hostile to the government, but had spoken simply from a sense of duty to the memory of Peel. The debate inevitably fuelled speculation over a reconstruction of the government. On the evening of 24 November, Derby was advised by the Peelite Lord Jocelyn that Gladstone and Herbert were speaking privately of the reunion of the Conservative party. Derby also received reports indirectly from some leading Peelites that they could not serve under Disraeli, but were ready to serve under Palmerston. Prince Albert, in conversation with the prime minister, observed that Palmerston 'was anxious to come into office again, he looked to becoming leader in the House of Commons and then to supplant Lord Derby very soon'.[207] Derby was advised that the Queen would have strong objections to such an arrangement. Prince Albert questioned whether Derby could depend on Disraeli's loyalty amid widespread speculation about Palmerston's exact intentions. The Prince was convinced that Palmerston was 'aiming at the leadership of the House of Commons in order to possess himself of *absolute power*' and feared Disraeli and Palmerston's settling between themselves a ministerial arrangement repugnant to the court.[208] But Derby reassured the Prince that Disraeli's capacity for independent negotiation was negligible. Disraeli knew well, the prime minister replied, that Derby possessed the confidence of 300 of his supporters, while Disraeli, if he struck off on his own, would very likely not carry five MPs with him.[209] No ministerial rearrangements could occur, Derby declared, without his endorsement. Nonetheless, the prospect of an eventual reconstruction of the government to include some Peelites did float before Derby's eyes.

On the evening of Saturday 27 November, Lady Derby hosted a party, during which the prime minister took Gladstone aside. Derby confided that his 'great object' was to get rid of all personal questions and consider how men, united in their general views of government, might come together. Gladstone replied that Herbert, Goulburn, and he looked to the government's budget as 'the next step'. In response to Derby's talk of rapprochement, Gladstone observed that 'there were many difficulties of a personal nature to be faced in conceiving of any ministerial continuation' and 'great difficulties arising from various causes, present and past relations, incompatibilities, peculiar defects of character or failures, in bringing them into harmony'.[210] Derby understood this conversation as a reaffirmation of the leading Peelites' disgust for Disraeli. They could neither forget nor forgive Disraeli for his humiliation of Peel in 1846. But Derby was convinced that 'he could not in honour sacrifice Disraeli, who had acted very straightforwardly to him'. Equally importantly, Derby did not favour Gladstone as a replacement for Disraeli. Prince Albert had enthusiastically proposed Gladstone as a substitute for Disraeli as Leader of the Commons. But Gladstone was, Derby judged, 'quite unfit' for such a position; 'he had none of that decision, boldness, readiness and clearness which was necessary to lead a party, to inspire it with confidence, and, still [more], to take at times a decision on the spur of the moment, which a leader had often to do'.[211]

Derby believed, however, that Palmerston would be an acceptable replacement for Disraeli, for whom Disraeli might, with honour, make way. Malmesbury agreed that Palmerston was a desirable catch, but disagreed with bringing Gladstone and Herbert in alongside him. In that event, Malmesbury feared, Derby 'would be overwhelmed by the Commons portion of his cabinet and lose his influence'. Moreover, while Malmesbury regarded Palmerston as a gentleman, he believed 'Gladstone cannot be *that*. He is a Jesuit *tout cachet*.'[212] Derby decided to do nothing further for the moment. Hopefully, support for Palmerston's amendment and Disraeli's budget would naturally lead to a reconstruction of the ministry during the Christmas recess.

As party alignment in the Commons awaited Disraeli's budget, which had now acquired a critical significance, Derby maintained a spirited defence of his government in the Lords. Following the Lord Chancellor's introduction of further reforms to the administration of the law on Tuesday 16 November, a long evening of intense debate ensued on Monday 22 November. Derby opposed Lord Panmure's plea against the Sunday opening of the Crystal Palace, now transferred to Sydenham. Rather than being a desecration of the sabbath, as suggested by Panmure, Derby believed Sunday openings to be a great benefit to the people of the overcrowded metropolis. As a Commissioner for the Great Exhibition he had consistently supported Sunday openings as encouraging the labouring classes to use their one weekly day of rest for educational and morally uplifting purposes.[213] Clanricarde then challenged Derby to clarify the government's intentions with regard to their financial policy. Noting that the commercial affairs of the country had been a matter of bitter controversy for many years, Derby declared it desirable finally to settle the matter at the earliest opportunity. Guided by the sense of the community at large, as expressed through its representatives, he reaffirmed the government's compliance with the electoral judgement that there should be no alterations in the present commercial system. In light of his public commitment to this position, Derby characterized Clanricarde's motion as factious. An ill-tempered exchange then occurred as the young Liberal Lord Wodehouse attacked Derby for his change of view. If the prime minister believed Protection to be best for the country he should resign. If, on the other hand, Derby now espoused Free Trade then he must relinquish any claim to consistency.[214] An infuriated Derby expressed his fierce objection to being lectured on matters of personal honour by the 26-year-old peer. Wodehouse promptly apologized and withdrew his remarks.[215]

Acrimony then spilled over into further debate, on Monday 6 December, of Clanricarde's resolution, strongly supported by Beaumont, committing the Lords to Free Trade. Derby declared his concurrence with Clanricarde's motion without the slightest reservation. But he felt compelled to point out that in 1839 Clanricarde had voted by proxy against Free Trade in corn and that, as recently as 1846, Beaumont had voted against repeal of the Corn Laws. He was not, Derby observed, the only member of the Lords to have changed his views. He also defied the opposition to find in any of his speeches or writings any expression derogatory to the character of Sir Robert Peel or impugning the integrity of the dead statesman's motives. Controversy over the nation's commercial policy, Derby insisted, should now be consigned to the oblivion of the past.[216] Clanricarde's motion was agreed by the Lords without opposition. On 6 December, Malmesbury also informed the Lords of the government's formal recognition of the new French Empire, observing that 'a people have a right to choose their own sovereign without the interference of any foreign power'.[217] He looked to maintain an unbroken friendship with France, he continued, and believed that Napoleon III fully appreciated the great folly which would be committed by any provocation to war. Derby thought that Malmesbury overdid his laudatory references to Napoleon III, however, and Lord Canning immediately criticized the Foreign Secretary for excessive personal compliments about the French Emperor.

Fractious debate in the Lords played itself out against feverish speculation over Disraeli's budget. The Chancellor of the Exchequer himself remained dispirited: 'I fear we are in a great scrape, and I hardly see how the budget can live in so stormy a sea.'[218] On the eve of his budget statement to the Commons, a shocked Disraeli received a request from the Admiralty for a further increase of £1 million to the Naval Estimates. Derby confirmed the cabinet's decision to reduce the proposed increase to the Naval Estimates for 1853/4 to £350,000. But by his own calculations this still required Disraeli to sacrifice some of his proposed reduction of the malt tax, while a reduction of 4*d*. instead of 6*d*. on tea duties would be necessary. Nonetheless, Derby remained hopeful that the budget 'would place [Disraeli] on velvet'. 'Put a good face on it', Derby urged his discouraged Chancellor, 'and we shall pull through: '—l'audace—l'audace—toujours l'audace'.[219] By agreeing with calls in the Lords to endorse Free Trade, Derby believed he had 'thrown a shell among the Free Traders' in the

Upper House, splitting the Peelites and securing Lansdowne's support. On the morning of Disraeli's budget speech, Derby again advised against the abolition of the advertisement duty and the necessity of the proposed house tax, which would allow, he estimated, the Chancellor to forecast a surplus of £1.6 million. Reluctantly Disraeli accepted Derby's last-minute proposals, though complaining that 'on the very eve of battle I should suddenly be called on to change all my dispositions'.[220]

In a speech lasting over five hours, Disraeli presented his budget to a packed Commons on the evening of Friday 3 December. The Chancellor was both ill from influenza and evidently nervous. Anti-Semitic characterizations in the press and a clearly plagiarized passage in Disraeli's Commons eulogy of the Duke of Wellington, drafted by George Smyth and delivered by the Chancellor on 15 November, had damaged his credibility. Even so, Derby remained hopeful as he sat in the gallery of the Commons, accompanied by Malmesbury, 'anxiously watching the effect produced'.[221] Disraeli began by acknowledging that the last general election had confirmed 'that unrestricted competition is entirely and finally adopted as the principle of our commercial code'. His subsequent statements marked the official unveiling of the Conservatives' fiscal strategy, intended to fracture a parliamentary majority united in its opposition to Protection. The revision of direct taxation was designed to provide a conciliatory substitute for import tariffs, as a means of restoring the constitutional balance disrupted by Free Trade. As a member of Commons Select Committees, chaired by the radical Joseph Hume during 1851 and 1852, Disraeli had come to accept the advisability of distinguishing between 'spontaneous' (unearned) and 'precarious' (earned) income for the purposes of revising the income tax, an amendment upon which Conservatives and radicals, for very different reasons, might agree. Indeed, the immediate effect of Disraeli's statement appeared favourable. Announcing a reduction in the malt tax, hop tax, and tea duties and attempting to distinguish between earned and unearned incomes, Disraeli proposed an increase in the income tax, extended to Ireland, and the house tax. Thus, in the absence of import tariffs, the burden of direct taxation might be equalized and a fiscal equilibrium restored within the national economy.[222]

Derby judged it 'a masterly performance'. Disraeli, he wrote to the Queen at midnight that evening, 'kept alive the attention of the House with the greatest ability, introducing the most important statements, and the broadest principles of legislature, just at the moments when he had excited the greatest anxiety to learn the precise measures which the government intended to introduce'.[223] The Irish part of the budget, Derby believed, Disraeli delivered 'with remarkable dexterity'. Though it was difficult to foresee the ultimate result, the prime minister thought 'the general first impression was very favourable'. The following day he congratulated Disraeli, declaring that he 'listened to the whole exposition with entire satisfaction, and admiration of the clearness and breadth with which you stated your views ... One ought not to be sanguine, or to trust too much to first impressions; but I think you have weathered the really dangerous point, and that the ship is now in comparatively smooth waters.'[224] The Queen also wrote to Disraeli to 'congratulate him on the very successful way in which he brought forward the budget'.[225] Derby's unreserved support in the Lords for Clanricarde's Free Trade motion, on Monday 6 December, affirmed his wish that the great controversy be navigated into the calm consensual anchorage offered by fiscal reform. Disraeli's budget, he informed the peers, was ample evidence of the intention of the government to adhere to the principles of Free Trade.

Yet, Derby's confidence quickly proved misplaced, first impressions belying the deep animus surging beneath the initial peaceful surface of events. Whigs, Peelites, and radicals adamantly refused to accept the Conservatives' fiscal strategy as a penitential liberation from the prejudices of Protectionism. Despite Greville's judgement that the first night of Commons debate had made the government safe, continued discussion brought forward powerful critics.[226] This exposed the paucity of Commons debating talent on the government front bench. While Herries and Henley remained conspicuously silent, Stanley pleaded pressure of Foreign Office business prevented him from speaking. Speeches from Walpole, Manners, and Pakington, meanwhile, failed to rally support. Loud cheering for Derby and Disraeli's speeches at the Lord Mayor's banquet on Wednesday 8 December could not disguise the fact that the government's fate now lay in the unpredictable hands of an increasingly hostile Commons.

When the budget debate resumed in the Commons on Thursday 10 December, Wood fiercely criticized every aspect of Disraeli's scheme, especially the proposed house tax, and urged the government to withdraw the budget for reconsideration. In response to these criticisms, with a bitter virulence, Disraeli declared that Wood 'should learn that petulance is not sarcasm, and insolence is not invective'. He rejected the 'vulgar insinuations' that he was 'clinging to office, if not power'.[227] In turn, the radicals Cobden and Hume indicated their contempt for the budget; the Peelite former Chancellor of the Exchequer Henry Goulburn condemned the principle of differentiation in assessing income tax; Gladstone privately stated the budget contained 'fundamental faults of principle which it is impossible to overlook'; and the Whig MP Thomas Macaulay derided the scheme as 'nothing but taking money out of the pockets of the people in the towns and putting it into the growers of malt'. In response, Edward Bulwer Lytton declared that, in the school where he had learnt the meaning of constitutional liberty, it was never considered a disgrace for a minister of England to regulate his political conduct according to the opinions of his time. Rather than the 'exclusive advocates of a single class, or the inert supporters of a retrograde policy', the government were the sincere proponents of responsible improvement and advancing welfare.[228] On Monday 14 December, Graham attacked the details of the budget, while Ralph Bernal Osborne (Liberal MP for Middlesex) pronounced it essentially anti-middle-class. Palmerston's absence from parliament on the grounds of ill health, which many correctly suspected to be a political pretext, moreover, removed the possibility of securing a cross-bench resolution. In the Lords that evening Derby declared that he might resign if his government were defeated over their budget.[229] He privately also threw out hints that if removed from office he might well withdraw from public life altogether. This, he hoped, would dissuade waverers from joining the opposition.

Mounting hostility prompted Disraeli desperately to seek additional Commons support from unlikely sources. Without Derby's knowledge, he sought aid from the fifty Irish Independent party MPs, in exchange for promises of reform to Irish tenant rights. Even more recklessly, on the evening of 15 December he invited the radical Bright to Grosvenor Gate and suggested that he, Cobden, and Thomas Milner Gibson, in return for a general vote for the budget, might in due course join Disraeli in the cabinet. Predictably, both rash undertakings failed. Bright laughed at Disraeli's proposal and left Grosvenor Gate convinced that the Chancellor was 'unable to comprehend the morality of our political course'.[230] For his part, Disraeli cynically believed that the Manchester School, although '*hot* for *organic* changes', only needed to be given office to be tamed.[231] Malmesbury, meanwhile, was receiving reports that Newcastle, through his brother Lord Charles Pelham-Clinton (Conservative MP for Sandwich), was canvassing the party, with some success, regarding the possibility of his succeeding Derby in the event of Derby's giving up politics.[232]

A suspicious Derby wrote to Disraeli on 15 December and firmly scotched desperate remedies to their predicament. Although Disraeli now believed the carrying of their budget as it stood was hopeless, Derby firmly opposed any concessions aimed at securing unnatural support. 'We may buy off a hostile vote before Christmas; but how shall one stand afterwards?' Having avowedly abandoned Protection and having proposed reduction of the malt tax as the *only* relief granted to land in the budget, to modify their financial plan further would expose the ministry to a double attack from both their friends and their opponents. 'We have staked our existence on the budget *as a whole.*'[233] Derby had bound the government to abide by the decision of the country on Free Trade. But, equally, he had committed the party to relieving the agricultural interest. Postponing parliament's decision on the amount of house tax to be levied and abandoning the malt tax might defer a crisis, but 'the temporary respite will be dearly bought'. It was better, Derby maintained, to 'be defeated honestly in a fairly fought field, than to escape under a cloud, to encounter defeats with alienated friends and sneering opponents'. If the principle of extending and increasing the house tax was accepted, Derby would consider deferring the decision on its precise timing and amount. But 'if the House have not so much confidence in us as to place us in a majority on these conditions, it is high time that the country should satisfy itself whether any other possible combination possesses *more* of its confidence'. If such a combination was formed, the current government would be defeated, but not discredited. If no such combination was realized, 'we must very shortly be returned to power, with increased means from the failure of our divided opponents'. Derby's resolution brought Disraeli firmly back into line.

At the beginning of the final climactic night of the budget debate, on Thursday 16 December, Disraeli called on the Commons to approve the extension and increase of the house tax in principle as an endorsement of the government's policy, the amount of the increase to be decided later. In an impassioned speech intended to close the debate, he forcefully defended his budget, castigating Wood for his policies as Chancellor of the Exchequer under Russell and denouncing Graham for inconsistency. Against the dramatic backdrop of a loud thunderstorm, Disraeli then, in a bravura performance, disparaged his opponents as a coalition whose triumph would be brief, pronouncing the famous phrase: 'This, too, I know, that England does not love coalitions.'[234] Rather than the factious intrigue of coalitions, the fate of the ministry should rest, he declared, on the mild and irresistible influence of public opinion, without which the most august and ancient institutions were but 'the baseless fabric of a vision'. With this speech, Lord Londonderry warned, Disraeli had 'outheroded Herod'.[235] Amid furious cheering from the Conservative benches Disraeli sat down. But availing himself of a procedural nicety, an incensed Gladstone refused to allow Disraeli the last word. Loftily condemning Disraeli's impassioned language as beyond the limits of discretion and forbearance, Gladstone proceeded, amid fierce Conservative taunts and fervent opposition applause, to decry the budget as the most subversive in its ultimate effects of any he had known.[236] Gladstone appeared 'choked with passion, for which he could find no vent in words'.[237] Listening in the chamber as Gladstone began his speech, Derby dropped his head down on his arms and muttered, 'Dull!'[238] But in the division called at 3 a.m. Whigs, Liberals, Peelites, radicals, and the Irish Independent party streamed into the opposition lobby. It was, Palmerston observed, 'an immense crowd'.[239] By a majority of nineteen Disraeli's budget was defeated by 305 to 286 votes. From the gallery Derby immediately pronounced: 'Now we are properly smashed; I must prepare for my journey to Osborne to resign.'[240]

Before retiring to bed, at 4 a.m. that night, Derby wrote to the Queen stating that this decisive Commons defeat left him no alternative but resignation. Later that morning Derby informed Malmesbury that he intended to advise the Queen to send for Aberdeen. But Malmesbury argued strongly against such a course. This would, Malmesbury warned, rob them of some Conservative support; better, he persuaded Derby, to suggest the Queen send for Lansdowne. This would keep Conservative MPs united under Derby.[241] After a brief cabinet meeting Derby left London and crossed by ferry to the Isle of Wight later that day, formally tendering his resignation to the Queen, who, though grave and anxious, received him cordially. Following dinner Derby advised the Queen and Prince Albert about the crisis they now faced. Critical of the factiousness of the opposition, Derby affirmed that the budget vote had now crystallized Commons party feeling. Against 286 loyal Conservative MPs stood 150 radicals, 120 Whigs, thirty Peelites, and fifty of the so-called Irish Brigade. Combined, the opposition outnumbered the Conservatives, but alone, none of the opposition parties comprised as much as half of the Conservatives' Commons strength. Derby received reports of the Whigs and Peelites coalescing who, by virtue of their recognized talent and experience, might provide a combination able to command the confidence of the House. But he advised the Queen, as Malmesbury had suggested, to send for Lansdowne. Derby requested the Queen not to send for Aberdeen straight away, as apprehension about his own retirement from public life might induce some Conservatives to join Aberdeen. At the same time, other Conservatives, indignant at their treatment by the Peelites, might attempt a reckless alliance with the radicals in order to avenge themselves on any new government.[242] In response, the Queen conceded to the extent that she proposed to send for Lansdowne and Aberdeen together. Whereupon Derby joked that any new cabinet would have to contain at least thirty-two ministers, so numerous were the various opposition aspirants for office. Upon Prince Albert repeating his suspicions about Disraeli's democratic inclinations, Derby loyally defended his colleague. Disraeli 'has better reason than anyone', Derby replied, 'to be attached to our constitutional system since he has experienced how easily a man under it may rise'.[243] That, just two weeks before, Disraeli had helped to secure parliament's agreement to the granting of £150,000 to assist in purchasing land in South Kensington for Albert's plan to establish institutions dedicated to science, technology, and music helped to temper the Prince's mistrust.

Upon returning to London a wearied Derby held a Conservative party meeting at Downing Street at noon on Monday 20 December. Attended by 160 of his followers, many Conservative MPs and peers having already left for the country, he spoke at length of his firm resolution, at whatever personal inconvenience, to continue to lead the party. 'The cordiality shown by those present', Stanley noted, 'was very great.'[244] Intense relief at Derby's not retiring from public life fuelled the acclamation when Lord Delawarr proposed a vote of confidence in their leader. 'The cheers, according to the hostile testimony of the *Daily News*, "could be heard three streets off".' That evening Derby delivered a defiant speech in the Lords attacking the discordant combination which had forced him from office. It was an opposition, he averred, composed of the highest aristocratic and most exclusive Whigs, to the wildest theorists and most extreme radicals; those representing the views of the Irish Roman Catholic clergy and holding the extreme doctrines of the Ultramontane School; and that eminent and respectable small party the Peelites, possessing considerable official experience and much talent. Over Villiers's motion this combination had fallen apart. Yet, undeterred, this same factious coalition had forced the government to a defeat over its budget. Derby understood that the Queen, because of Lansdowne's age and infirmity, had commissioned Aberdeen to form a government. But 'on what principle is the administration to be formed, how is it to be composed?'[245] The threat of Protection no longer provided non-Conservatives with a common cause. Only selfish political purposes held them together. As an avowed Conservative, Derby concluded, Aberdeen would be unable to remain faithful to his own principles alongside associates such as those with whom he proposed now to share power. The Conservative peers were delighted by Derby's pugnaciousness as he surrendered office to what he portrayed as a muddled coalition. The following morning *The Times*, coming out in strong support for Aberdeen's new ministry, fiercely denounced Derby for expatiating on the 'details of conspiracies, ill motives and anticipated perils to the constitution' that he suggested were represented by the coalition government.[246] Two days later *The Times* printed a letter by Gladstone forcefully denying that the ejection of the Conservative ministry was the result of concert or combination.[247]

Despite the hearty cheers of the Tory peers, an uncomfortable question now hung over Conservative heads. With Protection abandoned and Protestantism tempered, what principles sustained the party? Exercising the prerogative of old age, the 72-year-old Croker posed the unpleasant query directly to Lord Hardwicke:

> Why are you all turned out on—neither you or anyone else can say—*what*? You have not even hoisted a flag to rally round. You have been like some poor people I have read of in the late storm, buried under the ruins of your own edifice; but whether you were stifled or crushed—killed by a rafter or a brick—nobody can tell. You have died a death so ignoble that it has no name, and the coroner's verdict is *found dead*! Why did you not die in the Protestant cause—or something that some party could take an interest in.[248]

Croker's indictment was scathing. After 1852 his close correspondence with Derby fell away.

Yet strong loyalty to Derby among his parliamentary adherents endured, despite prevalent mistrust of Disraeli. The party was united, despite abandoning Protectionism. During 1852 the Conservatives began to restore their claim to being a party capable of moderate responsible government. Fiscal reform and the equalization of direct taxation replaced the hopeless cry of Protection. Defence of the Established Church was maintained, without surrender to bigotry. Administration of the law was reformed and the process of colonial self-government advanced. National defence, with increased naval and military expenditure, was strengthened. Cordial diplomatic relations with the major European powers were maintained, despite Austrian grievances and Louis Napoleon's apotheosis as Emperor; conciliation with the United States, over fishing rights and British protectorates in Central America, was pursued; and a treaty was concluded in London settling the dispute between the German States and Denmark over Schleswig-Holstein. This was a commendable achievement, albeit that negotiations with France over a commercial treaty ran out of time and a secret approach to the Vatican to establish diplomatic relations quickly came to naught. Yet real power, rather than mere survival, now depended upon the disunity of their opponents. Acrimonious discord, Derby believed, would be the probable fate of Aberdeen's motley, if distinguished, coalition.

CHAPTER 2

'Killing with Kindness': 1852–1855

It is difficult to imagine how a government can go on formed of such discordant elements as that which Aberdeen has brought together. ... The chance for Conservatism is the disruption of the cabinet from internal differences, which external pressure would rather tend to heal than otherwise.

(Derby to Liddell, 4 January 1853)

Released from office in December 1852, Derby escaped to Lancashire for the Christmas season, venting his spleen on the rabbit population of the Knowsley estate.

He immediately had recourse to his gun, and during a day's rabbit shooting gave vent to his feelings in the following characteristic manner. 'Ha!' he would cry, as a rabbit crossed the ride, 'There goes Gladstone; hope I haven't missed him. There, do you see that big fellow? That is Graham. He'll be none the worse for a few pellets in his ribs,' and so on through the rest.[1]

While Derby wreaked vicarious revenge at Knowsley, Aberdeen negotiated the formation of a coalition government in London and Woburn. The new cabinet proved to be, as Graham acknowledged, 'a tessellated pavement'.[2] An ill-tempered Russell agreed to serve, initially as Foreign Secretary, under Aberdeen, while assuming, after much evasion, the leadership of the Commons. Clarendon undertook to replace Russell as Foreign Secretary in due course. The elderly Lansdowne joined the cabinet as Minister without Portfolio, his presence, without official duties, promising Whig support. Gladstone was appointed Chancellor of the Exchequer, the Peelite Duke of Argyll was given the Privy Seal, Granville the Lord Presidency of the Council, the Duke of Newcastle the War and Colonial Office, Graham the Admiralty, Wood the Board of Control, Herbert became Secretary at War, and the radical Sir William Molesworth entered the cabinet as First Commissioner of Works. Initially, an ill Palmerston, walking with the aid of two sticks and in evident pain, had been displeased at the turn of events, fuelling speculation that he would join Derby in opposition.

But after entreaties from Lansdowne and Clarendon, on Christmas Eve, Palmerston, whose perilous financial situation made an official salary all the more attractive, agreed to serve as Home Secretary. Aberdeen and Russell, Shaftesbury commented in his journal, 'wanted to gag Palmerston' and 'they have succeeded; they have bound the wild one between two tame elephants'.3 Malmesbury heard rumours that Aberdeen was considering sending Newcastle out to Canada as Governor General. 'This is what they call *isolating* Lord Derby!'4

As Derby predicted, constructing a coalition ministry proved difficult and produced considerable ill feeling. Many Whigs at Brooks's were angered by the number of Peelites appointed to the cabinet. 'The exclusions', Greville noted, 'will be very painful.'5 Whig criticism of Russell's obstinacy and conceited self-interest grew, flaws generally attributed to the ambitious intrigue of his wife and her numerous relatives. The radicals, despite Molesworth's appointment, appeared 'exceedingly sulky and suspicious'.6 The Irish Brigade also assumed 'a menacing and half hostile attitude'. 'Hampered with difficulties and beset with dangers,' Greville concluded, 'it is impossible to feel easy about [the coalition's] prospects.' The surfeit of talent and ambition in the cabinet itself magnified Aberdeen's problems, despite Palmerston's seeming to be 'safely tethered within the peaceful pastures of the Home Office'.7 In the government 'are five or six first-rate men of equal or nearly equal pretensions, none of them likely to acknowledge the superiority or defer to the opinions of others, and every one of these five or six considering himself abler and more important than their premier'.8 An oversupply of talent and ambition intensified asperities, there being little distinction in being distinguished.

None of this was lost on Derby. On Christmas Eve, Malmesbury found him 'gay and good humoured'.9 Disraeli concurred that 'the existence of the coalition will be brief and its end ignominious'.10 Meanwhile, the mood at the Carlton Club was determined, it being anticipated that the new government would be unable to go on for even a short time, the Conservatives being very speedily let in again. The long-serving Liberal MP and former chief whip Edward Ellice, it was noted, predicted Aberdeen's failing and 'that it will end in Derby coming back, reinforced by Palmerston and some Peelites'.11 In the Carlton Club, Gladstone was insulted by enraged Derbyites, as dark resentment swirled around the negotiations set in motion by Aberdeen's commission. This confirmed Derby's conviction that the Conservatives' best hope was to let bad blood contaminate the coalition from within, allowing the opposition 'to kill them with kindness'.12 Over Christmas he repeated to his elder son that the Conservatives' most advantageous course was to 'wait—don't attack ministers—that will only bind them together—if left alone they must fall to pieces by their own division'.[13] In the New Year he privately confirmed that it was

> difficult to imagine how a government can go on formed of such discordant elements as that which Aberdeen has brought together … The great difficulty will be to keep the Conservative party together without the excitement of a systematic opposition which we must avoid as far as possible. The chance for Conservatism is the disruption of the cabinet from internal differences, which external pressure would rather tend to heal than otherwise.[14]

In an ill-delivered speech in the Lords, on Monday 27 December, Aberdeen presented the credentials of his coalition cabinet. Their common bond, the premier explained, was the prudent maintenance of Free Trade. In addition, national education would be extended, those law reforms instigated by Derby's ministry continued, and well-considered Reform of parliament undertaken. The latter policy was pushed by Russell as a condition of his presence on the front bench. While forcefully rejecting Derby's accusation that he had been overthrown by 'a species of combination or conspiracy', Aberdeen deliberately sought to blur the distinction between Conservatives and Liberals. These terms, he argued, no longer had any definite meaning. They suggested distinctions where there were no differences.[15] In reply, Derby ridiculed Aberdeen's attempt to erase party distinctions, which only created in the public mind, he insisted, a deep distrust of the principles upon which the ministerial alliance was constructed. The premier's intention to be conservatively liberal or liberally conservative, he sarcastically observed, conveyed no distinct ideas. With his target listening in the chamber, he then pointedly attacked Graham's recent 'radical' speech at Carlisle (advocating an extension of the borough suffrage and condemning Napoleon III as a despot who had trampled on the liberties of 40 million Frenchmen) as revealing the incompatible opinions entertained within the ministry and the inconsistency of Graham's career.[16] This attack on his erstwhile companion affirmed the distance that now separated the two men. Graham's denunciation of Napoleon III was a clear repudiation of the Anglo-French entente which Derby had pursued as prime minister. Yet, Derby assured the House that he was not opposed to safe Reform of the representative system. Judicious Reform, to remedy proven defects, would receive his cordial support. But any reckless extension of the suffrage would merely exacerbate those evils evident in large urban constituencies and deliver the Commons into the hands of the less informed classes of society. With Protection dead and buried and Protestantism an uncertain asset, Derby characterized, in responsible Reform, that 'Conservative progress' which, upheld by an opposition avoiding factious manoeuvring, might prove the solvent of an uneasy ministerial alliance. Silence followed his statement, whereupon parliament adjourned until 10 February 1853. Returning to Knowsley, in the relaxing company of Malmesbury, he enjoyed shooting on his estate during the course of January, also staying with Lord Hardwicke at his Cambridgeshire seat, Wimpole Hall, for a few days' shooting in mid-January.

Derby resolved to await events 'with his arms folded'.[17] He impressed upon Disraeli the importance of masterly inactivity. 'We shall have a difficult game to play. We must to a certain extent keep up the spirits of our party; but we must exercise, and get them to exercise, great patience and forbearance, if we do not wish, by an active and bitter opposition on our part, to consolidate the present combination between those who have no real bond of union, and those who must, I think, fall to pieces before long, if left to themselves.'[18]

> ... ever 'tis thy way
> Apart from me to weave thy secret schemes,
> Nor doest thou freely share with me thy mind.
>
> (Derby, *The Iliad of Homer*, i. 30)

'Civil war', Sir Walter Scott wrote, 'is a species of misery which introduces men to strange bedfellows.'[19] Certainly the Conservative schism of 1846 created an unlikely association between the aristocratic Derby and the parvenu Disraeli. Derby's coolness towards Disraeli sprang, in part, from their jarringly dissimilar temperaments. Derby assumed public pre-eminence as a duty and accepted office as an obligation of his birth. A near-recluse in London society, his passions lay in his library, translating Homer, or in the field, racing horses and shooting. His country estate and the racecourse, in the company of tenants, trainers, jockeys, and bookmakers, were those settings in which he appeared at his most natural. Disraeli, by contrast, had fought his way to prominence in the metropolitan milieu of fashionable salons. For rural pursuits, such as shooting and farming, Disraeli, who never learnt to ride a horse with ease, had 'no taste'.[20] Indeed, while visiting Yorkshire in January 1853, he confessed that 'the wild hospitality of the North and living much in the air' had 'demoralised my intellectual capabilities'.[21] Unable to share Derby's amusements, Disraeli never enjoyed the warmth of his leader's full acceptance. While admiring Disraeli's ability, Derby sneered at his lieutenant's extremes of alternate excitement and depression. The more so perhaps as he tried to cloak his own fluctuations of mood behind an insouciant manner. Certainly Disraeli's Romantic disposition and ironic postures grated on Derby's patrician sensibilities. In May *The Times*, while recognizing Disraeli's intellectual resources and skill as a debater, concluded that his mind resided in that mysterious borderland between truth and falsehood, between right and wrong, to which his imagination led him, and which was the natural habitation of the sophist.[22]

Derby was never fully to trust the exotic Disraeli. His lieutenant's patent ambition and tactical ingenuity prevented Derby from believing in his dependability, suspicions skilfully exploited by the court, particularly Prince Albert. Derby continued to regard Disraeli as responsible for the embarrassment caused in 1831 by Henry Stanley's temporary disappearance and eventual discovery among dissolute gambling company in 'the Hell' on St James's Street. In his biography of Lord George Bentinck published in December 1851, Disraeli, for his part, pointedly ignored Derby's contribution to the party. Disraeli nursed, Derby recognized, contempt for the Conservative backbenchers he led. As a body they were, Disraeli privately opined, politically apathetic and too easily distracted from parliament by the hunting season. Though possessing ability they 'wanted culture'. They 'never read' and 'their leisure was passed in field sports', the largely self-taught Disraeli complained, and, because of 'the wretched school and university system', they 'did not understand the ideas of their own time'.[23] While Disraeli was solicitously deferential in his exchanges with Derby, Disraeli's confidants suggested that he actually had little regard for his leader's abilities. Disraeli 'dislikes and despises Derby, thinks him a good "Saxon" speaker and nothing more'.[24] Certainly Derby's patrician aloofness inflamed the defensive barbs of Disraeli's insecurity. These sensitivities preserved that social distance which Disraeli encountered among most of his Conservative colleagues, although some younger acolytes, notably Derby's elder son, were drawn into Disraeli's intimate circle.

Derby's mistrust of Disraeli was exacerbated by the close friendship developing with his elder son. The possibility of Disraeli's influence contaminating the political views of his heir, having twenty years before corrupted the morals of his younger brother, was a deeply disquieting prospect. The shy Lord Stanley found much to admire in the flamboyant Disraeli. In particular, Stanley, keen to avoid being enmeshed in the atavistic prejudices of narrow Toryism, was drawn to Disraeli's colourful talk of party reconstruction. As an increasingly frequent visitor to Hughenden after 1850, Stanley provided Disraeli with intelligence concerning the mood at Knowsley. This intimacy introduced an unwelcome reserve into Derby's relations with his son. The affectionate feelings Derby had shown towards Edward during his elder son's youth became overshadowed by suspicions about Disraeli's hold over the young politician. Derby shared the belief that, in Malmesbury's words, Disraeli would 'do anything and act with anyone' in order to get office.[25] Greville ascribed 'the ruin of the party' to Disraeli, and 'Derby had now the mortification of seeing his son devoted to him.'[26]

Proof of Disraeli's cynical opportunism Derby saw in the myriad alliances Disraeli concocted in the early months of 1853. Already he had quashed Disraeli's attempt to establish an understanding with the Irish Brigade. However 'plausible and gentlemanlike' the individuals the Irish Brigade brought forward as their organs, he warned, 'if we lose the landed gentry of Ireland, and especially of the North, we are lost'.[27] Nonetheless, during January 1853, Disraeli carried on a confidential negotiation, through Sir James Tennent, with Gavan Duffy of the Irish Brigade, who indicated the support of thirty to thirty-three MPs for the Conservatives, if they launched an assault on the coalition.[28] The Irish Brigade, Disraeli believed, 'wanted only encouragement to join us'.[29] But Stanley shrewdly advised that 'the less we say about an alliance with the Brigade the better'.[30] During April, Disraeli was 'full of a project of alliance with Lord Grey and the discontented Whigs, Lords Carlisle, Clanricarde and Fitzwilliam'.[31] If such a union could be secured, Disraeli indicated, he would surrender the Commons leadership to Sir George Grey.[32] Through Lord Lonsdale, Disraeli received reports in late March of 'desperate conspiring' by the 'dissatisfied Whigs … to oust the Peelites'.[33] At a Conservative party meeting at St James's Square on 16 April, Derby himself joked that, with the Aberdeen coalition's speeches about Liberal Conservatism and their insistence that 'the black was not so very black, nor the white so very white', it 'was odd that the one colour carefully excluded from their union was that of Grey'.[34] Yet, he regarded Disraeli's hope of capturing high Whig support as 'simply impossible'. Stanley thought it absurd to envisage a cabinet with Derby and Lord Grey sitting alongside each other. Lord Grey, for his part, firmly rejected the suggestion floated by Disraeli that he might become party leader in the event of Derby's retirement. Undeterred, Disraeli also entertained hopes of joining forces with the radicals. By January 1853 some radicals were talking of forming an independent party, with their own whip and Milner Gibson as their leader. Disraeli entered unofficial discussions with Milner Gibson, while 'secretly fearing the effect on Lord Derby and the party if these confidences were known'.[35] Malmesbury bluntly informed Disraeli that he would 'as soon be seen walking to the House of Lords with a jack whore on my arm as appear politically intimate' with Cobden and Bright.[36]

In early 1853 Derby had good reason for mistrusting Disraeli. His suspicions were given further weight by Disraeli's launching of his new weekly journal *The Press* in May 1853. Under the editorship of Samuel Lucas, a former writer for *The Times*, *The Press* presented articles penned by Disraeli himself, and other Conservatives such as Stanley, George Bentinck, Edward Bulwer Lytton (a former radical and fellow novelist), Sir James Tennent, and George Hamilton. Derby privately strongly discouraged this journalistic initiative, which became another source of tension with his elder son. In mid-March, Stanley found his father 'decidedly hostile' to the whole venture. Derby feared the Conservative leadership being compromised and offence unnecessarily given by 'whatever appeared in a paper confessedly their organ', despite an inability either to acknowledge or to disavow such a connection. He repudiated the claim of any journal to represent his views, the probable effect of the publication being to divide the party into separate factions. He distrusted, he coldly informed Stanley, all the individuals engaged in the project and, while not publicly disparaging the initiative, wanted it clearly understood 'that his name was to be in no way used'.[37] Derby dissuaded the Duke of Northumberland from funding the new journal, while Malmesbury unsuccessfully urged Disraeli not to proceed with publication. In its first issue, on 7 May, *The Press* lampooned 'the motley crew of statesmen' clustered around Aberdeen, while subsequent numbers proposed 'a manly alliance' of Conservatives and Whigs, ensuring that moderate Reform remained a bulwark against democratic forces.[38] During the spring of 1853 Derby repeatedly voiced his dark suspicion that the ambitious and opportunistic Disraeli was 'aiming at the first place'.[39]

Derby never visited Hughenden. Disraeli only received his first invitation to Knowsley in December 1853. The invitation was not extended to Mary Anne Disraeli. Disraeli's verdict on Knowsley was predictably scathing. He deemed it 'a wretched house, yet very vast'. It was 'an irregular pile of many ages, half of it like St. James's Palace, low, red with turrets—the other like the Dutch façade of Hampton Court'.[40] Nonetheless, he admired the park, almost as large as Windsor, surrounding the house, which provided a setting of 'great beauty'. The grounds contained 'red deer, as well as fallow deer, oak forests, a splendid lake, great undulation, and in the moorland, or as it is called in Lancashire, Moss, the landscape is all rhododendron on a large scale'. In turn, Derby seemed bored by Disraeli's company. It obliged him to discuss politics with a visitor who had no interest in field or turf.[41] Following the exertions of the previous months, Derby's spirits remained low through much of 1853, melancholy clouding his assessment of political affairs. Disraeli's presence at Knowsley proved an unpleasant irritation. The social chasm between the two men never seemed greater than when they came together under the same roof at Knowsley. Disraeli retained the strong impression that Derby only employed him without trusting him. Disraeli's oratorical skills were useful to Derby, just as Derby's endorsement remained essential to Disraeli. Mutual need, rather than trust, remained the basis of their relationship.

When, in February 1853, Disraeli saw an opportunity to attack the coalition, over the offence given to France by the speeches of Graham and Wood describing Napoleon III as a despot, a wearied Derby was unenthusiastic. Nonetheless, on 18 February, Disraeli spoke at length in the Commons on the importance of a cordial understanding with France to British foreign relations. Aberdeen, Wood, and Graham were picked out by Disraeli for particular criticism, while Palmerston was largely spared. When he represented the Whigs as subservient to the Peelites and the radicals as the tools of both, Stanley admiringly judged it 'a most skilful and ingenious rubbing up of old sores'.[42] The speech raised the spirits of the Commons opposition and drew prolonged cheering from the Conservative back benches. But Derby refused to attach importance to it. The speech enhanced Disraeli's reputation for withering satire, but diminished his claim to the possession of prudence.

To keep good watch and still be near at hand.

(Derby, *The Iliad of Homer*, ii. 97)

In almost entire seclusion Derby spent much of the early part of the 1853 session at St Leonards in Windsor in very low spirits. The death of his eldest sister, Lady Charlotte Penrhyn, on 15 February, aged 52, overlaid physical incapacity with private grief. In early March he travelled to Liverpool to attend the formal opening of the Derby Museum, housing his father's zoological specimens in cramped temporary quarters in Duke Street. After a brief stay at Knowsley he returned south, visiting the

Northampton races on 31 March to watch his horse Longbow win the Delapre Stakes. But the strain of the previous twelve months, when the heavy burden of government had fallen largely on his shoulders and with his mistrust of Disraeli's intentions, left him much depressed. In early April his 82-year-old father-in-law, Lord Skelmersdale, having lapsed into unconsciousness, died at Lathom House, and an attentive Derby offered his grieving wife what consolation he could in her bereavement. Two deaths within the close family over a six-week period compounded Derby's dejection.

Throughout most of 1853 and 1854 Derby remained remote, weighed down by a dark mood of despondency. Only occasionally did he travel to London to attend debates in the Lords. Disraeli complained of 'the Captain's self-imposed isolation and their leader's reluctance to entertain his political supporters; particularly those numerous new Conservative backbenchers elected to parliament the previous July'. A 'great muster', Disraeli urged, would do more for Conservative morale than 'a great division'.[43] Yet in private conversation an ill and tired Derby expressed an expectation of never holding office again. If the coalition refused to bid for Liberal support, he thought, and proposed Conservative measures, 'they might, with their strength and prestige, destroy his party within two years'. With gloomy fatalism he repeated his conviction, 'which he said had been forced on him early in public life, that real political power was not to be had in England: at best you could only a little advance or retard the progress of an inevitable movement'. An English minister, he believed, 'had more responsibility, more labour and less authority, than the ruler of any people on earth', the only posts of power remaining being the Governor Generalship of India and the editorship of *The Times*.[44]

In early April, Derby's spirits and health partially recovered. Having arrived in London on Thursday 14 April, he urged Malmesbury, himself fresh back from a stay in Paris and a meeting with Napoleon III, not to give the impression of stifling any parliamentary inquiry into corrupt electoral practices, even if embarrassing to themselves. On Saturday 16 April he gave a party at St James's Square for his supporters, which was much better attended than the previous meeting in December.[45] The gathering, Stanley noted, was 'very crowded and enthusiastic', his father speaking to the assembled Conservatives for one and a half hours.[46] As usual, the Conservatives responded spiritedly to Derby's return to the fray. But the volatile nature of Commons party feeling had been evident on Friday 15 April, when Disraeli led the Conservatives in support of Milner Gibson's annual resolution to abolish the advertisement duty, an abandoned element in Disraeli's original budget plan of the previous session. Alongside the radicals and the Irish Brigade, the Conservatives carried the resolution repealing taxes on knowledge with a majority of thirty-one MPs, by 200 to 169 votes. Many Conservatives were annoyed, however, to be employed in carrying a radical objective. The dangers of which Derby had warned in undertaking hostile initiatives against the coalition ministry were affirmed. His successful gathering at St James's Square the following day was intended to repair Conservative unity prior to Gladstone's major budget statement on Monday 18 April.

Gladstone's budget, delivered in a speech of epic proportions lasting five hours and displaying a formidable technical mastery, was Peelism writ large. His ambitious Free Trade budget established the office of Chancellor of the Exchequer and national finance as central to executive politics. A wide range of indirect taxes and duties were reduced or abolished, the income tax extended until 1860, and the social base of those liable to pay income tax broadened. The cabinet, however, only reached agreement on Gladstone's budget the very day of his statement to the Commons. Palmerston and Wood, in particular, objected to various aspects of Gladstone's plan. Yet, in the Commons the budget was received well, with prolonged and enthusiastic cheering. Every party, except the landed interest, 'took away something in the way of a boon'.[47] The Manchester School radicals welcomed the extension of the legacy duty on land. The Irish Brigade praised the remission of debt for Ireland. Popular acclaim greeted Gladstone's delivery of cheaper tea and soap, while the press welcomed the reduction of the advertisement duty.

Despite their dislike of the succession duty, most Conservatives opposed a contest over Gladstone's budget. In turn, Gladstone's coup shored up the coalition in a characteristically Peelite demonstration of executive ability. In the wake of Gladstone's success, Derby called another party meeting at St James's Square on Monday 25 April, intended to sustain Conservative morale. By hinting that he would retire unless the party kept together, he preserved Conservative unity under the pressure of Gladstone's triumph, a financial scheme similar, in various aspects, to that which Disraeli had failed to deliver the previous December. Yet it seemed that the government were not about to fracture. Derby's opposition strategy of patient passivity was apparently not going to return the Conservatives to office in the near future. The hostile observer Greville noted the impotent rage of the Derbyites at Gladstone's success, the legacy duty bestowing a heavy blow on the landed interest.[48]

While Gladstone's budget occupied Commons attention, in the Lords, on Friday 22 and Monday 25 April, Derby criticized the coalition's first noteworthy legislation, the Canadian Clergy Reserves Bill. In 1840 Russell had extended the Clergy Reserves, comprising one-seventh of all Canadian land grants, to Protestants generally as well as Catholics, thereby breaking the Anglican monopoly established by Pitt in 1791. The new measure proposed to vest the Canadian legislature, rather than Westminster, with the power of securing this arrangement. After passing its Commons second reading on 4 March the Duke of Newcastle introduced the measure in the Lords on 22 April. Derby immediately opposed disturbing the 1840 settlement. The Canadian legislature, he feared, wished to secularize the church revenues and establish the principle of voluntarism. But not wishing simply to reject a bill possessing the sanction of the Commons, he warned of his intention to amend the measure in Committee. On 25 April he moved an amendment aimed at protecting the inalienable property of the churches of Scotland and England in Canada.[49] In what Aberdeen acknowledged was an 'ingenious and dexterous speech',[50] he argued that the bill rendered the Church dependent on the State and its revenues at the disposal of the State. Such a rule, he warned, might subsequently be applied to the Church in England, or still more to the Church of Ireland. His own 1833 Irish Church Temporalities Act, he reminded the Lords, while diminishing the number of Anglican bishops in Ireland, had also affirmed that the property of the Church was inviolate. The government's new measure, he argued, was inconsistent in claiming to provide for existing interests, while at the same time giving uncontrolled power to the colonial legislature. He was infuriated by the support of some ecclesiastical lords, particularly the conciliatory Bishop of Oxford, Samuel Wilberforce, for the measure. His chagrin led him to suggest Wilberforce's culpability on the issue, quoting the Shakespearian line 'A man may smile and smile, and be a villain.' Clarendon immediately accused Derby of unparliamentary language, whereupon barbed repartee followed. At the close of the debate Derby and Clarendon 'ended by drinking each other's health in water across the table' and Derby's amendment was defeated by 117 to 77 votes.[51] So was revealed Derby's intention to wound, but inability to topple, the coalition.

On Tuesday 10 May, Derby supported Lord Grey in attacking the government's announcement of the virtual abandonment of penal transportation without the matter being considered by parliament. But again he held back from mounting a decisive assault. He declared himself in favour of the discontinuance of transportation, but believed abandonment should be gradual. He thought that convicts had a much greater chance of permanent amendment in life in the colonies than at home. Without allowing parliament to discuss the matter the government were in danger of engaging in ill-considered changes. Yet, he concluded, he had no desire to cast a slur or censure on the ministry.[52] Grey's motion was defeated by 54 to 37 votes and in July the Lord Chancellor, with little parliamentary debate, reduced the number of crimes for which transportation remained a punishment.

Gladstone introduced his resolution, establishing succession duties, into the Commons on Friday 13 May. Aberdeen anticipated this being 'the most formidable part of the budget, especially in the Lords, although popular in the country'.[53] On Friday 27 May, Derby supported Malmesbury's motion for a Select Committee, the Commons having passed the resolution on its first reading without a division. The Lords should not, he urged, either legislate blindly or meekly comply with the behests of the other House. By examining the proposal in Select Committee, the Lords, he agreed, would enable the Commons to amend the bill in its later stages. He rejected Aberdeen's claim that Gladstone's financial plan had been an immense success, almost without precedence. Rather, he maintained, Gladstone had underestimated the amount to be levied under the terms of the duty and Derby believed that, in many cases, the tax would produce great hardship. Their lordships could not, he concluded, shut their eyes, bow their heads, and pass a bill that would work injustice, in passive obedience to the Commons.[54] Yet, Malmesbury's motion was defeated by 139 to 126 votes, all thirteen episcopal votes going with the government. The absence of a number of Conservative peers, others being shut out of the division, rescued the ministry from what some cabinet members feared was a probable defeat. In the Commons the Conservatives split over Pakington's motion, on 13 June, to postpone the succession duty, twenty-eight Conservatives supporting the government, with the Irish Brigade abstaining from the vote. By June, Conservative fragmentation in the Commons, exacerbated by deep dislike of Disraeli, was increasingly apparent. It was with a sense of relief that Derby left the Conservative squabbles of Westminster for the Epsom Downs in late May, where he watched his horse Dervish win the Two-Year-Old Stakes by a length.

During June and July 1853 parliament passed the Income Tax Bill, the Spirits Excise Bill, the Customs Duties Bill, and the Stamp Duties Bill, which, alongside the succession duty, comprised Gladstone's ambitious financial plan. In the Lords, on Tuesday 21 June, Derby accepted the income tax proposal as inevitable, though he objected to its principles and believed Gladstone's calculations were vague and illusory.[55] Similarly, on Wednesday 22 July he reiterated his objections to the succession duty, dubbing Gladstone 'a phoenix of the Exchequer, in whom Mr. Pitt rose from his ashes with redoubled lustre', but feared that the Lords had little choice but to bow to the injustice which the Commons was pleased to inflict.[56] His personal objection to the succession duty was fierce, but he reluctantly acknowledged his inability to block it. His opposition excited sufficient ministerial anxiety for the government whips to fetch peers from Paris, Brussels, and Dublin Castle to ensure a majority on the second reading. But, when the government whip Lord Bessborough enquired if Derby would oppose the third reading, Derby peevishly replied: 'The bill may go to the Devil, for all I care; I shall take no further trouble about it.'[57]

Conservative divisions in the Commons were painfully exposed in debate on Wood's cautious India Bill. Presented by Wood in a dull and prolix speech on Friday 3 June, the measure preserved the existing dual government of India, the cabinet and the East India Company jointly exercising control over the Governor General of India. Wood proposed to amend, however, the process of appointment to the Court of Directors and to curtail their patronage.[58] Bright immediately attacked the bill for merely tinkering with a matter which required far-reaching reform. Two days later Bright privately met Disraeli to coordinate opposition to Wood's legislation.[59] Then, on Thursday 23 June, during the measure's second Commons reading, Stanley moved for a postponement of legislation, until further information had been obtained.[60] But there was precious little Conservative support for Stanley's motion, the sharpest criticism of the bill coming from radicals such as Cobden, Bright, and Hume, while Graham and Macaulay spiritedly defended Wood's measure. Disraeli, on Thursday 30 June, attacked the bill, though acknowledging that many of his party supported it. In the event, the second reading was passed by 322 to 140 votes, eighty-seven Conservatives voting with the government.

Even before Wood presented his India Bill, Derby had been anxious about Conservative disunity over the issue. Many Conservatives, such as Lord Lonsdale, informed him that they looked upon the East India Company 'as a good Tory body' and that they favoured the maintenance of the dual system. Anticipating that the government hoped for the defection of a large number of Conservative backbenchers, he urged Disraeli to 'feel their pulse, before we take any irretrievable steps'.[61] On Monday 20 June he again urged Disraeli to exercise great caution, so as to prevent 'open mutiny in the camp'. Henley, Herries, and Lonsdale, meanwhile, communicated to Derby their support for Wood's measure. It was clear, he then advised Disraeli, that 'we have no chance of carrying with us anything like the united strength of our party'. A considerable portion of dissatisfaction, he suggested, was attributable to deep suspicions of any understanding with the radicals. Derby himself opposed overthrowing the government through a junction 'of the most conflicting elements'. He feared Disraeli was gradually withdrawing from his Conservative supporters and seeking alliances in quarters with which, Derby warned, he could not recognize any bond of union.[62] As Derby anticipated, Disraeli and Stanley's precipitous move, while failing to block Wood's India Bill, displayed the deep divisions within Conservative ranks. Stanley recognized that the defeat was the result of his own and Disraeli's unpopularity among the Conservatives. For Derby the spectacle was the more mortifying because he believed that the coalition cabinet had 'no elements of strength in itself, but the permanent disruption of our party in the House of Commons'. The declaration on Thursday 9 June, voiding Lord Adolphus Vane's election as Conservative MP for Durham because of bribery and the coercive influence exerted by Lord Londonderry on his employees, rubbed further salt in the open wound of Conservative dissension.

By the summer of 1853 the Commons Conservative party appeared to be falling apart. Less a strategic preference, patient passivity now seemed a disheartening consequence of party disunity. During the session over 100 Conservative MPs voted with the government against their opposition colleagues in at least one division. Over fifty-eight Conservatives supported the government in several divisions. Disraeli had neither the inclination, authority, nor skill to preserve Conservative unity in a pose of inaction. A restless urge to be constantly doing and a persistent flirting with radicals and Irish had created deep divisions within Conservative ranks. Disraeli supported Russell's Jewish Disabilities Bill, which was vigorously opposed by the Ultras, Newdegate, Inglis, and Sibthorp. The bill was subsequently rejected by a large Lords majority. Likewise, Disraeli abstained from the division on Spooner's annual anti-Maynooth grant motion and silently voted alongside the government in a division on church rates. As the Whig George Cornewall Lewis observed: 'The principal occupation of the Derbyites at present is … to vent maledictions against Dizzy.'[63] Cornewall Lewis interpreted Disraeli's increasing absence from the Commons, 'after his former pugnacious and censorious habits', as 'indicating a consciousness of defeat … A party can only be formed by some strong interest and opinion, or by a great personal popularity and qualities which inspire confidence. Disraeli has neither the one nor the other to trade upon … Nobody can say what his opinions are—and few believe he has any.'[64]

At the end of June 1853 Malmesbury suggested to Stanley 'that Disraeli could not be and ought not to be leader'.[65] Malmesbury hoped that Stanley might succeed Disraeli, if Stanley's sympathies for the Liberal side were held in check. But, while affirming his loyalty to the party as long as his father remained in politics, Stanley wished to retain his freedom, once Derby retired, to form any connection which might then seem suitable. 'From any wish to lead the Conservative party the fate of Peel is enough to set me free,' Stanley concluded.[66] Thus Disraeli remained the only credible Commons leader available to Derby. Yet, by 1853 Disraeli also appeared the single greatest obstacle to Conservative unity. Derby reprimanded Disraeli during June for leaving the chamber prior to a vote on the ballot, and for absenting himself from discussions on the succession duty.[67] Such behaviour clearly indicated, he remonstrated, that Disraeli wished to distance himself from his supporters. Yet with whom could he replace the maverick Disraeli? The paucity of Conservative talent, shorn of Peelite expertise, left an irritated Derby little choice but to cajole a man he neither liked nor trusted. After seven years the legacy of 1846, despite the abandonment of Protection, continued to constrain his political options. During July his despondency, which had partially lifted during April and May, returned. For his own part, Disraeli despaired that 'nothing can be more unsatisfactory than the condition of the Tory party'.[68] The dispatches he received from Knowsley, he complained, only took the 'shape of haunches of venison'.[69]

During August a downcast Derby approved the appointment of Sir William Jolliffe as Commons chief whip, in place of the discredited Forbes MacKenzie, unseated for bribery at Liverpool. Jolliffe was MP for Petersfield and had served as Under-Secretary for the Home Office in 1852. A popular landed gentleman with good connections among the Conservative gentry, the 53-year-old Jolliffe faced a formidable challenge in restoring harmony to the Commons back benches. Derby's endorsement was essential to any prospect of success. If he was seen as the nominee of Disraeli, Jolliffe warned Derby, 'I would not retain the post a moment.'[70] Derby hoped that Jolliffe's tact might repair the damage caused by Disraeli. Colonel Edward Taylor and the able Lord Mandeville, heir to the Duke of Manchester, were appointed as Jolliffe's assistants. So might 'the *dejecta membra* of our body politic', Derby urged Disraeli, be reunited.[71] But for Jolliffe's team to be effective there had to be an insistence on Disraeli's 'riding to orders'.[72] In 1848 the Conservative Commons opposition had descended into a disorganized throng, divided by mutual suspicion and devoid of effective leadership. After 1849 party unity was repaired and a brief spell in government restored their collective will. But 1853 saw a return of Commons disarray, which greatly eased the Aberdeen coalition's difficulties. In 1853, as in 1848, Derby's severe ill health allowed internal squabbles to fester, underscoring the importance of his personal authority to the preservation of Conservative solidarity.

While the fragmented Conservative Commons party presented a dispiriting political spectacle, on Wednesday 8 June 1853 Derby attended his triumphant ceremonial installation as Chancellor of Oxford University. Having arrived in Oxford on Tuesday 7 June as a guest of the Vice-Chancellor at Worcester College, Derby hosted a ball at the Town Hall, to which representatives of the University and city were invited. The same day he opened the theological training college at Culham near Abingdon, delivering an address in which he urged that moral improvement must keep pace with the material advancement of their age. The following day his installation, as part of the Encaenia ceremony, took place. The Conservative backbencher Sir William Fraser well remembered the imposing scene in Wren's Sheldonian Theatre. 'Lord Derby's appearance was magnificent. Dressed in his rich robes of black satin, with masses of gold; tall; of exceptionally dignified presence; no one could look the Chancellor better than he.'[73] Malmesbury believed nothing could exceed the enthusiasm with which Derby's installation was received by the University. Derby 'spoke magnificently, and did the whole thing with great dignity and grace, looking very distingué in his Chancellor's robes'. He delivered his Latin oration without notes, 'the learned critics' agreeing that 'they could only find two trifling faults in it'.[74] Loud cheering for Derby, it was noted, was especially strong from the undergraduates assembled in the upper gallery.[75]

During his speeches Derby expressed his unshakeable conviction that Oxford must remain a university of the Church of England, but, in addition to classical and mathematical studies, he hoped that the study of modern languages, modern history, comparative law, and the physical sciences would continue to acquire an increasing importance. Following his installation, the new Chancellor immediately bestowed a number of honorary degrees upon eminent literary and scientific men, such as Thomas Macaulay, as well as many of his former ministerial colleagues. The honorands included Disraeli, Stanley, the Duke of Richmond, Lord St Leonards, Malmesbury, Pakington, Walpole, Henley, George Hamilton, Edward Bulwer Lytton, and Lord Eglinton. The Tory historian and Protection publicist Sir Archibald Alison was also honoured. Such a list, *The Times* complained, showed the University to have become a final refuge for the discredited, formerly Protectionist, faction,[76] a confirmation

of Oxford as the home of lost causes. At the beginning of the ceremony
Disraeli looked pale and nervous. Derby had warned him that 'we shall
have to run the gauntlet of the public opinion of the undergraduates, who
on that occasion gave free vent to their political and personal feelings'.[77]
But a burst of loud cheering accompanied the bestowal on a relieved
Disraeli of an honorary degree of DCL. A great effect was also produced
when Stanley approached the new Chancellor, who declared slowly and
distinctly, 'Fili mi dilectissime!'[78]

At the celebratory Gaudy that evening, in the Hall of Christ Church,
Derby sat at high table beside the distinguished 74-year-old Greek scholar
Thomas Gaisford, long-serving Dean of Christ Church. Surrounded
by the Canons and Students of Christ Church, he recalled his own
undergraduate days at 'the House', reflecting on his elevation from high-
spirited gentleman commoner to acclaimed Chancellor. His predecessors
as Chancellor since 1792, the Duke of Portland and Lord Grenville,
had also been Christ Church men as well as prime ministers, while
Wellington's name was entered on the books of 'the House' (his brother
having been a distinguished Christ Church undergraduate) at his election
as Chancellor in 1834. Through Derby, Christ Church's pre-eminence
within Oxford and its direct association with the foremost public office
in the nation's affairs was maintained. As MP for the University and
a fellow Christ Church man, Gladstone proposed the toast to the new
Chancellor, quoting, by way of compliment, from Derby's own translation
of Manzoni's ode 'Il Cinque Maggio'. Depicting Napoleon on St Helena,
looking out on the turbulent ocean and imagining a vast army obeying his
command, Gladstone declaimed:

> He saw the quick-struck tents again:
> The hot assault: the battle plain.
> The troops in martial pomp arrayed:
> The pealing of the Artillery:
> The torrent charge of Cavalry:
> The hasty word,
> In thunder heard:
> Heard; and obeyed.[79]

While praising by analogy Derby's eminence, the depiction of united
ranks stood as ironic comment on the divided parliamentary troops
Derby commanded. Gladstone tactfully amended the final line of the
passage, which read as 'Heard and at once obeyed', although the allusion
to hasty words remained as a pointed personal reference. Nevertheless,

Gladstone noted that the applause for Derby after the dinner was especially tumultuous.[80]

The martial metaphor of Gladstone's tribute had wider resonance, as it echoed growing national anxiety about impending war in the Near East. During 1853 the gravest European crisis since 1815 confronted Aberdeen's government. Believing Turkey to be on the brink of collapse, Russia demanded, in May 1853, that the Sultan acknowledge Russian protection of his Christian subjects. When Turkey refused what was in effect an ultimatum, diplomatic relations were broken off and, on 3 July, Russian troops marched into Turkey's Danubian Principalities. The attempt by the European powers to negotiate a settlement, the so-called Vienna Note, failed. On 4 October, Turkey declared war against Russia. From the beginning Aberdeen's cabinet was divided over the crisis, with Clarendon, as Foreign Secretary, caught between contending ministerial groups. Both Palmerston and Russell believed Britain must defend Turkey, as a key element in the European balance of power, against the expansionism of anti-liberal Russia, Turkish misrule being played down. Aberdeen and Graham, meanwhile, opposed decisive support for Turkey as likely to precipitate wider hostilities. Under diplomatic pressure from Austria and France to shore up Turkey against Russian aggression, by June Aberdeen feared that 'we are drifting fast towards war'.[81] A conference of Austrian, French, Prussian, and British representatives, which produced the Vienna Note of 28 July as a basis for the settlement of the dispute, was rejected by Turkey and wilfully misrepresented by Russia. As popular Russophobia mounted in Britain, following Turkey's declaration of war, in January 1854 the French and British fleets were moved into the Black Sea. Then, with Russia refusing either to submit to an international conference or to evacuate the Principalities, on 12 March 1854 Britain and France signed an alliance with Turkey. On 28 March the Allies declared war against Russia.

As early as May 1853 Derby believed that 'matters look very threatening'.[82] On his prompting, Malmesbury asked Clarendon in the Lords for an account of diplomatic affairs, in response to which Clarendon was evasive. Derby and Malmesbury favoured a decided move by Britain to indicate support for Turkey. In conversation with Palmerston on 29 May, Malmesbury found the Home Secretary favoured 'decided measures against Russia', but learnt of Aberdeen's extreme reluctance to undertake such a move.[83] Again, on 30 May, Clarendon in the Lords and Russell in the Commons refused to comment on either the collapse of diplomatic relations between Russia and Turkey or British fleet movements. During the summer it was clear that the government was deeply divided. But

Malmesbury believed that Palmerston's more robust view would eventually prevail over Aberdeen's vacillation. During mid-July, Derby left Westminster for the Liverpool races, where he enjoyed much success, Longbow winning the Croxteth Stakes by a head, his horse Sortie coming first in the Produce Sweepstakes, and his 3-year-old Umbriel winning both the Triennial Produce Stakes and the Bickerstaffe Stakes. At Goodwood, on 29 July, he watched his 2-year-old colt Boiardo win the Rous Biennial Stakes.

In Westminster, meanwhile, dissatisfaction with the government's handling of the Eastern crisis increased. At the beginning of August Lord Clanricarde again pressed the government for information. This prepared the way for Malmesbury's call for the production of papers on 14 August. He emphasized the importance of good relations with France and the value of Turkish independence to Britain, and criticized the actions of Russia over the past months. It was Russia's doubts about Britain's maintaining an alliance with France in support of Turkey, he believed, that had encouraged the inconsistent diplomacy of the Tsar. This led Malmesbury into a retrospective vindication of his own policy as Foreign Secretary, which had made the alliance with France one of his principal objects, so discarding the old prejudices which for centuries had prevailed between the two countries.[84] Again, Clarendon refused to divulge information while the European powers were in diplomatic negotiations to resolve the conflict. Clanricarde, Lord Hardwicke, and Lord Beaumont subsequently registered their indignation at Russia's occupation of the Danubian Principalities. Privately, Malmesbury denounced the Vienna Note, whose details became known during August. It was 'a most disgraceful business', he declared, as the Note made no mention of evacuating the Danubian Principalities and contained terms which Britain and France had previously advised Turkey to reject. The government were, he noted, 'in great difficulties'.[85] Derby shared Malmesbury's concern that Aberdeen's indecisive diplomacy was endangering the Anglo-French entente, while at the same time misleading the Tsar over Britain's intentions.[86]

During the last day of the session, on Tuesday 16 August, the ministry faced blistering attacks in the Commons. For the radicals, A. H. Layard and Cobden pronounced Turkish misrule no less distasteful than that in Russia. Cobden believed Russian military strength, which was much exaggerated by the British press, posed no direct threat to British interests and he vigorously protested against any policy leading to war. The government was only rescued by Palmerston's interjection, forcefully arguing that the maintenance of Turkish integrity was both a desirable and a feasible object of British policy. The end of the session saved the government, Graham believed, from a breach on the ministerial benches soon spreading into a rupture.[87] Yet, apart from a mild speech by Pakington, the Conservative opposition took no part in the debate, a sullen Disraeli already having left London for Hughenden.

As, during the autumn of 1853, the Eastern crisis slid towards war and cabinet tensions increased, Derby watched for ministerial fractures. In early September, Malmesbury advised him that 'if Palmerston left the government there is no doubt that many of our staunchest supporters would follow him as leader of the Commons'.[88] Greville noticed that the Conservatives paid Palmerston 'every sort of court, never attack him, and not only defer to him on all occasions, but make all the difference they can between him and the rest of the government'. For his part, Palmerston did not 'discourage or reject these civilities', thinking 'the disposition towards him of that large political party enhances his value to his own friends and increases his power, besides affording him a good alternative in case anything should happen to break up the present government or separate him from it'.[89] This was a gradual fulfilment of Derby's plan of killing the coalition with kindness.

On Wednesday 5 October, Derby attended a banquet given in his honour by the Mayor of Liverpool. Speaking after the dinner he rejected recent declarations that the government of the country should be carried on independently of party. The nation could have little confidence, he pronounced, in a ministry whose elements were heterogeneous and differed from each other by a broad line of separation. While claiming credit for the prosperous position, commercially and otherwise, of the nation's finances secured under his own ministry, he concluded by declaring that, in the event of war, his party would 'uphold the dignity of the Crown and the sacredness of treaties'.[90] Then suddenly, on Monday 17 October at Knowsley, Derby suffered his most severe attack of gout for many years. In intense pain and scarcely able to move in bed, he languished for days in an agonizing state of extreme debility. Not until late November did he begin to recover. He occupied himself during his prolonged confinement by translating Homer's *Iliad* and pieces from foreign languages, including further sections of Alessandro Manzoni's 'Ode to Napoleon'. The gloom of earlier in the year returned, his own form of exile at Knowsley removing him from the political battle. Whether, as with Napoleon's escape from Elba, Derby would be able to return remained a pressing question for his Conservative colleagues.

On every side the circling ring of war
Is blazing all around thee ...

(Derby, *The Iliad of Homer*, ii. 39)

During Derby's confinement to his sickbed in October 1853, Turkey declared war on Russia. Fighting immediately broke out on the Danube and in the Caucasus. Aberdeen and Clarendon remained inclined to put pressure on Turkey, as Palmerston and Russell continued to portray Russia as the real menace. Aberdeen admitted to the Queen in early November that 'symptoms of great differences were apparent' within the cabinet.[91] At the same time, during November, Aberdeen's compliance with Russell's enthusiasm for a Reform Bill, also supported by Graham and Newcastle, put even more pressure on ministerial relations. A cabinet committee began drafting a measure for the 1854 session. While honouring Russell's pledge to parliamentary Reform, although the country seemed indifferent to the matter, it was anticipated that the issue would probably drive Palmerston further into the wilderness.

Reports of growing government disunity prompted an excited Malmesbury, on 15 October, to urge Disraeli to persuade an ailing Derby of the urgency for consultation. If Derby hoped to turn out the government, Malmesbury implored, he must set out a plan. 'To rush again into action without concert, every man with his own hobby and God against us all, will only seal the fate of a party which is all but in extremis.'[92] As a result, Disraeli wrote to a bedridden Derby, on 28 October, requesting his leader's 'general opinion as to affairs'.[93] Clearly the government's hope to 'weather the storm and meet parliament with peace', Disraeli observed, was dashed. If the ministry proposed a Reform measure based on 'territorial principles', he was inclined to support them, as this would lead to the break-up of the Liberal party. But if, on the other hand, the government's bill was a radical measure, the Conservatives would find the country on their side. Moreover, the recent appointments of Jolliffe as chief whip and Philip Rose as the party's new election agent, Disraeli believed, had brought greater efficiency to Conservative extra-parliamentary organization, with the constituency registration lists of electors in an improved state. Rose had established a new staff to manage future elections, replacing the discredited personnel overseen by Beresford, with Markham Spofforth as a paid agent. As a result, a combative Disraeli gauged that 'we could not be too quiet, and that the best course we could take was indirectly to sustain the spirit of our friends and to remove, as far as one could, socially any apathy or misapprehension among those who were in our ranks'. The difficulties of the government would assist them. To this end, Disraeli judged Derby's statement in Liverpool earlier in the month 'very judicious, spirited and apposite'. In conclusion, Disraeli commented on the strike by cotton operatives currently spreading throughout Lancashire. In response to a demand for a 10 per cent increase in wages in mid-October, the mill owners locked out the workforce. In Preston 80,000 hands joined the strike. As industrial conflict spread, Disraeli speculated, it might give the radicals the popular cry they currently lacked in calling for further parliamentary Reform.

Illness prevented Derby from replying to Disraeli until Monday 14 November. When he was finally able to do so, he sought to identify the rock upon which the government would split apart. Either foreign affairs or parliamentary Reform might sink the ministry. But he anticipated that Reform would prove the treacherous hazard upon which the coalition would founder. On this vital subject he urged Disraeli to amass current statistics on town and country representation, taking care not to count unrepresented towns as county population. Derby's particular concern remained the increasing intrusion into the counties of urban voters. He agreed that Jolliffe's tact and popularity would do much to restore party unity. But he seriously doubted whether, as Disraeli naively suggested, 'a single speech at the right moment in either House' would 'clear the skies'. The effect could only be temporary 'and the clouds will gather again, unless there is in the party a strong foundation of personal confidence, which must be maintained by constant attention, and even by some indulgence to the prejudice of those whom we lead'.[94] Derby impressed on his Commons leader the importance of diligently attending to backbench sentiment. The damage done by Disraeli's fanciful alliances and neglectful disdain for his own supporters, he implied, had largely created the dispiriting trough into which Conservative morale had slumped. Only by acting as a committed leader, sensitive to his followers' opinions, he believed, could Disraeli restore Conservative unity, an achievement requiring more than just one stirring speech. 'Manifest dissensions', Derby warned, 'indicative of internal weakness, react upon the country, and tend to deprive us of support which we should otherwise have.'

As far as the strikes by Lancashire cotton operatives were concerned, though serious and dangerous, Derby saw them as an 'irremediable evil—irremediable that is to say as far as any legislative provisions can go'. Ultimately, capital would always prove too strong for labour. After much suffering to themselves and loss to their employers, he predicted, 'the workmen will always have to give in'. If this were not so, a large portion of our manufacturing capital would transfer itself to other countries. The only remedy was increasing intelligence among the working classes and 'a more just appreciation of the relative positions, duties and responsibilities of themselves and their employers'. It was unfortunate, Stanley noted, that no personal intercourse between cotton masters and operatives paralleled those relations existing between rural landlords and tenants. But if urban unrest made manufacturers more decidedly Conservative, then that would bode well for parliamentary Reform.[95]

Derby's reproaches had an immediate effect. In consultation with Pakington and Jolliffe, Disraeli met with Walpole in early December to discuss how best to prevent 'a mortifying decomposition of our friends'.[96] As a result, Pakington was hopeful 'that when parliament meets we shall find a very large majority of those members of our House who have hitherto been followers of Lord Derby still disposed to regard him as the greatest and safest statesman of the present day, and no less willing to rally round [Disraeli] as their leader in the House of Commons'.[97] Disraeli's first invitation to Knowsley in early December was intended to steel his resolve. Though appearing thin and pale, Derby seemed somewhat improved, Disraeli noted, and looked younger than his 54 years. The gout remained in one ankle, which still rendered Derby housebound. And, although he appeared bored by Disraeli's presence, the visit served its primary purpose by giving Disraeli the impression that his leader 'was extremely anxious to come in again, and full of fight'.[98] Upon returning to London, Disraeli energetically refuted the rumours circulating Tattersall's and the clubs that Derby remained gravely ill. Following Disraeli's visit, Derby wrote to Walpole urging the critical importance of party unity. Over foreign affairs, he observed, the coalition government 'have got themselves and the country into a scrape from which they will find it very difficult to escape with honour'. But he doubted whether, if the coalition were broken apart by internal differences over foreign policy, the Conservatives could reconstruct a government with any prospect of permanence. But Reform, on the other hand, was a question which must cause the coalition 'very serious embarrassment'.[99] He had received accurate reports that Palmerston fiercely objected to Russell's proposals for Reform, as threatening to swamp intelligence and property among the electorate with ignorance and poverty. Over Reform, Derby believed, it was of the utmost importance that the Conservatives were thoroughly united.

Having identified Reform as the crucial question upon which the Conservatives must act together and having brought Disraeli firmly into line,

Derby looked to cabinet dissension to scatter the ministerial front bench. He did not have long to wait. On Tuesday 13 December, Disraeli informed him of an unofficial approach to the Commons whip Colonel Taylor by the Peelite Lord Jocelyn, on behalf of the conservative section of the cabinet, primarily Palmerston. The spendthrift and wild Lord Jocelyn, heir to the Earl of Roden, was married to Palmerston's illegitimate daughter Lady Frances Cowper. Already, on Saturday 10 December, Palmerston had informed Aberdeen of his deep objections to any material change in the organic arrangements of the House of Commons. Those within the cabinet who were anxious about extensive Reform, Jocelyn indicated to Taylor, were not the Peelites, but those with whom the Conservatives 'might act without any disagreeable feeling or inconvenience'.[100] Jocelyn, Stanley's fellow MP for King's Lynn, expressed his wish to communicate further with the Conservative leadership. In response, Taylor affirmed that the Conservatives were both united and resolved, not wishing to disturb the government if they were cautious over Reform, but ready to conduct an opposition on uncompromising conservative principles. For his part, Disraeli restated the distinction between measures for purifying and for reforming parliament. If the ministry doubled the county electorate, by extending the suffrage to £10 householders, then the aristocratic principles of the constitution would inevitably be diminished. But, a proposal to allow £10 householders in the counties to vote in contiguous boroughs, and the reallocation of seats disfranchised for corruption to rural constituencies, would receive favourable consideration from the opposition. As Derby advised, the insulation of county constituencies from an intrusive popular urban electorate was the essence of responsible Reform.

Then in sensational prose, on Wednesday 14 December, *The Times* announced Palmerston's dramatic resignation from the cabinet because of differences over the government's Reform measure. The coup, Derby responded, 'struck sooner than any one expected'.[101] Palmerston's resignation, he speculated, might prove fatal to the coalition. Jocelyn, now in direct communication with Derby, revealed that Palmerston had hoped to take Lansdowne with him. But, despite objecting to the Reform Bill, Lansdowne was persuaded to remain in office. Lansdowne chose to see the proposed government measure, introducing a £20 county franchise and extending the borough suffrage, as a desirable modification to the 1832 Act. Palmerston's departure alone, though a loss to the government, would prevent, Derby believed, any substantial support from gathering around the former Home Secretary. To his intermediary Jocelyn, Derby affirmed that his strongest objection to any Reform proposal would be to an assimilation of the county and borough franchise, which would have the effect of swamping the farmers with ten-pounders.[102] Malmesbury agreed that Lansdowne's refusal to resign had scuttled Palmerston's plan of placing himself at the head of 'the old and discontented Whigs'.[103] Indeed, Malmesbury suspected that the ministerial Peelites were very glad to be rid of Palmerston, his suggestions for amending the Reform plan being rejected by them at once, while Lansdowne's preferred modifications were willingly accepted 'as the price of his remaining'.[104] A belief prevailed that Palmerston had less resigned than been extruded from the cabinet. Certainly the court was delighted at his departure. 'If he is to go, as he most probably will, anyhow,' the Queen commented, 'let it be on the Reform question which is unpopular ground.'[105]

But, as news arrived in London of a devastating Turkish naval defeat at Sinope, which stimulated greater popular bellicosity in both Britain and France, Aberdeen feared that Palmerston had 'stolen a march by combining the Eastern Question with Reform'. Popular opinion refused to believe that Palmerston's quitting the cabinet had nothing to do with foreign policy. Grudgingly, an increasingly apprehensive Aberdeen acknowledged that 'truly [Palmerston] is a great artist'.[106] 'Love of war and hatred of Reform' were cleverly 'mingled in equal proportions' in Palmerston's protests, Graham noted.[107] As Palmerston, frustrated in his hopes of precipitating a wider cabinet breach, began to entertain second thoughts about his resignation, Aberdeen became increasingly anxious about bellicose press feeling rendering Palmerston a popular martyr to the coalition's hesitant diplomacy. Wood and Newcastle met Palmerston to explore the basis upon which he might return. Palmerston, for his part, welcomed their indication that the details of Reform were still open to modification and applauded the government's decision, in his absence, to send the British fleet into the Black Sea. This allowed Palmerston to register his wish, on Friday 23 December, to slip back into the cabinet, a desire with which, the following day, Aberdeen immediately complied.

The busy Jocelyn visited Derby at Knowsley on Tuesday 27 December and gave a detailed account of the ministerial crisis. Palmerston's reconciliation with his cabinet colleagues had clearly dashed Disraeli's early exultant speculation about the juncture of Palmerston and 'the old Whigs' with the Conservatives, leading to the creation of an opposition majority in the Commons. Nonetheless, Derby found much in the extraordinary episode to encourage them. It revealed those deep animosities churning just beneath the amicable surface of coalition collegiality. It was possible that Aberdeen, Russell, Graham, and Prince Albert had contrived the crisis in order either to expel Palmerston from the ministry or bring him to heel. That many Peelites reported that Palmerston had 'begged to be let in again' betrayed their sense of personal triumph. Equally, it was noted that, as soon as Palmerston resigned, he was 'congratulated by Lord Fitzwilliam and others of the discontented Whigs, who disliked the Peelites as much as they love their pocket boroughs'.[108] Some Whigs felt that the sole consolation in the prospect of war was that it would shelve Reform.[109] Resentment and self-congratulation exhibited precious little cordiality among the government. One of Palmerston's ministerial colleagues, it was heard at Knowsley, had delightedly pronounced that the Home Secretary 'had come to the door of the cabinet, whining like a dog to be let back in'.[110] Peelite exultation was implicit in the verdict that Palmerston 'has done for himself now'. As Disraeli reported to Derby, the Peelites were unabashedly 'crowing'.[111] Palmerston's confidants, meanwhile, saw the episode as proof of Palmerston's indispensability and a firm check on Russell's influence. Moreover, the pressure on Aberdeen to pursue a more robust policy against Russia mounted. Malmesbury was told by the Peelite Lord Clanwilliam that the cause of war in the Near East was Aberdeen's 'timid policy'.[112] Press attacks on Prince Albert attributed Aberdeen's ineffective diplomacy to unconstitutional Germanic royal influence. Events were forcing the ministry to follow the forthright policy Derby favoured. Malmesbury believed that Britain's active involvement in the war was now inevitable.

To this extent, the 1853 Christmas season brought Derby some warm political cheer. The dispiriting gloom of the previous year lifted. His health recovered with the New Year and his resolve returned. All other Commons parties, Stanley observed encouragingly, were now split. The Whigs and Peelites could no longer suppress their quarrels. The English radicals, approximately 100 strong, were divided into a war and peace party, the former led by John Roebuck and the latter represented by Cobden and Bright. Even the Irish Brigade had ended the previous session half sitting on one side of the Commons and half sitting on the other. Among the coalition cabinet, Russell was regarded 'as worn out in body and mind'; Clarendon wanted debating aptitude; Graham's talents were neutralized by his reputation for inconsistency; though admired for his financial mastery, Gladstone's verbosity, inscrutability, and religious views fostered mistrust; and Newcastle, despite being a favourite at court, lacked parliamentary standing.[113] Even Disraeli now agreed with Derby that their resignation from office, twelve months earlier, had 'proved to have been founded on a deeper knowledge of men and things than our critics gave us credit for'. In the approaching session Disraeli believed that Derby would 'not be much troubled any longer with grumblers in our party. The party's "confidence" is wonderfully restored.'[114]

With Jolliffe's support, a revived Derby urged Disraeli to hold regular meetings with the backbenchers. 'I cannot but think that much of the disorganisation which has prevailed has been owing to the want of unrestricted intercourse of this kind.'[115] Despite his own unquestioned overall authority, there was much, he confided in Jolliffe, 'that *must* be managed by the leader of the House of Commons'. Invitations were sent out for a dinner, given by Derby, for Conservative peers at St James's Square on Monday 30 January 1854, Disraeli hosting a gathering for Conservative MPs the same evening. With Jolliffe busily drawing up the guest lists, a purposeful Derby also agreed to give three dinners for a total of ninety-three Conservative MPs on 1, 4, and 8 February. In addition, Derby drafted a circular for distribution by Jolliffe to Conservative MPs, inviting them to meet with Disraeli at Grosvenor Gate each Saturday afternoon during the session to discuss the important questions being considered in parliament. Such frequent consultation would 'secure as far as possible a concurrence of opinion and uniformity of action amongst the members of the party'.[116] On Wednesday 11 January, Derby and Lady Derby were pleased to be guests of the Queen at Windsor, the cordiality of their reception interpreted as an indication of brightening Conservative fortunes. Then, returning to Knowsley, Derby characteristically celebrated his recovered health and new optimism by going 'out shooting in a heavy rain with 14 young gunners! Gout or manslaughter', Malmesbury brightly reported to Disraeli, 'must be his fate.'[117] On Friday 20 January a determined Derby arrived back in London. The following day Malmesbury confirmed that 'the Captain' was 'in great force' and 'would come to the post in prime order on the 31st'.[118]

Following Derby and Disraeli's dinners on Monday 30 January 1854, the next day, with parliament due to meet that evening, Derby held a party meeting at St James's Square, attended by about 150 Conservatives, to discuss the Queen's Speech. Speaking for one and a half hours, 'at times with great effect', Derby was received with much enthusiasm, despite the heat of the room and a shortage of seats.[119] He began by declaring that Aberdeen's government was formed upon less a fusion than a confusion of all principles. This unsatisfactory state of affairs was reflected in the Queen's Speech. The high price of food contrasted with ministerial boasts of prosperity, Derby suggesting that provisions would have been cheaper under Protection. Education, one of Aberdeen's main themes in the 1853 session and the subject of a bill which was dropped by the ministry without explanation, was not mentioned at all in the Queen's Speech. Derby's own view on education was that he was prepared to deal liberally with all sects, 'but no teaching could be worth anything that was not based on religion'.[120] He firmly dispelled the rumours that he hoped to introduce a Reform measure of his own; he preferred to abandon the cabinet to a predicament of their own making. With regard to foreign affairs, far from joining in denunciations of the Tsar, he 'thought the latter had been ill used, and had more reason to complain of Lord Aberdeen than Lord Aberdeen of him'. In consultation with Malmesbury, Disraeli, Walpole, and Stanley, Derby had already agreed not to attack ministers for resisting the warlike feeling as long as they could, 'but rather to blame them for general diplomatic blundering, and to point out the very slight difference between the terms offered by Russia and those which they would accept'.[121] He concluded his speech to the assembled Conservatives on 31 January by resolutely pronouncing on the favourable position of the party and the necessity of union. 'He eulogised Disraeli, who might have made mistakes, who dropped expressions which would have been better unuttered, but whose ability and devotion to their interests could not be doubted.'[122] The gathering concluded with a determined sense of renewed purpose.

A larger crowd than usual gathered to watch the royal procession opening parliament on Tuesday 31 January 1854, those outside the Palace of Westminster cheering vociferously the Turkish Ambassador.[123] In the Lords that evening a combative Derby launched a powerful barrage against the government. He targeted his anti-ministerial fire at the indefinite state of foreign affairs. It was a matter of conjecture, he fiercely declared, whether Britain was at peace or war. The government declined to declare Britain was at war, but talked of preserving peace. To the accompaniment of much laughter, he mockingly suggested this statement should be modified to say that before peace is preserved it must be restored. The ministry intimated that a state of warfare had ensued from the failure of negotiations.

> A state of warfare with whom? Are we engaged in that warfare? Are we belligerents? Are we partisans? Are we carrying on war openly and boldly, or are we carrying on that which is tantamount to war, but a war carried on in a pettifogging manner, and, I might almost say, in a manner discreditable to this great country? I know not ... [124]

British policy, he devastatingly continued, was shrouded in a dangerous obscurity. While the government had informed Russia that if their fleet left harbour this would be considered an act of hostility, the British fleet was conveying ammunition and troops to enable Turkey to prosecute the war.

Providing physical and moral support to Turkey was not a discreditable policy. But it meant that Britain was virtually engaged in war, with all the concomitant dangers and risks. Yet they remained without the dignity or moral effect of an open declaration of war.

To the accompaniment of loud cheering, Derby then delivered a pithy recapitulation of Russian policy over the last 150 years. Proceeding less by storm than by stealth, he averred, Russia had consistently pursued a policy of aggression. She fomented discontent among the subjects of subordinate states, then proffered mediation, then offered assistance to the weaker party, then declared the independence of that party, then placed that independence under the protection of Russia, and, finally, proceeded from protection to incorporation of that state into the gigantic body of the Russian Empire. Only when firmly opposed by Britain had Russia desisted from this creeping aggression. Yet, Derby observed, the Emperor of Russia had genuine cause to complain of being misled by the government's diplomacy. Ministerial ineptitude had led Russia to believe that under no provocation would measures of vigorous warfare be adopted and that there was no cordial union with France against Russia. If, however, war was inevitable, Britain's great object must be to carry it as soon as possible to a decisive and successful end. No time could be less opportune, he concluded, for the consideration of parliamentary Reform. His critique evoked earlier parliamentary triumphs. Razor-edged ridicule and caustic forensic skill combined with a devastating dissection of the coalition's equivocation. He carefully exonerated Prince Albert from unjust accusations of exerting an unconstitutional and un-English influence on foreign policy, prompted by his German sympathy for the Austrian and Russian emperors, as well as his detestation of Palmerston. The Conservative opposition themselves, he declared, were guided solely by a loyal and firm commitment to British interests and institutions. The speech, fired with partisan ardour, signalled his resolute return to the parliamentary fray.

During subsequent Lords debate Clanricarde also sharply criticized the ministry for inconsistency, while Lord Grey struck out on an idiosyncratic line of his own by dwelling on the horrors of war and his wish that Britain had not interfered in the Eastern crisis at all.[125] Such sentiments echoed Aberdeen's own profession that the concept that 'anything so horrible as war should ever be just and lawful' was 'the greatest proof of the corruption and depravity of human nature'.[126] Rocked by Derby's onslaught, Clarendon presented two volumes of Blue Books detailing the official diplomatic correspondence concerned with the Turkish question.

Carefully edited and omitting any private correspondence between the
Foreign Secretary and British ambassadors, the Blue Books encouraged
the view that Britain's representative in Constantinople, Stratford de
Redcliffe, had played a crucial part in Britain's involvement in the conflict.
On Tuesday 7 February the British and French ambassadors were recalled
from St Petersburg in the wake of the final collapse of peace negotiations
in Vienna.

On Tuesday 14 February, Derby was prominent in a second Lords
onslaught, prompted by Clanricarde's request for information regarding
the breakdown of diplomatic relations with Russia. Once again Derby
attributed the crisis to Aberdeen's dangerous indecision, which had misled Russia into believing that Britain would not check a disruption of
the status quo. Characterising Tsar Nicholas as the victim of Aberdeen's
vacillation had the political advantage of not alienating the more Rus-
sophile members of his own party such as Granby, Lord Lovaine (eldest
son of the Earl of Beverley and MP for Northumberland), Lord Claud
Hamilton (grandson of Lord Abercorn and MP for Tyrone), and Robert
Hildyard (MP for Whitehaven). Aberdeen, Derby privately commented to
Malmesbury, had become 'more old-womanish, ill-conditioned and impotent than usual'.[127] Aberdeen's inept comparison of the coalition's policy
to that of Sir Robert Walpole and Clarendon's utterance that the country was 'drifting towards war' were immediately seized upon by Derby.
To loud laughter, he scathingly observed that Aberdeen was Walpole
'without his peccadilloes', while Clarendon had invented a new state of
diplomatic relations, not peace, not war, nor neutrality, but a 'drifting
towards war'.[128] The Walpolean minister, Derby witheringly continued,
had allowed his anxiety for peace to frustrate the object. The published
official correspondence showed Russia's intent upon war to be apparent as
early as April 1853. But wavering ministers had preferred to rely upon the
delusion of the Tsar's friendly assurances. Moreover, by allowing Russia
to occupy the Danubian Principalities without official remonstrance, the
government had convinced the Russian Emperor that Britain lacked the
resolve to wage war. This had made war inevitable. That Aberdeen now
rested any vestiges of peace upon Russia's withdrawing, in the face of
British hostility, was an implicit condemnation of the government's earlier
conciliatory policy. Derby called for a decisive prosecution of 'a just and
righteous conflict'.

While Derby sustained a powerful onslaught against the cabinet in the
Lords during February 1854, the Commons heard mounting criticism of
ministerial policy from the government side of the House. On Friday 17

February the radical Layard and Peelite Lord Jocelyn bitterly attacked their own front bench. While pointing out that denunciation of the ministry was not being initiated by the opposition, Disraeli ensured debate was continued for a second night on Monday 20 February. This allowed him, in a fiercely pro-Turkish speech, supported by Lord John Manners, to denounce Clarendon for softness towards the Russians. Palmerston defended the ministry by outbidding Disraeli in his praise for the Turks and condemnation of the Russians. But Malmesbury heard that, at a dinner hosted by Palmerston later that evening, cabinet ministers 'were pictures of woe, and neither ate, talked nor smiled'. Disraeli, by contrast, arrived at a Conservative gathering 'radiant'.[129] But Stanley noted the variety of motives prompting Conservative MPs to support the firm prosecution of a just, if avoidable, war: 'some joined in the war cry out of mere thoughtlessness, some out of fear of Russia, some in order to annoy the government, some to stave off Reform: a few because they liked the prospect of popularity'. There were also, he noted, some who disliked any European disturbance and 'who object to fight where England has nothing to gain'.[130]

Russell's ill-timed introduction of his Reform Bill, on Monday 13 February, compounded the government's difficulties. The inopportune measure proposed a £10 household franchise in the counties, a £6 franchise (with a 2½-year residency requirement) in the boroughs, a wide range of 'merit franchises' for certain categories of taxpayers, university graduates, etc., and the redistribution of sixty-two seats from small boroughs. A total of twenty-nine seats from small boroughs were to be disfranchised and thirty-three others taken from boroughs with two Members. The plan, Stanley observed, 'seemed to startle the House from its magnitude'. Not one hearty cheer accompanied Russell's dry statement, which prompted but a few desultory comments.[131] Unmoved by Russell's Reform rallying cry and apprehensive about the war, government supporters evinced a deepening unease. They disliked the extensive redistribution proposed by the measure, were alarmed by the lowered borough franchise, and feared that it embodied not an extension, but a departure, from the principles of 1832. In the Lords, Whigs such as lords Grey, Beaumont, and Clanricarde attacked ministers for bringing in a needless Reform Bill in time of war. Whig and Liberal backbench hostility during 1854 at extending the borough suffrage and engaging in extensive redistribution, while supporting a lowering of the county franchise, was to influence Conservative thinking four years later when, during the recess of 1858, Derby embarked on drawing up a Reform Bill of his own. Russell's public endorsement of the idea of 'merit franchises', counteracting the numbers of newly enfranchised under a lower suffrage, moreover, provided another useful element in future Conservative thinking on Reform.

By the end of February 1854 Derby was 'confident of victory, planning future measures and framing his cabinet'.[132] Reports of angry divisions within the cabinet and Russell's obstinacy over Reform threatened to turn 'smouldering' ministerial differences into 'spontaneous combustion'.[133] When Disraeli dined with the Queen at Buckingham Palace on Monday 27 February, he construed 'the civilities received from the Queen and Prince' as 'proofs of political conciliation'.[134] Prince Albert had already appointed Disraeli as one of his Royal Commissioners to oversee his South Kensington museum scheme. In private, Derby and Disraeli drew up a Reform measure of their own, in anticipation of resuming office. The evil of the present system they saw as the enfranchisement of urban households residing in the counties. Derby's solution was to enlarge the area of the boroughs so as to include among them all the counties, thus establishing a double representation over the entire area of England. So might the dangerous intrusion of urban voters into the counties be contained. The scheme, however, was to be held in reserve until the disintegration of the coalition was complete.[135] Conservative hopes of government collapse remained pinned on Palmerston, who was 'intriguing busily' against Russell's Reform Bill.[136] Disraeli observed that Palmerston was 'playing fast and loose, throwing out hints that might mean much or nothing'.[137] But, if Palmerston remained obdurate over Reform, then his move into opposition would, Disraeli confidently predicted, bring over a number of Whigs. Such a junction, affirmed by private communications with Lord Grey, Sir George Grey, and Lord Seymour, Disraeli believed, was 'quite possible'. On Wednesday 1 March, Malmesbury informed Disraeli that he would be receiving 'a list of those who formerly having places of *all sorts* with us may this time be *left out*. This will shew at once what we can offer to an adhesive party and prevent the confusion to which we have twice been witness.'[138]

With Aberdeen's cabinet in convulsions, Derby became increasingly optimistic. But, on the verge of a rupture, frantic cabinet negotiations ensued. A reluctant Russell was finally forced by his alarmed colleagues to postpone the second reading of his Reform measure. Wood, in particular, pressed Russell hard, arguing that 'the country seldom entertains two ideas at the same time. It is now bent on war and will not trouble itself about Reform.'[139] On Friday 3 March a dispirited Russell informed the Commons that further consideration of Reform was postponed. 'The government have righted their ship', Disraeli immediately pronounced, 'by throwing over their cargo.'[140] Russell's concession bought the cabinet back from the brink of disaster. During March continuing pressure to abandon Reform altogether prompted Russell to threaten resignation from the government. On Tuesday 4 April, Graham advised him that neither the present House of Commons nor the present ministry could exist much longer.[141] Two days later, in a chronic state of vexation, Russell wrote to Aberdeen that it was now 'obvious there should either be a new parliament for the present ministers, or new ministers for the present parliament'.[142] But a dissolution, amid the onset of war against Russia, was a wholly unacceptable course for the prime minister. Palmerston, meanwhile, persisted in his fierce private opposition to Russell's Reform measure. Eventually, on Tuesday 11 April, Russell agreed to inform the Commons that the ministry's Reform Bill was abandoned for the current session. His emotional speech in the chamber that evening, on the eve of the Easter recess, was received with relief and gratitude by the government backbenchers. That a mortified Russell 'burst into a hysterical fit of crying' during his speech 'called forth the good feeling of the House and averted what might have been an angry debate'.[143]

As a lachrymose Russell relinquished his Reform measure, the government finally declared war on Russia on Monday 27 March 1854. Yet Greville judged the coalition were in 'a very weak and unsatisfactory state. They are supported in carrying on the war, but in every other respect they are treated with great indifference, and appear to have very little authority either in parliament or the country.'[144] The Whig Achitophel Edward Ellice predicted 'a breakup' of the ministry, the Peelite element being too strong, the Whigs in rebellion, and Russell and Aberdeen both disgusted from different causes.[145] On Friday 31 March, Derby spoke to the Lords, declaring his loyal support for the war, but maintaining his bitter tone towards the ministry.[146] He warned of the magnitude of the coming struggle, undertaken to abate the intolerable pretensions of Russia, who throttled the independence of weaker neighbours. Passing a warm eulogium on the conduct of France, he again accused British ministers of irresolution in their diplomatic communications, which had encouraged Russian pretensions. Nothing that had occurred, he asserted, would have taken place if Aberdeen had not been at the head of the government. Moreover, the ministry had introduced a budget in 1853 which, while initially applauded, had crippled the financial reserves of the country. As a result, the country faced the utterly impossible expectation of meeting the expenses of war out of yearly receipts. Unwise economy exposed the nation to a greater danger than it had ever faced. All efforts, he concluded, must be devoted to transacting successfully one of the most just wars in which Britain had ever engaged. With this forceful statement Derby donned Pitt's mantle. Just as the courage and firmness of the great patriot Pitt had safeguarded Britain's honour during the epic struggle with Bonaparte, so the Conservatives were committed to securing a victory of British arms in the righteous conflict against Russian aggression in which they were now engaged. Loyal dedication to the prosecution of a just war, in the greatest test of British arms since 1815, echoed bellicose domestic opinion. It pre-empted Palmerston's claim to champion patriotic fervour. The speech also established Derby's line of opposition argument, sustained throughout the Crimean War, combining loyal support for every exertion towards ultimate victory with persistent criticism of the inept diplomacy which had led to the regrettable necessity for war.

Derby's powerful attack was sustained by Disraeli in the Commons. On Monday 6 March, Disraeli protested against Gladstone's policy of paying for foreign emergencies by the enhancement of direct taxation. Again, on Monday 15 May, Disraeli derided the Chancellor for expatiating on Pitt's 'miserable policy' of 'loan, loan, loan'.[147] Disraeli scathingly advised Gladstone 'to give over these unworthy sneers levelled at the reputation of a Great Minister' who was 'dear to the people of England' and had 'held with a steady hand the helm when every country but Great Britain was submerged in the storm'. Privately, prominent Whigs, such as Russell, sneering at the premiership of Pitt, the opponent of Charles James Fox, were dismissive of the Conservative portrayal of the heroic self-sacrifice of 'the great patriot', Holland House preferring to caricature Pitt as a craven alcoholic. In May 1854 both Russell and Gladstone criticized Pitt's policy, prior to 1797, of financing the war against Bonaparte by raising loans, while approving his subsequent policy of resorting to taxation instead. In response, Bulwer Lytton denounced Gladstone for flavouring his comments on Pitt with sarcastic reproaches. Disraeli pointed out that Fox had forcefully opposed Pitt's policy of financing war by taxation. Pittite patriotism provided Derby and Disraeli with a powerful critique of vacillating diplomacy and niggardly financing. Even Greville, supportive of the coalition, noted during April that the very government, believed to be possessed of great administrative capacity, had 'turned out just the reverse of what was expected, for they commit one blunder after another, and nothing can be more loose, careless and ignorant than the way in which their business is conducted'.[148]

Russell's painful retraction over Reform and the rising tide of patriotic sentiment just barely kept the crippled coalition afloat during the critical months of April and May 1854. Riding the swell of national fervour, the ministry steered through the dangerous cross-currents of Manchester School pacifism, suspicion of royal Germanic sympathy, and opposition derision of inept diplomacy and inadequate national finances. As a result, Derby's hope of being carried back into power on a Pittite current of popular feeling gradually began to ebb away. Then, in mid-April, his health again dramatically failed him. Rheumatic neuralgic gout, as diagnosed by his physician, Dr Ferguson, forced him to his bed in excruciating pain. The intense exertion of the previous weeks, having failed to dislodge Aberdeen's damaged coalition, brought on a rapid physical collapse. During May, Derby was left feeling very low and weak. As a frequent visitor to Derby's bedside, Malmesbury ascribed his friend's debilitated state to his unwholesome lifestyle in London; 'he never walks or rides, but sits all day in a back room, without taking any exercise, until he goes to the House of Lords from St. James's Square'.[149] Reclusive inactivity while in town, Malmesbury believed, aggravated Derby's hereditary susceptibility. Certainly gout transformed Derby's bearing of sanguine expectation in March into weary incapacity by May. For the rest of the summer he remained an invalid. Only occasionally, during the remainder of the session, did he rouse himself to political exertion.

During 1854, while nursing himself back to health, Derby and Lady Emma moved from 8 St James's Square, their London residence since 1836, to the handsome house designed by Robert Adam in 1770–2 on the corner of King Charles II Street and the east side of the square, 23 (now 33) St James's Square. First occupied by the earls of Buckinghamshire, in 1805 the house was purchased by Lord Eliot, who in 1815 became Earl of St Germans. Between 1817 and 1823 Sir John Soane extended the house to provide more impressive accommodation and to enlarge the formal reception rooms. In 1854 Derby bought the house from the third Earl of St Germans. The elderly Charles Blomfield, whose official residence as Bishop of London was 22 St James's Square, became Derby's immediate neighbour. Certainly 23 St James's Square, renamed Derby House, provided a grander residence, now he had succeeded to his father's title, although his generally reclusive habits while in London persisted. The remaining lease on his grandfather's large townhouse, 23 Grosvenor Square, was sold and the imposing building designed by Robert Adam and decorated by Angelica Kauffmann was demolished.

Themselves with ardour fill'd, he thus address'd.

(Derby, *The Iliad of Homer*, ii. 3)

If patriotism superseded Protection as the mainstay of Conservatism in 1854, Protestantism survived. Yet, Derby consistently distanced himself from the visceral anti-Catholicism of MPs such as Charles Newdegate. The firm defence of the Established Church, he maintained, was distinct from anti-Catholic bigotry. As premier in 1852 he declared his commitment to upholding the rights of the Established Church, while desiring religious liberty for all, as long as it did not injure the Church of England. His cautious line over the Maynooth grant in 1852 reflected his wish not to offend Irish Catholics, nor to antagonize his own ultra-Protestant supporters. Nonetheless, the 1852 election gave popular expression to much anti-Catholic feeling by Conservatives that embarrassed Derby's bid for neutrality. Anti-Irish riots in Lancashire and Glasgow, during which Catholic chapels were burnt down, indicated the strength of popular anti-Catholic sentiment, endemic in communities where large-scale Irish immigration had occurred. The continuing strength of Protestant associations warned of the dangerous emotions stirred by sectarian animosity. During 1853 ultra-Protestant Conservatives in the Commons rallied around Spooner's unsuccessful call for the repeal of the Maynooth grant. Lord Winchelsea's request for an investigation into Maynooth College Derby was happy to have steered by the government into the safe waters of a Royal Commission. He assisted in the Lords defeat of Russell's Jewish Disabilities Bill (allowing practising Jews to sit in the Commons) in April 1853. But defence of the Protestant constitution was not to be inflamed into a coarse anti-Catholic crusade. He believed the vehemently anti-Catholic National Club, largely Conservative in membership, to be 'a mischievous body whose extreme pretensions and views must not be encouraged'.[150]

Derby's wish to avoid sectarian differences becoming the basis of party distinctions came under pressure during 1854, however, as Disraeli fashioned himself into an unlikely Protestant champion. In early 1853, while courting the Irish and radicals, Disraeli talked of a liberal and generous policy with regard to Catholicism. But, by the end of the year, through the pages of *The Press*, he was shaping fear of popery and High Church ritual into a weapon against ministerial Peelites. 'The middle classes of England are essentially Protestant. They shrink with unconquerable distrust from Puseyite Secretaries of State, from Jesuits in the guise of financiers, and from impassioned Oratorians in the garb of Secretaries of War.'[151] In

February 1854 *The Press* printed an ultra-Protestant diatribe. This prepared the ground for Disraeli, at the close of the 1854 session, during debate of Spooner's proposal to make the Maynooth grant subject to an annual vote by parliament, to laud the Protestant constitution. The acclamation of Protestant associations around the country immediately followed. In Liverpool, Burnley, Blackburn, and elsewhere, votes of thanks from Protestant association meetings expressed an 'indescribable pleasure' at Disraeli's stalwart defence of 'the Protestantism of England'.[152] In September, Disraeli wrote to the anti-papist pamphleteer the Revd Robinson in Blackburn of the 'intrigues of the Jesuit party' in parliament, undertaken with 'eminent ability and unhappy success by Lord Aberdeen, Sir James Graham, and Mr. Gladstone'.[153]

The predictable hostile reaction at Knowsley was communicated to Disraeli by Stanley, who recalled that their 'chance at the [1852] elections had been ruined by our taking up high Protestant politics'. Stanley warned that 'I fear you will burn your fingers with that infernal "Protestantism".'[154] Derby remained staunchly opposed to exciting Protestant prejudice as a Conservative rallying cry. Even when forged into a weapon against the Peelites, he sensed that the dangers of impassioned religious feeling outweighed any immediate party advantage. Crude animosity towards the Catholic laity, he feared, merely alienated sections of the population, without striking at what he saw as the real dangers of a political clerisy and the ultramontane tendencies of the Catholic hierarchy. The 'extreme pretensions' of the ultra-Protestants were to be discouraged, he insisted, 'by the negative means of avoiding in debate, or in meetings of the party, language which may unnecessarily *frossier* their ... views'.[155] Disraeli's championing of Protestant views during 1854 affirmed the persistent suspicions at Knowsley of an inveterate weakness for intrigue at Hughenden.

Yet one issue close to Derby, which had significant religious implications, reform of Oxford University, came to the fore during the 1854 session. In 1850 Russell appointed a Royal Commission to inquire into reform of the ancient University. Gladstone took a close interest in their proposals and, in consultation with Benjamin Jowett at Balliol, submitted a sketch of a bill to Russell in December 1853. This prompted Derby, as the newly installed Chancellor of Oxford, to write to Palmerston, as Home Secretary, in January 1854 requesting the government suspend any legislation until the University presented its own proposals.[156] Better, Derby advised senior figures at the University, that Oxford reform itself than have change forced upon it. In February an emergency meeting of Oxford's Convocation agreed, despite the opposition of the resident Fellows, to the repeal of those Caroline statutes restricting fellowships and scholarships and the setting-up of a new Hebdomadal Board. But this attempt by the University belatedly to reform itself was firmly rejected by the government, who believed the current Hebdomadal Board was too dominated by heads of houses, representing the narrow interests of the colleges, to see through effective change. On Friday 17 March, Russell introduced to the Commons an Oxford University Reform Bill that proposed the extension of the professorial system, the restriction of the presence of heads of houses in a reconstituted and more broadly representative Council, the establishment of private halls to accommodate economically additional students, the awarding of fellowships by competitive examination, and the appointment of parliamentary commissioners to frame new University statutes.[157] Conservatives immediately objected to this intrusion upon the University's self-government, while radicals called for the admission of Dissenters to Oxford, removing the requirement that all matriculands swear to the Thirty-Nine Articles of the Anglican Church. During June the Voluntary Liberal MP for North Lancashire, James Heywood, secured Commons support for allowing Dissenters both to matriculate at Oxford and to be given degrees without submitting to the Thirty-Nine Articles.

In early July, Derby, slowly recovering his health, spoke on the second reading of Russell's bill in the Lords.[158] While defending the University from the attacks of critics, he refused to waive his strong objections to the government's measure. The proposed Commission he described as a dangerous precedent destructive of the character of the University. The establishment of private halls would benefit the rich rather than the poor and withdraw many young men from the control of the University and the colleges. This would be particularly true, he believed, if Dissenters were admitted. If private halls became the nurseries of Dissent then the University would be destroyed, by diminishing the association existing between Oxford and the Church of England. While disliking the obligation matriculands faced of signing the Thirty-Nine Articles, he objected to modifying the rules of the University to the views of Dissenters. He was prepared, he declared, to propose a clause preventing Dissenters from holding fellowships and tutorships, or influence over the teaching and government of the University, but his principal aim was to impose further restrictions upon the arbitrary power of the Commissioners. Yet, despite an ailing Derby's spirited criticism, the government's Oxford University Reform Bill, championed by Lord Canning, was approved by the Upper House with minor modifications. Upon receiving the royal assent on 7 August 1854 it inaugurated a 'quiet revolution in Oxford life'.[159] Ancient oaths were annulled, preferences in the awarding of scholarships and fellowships were removed, the obligation of Fellows to take clerical orders done away with, and the professorial system reorganized. Moreover, most significantly from Derby's point of view, it pushed aside the prerogative of the ancient University to reform itself. The impulse of liberal meritocratic reform imposed upon Oxford change which the old Hebdomadal Board had been reluctant to countenance.

Late in the session Aberdeen's coalition also succeeded in passing legislation reforming electoral bribery. But much other domestic legislation, including reforms to the civil service, the law of settlement, divorce law, a Testamentary Jurisdiction Bill, and a Public Health Amendment Bill, had to be abandoned. When parliament prorogued, on 12 August, it was the progress of the war against Russia that preoccupied the nation. During June a still weakened Derby supported Lyndhurst's attack on the limited aims of Austria and Prussia in prosecuting the war. Only the complete removal of any possible aggression by Russia in the region was a suitable objective in undertaking the conflict to which Britain was now committed, Derby asserted. Yet his appearances in the Lords during the summer were occasional and brief. The gout, which had laid him low in April, rendered him a shadowy political presence for the remainder of the session. On 12 August *The Times* was pleased to observe that the Conservative opposition had, once again, lapsed into 'chronic and permanent disorganisation'.[160]

With stern resolve to wage unflinching war.

(Derby, *The Iliad of Homer*, ii. 52)

By August 1854 Disraeli was in a bitter mood of disillusionment, privately critical of the inadequacies of his invalid chief. 'We never see him,' Disraeli complained to the receptive Lady Londonderry. 'His house is always closed; he subscribes to nothing, tho' his fortune is very large; and expects, nevertheless, everything to be done.' Derby, he protested, is 'always at Newmarket and Doncaster, when Europe, nay the world, is in the throes of immense changes, and all the elements of power at home in a state of dissolution'.[161] While his lieutenant bemoaned his leader's incapacity, Derby spent the recess at Knowsley, enjoying the warmth of an Indian summer, and slowly nursing himself back to health. Not until early October was he able to walk with ease or shoot with his customary aim. The requirement of an emergency meeting of parliament before

Christmas, which was being pressed by Disraeli, he regarded with deep distaste. Conservative policy, he advised Malmesbury, would have to be guided by the successes or reverses of the war.[162]

News of the war against Russia was mixed. During August 1854 British and French naval forces destroyed a Russian fort in the Baltic, but failed to overthrow Russian control of the region. Meanwhile, the Allied army supported the Turks in forcing the Russians to withdraw from the Danubian Principalities, whose occupation had sparked off hostilities at the beginning of the year. Then, in mid-September, the Allied army landed in the Crimea and defeated the well-entrenched Russian forces at the Alma. But military deadlock followed victories at the battle of Balaklava on 25 October, scene of the gloriously futile charge of the Light Brigade, and the battle at Inkerman on 5 November. As vicious winter weather closed in, the protracted Allied siege of Sevastopol began and early elation evaporated amid the cold and disease ravaging the British camp. Vivid reports in *The Times* of the suffering of British troops and the inefficiency of military administration inflamed domestic frustrations over a campaign now apparently frozen into a prolonged and pitiless struggle. Derby deemed the Baltic operations 'a failure', though demonstrating Russia to be a less formidable enemy than was expected.[163] News of the victory at the Alma encouraged him to hope that Sevastopol would shortly fall. But by November such optimism was quickly fading. The report of the death of Jolliffe's eldest son of cholera in the trenches at Sevastopol (his second son having taken part in the charge of the Light Brigade) brought sharply home to the Conservative leadership the human tragedy now unfolding.

Visiting Knowsley at the end of November, Malmesbury was delighted to find Derby now 'in the strongest health (I never saw him better) and quite a different man from last year—evidently ready for any work'.[164] Derby agreed that, thanks to Dr Ferguson and Providence, he was considerably a better man than he had been twelve months before.[165] His recovery coincided with the government's announcement of a meeting of parliament on 12 December, the cabinet seeking authorization for the sending of reinforcements to the Crimea. He immediately advised Disraeli 'that our course is so clear as to leave little room for doubt'. The Conservatives should give cordial support to every exertion which the government could be induced to make in prosecuting the war, while being unsparing in their criticism of the government's lack of timely preparation for the exigencies of war.[166] At Knowsley, Derby and Malmesbury shared the latest news from the Crimea, that 'all the officers and men are in tatters like so many beggars, and all from the highest to the lowest covered with vermin. They have neither clothes to change nor water to wash with, having barely sufficient to drink.'[167] From his whip in the Lords, Colville, Derby acquired information about the campaign with which to prepare a major statement upon parliament meeting. Having regained his health, Derby also resumed those preparations for the approaching session which had lifted Conservative morale at the beginning of the year. A purposeful resolution once again replaced the despondency of the previous months. Arranging to return to London on Monday 11 December, he issued invitations to Conservative peers to meet at 23 St James's Square the following morning. Meanwhile, he sanctioned a circular to Conservative MPs requesting their attendance at a meeting hosted, for the first time, by Disraeli at Grosvenor Gate. Jolliffe had misgivings about assembling their MPs at Disraeli's London residence, believing only a meeting hosted by Derby would secure a full attendance. But Derby preferred a separate Commons meeting as an explicit endorsement of Disraeli's leadership.[168] The invitation to Grosvenor Gate required delicate handling on Jolliffe's part, as he drew on his diplomatic skills to ensure a respectable showing. Suggestions from Disraeli that the Conservatives might acquire 'extraneous support' Derby judged 'very useful', Jolliffe having floated the possibility of Richmond, perhaps with Lord Grey's support, sounding out 'the old Whigs' about an alliance. Derby, Disraeli now cheerfully informed Lord Lennox, 'seems to be full of his ancient spirit'.[169]

Derby's contribution to the Lords debate on Tuesday 12 December 1854 proved another memorable performance. The caustic edge, eloquent power, and weighty devastation of his speeches of the previous January and February returned. It was not the occasion, he trenchantly declared, for considering whether the war might have been avoided. Nor was it the moment to discuss reconstructing the constitution of parliament, as Russell had advocated during the previous session. War with Russia was the one issue upon which the hearts of the country were set. 'The nation, as one man, was pushing forward with an abnegation of self unparalleled in history.' With fluent passion, he reviewed the 'glorious achievements' of the British Army.[170] Numerically small, untested in war, their ranks thinned by disease, with barely sufficient equipment and provisions, British troops had invaded the dominions of a powerful enemy and by their indomitable courage defeated a veteran army occupying strongly fortified positions at the Alma; following which, while suffering from cold, hunger, and severe privation, they had repulsed a Russian force seven times their number. To loud cheering Derby pronounced that 'no words can do justice to the merits of such brave and heroic soldiers'. There cannot be a heart, he continued, that 'does not throb with honest and generous pride that these much-enduring, all-daring, all-achieving, men were our countrymen.' But, while British troops were performing heroic deeds under appalling conditions, the government had shown a total want of prescience. 'The fatal words "too late" had adhered to the whole conduct of the war.' With no reinforcements and no army of reserve, 25,000 troops had been sent to the Crimea to settle the question of Russian supremacy, a force totally inadequate for that purpose. Blundering had hampered the shipment of stores and created chronic shortages of medical supplies. A ferocious gale had sunk the Allied supply ships in the harbour at Balaklava, including the steamship *Prince*, which went down with almost all hands, while the results of the naval campaign in the Baltic were practically nil. Only belatedly had the government recalled parliament to ensure adequate reinforcements were available. All this, he insisted, revealed the ministry's complete lack of foresight. It was, Greville noted, 'a slashing, effective philippic on the text of "too late"'.[171]

Newcastle's reply was feeble and dull, the Secretary for War proving 'totally unequal to meet Derby in debate'. Ellenborough supported Derby's powerful attack, while Argyll injected as much vigour as he could muster in defence of the coalition's policy. During subsequent debate the Foreign Enlistment Bill and the Militia Bill, introduced by the ministry, received a mauling in both Houses. Not until 23 December were both bills approved, whereupon parliament adjourned for a month. It had proved, Disraeli observed, 'a brief, but hot campaign'.[172] Significantly, on 19 December *The Times* forsook its former support for Aberdeen's ministry by forcefully denouncing the utter mismanagement of the Crimean expedition.[173]

The convulsive death throes of Aberdeen's coalition government quickly followed. It was, the radical John Bright declared in the Commons on Friday 22 December 1854, an 'incapable and guilty Administration'.[174] Greville believed the ministry to be 'weak, unpopular, dispirited and divided'.[175] Conservative emotions, meanwhile, were stirred by Derby's powerful denunciation of government ineptitude. He believed the difficulty remained, however, that no clear perception existed of how a strong ministry might replace the discredited coalition. The Conservative back-benchers were excited and restless. But he still favoured a 'patience policy', in order to prolong the coalition's agonies. To Eglinton he commented that 'it is not my policy to hazard a division, though I may any day be forced into one'.[176] For once, Disraeli agreed that holding back would best serve their purposes. He feared that the Conservatives still lacked sufficient

talent and weight in the Commons to form a powerful ministry.[177] Derby
explained his own thinking to Jolliffe:

> Our Irish friends, and very likely some of our English ones too, are as
> impatient that we should make a general attack on the Govt., as the latter
> are said to be that Lord Raglan should make an immediate assault on
> Sebastopol. Lord R. seems to think that there would be more probability of
> his knocking the heads of his army against stone walls, than of achieving
> a great success; and accordingly proceeds in a more methodical, though
> perhaps less striking, course; and I am very much more inclined to think
> that we should follow his example, and not risk an assault leading to a
> great action, in which we should probably be beaten, and in which, if not,
> our success would be very embarrassing to ourselves and still more to the
> Country. Our own strength is not sufficient to form a Govt… and it is
> obvious that if we succeeded in carrying a vote of censure on the whole
> management of the war, such a vote would render it impossible for us to
> obtain a reinforcement from any part of the present Administration; and
> with Bright & his friends we can have no sympathy, and no possibility of
> combination.[178]

Jolliffe agreed with Derby.[179] He warned Disraeli that an abortive attack
on the coalition 'would have the effect of strengthening the government
and patch up their internal differences—to which we must look for our
best chance of succeeding to and retaining power'.[180] Malmesbury also
concurred. The whole country was 'in a state of fever', he observed, but
the 'Commons would not turn out this government at such a moment
without stronger indications than now exist of what a new one would be
made of, nor can I conceive anything more disagreeable than taking office
under the difficulties we must find'.[181] After spending the holiday season at
Knowsley, Derby returned to London alone on Monday 22 January, Lady
Derby remaining in Lancashire because of illness. That evening Disraeli
visited St James's Square, where it was agreed not to give notice on the first
day of the session inculpating the whole conduct of the war and forcing a
vote on the fate of the government. Malmesbury supported the decision,
while advising Derby not to remain silent when parliament met and so
seeming to 'play second fiddle to Grey… *You* ought to be at the head of
every demonstration even if you don't *charge.*'[182]

When the parliamentary session resumed on Tuesday 23 January 1855,
Westminster was rife with rumours of deep divisions within the cabinet.
Straight away it became clear that hostile motions were to be proposed
by opponents of the coalition, despite Derby's wish not to force matters immediately to a head, the government being supinely compliant in

response. The ministry acceded to Lord Grey's address on the maladmin-
istration of the Army, 'to Ellenborough's motion for returns, impugning
the whole outcome of the campaign, and to a motion from Lord Salisbury
demanding the correspondence relating to the non-blockade of the Black
Sea ports'.[183] Most significantly, the pugnacious radical John Roebuck,
recovered from serious illness, gave notice in the Commons of a motion
demanding a Select Committee to examine the condition of the Army
before Sevastopol. Though Derby regretted Roebuck's initiative, fearing
it might yet galvanize support for the coalition, he reluctantly advised
Disraeli that the Conservatives must back it. It was the dramatic news
of Russell's resignation from the government on Thursday 25 January,
however, that pushed the situation to crisis point. Russell's departure,
Stanley noted, was 'a dexterous leap out of a sinking boat'.[184] Debate
on Roebuck's motion in the Commons, begun the following day, now
stood as a vote of confidence in Aberdeen's disintegrating ministry. With
many Conservatives still in the country, Disraeli urged Jolliffe to secure an
adjournment if possible.[185]

   The possibility of an imminent resumption of office now opened up
before Derby. While Malmesbury, Stanley, and Walpole were pessimistic
about forming a government without support from non-Conservatives,
Disraeli characteristically urged Derby on. To Malmesbury an excited
Disraeli threatened: 'He must do it. I will make him—if he does not I will
break up his party.'[186] In discussion with Ellenborough, Derby prepared
an immediate course of action, in the event of occupying Downing Street,
with regard to the war; Lord Raglan, commander of the British Army
in the Crimea, would be instantly recalled and a prohibitory duty placed
on all Russian goods so as to destroy the enemy's economy. Stanley
believed his father to be 'inclined to try the experiment of forming a
government even if unsupported by any other party than his own'.[187]
Jolliffe reckoned on 267 reliable Conservative votes in the Commons,
with forty-five 'Regular Peelites' and twenty-six 'doubtful Conservatives'
as possible adherents.[188] The first night of debate on Roebuck's motion
was poorly attended by the Conservatives, some still absent from London,
others objecting to supporting a radical motion. But the second night of
debate, on Monday 29 January, found the Conservatives at full strength
and the Commons benches on both sides crowded. Walpole spoke for
an inquiry and a reconstruction of the cabinet, but opposed forcing the
coalition out of office. Though uncertain that a division would occur
that night, Derby pressed Disraeli to speak as late in the proceedings as
possible, preferably after Palmerston. In the event, Disraeli rose to his feet

before Palmerston to pronounce that the ministry lacked the confidence of the House because ministers had no faith in each other. Aiming his fiercest invective at Russell and sparing Palmerston, Disraeli described Russell's explanation of his resignation as 'an all-unconscious admission of profligate intrigue'.[189] Palmerston spoke only briefly in reply. Roebuck's motion was subsequently carried by an overwhelming majority of 305 to 148 votes. 'When the numbers were announced,' Stanley observed, 'there was no cheering but a slight incredulous laugh: the extent of the victory had astonished one party and stunned the other'.[190] Under orders from Derby, the Conservatives refrained 'from giving the cheer of triumph which usually issues from a majority after a vote upon an important occasion'.[191]

Conservative unity and Whig, Liberal, and radical disarray brought Aberdeen's coalition down. All but six or seven Conservative MPs, about 220 in all, voted for Roebuck's motion, some seventy to eighty Whigs and Liberals voted against the government, while Cobden and Bright stayed away. The following day a broken Aberdeen travelled to Windsor to offer his resignation as premier. Aberdeen was now discredited, Russell regarded as devoid of loyalty or principle, and Palmerston feared by the court as an unpalatable final resort. The 'difficulties are enormous', Greville concluded.[192] Among the press *The Times*, *Morning Post*, and *Morning Advertiser* were calling for a Palmerston government. While the *Daily News* defended Russell, as the only real Liberal leader, the *Morning Chronicle* lamented the downfall of Aberdeen, and the *Morning Herald* declared for Derby. That Tuesday evening Derby received a letter from the Queen asking him to attend her at Buckingham Palace the next morning. Dining at St James's Square with Stanley and his brother-in-law Colonel Edward Wilbraham, he was reading aloud to the group when the royal messenger arrived at about 9.45 p.m. He read the royal communication, handed it round, and then calmly resumed his book, finishing the chapter. Stanley was then dispatched to Grosvenor Gate to inform Disraeli. Visiting the Carlton Club en route, Stanley found a general expectation that Palmerston would be sent for by the Queen. But Disraeli was dismissive of Palmerston's claim to the premiership: 'Palmerston would be deterred by age, infirmity and the consciousness of an overrated reputation', he believed, 'from undertaking the government.'[193] The possibility of Palmerston's leading the Commons, under Derby's leadership, bringing Gladstone and Herbert with him, on the other hand, promised necessary accessions of support. Derby concurred that this was the best hope for a strong Conservative administration.

On Wednesday 31 January 1855 Derby attended his audience with the Queen at 11.30 a.m. She immediately asked him, as head of the largest and most unified party in the Commons, to undertake the formation of a government. Distancing himself from responsibility for Roebuck's motion, he replied that any ministry he formed would have to contain Palmerston, who was popularly, if erroneously, perceived as the man capable of prosecuting the war with success. Personally Derby doubted Palmerston's capacity. Whatever 'the ignorant public might think', he observed, 'Palmerston was totally unfit for the task. He had become very deaf as well as very blind, was seventy-one years old, and … though he still kept up his sprightly manners of youth, it was evident that his day had gone by.'[194] But public expectation required Palmerston's presence on the ministerial front bench, and Disraeli was willing to surrender the Commons leadership to him. Derby hoped Ellenborough, who was popular with the Army, but who would also require managing, might head the War Office. Malmesbury would be offered the Foreign Office. Derby believed that Malmesbury 'had done well before, and now had additional experience'.[195] Lord Raglan and his staff would be recalled, but the Commander-in-Chief might be given the sop of a position in the cabinet. Derby believed the presence of some Peelites in the ministry was a critical requirement for success and Gladstone and Herbert's acceptance of office would give his government necessary credibility. For though he led a party of about 280 MPs, Derby confessed, 'he had no men capable of governing the House of Commons'.[196] The Queen advised him that the Peelites would oppose a Russell government but support a Derby ministry. Looking to play the longer game, Derby concluded the audience by reserving his position in the event of initial failure. Any reconstruction of the old government, he believed, would be unacceptable to the country. But, should support for a Conservative ministry at this first attempt be unforthcoming and his commission relinquished, he would be prepared to come forward a second time with such materials as he had. The unpopularity or incapacity of rival claimants, such as Russell or Palmerston, would then have been shown and compelling patriotic duty would substantiate Derby's claim to office.

Having prepared his ground with the Queen, Derby left to consult Palmerston, as news of his summons to Buckingham Palace circulated around the clubs. At Cambridge House he offered Palmerston the Presidency of the Council and leadership of the Commons, contingent on Gladstone and Herbert's also joining his cabinet. For his own part, Palmerston immediately accepted, but added two conditions of his own.

First, that an attempt should be made to retain Clarendon at the Foreign Office, and, secondly, Palmerston must consult Gladstone and Herbert.[197] These requirements, particularly the first, did not, as Palmerston must have known, suit Derby at all. Derby knew that Clarendon's inclusion in a Conservative ministry as Foreign Secretary would be ill-received by his backbenchers. It is possible that Palmerston, while appearing compliant, hoped to sabotage Derby's commission. Certainly Palmerston's own claims to the premiership, once it was demonstrated that neither Derby or Russell could form an administration, would be strengthened. Nonetheless, Derby remained confident of success. He reported Palmerston's favourable initial response to the Queen that same afternoon. Even the hostile Greville conceded that, in the current circumstances, a Derby government 'must be allowed the fairest play, and be supported unless and until it commits some flagrant errors'.[198]

During the afternoon, however, Derby's provisional arrangements quickly unravelled. As heavy snowstorms and bitter winds swept through London, there existed 'little disposition to discard prejudices, antipathies and personal feelings and interests'.[199] Palmerston met Clarendon, who refused outright to serve under Derby, so deeply did he detest the Conservative leader's want of principle. Gladstone and Herbert likewise indicated to Palmerston their reluctance to join a Conservative cabinet. That evening Palmerston wrote to Derby conveying the difficulties he now envisaged in serving under him.[200] Gladstone and Herbert also wrote to Derby promising him 'independent support', but stating the impossibility of their taking office in his administration. Gladstone went so far as to say that 'the formation of a government from among your own political friends would offer many facilities at this moment, which other alternatives within view would not present'.[201] But the true definition of 'independent support', Derby caustically observed, was backing which could not be depended upon. On receiving Palmerston's letter at 9 o'clock that evening, he 'wrote to the Queen advising her that someone else should be called in, and for the present declining the duty of forming an administration'.[202]

The next morning, on Thursday 1 February, Derby travelled to Windsor and, at 11 a.m., had another audience with the Queen. He was anxious to know what sort of statement Aberdeen would make in the Lords that evening. In particular, he wished 'that it should not appear that the administration had gone from Aberdeen through any other hands than the ones which should finally accept it'. While it was well known that Derby had been consulted, he hoped 'there was no necessity for making it appear he had undertaken to form an administration'.[203] The concealment of his initial failure was crucial to his hope of eventual success. Russell was unacceptable as a premier, while he believed the old and infirm Palmerston, despite popular support, was incapable of leading a strong ministry. But Derby's success in any renewed attempt to form a government, after being recalled by the Queen, required avoiding any public acknowledgement of his initial failure. Disraeli was deeply angered by Derby's 'throwing up the cards so soon'.[204] Surrendering the Queen's commission, he complained, might appear to be a confession of incompetence. To counter Disraeli's low spirits and fear of Conservative desertions, Stanley reminded him that Palmerston's health was failing, and predicted that Palmerston's overrated reputation would collapse under the weight of the premiership. Those Whigs now gathering around Russell were unfriendly to Palmerston, while radicals such as Cobden and Bright hated Palmerston even more than did the court. To his father Stanley observed: 'I don't give up the game yet: if it is lost "vendetta" must be our consolation, and of that we shall have enough.'[205] During the day Jolliffe also reported the deep revulsion felt by many Conservative backbenchers at any prospect of union with Gladstone. The recruitment of Gladstone to a Conservative cabinet, Stanley agreed, 'would be to us a source not of strength but of weakness'.[206] Derby's verdict was conclusive:

> Gladstone's refusal has saved us from imminent disaster, for such is the intensity of feeling among the best of my supporters against him, partly on account of his religious tendencies, partly in consequence of the bearing of his financial measures, that had he joined me, I should not only have had to encounter great dissatisfaction, but possibly the loss of fifty or sixty votes and some of them men I had destined for office.[207]

He now waited to be recalled, relying upon the failure of his rivals as proof of his indispensability.

The gamble Derby took by relinquishing his commission, thereby throwing responsibility back onto his divided opponents, was a high-risk tactic. It assumed Clarendon, Russell, Palmerston, and the elderly Lansdowne were inadequate to the challenge. It was also important that knowledge of his initial failure be concealed. Almost immediately the latter advantage was lost when, during the evening of Thursday 1 February, Derby was required to admit in the Lords that he had been asked to form a ministry. Speaking to the Upper House, Aberdeen referred to Derby's invitation from the Queen to undertake the construction of a cabinet. This compelled Derby, who had intended not to speak, to make a brief statement. The emphatic defeat of the coalition, he asserted, had not been caused by the direct opposition of the Conservatives or any one party. Declining to go into details, he acknowledged his 'inability to discharge the duties this arduous position would have imposed upon me'. Without commenting on the merits of his own party, he merely observed that 'in the present state of parties and in the present condition of the House of Commons, the task of forming a government was unacceptable.'[208] This, he hoped, still left the door open to being recalled. The Queen's subsequent consultations seemed initially to corroborate his hopes of affirming the incapacity of his rivals. The Whig patriarch Lansdowne was called to Buckingham Palace late on 1 February and the possibility of a Clarendon ministry discussed. But the following afternoon a dispirited Lansdowne returned to report that deep asperities prevented cooperation among the former cabinet. Clarendon lacked the weight to assume the premiership, Gladstone refused to serve under Russell, while Russell refused to serve under Palmerston. Lansdowne saw no way out of these difficulties. At 5 p.m. on Friday 2 February the Queen met Russell. But during the following day Gladstone, Graham, and Sir George Grey informed Russell of their disinclination to join a ministry under his leadership. Clarendon bluntly informed Russell that any ministry formed by Lord John would be 'still born'.[209] On Sunday 4 February a dejected Russell advised the Queen of the impossibility of his forming an administration. Lansdowne counselled the Queen that Palmerston would have equal difficulty in forming a ministry, 'but when that had failed some solid combination would become possible'.[210]

By Sunday 4 February, after six days of inconclusive consultation, the prospect of Derby's being recalled appeared increasingly likely. Pakington believed 'it must be Derby ere long'.[211] All depended on the final untested option of Palmerston being asked to construct a ministry. That evening, the Queen, despite her personal aversion, wrote to Palmerston.[212] During Monday 5 February alarmed Whigs, Liberals, and Peelites recognized this critical moment as their last opportunity to avoid a Derby administration. Clarendon, Granville, Sir George Grey, Charles Wood, and the elderly radical Sir William Molesworth immediately agreed to serve under Palmerston. After initial hesitation, on Tuesday 6 February, Gladstone, Graham, and Herbert, encouraged by Aberdeen, also consented to taking office under Palmerston's leadership. That evening Palmerston kissed hands with the Queen as prime minister. Malmesbury believed that the French Ambassador, Count Walewski, had been busily intriguing against both Derby and Russell, so as to secure Palmerston's assumption of the premiership.[213]

For the highest stakes Derby had wagered on Palmerston, as well as
Russell, failing. He never regarded Palmerston as a credible prospective
premier. Popular adulation of Palmerston he dismissed as a fickle illusion.
To Malmesbury he confided 'that no one but himself could form a
government after Lord John and Lord Palmerston had failed, and that he
would come in on his own terms. He said to me, "I shall then be a most
powerful minister." '[214] But the gamble was lost and a bitter debt paid in
terms of Conservative recrimination. The Derbyites, Greville observed,
were 'sulky and angry to the greatest degree'.[215] The Carlton Club was
reportedly 'frenzied with rage'.[216] Disraeli was inconsolably caustic: 'he
saw no prospect for the future: this failure was final'.[217] All this Disraeli
deemed to be Derby's fault.

But calmer Conservative voices endorsed Derby's judgement. Pakington
told a scathing Disraeli that he thought 'Lord Derby was, on the whole,
right in his late difficult decision.'[218] Similarly, Malmesbury wrote to
Derby: 'I believe that we could have gone on with the *old lot*, attaching to
them Ellenboro', Lytton etc., for a time, but that your present fame is the
best.'[219] Endorsing the view of events from Knowsley, Stanley told Lennox
that 'Derby did right in refusing; that the [Palmerston] government cannot
stand; that then *every* combination will have been tried and failed.'[220] This
would clear the way for Derby's assumption of office, not on sufferance,
but with the assurance of power. Tellingly, a radical observer, Richard
Cobden, concluded that 'Lord Derby seems to me to have played a clever
game for the future.'[221] On 12 February an unruffled Derby calmly informed
Malmesbury 'that if the Conservatives would only be patient, we should
certainly be in office before long'.[222]

The Conservative back benches, who largely failed to appreciate Derby's
view of events, were further incensed by Derby's explanation of his conduct
to the Lords on Thursday 8 February. He could not, Derby stated, have
governed with his own party without extraneous aid.[223] While disparaging
his own supporters he praised the Peelites and produced in Disraeli a
'state of disgust beyond all control'.[224] Yet, such was Derby's authority
that, despite deprecating their collective talent in public, he could, with
one rousing call, rally his party around him. At a large meeting of over
230 Conservatives on Tuesday 20 February, at Lord Eglinton's house
at 10 St James's Square, with 'frankness and dexterity'[225] he explained
his recent conduct and assessed the party's prospects. Disraeli reported:
'I never heard a finer speech than Derby's: the ablest he ever made.'[226]
Conservative patience and unity were now essential, Derby urged, as
the party awaited the collapse of Palmerston's attempt to govern. The

speech was enthusiastically received, a unanimous vote of confidence in Derby's leadership was immediately passed, and the gathering dispersed, Malmesbury noted, 'quite satisfied'.[227] The 'grumblers', Taylor observed to Jolliffe, were effectively silenced.[228]

Belief that the 70-year-old Palmerston's fragile grasp on the premiership was a provisional arrangement underpinned Conservative hopes. Hamilton confidently advised Disraeli that 'Palmerston will prove a failure.'[229] Swift support for Derby's expectations came the following day, Wednesday 21 February, when the startling news was received that Gladstone, Graham, and Herbert had suddenly resigned from Palmerston's cabinet, having accepted office only two weeks before. Six additional Peelites outside the cabinet, including Cardwell, also promptly resigned from the ministry. Objecting to Palmerston's agreement to continuing with Roebuck's Committee of Inquiry into the conduct of the war, the Peelites 'now leave [the premier] in the lurch at a moment of great danger and difficulty'.[230] 'Bad as Lord John's conduct was,' Malmesbury observed, 'this is a thousand times worse.' During Gladstone's diffuse speech in the Commons on Friday 23 February explaining his resignation, Malmesbury noted that Palmerston fell asleep. 'He appears to be failing under the fatigue and difficulty of his position,' Malmesbury concluded.[231] Palmerston subsequently patched up his cabinet by appointing Russell to the Colonies, Wood to the Admiralty, and Sir George Cornewall Lewis to the Exchequer. But this left his front bench far short of being a distillation of talent.

'The political volcano still heaves and vomits forth its lava,' Disraeli noted, whose streams 'are not yet cool and are even still flowing'.[232] A strong government, he decided, must be 'preceded by a period of parliamentary anarchy and spasmodic weakness'. Judging Palmerston's statements to the Commons to be 'flat and feeble', Greville found 'the House is in complete confusion and disorganisation, and, except the Derbyites, who are still numerous and act together in opposition, in hopes of getting into power, nobody owns any allegiance or even any party ties, or seems to care for any person or any thing'.[233] General distrust, Greville anticipated, must render Palmerston's makeshift premiership a short-lived expediency.

CHAPTER 3

War and Peace: 1855–1858

For myself, I *never* was *ambitious* of office, and am not likely to become more so as I grow older; but I am now, as I have been, ready to accept the responsibility of it if I see a chance not only of taking it but of keeping it.

(Derby to Malmesbury, 15 December 1856)

Few politicians in February 1855 believed Palmerston's ministry could last long. Palmerston seemed old, infirm, and tired. The Peelites were alienated and bitter, the Manchester School radicals deeply hostile, Russell unpredictable and resentful, and the court, particularly Prince Albert, profoundly mistrustful of the new premier. Most within Westminster perceived Palmerston's extra-parliamentary popularity as fragile. 'Never', Greville commented, 'was there a greater delusion.'[1] On 10 March he observed that 'Palmerston's government does not seem to take root or gain much strength; every day seems to prove the more clearly that he is unfit for the task he has taken on himself. He inspires neither respect nor confidence, and is totally unable to manage the House of Commons.'[2]

All this consoled Derby. Yet, Palmerston's great triumph in 1855 was to defy such expectation. This, in turn, made Derby's provisional rejection of office look, in retrospect, like an acknowledgement of incapacity. Luck played a part in Palmerston's survival. Following Tsar Nicholas's death in March 1855, a turn of military events in the Crimea, the capture of Kerch in May and the eventual fall of Sevastopol four months later, allowed Palmerston to garner the acclaim of a revived national self-respect. The frail elderly premier stepped forward as the personification of British pluck. His unexpected resilience and sheer dogged diligence enabled him slowly to win over parliamentary support. Russell's ill-tempered resignation from his cabinet in July 1855 greatly helped.

After February 1855 Derby found himself grappling with three persistent difficulties: first, how to oppose Palmerston; secondly, how to handle Gladstone; and finally, how to bolster Disraeli. Derby's relations with

Palmerston were complex. He saw Palmerston, who was thirteen years his senior, as the surviving product of an earlier age, a representative of those Regency mores associated with his own grandfather, the 12th Earl, rather than the world of his evangelical mother and father. Palmerston, he observed, belonged to the pre-moral, while he belonged to the pre-scientific, school. In the late 1820s both the young Derby and the Regency buck Palmerston associated themselves with Canning's legacy. As members of Lord Grey's ministry, both exhibited distaste for the advanced reform enthusiasms of their colleagues Durham, Russell, and Althorp. But, while Derby followed a Canningite line in domestic politics during the 1830s, Palmerston assumed Canning's mantle in foreign policy. After 1830 Palmerston became the Foreign Office expert, championing liberal change and nationalist causes in Europe, while savouring his image as a dashing dandy. In the early 1840s and particularly in 1850, over the Don Pacifico affair, Derby defined Conservative foreign policy in terms of a rejection of Palmerston's diplomacy. This forged a bond between Peelites and Conservatives, offering up the possibility of Conservative reunion. Thus, when attempting to form a Conservative cabinet in February 1851, Derby made approaches to the leading Peelites, but did not extend a similar invitation to Palmerston. The leading Peelites, however, rejected Derby's overtures. Thereafter, Derby came to regard the leading Peelites as a lost cause, despite many less prominent Peelites' quietly rejoining the Conservatives.

Merger with leading moderate Whigs now appeared to Derby a more promising prospect. Palmerston's conservative views on domestic issues, particularly parliamentary Reform, suggested a potential compatibility, despite their differences over foreign policy. If Palmerston was kept away from the Foreign Office, shared domestic political views might provide the basis for junction. Derby saw Palmerston as a political chameleon, who assumed different colours according to the setting in which he was placed. In February 1852 he sought to bring Palmerston into his cabinet as Chancellor of the Exchequer. But Palmerston declined the approach because of Protectionism. Similar discussions came to naught in July 1852, although during November and early December Palmerston offered independent aid to Derby's ministry in the face of radical and Peelite attack. In December 1852 Aberdeen achieved what Derby desired, by bringing Palmerston into his coalition cabinet as Home Secretary. When subsequently Palmerston briefly resigned from Aberdeen's cabinet in December 1853 over parliamentary Reform a Derby–Palmerston alliance was widely mooted. Derby's strong Pittite line over the Crimean War during 1854 added patriotism as a basis for union, underscored by Russell's putative radicalism and

Aberdeen's dangerous vacillation. Yet, when Derby invited Palmerston to join a Conservative cabinet in January 1855 Palmerston responded with unacceptable conditions. Palmerston looked to assume the premiership himself, his ambition reaching beyond becoming a Conservative minister. As a result, after February 1855, Derby found himself in opposition to the non-Conservative most acceptable to Conservative backbench sensibilities. Combining courtship with opposition was to prove a difficult tactical balance to maintain.

The turmoil of February 1855 also forcefully revealed the revulsion felt by many Conservatives at the prospect of association with Gladstone. Of all the leading Peelites Gladstone was most strongly disposed towards Conservative reunion. Aberdeen and Graham believed Gladstone's future lay with Derby, rather than with Palmerston or Russell. This was seemingly confirmed by Gladstone's abrupt resignation from Palmerston's cabinet in February 1855, just two weeks after accepting office. Yet, because of his overbearing manner, religious views, and verbose inscrutability, Gladstone was deeply distrusted by most Conservative backbenchers. Malmesbury characterized Gladstone as a political Tartuffe, Molière's pedantic hypocrite, who was 'hated by some of our best friends'. The Conservatives 'already have one man [Disraeli] whose eloquence is his only respectable quality'; Malmesbury, therefore, had no regret that Gladstone remained aloof.[3] The highly strung Gladstone was more an aggravation than a solution to Conservative problems. Gladstone's refusal to join him in February 1855, Derby concluded, saved him from an 'imminent risk of great disaster'.[4]

Finally, Disraeli remained deeply mistrusted by many of the Conservative rank and file, and only Derby's endorsement preserved his Commons leadership. Despite his own private misgivings, during 1853 and 1854 Derby publicly propped up Disraeli's authority, recognizing that he provided the best debating talent the Commons party possessed. Yet Disraeli's incessant intriguing, his pursuit of unholy alliances, and his temperamental volatility aroused distrust. His exoticism, although increasingly muted, remained a potent irritant to the country squires on the Conservative back benches.

Confronting a possible ally, distancing an unacceptable suitor, and shoring up the authority of a mistrusted lieutenant imposed on Derby a complex web of constraints, enforcing difficulties, rather than offering up solutions. Consequently, as Palmerston grew into his new role, slowly strengthening his hold on office, Derby was forced to make the best of doing little.

Contend with one thy better far confess'd.

(Derby, *The Iliad of Homer*, ii. 167)

In early March 1855 Greville observed that 'the Derbyites are quite confident of forcing their way to office, and quite determined to do so; but it is their game to damage the present government as much as possible, and they will do everything in opposition but what may recoil upon themselves after they have got into office'.[5] Palmerston, meanwhile, passed to Russell the poisoned chalice of appointment as British plenipotentiary to the Vienna Conference called, at Austria's behest, to explore a negotiated Crimean peace. Palmerston, Clarendon, and Napoleon III, however, had little commitment to the discussions and Russell quickly became mired in diplomatic manoeuvring. A successful state visit to England by Napoleon III during April cemented the Franco-British alliance and strengthened Palmerston's determination to wrest further concessions from Russia by force of arms. The final collapse of the Vienna Conference in May left Russell isolated and embittered, enraged by the discovery that Palmerston had privately encouraged the British Ambassador in Paris, Lord Cowley, to make statements undercutting his negotiations. On 21 May the radical Milner Gibson proposed and then withdrew a Commons motion regretting the failure of the British government to accept Russia's peace terms. The patriotic radical Layard, meanwhile, gave notice of a motion demanding the vigorous prosecution of the war. The maverick Lord Grey brought forward a Lords motion deploring the failure of the Vienna talks. In response to Milner Gibson and Layard, Palmerston declared the Vienna Conference merely suspended, not ended. This, in turn, prompted Disraeli to give notice of a resolution for 24 May expressing dissatisfaction with the government's 'ambiguous language and uncertain conduct'.

Having returned at the end of April to London from the first spring meeting at Newmarket, where he had been wholly immersed in the racing and watching his 3-year-old colt De Clare winning the sweepstakes, Derby met Ellenborough and Malmesbury at St James's Square on 6 May. It was agreed that Ellenborough should move a Lords motion pronouncing a want of confidence in the government's policy with regard to the war.[6] Palmerston adroitly pre-empted the Lords debate, however, by quickly announcing reforms to the ordinance, commissariat, and medical departments of the Army. As a result, Ellenborough's speech, in a crowded Upper House, fell flat and his motion was decisively defeated. Malmesbury concluded that the impression left was 'that the attack was not on the present government, but on the last'.[7] Nonetheless, Derby conveyed to Disraeli, via Ellenborough, his view that 'the primary object should be to make Foreign Powers understand we were determined to go on with the war'.[8]

Disraeli had high hopes for his own Commons motion, introduced on 24 May, accusing the government of unclear objectives in their pursuit of the war. If the Conservatives remained steady, he anticipated its placing the party in a clear and intelligible position before the country, reducing Palmerston's Commons majority and preparing the way for a Conservative resumption of office. But a host of hostile amendments descended on Disraeli's motion, proposed by Sir Francis Baring for the Whigs, Sir William Heathcote for the Peelites, and Robert Lowe on behalf of the Liberal Reformers. Baring's amendment was passed by 319 to 219 votes and Disraeli's motion was slowly smothered. In all thirty-one Peelites, including Gladstone, Graham, and Herbert, supported Baring. More ominously, twenty-one Conservatives voted with the majority and a further forty Conservatives abstained. Derby's analysis of the division estimated the total strength of the Conservatives in the Commons at 292, while he calculated that a total of 359 MPs, including Peelites and Irish Independents, comprised the Liberal majority.[9] That over sixty Conservative MPs failed to support Disraeli clearly demonstrated the dislike of their Commons leader and the sympathy for Palmerston existing among the back benches. Four further nights of debate led to discussion ending with a dispiriting whimper, rather than a bang, on 8 June. This kept Palmerston's ministry afloat and left a frustrated Disraeli railing at being 'vexed, every moment, with sad stories of crotchety idiots'.[10] Reports on 24 May of the bombardment and capture of Kerch by an Allied fleet, securing control of entry to the Sea of Azov, further bolstered Palmerston's position. The ministry, Greville concluded, while not gaining permanent power, had at least averted immediate danger.[11] An imminent Conservative accession to power, following the collapse of Palmerston's premiership, appeared increasingly less likely.

On 31 May, Derby and Lady Emma celebrated their thirtieth wedding anniversary. A week later they attended Ascot, where Derby's horse Poletot came first in the St James's Palace Stakes and his 3-year-old colt The Professor easily won the Windsor Castle Stakes by a length and a half. On 19 June they travelled to Oxford from St James's Square, so that Derby could preside as Chancellor over the laying of the foundation stone of the new University Museum. After a crowded soirée in the Radcliffe Camera that evening, at the following morning's Encaenia ceremony in the Sheldonian Theatre he conferred honorary doctorates on the leading scientists Charles Lyell, George Stokes, and Humphrey Lloyd. A hurried lunch at Worcester College then preceded the stone-laying ceremony in the University Parks, the site chosen for the little-known Benjamin Woodward's Museum design, a remarkable exercise in Continental Gothic. Oxford's Hebdomadal Council had preferred Woodward's Rhenish Gothic structure, influenced by the views of John Ruskin and incorporating a spectacular vaulted iron and glass roof, to an alternative more conventional classical design. A replica of the fourteenth-century kitchen at Glastonbury Abbey was built alongside the Museum, modified to provide the University's first purpose-built chemistry laboratory. Thus Oxford embraced the natural sciences, while dressing them in a medieval aesthetic. Only a long and tedious prayer from the Vice-Chancellor marred the occasion, which offered a brief ceremonial respite from the events unfolding at Westminster.

During July an increasingly confident Palmerston abandoned the humiliated Russell to his parliamentary enemies. Between Westminster and Vienna, Russell stumbled into a maze of contradictory diplomatic pressures. His statements in one context conflicted with the positions he espoused in other settings, as he seemed to be both walking towards and moving away from the feasibility of peace. He was driven to attempting to draw fine distinctions in parliament between diplomatic understandings of limitation and counterpoise. Such sophistry could only have one result. Derby agreed with Disraeli that the Conservatives should firmly denounce Russell's dissembling.[12] On 10 July, Bulwer Lytton gave notice of a Commons motion of censure against Lord John. When Palmerston suggested to the Commons that Bulwer Lytton's motion was 'much ado about nothing', Lytton immediately reminded the premier that *Much Ado About Nothing* came just after *The Comedy of Errors*. Malmesbury predicted that, if the government attempted to rally around Russell, 'then there is no one left but Lord Derby for prime minister'.[13] Promptly, Palmerston privately advised Lord John that the storm could not be withstood. On 16 July a mortified Russell announced his resignation to the Commons.

Jettisoning Russell enabled Palmerston to save his government. On Derby's advice Bulwer Lytton withdrew his motion. To persevere, Derby warned, would only strengthen the remnant of the ministry.[14] Roebuck's subsequent motion drawing on the recently submitted report of the Sevastopol committee, charging the Aberdeen coalition with responsibility for the military catastrophes in the Crimea, was decisively beaten on 19 July. The opportunity to bring fresh blood into the administration also provided Palmerston with the chance to patch up his ministry. Appointing the utilitarian Liberal Robert Lowe as Paymaster-General helped to tame *The Times* as a virulent critic of inept aristocratic government. In his capacity as leader writer Lowe had spearheaded the paper's assault, sustained since the autumn of 1854, against the mismanagement of the Crimean campaign as an exemplar of feeble aristocratic government, merit being smothered by nepotism and inefficiency. Lowe's appointment paid immediate dividends. By August, Palmerston's links with Delane were strengthened and *The Times* was bringing a new orthodoxy to the breakfast tables of the political public: 'The country had needed a man, and in Lord Palmerston it found the man it needed.'[15] The entry into the cabinet of the elderly radical Molesworth as Colonial Secretary further muzzled popular anti-aristocratic critics. By the end of the year the Administrative Reform Association, formed in May 1855 and supported by forty radical MPs and many London commercial and professional men, with its watchword of 'efficient government', had fallen mute. Parliament was prorogued on 14 August and Derby left for a tour, with Lady Derby, of Scotland. The final capture of Sevastopol on 9 September by French and British troops, after a protracted year-long siege, appeared a triumphant vindication of Palmerstonian resolve.

So Palmerston survived the political storms of 1855. The failure of Ellenborough and Disraeli's motions in May and June, followed by the abandonment of Bulwer Lytton's motion in July, kept Palmerston afloat. Yet Derby judged that 'Palmerston may be able to save himself for a time by throwing Johnny [Russell] overboard, but it will be only for a time.'[16] An embittered Russell now privately condemned Palmerston's ministry as a concern 'doomed to rottenness'.[17] Russell's resentment blended with Peelite enmity and Manchester School hostility to produce a rich brew of antipathy. Palmerston's possession of power, Stanley believed, was acquiesced in by the nation, 'though his personal following is small, and he can scarcely rely on a working parliamentary majority'.[18] Yet the Peelites themselves were unpopular because of their opposition to the war. While Cobden retreated into rural seclusion in Sussex, Bright was suffering from the onset of a nervous breakdown. Disraeli's restless mind, meanwhile, began to speculate on a Conservative, Peelite, and radical alliance, based on a call for peace, now that Sevastopol had fallen. He hoped to begin 'scaring the Ministers ... by holding up the bugbear of an understanding with Gladstone and Bright'.[19] England and France, *The Press* proclaimed in late September, no longer had an object in continuing the war.

At festivities in Liverpool in early October, celebrating the Crimean victory at Sevastopol, Derby maintained the Pittite party line of the firm prosecution of a just war. Derby's speech, Lennox reported to Disraeli, 'was the *old roar* of the British Lion!'[20] The Queen's first cousin, the Duke of Cambridge, attended the celebrations and was given a lavish reception by Derby at Knowsley on 9 October. As a Lieutenant General, the Duke had led troops at the Battle of the Alma and had his horse shot from under him at Inkerman, subsequently returning to England to recuperate. Against a popular mood of patriotic celebration, on 10 October, Derby accompanied the Duke into Liverpool where the streets were decked with flags, banners, and bunting, and the crowds were swelled by those brought in by special trains from neighbouring manufacturing districts. Alongside the Union Jack, French and Turkish flags were raised, and loud cheering greeted the party as they travelled through the town. Against the backdrop of the recently completed St George's Hall, located opposite Lime Street station, the Hall's façade of giant Corinthian columns evoking the Roman Forum and expressing the civic confidence and growing prosperity of the rapidly expanding town, enthusiastic crowds extended a warm welcome to the royal Crimean veteran. The Earl of Hardwicke and Spencer Walpole joined Derby at the elaborate banquet held in the Town Hall that evening to honour the Duke, during which fulsome tributes to the bravery of British troops in the Crimea were delivered. This patriotic mood matched the feelings of most, if not all, the country gentlemen of the Conservative rank and file, Stanley noted, who connected 'the idea of war with prosperity and high prices' and so supported Derby 'to a man'.[21]

It was, therefore, with intense fury that Derby learnt of Disraeli's peace initiative. Their fragile relationship entered a new crisis. Jolliffe was immediately dispatched to Buckinghamshire to remonstrate with Disraeli. He was armed with a letter from Derby fiercely complaining of pro-peace articles in *The Press* which were 'eminently calculated to injure the Conservative party'. Derby declared that 'nothing could be more fatal' to the reputation of the Conservative party 'than a suspicion ... of an intention to combine with the various subdivisions of the Peace Party ... for the purpose of embarrassing the government by urging upon them an impossible peace'.[22] At Hughenden, on 20 October, Disraeli argued with Jolliffe 'that is impossible for a party to exist without a policy, and still less possible for an Opposition to be of the same policy as the Government to which it is opposed'. Having shrunk from conduct of the war, Disraeli declared, the Conservatives 'were bound to prepare the public mind for a statesmanlike peace; that a war Opposition and a war Ministry could not coexist'. Otherwise, the Conservatives would be degraded 'to the level of the mob who will huzza Lord P. through the City on the Lord Mayor's Day'.[23] When Jolliffe reported Disraeli's conversation to Derby on 23 October it drew from the Conservative leader a furious rebuke. Derby did not deny that the position of the Conservatives was one of extreme difficulty, requiring 'no little patience on all sides to keep any party together without some definite object to aim at'. But he adamantly refused, he wrote to Disraeli on 25 October, to 'admit that we shrank from *conducting the war*'. On the contrary, the war and its general popularity 'have given us our best chance of carrying on the government ... We cannot with honour, or even with regards to party interests, constitute a peace opposition.'[24] He sharply declared he would never consent to weakening an administration by increasing their difficulties in carrying out a just war. In 'the present temper of Russia', he insisted, 'the greater anxiety we show for peace, the less our chance of obtaining it'. Higher motives than narrow party advantage prevented him, he lectured Disraeli, from adopting the peace cry. 'If the Conservative party cannot be kept together on any other grounds, it is time that it should fall to pieces, or at least that I should retire from the scene.'

A tense silence in Derby's relations with Disraeli followed this epistolary salvo. Malmesbury also fiercely rejected Disraeli's peace initiative and an iciness subsequently descended on communications between them. '*Disraeli must not prate peace*,' Malmesbury fulminated to Derby.[25] To Lennox a sullen Disraeli complained that the 'Conservative party is entombed in the same sepulchre as that Protectionist party at which it used to sneer'.[26] Derby, meanwhile, became the more furious at the lack of any reply from Hughenden to his reprimand. Not until 7 November, two weeks later, did Disraeli, prompted by Jolliffe, finally acknowledge Derby's letter. The reply tersely conveyed Disraeli's intention to refrain 'from saying, doing or writing anything which should bring my views, or even name, before the country'.[27]

The Conservative party now lurched towards a debilitating crisis. Opposition to a resourceful Palmerston brought Derby's relations with Disraeli to a chilly low. All Derby's suspicions about Disraeli's scheming, naked ambition, and narrow selfishness were confirmed. The Conservative rank and file, as well as colleagues such as Malmesbury, were committed to a vigorous prosecution of the war. Taylor reported to Jolliffe that the back benches were outraged by widespread rumours of a 'junction of planets and the mooted triumvirate of Disraeli, Gladstone and Bright'.[28] Only the absence of an alternative leader compelled Derby to tolerate Disraeli's continued leadership of the Commons party. For his part, Disraeli was forced to accept that only Derby's endorsement preserved his influence, keeping widespread personal hostility at bay. Necessity, in the absence of trust, just barely maintained arrangements during the succeeding months, but seriously impeded effective Conservative opposition to Palmerston. The crisis also estranged Malmesbury from Disraeli. Formerly, the two men had enjoyed cordial relations, but Disraeli now nursed a strong jealousy of Malmesbury, deeply resenting Malmesbury's close friendship with Derby. After 1855 Disraeli took to portraying Malmesbury as incompetent. To Greville, in January 1856, Disraeli sourly complained that 'Derby with all his talents had no discretion, and suffered himself to be led and influenced by some of the weakest and least capable men of his party—Malmesbury in particular ... '.[29]

Derby's elder son now appeared to some, including Malmesbury, to be a desirable replacement for Disraeli. But by 1855 filial piety could not protect Stanley from suspicion among the Conservative back benches. His close, though waning, friendship with Disraeli, his well-known liberality of views, and his disdain for the rural fatuousness of the Tory squirearchy increasingly alienated him from the Conservative rank and file. Derby's 29-year-old heir had shown himself to be a high-minded and conscientious politician, although his shyness and earnestness did not endear him to party backbenchers. In his banter with Disraeli, Lord Henry Lennox dubbed him 'Young Morose'.[30] A reclusive isolation, partly enforced by ill health, reflected Stanley's scorn for Tory bigotry. During 1855 he found congenial company in the friendship of the progressive Conservative Sir John Pakington, their conversation dwelling on social reform and working-class education. Pakington, encouraged by Stanley, successfully irritated Disraeli and stole some of Russell's thunder during the 1855 session by raising the issue of education as a private member.[31] On 18 August, Derby, while away in Scotland, made Knowsley available for a meeting of the Mechanics Institutions, linked with the Institutional Association of Lancashire and Cheshire. Members not only enjoyed the grounds, but were allowed free access to the picture gallery and formal rooms of the Hall. From the south colonnade of the Hall, Stanley addressed the gathering, declaring his enthusiastic support for educational reform and all measures conducive to the moral and intellectual welfare of the people. The speech was received with loud applause and hearty cheers given for Stanley, Derby, and Lady Derby. The excursionists, *The Times* reported, 'returned at the appointed hour by the train to their respective localities, highly delighted with the day's pleasurable enjoyment, and with the courtesy they had experienced at the hands of the noble house of Stanley'.[32]

On 31 October 1855 Palmerston attempted to bring Stanley into his cabinet as Colonial Secretary. Surprised by the invitation and doubtful about accepting, Stanley immediately travelled to Knowsley to discuss the matter with his father. Derby allegedly greeted his son with the caustic remark: 'What the devil brings you here Edward? Are you going to be married or has Disraeli cut his throat?'[33] This pointed welcome betrayed Derby's abiding anxiety about Stanley's single status and Disraeli's baleful influence. That Stanley was, as yet, unmarried and therefore unable to produce an heir, added to their strained relations. Subsequent conversations with his father that evening and early the following morning confirmed Stanley's inclination to decline Palmerston's offer. To Palmerston, Stanley refused on the ground of differences over foreign policy. Privately, he confessed to more extensive considerations. The ageing Palmerston had an uncertain hold over the Whigs. Meanwhile, radicals and Peelites 'agree on nothing more cordially than a dislike to the present premier'.[34] Moreover, a political separation from his father would probably result in a personal breach; a 'great House divided against itself' not being 'a seemly spectacle'. Thus, 'the proposed junction', he concluded, would be 'on my part a secession from the stronger to join the weaker side—a sacrifice of permanent results for temporary distinction'. Derby was pleased by Edward's decision, although Stanley, suffering from problems with his eyesight, remained depressed during the following months at his lack of political prospects and privately contemplated retiring from parliament and devoting himself to 'good works' of a public nature.[35] For his part, Derby recognized that his elder son was not to be relied upon 'with too much confidence as an out and out party man'.[36] Derby's own hopes for assuming office were, by November 1855, also fast fading. He seemed content, Stanley noted, 'to watch events, keeping under his command as large a body of Conservative peers and MPs as will remain satisfied with inaction'.[37] Now doubting the probability of an early dissolution, Derby agreed with Jolliffe that 'the feeling of the country' was 'altogether in favour of the prosecution of the war. I should be sorry to say or do anything to influence this feeling,' he affirmed, 'but it would be very bad policy on our part to run counter to it.'[38] A chastened Disraeli, in turn, concurred with Jolliffe that 'silence and inertness appear to me our wisest course'.[39] This subdued mood prevailed into the New Year. In early January, Derby suffered a slight attack of gout, although he reassured his elder son that 'it was not an attack in force, only a reconnaissance by the enemy, and I think will lead to nothing'.[40]

Disraeli's sullen withdrawal and Derby's despondency left the Conservatives drifting dangerously towards fractious impotence. News of the capture of the fortress at Kars by Russian forces on 28 November 1855 reached London in early December. Diplomatic reports of Russia's unwillingness to resume the negotiation of a peace settlement, on terms proposed by the Austrians, meanwhile, were apparently received favourably by Napoleon III. Palmerston and Clarendon resisted the gathering momentum for peace until, suddenly on 16 January 1856, the dramatic news arrived that Russia had accepted the Austrian ultimatum, without qualification, as a basis for negotiations. Nonetheless, Palmerston remained reluctant to abandon the military campaign. 'We stand on the brink of a slope' and 'if we allow ourselves to be dragged down at the tail ... we shall be drawn into the mire at the bottom', he warned Clarendon.[41] Yet Britain could not fight on alone. Protocols were signed in Vienna on 1 February and the Congress of Paris began on 25 February.

Unsurprisingly, Jolliffe had great difficulty in rallying the Conservatives for the beginning of the 1856 session. Having arrived in London on 26 January, Derby met four days later with a small group of MPs and peers at St James's Square, a number of Conservative MPs ominously refusing or not replying to the invitation to dine with Disraeli that evening. The following day, in the debate on the Address, Disraeli made a brief speech welcoming the prospect of an early peace. In a longer statement in the Lords, Derby extensively criticized the Queen's Speech, deploring the lack of any reference to Kars, the deterioration of relations with Persia, and the avoidance of mention of the diplomatic crisis with the United States over the foreign enlistment issue. But he concluded his strictures with the declaration that he would not offer the 'slightest opposition' to the Address.[42]

While remaining passive over party politics during February 1856, Derby was roused to action over the privileges of the peerage. During 1855 he had opposed Palmerston's proposal to revive the Irish barony of Fermoy. In October 1855, in response to popular radical criticism of aristocratic government, he had spoken to a Liverpool audience of the virtues of the House of Lords. The Upper House, he pronounced, 'performed an important and useful function in checking hasty legislation', while 'it presented no barrier to freedom and improvement'. By infusions of new blood the Lords was open to those who showed themselves worthy of entering that distinguished assembly. 'But heavy would be the responsibility of that minister', he warned, 'who should recommend his Sovereign to raise improper and unworthy objects to the dignity of the peerage.'[43] The premier's wish to confer a life peerage, as Lord Wensleydale, on the lawyer Sir James Parke, in February 1856, again brought Derby to his feet. Derby regarded the matter as 'a very grave constitutional question' of doubtful legality and exercising, without the slightest necessity, a prerogative which had been dormant for 300 years.[44] After consulting Lord St Leonards, he decided to challenge the practice upon parliament meeting. As he saw it, the proposed life peerage threatened the Lords' independence of Crown and Commons, disrupting the 1688 settlement. His opposition to the Wensleydale peerage elicited warm support from the great majority of the Upper House, lords Lyndhurst, Campbell, and St Leonards also speaking against it. That the maverick Lord Grey supported the ministry did more harm than good to the government's cause. With the prerogative in the hands of ministers rather than the Crown, Derby argued in the Lords on 7 February, life peerages constituted a political bait, dangled before father and son to keep a family loyal to the government.[45] So would life peerages destroy the independence of the Lords, leave the throne isolated, and expose the institution of aristocracy to the vagaries of volatile public feeling. If not absolutely illegal, the proposed creation was inexpedient and improper, threatening the political power of the hereditary peerage. The government's argument, that this particular creation was merely a specific remedy to the shortage of law lords to hear appeals, ignored dangerous broader implications. Parke's personal reputation for being fussy and pedantic did not help the ministry's case. Greville judged Derby's argument 'very difficult to meet' and considered the premier's proposal 'a blunder'.[46] On 22 February, Derby handsomely defeated Lord Glenelg's motion to refer the matter to the judges.[47] Lyndhurst then immediately carried successfully a motion affirming that precedent did not allow a life peer to sit in the Lords. Conservative, Peelite, Whig, and cross-bench peers warmly supported Lyndhurst's motion.

Dining with the Queen on 27 February, Derby was informed that Her Majesty would not have granted Palmerston's request had she known it would create such a furore.[48] Prince Albert was enlisted as an intermediary to secure a compromise settlement. As a result of the Prince's conversations with Derby, the Lords agreed to set up an investigating committee, Derby to work with Granville, as government leader in the Lords, to resolve the crisis. Derby produced a proposal on which he and Granville might agree, which formed the basis of the committee's report, drafted at the end of March.[49] The Lords' agreement to legislation based on the report quickly followed. But in the Commons the legislation fell foul of bitter anti-Palmerston feeling. Russell, Gladstone, and Graham fiercely opposed the measure. Thus the Lords' attempt to secure a compromise was killed off, not by aristocratic reaction, but by Commons hostility to the premier.[50] In June, Wensleydale received a hereditary peerage, and not until 1887, under the terms of the Appellate Jurisdiction Act, did life peers acquire the right to sit in the Lords.

The outcome of the Wensleydale peerage case was a victory of sorts for Derby, illustrating Palmerston's vulnerability in the Commons. The subsequent legislative output of the 1856 session was meagre. In April, Palmerston shelved the Local Dues Bill in a Select Committee. The question of the purchase of military commissions was laid aside. When Palmerston 'gagged' Russell's education resolutions in April, Lord John was reportedly 'a concentrated essence of Lemon'.[51] By the end of the session the ministry had discarded a Limited Liability Bill, a Public Health Bill, and an Agricultural Statistics Bill, and had postponed law reform. The government's legislative programme, as Derby characterized it at the beginning of the session, was 'redolent of water gruel'.[52] On 30 March 1856 Britain, in the person of Clarendon, signed a peace treaty in Paris concluding the Crimean War. In early May lengthy resolutions, expressing 'joy and satisfaction' at the securing of an honourable peace, were approved in both Houses with little debate and scant opposition. Only Malmesbury and Derby in the Lords voiced any extensive criticisms of the Treaty for the Conservatives. Derby accepted the peace 'without enthusiasm, but without opposition'.[53] Regretting the surrender to Russia of territory in Bessarabia, he characterized the Treaty as 'a peace that might have been worse, but which might have been far better'. Certainly, it failed to compensate for 'the sacrifices, the sufferings, the labour, and the expenses of the war'. Privately, he thought it would not be long 'before our government will have cause to be heartily ashamed of the terms and results of the peace they have "patched up"'.[54] Nonetheless, he refrained from voting against the Treaty, which comprised the most notable achievement of Palmerston's government in a lacklustre session.

Palmerston's success during the 1856 session was scant and his parliamentary support fragile. But the Conservative opposition presented an even sorrier spectacle. In the Commons the Conservative party remained chronically divided. Derby's communication with Disraeli fell away, only the occasional letter passing between them. The regular Saturday meetings of MPs hosted by Disraeli during the session, held during 1854 and 1855, lapsed. As a result, frontbenchers such as Walpole, Pakington, and Stanley took off on independent courses of action over the Maynooth grant, national education, and church rates. Cleavages of opinion and acrimonious resentment multiplied. Reflecting on the state of his party in December 1856, Derby acknowledged that the Conservatives' disorganization was not to be wondered at. 'Indeed', he confessed to Malmesbury, 'I am disposed to be rather surprised to find how mere fidelity to party ties, and some personal feeling, has for so long a time kept together so large a body of men, under most adverse circumstances, and in the absence of any cry or leading question, to serve as a broad line of demarcation between the two sides of the House.'[55] Following the Conservative schism of 1846, the leading Peelites had refused to give Derby any fair support, or even remain neutral, a breach widened by the formation of Aberdeen's coalition in 1852. Since assuming the premiership Palmerston 'has adroitly played his cards, so as to avoid, with one or two exceptions, making any attacks on our institutions, or affording much ground for censure from a Conservative opposition'. In other words, Derby concluded, Palmerston 'has been a Conservative Minister working with Radical tools, and keeping up a show of Liberalism in his foreign policy, which nine in ten of the House of Commons care nothing about'.[56] Only 'some very gross blunder' by Palmerston, he believed, could threaten the premier's position, Conservative hopes otherwise resting upon 'active exertions' at the next general election.

In November 1855 Disraeli declared to Malmesbury that the Conservatives 'are off the rail of politics'.[57] The 1856 session fulfilled this judgement. Disraeli's attack on the government over the loss of Kars, in March 1856, failed. His opposition motion was defeated by an overwhelming majority of 303 to 176 votes, Jolliffe having hoped that the Conservatives would muster at least 200 votes.[58] Disraeli chose not to speak in the Commons on the Treaty of Paris at all, Lord John Manners being the only prominent Conservative MP to criticize, though not oppose, the terms of the peace. Disraeli's hope of reuniting with the Peelites appeared increasingly unlikely and unpopular. 'The reconstruction of the Conservative party', he lamented in June, 'goes on at about the pace of a Tertiary formation.'[59] His attempt to end the session on 25 July with a comprehensive review of the failures of Palmerston's government proved a damp squib. Meanwhile, seething hostility swirled around Disraeli among his Commons rank and file. The recently elected Conservative MP Sir Stafford Northcote, formerly Gladstone's private secretary, despaired of the party's 'indecisive manoevring'.[60] The High Anglican and acerbic Lord Robert Cecil, MP for Stamford, openly ridiculed Disraeli's leadership in his journalism. With devastating scorn Cecil dismissed Disraeli as 'damaged goods', Disraeli's Conservative convictions being an accident of his career.[61] The Tory MP for Norfolk, George Bentinck, familiarly known as 'Big Ben', popularized the fashion among the anti-Disraeli clique of referring to their Commons leader as 'the Jew'. Stanley also increasingly moved away from Disraeli's orbit, finding more congenial company in the sophisticated companionship of Lady Salisbury at Hatfield House, while Pakington continued to push forward education reform as an inconvenience to Disraeli.

A party meeting called by Derby in late April 1856 'was not a very full one; Lord Granby was present, and, as usual, made difficulties, as did also Mr Bentinck, without anything leading to it'.[62] By the end of the session, in August 1856, a dispirited Disraeli promptly left England for Belgium, and, after returning briefly to Hughenden, journeyed to Paris in December. In the French capital fellow visitors found 'Dizzy ... very low and his more open-mouthed wife anything but complimentary about Lord Derby'.[63] Meanwhile, in London rumours of 'a great intrigue to shelve Dizzy' were rife.[64] One senior Conservative backbencher declared to Jolliffe that their party was 'extinct for useful purposes'.[65] It was little wonder that Graham believed 'there is not one man in the House of Commons who has ten followers, neither Gladstone nor Disraeli, nor Palmerston'.[66] The 'total destruction of parties and of party ties and connexions' appeared imminent.

Derby's despondency reflected this parlous state of affairs. During the latter half of the year his mood again darkened, melancholy and seclusion overtaking his active engagement in the Wensleydale peerage debates. He remained committed to resuming the premiership, if he saw a realistic prospect of exercising real power. But the fractious condition of the Conservatives made this unlikely. They were, Malmesbury confirmed, in a 'destitute condition'. It was 'impossible to conceal from ourselves that the *animus* of our party is very unsatisfactory'.[67] The Conservative party, Malmesbury concluded, 'can never be an active one except in office, or in opposition against a Minister who attacks our institutions, and that we are now without either of these stimulants and therefore dormant'. In November, Derby threw cold water on Samuel Warren's suggestion of Conservative support for a rumoured attack by Roebuck on the Royal Address over Naples. Such a move, he stated, 'will assuredly do more to strengthen Palmerston ... There is no occasion on which a great parliamentary battle is fought to so much disadvantage as an amendment to the Address.'[68] A large group of MPs were ready to condemn the

Palmerston policy of 'barking without biting', but the very fact that such an amendment was brought forward by Roebuck would deprive it of much Conservative support. The result, Derby believed, would be 'a signal triumph of the government'.

The sour dejection of Conservative backbenchers even threw up criticism of Derby himself, a striking measure of the disaffection infecting the party. His remoteness from MPs and reclusive social habits while in London, leaving management of the Commons to Disraeli, Jolliffe, and Taylor, became an increasing cause of complaint. Malmesbury noted how *The Press* avoided mentioning Derby's name, while lavishing fulsome praise on Disraeli. Malmesbury was even approached in late April 1856 by a Conservative sounding out his opinion about making Disraeli or Stanley leader of the party; 'but I do not think the person to whom I allude will ever do so again', the loyal Malmesbury recorded.[69] Nonetheless, Malmesbury feared that Derby 'has certainly lost a great deal of his influence by refusing office last year'.[70] The 'best men' of the party, Malmesbury warned, such as Lonsdale, Hardwicke, Pakington, Salisbury, and Lord Wynford, suspected Derby had no appetite for office. 'This impression', Malmesbury advised Derby, 'and the unpopularity of Disraeli are distracting our party.'[71] In November, Taylor grumbled to Jolliffe that, if Derby 'continues to hold aloof, does nothing, and communicates with nobody, it is only natural that many of our best men should complain, and finding no redress, and receiving no explanation, should ride off on their own hobbies'.[72] Pakington, with his enthusiasm for education reform, was the main object of Taylor's disquiet. Pakington, in turn, lamented that the party was constructed on 'the peculiar principle of nobody ever communicating with anybody'.[73]

Pleas for Derby to exercise a more active leadership had their effect. Unlike Disraeli's, Derby's status was such that any gesture of command was greeted with immediate expressions of loyalty. Criticism of Disraeli was a symptom of deep distrust. Conservative complaint about Derby was intended to prod their leader into action. As his health recovered, Derby roused himself. As a result, the party's debilitating drift towards fractious impotence was stemmed. The visit of the French Ambassador, Count Persigny, to Knowsley during November, accompanied by the Duke of Richmond and Lord Wilton, occasioned a ceremonial visit to Liverpool where, at a luncheon in the Town Hall, Derby declared peaceful Anglo-French relations crucial to the stability of Europe. Over Christmas, Derby then began discussing with Malmesbury and Jolliffe how best to restore Conservative morale. Malmesbury exhorted Derby that 'the present and future require all your energy and abilities if during *our lifetime* the Conservatives are to remain an organised class of the political comity of England'.[74]

While visiting Hatfield House on 19 December, Derby took the opportunity 'to talk over quietly' with Malmesbury and Jolliffe 'the position and prospects of the Conservative party'.[75] This 'consultation and conference in high quarters' lifted Jolliffe's spirits. Derby, he believed, had 'set the wheels going'.[76] 'I am afraid it will be very difficult to keep the party together, and still more to satisfy them,' Derby confided to Jolliffe, 'but I will do my best.'[77] The danger was, Jolliffe warned, 'whenever a peer shall be the leader of a political party, a somewhat divided leadership in the House of Commons will naturally result'. But he confirmed 'that there is no peer or commoner who can unite a larger portion of Conservative political opinion of the country than your Lordship does'.[78] Jolliffe conveyed the inclination of those 'independent' MPs, 'below *our* gangway', such as Sotheron-Estcourt and Lord Hotham, to join the Conservatives. 'What is wanted to unite all our sections', he urged, 'is a certainty that it is your Lordship who directs.' Malmesbury pressed for a resumption of those regular meetings during the session which Disraeli had allowed to lapse during 1856.[79] Malmesbury and Jolliffe's encouragement stirred Derby into action. Palmerston, 'who at home is acting on a Conservative policy with radical instruments', Derby declared, 'is at his old game of currying favours with the "Liberals" of this country by meddling and interference with the internal affairs of other countries'.[80] In response to Malmesbury's complaint that a 'miserable £500 a year' had been all that was collected from twenty Conservative peers, Derby donated a sum of money to the party's electoral fund.[81] Preparations were undertaken for a conference at Knowsley, attended by Stanley, Jolliffe, Malmesbury, Pakington, Walpole, and Bulwer Lytton. Disraeli was invited, but as he was still abroad it was anticipated that he would be unable to attend. Characteristically, Derby kept these counsels confined to a small, close circle, his bluff social manner being all that was exhibited to the excluded or the suspect. Disraeli's confidant the scurrilous Lord Henry Lennox spent a week at Knowsley over the New Year and left exasperated. 'As a leader of the party [Derby] is *more* hopeless than ever!! Devoted to Whist, Billiards, Racing, Betting and making a fool of himself with his female guests', Lennox reported to Disraeli, '*Derby* is the great bar to Conservative consolidation.'[82] But this was more comment on Lennox's exclusion from Derby's confidence than an insight into Derby's real purposes. In truth, a new resolve now suffused Derby's thinking.

At Knowsley on 19 January 1857 Derby firmly reminded Stanley of his filial obligations, although this did not prevent Stanley from refusing Disraeli's invitation to a pre-session Commons dinner later that month. A painful crisis with his eyesight enforced Stanley's withdrawal from political society. Unable to consider himself a representative of 'agricultural Conservatism', he privately speculated on the possibility of 'a coalition that all moderate politicians might join';[83] his 'real reason' being 'simply a wish to be free as regards political action, especially on the subject of income tax'.[84] As a fellow spirit to Stanley, Pakington entertained both Cobden and Gladstone in turn at his country residence during January 1857, affirming the reach of more progressive Conservative minds beyond agricultural Toryism. Pakington rejected Derby's proposal to regard education reform as an 'open question', but was appeased by the promise of further discussion and the possibility of conciliation in the arrangement of details.[85] So Derby began to pull together the dispersed fragments of Commons Conservatism scattered by inaction and disaffection. The death of the elderly Duke of Rutland in mid-January raised Granby to the Lords; an unforeseen, but positive, further step towards restoring Conservative amity in the Commons.

Palmerston's unpopularity among Whig, Peelite, and radical MPs also proved a tonic for Conservative morale. Aberdeen and Graham saw the embittered Russell as the one man who could give the *coup de grâce* to Palmerston. Gladstone, hankering after Conservative reunion, looked to an assault on the government's financial policy, represented by the careful Chancellor of the Exchequer, Cornewall Lewis, as the best means of overthrowing Palmerston's ministry, an administration Gladstone privately denounced as 'an organised hypocrisy'.[86] Yet Conservative revulsion at any junction with Gladstone and Palmerston's appeal to his own back-benchers remained Derby's greatest difficulties. Many Conservatives in the Commons clearly preferred a Palmerston government to the objectionable prospect of being led by Gladstone.

Between October and December 1856 a brief triangular correspondence revealed the readiness with which Gladstone looked to an understanding with Derby, and the circumspection Derby felt at concert with Gladstone. Seizing upon a polite response from Derby about Conservative reunion, the Revd Elwin, the anti-Disraeli editor of the *Quarterly Review*, took upon himself the role of broker. In late October, Elwin wrote to Gladstone as 'the competent leader' under whom 'the hollow alliance' of the Conservative party might 'be broken up that it may be remodelled and united'.[87] In response, an eager Gladstone stated to Elwin he was 'ready to speak to [Derby] in confidence and without reserve on the subject of public affairs'.[88] But Elwin had overstepped his mark. Derby failed to react with the promptness Elwin desired or Gladstone had been led to expect. Only after the lapse of a month did Derby eventually relay to Gladstone a non-committal 'pleasure' at the possibility of an interview.[89] He revealed his real feelings to Jolliffe:

> Gladstone is, I know, expecting to hear from me, and *very hungry*, though very cautious. I shall write to him shortly, but only to express my readiness to talk with him confidentially upon the state of public affairs. I am sure it is good policy not to seem too eager to effect an understanding at which, after all, we may never arrive.[90]

'So far so well!' was the chief whip's succinct response.[91] In truth, the Conservative party had become more important to Gladstone than Gladstone was to the Conservative party. Malmesbury recalled that when, in February 1855, Derby offered office to Gladstone, 'no less than eighty members of the House of Commons threatened' to abandon the Conservative leader.[92]

If Gladstone's desire for reconciliation was gratifying, though problematic, the growing disposition among anti-Palmerston sections for a decisive showdown with the premier was encouraging. Having returned from the Continent, Russell, it was reported, was 'getting up materials for an anti-ministerial display on Italy' and was in 'open rebellion'.[93] While writing a biography of Charles James Fox, Russell furbished his Whig inheritance as an antidote to Palmerston's sham liberalism. An outcry roused by Russell over the corrupting temporal power of the Papal States and Neapolitan tyranny would expose Palmerston's vulnerability to revived Liberal rectitude. Lord Grey privately declared his intention to make Britain's declaration of war against Persia, intended to stop encroachments into Afghanistan, 'his great "cheval de bataille" '.[94] The government sought to expel the Persians from the frontier principality of Herat, while inciting the Afghans to attack their historical Persian enemy. Meanwhile, Aberdeen, Graham, and Gladstone agreed that, in obstructing Palmerston, there was 'no safety but in the stoppage of supplies, so as to make a war expenditure impossible'. Forcing Cornewall Lewis to reduce income tax to the level proposed by Gladstone in 1853 offered the opportunity to shackle Palmerston.[95] But, while Aberdeen and Graham saw a financial assault on Palmerston as the prelude to enlisting under Russell, Gladstone perceived it as a prologue to Conservative reunion. Reports in January of the British bombardment of Kuang-tung, as retaliation for a technical insult to the British flag, excited the Peelites and radicals to greater fury against the prime minister. With Gladstone 'overflowing with economical venom', Graham intent on doing 'all the mischief he could', and Russell 'coming home to run out Palmerston',[96] it was with justifiable anxiety that Clarendon feared that 'Persia, Naples and China stand in awful array next to each other.'[97] The Conservative George Hamilton, a junior minister in Derby's 1852 government, pressed home the obvious point on Jolliffe. If 'Lord John comes home with mischievous intent and Gladstone has the same intent as regards the government', then it was 'the more desirable that [Derby] should be at the head of his army'.[98]

Disraeli returned from France in mid-January 'in the highest exultation' over intelligence gathered in Paris of a 'secret treaty' between Britain and Austria safeguarding Austria's Italian dominions. Disclosure in parliament of this treaty would, he excitedly predicted, return the Conservatives to office within a fortnight.[99] He refused to consider an initiative over education, as pressed by Pakington. Russell's education resolutions of the previous year had been 'the climax of confusion', he argued; 'I cannot bring my mind to education at present. I am as sick of it as the country is.'[100] Disraeli did, however, prepare a financial resolution designed to complement Gladstone's call for reducing the income tax and restoring the financial settlement of 1853. Derby regretted Disraeli's hostility to Pakington and seriously doubted the force of Disraeli's revelation of Palmerston's diplomatic duplicity. But Derby, who was now 'in high force', was prepared to endorse Disraeli's fiscal resolution as part of an 'intended financial attack upon the enemy'.[101] On the eve of the session the debilitating despondency among Conservatives rapidly lifted. Greville noted the 'striking fact' that the Conservative opposition, 'of whose disunion we have heard so much, and of the internal repulsion supposed to prevail among them, seems to be as united as ever'.[102]

> ... through the ranks assenting murmurs ran.
>
> (Derby, *The Iliad of Homer*, i. 2)

Palmerston met parliament, on Tuesday 3 February 1857, ill from gout and with a Royal Address which, Malmesbury observed, 'told us nothing'.[103] In the Lords, a revitalized Derby characterized the 'meagre bill of fare for the coming session' as a mere 'vague and shadowy portraiture of the measures' the government planned to introduce. He challenged the ministry to make 'a positive pledge that, beyond the year 1860, the income tax should not be maintained'. He also delivered a general indictment of Palmerston's diplomacy, which had brought on hostilities in China and Persia. As Derby predicted, Disraeli's revelations in the Commons of a secret treaty with Austria fell flat, while Gladstone excitedly denounced Cornewall Lewis's financial policy for destroying his 1853 settlement, and Russell discomforted ministers by criticizing their policy over Naples. It was 'obvious from the whole tone of the proceedings in both Houses that the government' was 'threatened with very serious difficulties'.[104] On Friday 6 February, Derby joined Malmesbury at Heron Court for a weekend of wildfowl shooting, convinced that 'Palmerston's government is becoming very unpopular.' Derby, his host noted, 'seems very sanguine about turning out the government in the course of the session; if we could do it on the income tax, that would be the best, as they would not dissolve parliament on that question'.[105] The tactical difficulty remained, however, that a fiscal offensive against Palmerston would bring the Conservatives into closer alliance with Gladstone.

Two days earlier, on Wednesday 4 February, a wary Derby held a 'strictly confidential' three-hour meeting with Gladstone at St James's Square. With disarming candour, the highly strung Gladstone declared he was willing to act against Palmerston without enquiring who was to follow. He decried his isolated position, denounced the Peelites as 'great evil', and described himself 'as a public nuisance'. To his 'separate position', Gladstone confessed, he 'felt most anxious to put a period'. In a cautious reply, Derby drew attention to 'much bitterness' felt towards the Peelites 'among a portion of his adherents'.[106] Overtures made to the Peelites, rejected in 1851 and 1855, had angered his supporters. Moreover, Derby saw significant differences of intent between Gladstone and his colleagues Aberdeen, Graham, and Herbert. The meeting ended inconclusively. Two days later Derby reported to Malmesbury that the Peelites apparently wished to make up their differences with the Conservatives. But he remained cautious.[107] Disraeli confirmed that some Conservatives were threatening to abstain from any financial offensive against Palmerston because of the alliance with Gladstone it would entail. This was the sort of 'undercurrent', he warned, 'which leads to shipwreck'.[108]

Derby decided to call a meeting of the Conservative leadership, 'both peers and Commons, but only four of each—*not* including Henley'.[109] Henley's absence, he hoped, would reassure Pakington. On Wednesday 11 February he also wrote to Gladstone, following another visit by Gladstone to St James's Square the previous afternoon, expressing reservations about Gladstone's financial resolutions, which suggested that the income tax might become permanent, rather than ceasing in 1860 as proposed in his 1853 budget. To support such a move, Derby stated, would be 'alike inconsistent with good faith and policy'.[110] An anxious Gladstone immediately again called on Derby at St James's Square that afternoon to review his draft resolutions with the Conservative leader. However, Derby remained insistent that, while he would welcome Gladstone's 'spontaneous support' of Disraeli's financial resolution, he would not commit Conservative support to any Peelite motions. Their conversation, he insisted, could not interfere with the Conservatives' 'entire freedom as to our future course'.[111] So Derby continued to hold an anxious Gladstone at bay, while ensuring that the financial offensive against the government stood on Disraeli's resolution, rather than under Gladstone's banner.

In the event, the Conservative meeting requested by Derby was postponed because Disraeli insisted he was too preoccupied with his secret treaty accusations to attend. Meanwhile, the government brought on their budget statement earlier than anticipated. On Friday 13 February, Cornewall Lewis announced to the Commons a budget designed to take the wind out of Gladstone and Disraeli's sails. Proposing a reduction of the income tax from 16d. to 7d. in the pound (the fixed rate, Cornewall Lewis noted, originally introduced by Peel), the Chancellor recommended a gradual diminution of the tea and sugar duties. Generally well received by the Commons, the budget dramatically pre-empted opposition attack. Yet Gladstone's hostility remained unabated. With Cornewall Lewis refusing to offer an easy target in terms of policy, Gladstone's attacks became increasingly personal. But vehement abuse of Cornewall Lewis only emphasized his impotent isolation. The deferred meeting of the Conservative leadership finally occurred at noon on Saturday 14 February, at which it was agreed that Disraeli's financial resolution should not be withdrawn. If rejected, Derby argued, it would shield from responsibility those who voted for it if they should come into office. Later that afternoon Gladstone visited Derby to confirm he would support Disraeli's resolution.[112] But Jolliffe was receiving impassioned warnings from Conservative backbenchers that they would 'almost sooner keep away from the [financial] division, than help to be the means of restoring [Gladstone] to office'.[113] Derby wrote to Ben Bentinck expressing surprise and displeasure at reports of Bentinck's efforts to lead Conservative MPs in opposition to Disraeli's financial resolution. Bentinck's belated reply, eight days later, firmly reiterated his public warnings of 'the dangerous consequences to the welfare of the party, if certain *rumoured coalitions* should be carried out'.[114]

As a result, after 13 February, Derby looked to the China question as the more effective ground on which to dislodge Palmerston. The conclusion of the budget debate in the Commons, on 20 and 23 February, produced a defeat for Disraeli's resolution, 286 MPs voting with the government and 206 MPs, including Gladstone, voting for the Conservative motion. The cabinet viewed the victory as the result of 'a junction between the haters of Gladstone and the haters of Disraeli'.[115] All this strengthened Derby's conviction that the Conservatives '*must* bring forward the case of China, in some shape or other'.[116] While in private Disraeli threw 'cold water on the China question', still believing that his revelations about the Austrian Treaty would topple Palmerston,[117] Russell delivered his widely anticipated blow against the government. On Thursday 19 February the radical Locke King brought forward a motion, proposed annually and previously promptly rejected, to establish an identical £10 parliamentary suffrage in both counties and boroughs. Declaring his unqualified support for Locke King's motion, Russell led 157 Whig, Liberal, and radical and eight Peelite MPs into the division lobby, leaving a frontbench Palmerstonian rump of thirty-seven MPs opposing the proposal. Only the unified opposition of the Conservatives secured the defeat of Locke King's motion. The message for the ministry was clear. On Reform Russell's influence over government votes surpassed that of the cabinet. Russell, at a stroke, revived the issue of parliamentary Reform and forcefully demonstrated its disruptive power on Palmerston's Commons majority. Subsequent discussion of the Maynooth grant revealed further divisions within government ranks. With Palmerston's Commons majority rapidly dissolving, Derby launched his attack on the ministry's policy in China, despite Disraeli's indifference.

In what Gladstone judged a 'very powerful and admirable speech',[118] on Tuesday 24 February, Derby delivered in the Lords a ferocious denunciation of British policy in China. The British representative in China, Sir John Bowring, had bombarded a defenceless Kuang-tung and demanded reparations, in response to the Chinese authorities' boarding a British registered vessel, the *Arrow*, to take off a pirate. A dozen of the crew were also imprisoned. Lorchas like the *Arrow* were commonly used for smuggling in the region, the crew were quickly released, and the vessel's British registration had in fact lapsed. Nonetheless, Bowring seized the opportunity to assert, by force of arms, British power. Having spent the previous days closeted with Lord Lyndhurst examining the Blue Books, Derby declared that 'proceedings of a most violent kind had occurred at Canton', exhibiting behaviour by British officials that was 'menacing, disrespectful and arrogant'.[119] The young Conservative peer Lord Carnarvon disavowed the acts committed at Kuang-tung on every principle of humanity and justice. Malmesbury, on grounds of policy and morality, condemned British actions as shaming and unjustifiable. In response, Clarendon argued that Derby's censure would endanger the lives of all British subjects in China, cast dishonour on the British flag, and bring ruin on the oriental trade. Derby's motion of censure was defeated by thirty-six votes, but both Aberdeen and Grey accompanied him into the division lobby. His attack proved the opening salvo in a 'grand onslaught' against Palmerston's ministry.[120]

The *Arrow* incident, as Derby hoped, provided a righteous common cause for all Palmerston's enemies. 'The long looked for coalition', *The Times* commented, which had 'been impending from the first night of the session', assumed a reality.[121] As the minister Robert Lowe described it, in the *Edinburgh Review*: 'The war cloud under which they had cowered had drifted by,' and Gladstone, Graham, Herbert, Russell, and Disraeli 'raised their heads, like Milton's fallen angels, from the oblivious pool, to plot anew for the recovery of all that the last two years had cost them'.[122] The radical Cobden moved a Commons motion denouncing government policy in China, which, he declared on Friday 27 February, violated international law and common humanity. In an 'exceedingly bitter' speech, Russell vilified Palmerston's policy in China in terms of 'unqualified hostility'.[123] The Conservatives Bulwer Lytton and Lord Robert Cecil expatiated on international law to demonstrate the injustice of the bombardment of Kuang-tung. Disraeli, meanwhile, sulking over the failure of both his secret treaty revelation and his financial resolution, remained silent. Straight away, on Saturday 28 February, Derby called a meeting of the Commons Conservative party at Eglinton's residence at 10 St James's Square, attended by 160 MPs. The response to Derby's call for party loyalty was, as always, immediate and enthusiastic. Derby began his rousing speech to the assembled MPs by alluding to the defection of some Conservatives over the budget, caused by reports of his having coalesced with Gladstone. 'He denied such being the case, but declared in the most emphatic manner that should any member of the Conservative connection attempt to dictate to him the course he should pursue with regard to any political personage whatever, he would regard it as an insult, and no longer recognise that member as attached to his party.'[124] No one was more opposed than himself, he continued, to coalitions effected in defiance of political principle. But neither should the party refuse to acknowledge support based on a genuine identity of sentiment. Derby then repudiated the impression prevailing in some quarters that the interests of Protestantism might suffer in his hands. His past career and well-known principles, he insisted, were sufficient disproof of such suspicions. This forceful declaration was received with long-continued cheering 'and the most complete confidence in Lord Derby was expressed'. Spooner, Newdegate, Lord March, and Colonel Gilpin (MP for Bedfordshire and a close colleague of Newdegate) expressed their loyalty and confidence in Derby to the accompaniment of loud cheering. Conservative unanimity during the continued Commons debate over Cobden's motion was thus assured and Disraeli's active compliance demanded. Disraeli 'clung to his leadership with desperate tenacity', *The Times* observed, 'and his party ... have acquiesced discontentedly in his pretensions'.[125]

Four nights of impassioned Commons debate on Cobden's motion followed and many, including Gladstone, Herbert, and Conservatives such as Warren and James Whiteside, maintained the opposition onslaught. The 'future historian, if by patient research he makes himself acquainted with the opinions of noble lords and hon. gentlemen who will then have passed into oblivion', *The Times* commented, 'will perceive that the battle has merely been one between those immemorial enemies the "Outs" and the "Ins"'.[126] At a meeting of ministerial backbenchers, called by Palmerston on Monday 2 March, open dissent was voiced. During the final night of debate on Tuesday 3 March an ill and tired Palmerston performed poorly. The radicals Milner Gibson and Roebuck lampooned Palmerston for forsaking the watchword of 'Peace, Retrenchment and Reform' for the motto 'Bombardment of Canton and No Reform'.[127] Finally coming to his feet to close the debate, Disraeli portrayed Cobden's motion as a vote of confidence in the government. He challenged Palmerston to appeal to the country with the cry 'No Reform! New Taxes! Canton blazing! Persia invaded!'[128] Cobden's motion was then carried by 263 to 247 votes, a majority against the government of sixteen. Derby's belief in the China issue as the most effective ground on which to destroy Palmerston's Commons majority was triumphantly vindicated. In his analysis of the division Jolliffe counted thirty-six Whigs and radicals who had voted with Cobden, accompanied by nine Irish Brigade MPs and eighteen Peelites. On the other side Jolliffe identified twenty-four Conservatives who had supported the government.[129] Eleven of these MPs regularly voted with the ministry, while a further thirteen including Bentinck, who usually supported the opposition, had also voted with Palmerston.

As in January 1855, so in March 1857, unified Conservative support for a radical motion put the government in a minority. As in 1855, so in

1857, the fracturing of ministerial support swelled opposition votes. Over the *Arrow* affair a significant number of Whigs, Liberals, Peelites, and radicals joined Disraeli's forces, affirming Derby's belief in the inherent instability of Palmerston's non-Conservative coalition. *The Times* believed that Palmerston's government had 'passed through a complete phase of its existence'. There was 'a kind of dramatic unity in its rise, its popularity, and its defeat within the space of two years'.[130] The Conservatives now clearly formed the single largest unified body of votes in the Commons. In March, by immediately calling a general election, Palmerston challenged his opponents to take their cry to the country. The cabinet portrayed those arrayed against them as 'a combination among all the scraps and debris of parties which had resulted from many fractures and which had nothing in common except an unreasoning antipathy to Palmerston'.[131] In the few remaining weeks of the session, until parliament was prorogued on Saturday 21 March, ministers carefully cleared the way for a personal electoral appeal based on Palmerston's popularity in the country. A debate on revenues for the war in Persia was deferred and Clarendon placed before the Lords the terms of a treaty recently signed by the British and Persian governments. Rumours of peace negotiations with the Chinese government were also circulated. Possible contentious distractions from Palmerston's personal reputation were thus removed. Never, Argyll observed, was 'a personal dissolution more thoroughly deserved'.[132] Palmerston's popularity, Clarendon confidently believed, was 'red hot'. [133] In response, Derby declared to the Lords his deep repugnance for Palmerston's 'mischievous interference with the affairs of foreign countries'.[134]

> On rush'd, with joyous shout, the sons of Greece,
> In hope to seize the spoil.
>
> (Derby, *The Iliad of Homer*, ii. 66)

'Public appeals in favour of a *name* and not a *policy* are convenient,' Disraeli observed to a lady admirer in late March 1857, 'but at the same time deceptive.'[135] Certainly it was not in the nature of mid-Victorian general elections to be popular plebiscites on the current government. In the 1847 general election 368 Commons seats, over 55 per cent of the Lower House, had been uncontested. In 1857 over 50 per cent of the Commons, 328 MPs, were returned without facing a contest. Where contests did occur national issues remained a gloss overlaying local politics. Constituency contests remained largely a function of intense local allegiances, with traditional emblems of colours, clubs, and flowers accompanying the noisy rituals, part carnival and part ceremony, of voter registration, nomination husting, canvassing, the public polling of votes, and the chairing of the successful candidate. Public meetings, private dinners, treating and toasting, bands and processions, as well as incidents involving beer and brawls, including both electors and the unenfranchised, accompanied these mock and official rituals. The election day and its humours, with its cast of local notables, the novelist George Meredith observed, 'are those of the badly-managed Christmas pantomime'.[136] Electoral tradition, *The Times* affirmed, required that hustings speeches should be 'scintillating with an appropriate jocularity'. Candidates were expected to exchange jokes and repartee with their constituency, and when argument must be attempted, it should 'be made as short as possible, and even what there is must be in the form of some very, we will not say coarse, but *strong* illustration, which brings the whole to a head instantaneously with a loud report like that of a pistol'.[137]

Following the 1832 Reform Act constituency organization increasingly focused on the registration of voters. The processes of registration were time-consuming and expensive, procedural complexities reflecting the intricacy of varied qualifications to vote in both boroughs and counties. Every voter had to pay a shilling to be registered. This was a one-off payment in the counties and an annual payment in the boroughs. Individual registrations, moreover, could be challenged on a number of grounds—change of address, failure to pay rates, or simple ineligibility—and the objection was automatically upheld if the elector did not appear in person to defend his claim. Thus, after 1832 registration disputes in the revision courts became the battlefield of local partisans, control of the electoral register being essential to the outcome of constituency contests.[138]

Under Peel in the 1830s Francis Bonham had, as the first full-time agent for the Conservative party, from his desk in the Carlton Club encouraged the organization of Conservative associations in the constituencies. But the registration of voters, selection of candidates, organization of the canvass, and the payment of expenses remained firmly in local hands. Bonham and his Carlton Club election committee provided information and support, but were forced to respect the power of the local gentry and party activists. In the 1841 general election their efforts helped to produce a Conservative majority of 106 MPs in the Commons. After 1846, however, central support for local Conservative organization in the constituencies fell away. The retirement of Bonham and the loss of the party's official corps over Corn Law repeal left local Conservatives more reliant than ever on their own resources. Neither Lord George Bentinck nor Disraeli took a close interest in constituency matters. Registration, Bentinck declared, was 'old woman's work'.[139] The void was filled by Protectionist societies and Protestant associations, to the discomfort of Derby. Beresford's injudicious efforts to galvanize popular support in 1852 produced damaging accusations of corruption and bribery. As a result, in 1853 Disraeli vested electoral party management in the hands of his solicitor Philip Rose, aided by Markham Spofforth as party agent. The capable and discreet Rose had managed Disraeli's debt-ridden private finances since 1846, bringing a stability to Disraeli's affairs critical to his claims to respectability. The 28-year-old Spofforth, as a solicitor in Rose's London law partnership, loyally supported Jolliffe and Rose's activities. As chief whip Jolliffe, after 1853, sought to repair Conservative constituency organization and encouraged local gentry to give attention to the registration of voters. Under Jolliffe, Rose, and Spofforth, Conservative electoral organization was reinvigorated and the damage caused by Beresford's inept handling of constituency matters slowly repaired. The 1857 general election was the first real test of Rose, Spofforth, and Jolliffe's regime.

Derby firmly endorsed Jolliffe's authority, of whom he thought highly, and consistently supported his work. He ensured that Jolliffe was regarded as much his own choice as Disraeli's appointment. In turn, Jolliffe recognized that Derby's endorsement was critical to his own effectiveness and the necessary counter to accusations that he was merely Disraeli's fixer. As a peer Derby was inevitably distanced from the electoral struggles of his Commons rank and file. By convention members of the House of Lords did not campaign on behalf of their party in the constituencies. Nonetheless, he did not regard Conservative electoral business with remote indifference. Indeed, Jolliffe after 1853 had a more extensive correspondence with Derby on electoral matters than he maintained with Disraeli. Derby's Whiggish aristocratic instincts, in turn, fortified his belief, learnt from Lansdowne and expressed during the Reform debates of 1831–2, in the legitimacy of the influence exercised by responsible local landed elites. Therefore, patronage remained indispensable to encouraging and rewarding loyal efforts. To these matters Derby gave an active interest. In 1854, for example, he recommended Lord Portarlington for a vacancy in the Irish representative peerage for his part in securing a Conservative electoral victory in the Irish borough of Portarlington and as a guarantee of support at the next election. As a result, in 1857 Lord Portarlington contributed £100 to the party election fund.[140] Similarly, Derby kept Jolliffe well informed on the health and circumstances of his fellow peers in cases where this would affect constituency matters, while the mundane details of constituency organization were left to Jolliffe and Rose's team. A necessary delegation, not disregard, of electoral matters characterized Derby's relation with his party's activities. His support for Jolliffe and Rose's efforts remained crucial to their effectiveness.

After 1853 Rose, Spofforth, and Jolliffe concentrated their attention on the English and Irish boroughs, content to rely on the loyalty of the Conservative gentry in English counties, and recognizing the strength of Whig and Liberal control in Scotland. In March 1855 Rose reported to Jolliffe that communication had been established with 'confidential parties' in 114 boroughs.[141] A newly founded Conservative Association in Leeds, for example, was getting Conservative voters onto the electoral registers in both the borough constituency and the West Riding, as well as identifying prospective candidates. Though this was satisfactory progress, Taylor reported that lack of adequate funds to support sustained organization in English constituencies and the partisan culling of the electoral registers hampered their efforts. As a result, Derby initiated the setting-up of a general election fund. During 1856 twelve Conservative peers subscribed a total of £9,000 to the fund. Derby's own contribution in December 1856 was seen as proof of his renewed commitment to overthrowing Palmerston. Similarly, he led the subscriptions to cover Lord Chelsea's election expenses in unsuccessfully contesting Middlesex in April that year. In March that year Derby also made personal efforts to defeat Ben Bentinck's candidature in West Norfolk. Alarmed by reports that the loyal Conservative William Bagge was going to give way to Bentinck's nomination, Derby immediately wrote to the Norfolk landowner Lord Sondes. Bentinck's recent conduct, he stated, was 'wholly inconsistent with the ordinary obligations of party'.[142] But the preferences of local activists prevailed, Bentinck being returned as one of the two MPs for the county constituency in an uncontested election.

In the event, the overall number of candidates of all parties standing at the 1857 election was the lowest of any general election since 1832. Similarly, the number of uncontested elections was higher than in any general election since 1832, with the exception of 1847. While the government portrayed the election as a national plebiscite on Palmerston's popularity, the more complex reality was firmly rooted in the partisan dynamics of locality. In Wales religious issues dominated the hustings. In Ireland the Maynooth grant and patronage, in the form of tenant rights, prevailed.

The efforts of the Irish Central Conservative Society, however, secured forty-six seats for the party (a gain of six seats over the 1852 election), with twenty of these seats won outside Ulster. Lord Donoughmore, long active in registration work in Tipperary, Cork, and Waterford, exploited the disruption of Liberal partisans in Munster, caused by the bankruptcy and suicide of Jon Sadleir, the long-serving O'Connellite MP, while, as the acknowledged Conservative expert on Irish electoral matters, Lord Naas undertook delicate negotiations with members of the Irish Brigade to secure a common opposition to Whig candidates in Mayo and Tipperary. English elections alighted on a variety of issues, embracing religion and Reform as well as diverse appeals to Palmerston's dogged defence of British interests abroad. To his constituents in Tiverton Palmerston denounced the Commons opposition for making the humiliation of the country a stepping stone to office. A number of prominent radicals, including Cobden, Bright, Milner Gibson, Miall, and Layard, lost their seats. But in Greenwich, Bolton, Bristol, Carlisle, Stockport, Stoke, and Sheffield anti-Palmerston radicals were returned. In London, on Thursday 19 March, Russell announced a further instalment of parliamentary Reform as the real proof of Whig and Liberal commitment to progress.[143] As intended, with many Liberal and radical candidates subsequently pledging themselves to Reform, this put Palmerston in an embarrassing position.

As the elections drew to a close in mid-April the appearance of a ministerial triumph seemed obvious. It was particularly disappointing to the Conservatives that many seats in small English and Welsh boroughs were lost, despite the efforts of Jolliffe, Spofforth, and Rose. Indeed, while gaining seats in Ireland, a significant Conservative loss of seats in England and, to a lesser extent, Scotland more than offset these successes. Rebuilding the efficiency of Conservative constituency organization enjoyed under Bonham in 1837 and 1841 was a formidable long-term task, with revived Conservative associations in the English boroughs still labouring under the difficulties of restricted funds and inexperienced personnel. In all 367 Whig, Liberal, and radical MPs were returned; 260 Conservative MPs were elected, and twenty-seven Peelites were returned to Westminster. But appearances were deceptive. The nominal Whig, Liberal, and radical majority was deeply divided. In particular, pledges given to parliamentary Reform by many Liberal and radical candidates suggested the vulnerability of Palmerston's leadership to Russell's progressive rectitude. Russell had burnished his Liberal credentials in his City of London hustings speech on 19 March, delivering an extended argument for Reform and the promotion of 'progress', seeing off the challenge of the Palmerstonian candidate, the banker and East India proprietor Raikes Currie. As government leader in the Lords, Granville recognized that the 'danger consists in the probable formation of a numerous and respectable Liberal party opposed to the present government'.[144] Acute observers predicted that ministerial exaltation would be short-lived, as discord among the Liberals fermented. Supporters of Russell believed the implications of the election to be clear: 'the immediate victory is Palmerston's, the second is the Liberal party's, and the third will be Lord John's'.[145]

Derby's response to the election drew directly on antipathies festering within the government's Commons majority. After watching his horse Fazzoletto win the Port Stakes at Newmarket on 16 April, he turned his mind to the Conservatives' future strategy. 'The elections have undoubtedly given Palmerston a large majority,' he wrote to Disraeli on 24 April, 'though one of a heterogeneous character.' He outlined an opposition strategy calculated to breed ministerial differences.

> The Peelite and Manchester parties are obliterated, but it would be a mistake to say that the House is divided into two parties only; among the Liberals there are two divisions, the differences between whom must shortly become more marked than they are at present. The old Whigs are far less numerous than the radicals, and are proportionately afraid of them. Pam has ousted Johnny from the command of the Whigs, and the necessities of the latter's position will make him bid for the support of the radicals, with whom, however, he will never obtain a cordial acceptance. Palmerston, on the other hand, would not be sorry to see him take this course, and, if he finds him committed to it, will take the line of great moderation, and lean upon Conservative support. To encourage this tendency on his part, if it exists, and to foment divisions and jealousies between the discordant elements of the Government majority, must be our first object; while we should carefully avoid multiplying occasions for their voting in concert, in opposition to motions brought forward by us.[146]

Though Palmerston might at present have the game in his hand, the Conservatives' primary object 'must be to make him play it in our sense'. Many Conservatives were favourably disposed to Palmerston, while among the Palmerstonians proper 'there are as strong Conservatives at heart as any in our ranks'. Looking 'to Palmerston's age and increasing infirmities, the oftener there can be radical moves, the better for us and the country'. This must be, Derby pronounced, the leading principle of Conservative strategy in the forthcoming session. They should seek to 'avoid attacks on the government, and especially on Palmerston individually, to profess a readiness to consider candidly any measure of internal improvement which he may recommend; and to intimate, rather than profess, our readiness to support him in resisting violent counsels forced upon him by his colleagues or supporters'.

With characteristic restlessness Disraeli advocated an immediate Conservative move over parliamentary Reform at the meeting of the new parliament, exploiting Liberal differences and laying a Conservative claim to Whig policy. A bold course, he urged, would 'put us on our legs'.[147] But Derby firmly reined in Disraeli's impatience.

> With the knowledge that there are two rival chiefs in the field, and the probability that the question [of Reform] will be adversely discussed between them, I think our obvious policy is to wait till both of them have opened their budget, or at all events committed themselves to some course; and on this account I should deprecate the giving of any notice, from our side of the House, on the subject of Reform.[148]

Patient vigilance was contrary to Disraeli's mercurial temperament. But Derby pronounced prudent caution as the party's best strategy. He anticipated no Reform Bill in the forthcoming session, 'but that Palmerston will try to turn John Russell's flank by compelling him to show his cards, and then promise to bring forward the subject of Parliamentary Reform, after mature consideration by the Government, in the session of 1858'. The Conservatives ought to support Palmerston in this line, he advised, if the premier chose to take it. Over further parliamentary Reform he proposed two principles to guide Conservative thinking: adherence to the present borough and county suffrage, and approximation to a just proportion between the number of representatives allotted to each. Lowering of the franchise, the abolition of rate-paying clauses, and the introduction of the ballot should be resisted. But public silence remained their best immediate course. To Malmesbury, on 30 April, Derby stressed the importance of impressing 'upon all our friends in both Houses, and especially on Disraeli, the necessity in mind of being very guarded in their language on the subject of Reform, and of not committing the party hastily to the adoption of any cause'.[149]

Conservatives' initiatives over Reform, while in opposition, Derby warned Disraeli, would anger their Commons rank and file. This mattered because both believed that their party, in contrast to the Whigs and Liberals, had emerged from the election 'much more compact and united'.[150] Many doubtful Conservative votes in the Commons had been purged. Although the Conservative party had 280 MPs on its muster-roll prior to the election, Disraeli observed, 'when the hour of battle arrived, we could never count on more than 220, the rest absent, or worse, against us'. After the election Jolliffe identified 260 MPs, 'good men and true', who were loyally supportive of the Conservative leadership. On 16 April he wrote to Derby that 'it is something to have got over the elections without the loss of one man who was absolutely necessary to our party'. Taylor's success in Dublin, 'against all the government could do', was 'a great satisfaction'.[151] Already, during March, Pakington had written to Derby declaring his firm allegiance.[152] Taylor's calculations showed 256 reliable Conservative votes in the Commons prior to the election, with an additional seventy-three MPs as Liberal Conservatives or 'doubtfuls'. After the election he calculated that there were 260 secure Conservative votes, with the section of Liberal Conservatives and 'half-government men' reduced to thirty-six MPs. Three reliable Conservative MPs had been gained in England and Wales, and an additional few gained in Ireland, offset by three losses in Scotland.[153] 'All the sections, all the conceited individuals', Disraeli celebrated, 'who were what they styled themselves "independent", have been swept away, erased, obliterated, expunged.' This was a state of affairs 'much more wholesome, and more agreeable'.[154] In particular, as Herbert bluntly declared to Aberdeen, the Peelite party was now 'extinct'.[155] Graham agreed that the 'Peelites as a party are gone'.[156] 'A small knot of men may go on for some time flattering itself upon its esoteric correctness and exclusive possession of truth in the midst of the whole mistaken world,' The Times pronounced, 'but sooner or later, it has to give up its position.' The Peelite party, it concluded starkly, 'is no more'.[157] Floundering in dark desperation, an isolated Gladstone thought his future lay with Derby's Conservatives, while Aberdeen and Graham looked to join those 'honest reformers' gathering around Russell.[158] Malmesbury informed Derby of Graham's declaration that he was 'an isolated man and that Peelism was at an end'. The election, Malmesbury continued, 'has shown the feeling against Gladstone in a very remarkable manner. The hatred of him among all classes is such as to be unjustified by anything [Gladstone] has done, but still is even stronger than the popularity of Palmerston.'[159]

Given the discord brewing within the government majority, Conservative consolidation augured well for the future. Hamilton advised Disraeli that 'an advent to power is almost a certainty' if the Conservatives did not 'run at it too soon'. It seemed impossible, he predicted, 'that the two sections of which the Palmerstonians are made up can hang together after the commencement of the 1858 session'.[160] Similarly, Jolliffe wrote to Derby anticipating that, with a ministerial Reform Bill now apparently inevitable, the 'government will not last six months!!!'[161] Though disappointed by the loss of three or four more county seats than they had anticipated, Malmesbury concurred that a ministerial Reform Bill was certain. He agreed, however, with Derby's view that it was best for the Conservatives not to initiate a Reform debate, while deprecating any further lowering of the suffrage. 'The five pounders would I believe be practically even worse than universal suffrage as they are a class ignorant and ill-disposed and removed from all aristocratic influences.'[162] Derby's own conviction, that the Conservatives could be 'a very formidable opposition' if they remained 'united and moderate and not crotchetty', matched the judgement of calmer voices in Conservative counsel. 'On the whole,' he informed Manners, 'considering the Palmerston fever now raging, we have not done badly, and shall still be able, I hope, to show a good compact front, while Pam and Johnny fight it out for the liberal leadership.'[163]

Doing little was all the more conducive to Derby as, at the end of March, his health again failed. The exertions of the New Year took their familiar toll. A violent attack of gout inflamed both ankles, both knees, and both elbows. During April he was confined to his bed. News that Palmerston was also bedridden with gout, unable to ride or walk, further fuelled political speculation. From Lancashire, Derby begged Malmesbury to send news, Lady Derby adding that the mood at Knowsley was 'very *triste*'.[164] Malmesbury reported 'from *undoubted* authority' that Lady Palmerston was very anxious about her husband's health. 'He is so weak as to be unable to take any exercise even on horseback and he has an open sore on his foot very dangerous at his age.' Only Lady Palmerston's ambition, Malmesbury wrote, had prevented her husband from retiring following the signing of the Treaty of Paris, 'and she now reproaches herself with it'. If Palmerston went, he speculated, the Queen would probably send for Clarendon, and Russell would become leader of the Commons.[165] But Malmesbury found it difficult, in Derby's absence, to engage Disraeli in consultation over the party's tactics upon parliament meeting. Disraeli's sullen isolation, his proposal for a Reform initiative having been quashed by Derby, seriously hampered the party's preparations.

Following the opening of the new parliament at the beginning of May 1857, Derby struggled down to London on 16 May. In his absence, consultation between Disraeli and Malmesbury had not gone smoothly. Despite looking weak and ill, he insisted on going to the House of Lords, combatively commenting to his whip Lord Colville: 'Palmerston says I am dying, but I'll show him I'm alive.'[166] But, despite this stubborn pugnacity, he remained a low-key presence during the remainder of the session. His occasional statements to the House were brief interjections of conventional sentiment. His arrival in St James's Square, however, did force Disraeli to be more cooperative. By early September, Derby appeared to be 'in very low spirits—quite without his usual *entrain*'.[167] As a semi-invalid, he remained committed to a strategy of vigilant inactivity, which he pressed upon the restless Disraeli. Not until the late autumn did he recover the resolve he had exhibited at the beginning of the year.

As Derby predicted, Palmerston also sought refuge in quiescence. The Queen's Speech of Friday 1 May said little, ignoring Reform and dwelling much on foreign affairs. The session, Derby affirmed, was 'likely to be a quiet one'.[168] The election of a new Speaker for the Commons passed without contest, despite Walpole's earnest wish for the position. The government nominee, the old Etonian and Derby's Christ Church friend and companion on his North American journey in 1824 John Evelyn Denison, was elected without opposition. Walpole's bitter disappointment, however, remained a tart irritant in Conservative counsel. Malmesbury, assuming the leadership of the Conservatives in the Lords in Derby's absence, concurred that there would not be a question of consequence in the Upper House for a long time. In response to an enquiry from a Palmerstonian backbencher, the premier took the opportunity to reassure the Commons that the government would introduce a Reform Bill in the next session, it being 'highly inexpedient' to engage in discussions about constitutional change before then. Thus was parliamentary Reform deferred. Russell and his supporters appeared willing to wait until the 1858 session to challenge Palmerston's authority, watching, in the interim, for further signs of Palmerston's physical decline.[169]

During May, over the proposal to grant an annuity and dowry to the Princess Royal in anticipation of her marriage to Prince Frederick of Prussia, Derby informed Disraeli that 'we must "combine" with the government to protect them against their radical supporters'.[170] Thus Roebuck's objection to the annuity was defeated and, on 25 May, a dowry of £40,000 was approved. A placid calm then descended on parliament, as Derby, as well as much of fashionable London society, spent the week of 8 June watching the races at Royal Ascot. In this lull religious questions came to the fore. A bill introduced by Palmerston to allow practising Jews to take a seat in the Commons, as the premier expected, was rejected by the Lords. This was the one issue which animated Derby during June. But Pakington's announcement of his conversion to removing the bar to practising Jews entering the Commons, a view known to be shared by Disraeli and Stanley, suggested to many that the Conservatives' objection to such legislation, vigorously maintained since 1848, must shortly be abandoned. Gladstone, meanwhile, tested the patience of the Commons by his prolix objections to the government's Divorce Bill.

Then dramatic reports in late June of a mutiny by native troops in India, the mutineers' seizure of Delhi and Cawnpore, and the siege of Lucknow, accompanied by horrifying tales of torture inflicted on British women and children, whipped up popular outrage against native barbarity during July and August. The distribution of cartridges greased with beef and pork fat for the new Lee Enfield rifles had triggered a horror at loss of caste among Bengal sepoys, leading to mutiny by the native army and a collapse of British authority. The Governor General of India, the Peelite Lord Canning, was taken unawares by the uprising. But Palmerston responded with unruffled assurances that all that need be done to suppress the Indian revolt was being done. Attempts by Disraeli in the Commons and Ellenborough in the Lords to initiate a broad debate on the Indian crisis, as less a military mutiny than a national rebellion, fell on deaf ears. After parliament prorogued on 28 August ministers quickly vacated London. Derby spent the end of July at Goodwood watching Fazzoletto win the Sweepstakes and his 2-year old filly Target come first in her race the following day. At York, on 21 August, he watched Target repeat her success in the Juvenile Stakes. During September and October hardly a single member of the cabinet stayed in town.

But beneath the smooth surface of events those disruptive undercurrents, evident at the beginning of the year, continued to churn. Remaining 'very hostile' to the government and 'long[ing] to supplant Palmerston', Russell established during September the basis upon which Liberals and Peelites such as Graham might agree over parliamentary Reform, while awaiting Palmerston's measure.[171] 'His game', Graham reported, 'is to wait on Palmerston, compel him, if he can, to produce the government bill and then tear it to rags as worthless and inefficient.'[172] Roebuck during the late summer, with Cobden in rural seclusion in Sussex and Bright recovering from a nervous breakdown, undertook the marshalling of radical parliamentary forces over Reform; while Disraeli continued to brood over the Indian crisis as 'one of the mainsprings on which any ministry must be formed'.[173]

Just as in September 1855, when news of the fall of Sevastopol bolstered Palmerston's political position at home, so two years later, in September 1857, reports of the recapture of Delhi and the first relief of Lucknow appeared momentarily to ease the cabinet's domestic difficulties. Palmerston's calm optimism seemed vindicated. Equally importantly, it allowed

Palmerston to steer the Indian issue away from an awkward post-mortem into the cabinet's handling of the crisis, into the safer waters of discussion about administrative reform. Palmerston talked of abolishing the East India Company's governing powers and establishing in its place government by the Crown. Granville discerned that 'one of Palmerston's motives' was 'to do something great which will distinguish his premiership', while another aim was 'to have something that will act as a damper to [parliamentary] Reform'.[174] During October the premier drew up a ministerial Reform Bill. It was a moderate measure, keeping the borough franchise at £10, lowering the county suffrage to £20, and granting the vote to officers of the Army and Navy, lawyers, physicians, clergymen, and the clerks of merchants, bankers, and manufacturers. Disraeli believed Palmerston's Reform measure would 'only be *pour rire*: it will not pass, nor will it be intended to do so, but it will keep J. Russell in the background'.[175] Palmerston saw it as sufficient to honour his Commons pledge and secure moderate Whig and Liberal support, while being cautious enough to enlist Conservative sympathies. It reflected Palmerston's wish to avoid extensive redistribution and any lowering of the borough franchise, while securing an enfranchisement of property and intelligence through a lowered county suffrage and 'merit franchises'. These were proposals, Palmerston anticipated, moderate Liberal opinion might endorse. So Russell and the radicals would be isolated and the issue of India exploited as a 'damper' on Reform.

A financial crisis, however, forced Palmerston to call an emergency session of parliament in December to approve a bill of indemnity authorizing the Governor of the Bank of England to issue extra banknotes. A banking crisis in the United States precipitated a severe drain of bullion reserves, leading to several banks in Britain stopping payment. The premier had hoped to avoid meeting parliament until February 1858. But, with 'a feverish anxiety pervading the mercantile classes', and the extensive stoppage of banks in Europe and the United States, the cabinet were forced to confront parliament far sooner than they preferred.[176]

Fill'd them with strength and courage.

(Derby, *The Iliad of Homer*, ii. 4)

By November 1857 Derby was again 'in high force'.[177] The success of his promising young filly Target in the Sweepstakes at Newmarket on 30 October lifted his spirits. Fully recovered from his infirmities of the

previous seven months, he sensed a renewed gathering of hostility against
the government. It was now Derby who urged Disraeli to action. The
emergency session, he pressed Disraeli on 15 November, must not be
confined to discussion of the financial crisis. 'We must have a Queen's
Speech and the whole policy of the government, foreign and domestic,
must be laid before us.'[178] They had reached a stage in Indian affairs,
he believed, in which there must be a full inquiry into both the past
and the future. Disraeli, on holiday in Torquay, pressed the same point
on Lord Henry Lennox. 'The government, of course, wish to make the
Co. a scapegoat, and are feeling their way to that end. This must not be
allowed.'[179] He agreed with Derby that 'the whole policy of the government
must be opened'.[180]

Consulting with Ellenborough, Derby's views on future policy in India
crystallized. Ample punishment must be meted out to the leading partici-
pants in the revolt and British power re-established. The British Army in
the subcontinent should be increased and a higher proportion of British officers appointed. Moreover, greater discretionary powers might be granted
to the Governor General and interference by parliament reduced. At the
same time, non-interference with the internal administration of native
princes should be adopted, respect for local laws and customs shown when
not at variance with morality, the free exercise of all religious rites protected
under the same restriction, and toleration extended to the prejudices of
caste where they did not affect military discipline. Expenditure on works
of public utility of a remunerative character should also be approved.[181]
Without laying themselves open to any imputation of faction, he informed
Disraeli, 'we may fairly challenge the government to vindicate the measures
they have adopted in the East, including the forgotten China!'[182] A full
discussion of the government's financial policy should also be secured. 'I
am afraid that we shall have some difficulty in getting our forces together
at this time of year and on so short a notice,' he confessed, 'but I think you
will agree with me that we ought not to allow this early session to be made
a mere matter of form, to suit the convenience of the government.'

A recovered Derby also fired Jolliffe's resolve. In response to the
chief whip's request for an outline of his views, so as to ensure 'a good
understanding with our friends',[183] Derby wrote on 25 November two
substantial letters to Jolliffe dealing with the banking crisis and the Indian
revolt.[184] Over finance, he pronounced: 'we shall have to go much further
and deeper than the Act of Indemnity', while India 'must be the paramount
question with every man'. They would be failing in their duty, he urged, if,

... from fear of embarrassing the government, we abstain from insisting on a full enquiry into the causes which have led to this revolt, the degree of unpreparedness in which it found the government, the warnings they received and neglected; and how far loss of time in the first instance, even after they took the alarm, has rendered the state of affairs, to say the least of it, much more critical than it would otherwise have been.

Though a vote of censure was best avoided while fighting in India continued, a 'day of reckoning', he insisted, must accompany the restoration of order. Their main point of attack must be the government's 'utter unpreparedness, and their obstinate disbelief in the magnitude of the danger, 'til it had grown almost too strong for them'.[185] He doubted the government would introduce parliamentary Reform into the Queen's Speech, but if it was absent 'the radicals will be open-mouthed'; while, as regarded foreign affairs, the government's policy in neither Persia nor China appeared dignified.

On Thursday 3 December a combative Derby delivered in the Lords, in answer to the Address, a comprehensive indictment of the government's policies. His speech, Malmesbury judged, 'was very good, some parts extremely eloquent'.[186] Never, Derby declared, had parliament been faced with 'such varied anxiety and almost unvaried gloom'.[187] A 'complication of misfortune' confronted the country. An overwhelming commercial crisis accompanied a rebellion shaking the very foundations of the Indian Empire. The enactment of certain clauses of the Treaty of Paris was outstanding and the Address omitted any mention of China. Their sole comfort was the peace currently prevailing in Europe, but this, he sarcastically suggested, might be a source of disappointment to the ministry. 'If the noble Viscount at the head of the government cannot disturb the peace of Europe', he averred, 'no one else can.' The operation of Peel's Bank Charter Act of 1844 had aggravated the commercial crisis and produced widespread suffering in British manufacture, especially in Lancashire. Factory operatives were being put on short time. Yet, the ministry offered no explanation of the causes of commercial distress. Meanwhile, the whole framework of empire in India was being rudely shaken. He roundly condemned the policies of the Governor General. Lord Canning had done little to disabuse the sepoys of their alarm at rumours of cartridges greased with beef and pork fat, an egregious violation of native religious belief. The government had shown no foresight, promptitude, or vigilance, while, from first to last, refusing to believe in the seriousness of the revolt. Complacent levity had characterized Palmerston's response to this grave crisis.

Granville offered little defence to Derby's attack. Ellenborough supported Derby's offensive, while Argyll and Panmure (speaking with his usual awkwardness) offered unpersuasive responses to the Conservatives' accusations. Commons debate during December, however, did focus almost solely on the commercial crisis. This was as Palmerston intended. Disraeli, ill with influenza, oriticized the suspension of the Bank Charter Act, but his denunciation of government policy in India failed to ignite a broader assault. News of military successes in India, meanwhile, bolstered the government's standing. Disraeli's amendment to Cornewall Lewis's motion to reappoint a Select Committee to inquire into the operation of the Bank Act was defeated by a majority of 178 votes. What did emerge, however, were tangible signs of Palmerston's growing unpopularity. Derby issued a dark warning. The present moment, when all were engaged in putting down the revolt, was not an appropriate time for an inquest. But once the revolt was successfully repressed, he cautioned, it was the bounden duty of parliament to inquire fully into its causes.[188]

Rattled ministers became increasingly apprehensive. The government whip in the Upper House, Lord Bessborough, noted that the tone of the opposition was 'more than ordinarily bitter, Derby especially'.[189] Bessborough warned that 'when our blessed Reform bill is launched we shall have very few friends'. Granville began to 'dread' the resumption of the session in February 1858 'as a great breaker up of parties', making 'the future very difficult'.[190] Ministerial foreboding was, in part, an acknowledgement of Russell's predicament; 'waiting for an inheritance at 66 years of age is a sorry game'.[191] It was also a recognition of Derby's revived determination and greater Conservative unity. During December anxiety became a contagion among cabinet ministers. When Disraeli, in conversation with Greville, described Palmerston's popularity to be of an entirely negative character, resulting from the unpopularity of every other public man, rather than any particular attachment to him, Greville repeated the comment to Cornewall Lewis. Disraeli 'estimated Palmerston at his real worth' was the Chancellor's succinct response.[192] Argyll, meanwhile, shared with Clarendon his deep unease that their measure for reforming the government of India was barely considered and hastily drafted while the premier only procrastinated over parliamentary Reform. The terminal disease of chronic self-doubt now began to infect the government.

To universal indignation it was at this precise moment that Palmerston appointed the scandal-ridden Lord Clanricarde to be Harrowby's successor as Lord Privy Seal. Reportedly, Lansdowne promptly asked Palmerston 'if he was out of his senses'.[193] Parkes described the appointment as 'an outrage of public opinion'.[194] From an old Irish family with estates in Co. Galway, Clanricarde had served as Postmaster General in Russell's cabinet from 1846 to 1852. Excluded from Aberdeen's coalition cabinet, he had taken a strong anti-Russian line during the Crimean War. During 1855 he was then implicated in a scandalous Irish court case involving the sexual abuse of children and alleged murder. Although Clanricarde was not directly charged, Lord Grey considered it 'the worst case, by many degrees, against a man of rank that had come out in our time'.[195] Disraeli reported the rumours that Lady Palmerston had been primarily responsible for the successful selection of her 'protégé'.[196] The appointment seemed to suggest Palmerston's contempt for wider opinion. Lord and Lady Palmerston, Parkes concluded, had become 'intoxicated with their supposed popularity', and were 'too old to recollect its treachery'.[197] Clanricarde, as brother-in-law to Lord Canning, Governor General of India, made the abolition of the East India Company a precondition to his accepting the Lord Privy Seal. This he pressed as a just vindication of his brother-in-law's actions during the revolt. Palmerston agreed to Clanricarde's demand and cabinet anxiety assumed a new intensity. Over Christmas and the New Year, Russell and Graham prepared for an all-out assault on what they anticipated would be an ill-digested India Bill and a sham parliamentary Reform Bill. During January 1858 Aberdeen was drawn into their discussions. Palmerston, meanwhile, indicated no definite views on the revised form of government in India, except that the Crown should replace the East India Company's Board of Directors.

With ominous parliamentary storm clouds gathering, the cabinet received reports, on 15 January 1858, of the attempted assassination of Emperor Napoleon III outside the Paris Opera House. Though the Emperor and Empress were unhurt, the three grenades thrown at the imperial carriages killed all the horses and left 102 bystanders wounded. The Italian leader of the plot, Felice Orsini, it was discovered, had travelled to France with a British passport in an assumed English name, carrying bombs manufactured in Birmingham. Violent Anglophobia erupted in the French press. Count Walewski, the French Foreign Minister, sent Clarendon a dispatch on 21 January calling on the British government to assist France in suppressing revolutionaries who violated the right of asylum. Clarendon sent no formal reply. The cabinet suddenly found itself caught between the contrary demands of diplomatic necessity abroad and political caution at home. Clarendon feared French outrage would forge an anti-British alliance in Europe led by France and Russia. In England, meanwhile, opinion was enraged at the prospect of French diplomatic pressure forcing an amendment of British laws in response to Gallic dictate. In late January ministers framed a Conspiracy to Murder Bill introducing no new laws but increasing the existing penalties for proven conspirators. This, Palmerston hoped, would square the circle of securing the diplomatic maximum and political minimum that need be done.

Palmerston looked to guarantee passage of his Conspiracy to Murder Bill by securing Derby's prior support. To this end, during the evening of Saturday 30 January, Clarendon 'had a long and upon the whole satisfactory conversation' with the Conservative leader. Clarendon emphasized the importance of maintaining the Anglo-French alliance by placating public opinion in France.[198] Though doubtful that parliament would invest the government with the powers they sought, Derby declared his willingness to treat the question as a national, rather than party, matter. He was prepared, he informed Clarendon, to consider with the cabinet beforehand any measure which the government wished to introduce. Maintaining friendly diplomatic relations with France remained an important element in his view of Britain's foreign policy. Derby's 'handsome offer' temporarily bolstered cabinet confidence.[199] But, when Sir George Grey, as Home Secretary, sent details of the bill to Russell, on Tuesday 2 February, in the hope of also obtaining Russell's prior approval, the immediate response was that Russell would oppose it 'to the utmost of [his] power'.[200] Though Palmerston cheerfully dismissed Russell's reaction as 'childish', it was a forceful indication of the opposition gathering against him.[201] It also provided the broader context for Derby's amenable response to the Conspiracy to Murder Bill.

Apprehension about legislation over India, outrage at Clanricarde's appointment, and the imminence of fractious debate on parliamentary Reform allowed Derby to extend a friendly hand to Palmerston over the Orsini crisis. In this way, the premier might be reminded that his real friends sat opposite him in the Commons, while his implacable enemies were arrayed on the benches around him. Greville could 'never remember parliament meeting with greater curiosity and excitement'. The situation of the ministry 'is generally regarded as so precarious and the revolution in Palmerston's popularity and therefore his power so extraordinary, that everybody is expecting some great event will occur, and the hopes of all who wish for a change and who expect to profit by it are reviving'.[202] This volatile public mood was intensified by the elaborate preparations for the first royal wedding in eighteen years, the marriage of the Princess Royal to Prince Frederick of Prussia in the Chapel Royal at St James's on 25 January; news from

India of the second relief of Lucknow and graphic details of the bloody mas-
sacre at Cawnpore, revived anguished outcries against the barbarous sepoy;
while inflammatory statements from France, in the pages of the *Moniteur*,
attacking English asylum law, enraged British patriotic sensibilities.

Palmerston's announcement to the reassembled Commons on Friday 5
February of the government's intention to amend the law of conspiracy
was received with an ominous lack of enthusiasm. The Conservatives
watched the government's Commons majority dissolve into anarchy. The
radical Roebuck condemned the French press for stigmatizing England
as 'a den of conspirators'.[203] After the introduction of the Conspiracy
to Murder Bill on Monday 8 February, the advanced Liberal Alexander
Kinglake denounced the government for surrendering to French bullying.
Roebuck portrayed Emperor Napoleon as the failed assassin of the Duke
of Wellington. It was Roebuck's boast, Derby noted, that the result of
his speech will be war with France in six weeks 'and the formation of
a government of which Lord J. Russell should be the head, and he
himself a member'.[204] Russell, speaking with 'extraordinary vehemence
and anger', denounced the measure as contrary to the whole course of
'modern enlightened legislation'.[205] Disraeli remained content to point out
that a vote to allow the bill its first reading was a vote to discuss, rather
than approve, the measure.[206] On Tuesday 9 February the first reading of
the Conspiracy to Murder Bill was passed by 299 to 99 votes, Russell and
Roebuck leading a large body of radicals and Liberals into the opposition
lobby.

Further demonstrations of the disarray convulsing the government
benches quickly followed. Greville found the aspect of public affairs 'like
the figures in a kaleidoscope', each 'fleeting symmetrical arrangement
giving way immediately to another equally fleeting'.[207] Objections to
the inclusion of Lord Canning's name among those commended for their
energy in suppressing the revolt in India foreshadowed acrimonious debate
on the reform of the administration of the subcontinent. On Friday 12,
February, Palmerston introduced the ministry's India Bill, which proposed
doing away with the existing 'double government', jointly exercised by the
East India Company and the Governor General, by abolishing the East
India Company and making India a Dominion of the Crown. Bringing
no accusations against the East India Company, neither did Palmerston's
speech, Malmesbury observed, give 'any intelligible reason for this act
of spoliation'.[208] While Conservative backbenchers defended the record
of the East India Company, Russell held back. That same evening, in
the Lords, Grey presented a petition protesting the abolition of the East

India Company. The India Bill passed its second Commons reading on Thursday 18 February by 318 to 173 votes. Into the opposition lobby 132 Conservatives were accompanied by thirty-seven Whigs, Liberals, and radicals and four Peelites. The Attorney General, Sir Richard Bethell, promptly suggested that Palmerston, like a Roman consul at a triumph, should be accompanied by a slave to remind him that he was 'a minister mortal'.[209] The collapse of Palmerston's popularity, Greville noted, 'was visible universally'.[210]

The following day, on Friday 19 February, Palmerston moved the second Commons reading of his Conspiracy to Murder Bill. The premier defended the cabinet's failure to answer Walewski's dispatch by assuring the Commons that a reply had been given orally. A written communication of their intention to amend the law, he maintained, would only have led to the appearance of the government submitting to a foreign power. Fierce Commons opposition to the ministry immediately erupted. In a speech Palmerston admitted to be of 'considerable ability',[211] the radical Milner Gibson denounced the government for failing to answer Walewski's dispatch. By their silence, Milner Gibson charged, the ministry had admitted that they sheltered assassins. He then introduced a motion criticizing the government for not refuting in writing Walewski's accusations. Derby immediately recognized the significance of this radical move. It 'is of the utmost importance', he advised Disraeli, 'and requires the most wary walking on our part'.[212] It was rumoured that Graham had suggested the motion and that Russell had drafted its precise wording. Milner Gibson's amendment 'was received with cheers from all sides, and Baines who got up to answer him was very little listened to'.[213] From the Conservative benches, both Disraeli and Walpole spoke in favour of Milner Gibson's motion. Gladstone, likewise, made a 'vehement and eloquent speech' against the government's measure.[214] Russell remained ominously silent. Derby portentously observed to Disraeli, 'C'est le commencement de la fin.'[215]

At the close of the debate Palmerston, refusing an adjournment, lost his temper, waved his fist at the radical benches, and violently attacked Milner Gibson. Clanricarde's conspicuous presence in the Commons gallery enraged many MPs. Confident of a majority on the second reading, the government whips, lulled into a false sense of security, had allowed some of their people to leave Westminster unpaired. Milner Gibson's motion, however, threw their calculations into disarray. The cabinet subsequently accused Derby of reneging on his undertaking to safeguard the Conspiracy to Murder Bill. Seeing the effect of Milner Gibson's speech, ministers asserted, Derby 'gave the word "charge"'.[216] But Derby defended his action to Clarendon the following day by pointing out that Milner Gibson's motion did not attack the principle of the bill. Rather, it denounced the ministry for its official silence in response to Walewski's dispatch. The motion was 'most skilfully framed', he informed Clarendon. 'It did not interfere with the passing of the bill. It did hit the weak part of [the government's] case.'[217] As proof of his good faith, Derby reminded Clarendon that, of the 299 MPs who had supported the first reading, at least 112 were Conservatives. The Conservatives had not, he declared, had any communication with Milner Gibson prior to the debate. Notice of Milner Gibson's motion had taken him by surprise. Nor was there a whip on the motion. Voting had been the result of 'spontaneous conviction'. If the Conservative leadership had induced their followers to stay away from the vote on Milner Gibson's motion, then it would have been impossible, Derby claimed, to persuade their backbenchers to give cordial support to the Conspiracy to Murder Bill during subsequent debate. 'No measures were taken on our side of the House', Derby insisted, 'to obtain an attendance hostile to the government.' Nor were any steps taken, ministerial critics might have retaliated, to secure support for the ministry against Milner Gibson's motion. Prior to the debate Derby talked to Disraeli of passively allowing 'the party to commit itself'.[218] This allowed Derby to portray Conservative backing for Milner Gibson as a spontaneous expression of rank-and-file opinion, over an issue peripheral to the principle of the legislation proposed by the ministry. Derby wrote to Palmerston directly on 22 February making the same points.[219] But for cabinet ministers this smacked of sophistry. An infuriated Palmerston believed that Derby 'had caught at an opportunity of putting the government in a minority', having seen that nearly 100 MPs, who formerly had supported the ministry, had opposed the first reading of the bill.[220]

Late on 19 February, Milner Gibson's motion was carried by 234 to 215 votes, a majority against Palmerston's ministry of nineteen. Announcement of the vote was met with a 'burst of cheering'.[221] 'Disraeli's face', Malmesbury observed, 'was a mixture of triumph and sarcasm that he could not repress.'[222] Graham, in raptures, seized Bright's hand, 'as if he had met with a great deliverance'.[223] Bright celebrated that 'the impostor is once more overthrown'. While Lord Grey, with characteristic indiscretion, reminded Russell, who had voted with Milner Gibson, of 1852, 'when Palmerston had tripped up Lord John's heels ... saying [Russell] had now paid off Palmerston—a joke [Russell] by no means like[d]'.[224]

Consistently with Derby's account of the vote to Clarendon, only 158 Conservatives took part in the division on Milner Gibson's motion, over 100 Conservative MPs being absent from the Commons. No concerted effort was made to bring them to Westminster. One hundred and forty Conservatives, including Disraeli, voted for Milner Gibson's motion. Eighteen Conservatives, led by Bentinck, 'whose most lively apprehension is that of a union with Gladstone', voted with Palmerston.[225] It was the hostility of non-Conservatives, over a radical initiative, that brought about Palmerston's defeat. Russell, Gladstone, Graham, Cardwell, and Bright all voted with Disraeli in support of Milner Gibson.

In a cabinet meeting on the afternoon of Saturday 20 February ministers agreed, with the exception of Vernon Smith, to resign. Yet this decision should not be accepted as dutiful compliance with what Palmerston insisted was a chance defeat. Of all the questions confronting his government, the Orsini crisis, India, forthcoming debate on Clanricarde's appointment, and parliamentary Reform, the first arguably offered Palmerston the most favourable ground on which to surrender office. Resignation, before damaging splits over India and Reform occurred, could be construed as an act of retribution, intended to embarrass 'the accidental combination of parties' gathered behind Milner Gibson's motion. Certainly Lady Palmerston, glad there was no time to bring in a Reform Bill, was gratified that their enemies 'should find the difficulties of what they have done', Milner Gibson's motion being 'merely a sham reason and an excuse used by the crafty to catch the fools'.[226] Among the Palmerstonian Whigs at Brooks's there was a belief that, like Lord Grey in May 1832, Palmerston was stepping down expecting to be quickly recalled, once the impossibility of forming an alternative government had been proved.[227] Derby also suspected Palmerston's resignation 'might only be for the purpose of going through a crisis in order to come back again with new strength, for there existed different kinds of resignation'.[228] It might, he confided to his elder son, be 'a ruse'.[229] He remained wary. But equally, he was determined that, if Palmerston was entertaining such hopes, they should, if possible, be dashed. The ruse should be unmasked. While staying with Malmesbury at Heron Court for some wildfowl shooting, on Wednesday 17 February, Derby made it clear to his host that he would 'not refuse office if it [was] offered him'.[230]

CHAPTER 4

Derby's Second Premiership: 1858–1859

My Lords, in politics, as in everything else, the same course must be pursued—constant progress, improving upon the old system, adapting our institutions to the altered purpose they are intended to serve, and by judicious changes meeting the demands of society.

(Derby, 1 March 1858, *Hansard*, 3 ser., cxlix. 41)

The 58-year-old Derby made the short journey in his coach from St James's Square to Buckingham Palace late in the afternoon of Saturday 20 February 1858. He had an audience with the Queen, who was accompanied by Prince Albert, a little after six that evening. It was a delicate conversation. Expressing surprise at Palmerston's resignation, Derby ascribed the government's fall to Russell and Graham's intriguing in the interest of the radicals, and blamed the ministry for not answering Walewski's dispatch. Proceeding carefully, he asked the Queen to consider further before asking him to form a cabinet. 'After what happened in 1851 and 1855, if the Queen made the offer he *must* accept it, for if he refused, the Conservative party would be broken up for ever.'[1] But he faced considerable difficulties. The Conservatives, though the single largest party in the Commons, were in a minority. Both the external and internal relations of the country were 'in a most delicate and complicated position'. There was armed conflict in India and China and a crisis with France, an Indian Government Bill had been introduced, and a parliamentary Reform Bill promised. Only 'the forbearance and support of some of his opponents', he informed the Queen, 'would make it possible for him to carry on any government'. Moreover, he suggested, Palmerston may have resigned in order to return to office with renewed strength. The truth was that 'the person who was asked first by the sovereign' to form a ministry in such circumstances was at a great disadvantage. Perhaps other combinations were possible. Only when the alternatives were found wanting would a Conservative ministry be readily accepted by the country.

The Queen agreed to defer the commission so as to allow time for further reflection.

That evening Stanley found his father back at St James's Square depressed and anxious, rather than sanguine of success.[2] To decline office again, if it was offered, was impossible. But success would only be secured by assuming power on his own terms, rather than under conditions dictated by his opponents. Typically, Disraeli was irritated that Derby had not immediately accepted office. But, with good reason, Derby was wary. During the evening Prince Albert talked to Clarendon, who convinced the Prince that Palmerston's cabinet had resigned from a genuine conviction that it was impossible for them to go on with honour and success. Derby was, Clarendon insisted, 'the only man who could form a government' and Gladstone 'would probably join him'.[3]

The following morning, on Sunday 21 February, the Queen again wrote to Derby repeating her wish that he attempt to construct a cabinet. Palmerston's sudden resignation was 'the result of a conscientious conviction' she declared. Derby was 'at the head of the only party which affords the materials of forming a government'.[4] Exchanges of correspondence between St James's Square and Buckingham Palace followed during the day. Derby finally accepted the Queen's commission, although he warned that he could 'hardly hope, in the formation of a government, for much extrinsic aid'.[5] The Queen's indulgence in giving him freedom to offer particular offices to individuals not associated with his party might be necessary. The Queen responded that she wished for close consultation over his appointments to the Foreign and War offices. These understandings were confirmed at Derby's audience with the Queen that same evening.

Stanley listed in his journal the difficulties confronting his father. The Conservatives lacked a firm majority in either the Commons or the Lords.[6] The creation of peers or a dissolution, so soon after the 1857 election, were not available options. Disraeli did not command confidence. Gladstone was unpopular. The radicals would welcome a Derby ministry as an opportunity to unite the Liberal party in opposition. The prospect of a parliamentary Reform measure might encourage the Liberal opposition to stir up agitation in the country. The successful suppression of the Indian revolt, moreover, weakened the plea of urgent public necessity as a reason for governing without a majority. There also existed the suspicion that the object of the court was to give time for the reconstruction of a prospective Liberal administration on a broad basis, most effectively done out of office. But, as Derby informed the Queen, his refusal of office, after the events of February 1855, was impossible. As he observed to the Duke of Northumberland, declining the Queen's commission 'would have been the signal for the utter and final dissolution of the party'.[7]

Remit not now; but rouse each sev'ral man.

(Derby, *The Iliad of Homer*, ii. 13)

Derby undertook the formation of his second administration with a heavy sense of duty, rather than elation. But he did not allow his doubts to sap his determination. He believed that at least he undertook the task, '*as regards the Court*, to more advantage than if [he] had at once, and without giving [the Queen] time to weigh the difficulties', accepted her commission.[8] He was 'anxious to frame the new cabinet upon a comprehensive basis, availing [himself] of the services of eminent men of Liberal Conservative opinions, who are not ... fettered by engagements, which would render their cooperation hopeless'. The going would be heavy, but on this occasion he was resolved to stay the course.

The first fence to clear was to establish whether any Whigs or Peelites could be brought into his cabinet. Derby immediately wrote to Lord Grey, the Duke of Newcastle, and Gladstone. But Grey 'had no hesitation' in declining, because of 'the wretched leaders Derby [had] for his party in the H. of C.—had there been a different set of these and especially if Disraeli had been out of the way, [his] view of the question would have been altered'.[9] Surprised by Derby's invitation, Newcastle declined on the grounds that, by joining a Conservative government, he would neither give strength to the ministry nor render any real service to the country. In private Newcastle admitted that he 'could not tell Derby the real reason for my refusing to join him. I could not say one of your colleagues is a rogue and the other a fool—Dizzy and Malmesbury to wit.'[10] Gladstone consulted with Aberdeen, Graham, and Herbert over Derby's invitation. Their advice resulted in a more forthright refusal than Gladstone had originally intended. A passage in Gladstone's draft reply expressing his willingness to have a private interview with Derby was deleted. A promise of qualified support from outside the government was retained. Gladstone noted those circumstances of which Derby was well aware. 'There is a small but active and not unimportant section who avowedly regard me as the representative of the most dangerous ideas. I should thus, unfortunately, be to you a source of weakness in the heart of your own adherents, while I should bring to you no party or group of friends to make up for their defection or discontent.'[11] This was corroborated by Delane's remark to Disraeli that a Derby ministry would do much better without Gladstone. The Conservative Irish peer Lord Galway (MP for East Retford) enforced the point on Jolliffe: 'What rascals these Peelites are, a thorn in the side of *both* parties. Shall we lose much by Gladstone not joining?'[12] Little would be lost, Galway believed, by Gladstone's absence. Despite regarding his refusal as not 'very conclusive', Derby did not pursue the matter with Gladstone further. 'This small clique', Grey noted of the Peelites, 'remain consistent to the end in making any strong government impossible by refusing to go into or succeed another they have destroyed.'[13] 'Our time has been spent, the last eight and forty hours,' Disraeli observed on Monday 22 February, 'in making fruitless overtures, but they have not been disappointments, never calculating for a moment they would be accepted, but calculating, that the *refusals* would work for our advantage in public opinion.'[14]

A heavier blow was Stanley's reluctance to take office under his father. Without names in the cabinet to refute the charge of intractable Toryism, Stanley feared, the Conservative bid to govern would prove untenable. Yet Stanley's ministerial presence was the one appointment most likely to negate accusations of Tory obduracy. In October 1857 Stanley had taken a prominent part, alongside Brougham, Russell, and Pakington, in the inaugural meeting at Birmingham of the National Association for the Promotion of Social Science. He had spoken on the need for sanitation legislation and the importance of public health. His hesitation in accepting office under his father drew a flood of indulgent prose from Disraeli in his correspondence with Derby: 'There is really only one sorrow in all this: it draws tears from my eyes, and from your heart, I am sure, drops of blood. What mortifies me most is that I feel [Stanley] is making a great mistake.'[15] Derby immediately deputed Malmesbury to talk to his elder son and persuade him to join his cabinet.

Meanwhile, Derby stayed in the saddle, relying on the familiar names of 1852 to keep his mount on its legs. The loyal Malmesbury accepted the Foreign Office. The elderly Lord Salisbury, who had been Lord Privy Seal in 1852, became Lord President of the Council. The 69-year-old Earl of Hardwicke consented to become Lord Privy Seal. After the 65-year-old Pemberton Leigh refused a peerage and the Lord Chancellorship on account of his age, Derby appointed the popular 64-year-old Sir Frederick Thesiger with the title Lord Chelmsford to the Woolsack. Thesiger was one of many Peelite MPs who, after 1846, slowly made their way back to the Conservative party. Henley, as a representative of Ultra

Tory sentiment, accepted the Board of Trade. Still bitter at his failure to become Speaker, Walpole initially raised objections to Derby's offer of the Home Office, the position he had held in 1852. The failure to secure any leading Peelites, Walpole argued, deprived the Conservatives of sufficient authority to govern. Moreover, he feared the Conservatives were divided over the three main questions of the forthcoming session: the Bank Charter Act, the government of India, and parliamentary Reform.[16] But Derby eventually prevailed on Walpole to lay aside his misgivings. The progressive Conservative, champion of education reform, and Derby's Secretary of State for War and the Colonies in 1852, Pakington, who had no previous experience of naval affairs, accepted the Admiralty, and the joke circulated the clubs that Derby chose him 'because he is sure to be at sea when he gets there'.[17] Lord John Manners returned to the office he had held in 1852 as First Commissioner of Works. Likewise, Disraeli, as leader of the Commons party, returned to the Chancellorship of the Exchequer.

As well as the familiar faces of 1852, Derby brought fresh blood into the government, young Conservatives destined for future prominence in the party leadership. The 40-year-old evangelical and austere Ulsterman Sir Hugh Cairns, MP for Belfast, having become a QC in 1856, was appointed Solicitor-General. As a pious Low Churchman and a pungent legal advocate, the humourless Cairns followed a strict observance of the sabbath and was drawn to the revivalist meetings of the American preachers Moody and Sankey. The 44-year-old Gathorne Hardy, MP for Leominster, an eloquent and successful lawyer, the owner of 20,000 acres in Kent and part owner of an ironworks, became Walpole's Under-Secretary at the Home Office. A devout Anglican High Churchman, good-natured and agreeable, Gathorne Hardy was to prove a passionate ministerial orator, his rhetorical intensity giving backbone to the government's case in the Commons. Thomas Sotheron-Estcourt, MP for North Wiltshire, was appointed President of the Poor Law Board. A Gloucestershire landowner who had married a wealthy heiress, Sotheron-Estcourt espoused progressive Conservative views.

Most importantly, however, on 25 February, after pleas from Malmesbury and Pakington, Stanley finally agreed to join his father's government. The impetuous and short-tempered 68-year-old Lord Ellenborough, who had served under Peel as Governor General of India until recalled in 1844, had already accepted the Presidency of the Board of Control. At first, it was intended that Stanley serve as Ellenborough's subordinate in the Commons. This Stanley understood as a preliminary to his becoming Governor General of India in the near future. But this arrangement was quickly abandoned and Stanley entered the cabinet as Secretary of the Colonial Office. Aged 34 his father had first assumed the same office in Lord Grey's cabinet; Stanley now took up the appointment aged 32. Discussions about the Colonial Office had already taken place with the flamboyant, coiffeured, and perfumed best-selling novelist Edward Bulwer Lytton. A radical dandy in his youth and haunted by a scandalous estrangement from his wife, despite his increasing deafness and susceptibility to hypochondria Bulwer Lytton, following his election as a Conservative MP in 1852, had established a reputation as an effective, if somewhat eccentric, speaker in the Commons. But the temperamental Bulwer Lytton, in response to Derby's ministerial offer in February 1858, indicated difficulties regarding his re-election for Hertfordshire. Derby interpreted this as an impertinent attempt to secure a peerage and a disappointed Bulwer Lytton was immediately dropped.[18] Stanley's subsequent placement at the Colonial Office was an important counterweight to more Tory cabinet appointments.

The able and devout 26-year-old Anglican Lord Carnarvon was secured as Stanley's Under-Secretary. In his maiden speech to the Lords in January 1854, Carnarvon had elaborated on his belief in the Empire, Britain's colonies living in close harmony with the mother country. He also pursued a strong interest in penal reform and a private passion for classical scholarship. After some hesitation, General Jonathan Peel, MP for Huntingdon, younger brother of the former Conservative leader and, like Thesiger, a former Peelite, also joined the cabinet as Secretary of State for the War Office, availing the government of the political asset his name provided. The 44-year-old progressive landowner Charles Adderley (Conservative MP for North Staffordshire) was appointed President of the Board of Health and vice-president of the Privy Council Education Committee. A passionate horseman and accomplished musician, Adderley was a strong Broad Churchman, on cordial relations with Gladstone, as well as a leading member of the Colonial Reform Society. While overseeing the planning of the new town of Saltley, on his estates near Birmingham, he had become, during the 1850s, an advocate of reformatory schooling for young criminals, believing in education, rather than penal punishment, for child offenders.

Disraeli's insistence that the staunch defender of the Church of Ireland George Hamilton, MP for the University of Dublin, and Lord Henry Lennox, the flighty second son of the Duke of Richmond and MP for Chichester, receive office secured a Financial Secretaryship to the Treasury for the former and a Junior Lordship of the Treasury for the latter. Both posts were associated with Disraeli as Chancellor of the Exchequer. Lennox took the post dealing mainly with Scottish business, despite warnings of ill feeling among Scottish Conservatives at an Englishman sitting for an English borough being in charge of Scottish affairs. Irish feeling was treated more sensitively, however, by the appointment of the astute 36-year-old Lord Naas, eldest son by the Earl of Mayo, as Chief Secretary for Ireland. Naas's tact and sound judgement were complemented by his good humour in disarming opposition. Lord Eglinton returned as Lord Lieutenant and the effective Irish executive team of 1852 was reinstated.

On Monday 22 February, prior to Stanley's appointment, Disraeli secretly sent Delane a provisional list of ministerial names, which *The Times* on Wednesday 24 February, without disclosing the source of its information, described as 'a penitential sheet'.[19] Undeterred, on Thursday 25 February, Disraeli sent Delane the final cabinet list, including Stanley, commenting that he did not think 'at any time the secondary appointments were so strong. Hardy, W. Fitzgerald [Under Secretary to the Foreign Office], Sotheron-Estcourt, Carnarvon, Hardinge [Under-Secretary to the War Office]—all very good. Legal—good. Irish good.'[20] In *The Times* leader on Friday 26 February the government's appointments were reviewed cordially and Disraeli was singled out for special praise. By 16 March, Malmesbury noted that *The Times* was 'most complimentary' towards the government.[21] In the privacy of his journal Greville endorsed the judgement of *The Times*. 'The first class of this government is not worse than that of the last, and the second class is a good deal better.'[22]

His words fresh courage rais'd in every breast.

(Derby, *The Iliad of Homer*, ii. 9)

On 28 February severe storms and freezing temperatures swept the country, followed by heavy snow during early March. But, when the Commons reassembled on Friday 5 March, the Conservatives, after six years of frigid opposition, were once again 'on the sunny side of the House'.[23] The move 'seemed to have imparted new life to them'. As Disraeli informed Delane: 'we have no absurd pledges to hamper us; we shall be able to settle France admirably; and we have a dissolution in our pocket which, as in 1852, we shall not be forced immediately to make use of'.[24] The government drew comfort from the divisions afflicting other parties. Palmerston sat directly across from Disraeli. Graham, Gladstone, and Herbert placed themselves below the gangway on the government side of the House. Around them sat the rump of the Irish Brigade. Russell, arriving late, appeared unsure where to sit, but eventually placed himself on the opposition front bench below the gangway, among the radicals and 'independent' Liberals. This arrangement reflected the deep antipathies dividing the opposition.

Already, on Monday 1 March, Derby had sounded the keynote of his government's policy. '[T]here can be no greater mistake', he informed his fellow peers, 'than to suppose that a Conservative ministry necessarily means a stationary ministry.'[25] Moderate progress, improving on the old system and by judicious changes meeting the increased demands of society, was to be combined with resistance to radical innovation. Opportunities for the varied sections of the opposition to combine in criticism of government policy were to be avoided. This might bring Whigs and Liberals into concert with the ministerial front benches. He pronounced his government ready to introduce safe improvements of every sort. Lord Grey, for one, found Derby's statement 'very reasonable'. Derby declared that the former broad demarcation of political parties no longer existed. Subtle distinctions between Tories, Conservatives, Liberal Conservatives, Whigs, Liberals, and radicals blurred the alignment of political sentiment in parliament. Like the various ranks in society at large, while there was a broad interval between the highest and the lowest, the gradations by which one melted into the other were so gradual as to be often imperceptible. Thus he hoped to earn the support of those not usually associated with him.

With regard to the Orsini affair Derby promised that, without exception, the right of asylum in Britain would be maintained inviolable, although it was an intolerable grievance that persons having that protection should by their acts embroil Britain with her allies. This led to a restatement of those principles which had guided his foreign policy in 1852. Friendly relations with other nations would be maintained, with neither 'a tone of haughty intimidation or a tone of servile submission' being adopted towards other governments. Interference in the purely domestic affairs of foreign powers would be avoided, international disputes being resolved by frank and amicable communications. He stressed the importance of cordial Anglo-French relations, a permanent good understanding with Britain's nearest and most powerful neighbour being necessary to their mutual welfare. To this end, he would calmly work towards removing causes of irritation between the two nations. On India he declared his intention, in accordance with the expressed opinion of a majority of the Commons, to transfer executive authority from the East India Company to the Crown. With regard to parliamentary Reform it was 'highly inconvenient' that 'it should perpetually be kept dangling before the legislature'. Avoiding any specific pledge, he hoped, as soon as the pressure of business allowed, to introduce a Reform Bill during the next session, which might be accepted 'as fair and reasonable' by 'all moderate, impartial and well-educated men'. With a sense of grievance, rather than vindication, Palmerston commented that Derby 'adopted all my measures with more or less modifications'.[26] While praising the eloquence of Derby's statement, *The Times* noted that the new premier had entered the citadel of office by default of the defenders. The political property of the late government, therefore, was not condemned, but sequestered, and placed in the hands of Derby's cabinet as assignees.[27]

The spirit of Derby's speech was echoed in the hustings speeches of Commons ministers seeking re-election. In Belfast, Cairns denied that Conservatism was opposed to improvement. Rather, the new government had a wish to safeguard progress.[28] At Droitwich, Pakington declared true reform to be the careful improvement of all institutions.[29] Sotheron-Estcourt in North Wiltshire emphasized his independence of party and his liberal views by way of endorsing Derby's policies.[30] Stanley's speech in King's Lynn and Disraeli's statement in Aylesbury were reworkings of the established text. To his constituents Stanley declared it to be a matter upon which 'men of all parties agree' that, 'as a matter of reason rather than feeling', a 'close and intimate alliance between Britain and France' provided 'the best hopes of European civilisation'.[31] Significantly, unlike Aberdeen's ministers in early 1853 and Palmerston's government in 1855, none of Derby's appointments were opposed when seeking re-election. In the Commons, on Monday 15 March, Disraeli seized on the Liberal Bernal Osborne's challenge to state the new government's principles as an opportunity to extol their moderate aims. 'We believe that the best way to maintain the institutions of the country is to improve them; and therefore we cannot permit the Hon. Gentleman to be such a monopolist of all plans for the amelioration of society as he and his friends, in a manner so greedy and covetous, aspire to be considered.'[32] The taunt was well aimed. Derby's cabinet intended to prick Liberal pretensions to being the monopolists of progressive wisdom.

As in 1852, Derby exercised an unchallenged authority over his cabinet. Once again he was *primus inter impares*. He took a close interest in all departmental business and conferred constantly with Malmesbury over foreign policy. As in 1852, he believed Britain's diplomatic interests were best served by maintaining as cordial relations as possible with European powers. Derby and Malmesbury, in discussion with the French Ambassador, de Persigny, and through the efforts of the British Ambassador in Paris, Lord Cowley, swiftly arrived at a settlement of the disagreement between Britain and France over the Orsini affair. Through detailed recommendations to his Foreign Secretary, Derby ensured that national dignity was preserved on both sides. Malmesbury sent a conciliatory answer to the Walewski dispatch, to which the French government replied on 12 March in a similar spirit. Malmesbury found the French response 'very friendly, and must be considered as giving full satisfaction to England'.[33] He immediately conveyed the dispatch to Derby, who was 'much pleased'. Disraeli rushed to join them in the Treasury 'in such a desperate hurry that he nearly knocked over the messenger, and entered the room in a great state of excitement'. When he read the French response Disraeli's 'delight was indescribable and amazingly demonstrative, considering the usually phlegmatic manner in which he receives news of all kinds'.[34] In the Commons his announcement of the French dispatch elicited loud cheering from the Conservative benches, while on the other side of the House, Malmesbury observed, 'not a word of satisfaction was expressed by the opposition at the settlement of the quarrel with France'.

Another diplomatic dispute, the *Cagliari* affair, was also resolved during these first weeks. The *Cagliari*, a Sardinian ship freighted and manned by the Carbonari, had been sailing to Calabria to stir up revolution. When the Naples government seized the ship two British engineers, Watt and Park, were taken into custody and placed in a Neapolitan prison. Derby urged Malmesbury to seek an amicable settlement. No gunboats were dispatched to the Bay of Naples. The cabinet, Disraeli reassured the Queen, were 'agreed to take a temperate course'.[35] On 15 March the government informed the Commons that they intended to submit the matter to the Crown's legal advisers and follow their advice. From the opposition benches Edward Horsman expressed the wish of moderate Liberals that the government be given a fair trial. London having witnessed an almost total eclipse of the sun that day, Disraeli took up the metaphor to observe that the government now felt that their own 'eclipse was over'.[36] With 'the opposition … in a very anarchical state', he reported, 'our foreign policy is popular, and when our domestic measures are fairly before the country, I think they will obtain public support'.[37] Four weeks later, on 16 April, the ministry were able to announce that Watt and Park were to be released and compensation of £3,000 paid by the Neapolitan authorities. Palmerston and his colleagues, Malmesbury observed, did not even pretend to be pleased that the crisis, 'which had seemed to threaten war in the Italian peninsula, had been concluded in such a satisfactory manner'.[38]

Initial disdain for the Conservative ministry among the opposition slowly began to shift to grudging respect. Broughton noted 'the general impression' that Derby might '*pull through* the session'.[39] Greville recorded 'a growing opinion that [Derby] ought to have fair play and no vexatious opposition'. Granville now thought Derby 'would get on very well'.[40] The US ambassador G. M. Dallas believed 'parliament has got along with the new ministry pretty well. Prodigious efforts to propriate members by the attentions and blandishments of private intercourse are obviously unremitting. They will have their effect.'[41] Lady Derby consulted closely with Jolliffe over invitations to the parties she regularly hosted, despite her fragile health, at Downing Street, Lady Salisbury and the Duchess of Northumberland also consulting Jolliffe carefully when hosting their own social gatherings. On 18 March, Disraeli relayed to Derby a private conversation with the Whig Henry Labouchere, who informed the Chancellor: 'You have nothing to fear from us. No intention and no inclination to disturb, or annoy, you. In a year's time, perhaps, we shall enquire how you are getting on.'[42] The result, Dallas concluded, 'will be first seen in the care with which a test question will be avoided by the extreme Liberals'.[43]

Stand forth, and urge the rest, to face the foe.

(Derby, *The Iliad of Homer*, ii. 98)

Derby saw the promise of safe improvement as the best basis for his minority government to apply subversive pressure on the divided opposition majority. Reform of the Indian government emerged as the immediate test of this strategy. The Indian Government Bill to which his cabinet agreed revealed the lengths they were prepared to go to demonstrate the absence of reactionary inclinations. The bill bore the marks of its author, Lord Ellenborough, whose air of enlightened opinion was only marred by a putative weakness of judgement. In transferring executive power to the Crown, the measure introduced the elective principle into the selection of the Indian executive and recommended representation of the commercial interest. The existing system of 'double government' was to be abolished and a Minister of the Crown, occupying the rank of a Secretary of State, would be President of a Council of India. The composition of this Council characterized the government design. Half the Council of eighteen would be nominated by the Crown, the other half elected. Originally Ellenborough proposed to give three elected members to large cities in India. But, upon Stanley's advice, the constituencies were transferred to urban areas in Britain and their number increased to five, namely London,

Manchester, Liverpool, Glasgow, and Belfast,[44] the electorate to be the same as the existing parliamentary franchise. The remaining four elected members would be chosen by an electorate made up of British males resident in India for ten years who had been either in the Civil Service or resident proprietors of £2,000 stock—a constituency estimated at about 5,000 persons.

The introduction of the Conservative measure (India Bill No. 2 as it became known) in the Commons on Friday 26 March failed, however, to elicit cross-bench support.[45] Incredulity typified most MPs' response. Roebuck attacked the bill as 'a sham'.[46] Bright declared the electoral provisions 'clap-trap'.[47] He privately denounced the measure, like Ellenborough, as 'all action and no go'.[48] Broughton dismissed the bill as 'a crazy scheme'.[49] Junior ministers, such as Gathorne Hardy, were 'startled' by the plan. 'Such a measure from the collective wisdom of our cabinet amazes me.'[50] The Times likened Derby's situation to those ancient generals who relied on elephants as their surest auxiliary in battle. Just as the elephant was frightening in aspect and possessed of an almost impenetrable skin, yet also wild and capricious and so likely to turn and trample underfoot those who drove, rather than those who confronted it, so Ellenborough was proving a dubious asset.[51] As the Commons dispersed for the Easter recess after 26 March, the opposition prepared to dismember the government's Indian Government measure. But the rivalry between Palmerston and Russell, Peelite reluctance to overthrow Derby's government so soon, and radical hopes of exploiting opposition divisions so as to enhance their own influence, prevented a unified attack. Derby sensed the opportunity to prise apart the opposition through modification of their bill.

Disraeli's private secretary, Ralph Earle, identified Roebuck, Ayrton, Horsman, and Kinglake as Liberals and radicals who wished, if possible, to support the Conservatives' Indian Government Bill.[52] Derby approached Bulwer Lytton, as a Conservative enjoying social connections with many radicals, to ascertain what Bright and Milner Gibson objected to in the measure and what changes they would find acceptable. Both Bright and Milner Gibson conveyed their abhorrence of an early restoration of Palmerston to office, the most likely result, they feared, of a swift rejection of Ellenborough's measure.[53] Russell, it was learnt, also feared Palmerston's grasping at the quick defeat of the Conservative bill as the opportunity to resume power. Reports of meetings at Cambridge House urging an early rejection of the bill heightened Russellite and radical alarm. This prepared the way, during the Easter recess, for Derby to extend the hand of compromise.

Ellenborough was obliged to agree with Derby that the five popularly elected Council members formed the weakest part of his bill.[54] It was decided that they should be reduced to two, which would, nonetheless, allow some 'commercial men' to be retained. Then, on 5 April, Derby delivered a speech at the Mansion House courting the cooperation of parliament and the country. The premier deprecated the fact that the government of India 'should be made the sport of political parties or the battlefield of rival disputants'.[55] Palmerstonian hostility was branded as narrow factiousness and the door opened to Russell and the radicals to engage in negotiation. Derby announced the ministry's readiness to relinquish popularly elected membership of the council. Clarendon understood Derby's speech as a declaration that their India Bill was 'no life and death question for the government and that it may be safely cut up or kicked out'.[56]

During the following days Russell and the radicals, with the support of the remaining leading Peelites, accepted the invitation to devise a compromise settlement. Russell estimated that Gladstone, Milner Gibson, and 100 other opposition MPs were determined to block Palmerston's return to office. Disraeli corroborated that 'the independent Liberal party', who now looked to Russell for leadership, were most anxious to prevent the triumph of Palmerston.[57] Stanley undertook conversations directly with Russell. In cabinet on 7 April, Derby led ministerial discussion to agreement to abandoning their bill and proceeding by resolutions.[58] When parliament reassembled on 12 April the agreed plan of conciliation, confirmed in cabinet the previous day, was played out. Disraeli opened the Commons debate with a statement that the second reading of their India Bill would be moved as soon as possible. Immediately, Russell proposed that both India bills (Palmerston's bill and the Conservative scheme) be withdrawn and that resolutions be discussed in a Committee of the Whole House as a basis for a new government measure. Disraeli immediately welcomed Russell's conciliatory proposal. Considering Russell's experience and ability, Disraeli courteously declared, proceeding by resolution could not be in better hands.[59] Wood, for the Palmerstonians, then quickly tried to sabotage Russell's mediation by accusing the government of abdicating its duties.[60] In response, Disraeli, with a copy of the resolutions already privately received from Russell, agreed to move them from the Treasury bench.[61] Although mortified at not moving the resolutions himself, Russell, nonetheless, successfully forestalled Palmerston's restoration. The episode revealed, Disraeli reported to the Queen, 'a marked discordance between Lord John and Palmerston, not concealed by the latter chief, and strongly evinced by some of his principal followers, for example, Sir C. Wood,

Sir B. Hall, Mr Bouverie'.[62] Bolstering Russell's authority and maintaining the government's existence had become mutually supportive considerations. It was only left to Palmerston to jeer that Disraeli 'like Antony came to bury his bill and not to praise it'. The Chancellor of the Exchequer, it appeared, was 'assisting at a sort of Irish wake'.[63]

Derby's policy of compliant moderation shaped the cabinet's response to other pressing issues. As Disraeli warned Pakington, there were 'plenty of rocks ahead' and the government must avoid 'sinking ships to increase their difficulties'.[64] The question of church rates bitterly divided the cabinet. Both Walpole and Pakington were devising their own schemes for settling the issue. But agreement would be impossible, Disraeli complained, even if 'the Angel Gabriel were to draw up a Church Rates bill'.[65] As a result, ministers postponed legislating on the question during the current session. A deputation from the Protestant societies, campaigning for repeal of the Maynooth grant, was received by Derby on 27 April with studied aloofness. The composition of an Education Commission alarmed Henley, who threatened resignation. But with consummate tact Derby placated both Henley and Pakington, while appointing the Peelite Duke of Newcastle as head of a commission that included the economist Nassau Senior, the radical Dissenter Edward Miall, the Revd William Rogers, a champion of elementary education in London's East End, the reformer Goldwin Smith, whom Derby had just appointed as Regius Professor of Modern History at Oxford, and William Charles Lake, later Dean of Durham and a friend of Gladstone.[66] When the radical Locke King introduced a private bill abolishing the property qualification for English and Welsh MPs, Walpole, as Home Secretary, supported the proposal.[67] Walpole's grounds for approving the bill were that the existing law required no such qualification from Scottish MPs and it was unbecoming to parliament to maintain a regulation universally understood to be a sham. *The Times* agreed that the requirement had become 'a complete farce'.[68] Despite the public opposition of one cabinet minister, Henley, and backbenchers such as Newdegate, Knightley, and Bentinck, the measure quickly passed through the Commons and was subsequently supported by Derby in the Lords. Thus was secured a Chartist demand from the 1840s. It must 'astonish the shade of poor Feargus O'Connor', the deceased Chartist leader, *The Times* observed, 'to find his old opponents the Tories so busy in passing the Five Points of the Charter. Which one will Lord Derby take next?'[69]

It was Disraeli's budget in April 1858, however, that proved the most important substantiation of the government's moderate intentions.

Sir Stafford Northcote saw the 1858 session as 'the critical moment for deciding whether the scheme of 1853 should or should not be carried into effect'.[70] Faced with a deficit of £3½ million, incurred by war expenditure and the interest on loans raised by Cornewall Lewis, Disraeli's choice lay between liquidation of the debt or the abandonment of Gladstone's 1853 fiscal plan. Disraeli delivered a Gladstonian budget without Gladstone. As Ralph Earle confided to Disraeli, 'a Tory government can only exist by Liberal budgets'.[71] Deciding to write off the debt, Disraeli proposed a return to the rate of income tax Gladstone had proposed in 1853. On Saturday 17 April the cabinet approved Disraeli's financial plan. The increased liabilities arising from the Crimean War, Disraeli declared to the Commons on Monday 19 April, did not 'furnish reasons strong enough to make [parliament] regard the scheme of 1853 as visionary or fantastic'.[72] Gladstonian in substance, but Conservative in authorship, Disraeli's budget was 'received with favour and excited no opposition in any quarter'.[73] While warning against excessive expenditure, Gladstone expressed his general approval of Disraeli's policy. The following day Derby wrote to congratulate the Chancellor on 'the signal success of the budget'.[74] From Liverpool, Manners reported to Derby that 'the budget is universally approved of down here by all parties'.[75] The timing of Disraeli's budget did not pass unnoticed by Cornewall Lewis. That the Chancellor announced his budget before debate on the Indian resolutions suggested he thought he had something 'captivating'. If the budget was 'a tolerably safe and quiet one', the House would agree to it, and the stage would be set for the reconciliation of differences over India.[76] A simple restoration of the late Palmerstonian ministry now appeared increasingly unlikely. Dallas noted the growing impression that 'the ministry is gradually getting firmer in their seats … They have dodged on open breach with France. They have steered their India bill, piloted by Lord John Russell, into smooth "no party" waters,' while Disraeli's budget was 'praised and accepted by the practical financiers of the City'.[77]

On Saturday 10 April, Derby's cabinet considered the Indian Government resolutions to be brought before parliament. Using Russell's proposals as a framework, a form of words was agreed which Derby 'laboured' to 'impress upon the minds of the party' as that 'without which we cannot go on'.[78] When Russell attended a party given by Lady Derby at Downing Street on Wednesday 14 April, the premier, in his characteristically bantering manner, greeted Russell with the announcement, 'Here comes my confederate.' It was a joke at which Russell did not laugh.[79] Following Disraeli's introduction of the Indian resolutions to the Commons on Friday 16 April, to Derby's great pleasure, Stanley performed impressively in the subsequent debate. 'Stanley's success', he commented, 'was in every sense, private and political, most gratifying to my feelings.'[80] At a party gathering on 30 April, Derby spoke to nearly 200 Conservative MPs who were, at first, 'in a somewhat hesitating mood, but the fiery and impassioned address of Lord Derby really produced a feeling of enthusiasm, and they resolved unanimously to support him in his Indian struggle without flinching'.[81] Meanwhile, the bitter antagonism between Palmerston and Russell smoothed the way. Palmerston was 'not disposed to abdicate his Throne—Johnny to usurp it', and while 'the game lasts', Edward Ellice lamented, 'Derby is quite safe.'[82]

This comforting prospect, however, was suddenly shattered when Ellenborough received from Lord Canning, as Governor General of India, the draft of his proclamation to the people of Oudh threatening the imminent confiscation of private property in the province by the British Crown. As yet unaware of the change of ministry, Canning sent his dispatch explaining the proclamation to Vernon Smith, in the belief he was still the responsible minister. Thus Ellenborough received the apparently punitive proclamation with an incomplete understanding of its purpose and character. Ellenborough's reaction was as severe as his interpretation of the proclamation's intent. Threatening the disinheritance of a whole people, Ellenborough thundered, would create insurmountable obstacles to the restoration of peace in India. He immediately fired off a powerful rebuke to Canning. The reprimand was sharp, severe, and, in retrospect, appeared heavy-handed. Ellenborough had shown his censure of Canning to Derby on Saturday 17 April, the day after the cabinet had discussed the matter.[83] Derby, as Ellenborough remembered, approved it 'saying it was very proper and not too strong for the occasion'. Disraeli, Pakington, and Manners also read Ellenborough's response later that evening or during the following morning. Pressure of business, however, prevented Ellenborough from submitting his dispatch to the whole cabinet on Saturday 24 April; nor, more seriously, was the communication submitted for the approval of the Queen. Misjudgement then compounded procedural oversight when Ellenborough sent copies of his dispatch, in anticipation of agreement, to Granville in the Lords and Bright in the Commons. Publication of the dispatch became inevitable and it was immediately exposed to hostile public scrutiny.

Ellenborough's intemperate, if partially uninformed, reprimand of Canning provided all sections of the opposition with an opportunity for concerted attack. Canning was immediately cast as an abused martyr to Conservative folly and Ellenborough's immoderate rebuke cited as proof of ministerial incapacity. Hostile moral rectitude was further inflamed when, in early May, different versions of Ellenborough's dispatch were laid before the Lords and Commons. Presented *in extenso* in the Commons, the dispatch was given to the Lords with omissions. Ellenborough's confession that this was an administrative accident dealt a further blow to his credibility. The City and the directors of the East India Company were outraged by his behaviour towards Canning. 'All the government people', Granville noted with satisfaction, 'say it is a very bad case'.[84]

During early May the opposition marshalled itself for an all-out assault on the government. Palmerston and Granville agreed that an independent member of each House, Cardwell in the Commons and Shaftesbury in the Lords, should move a motion condemning Ellenborough's conduct. Russell indicated his willingness to support Cardwell's motion. The timing was critical. The ten weeks the Conservatives had been in office was sufficiently short a period for Palmerston to believe he was acting before his authority was irretrievably dissipated. Equally, it was sufficiently long a period for Russell to hope it was an appropriate moment to assert his leadership over a divided opposition. While disparaging any suggestion of having entered into an alliance with Palmerston, Russell affirmed his intention to vote with Cardwell against the government. The leading Peelites dutifully followed Russell's cue.

Intense partisan feeling quickly suffused Westminster and St James's. 'Language almost transgressing the borders of decency', the Conservative Sir William Fraser recalled, 'was used'.[85] The crisis dominated the meetings of cabinet, held as usual since the formation of the government in 11 Downing Street, on Saturday 1, Wednesday 5, and Saturday 8 May. Derby now had to judge whether his government could survive the storm, or whether Ellenborough, as the Jonah of the cabinet, should be thrown overboard. When the Duke of Bedford visited Lady Derby at St James's Square she observed that her husband had three courses open to him, resign, dissolve, or turn out Ellenborough. As they wished to be in office for a little longer, Lady Derby concluded, 'she preferred turning out Ellenborough'.[86] A packed Lords debated Shaftesbury's motion during the evening of Monday 10 and Tuesday 11 May. Shaftesbury, Disraeli recounted, like 'Gamaliel himself, came down ... bearing the broad phylactery of faction on his brow'.[87] Ellenborough calmly defended his conduct, declaring himself for 'discriminatory amnesty'. But when pressed by Grey,

Ellenborough was forced to admit that the government were not certain that Canning's proclamation to the people of Oudh had been issued. They had received no direct communication from the Governor General for nearly a month.[88] This led to an impassioned debate on Vernon Smith's conduct. Both Derby and Malmesbury accused Vernon Smith of failing in his bounden duty to furnish Ellenborough with the information contained in Canning's correspondence. Granville's riposte, that Vernon Smith received Canning's letter too late to influence Ellenborough's condemnation, was swiftly refuted by Ellenborough's detailing the dates of subsequent correspondence. Nevertheless, Ellenborough accepted full responsibility for the tone of his dispatch and announced to the Lords that his resignation had already been accepted by the Queen. Shaftesbury's motion was then defeated on Friday 14 May by a majority of nine votes.

Such acts of immolation, *The Times* observed, were rare in British politics.[89] Derby hoped that Ellenborough's self-sacrifice might yet scuttle Cardwell's motion in the Commons. As a further safeguard he visited the Queen on Tuesday 11 May to request a promise that a dissolution would be granted if his government were censured in the Commons. Commenting on the inconvenience of frequent dissolutions, the Queen, however, refused to commit herself. She informed the prime minister she would take advice. The cabinet, meeting at 11 Downing Street on Wednesday 12 May, were unsettled by Victoria's response. Derby, 'very much disappointed and mortified', waited upon the inclination of the Queen's advisers.[90] She turned to Aberdeen. The Peelite leader informed the Queen that, if Derby resigned, Palmerston would have to be recalled. Moreover, Aberdeen could think of no precedent that would justify refusing a dissolution, if it would automatically dismiss the prime minister.[91] Derby had a second audience with the Queen on Sunday 16 May. Fearing defeat by between fifteen and thirty-five votes on Cardwell's motion, Derby hoped he could be saved if it were known that the Queen did not preclude the possibility of a dissolution.[92] She maintained that it was unconstitutional to threaten parliament and to use her name for that purpose. He disavowed any such intention, but suggested that there were modes of letting the fact be known without any risk. Eventually, the Queen indicated that a dissolution would not be refused, but trusted that her honour would be safe in Derby's hands as regards the use he made of that knowledge. Greatly relieved, he indicated his firm belief that an election would produce a great gain in Conservative strength in the Commons. He thought the country was tired of the 'Whig family clique', while radicals such as Milner Gibson and Bright would support a Conservative government.[93]

With his options secured in the event of a defeat, Derby squared up to the Commons. Palmerston was determined to press ahead with Cardwell's motion and called a meeting of his Commons supporters at Cambridge House on Friday 14 May. That evening, while Shaftesbury's motion was being defeated in the Lords, Cardwell introduced his motion to the Commons. Despite Ellenborough's chivalrous declaration in the Lords, Cardwell insisted, his inept condemnation of Canning's conduct was the collective act of the ministry. The young Cairns coolly countered Cardwell's attack with legalistic precision. The motion, he contended, contained a complex proposition. It expressed no opinion on Canning's policy, but it censured the government for having been critical of Canning. But, if the House avoided a judgement on Canning's policy, then it was, Cairns proposed, impossible to address the other portions of the resolution.[94] Cairns's speech shifted scrutiny onto the Governor General. Disraeli prolonged the debate so as to increase the pressure on the opposition. Conservative backbenchers provided a counterpoint of ironic cheering, groaning, and cheering to every opposition speaker. By Sunday 16 May the threat of a dissolution was pulling apart the opposition. During the second and third nights of debate, on Monday 17 and Thursday 20 May, Roebuck delivered a violent speech against Cardwell and the Whig party. Bright denounced Cardwell's motion as a cynical party manoeuvre. Graham condemned Canning's dispatch and pronounced Ellenborough's response as harsh and impolitic, but nothing more. Clearly there was 'some solvent at work that [was] rapidly disintegrating the opposition'.[95] As Derby travelled to Epsom on Wednesday 19 May to watch his horse Toxophilite run, as favourite, in the Derby, the Commons opposition continued to unravel. The arrival of further mail on Thursday 20 May showing that Sir James Outram, the military commander in India, also disapproved of Canning's proclamation was, at Derby's insistence, immediately laid on the table of the Commons.[96] It exercised, he observed, 'a powerful influence' on the opinion of the House.[97]

Events on Friday 21 May produced a remarkable denouement. During the morning Cardwell requested Disraeli's agreement to the withdrawal of his motion.[98] Disraeli refused, insisting that Cardwell's abandonment of his censure of the ministry must be public and self-avowed. That evening the opposition attack spectacularly collapsed. Disraeli likened the scene to 'one of those earthquakes in Columbia or Peru of which we sometimes read. There was a rumbling murmur, a groan, a shriek, distant thunder; and nobody knew whether it came from the top or the bottom of the House. And then the whole of the opposition benches become one great dissolving view of anarchy.'[99] To a lady admirer he exultantly reported that, 'when it was thought that the very heat of the fight was to rage: the enemy suddenly fled in a manner the most ignominious. Never was such a rout!'[100] A greatly relieved Derby believed that 'no exaggeration could be applied to that extraordinary scene'.[101] The radical James Clay called on Cardwell not to press his motion to a division. The Irish Reformer George Bowyer seconded Clay's appeal. A succession of radical and Liberal MPs, to the accompaniment of Conservative jeering, urged that the motion be withdrawn. From the Conservative backbenches an elated Sir William Fraser shouted, 'the Lord has delivered them into our hands'.[102] Eventually, Palmerston himself rose to ask Cardwell to retract his motion. A crestfallen Cardwell complied. Immediately, Disraeli pointed out that it was the action of men unconnected with the ministry that had led to the strange result at which they had arrived.

Cardwell's humiliation provided a watershed for the Derby ministry. Gathorne Hardy celebrated that the opposition 'bubble is burst'.[103] Derby found the debate analogous to 'the explosion of a well-constructed mine under the feet, not of the assailed, but of the assailants'.[104] In a mood of triumphant elation ministers gathered in cabinet at 11 Downing Street on Saturday 22 May. As a 'faction fight' which had 'ended in a farce', Graham privately concurred that the opposition debacle would 'carry Derby over the session if he made no great mistakes'. For 'Johnny will think twice, if he ever thinks twice, before he embarks on a second Cambridge House foray.'[105] Dallas discerned three effects of the 'abortive impeachment'.[106] First, it had 'permanently split and so kill[ed] the Peelite party'. Secondly, it postponed for 'a considerable time any further assault'. Finally, it went 'very far to produce throughout the country the impression that the men at present at the helm understand steering at little better than their opponents and can safely be permitted to command the ship until some other enquiry occurs'. Only an exaggeratedly vivid speech by Disraeli at a banquet in Slough on 26 May disturbed the new-found calm into which the ministry now found itself sailing. Disraeli's claims that the Conservative government had speedily resolved those difficult issues, such as the Orsini crisis, the rule of India, and the *Cagliari* affair, which had been bequeathed to them by their predecessors, drew predictably scathing fire from a frustrated opposition.

I feel fresh spirit kindled in my breast.

(Derby, *The Iliad of Homer*, ii. 5)

Following the failure of Cardwell's censure Derby's 'government floated on top of the wave. We suddenly found ourselves', Carnarvon rejoiced, 'in the confidence apparently of the country, the newspapers, and the House of Commons, where we hardly ever', for the remainder of the 1858 session, 'meet with a defeat.'[107] Party government, *The Times* observed, seemed in abeyance. The 'independent' Liberal Sir Robert Peel, eldest son of the former Conservative leader, suggested that Derby had shown himself to be an abler, wiser, and, above all, a more liberal premier than Palmerston had proved, and that his government 'was equal to the conduct of public affairs'.[108] In record summer heat, assaulted by an evil stench from the Thames that forced MPs to abandon the Committee Rooms, parliament slumped into acquiescence. Lyndhurst's reflection in July that the 'Tories are getting on admirably', with 'nothing to oppose them and majorities in every division', accurately summarized the remainder of the session.[109] 'The government party', the radical Trelawny confessed despondently to his diary in late July, 'is a well disciplined phalanx.'[110] Resumption of debate on the government of India during June, by contrast, revealed the deepening dissension ravaging Whig and Liberal ranks.

Following the triumph over Cardwell's motion and with the opposition in increasing disarray, Derby reshuffled his cabinet, adjusting to the ministerial loss of Ellenborough. On Wednesday 26 May, Derby left Southampton Docks on the royal yacht *Elfin* for Osborne, where he consulted with the Queen. At a cabinet meeting at 11 Downing Street on Saturday 29 May he discussed arrangements with his ministers. A second invitation was sent to Gladstone. With Derby's authorization, Walpole offered Gladstone either the Board of Control or the Colonial Office as proof of 'the wish of the government progressively to extend its basis'. Disraeli's journal *The Press* declared that there was no 'solid difficulty in the way of a junction on the part of Mr. Gladstone with the present government'.[111] Gladstone agreed to discuss the offer with Graham and Aberdeen before giving a final answer. Graham recognized that Derby's invitation was 'a tempting one' and the moment chosen 'opportune'. Gladstone complained of being 'at the bottom of a well, waiting for a ladder to be put down ... Derby tenders this ladder.'[112] The truth, Graham confided to Aberdeen, was 'that Gladstone wishes to join, and to carry with him Herbert and his most intimate friends'.[113] On Tuesday 25 May, Disraeli wrote directly to Gladstone, declaring his readiness to 'make every sacrifice of self for the public good', a consideration Disraeli thought consistent with Gladstone's joining the Conservative government.[114] Gladstone's frigidly aloof reply Derby interpreted as a *réponse argumentative*, rather than a *refus catégorique*.[115] He saw it as an attempt to prompt him to invite Aberdeen into his cabinet as well. Gladstone's sense of his own worth to Derby, however, exceeded the premier's estimation of Gladstone's value. Derby could not think of any offer to Aberdeen which would not be either an insult or degradation to the ministry. He let the approach to Gladstone lapse, leaving Gladstone 'more isolated than ever, estranged from his present friends, and cut off from a new alliance'.[116]

Reorganizing his cabinet without Gladstone, Derby appointed Stanley to the Board of Control. Bulwer Lytton was brought into the ministry as Stanley's successor at the Colonial Office. As the flamboyant face of progressive Conservatism, Bulwer Lytton, despite his incapacity for detailed administrative business, affirmed the moderate complexion of Derby's ministry. During the following weeks Stanley successfully steered the Indian government resolutions through the Commons, enhancing his rising reputation for integrity and talent. Disraeli came to recognize his 32-year-old colleague as a man of first-rate abilities, Stanley distinguishing himself in the Commons, and Russell lavishing high praise on him: 'There was a fairness and candour about him, coupled with an evident determination to apply his high abilities to the consideration of the most important question, which eminently entitled him to the best confidence of the House and the country.'[117] Stanley's indefatigable industry and his businesslike qualities, Greville noted, rendered him 'completely *the man* of the present day'.[118]

Derby, meanwhile, maintained an enlightened legislative line, demonstrating that Conservative ministers provided safe hands to which to entrust the national interest. Russell's Oaths Bill, allowing practising Jews admission to parliament, survived a hostile Commons motion moved by Newdegate and seconded by Spooner. Approved by the Commons, in April the measure came up for debate in the Lords. Modifying his former staunch opposition, Derby declared his willingness to support the view of the bill taken by the Lords in Committee.[119] The second Lords reading was approved on Thursday 22 April. But five days later the Chancellor, Lord Chelmsford, carried a hostile amendment by 118 to 80 votes, striking out the crucial fifth clause of the measure omitting the words 'upon the true faith of Christian' from the parliamentary oath. Subsequent Commons debate reinstated the fifth clause, rejecting Chelmsford's amendment, and appointed a Committee to examine the issue. Provocatively, Lionel de Rothschild was made a member of the Committee as the elected member for the City of London, despite his official exclusion from the Commons. A confrontation between the Commons and Lords now threatened to become a constitutional crisis.

Privately Derby quickly sought a compromise, while publicly saying as little as possible, so as not to inflame the Anglican sensibilities of his backbenchers. During early May he encouraged Disraeli to negotiate a reconciliation, but approaches to Russell proved unsuccessful. On Tuesday 18 May, meanwhile, Lord Ellesmere suggested to Derby that the Commons should be allowed to admit Jews while the Lords continued to exclude them from their counsel.[120] Derby accepted his friend's proposal as the basis of a compromise settlement. On Monday 31 May, a week after the withdrawal of Cardwell's Indian motion in the Commons, Lord Lucan presented an amendment to the Oaths Bill in the Lords enabling each House to alter the parliamentary oath with regard to its own members.[121] An alternative scheme, proposed by Lyndhurst, empowering each House to admit not only Jews, but all non-Christians, was discarded in favour of Lucan's more limited proposal. This was consistent with Derby's wish to avoid, as far as possible, offence being given to Ultra Tory feeling.[122] Derby also wrote to known zealous Anglicans highlighting the dangers of a constitutional crisis. The 'question has resolved itself', he warned, into one 'whether it is desirable to continue without attempt at compromise … or whether a solution may be formed which may save the dignity, and to a certain extent maintain the principles, of both Houses'.[123] Lucan's proposal, he urged, offered a safe solution. Derby and his ministerial colleagues ensured the success of the second Lords reading of Lucan's measure with a majority of forty-six votes. In the Commons, Newdegate and Spooner launched one last unsuccessful attack upon the bill. But by 21 July, with Russell's support, it passed both Houses. So Derby skilfully avoided a constitutional crisis. A significant legislative reform was secured and the ministry's claim to responsible governance strengthened. The Parliamentary Oaths Act, as one historian has remarked, stands as 'the most symbolic religious liberty measure of the 1850s'.[124]

Religious concessions were also made to Catholic demands, which gained the support of the Irish Brigade for the ministry during the 1858 session. From Phoenix Park the astute Lord Naas affirmed his reputation for calm, authoritative, and courteous tact. On 25 March he skilfully defeated Roebuck's Commons motion to appoint an Irish Secretary of State to replace the offices both of Lord Lieutenant and of Chief Secretary. Lord Eglinton, in Dublin Castle, also proved a popular and capable member of Derby's accomplished Irish team. By mid-June, Disraeli noted that the position of the government in Ireland 'is very favourable—and, except for a few of the Ultra Orange party, all classes and sections unite in evincing their confidence in them'.[125] In Ireland, Derby again advocated careful reform. Catholic chaplains in the Army were given permanent rank and salary; a contract was negotiated for a direct mail service between Ireland and America which was expected to create a commercial boom in Galway; the Home Secretary allowed easier access to prisons and workhouses for Catholic priests; and it was made known that the cabinet was considering reform of the Irish landlord and tenant law. In early May, James Whiteside, as Irish Attorney General, introduced the ministry's Sale and Transfer of Irish Land Bill, which passed its second Commons reading on 25 May with little discussion. The measure proposed a Landed Estates Court, in place of the Encumbered Estates Court established by the Whigs in 1849, to examine property claims. After the bill's third Commons reading on 9 July, the measure received the royal assent on 2 August. *The Times* immediately welcomed the Act as 'one of the most beneficial that has emanated from the Derby government'.[126] To save Catholic sensibilities Walpole also curtailed debate over Spooner's annual motion to repeal the Maynooth grant.

Seldom, Disraeli rejoiced at the end of July 1858, had there been a session 'in which a greater number of excellent measures have been passed than the present'.[127] As parliament prorogued on 2 August, the government's India Bill, Sale and Transfer of Irish Land measure, and Scottish Universities Bill (unifying the colleges in Aberdeen), all received the royal assent. They joined the legislation amending the parliamentary oath and abolishing the property qualification for MPs passed during the session. The traditional Fish Dinner at Greenwich attended by ministers at the end of the session was a convivial affair. A witty and eloquent Whiteside chaired the dinner, at which Pakington was presented with a wooden spoon for being the minister who had attended the least number of Commons divisions. Derby concluded the celebration with the toast 'Whiteside and Whitebait!'[128] Ministerial spirits were high. Dallas directly attributed this success to the prime minister.

> Lord Derby has shown wisdom, tact and statesmanship, far beyond what was expected of him, and the natural result is a corresponding triumph over public opinion. The spirit of exterior conciliation is quite distinct. He soothes and satisfies everywhere: France, United States, Naples. At home he has ceased to fight with the age, concedes more liberally than he ever promised ... Surely, there is nothing equivocal in these traits of a six months' policy; shown, too, in the midst of difficulties, which might have provoked their angry relinquishment without exciting surprise.[129]

Dallas found no traces of Toryism in Derby's policies. This would, he predicted, bring rich rewards in any future election. Lord Campbell concluded that 'Democracy has made more progress in England during the last three months than during twenty years of Whig rule.'[130] On 2 July *The Times* conceded that Derby had shown the wisdom of graceful concession.[131] The Conservative daily newspaper *The Standard* celebrated Derby's prudent sense of compromise.[132] The arrival in London, on 20 August, of news of the signing of the Treaty of T'ien-chin, concluding hostilities in China, raised ministerial spirits further. By mid-August society had abandoned London to the sweltering heat and malodorous Thames. The clubs were vacant, the Queen and Prince Albert left for a state visit to Prussia, and political hosts journeyed north to the grouse moors of Scotland. Even the press, Dallas reported, fell into an uncharacteristic somnambulism. As Disraeli began his annual retreat at Hughenden, Derby visited Lord Jersey at Osterley Park and then travelled on to Knowsley to resume his seasonal sport with the wildfowl of Lancashire.

Yet Derby's other great recreational passion had not matched his political success during 1858. His 3-year-old Toxophilite won at Newmarket twice during April and was regarded by the bookmakers as the clear favourite for the Derby on 19 May. But Toxophilite was beaten into second place at Epsom by Sir Joseph Hawley's Beadaman. A sorely disappointed Derby was denied the double triumph of holding the premiership and winning the Blue Riband of the turf in the same year. Nonetheless, the racing world was surprised by his sudden announcement in September that he intended to put up his horses in training for auction, though keeping his stallion Longbow, his brood mares, and foals as a *point d'appui* for the future. Initially, rumours circulated that the decision was brought on by Derby's disgust at the failure of his efforts to reform the nation's race courses, his public letter of the previous year to the Jockey Club having denounced the shadier activities of certain owners and trainers. Derby quickly rebutted these reports, however, by stating that the sole reason for the sale was that affairs of state left him with little leisure for actively following his passion for the turf. He had decided, therefore, to retire from racing. On 18 September the racing fraternity, including Derby's trainer John Scott, gathered at Tattersall's in Doncaster to bid for the twenty-two horses put up for auction. The bids for Paletot, De Clare, and Fazzoletto, however, failed to reach their reserve price, and Toxophilite, 'the lion of the sale', was bought in.[133] Twelve yearlings, colts, and older geldings, including Target, were sold. The auction marked Derby's gradual withdrawal from the sport from which he had derived, over nearly thirty-five years, immense pleasure.

Disappointment at the result of the Derby and the pressure of political affairs, which he anticipated would continue for the foreseeable future, undoubtedly influenced him. His concerns about his health may also have contributed to this decision. Aged 59, in June he had suffered a particularly serious attack of gout and his health remained fragile throughout the autumn. Political duties, he concluded, must exercise the strongest claim upon his time and energy, although Toxophilite's victory, in the Grand Duke Michael Stakes at Newmarket on 28 September, provided some consolation for earlier disappointment.

Despite his illness during June, Derby's spirits untypically remained high during the recess, although another attack of gout in early September forced him to his bed. It was, therefore, with difficulty that he honoured his duty to attend the Queen at Balmoral on 13 September; his memories of the spartan accommodation and dull routine of his first official visit to Balmoral six years earlier made the journey no easier. His reception, however, was cordial and the arrival of the Prince of Wales enlivened the evenings. Derby was relieved to discover that the major rebuilding of the original cramped accommodation, under Prince Albert's close direction, now provided far more comfortable lodgings. Accompanying Prince Albert on deer-stalking expeditions, his health slowly improved. Only the Queen's continued preference for court appointments from among the Whig clique caused him irritation. On returning to Knowsley from Balmoral, however, he suffered yet another attack of gout, which laid him up for most of early October. But by late October, Malmesbury found his old friend once again 'in great force'.[134] Returning to London for the first cabinet meeting of the recess, held in 11 Downing Street on Wednesday 3 November, Derby appeared fully recovered.[135] Later that month, when he encountered Derby at Hatfield House, Clarendon found the prime minister 'in great spirits and endlessly making jokes'.[136] As younger guests enjoyed 'endless polkas', Derby engaged in light-hearted banter and chaffing.[137] During the course of the evening he learnt of the engagement of Jolliffe's second son and heir to Lady Agnes Byng, the eldest daughter of Lord Enfield. The next morning, at Downing Street, Derby was amused to be able to share the news with Jolliffe, 'who heard it from the prime minister for the first time!'[138]

Derby's high spirits were a fair reflection of the Conservatives' reviving fortunes. It was also comment on the parlous state of the opposition. The Duke of Argyll believed that the Whigs and Liberals were 'in chaos and [with] no prospect of an end to this condition of things'.[139] The Observer lamented 'the schism' which divided the opposition, while noting that 'the Conservative ministry have now got regularly warm in office, and every day adds more to the strength of their position'.[140] Russell grudgingly acknowledged that 'Public events have been favourable to this country and consequently to the government.'[141] When, amid widespread criticism, Palmerston visited Napoleon III at Compiègne in October, Liberal detractors declared Palmerston's political career at an end. Eloquent about 'the miserable condition' of the Liberal party, Wood pronounced over the dinner table that Palmerston 'would *never* again be prime minister'.[142] Herbert saw only 'chaos on the opposition benches'.[143] Graham confirmed that the 'broken fragments of the old Whig party are so shattered that they cannot be pieced together again'. They had known each other too well and for too long, Graham lamented, 'and they dislike each other too much'.[144] Clarendon's radical brother Charles Villiers judged the Liberal party 'too much divided and scattered' to hope for an early return to office.[145] Palmerston himself, during August, admitted that if he 'was to make a bet about the government's chances I would rather back them in, than out, for next session'.[146]

What was certain about the forthcoming session was Derby's pledge to introduce a Reform Bill. In March 1858 he had promised a moderate and reasonable measure deserving the support of all well-educated men. What precise form such a bill might take, however, was unclear. During the recess he deliberately kept the opposition guessing. In October he reminded Disraeli of the merits of ministerial evasiveness: 'Nothing has so disconcerted our opponents, especially of the peers, as the silence we have kept as to all our intended measures.'[147] As Disraeli prepared to give a speech to his constituents, Derby wrote: 'I need not urge on you the advantage of saying *nothing* in your speech.' All that Clarendon could extract from Derby at Hatfield House in November was that the government's measure would 'not be a sham, otherwise we will create an angry feeling and an extensive demand'.[148] At the same gathering Hardwicke informed Clarendon that their legislation would settle the Reform question for many years to come. Such sentiment, Clarendon observed, 'showed progress in a man who a year ago was the Toriest of all living Tories'. The 'only *fact*' Parkes could garner during the recess was a speech by Henley which merely 'committ[ed] his colleagues to a measure' intended 'to influence the stiffer Tories out of doors'.[149] Even the Ultra Tories, Clarendon noted, 'seem determined to give the government a generous confidence which means eating the same dirt as them'.[150] In December, Clarendon confessed to still knowing nothing about the details of the forthcoming Conservative Reform Bill; 'but if it is a tolerably decent one—not a sham on the one hand nor on the other courting radical popularity—the chances will be greatly in favour of its passing in preference to any other measure come from what quarter it may'.[151]

While keeping his cards close to his chest, privately Derby was giving serious thought to Reform. Philip Rose came away from a meeting with the prime minister in London on 11 August 'quite convinced that no one ought to venture to talk to Lord Derby who does not thoroughly understand the subject'.[152] Since 1851 Derby had indicated his willingness to modify the 1832 Reform settlement, as long as it did not involve any uncalled-for extensive alterations. During the Crimean War he argued for deferment as long as hostilities lasted. Then, in 1857, he confided to Disraeli his readiness to amend the defects of the existing system. The preservation of the distinction between the county and borough electorates, however, he felt was essential. The intrusion of urban freehold voters into county constituencies was a dangerous distortion of the representative system that required remedy. During 1854 many Whig and Liberal backbenchers had expressed alarm at Russell's proposed lowering of the borough franchise and extensive redistribution, while favouring a lowering of the county franchise complemented by 'merit franchises'. In October 1857 Palmerston privately endorsed these views as the basis for further Reform. Two Commons votes in June 1858, meanwhile, further defined Whig, Liberal, and radical feeling on the subject. Non-Conservatives were united in support of Locke King's proposed equalization of the county and borough suffrage, while being bitterly divided over the ballot. These considerations formed the background to Derby's thinking about Conservative Reform during the autumn of 1858.

At the beginning of August, Derby, in consultation with Jolliffe, decided to appoint a cabinet committee to draw up the government's Reform Bill. Disraeli, who had already left London for Hughenden, was unaware that the premier's thoughts were 'so advanced' on the subject and found consideration of Reform initiated in his absence, without being able to prepare cabinet colleagues for his own views.[153] Derby's appointments to the cabinet committee, meanwhile, revealed his expectations of the measure. The committee was made up of Disraeli, Stanley, Pakington, Manners, Salisbury, Jolliffe, and himself.[154] More recalcitrant cabinet ministers—Walpole, Henley, Hardwicke, Chelmsford, and Peel—were excluded. Malmesbury was not appointed because of the pressure of work at the Foreign Office. The progressive character of the committee pointed to the nature of the bill to be framed. Derby was keen to rebut accusations of a sham and to propose a moderate measure. Hopeful of an enlightened proposal, Stanley noted that his father spoke 'in terms of warm praise of Rose which is a good sign'.[155] Derby conveyed optimism to Disraeli. He indicated flexibility on the question of any new suffrage, being prepared to adopt an £8 rating franchise in the boroughs, though personally favouring a £25 county franchise. This fell short of Rose's wish for a £6 rating borough franchise, but was a significant concession to progressive opinion within the cabinet. The 'keystone of the whole' for Derby, however, was 'making freeholders in boroughs voters for the boroughs and not for the counties as at present'.[156] This was the Conservative version of the argument propounded by radicals, such as Cobden and Bright, that it was the distribution of voters, rather than their number, that mattered most. In the early 1850s Derby opposed an identity of suffrage in both counties and boroughs. But, accompanied by the transfer to borough constituencies of county votes entitled by urban freeholdings, he now began to see it as the basis for a permanent settlement.

As Derby travelled north to Lancashire and then on to Balmoral, cabinet colleagues reacted to his initiation of discussion of Reform. Disraeli agreed that the level of any borough franchise should be dependent upon the general character of their measure. He also supported Derby's view that urban freehold voters should be confined to the boroughs, as the only mode by which a tolerable balance could be maintained between urban and rural constituencies. With this in mind, Disraeli suggested that a uniform £10 franchise was their 'wisest' course.[157] But Walpole was alarmed that the ministry were preparing 'for *Radical* Reform'. A uniform franchise would, he believed, be 'a fateful step'.[158] Disraeli's justification was that the assimilation of the county and borough franchise would provide 'an intelligible principle' offering 'a fair settlement of this important question'. But if permanence was their aim, Walpole retorted, then he favoured a county franchise for all who paid the house tax and the borough franchise for tenants rated at £6 upwards, with proof of eighteen months' or two years' residency. In addition, he proposed the enfranchisement of 'all who had realised a sum in Public Securities as would yield an interest of £6 per year'. The Conservative purpose of such a suffrage would be best served, he argued, by the promise of permanence. Otherwise, Russell would bid for a £6 rating borough franchise, Palmerston would be satisfied with £8, and the radicals would demand household suffrage. Other ministers shrouded their views in ambiguity. Pakington reported to Derby a conversation with Walpole during which he was 'glad to find that our views were very similar—in principle quite so'.[159] At the same time, Pakington expressed his suspicion to Disraeli that Ellenborough, Stanley, Disraeli, and himself

had 'little in common with the party behind us ... [and] little in common
with Derby, Walpole, John Manners and Henley'.[160] Until commitment
became necessary Pakington appeared to be attempting to please all.

The prospect of Reform triggered widespread speculation outside the
cabinet. At the beginning of September, Russell invited Stanley to
Woburn, hospitality which the Duke of Bedford understood as a preliminary to a 'fresh organisation and combination' of parties.[161] In late
August, Disraeli had been anxious to have it known publicly that Stanley
was also visiting him at Hughenden, in order to counter rumours of an
impending ministerial rift. In mid-October, Russell travelled to Liverpool
to address a meeting of the Social Science Association and stayed for two
days at Knowsley in the company of the prime minister and his elder son.
Russell found Derby 'in boyish spirits ... but not one word of politics'.[162]
Derby believed Russell had his eye on Stanley in the event of a break-up
of the Conservative cabinet over Reform, and had been amused when,
while at Balmoral in September, the Queen had appeared startled when
he informed her of Russell's proposed visit. Russell left Knowsley with
the impression that Derby would not comply with any 'democratic movement' such as Stanley and Disraeli might suggest. A forthcoming split
in the government, he concluded, was therefore a probability.[163] During
August, Russell had been tempted to declare his hand on Reform. After
visiting Knowsley, however, he decided to hold back from any public
pronouncement, his silence allowing Conservative differences to emerge.
Yet the government were constructing 'a trap', Whigs feared, 'by trying to
win over Johnny' and proposing a Reform Bill he could support, a trap
Russell might fall into 'out of spite to Palmerston'.[164] It was 'wiser to await
than to seek the storm', Graham advised Lord John. 'Derby will soon find
himself in the midst of it without chart or compass; and friend Bright is no
helmsman in extremity.'[165] But who was offering to take whom on board
was unclear. During October, Jolliffe invited Stanley to stand as MP for
Manchester. The sitting Liberal MP, Sir John Potter, was known to be
dying, and Jolliffe believed 'a requisition of Liberals to oppose the League
which was beaten at the last election' would make Stanley's victory 'a
certainty'.[166] The acquisition of a seat formerly associated with Free Trade
radicalism had obvious political benefit. But Derby confirmed his son's
own inclination not to accept the invitation. 'As a general rule', the prime
minister observed, 'it is not desirable that a cabinet minister should represent a very large borough constituency, and be exposed to the consequences
of sudden popular caprice.'[167] On 27 October, Stanley declined Jolliffe's
offer. The Liberal Thomas Bazley was subsequently elected without a

contest as Potter's successor. The proposal was further proof, however, of the value of Stanley's known liberal views to the rehabilitation of the Conservative party.

That Bright broke ground in October 1858, undertaking over the next weeks a series of widely reported public addresses outlining his hopes for Reform, affirmed the wisdom of Derby's reticence and Russell's restraint. 'The present position of Parliamentary Reform is that of a triangular duel, in which the Conservatives, Whigs and Radical Reformers are the belligerents,' *The Times* observed in late November. There was, however, one 'novelty in the arrangement—that the one who has the privilege of the first shot has immediately to receive the fire of both the others'.[168] In speeches at Birmingham, Manchester, and Glasgow, during October and December, Bright staked out the radical terrain on Reform. His carelessness with electoral statistics gave ready ammunition to his Whig and Conservative critics; while his advocacy of a borough franchise conferred on all who were rated to the relief of the poor and a county franchise for all lodgers who paid a rent of £10 gave tangible form to the radical threat which moderate Conservatism might stave off. That Bright also pleaded for the revision of the law regarding primogeniture, which kept vast estates in single ownership through successive generations, helpfully stoked widespread fear of impending class warfare. Opponents eagerly seized on Bright's pronouncement as betraying the fundamental threat to the landed constitution that Manchester School radicalism posed. The Tory *Saturday Review* denounced Bright for wishing to exchange 'our regulated liberty for an unmixed democracy'.[169] Conservatives welcomed Bright's radical declarations as encouraging a more moderate reaction. A polarization of sentiment excited by Bright, ministers hoped, would force Russell either to embrace radical company or to assist in a Conservative settlement. The country did not want, *The Times* affirmed, 'to jostle the units of society into new relations or to wipe the whole surface smooth and clean for a new scheme of local and private as well as public arrangements'. The legitimate object of a Reform Bill should be 'to represent more truly than is now done the existing state of the country—not only its numbers, but its property, its usages, its social relations, its education, its actual influences, and whatever goes to make up the country'.[170] Moderation and finality, extending rather than subverting the principles of the 1832 Reform Act of which he had been a prominent advocate, informed Derby's own wishes for his Reform legislation.

Gladstone's acceptance, during October, of the invitation to be the government's envoy, heading a mission charged with negotiating a new constitutional arrangement for the Ionian Islands, also suggested a shift of support to the ministry. During the recess Graham observed in Gladstone 'a restless anxiety for a change of position'.[171] Through journalistic attacks in the *Quarterly Review* on the policy of shoring up the Ottoman Empire, Gladstone sustained his anti-Palmerstonianism. On Reform he hoped for a Conservative settlement. When Bulwer Lytton invited Gladstone to lead the Ionian mission Aberdeen recognized 'the means it might afford [Gladstone] of drawing closer to the government and of naturally establishing [him]self in a more suitable position'.[172] Gladstone himself perceived his 'Lilliputian die' was cast.[173] Graham understood Gladstone's acceptance was 'regarded by the ministers as an open act of adhesion'.[174] Cardwell observed 'that all Gladstone's leanings are towards the government and that this is regarded by him as an approximation ... obviously Gladstone is tending rapidly towards a more decided connection with the Conservative party'.[175] The ministry, the Whig man of letters Abraham Hayward noted, 'pride themselves on having made a prize of Gladstone'.[176] From November 1858 to March 1859 Gladstone was preoccupied abroad. Many suspected that the Ionian mission provided him with a convenient excuse for absenting himself from domestic discussion of Reform. Puzzled by Gladstone's motives for accepting the commission, *The Times* suggested his only reward would be that, having returned after the Easter recess to a Commons wearied by debate on Reform, 'like Desaix at Marengo', he hoped to 'give victory to the side to which he carries his support'.[177]

During late September 1858 Disraeli endeavoured to keep 'the Knowsley gout ... secret'.[178] Nothing, he feared, disheartened a party so much as an invalid chief. After visiting Balmoral and suffering another attack of gout in early October, Derby was confined to the house at Knowsley and unable even to walk around the estate. His recovery by mid-October, however, quickly set the ministerial wheels moving. Sotheron-Estcourt came away from a meeting with Derby fired with a determination 'to show people that we are in earnest; so resolved to proceed for a [Reform] bill forthwith'.[179] By the end of October, Derby, now recovered, was preparing to return to London, determined to put the cabinet Reform committee actively to work. At the cabinet meeting of Wednesday 3 November, the prime minister appeared 'in great spirits'.[180] It was 'a favourable moment', Manners exalted, for settling the Reform question 'for this generation, and Bright's violence and his promised bill assist us to carry a less sweeping measure'.[181] Walpole feared the prime minister being hijacked by his committee. He advised Derby that the committee should restrict itself to collecting facts and statistics, leaving the discussion of principles to the whole cabinet.[182] But, in truth, the disruptive debate of broad principles in cabinet was precisely what Derby wished to avoid.

On Sunday 21 November, with London swathed in dense fog, Derby drafted the cabinet Reform committee report himself. It laid out those propositions which, despite individual differences, had the sanction of a large majority of committee members.[183] First, he proposed that the bill should be concerned solely with England and Wales. Though it might become necessary to consider Scotland as well, it was desirable not to disturb the representative system in Ireland. Secondly, both franchise and redistribution should be dealt with in one bill. Thirdly, he proposed to retain the existing borough franchise and to lower the county franchise to a £10 rated suffrage. Pakington had dissented from the majority decision on the borough franchise, while Stanley gave a conditional assent.[184] As a concession a lodger franchise, based upon a £20 rental and a year's residence, was recommended which, in the towns, would extend the vote to 'a very large and in many respects, a very respectable class'. Most importantly, Derby secured majority agreement to his central concern that freeholders, enfranchised by property within the limits of a borough, should be confined to voting in the borough, although again Pakington dissented. With regard to redistribution, while rejecting any attempt at absolute equality, the committee adopted population, as reported in the 1851 census, as a basis for removing the worst anomalies. A limited number of boroughs with a population of less than 500 might be totally disfranchised. Some boroughs with a population of between 5,000 to 15,000 would lose a member. This made seventy-three seats available for redistribution. No new constituencies were to be created, with the exception of the West Riding and South Lancashire. But every county constituency with a population above 100,000 was to be given three MPs. County constituencies with a population greater than 50,000 were to be given two MPs. This created an additional forty-eight county seats. It was to be anticipated that many of these seats would be won by Conservatives. A further eighteen seats were to be given to borough constituencies, the remaining seven seats being granted to the University of London and the Inns of Court. Thus redistribution was to provide comfort to those Conservatives unsettled by franchise reform. Finally, it was agreed to disfranchise the dockyards, to recommend the use of polling papers for postal votes, and to resist the ballot in any form.

The Reform scheme recommended by the cabinet committee was the measure for which Derby had hoped. It restricted urban freehold votes to the borough constituencies. It adopted the suffrage annually proposed by the radical Locke King, which had received broad opposition support in July 1858, mitigated by a redistribution of seats favourable to the Conservatives. Those proposals preferred by Stanley fared badly. The borough franchise was not lowered and the ballot was rejected outright. But Derby's hope that proceeding by committee would pre-empt cabinet dissension signally failed. Even members of the committee subsequently pulled away from aspects of the report. On Tuesday 23 November, Pakington lobbied the prime minister for a uniform borough and county franchise at an £8 rated level. The Commons, Pakington argued, would not approve a measure which left the borough suffrage untouched. An identity of suffrage at the £8 rated level would be 'real and complete', rather than the mere adoption of 'the long-disputed motion of Locke King'.[185] Pakington privately sought Walpole's agreement to an attempt to defer any Reform measure, and the concentration of legislative attention on an Indemnity Bill and India.[186] Jolliffe regretted the omission of Scotland and Ireland from the measure. He also favoured a uniform £8 rated franchise and hankered after the further disfranchisement of 'inconsiderable places' with only one Member.[187] Pakington and Jolliffe's doubts revealed the vulnerability of the committee report in cabinet.

Derby presented the committee's recommendations to the full cabinet on Thursday 2 December. He declared it 'difficult to exaggerate their difficulty or the importance' of the question.[188] But pressure to modify the committee's scheme immediately came to bear on him. Walpole promptly rejected the committee's plan. Malmesbury was pessimistic and doubted the cabinet could devise a measure satisfactory both to themselves and the public. Yet enquiries in Hampshire and Dorset convinced him, 'from a careful study of "the idiosyncrasies of the various decades", that £10 [was] quite as conservative, if not more, than any of the tens under fifty'.[189] During December, Derby requested information from Conservative peers, such as Lord Redesdale, on the effect in their own regions of a £30, £20, or £10 county franchise. The responses were 'very contradictory'.[190] Rose's enquiries regarding the desirability of transferring freehold votes from the counties to the boroughs revealed more difference of opinion than Derby liked. Jolliffe, meanwhile, continued to advocate an £8 rated borough suffrage.[191] Then, on Monday 27 December, Henley forwarded to Derby an eighty-seven-folio memorandum on Reform 'as long as a Chancery brief',[192] written by Walpole. Walpole strongly objected to the assimilation of the county and borough suffrage and to any total, or more than very partial, disfranchisement. He did not reject the principle of transferring freehold votes to the boroughs. But, if it was accompanied by a £10 franchise, he objected to both. Henley and Peel also indicated their opposition to assimilation and transfer. Pakington, meanwhile, reiterated his views in cabinet that 'making no concession whatever to the working classes ... will be considered a great defeat in our plan'.[193] Derby came to fear that Walpole, Henley, and Peel would be joined in their opposition to the transfer of the urban freehold vote by Pakington, Salisbury, and possibly Stanley. He had framed the measure upon two principles: the adoption of Locke King's proposal for a uniform £10 county and borough franchise, and the transfer of urban freehold votes to borough constituencies. By early January 1859 both principles were being questioned by ministers. This was despite the transfer of the urban freehold vote, according to overwhelming evidence given to Derby by Rose, being 'the most Conservative provision in the bill'.[194]

For Derby, political difficulties were aggravated by family bereavement. On 16 December his aunt Lady Wilton, who had devotedly nursed the 12th Earl of Derby during his final years, died aged 57. For a number of years her husband, Lord Wilton, had been having a semi-public affair with the disreputable Caroline Cook (also known as Nelly or Lilly Cook) as well as Lady Ailesbury. The social hostess Lady Waldegrave took to referring to Wilton as 'the wicked earl'.[195] Derby became estranged from Wilton because of this scandal, despite their earlier close friendship. Privately, the family attributed Lady Mary's demise to the strain of her husband's public indiscretions. On Thursday 16 December, the same day as Lady Wilton's death, Bulwer Lytton, a well-known hypochondriac, informed Derby of his wish to resign from the government because of ill health.[196] The prime minister entreated Bulwer Lytton to stay.[197] In response, the Colonial Secretary forwarded notes from his doctor.[198] Disraeli, who with his wife visited Knowsley on 17 December, remained calm about the possible loss. The secession of Bulwer Lytton, he advised Derby, would be interpreted as proof that their forthcoming Reform Bill was insufficiently liberal. This inference, in turn, would reassure the Conservative back benches and help keep them together.[199] Derby looked to Sotheron-Estcourt as the best man, currently outside the cabinet, as a replacement for Bulwer Lytton. Jolliffe, who was equal to any post, was invaluable in his current position. Derby also considered replacing Bulwer Lytton with Walpole, who would be much gratified, and therefore appeased, by such an appointment. In a similar spirit, Disraeli suggested Henley, whose promotion to the Colonial Office would abate his 'crotchety churlishness'.[200] Derby acknowledged that such a move 'might smooth down [Henley's] bristles for a time—though he could never be secure against his snapping at one's fingers at any moment'.[201] The remark proved prescient. On Christmas Eve, Henley wrote to Derby offering to resign.[202] This 'ominous communication' Derby ascribed to Henley's 'dogged feeling as to the details of the Reform bill'.[203] Picturing Henley's 'grim smile', Disraeli pronounced Henley's mode of wishing the prime minister Merry Christmas, entirely characteristic.[204] That Henley subsequently forwarded Walpole's 'Chancery brief' on Reform suggested that their unhappiness would be less easy to deal with than Derby had hoped. Over Christmas, Bulwer Lytton also continued to send 'pathological epistles' to both Derby and Disraeli, listing his symptoms under the ailments consumption, dropsy, and paralysis.[205] During the week following Christmas, however, feelings were soothed. On Monday 27 December, Henley agreed not to resign. Likewise, on Saturday 1 January, Disraeli persuaded Bulwer Lytton to remain in post. With heavy irony he reported to Derby that Bulwer Lytton had agreed to sacrifice 'his life to his party'.[206]

While colleagues grew restive over Reform, Disraeli again pressed forward finance as an imperative concern. In September he assured Malmesbury that, although 'the difficulties of the Reform bill [would] not decrease ... the revenue flourishes and a popular budget will carry us thro'.[207] During October, Disraeli urged Derby to hold 'an early cabinet on finance'.[208] The Chancellor was encouraged 'by the state of the country, which I believe is as generally prosperous as it ever was at any period in its history. Everything succeeds, foreign and domestic, and the Exchequer is overflowing.'[209] In response, Derby insisted that Disraeli must allow for sufficient naval and military expenditure. National defence could not be sacrificed to a financial coup. New screw-driven battleships, for example, must be built for the Navy. The Queen reinforced Derby's message. Nevertheless, Disraeli anticipated 'a brilliant budget', as a sequel to his successful 1858 fiscal statement, securing him the mantle of financial mastery donned by Gladstone in 1853. Derby, however, kept ministerial attention focused on Reform. It was Reform, not the budget, he saw as crucial to his government's survival, as opposed to Disraeli's personal success.

In early January 1859 Derby, in response to Walpole's 'Chancery brief', reminded his Home Secretary of the practical requirements of the government's situation. They must deliver 'a fair and reasonable compromise which will for many years, at least, put a stop to agitation for further Reform'.[210] Concession by all was necessary. The cabinet had agreed to two propositions: that property was to confer the vote in both counties and boroughs and that the same privilege should be extended to lodgers. This commitment, he insisted, made it impossible to retain a distinction between the *character* of the borough and county franchise, as Walpole wished. Over redistribution their differences were ones of degree, not principle. As Derby reminded Walpole of practical requirements, his elder son also 'broke ground'.[211] Stanley forcefully denounced Walpole's views. A measure proposing a £20 county franchise had not a hope of passing the Commons, Stanley declared.[212] A majority of the Commons had committed themselves to Locke King's motion and would reject a bill not adopting that principle. Moreover, a measure based on Walpole's preferences would be certain of failure and those who advocated it would be accused of insincerity and acting in the expectation of defeat. The rejection of a Conservative bill would then be followed by a more radical measure from Russell which, in all likelihood, would be supported by the Commons.

On 11 January 1859 the Queen held a Privy Council meeting at Windsor at which it was agreed to extend the prorogation of parliament from 13 January to 3 February. Derby faced a seemingly irreconcilable ministerial split over Reform. His attempt to finesse cabinet differences through committee had failed. The crisis was grave:

> Any secession from the cabinet ... on the liberal or conservative side ... would enlist in its favour a certain amount of sympathy and encourage opposition on the part of many who would be willing to accept, even if they did not wholly approve, a measure which was sanctioned by a unified cabinet.[213]

Derby prepared to sacrifice the principles he had secured in committee on the altar of cabinet unity. He promptly laid before the cabinet an alternative Reform scheme comprising an £8 rating borough franchise and a rating franchise of £16 for the counties. He also reluctantly indicated his willingness to surrender his hitherto firm commitment to confining urban freehold votes to the boroughs. His continuing as head of the government, he then declared, was dependent upon the acceptance of this alternative plan by the whole cabinet.

It was a brave gamble. It too failed. Two events prevented the revised Reform plan from becoming a basis upon which to preserve cabinet unity. First, both Walpole and Henley persevered in their decision to resign, undeterred by Derby's reformulation of the measure. As 'a conscientious man and a Tory', Walpole declared it 'utterly impossible' for him to countenance the revised plan. The 'shrewd and clever, but crotchety and easily offended', Henley pronounced that his worst apprehensions were now confirmed.[214] As a concession, both ministers agreed to postpone their resignations until after the meeting of parliament. In the meantime, their resignations were to be kept 'a profound secret'.[215] Secondly, Rose submitted a memorandum to the cabinet summarizing the responses of Conservative organizations and landowners in the constituencies. Rose's intelligence supported the original principles Derby had advocated in committee. The assimilation of the borough and county franchise, Rose concluded, would substantiate the government's claim to have secured finality. It allowed for 'a broad and comprehensive measure', embracing 'the influence of property, station and intelligence, without regard *solely* to population'. A lowering of the borough franchise, however, '*would only be a certain step* on the road to universal suffrage and *democracy*'.[216] In the light of Walpole and Henley's insistence on resignation, Derby seized on Rose's memorandum as authoritative. The promise of permanence, the restriction of urban freehold votes to borough constituencies, and the redistribution schedule accompanying the Reform Bill would mitigate the effect of an identity of suffrage. In late January, Derby reverted to his original Reform plan, proposed by the cabinet committee, as the only basis upon which the government should now proceed. If ministerial resignations were unavoidable, then the merits of the committee plan were compelling.

On Saturday 29 January, Derby travelled to Berkshire for the inauguration, by the Queen, of Wellington College. The founding of the college had been Derby's proposal to the Queen six years earlier as a suitable commemoration of 'the Iron Duke', the public subscription being supplemented by the gift of a day's pay from every officer and soldier in the British Army. On behalf of the president, Prince Albert, and the governors of the school, Derby welcomed the Queen and declared his hope that the young men educated at the institution would follow the great Duke's example in their loyalty to the Crown, their service to the country, and their obedience to the call of public duty. The Revd Edward Benson, formerly a master at Rugby and future Archbishop of Canterbury, was installed as the energetic and diligent founding headmaster. The following day Derby returned to London. At his eve of session dinner for Conservative peers, held at 10 Downing Street on Wednesday 2 February, he called for strict party unity in the coming session. At the concurrent dinner, hosted by Disraeli at 11 Downing Street for Conservative MPs, the plea for party unity over the critical forthcoming weeks was equally insistent.

Of different nations and discordant tongues.

(Derby, *The Iliad of Homer*, i. 76)

Anglo-French relations and Italy saved Derby's cabinet from an exclusive preoccupation with Reform during the recess. But, in contrast to sharp differences over Reform, the question of Italy suggested a broad consensus within Westminster. Three considerations shaped common thinking among Conservatives, Whigs, Peelites, and Liberals on the Italian question during the winter of 1858–9: distrust of Napoleon III, a concern for the European balance of power in the event of military and political humiliation for Austria, and the perception of papal temporal sovereignty as a glaring example of illiberal corruption, as personified by Pope Pius IX. Sympathy for liberal Italian nationalism, leading to local reforms, existed. But Napoleonic aggrandizement and Austrian defeat, without eradicating the repression endemic in the Papal States and the Kingdom of the Two Sicilies, would be an undesirable disruption of European relations. After Napoleon's meeting with Count Cavour, prime minister of Piedmont, at Plombières on 21 July 1858, it appeared that France intended to provoke a war against Austria. Indeed, the secret pact concluded between Napoleon III and Cavour at Plombières comprised a cynical agreement that Piedmont, over the next year, would deliberately draw Austria into a war, preferably with Austria's appearing the aggressor. France would immediately send an army to support Piedmont and, with the Austrians forcefully expelled from Lombardy and Venetia, northern Italy would be absorbed by Piedmont. In return, France would receive Nice and Savoy. So Austrian influence would be diminished, Napoleon III would step forward as the champion of repressed nationalities, and the constitutional monarchy of Piedmont, as part of the Kingdom of Sardinia, greatly enlarged. The arrangement of the marriage between the King of Sardinia's daughter and Napoleon III's cousin cemented the alliance.

On 4 August the Queen and Prince Albert, accompanied by Malmesbury, Pakington, and Lord Hardwicke, visited the recently expanded French naval base at Cherbourg, of which Napoleon III gave them a formal tour. The state visit confirmed France's well-advanced plans for modernizing her navy and, while Napoleon III was very friendly in his manner, he complained to Malmesbury of criticisms in the English press about French military and naval expansionism.[217] A few days later General Peel, as War Secretary, warned Derby that France had begun to import large quantities of saltpetre and sulphur in preparation for a military campaign. Peel's reports were confirmed by Malmesbury. On 16 August, Derby wrote to Malmesbury: 'though I do not believe our trusty ally has any hostile feelings or intentions at this moment, it is clear that he means to place himself in a position to make his power to be felt, whenever it suits him that we should feel it'.[218] In response, Malmesbury worried that Britain was 'very deficient in materials of war' and that 'our population is defenceless'.[219] By 2 September, Derby correctly believed that French military preparations had primary reference to Italy. On behalf of Piedmont-Sardinia, the French Emperor apparently looked to drive Austria out of Lombardy and Venetia, thereby overthrowing the Vienna Settlement of 1815. But Italian nationalism, British politicians largely agreed, merely supplied Napoleon with a flag of convenience. Italian liberty was a pretext, not a motive. A strong wish for non-intervention prevailed consistently with Derby's view that Britain should not disrupt the Concert of Europe established in 1815. In 1855 Russell had brought forward the question of the Papal States as an embarrassment to Palmerston. But Russell also regarded Napoleon III as a tailless rocket, whose destructive force would produce unpredictable results. Altering the provisions of a treaty by force of arms, moreover, could not be condoned. Clarendon and Palmerston both argued for British neutrality in the event of France's picking a quarrel with Austria on behalf of Piedmont-Sardinia.

On 1 January 1859 Napoleon III openly snubbed the Austrian Ambassador, as tensions between Paris and Vienna increased. Malmesbury and Derby's diplomacy, meanwhile, conformed with the prevalent British wish to stand aloof from French intrigue in the Italian peninsula. Malmesbury reported to Derby his attempts at 'smoothing down the quarrels' between Count Walewski, the French Foreign Minister, and Count Buol, the Austrian prime minister.[220] He also advised the Austrian Ambassador in London, Count Apponyi, that Britain would never support Austria against Italians in 'a purely Italian war', although French aggression against Austria would raise a more difficult diplomatic dilemma. While British public opinion supported Italian nationalism, 'it would be equally strong against any wanton aggression of France or Russia, so Austria must take care to be forbearing and always in the right'.[221] As Derby advised Malmesbury on 5 January:

> The worst is that with France longing to pick a quarrel, and Sardinia too much inclined to be made a catspaw of, Austria, or rather Buol, is only too likely to give them a fair pretext.[222]

Malmesbury agreed that nothing would be more fatal to the Kingdom of Piedmont-Sardinia than a shift of power between France and Austria.

> The part that [Piedmont-Sardinia] would play in a war between France and Austria would be secondary, and she may be well assured that, like other small states acting in concert with a more powerful ally, her interests would not be consulted either in the prosecution or the conclusion of the war. The internal prosperity which Sardinia has acquired would disappear before the march of a friendly army; and the Sardinian government must know, even by recent experience, that the liberal institutions on which she justly prides herself would be equally distasteful to friend and foe, on whichever side she might be found in an Italian war.[223]

Malmesbury's analysis was shrewd and, over the next six months, proved penetratingly prescient.

The only internal cabinet difficulties over foreign policy during the recess arose from Disraeli's persistent private attempts, through his correspondence with Derby, to discredit Malmesbury. Through his secret informants in Paris, initially Ralph Earle and then the shadowy figure of Georg Klindworth (a former secret adviser to Frederick IV of Prussia), Disraeli prided himself on having diplomatic intelligence unknown to the Foreign Office. From October 1858 Disraeli sought to use this information to raise questions in Derby's mind about Malmesbury's competence. Disraeli claimed to possess a special insight into European realpolitik. During the recess he also feared Reform would overshadow any personal triumph he might achieve with his forthcoming budget. Disparaging Malmesbury would enhance his own personal position and insert his influence into Derby and Malmesbury's close consultation on foreign affairs. In early January, Disraeli suggested to Derby that Malmesbury felt 'an incipient reserve and jealousy' towards him over foreign policy. The accusation, however, revealed more about Disraeli's insecurity, rather than being an accurate comment on Malmesbury's state of mind. Certainly Malmesbury's reputation as Foreign Secretary, at the time and in subsequent historical judgement, has been unduly maligned. His diplomatic successes were substantial. His analysis of the Italian situation in January 1859 was astute and vindicated by subsequent events. Moreover, despite Disraeli's insinuations, Derby's relationship with Malmesbury during 1858–9 remained one of close cooperation and genuine mutual respect. Derby firmly dismissed Disraeli's unwelcome interventions.[224]

When parliament met on Thursday 3 February 1859 Derby committed his government to maintaining inviolate the faith of public treaties and

preserving the general peace. There was, he assured the Lords, no justification for recourse to war.[225] He recognized the Pope's temporal power
as 'the real plague spot of Italy'. But French incitement to armed conflict
was a dangerous diversion from desirable local reform. It was also the
case that Britain had 'no direct concern' in the 'state of apprehensions
under which Europe at the present moment labours'. Both Grey and
Brougham endorsed his opinion. Aberdeen agreed that 'French pretensions are scandalous … and unjust.'[226] In the Commons, Disraeli echoed
Derby and Malmesbury's views. He acknowledged the value to Britain of
the French alliance, but announced that the government would pursue a
policy conducive to peace. While referring to the desirability of reform
in the Papal States, both Russell and Palmerston also broadly approved
of the ministry's course. Their speeches were concessions to the tone of
the House, which was strong for peace. With Malmesbury's permission,
prior to the debate, Lord Cowley wrote privately to Palmerston from
Paris, aware that Palmerston's public statements would be scrutinized
closely in foreign ministries throughout Europe, urging support for the
government's policy.

> If our parliament takes the line of justifying the ejection of Austria from
> Italy, the probability is that we shall have war in the Spring. If on the other
> hand a determination is shown to stick to existing treaties, under which the
> peace of the world has been maintained for nearly half a century, I shall
> not fear the results of the present crisis. The internal state of Italy is indeed
> deplorable, but will war ameliorate it, is the question I cannot help asking
> myself.[227]

Cowley's influence helped to preserve consensus within Westminster.

On 4 February *The Times* affirmed that 'the national sentiment' on the
Italian question was strong and unanimous. The view of Englishmen was
'the same under all the guises of faction'. There were 'no serious or incurable
differences upon continental politics'. To cultivate friendly relations with
the European Powers, to maintain the faith of public treaties, and to
preserve the general peace was Britain's unanimous message to Europe.[228]
Subsequently, Russell opened private discussions with Palmerston, looking
to press the government to a more active diplomatic role in the Italian
peninsula. But, rather than opposing Malmesbury's policy, he sought
to suggest that Derby's cabinet was lax in pursuing its own avowed
aims. As a result, on Friday 25 February, Palmerston challenged the
government to describe their efforts to preserve peace and to define their
attitude to foreign military occupation of the Papal States as the main

obstacle to real political reform in Italy.[229] In an effective *coup de théâtre* Disraeli replied by announcing the dispatch of Lord Cowley to Vienna on a mission to effect peace and conciliation.[230] This was a diplomatic initiative Malmesbury, as encouraged by Derby, had eagerly proposed. Cowley's instructions were to seek a Franco-Austrian withdrawal from the Papal States, reform of the Papal States, a general declaration of peaceful intentions, and the annulment or revision of Austria's treaties with the Italian states, which permitted Austrian interference in the region. Prolonged and loud cheering greeted Disraeli's announcement. Russell could only offer congratulatory remarks and support Disraeli's recommendation to postpone further discussion until Cowley's mission had been concluded.[231]

During February 1859 Derby's grip on power appeared to strengthen. Malmesbury's authority at the Foreign Office was enhanced by Britain's successful diplomatic mediation in resolving the dispute between France and Portugal over the latter's commandeering of the French ship *Charles et Georges*. Just as Cowley's mission abated fear of an impending Italian war, so Malmesbury's constructive engagement in French and Portuguese negotiation, as urged by Derby, reinforced the perception of Derby's cabinet as providing safe hands for the management of the national interest. This view was strengthened by domestic legislation introduced to the Commons during February. Cairns, as Solicitor-General, brought forward two bills to simplify the title to landed estates. This complex subject had long received the attention of parliament. Several unsuccessful earlier attempts had been made to remedy the expense and difficulty of the transfer of landed property. Cairns's sensible measures and personal capability won approval.[232] On Monday 21 February, Walpole announced a Church Rates Bill which he believed to be 'a just, moderate and reasonable settlement of the question'.[233] The government proposed to establish a permanent substitute for the church rate by encouraging landlords to commute the rate into a rent charge on their lands, similar to the commutation of the tithe. Dissenting tenants could deduct the charge from their rent, leaving payment to their Anglican landlords. Provision for aiding this rent charge was to be provided by voluntary assistance. This was a significant concession to Dissenters on the part of the government, although Pakington wished the cabinet to go further. The radical champion of church rates reform, Sir John Trelawny, acknowledged the conciliatory spirit of the plan, as did Russell, who, nonetheless, criticized the measure. Revealing a degree of embarrassment over the proposal Sir George Grey and Cornewall Lewis deferred judgement so as to allow time for further consideration.

Conservatives supported Walpole's bill as an acceptable compromise. Meanwhile, Pakington's introduction of the Naval Estimates drew guarded approval from Wood. Jolliffe reported to Disraeli that 'things appear to have gone well in the house of Commons'.[234] But consensus over Italy, resolution of the *Charles et Georges* affair, successful law reform, concession over church rates, and approval of the Naval Estimates were only an engaging prelude, prior to the curtain lifting on the main drama of Reform. By 19 February *The Times* was impatiently declaring that peers and MPs were 'doing absolutely nothing' and that their 'residence in town just now is all a sham'. Waiting was not an Englishman's usual or most congenial occupation.[235]

> ... but if ye
> **Shrink from the perilous battle, then indeed**
> **Our day is come ...**
>
> (Derby, *The Iliad of Homer*, ii. 6)

Reference to Reform in the Queen's Speech of 3 February 1859 was cursory. Disraeli gave the impression of 'pooh-poohing Reform as a secondary affair which must wait until other measures of more importance were settled'.[236] In the Lords, Derby concentrated on foreign affairs. Argyll confessed himself 'astonished at Derby playing so loosely and lightly with the question of Reform'.[237] This reticence reflected persistent cabinet difficulties. Despite Disraeli's brief assurances to the Commons, the government met parliament without a measure fully framed.[238] On Monday 7 February, Derby circulated a memorandum to the cabinet pressing for final agreement.[239] Given Walpole and Henley's determined, though publicly deferred, intention of resigning, he now regarded the suffrage and the transfer of the urban freehold vote as settled. The recommendations made by the cabinet committee were to be implemented. The issue of redistribution, however, remained unresolved. The wisest course, he now suggested, would be to omit redistribution altogether from their bill.

> The omission of all disfranchisement will disarm much opposition; the large additions we make to the constituencies will secure much public support; the equalisation of the franchise will, partially at least, meet many demands; and the general character of the measure will commend itself for the better class of public opinion.[240]

During the following morning he had separate interviews with his ministerial colleagues, followed by a long cabinet meeting. Disraeli, Bulwer

Lytton, Walpole, Salisbury, Peel, and Hardwicke supported the omission of redistribution. Stanley, Pakington, Manners, and 'Henley (by proxy)' dissented.[241] Separating the suffrage bill from a redistribution scheme, Stanley, Pakington, and Manners feared, would prevent their franchise bill from being accepted as a final settlement of the question.

Following the cabinet, during the afternoon of Tuesday 8 February, Stanley, Pakington, and Manners pressed for an extensive redistribution scheme, partially disfranchising forty-seven seats. Derby, supported by Disraeli, rejected this proposal, favouring a smaller redistribution plan affecting only fourteen or fifteen seats.[242] While Manners and Pakington seemed ready to accept this compromise, a discontented Stanley continued to hint darkly at resignation.[243] At another cabinet meeting on Saturday 12 February all, with the exception of Walpole and Henley, agreed to a £10 county franchise and a £10 borough franchise, with 'merit franchises' given to the occupiers of lodgings to the amount of £20 p.a., those receiving pensions of superannuities of £20 p.a., those with deposits of not less than £60 in savings banks, and graduates, ministers of religion, barristers, attorneys, registered medical men, and certificated schoolmasters.[244] These 'merit franchises', it was anticipated, would offer the entitlement of the vote to respectable working men in the boroughs. They were similar to the 'merit franchises' Russell had proposed in his 1854 Reform scheme and those considered by Palmerston in 1857.

> Even if it is argued that intelligence and not property, should be the basis of the franchise, it may be answered that a well-directed intelligence will enable any man to lay by his £50 in a Savings Bank or invest £66 in the funds ... or £50 in India Stock, or any Joint-Stock Company paying a dividend of four per cent; and if this degree of Property is made to confer the franchise, no skilled workman or labourer earning high wages need be long excluded from possessing a vote.[245]

Moreover, it was agreed by the cabinet that equalization of the franchise and the transfer of the urban freehold vote were 'inseparably connected'.[246] Thus, at the cost of two ministerial resignations, Derby finally won cabinet agreement to those central propositions he had secured in committee in December. It was also agreed by the cabinet on Saturday 12 February to confine the redistribution of seats 'within *very* narrow limits' and 'to resist more extensive changes'.[247]

On Wednesday 16 February, Derby circulated among the cabinet a memorandum on disfranchisement, drawing on Rose's research into the claims of unrepresented towns. Proposing to give one MP to Barnsley,

Stalybridge, Birkenhead, West Bromwich, Croydon, Hartlepool, and Gravesend, he approved of the division of South Lancashire and Middlesex into two constituencies and the division of the West Riding into three, while rejecting Rose's suggestion of giving a third MP to Liverpool, Birmingham, and Manchester.[248] This arrangement disposed of the fifteen seats Derby considered it necessary to disfranchise. To this limited redistribution scheme the cabinet, despite Stanley's misgivings, unanimously agreed. Only the granting of the vote to clergymen and schoolmasters remained contentious. By mid-February cabinet acceptance of a Reform Bill following the broad outlines Derby had indicated in November 1858 was secured, at the price of Walpole and Henley's resignations. Clarendon noted that Derby, while attending a dinner given by the Prussian Ambassador, Count Bernstorff, 'was in high spirits'.[249]

Derby was now forced 'to reconsider [his] *personnel*'.[250] The sudden resignation of Lord Henry Lennox as a junior lord of the Treasury broadened the review. On Monday 14 February, Derby offered Pakington the Home Office, as successor to Walpole. With polite firmness Pakington declined.[251] Derby considered offering the office to Lord Chandos. But on grounds of financial difficulty and wishing to retain his railway chairmanship, Chandos also declined.[252] Finally, Sotheron-Estcourt was moved from the Poor Law Board. This promotion ensured that the cabinet did not lose its' '*bucolic* character' and might 'control Walpole' once he was outside the cabinet.[253] With a similar view to backbench feeling, Lord March was appointed to the Poor Law Board. Disraeli understood there to be 'a cabal brewing by Newdegate'. Lord March's adhesion, he hoped, would neutralize this dangerous intrigue.[254] Derby chose Lord Donoughmore, 'a man of the world, a sound partisan' and prominent in the Lords, to replace Henley at the Board of Trade.[255] The 41-year-old Northcote was appointed as Financial Secretary to the Treasury. A pious and intelligent Anglican, Northcote, while acting as Gladstone's private secretary prior to 1850, had favoured Free Trade. But by 1851, though not yet an MP, he was moving towards the Conservatives, privately declaring himself in 1852 to be a warm supporter of Lord Derby. He was joint author of the Northcote–Trevelyan Report in 1854, recommending meritocratic recruitment to the Civil Service, becoming a Liberal Conservative MP for Dudley the following year. Defeated at Dudley in 1857, he returned to the Commons, at Disraeli's prompting, as Conservative MP for Stamford in July 1858. Northcote, therefore, followed the path many expected Gladstone to travel. Northcote's appointment further strengthened Disraeli's authority at the Exchequer. As a final placation of personal feeling, Lord

Lovaine, who seemed 'very sulky' and 'bent on going', was promoted to replace Donoughmore as Paymaster-General.[256] These ministerial rearrangements were designed both to reassure backbench opinion and to suggest executive capability in anticipation of the decisive parliamentary battle over Reform.

With their Reform Bill finally settled and personnel adjusted, the cabinet decided to introduce their Reform measure to the Commons on 28 February. In the meantime, it was agreed to have it believed that their Reform scheme was 'rather an extreme one, so that the Palmerstonians may go on talking conservatism'.[257] Arrangements were made for Derby to hold a large meeting of his supporters on 1 March, so as to ensure party unity in the forthcoming debate. With these preparations completed, on Sunday 27 February Derby declared himself 'more sanguine of success than I have yet been'.[258]

Derby's composure was then sharply jolted by the publication in *The Times* on Monday 28 February of the franchise proposals of their Reform measure. Infuriated, he immediately suspected Disraeli of giving details to Northcote, who, in turn, had informed Delane. Since the beginning of the session there had existed a dark suspicion that *The Times* was 'writing from distinct information from *within the cabinet*'.[259] The revelation certainly bore Disraeli's fingerprints, even if there was no hard evidence forthcoming. Ralph Earle may possibly have been the source. Disraeli vehemently denied he was guilty of the leak, melodramatically declaring to Derby that the scoop had 'destroyed' him and left him 'half inclined to resign'.[260] Delane admitted to Disraeli that he had learnt of the suffrage proposals from Edward Ellice during the evening of Sunday 27 February. But the source of Ellice's knowledge, most probably Earle, was never ascertained. If the revelation unsettled Derby, the response to *The Times*'s intelligence was encouraging. Privately, Delane declared that he would give Derby's bill 'every support'.[261] He expected the Palmerstonians to do the same. Lowe's anonymous leader, accompanying the disclosure of the franchise proposals on 28 February, was complimentary. The measure, Lowe stated, was 'proof of the wish of ministers to deal with the question, if not on very wide, at any rate on honest and intelligible principles'.[262] Certainly the Conservative measure was 'as strong as any government would be able to carry in the present temper of the House of Commons and the public mind'. When Lowe fell in with Gathorne Hardy, immediately prior to the Reform debate on the evening of Monday 28 February, he praised the measure as 'a capital bill' and avowed his support.[263] Delane and Lowe represented precisely that moderate body of opinion that Derby hoped to secure.

What Disraeli's adroit presentation to the Commons lacked in surprise, on Monday 28 February, was made up for in deliberate conciliation. Just hours before his speech Derby urged Disraeli to 'avoid depreciating the *extent* of the measure. Prove that it is *Conservative* as much as you will, but do not let it be inferred that it is *small* ... I think our friends in general are well disposed.'[264] The Reform Bill, Disraeli declared, provided a lasting settlement, consistent with the spirit and principles of 1832, ensuring the representation not only of the numerical majority and the influence of predominant property, but of all the various interests of the country.[265] The Chancellor paid tribute to Russell, attacked the doctrine of 'Brightism' which advocated representation based solely on population, and announced the transfer of urban freehold voters to the borough constituencies. Both the county and the borough franchise would be established at a uniform £10 level. 'Merit franchises' would extend the vote to those not intimately linked to either agriculture or manufacture. Voting papers (which had been introduced to municipal elections in 1835) would be an option available to the enfranchised, while a limited redistribution of fifteen seats would be effected by the partial disfranchisement of boroughs with less than a 6,000 population. Disraeli's speech, Granville observed, produced 'immense relief' in the House. All 'the 130 members to be disenfranchised by Bright's bill were enchanted with the reprieve'.[266]

Following Disraeli's statement the Whigs sat largely silent. The Palmerstonians were 'still and impenetrable'.[267] Only Bright and Russell promptly spoke out against the bill. Bright denounced the 'merit franchises', or 'fancy franchises' as he derisively dubbed them, as well as the transfer of urban freehold votes to the boroughs. Russell declared that the bill said little or nothing about the working classes. This was language, Whigs nervously noted, 'smacking of the Bright school'.[268] Ellice was alarmed that Russell 'chimed in with Bright, Roebuck and Fox' by complaining 'of the *larger bodies* of the working classes not enfranchised'.[269] Such expressions, Argyll warned Russell, 'rather *frightened* the House'.[270] But the plaudits of the press countered the cavils of Russell and Bright. In its editorials *The Times* welcomed the Conservative Reform measure. It argued for the bill to be given 'a fair trial on its own merits'. Bright's accusation, that it would give no power to the working classes, it dismissed as 'a conclusion suggested only by blind prejudice or wounded vanity'. The Conservative bill was 'substantial and important', offering the vote, by its various franchise clauses, to almost anybody who thought it worthwhile.[271] The *Morning Herald* felt the bill was in 'the interests of all classes'.[272] The *Morning Chronicle* was fulsome in its praise.[273] *The Globe* was generally complimentary.[274] These journalistic opinions complemented the uncertainty shrouding Palmerston's intentions. Abraham Hayward came away from a conversation with Palmerston believing that 'a large body of moderate Liberals' had 'already declared for the second reading and the country seems perfectly indifferent'.[275] Disraeli received a report that Palmerston thought 'le bill est trop liberal'.[276] Clarendon believed it was 'of unspeakable importance to the country that a tolerably moderate bill should be passed this session and that can only be done by the present government'. He recognized that 'it will be difficult steering and require skill *but it is to be done* because there is no real union in the liberal party and a great contempt for authority, each scrubby fellow thinking himself fit to be a leader'.[277]

With opposition responses 'a Tower of Babel',[278] Derby concentrated on holding together his own back benches. He was pleased that Walpole and Henley's announcements of their resignations during the Reform debate on 28 February, despite being 'full of half-suppressed bitterness towards their colleagues', were judged to have 'exhibited weakness on the part of the retiring ministers'.[279] The seceding cabinet ministers, *The Times* declared, seemed 'possessed with terrors resembling that of the unhappy lunatic'.[280] Walpole and Henley, Malmesbury concluded, were like the men 'who deserted their ship at Calais the other day, thinking she was going down; they were drowned, but the ship was saved'.[281] At a party meeting at 10 Downing Street, on Tuesday 1 March, attended by over 200 MPs, Derby 'detailed the pros and cons' of the measure. Clauses, which in isolation might appear liberal or extreme, he assured his MPs, had to be viewed in the context of the measure as a whole. He then 'plumply informed the assembled gentlemen that everyone of them must vote for every part and the entirety of the measure unflinchingly'.[282] If the bill failed, he warned, he would dissolve parliament. This declaration had its desired effect. Despite Newdegate, Palmer, and Trollope's voicing a preference for a £20 county franchise, all present indicated their firm support for the bill. Conservative unity in the Commons appeared secured. The gathering was 'certainly larger than could have been obtained by any other statesman, or probably, by the two Whig leaders combined', *The Times* judged, 'and it gives reason to suppose that the measure of the cabinet will be at least read a second time'.[283] On Saturday 5 March, Derby held a meeting of Conservative peers, who also unanimously endorsed the measure. 'There is no fear *there*, he informed Disraeli.[284]

Newdegate and other irascible Ultras, however, persisted in sniping at the measure. On Wednesday 9 March a meeting at the Carlton Club, chaired by Newdegate, agreed to petition the premier for the withdrawal of the clause transferring urban freehold votes to borough constituencies. Such a change, Newdegate subsequently informed Derby, would excite the asperity of class distinction and strengthen the claim of large towns to additional representation.[285] Derby deemed Newdegate's objection perverse. 'If there was one constituency which, in a Conservative sense, would benefit more than any other by the transfer of the borough freeholds it was Newdegate's constituency of North Warwickshire.'[286] The bill would remove intrusive Birmingham freehold votes from Newdegate's county constituency. Nevertheless, at a cabinet meeting on Thursday 10 March, Derby floated the idea of giving urban freeholders the option of voting either in the borough or in the county.[287] Newdegate, however, received this compromise with ridicule. He portrayed the measure as Disraeli's clumsy attempt to eject 'such stiff old Tories' as himself from the party.[288] A group of twenty backbench malcontents, including Newdegate, Bentinck, and Palmer, met on Tuesday 15 March and decided to urge the withdrawal of the whole Reform Bill. But when Derby met Bentinck and Palmer on Thursday 17 March they were unceremoniously 'snubbed'.[289] Clearly no cabinet concession, short of complete withdrawal of their Reform measure, would appease Ultra Tory sensibilities. Any further attempt to tailor the bill to backbench opinion was, Derby decided, out of the question. He now paraded a firm resolve that brooked no compromise. 'There shall be no mistake!' he instructed Disraeli. 'We must command this parliament, or throw the die for the next—and let our friends know that it is the last card.'[290]

Derby's renewed resolution was also a response to Russell's organization of Commons opposition to the bill. During early March, Russell carefully drafted a hostile motion protesting against the transfer of freehold votes. Without a residency requirement, Russell argued, a large number of faggot votes would be created in the boroughs, a violation of the 1832 Reform Act's emphasis upon occupation and residency as a requirement for possession of the vote. The motion did not contain a broad objection to the measure, although it regretted the failure to lower the borough franchise. Parliamentary convention decreed that the second reading of a bill was an invitation to consider the general character of the legislation, while objections to specific clauses were usually left to the committee stage. But by immediately focusing attack on the transfer of urban freehold votes, Russell hoped to conciliate disparate Whig and radical sections. Palmerston tolerated the motion, while giving it to be understood that, although he 'did not mean to "throw over Johnny" ... he would bear it with great fortitude if others [did] so'.[291] Russell's announcement of his motion, prior to the second reading of the Reform Bill, on Thursday 10 March, sought to pre-empt a general consideration of the measure. In a speech at Birmingham, Bright announced his intention to throw out the Conservative bill. In response, *The Times* attacked the two extreme factions, one radical, the other Ultra Tory, opposed to the bill, asserting that 'the great body of the nation wants a safe and constitutional Reform' and that the government had created 'a great opportunity' by giving the country exactly what it looked for—a Conservative Reform Bill.[292] In distinguishing 'an artificial clamour from the expression of a serious popular conviction', *The Times* concluded, both the country and the House of Commons desired to terminate the existing agitation by the enactment of a measure which might, for a time, be considered final, 'and any statesman who will achieve the task will be rewarded by general confidence for the performance of a great and truly urgent public duty'.[293] In *The Times* on Tuesday 15 March, Lord Grey published a letter denouncing Russell's motion 'as an invitation to the Whigs to affirm what is superfluous or vague'.[294] Derby's own rejoinder, confirmed in cabinet on Saturday 19 March, was unflinchingly to confront Russell without concession. Government resolve, he anticipated, would scuttle the move to secure opposition unity over a specific aspect of the bill. It was to be made clear, he informed the Queen, 'that the success of Lord John's motion will be fatal to the bill'.[295] By standing firm, he believed, ministers might scatter the fragile opposition alliance.

Russell's targeted attack on Conservative Reform in late March avoided a broad denunciation of the measure. His assault focused on the trans-fer of the urban freehold vote. So might a general consideration of the Conservative bill, during its second reading, be deflected by an attack on one particular proposal, opposition to which, Russell calculated, was shared by Whigs, Liberals, and radicals. In retrospect, Clarendon char-acterized this behaviour as 'shameful factiousness'.[296] The narrow pass of Russell's motion proved the Thermopylae of the Reform debate, as Derby's outnumbered Spartan force faced the massed Persian ranks of the opposition. Firmly drawing a line in the sand, Derby hoped defi-ance would cause Russell's fragile alliance to falter and then fracture. On 20 March he advised Disraeli that going to the country, immedi-ately after a defeat on Russell's motion, would allow the government to appeal against 'a factious opposition to the whole bill, in an un-usual and unparliamentary form'.[297] But, as at Thermopylae, the danger of unexpected flanking movements was to expose Derby's position to encirclement.

Russell's introduction of his motion on Monday 21 March fell flat. Personal allusions to himself, as the champion of genuine Reform, were coolly received. During the first night of debate the independent Liberal Edward Horsman spoke against Russell's resolution, while calling for other friendly amendments to the measure. Disraeli privately pressed the moderate Whig MP Lord Elcho to voice opposition to Russell. Moderate Liberals, Derby urged, must not be allowed the comfort of believing they could vote for Russell's motion, while intending to support the government on the second reading. The success of Russell's resolution, the premier insisted, would be a rejection of the whole bill.[298] By making it 'the main question' they would force Whigs, Liberals, Peelites, and radicals to recognize that 'there was hardly a single point on which the various sections of the opposition could come to an agreement'.[299] Derby urged the prolongation of Commons debate. This would allow divisions within the opposition camp, he believed, to multiply. He also hoped that the settlement of a European Congress on the Italian question would provide a diplomatic coup with which to enhance the government's authority. This would affirm 'the hollowness of the union' opposed to them.

During the following days, debate remained focused on Russell's motion, Conservatives elaborated on the rifts within the opposition, and discussion was prolonged. Bulwer Lytton described Russell's motion as 'a rope of sand' patching up the quarrels of years for the division of a night.[300] Bulwer Lytton's accompanying description of the English constitution, Disraeli reported to the Queen, was 'as rich and more powerful than Burke'.[301] Pakington combatively denounced Russell's raising of an abstract resolution upon the second reading of their Reform measure as unparliamentary. Cairns challenged Russell to demonstrate why freehold property in a borough should be dealt with differently from other property. As intended, this perplexed the wavering. Gladstone, recently returned from his Ionian mission, stated he would give his vote neither to the government nor to the party when he voted against Russell's motion; his 'clever speech ... full of inconsistencies' was received with puzzled amusement.[302] While denouncing the bill for being 'too clever by half', Graham urged ministers to withdraw their measure and redraft it in accordance with the opinion of the House.[303] On Friday 25 March, Palmerston declared his support for Russell's motion, on the understanding that the government would persevere with the rest of their bill and allow consideration of every part of the measure in committee. Anxious to 'repress the expanding glories of his rival', Palmerston suggested that the success of the motion need not require the government's resignation or a dissolution.[304] Thus he sought to drain Russell's motion of its venom. From the government benches Whiteside firmly rejected the comforting option of Russell's success not being fatal to the bill. Privately, Derby commented that he had 'the misfortune to hear Palmerston, that it was clever, but the most provoking and aggravating speech he had ever heard'.[305] On 28 March *The Times*, in an equine metaphor, asked: 'How say you Lord Derby? ... Will you be stalled and stabled, and mashed ... in Lord Palmerston's stables?'[306] In the Commons the radical Roebuck, in the role of peacemaker, invited the government to consider a £6 borough franchise, in return for his support for the second reading, while Bright continued to pour scorn on the 'fancy franchises' proposed in the bill, unsuccessfully trying to broaden the discussion.

As the Reform debate unfolded, Derby became more optimistic about the outcome. 'Already many defections are spoken of from the ranks of the opposition, while the Conservative party are becoming more consolidated, and sinking minor differences as they begin better to understand the provisions and bearing of the measure.'[307] *The Times* criticized Russell for acting rather 'as the chief of a party than the member of a legislature in interposing to prevent the discussion and amendment of a measure which borrows some important features from his own'.[308] In cabinet, on Wednesday 23 March, ministers reaffirmed their intention to dissolve parliament if defeated over Russell's motion. Derby assured Eglinton that, whatever the result, he would 'not be in such a breathless haste to resign my office'.

> We shall at once drop the Reform bill, which will accordingly be lost for the session; but our accounts from the country are so favourable that I shall have no doubt whatever as to having recourse to a dissolution before I give in; and I do not apprehend any difficulty on the Queen's part ... But there may, and no doubt are, difficulties arising out of the critical state of Foreign Affairs, which may render an immediate dissolution inadvisable. In that event it is possible that we may go on for a short time, with the present House of Commons ... There is no concert among the opposition and no chance of their being able to form a government except one of extreme opinion which the country will not have.[309]

In such a situation Russell could be portrayed as the selfish saboteur of moderate Reform.

Disraeli closed the Reform debate on Thursday 31 March with a calm, almost solemn, speech, deliberately avoiding flashes of sarcasm or ingenious phrases. By bringing on his motion during the second reading, Disraeli observed, Russell had forced debate onto a matter of detail, more suitably considered in committee, rather than allowing a broad consideration of the measure to occur.[310] The bill adhered to three basic principles: first, that the constituent body of the country should be increased by the enfranchisement of a large number of responsible persons; secondly, that large communities were entitled to representation in the Commons; finally, that the existing borough franchise should be preserved. By jointly opposing this moderate settlement, Disraeli concluded, the House was forced to believe that Bright, Graham, Russell, and Palmerston were in agreement. But he could not reconcile 'the mild Conservatism' of Palmerston with the radicalism of Bright. The narrow terms of Russell's motion, he concluded, were a convenient device, bringing together an opposition deeply divided over all other aspects of Reform. 'There are wars in which nothing is done but mutual injury and common loss,' *The Times* concluded; 'there is no position to defend, no territory to occupy, and, as matters get worse and worse, no cause to maintain. That appears to have been the case in this discussion.'[311]

In a packed Commons, at 1 a.m. on Friday 1 April, the division on Russell's motion was taken. Derby's sanguine hopes were dashed. Russell's resolution was carried by 330 to 291 votes, with an opposition majority of thirty-nine. Uproar and confusion followed the announcement of the vote. The Conservatives had remained loyal. But only twenty-six non-Conservative MPs (sixteen Whigs and Liberals and ten Irish Brigade) opposed the motion. The size of the opposition majority surprised Derby. 'Some of the other side who had promised to vote had not kept faith.'[312] Palmerston's effective blunting of the motion and the belief that there would be no dissolution, unless the majority was a slender one, had dulled the ministerial portrayal of the resolution as a decisive vote. Derby faced a choice of resigning, dissolving parliament, or staying in office with Reform deferred and foreign affairs pressing. At a cabinet meeting at midday on Friday 1 April he led discussion towards a dissolution. Only Stanley and Sotheron-Estcourt were for resignation.[313] Some opposition leaders, such as Granville and Clarendon, feared resignation would acutely embarrass the supporters of Russell's motion. The announcement of the dissolution of parliament on Monday 4 April, however, scotched further speculation. Derby remained confident of an appeal to the country. Queen Victoria encouraged him by condemning Russell for a factious manoeuvre, which showed Lord John was 'ever ready to *make* mischief and do his country harm'.[314] In *The Times* Derby's ministers were praised for 'their industry, their readiness to take a fair view of subjects, and their general courtesy in the conduct of business, both in and out of parliament', which was 'freely acknowledged by men of all opinions'.[315]

In a full House of Lords, on 4 April, Derby elaborated the Conservative electoral text. The distracted state of parties made it impossible to administer the affairs of the nation.[316] This, in turn, threatened the very basis of parliamentary government. If no future government was able to obtain a permanent majority in the Commons strong enough 'to prevent it being overborne by other conflicting parties, not themselves bound by any common tie'; if the Commons was to be 'divided into a number of little parties, none capable of exercising a permanent influence on the affairs of the country, but able collectively to thwart the measures and impede the business of the ministry that has been formed'; then 'the system of government by parliament itself will have a very heavy shock to encounter'. If every year brought on another ministerial crisis, involving constant party fluctuations, then the authority of parliament would be undermined. Over Reform the diverse sections of the opposition had preferred the narrow advantages of faction to the broad interests of the nation. These 'motley and heterogeneous materials' had defeated the government not by fair parliamentary process, but by an ingenious manoeuvre. In reviewing Russell's political career Derby plotted a lifetime of self-interested intrigue. In 1835 Russell had turned out Peel on an 'impracticable pretext'. In 1852 he overthrew Derby's ministry with 'an objectionless coalition'. In 1855 he ejected Aberdeen from office in 'a personal *coup d'état*'. In 1858 he overthrew Palmerston, only to combine with Palmerston in 1859 over 'a cunning resolution' to sabotage a moderate Reform settlement. Rather than a noble memorial to enlightened progress, Derby presented Russell's career as a sordid tale of selfish subterfuge.

Nonetheless, Russell prepared to step forward as Derby's successor as prime minister, bringing together those parliamentary forces he had gathered at Lichfield House twenty years before, with the added element of Peelite Conservatism. But, ominously, Palmerston cloaked himself with ambivalence. When, during Commons debate on 4 April, Russell proposed his own Reform scheme, a £10 franchise for the counties, a £6 borough franchise, and a modest redistribution of thirty seats, Palmerston declined to endorse it. Those at Cambridge House refused to admit that 'the Derby Reform bill was a bad bill'.[317] Confusion prevailed among the opposition benches. Wood unsuccessfully canvassed Lord Grey's claims to the opposition leadership. Argyll and Clarendon also cast their eyes towards the premiership. But, as before, it was the rivalry between Palmerston and Russell that dominated speculation. By sharply attacking Whig claims to patriotic disinterestedness, Derby again relied upon his opponents' divisions to secure Conservative success.

Prior to the dissolution of parliament on Tuesday 19 April, foreign affairs, in particular Italy, did not divide the parties. All supported strict neutrality and the avoidance of any statements that might excite France, on behalf of Piedmont-Sardinia, to instigate a war against Austria. As Clarendon privately advised Cowley in Paris: 'at present no minister here could stand a week who was thought to be favourable to war'.[318] Derby was content that this seemed to be so. The government were encountering difficulties in securing foreign agreement to a Congress. Austria was making the disarmament of Piedmont-Sardinia, as well as France and Austria as urged by Britain, a prior condition to negotiation. Austrian insistence encouraged France to adopt a more intransigent attitude. Gloomy reports from Cowley in Paris led Malmesbury to expect war as almost certain. The French refusal to urge Piedmont-Sardinia to disarm was interpreted by Derby as a cynical attempt by Napoleon III to scuttle the Congress, while preserving a pacific pose. When the Piedmontese Ambassador, Emmanuel d'Azeglio, complained to Malmesbury of an Austrian dispatch insulting to Piedmont-Sardinia, Malmesbury saw it as 'fresh proof of the insincerity of France'.[319]

In the Lords debate on Italy, on Monday 18 April, Malmesbury reiterated Austria's rights by conquest, inheritance, and treaty to the province of Lombardy. But he recognized a legitimate cause of complaint arising from Austrian interference in other Italian states.[320] He acknowledged the strong feeling in Britain in favour of Piedmont-Sardinia's assimilation of her own independent institutions. But he found it difficult to understand why France should meddle in the question. In seeking a Congress, the government was making every effort to avert a war that would be 'a theatre for the dreams of the wildest theorists and the most unprincipled adventurers'. Derby supported Malmesbury with the pronouncement that neutrality, as the object pursued by his cabinet, had to be an armed neutrality. The chances of peace would be immeasurably strengthened if it was known that Britain would not remain a passive observer of any events in which her honour was involved.[321] Clarendon had already privately shared with Malmesbury his approval of the government's Italian policy.[322] In the Lords, Clarendon made a friendly speech. To the Queen, Derby reported that Clarendon had succeeded in 'laying down, in point of fact, every principle to which we had adhered'.[323] The debate, Malmesbury concluded, 'was altogether in our favour'.[324]

Consensus over Italian affairs effectively constrained both Russell and Palmerston. In a speech in London on Friday 15 April, Russell dwelt on Reform, declaring in a postscript that he had no reason for distrust with respect to Malmesbury's Italian policy.[325] Similarly, Palmerston, although he believed insistence on disarmament prior to a Congress was 'putting the cart before the horse', shared the government's desire to preserve peace.[326] Further Commons debate on foreign policy on Monday 18 April affirmed a broad agreement. But the following day dramatic diplomatic events shattered this consensus. On Tuesday 19 April, Malmesbury learnt of Piedmont-Sardinia's agreement to disarmament as a precondition to participation in a Congress.[327] But Austria, unaware of Piedmont-Sardinia's sudden compliance, the same day sent an ultimatum to Turin demanding disarmament in three days or else open hostilities would ensue. Advised by the French to give a defiant reply, Piedmont-Sardinia portrayed the Austrian ultimatum as an insult. As gloom descended on the diplomatic corps in London, preparations on the Continent for war were immediately begun.[328]

Austria's untimely diplomatic blunder immediately cast her as the aggressor. It also threw a damaging light, in retrospect, on earlier British ministerial statements, made in the belief that France would prove the instigator of hostilities. As Aberdeen observed, 'the tables are altogether turned' and Napoleon III, 'who was preparing for war without the shadow of a pretext', now assumed the part of an injured innocent.[329] Palmerston quickly seized on the apparent misguidedness of the ministry's policy. Before 19 April ministers were 'open-mouthed about the aggressive attitude of France and Sardinia, about to pounce on the innocent lamb of Austria'.[330] It now appeared, he declared, that 'Austria is the aggressor, and it is Austria that is fully prepared.' Even so, Palmerston found it hard to believe that the Austrian government would 'be so insane as to begin hostilities'.[331] The Viennese ultimatum dramatically wrong-footed the Derby cabinet. It transformed the Italian question into a partisan issue, exposing the ministry to hostile censure.

Parliament dissolved in mid-April with the government delivering definitive statements of their foreign policy within the common assumptions then prevailing. Three days later, with the flawed nature of those assumptions apparently shown, hostile electoral addresses were pronounced on dramatically altered diplomatic circumstances. In London, on Saturday 23 and Monday 25 April, Russell delivered speeches saying little about Reform. He now spoke at length on Italy. It appeared that Derby's professed 'armed neutrality', Lord John asserted, disguised a pro-Austrian policy.[332] Britain, alongside France, he continued, should support the desire of the Italian people for liberty and freedom. Derby quickly responded to Russell's Liberal clarion call. At the Mansion House, on Easter Monday

25 April, Derby publicly criticized Austria for opening hostilities and reaffirmed his government's policy of strict, though armed, neutrality.[333] He pointedly disclaimed Russell's accusation of ministers hoping to take the part of Austria in the impending conflict. That, at one point in his speech, in his eagerness to establish that he did not harbour strong pro-Austrian sympathies, Derby described Vienna's action as 'criminal', however, was regarded by some as an excessive condemnation. But the following day Derby reported to Malmesbury that he had been '*very* well received' and that 'the country is all for peace—almost *à tout prix*'.[334]

Palmerston had drafted his hustings speech on 7 April. It contained 'no foam or fury' and 'little more than the constitutional question as to whether the government ought to have resigned rather than dissolved parliament'.[335] After 19 April, however, he rapidly rewrote his speech, haranguing the cabinet for diplomatic incompetence and largely concentrating on the Italian question. Aberdeen recognized Palmerston's revised speech as a 'brilliant stroke' which, by shifting his opposition onto the issue of Italy, offered an isolated Gladstone justification for joining him.[336] Privately, Derby informed the Queen that by sending the ultimatum Austria deprived herself of all claims to the support or countenance of England.[337] A formal protest was sent to Vienna, while Piedmont-Sardinia was advised to appeal to the Protocol of Paris. Malmesbury believed there was 'not a pin to choose between the merits of the antagonists'.[338] But the sudden turn of events enabled Russell and Palmerston to portray the government's policy of neutrality as a cloak for pro-Austrian partiality.

As Russell and Palmerston drew the question of Italy into the arena of antagonistic debate, fears grew of a hostile Franco-Russian alliance threatening British interests. In late April, Derby encouraged Pakington to undertake further naval preparations so as to discourage an anti-Austrian alliance between Paris and Moscow,[339] although the British Ambassador in Moscow, Sir John Crampton, was assured that Russia did not wish, nor was prepared for, involvement in the war. Popular fears in Britain of a French invasion prompted the Volunteer Rifle Movement, with members of the public coming forward to train with arms, the mood being caught by Tennyson's poem 'Riflemen Form!', printed in *The Times* on 9 May. Three days later the War Office gave official sanction to the Volunteer Movement. A panic collapse at the Stock Exchange heightened the sense of crisis. But Derby's Mansion House speech allowed those who wished to do so to claim that a domestic consensus survived. He believed that 'Austria's intolerable stupidity has completely turned the scale.'[340] Tellingly, Ellice believed that Britain's position in the Italian crisis 'was equally well stated by Derby in his amended speech', as 'by John Russell in his excellent speech to the electors in the City. There seems no difference of opinion with respect to a national policy.'[341] *The Times* praised Derby for earnestly labouring for peace, even though he found that, in return, the antagonists only prepared themselves for war.[342] It was left to Russell and his supporters, such as Graham, to insist that recent events required the government to be brought to book for wanting in both sincerity and firmness. But Newcastle believed that 'the certainty of war would be in the government's favour where parties are equally divided—so many thinking it right to support *any* government at the commencement of a war'.[343]

As the general election began, Derby remained hopeful. Matters were 'going on as well as could possibly be expected, or even better'. He advised Disraeli that 'the Whigs are disgusted with Johnny and hanging back. We must avoid irritating them by supporting radicals against them—at least in England.'[344] It was noted that, under Jolliffe, Spofforth, and Rose's direction, the Conservative activists in the constituencies had been working more effectively than their opponents in the registration courts, while the dispensing of that patronage which came with office had been exercised with care. In April 1859, for example, three major contributors to the Conservative election fund were raised to the peerage, Sir Charles Morgan as Lord Tredegar, Tatton Egerton as Lord Egerton, and Colonel George Wyndham as Lord Leconfield. At Aylesbury, Disraeli reinforced the ministry's electoral message. Conservatives offered moderation, stability, and good government in both foreign and domestic affairs. In his electoral address Pakington presented the voters with a simple choice, between reform and progressive improvement on one hand and democratic innovation and revolutionary change on the other. On Saturday 30 April at King's Lynn, Stanley portrayed moderate parliamentary Reform as part of the Conservatives' broader agenda of good government and constitutional stability. The prospective European conflict, he declared, was the product of the ambition of a few scheming men, in particular Napoleon III. The independence of Italy was nothing more than a convenient plea, seized upon by a frustrated Liberal opposition. A broad consensus over Britain's foreign policy, he insisted, still survived. But electoral disappointment followed.

On Monday 2 May, Derby noted that 'many of the elections have been singularly unfortunate; the government candidates having been defeated in 11 places by less than ten votes'.[345] Nonetheless, he hoped for a gain of at least twenty-five seats, giving the Conservatives rather more than 300 Commons votes. To these might be added a number of 'independent

Liberals' who had promised their support. As the election closed in mid-May, Jolliffe calculated a total of 306 Conservative MPs, a striking gain of thirty-one seats.[346] Against this tally he listed 349 members of a disunited opposition. The final result, therefore, represented an electoral gain for the Conservatives. In England and Wales an additional twenty-three seats had been won, eleven of these successes secured in those small boroughs upon which Jolliffe, Rose, and Spofforth had focused their resources. A further nine seats gained in Ireland vindicated the government's concession to Catholics, as well as bearing testimony to the efforts of the Irish Central Conservative Society. The fifty-five Irish seats won by Conservatives in May 1859, twenty-six of those seats outside Ulster, marked a high point of Conservative electoral success in Ireland during the Victorian period. Both Cardinal Wiseman and Bishop MacHale of Tuam called on Catholic voters to support Conservative candidates. In his election handbill for the electors of the city of Waterford, John Blake, an Irish Reformer who had voted for the government against Russell's motion, quoted extracts from a letter sent by Cardinal Wiseman stating that, with regard to their sacred interests, he hoped that Catholic electors would not vote for a change of ministry.[347] From Phoenix Park, Lord Naas worked closely with influential Irish Catholics. Although, contrary to what some newspapers suggested, the ministry had no 'compact' with Cardinal Wiseman, Derby was pleased that the Conservatives had received 'a considerable amount of R.C. support'.[348]

The Conservatives, however, were still short of a clear Commons majority, although the rancour dividing non-Conservatives might induce some to join the ministerial side. Derby judged that 'very much will depend on the skill with which we play our game'.[349] He encouraged his Irish Lord Lieutenant, Lord Eglinton, to appoint 'one of two R.C.s even to second rate offices', a move which would be 'of considerable advantage' to the government. 'The Irish "independents" *want* nothing for themselves and would forfeit their positions by accepting anything: but they do want an answer to their co-religionists who taunt them with their support of a government who, as it is represented, zealously excludes R.C.s from offices of profit.'[350] Courting the Irish Catholic vote, however, brought with it the danger of Ultra Tory fury. Walpole, Newdegate, and Beresford long suspected Disraeli of pursuing 'an Irish Papist alliance'.[351] The strong anti-Semitic views of Walpole's ambitious wife, daughter of the assassinated prime minister Spencer Perceval, intensified their distrust. Diehard sensibility might yet offset Irish Catholic support.

Palmerston continued to be the most acceptable recruit from outside the party. He remained the most able Commons Conservative leader the party never had. On 3 May, Disraeli privately suggested to Palmerston that, if he joined Derby, bringing with him twenty or thirty MPs, the government would have an absolute majority. 'The union between Lord Derby and yourself would establish an enduring government.'[352] Disraeli invited Palmerston to state his terms. As well as influence over foreign policy, Disraeli indicated, Palmerston could propose his own Reform scheme, which the Conservatives would willingly support. Palmerston would be 'entire master of the situation'. Independently, Graham recognized the seductive attractions for Palmerston of such a proposition, anticipating the union of Derby and Palmerston as 'the most probable solution of existing difficulties': 'Whether Lord John and [Palmerston] will come to terms is more doubtful. But Palmerston, *with Tory support*, will be strong enough to conduct the government without [Russell].'[353] There was not, Graham concluded, 'much to choose between Derby and Palmerston: the one was a Whig and became a Tory; the other for half a century has been a Tory at heart and is so still'. Finding everything 'in a mess', Ellice separately concurred that the likely outcome would be 'some understanding between the Conservatives and Whigs under Palmerston'.[354] Failure to join the Conservatives, Disraeli suggested to Palmerston, would only leave him the unpalatable option of membership of a Russell cabinet—an uncomfortable and solitary predicament.[355]

Yet, in his brief reply to Disraeli on Tuesday 3 May, Palmerston politely refused the Conservative invitation.[356] This reflected Palmerston's growing hope of resuming power on more favourable terms, if events were allowed to unfold. He declined to commit himself prematurely. But parallel conversations between Malmesbury and Clarendon sustained the prospect of centrist merger. On Thursday 12 May, Clarendon visited Malmesbury for a 'long conversation about parties'.[357] Believing Russell and Palmerston would never combine, Clarendon 'agreed cordially' with Malmesbury that 'it would be a great benefit if moderate Whigs and Conservatives would join—there was little difference if any between them'. For good measure Clarendon 'abused Palmerston's speech at Tiverton'. Disraeli, meanwhile, sounded out the 'independent Liberal' Edward Horsman and pointed to the MP for Tynemouth, William Lindsay, as 'the type of some dozen men of doubtful Liberal allegiance' who might be brought over to the Conservative side.[358] Following a confidential meeting with Disraeli in early May, Lindsay acted as an intermediary, ascertaining Roebuck's requirements over Reform as a basis for supporting the ministry. A private statement of support for the Conservative government, drawn up by Lindsay on 23 May and shown to Disraeli, was signed by seventeen opposition MPs, with another six MPs indicating their assent. The signatories included Irish MPs such as George Bowyer, Matthew Corbally, Edward McEvoy, and John Maguire, as well as independent radicals such as John Roebuck, John Cobbett, William Lindsay, and Joseph Crook.

With little enthusiasm Derby made one more overture to Gladstone. The exchange had the tired air of a necessary ritual, in which neither invested much expectation of success. Disraeli suggested the India Office might absorb Gladstone's 'superfluous energies'.[359] But Derby waited until Thursday 19 May before writing to Gladstone and inviting a private discussion on public affairs. Privately, he doubted whether Gladstone was 'a desirable acquisition', as his 'extreme opinions on Italian affairs' would prove 'very embarrassing'.[360] In a characteristically non-committal reply, Gladstone declared himself ready 'to speak without reserve' to Derby, but questioned the value of such discussion.[361] Derby did not pursue the matter further, taking Gladstone's ambivalence as his cue promptly to drop communication. As he commented to Disraeli, 'it would have been useless to waste time by an unmeaning conversation, leading to nothing. I own I hardly regret it.'[362] Palmerston and the moderate Whigs promised a more acceptable accession of parliamentary strength. Gladstone could be left as the 'one remaining Ishmael in the House of Commons'.[363] As a postlude, in a continuation of his ineffectual private campaign to dislodge Malmesbury from the Foreign Office, Disraeli proposed inviting Lord Elgin, who had served as a popular Governor General of Canada from 1846 to 1855 and had headed the special mission to China in 1857 to negotiate a treaty following the *Arrow* incident, to become Secretary of State for Foreign Affairs. Derby immediately quashed the proposal. It was 'of great importance', he replied, 'to have a man there who has at his fingers' end the whole thread of the complicated negotiations in which we have been engaged'.[364] Another attempt to prise apart Derby and Malmesbury signally failed.

> And threat'nest now to wrest from me the prize
> I labour'd hard to win.
>
> (Derby, *The Iliad of Homer*, i. 9)

June 1859 was a landmark in Victorian parliamentary politics, those strategic factors shaping the party struggles of the 1850s coming to a head. Since

Peel's accidental death in 1850, Peelite, Whig, Liberal, and radical relations had revolved around the powerful rival ambitions of Palmerston and Russell. Derby refused to believe in the long-term compatibility of Peelite self-regard, patrician Whig progressivism, Liberal reform, and radical enthusiasm. He forsook Protectionism and subdued militant Anglicanism, so as to welcome the dejected refugees of the divided forces opposing him. A measure of his success was the seventy backbench Peelite MPs who, having voted for Corn Law repeal, rejoined the Conservatives after 1846. In office, he demonstrated that the Conservatives possessed safe hands to which to entrust the nation's prosperity and stability. As premier, since February 1858, he showed the Conservatives capable of responsible government. The reward he looked to, in May 1859, was an accession of moderate opposition support, leaving advanced Liberals and radicals to be led by Russell. The parliamentary arithmetic was beguilingly close. An additional twenty to thirty Commons votes would give the Conservatives a Commons majority. Clarendon's confidences, Peelite demise, Whig malaise, Liberal confusion, and radical division gave the aspiration substance. Disraeli's confidential communication with Lindsay and Roebuck, of which Derby remained unaware, encouraged the acquisition of a critical number of opposition votes. But, like the Greek god Tantalus, son of Zeus, who, for revealing divine secrets, was condemned to prolonged starvation surrounded by succulent grapes that withdrew from his reach, the imminent object of Derby's desire eluded his grasp.

In June 1859 the unlikely alliance of leading Peelites, Whigs, Liberals, and radicals, which Derby discounted, took shape. This was the progressive coalition which Russell had been anticipating, promising his triumphant personal apotheosis. But the events of early 1859 dashed Russell's hopes. Derby's cabinet proposed a more moderate Reform Bill than Russell expected. Russell pre-empted general discussion with a motion focusing debate on the borough freehold franchise. But radicals, such as Roebuck and Bright, refused to endorse Russell's authority. Palmerston supported Russell's motion in a manner intended to scuttle its author's ambitions. Forced into an election and quickly taking advantage of unexpected European events, Russell took up the lofty cry of Italian liberty. But he failed to dislodge an electoral preoccupation with Reform. His worsening plight brought the engaging subplot of Palmerston's intentions back into centre stage. By late May, Russell faced a critical challenge. The longer his difficulties persisted, the better Palmerston's prospects became. Intense opposition negotiation during late May and early June eroded

Russell's position further. Radical differences, Bright's silence, Graham's ill health, and Gladstone's ambivalence critically weakened Russell's hand. He entered discussion insistent upon a radical presence in the next government and his own freedom on all matters connected with the acceptance of office. After meeting Russell on Friday 20 May, however, Palmerston applied increasing pressure. Other leading Whigs and Liberals also pressed for unification. Russell had 'a vocation for splendid failures', *The Times* scathingly commented on 24 May, there being nobody who can smash his own cause 'with such heroic grace and facility'.[365]

While in late May busy intermediaries journeyed between Pembroke Lodge and Cambridge House, Derby's cabinet prepared for a Commons confrontation. The radical Roebuck informed the Conservatives that Brooks's was 'in open revolt' and the government's prospects 'good'.[366] Dubbed 'the Diogenes of Sheffield', the pugnacious Roebuck was too irritable and vain, ministers surmised, to play second fiddle to Russell and Bright, a judgement confirmed by Roebuck's confidential communications, via Lindsay, with Disraeli. At Milford, on 29 May, Roebuck declared Palmerston's posturing as a Liberal to be 'false and hollow', and the prospect of Palmerston and Russell combining 'a great mischief'.[367] At Leeds the Liberal MP Sir John Ramsden stated his intention not to vote for the dismissal of Derby's government, because the divided state of the opposition leadership did not offer the prospect of a stronger ministry.[368] Ministers discussed, meanwhile, approaches to Lowe and Horsman. Gladstone was advised that support for a motion of no confidence would be incompatible with his earlier support for Conservative Reform. At the same time, ministerial conversations with Conservative backbenchers sought to ensure that the Commons party remained disciplined and that no Ultra Tory splinter groups disrupted the government's ranks. Ralph Earle reassured the Chancellor that '*the game is still alive*'.[369]

A series of cabinet meetings at the end of May, under Derby's firm guidance, shaped the policy with which the government agreed to meet the new parliament. On Friday 27 May ministers decided not to raise any loans, so keeping financial policy in line with Gladstonian practice. At subsequent cabinet meetings, on Monday 30 and Tuesday 31 May, it was agreed to avoid any detailed reference to Reform in the Queen's Speech, but to express a non-committal readiness to consider a new scheme if it seemed desirable. If the bulk of moderate Liberal opinion in the Commons deemed the lowering of the borough franchise to be a necessary part of an acceptable Reform measure, the government would not put their face against it. It was also decided to counter the general impression, industriously cultivated by the opposition, that the court and government were pro-Austrian in their foreign policy. Disraeli was insistent that all 'distrust in the public mind' on this matter should be 'averted', so as to prevent the opposition from raising 'a colourable point on Austrian bias, or imminence of war from our policy'.[370] Derby informed the Queen that the Austro-French war was 'one subject on which, more than any other, the mind of the country was unanimous' in favour of 'an entire abstinence from participation in the struggle now going on in Italy'.[371] The Queen's Speech pledged the cabinet to strict neutrality, as long as the conflict remained confined to the present combatants. Gladstonian finance, compliance on Reform, and strict neutrality over Italy, he hoped, would wreck an opposition merger. On 1 June, Derby enjoyed a brief respite from his political labours by travelling to Epsom for the Derby. But, by the following day, he was again back in London busily preparing for the critical contest that awaited the opening of the new parliament. When, on Sunday 5 June, Clarendon again called on Malmesbury, the prospect of 'fusion', in the event of an opposition attack failing, was discussed, Malmesbury observing that the opposition appeared to be being pushed by its radical tail.[372]

On the eve of parliament meeting, however, the opposition mustered at Willis's Rooms on St James's Street to avow their unity of purpose. About 280 Whigs, Liberals, and radicals met, during the evening of Monday 6 June, to be addressed by Russell, Palmerston, Herbert, Milner Gibson, Ellice, and Bright. That, at the beginning of proceedings, Palmerston had to help the diminutive Russell up onto the stage was a moment of poignant symbolism, greeted with sarcastic cheers and droll laughter from the floor. Palmerston and Russell declared their readiness to cooperate, without prejudging who might succeed as premier. It was proposed to move a motion of no confidence on the Address, as Peel had done in 1841, without pledging any commitments on either Reform or foreign policy. Such a broad motion, it was hoped, would accommodate all shades of anti-Conservative feeling. Only Roebuck, Horsman, and Lindsay spoke against a motion of no confidence. Roebuck lobbed his shell into the gathering by rejecting the possibility of any cordial combination among the sections of the opposition and doubting whether Russell and Palmerston could cooperate in the same cabinet.[373] Palmerston adopted a smile of half-astonished curiosity as Roebuck spoke; Russell merely sighed deeply. By an overwhelming majority, those present endorsed an immediate attack on Derby's ministry.

The Conservatives consoled themselves 'with the certainty that the division must be so close, that the successful Whigs will be able to form no government which will have a certain working majority'.[374] There was still much to play for. However, the defeat of the Austrians by French and Piedmontese forces at the bloody Battle of Magenta on 4 June, and the Austrian loss of the plains of Lombardy, complicated the state of foreign affairs. The odds on the Conservatives defeating a no-confidence motion appeared to be lengthening. Derby and Disraeli decided to cut short debate on the Address so as to force a quick vote on an unprepared opposition. When the Commons met to debate the Address on Tuesday 7 June, Disraeli ensured all Conservative MPs were present. As seventeen new opposition MPs had not yet taken their seats, he hoped to catch the enemy napping. The young Whig Lord Hartington dutifully proposed a motion of no confidence that evening. Disraeli responded by calling for an immediate division. This manoeuvre was reported by the *Saturday Review* as a 'brilliant piece of trickery in the style of Vivian Grey'.[375] With Conservatives declining to speak, the opposition whips frantically scoured the Commons tearooms enlisting MPs to keep the debate open. By a close margin they eventually secured an adjournment. So deliberation was prolonged and Disraeli's tactical manoeuvre foiled. A dramatic set-piece debate then followed over the two successive evenings of Thursday 9 and Friday 10 June.

Foreign policy was now the focus of attack. Palmerston accused the government of an alarming ignorance. Ministers had believed France and Piedmont-Sardinia would instigate war against Austria, whereas the reverse had proved the case. Bright also devoted the greater part of his speech to foreign affairs, citing a general European suspicion of pro-Austrian bias in Malmesbury's diplomacy. To the surprise of the ministerial front bench, Horsman also announced his support for Hartington's motion on the grounds of foreign policy. Clearly Italy now offered a bond of union among opposition groups deeply divided over Reform. Graham denounced the recent dissolution which had risked the national interest, postponed measures of importance, and forestalled decisions upon 'questions of the gravest kind',[376] while Milner Gibson expressed radical distrust of the government's vague professions on Reform. The trial of the government by the national jury of parliament, *The Times* concluded, was one of character, conducted with little reserve. 'The winnowing machine has been plied hard, and the chaff and the dust have been flying about, till it seemed as if nothing would be left on the barn-floor,' as there occurred 'a great ripping up of reputations on all sides'.[377]

Through the haze rumours swirled around Westminster about the uncertain outcome of the debate. Clearly moderate Liberal and Irish

Brigade votes would determine the result. Horsman's speech indicated the loss of some potential government support. Lindsay, however, privately affirmed that there were '15 or 16 of us who are determined to pull you through, but you must give us time—we cannot vote with you without making speeches for our constituents'.[378] Disraeli consequently kept debate open and Lindsay duly declared to the Commons that, as an advocate for Reform, he would best discharge his duty to his Liberal constituents by voting against Hartington's motion. Rapturous cheers from the Conservative benches accompanied his statement. Safe, yet substantial, Reform, Lindsay argued, was more likely to pass at the hands of the party now in power, than if proposed by Russell. By ignoring Palmerston, Lindsay presented a stark choice between the moderate Derby and the unpredictable Russell. The prime minister, meanwhile, sought to keep the Irish Brigade up to the mark. Together with Jolliffe, he compiled a list of forty-four opposition MPs who might support them in the forthcoming division.[379] Of the Irish Brigade, Derby counted on Blake, Bowyer, Brady, Ennis, McEvoy, and Maguire as certain votes. Combined with Lindsay's dissident band, the government, with Irish support, might yet survive a concerted Liberal and radical onslaught.

During debate on Friday 10 June, Roebuck extended a radical hand of friendship to the Conservative government. The opposition, he declared, were riven with deep differences over Reform. The Conservative cabinet, he continued, would introduce as satisfactory a Reform measure as either Palmerston or Russell, with the additional merit of certain acceptance by the Lords. In an impassioned response, Russell reiterated Liberal wisdom on Reform and delivered a markedly moderate statement on foreign affairs. He characterized the failed Conservative Reform Bill as a regression from the 1832 Reform Act, diminishing popular strength in the constituencies. Britain's diplomatic influence in Europe had been weakened and Conservative ministers were not sufficiently competent to maintain the strict neutrality desired by the country. Such failure, he declared, warranted a verdict of no confidence. Derby was now experiencing alternating confidence and doubt. On Wednesday 8 June he optimistically observed that 'the hopes of a majority on the part of the opposition are not as high as they were', while Gladstone's course was 'said to be unknown even to himself!'[380] The following day, however, he felt that the 'junction' between the sections of the Liberal opposition made it difficult to achieve what he earnestly desired, 'a reconstruction of the government on such a basis as should include some of the leading *Whigs*, as contradistinguished from the more advanced Liberals'.[381] It now appeared that even men as moderate as

Lord Euston were 'prepared to join in overthrowing the government'. In any event, although the 'majority either way will be very small … the result will be very decisive'.

By Friday 10 June the tone of the government whips in the Commons was 'less sanguine'.[382] At the eleventh hour, Disraeli's ingenuity gave a new form to reconstruction. Unable to 'tell how this thing will exactly end' and certain that sending 'for Palmerston or John Russell is no solution of the difficulty', there existed an opportunity 'for a third man'. Disraeli bluntly suggested to Derby that there was 'only one man … who could combine the whole of the Conservative party and would immediately obtain a considerable section of the opposition. *It is Stanley*. He would reconstruct the cabinet: which you cannot.' His own and Derby's 'united withdrawal', Disraeli proposed, 'would give authority and sanction to Stanley' and 'would entirely sell all the Whigs'.[383] Clarendon could replace Malmesbury and a considerable body of Liberal votes would be secured. The advantage of such a course, Disraeli concluded, would be that, despite their being out of office, both Derby and he would have influence over the new premier. It 'is better than Mr Addington, for Stanley is a clever fellow, and his Pitt and Dundas would be his father and his friend'. But neither Stanley's temperament nor opposition intention lent real credibility to Disraeli's fancy and yet another attempt by Disraeli to oust Malmesbury from the Foreign Office failed. Another facet of Conservative frontbench anxiety was revealed by Malmesbury's private advice to Clarendon that 'a large number of Conservatives' might support a Palmerston government, if the 'opposition leaders do not in debate use language towards the party which would make it dishonourable for them to quit their ranks—in fact a bridge should not be lost sight of'.[384] For good measure, Malmesbury added that 'he was dead sick of office, which he only retained out of deference to Derby'.

After three nights of impassioned debate, on Friday 10 June, preparations were made for the division on Hartington's motion. By 2 a.m. Cairns, winding up the debate for the government, was met with weary cries of 'Divide, divide'. Granville thought it 'almost certain that there will be a majority against the government', although 'Lord John is still supposed to decline serving under Palmerston' and there was 'a good deal of heart-burning already'.[385] As a vote was called there were 'many anxious faces flitting about the doorways'.[386] In the crammed division lobbies, packed by a full Commons, 323 MPs supported Hartington's want of confidence motion, while 310 MPs stood by the government. The influence of Lindsay and Roebuck was revealed by the presence of fourteen opposition

MPs in the ministerial lobby. Horsman, Lindsay, and Roebuck, as well as Gladstone, voted against Hartington's motion. The effectiveness of Eglinton and Naas's regime in Ireland was evident in the fact that sixty-three out of 102 Irish MPs voted for Derby's government. The Conservatives had remained disciplined and united. But the victory of Palmerston and Russell, though close, was decisive. As the announcement of the vote was greeted with loud cheers from the opposition, in the lobby outside, Malmesbury noted, the Piedmontese Ambassador, Azeglio, threw his hat into the air and jumped into the arms of the French attaché. 'We have now been turned out by a mere trial of strength,' Malmesbury concluded. 'Nothing serious has been brought against us, only vague and general accusations of having mismanaged Reform and *not preventing war*.'[387]

The factious behaviour of the opposition in 1859 left a livid scar on Conservative consciousness. In subsequent speeches Derby constantly referred to the unpatriotic conduct of the Whigs, Liberals, and radicals in ejecting him from office, upon what he insisted was a partisan pretext. He evoked this grievance by way of contrast with the forbearing and patriotic behaviour of the Conservatives. The Liberal party had pursued power rather than principle, choosing selfish advantage over the national interest. By doing so, they revealed those narrow purposes which lurked behind their pious rhetoric. As a result, a moderate settlement of Reform was dashed, an unwarranted slur cast on Conservative foreign policy, and the dangerous forces of radicalism given new life.

A dejected cabinet, called by Derby on the morning of Saturday 11 June, quickly agreed on resignation as the only course open to them. Derby seemed, Malmesbury noted, exhausted by incessant labour and worn out by repeated attacks of gout.[388] By midday he was with the Queen tendering the resignation of his ministry. He seemed tired and 'much agitated', but informed his monarch that the Conservatives 'had never been more united ... and would therefore be powerful'.[389] Victoria appeared genuinely distressed at his ejection from office. As a mark of her esteem she conferred on him the Order of the Garter, an honour bestowed as a mark of personal regard by the monarch. The Queen also conferred the Order of the Bath on Malmesbury and Pakington. In 1851 Derby had found the Queen and Prince Consort suspicious of him, a feeling he attributed to the influence of Peel, who had tainted their views. By 1859, after holding the premiership twice and demonstrating the moderation of Conservative government, he enjoyed the hard-earned respect of the Queen, who treated him with increasing affection. *The Times* concurred that Derby had been a great ornament of the House of Commons and was now a great ornament of the House of Lords.[390] The winning over of royal support, aided by Victoria's dislike of Palmerston and Russell, was a significant achievement.

By 1859 Derby had also restored the Conservative majority in the House of Lords. In 1846 only 146 Conservative peers followed him in opposing Corn Law repeal. That the ecclesiastical peers, twenty-six archbishops and bishops from the Church of England and from the Church of Ireland, were reluctant to follow his lead after 1846 exacerbated his difficulties. In 1850 he estimated that there were about forty Peelite peers, led by Aberdeen, who held the balance of power in the Upper House. Through the 1850s, assisted by his chief whip, the conscientious Lord Colville, he devoted considerable effort to marshalling support. Among the Scottish and Irish peers, in particular, through the efforts of lords Redesdale, Eglinton, and Naas, Conservative votes were carefully consolidated. By 1859 these labours were rewarded by his effective control over Conservative peers, who, partly because a number of Peelite peers had rejoined his party, enjoyed a majority in the Upper House. After 1859 he was to secure a number of critical victories over the Liberals in the Lords. He used this majority carefully over the Paper Duties Bill in May 1860, the Danish censure motion of July 1864, and the Roman Catholic Oath Bill of June 1865. But it had been a resource often denied him during the early 1850s. This, as he commented to the Queen in June 1859, complemented the greater unity and discipline of Conservative MPs in the Commons. In July 1858 Malmesbury observed that Conservative MPs were now 'better disciplined than ... even in Peel's time'.[391] Granville reminded Palmerston, in June 1859, that 'the close attendance of [Derby's] supporters both in and out of office was very remarkable. This was probably owing not merely to a stricter system of discipline, which is characteristic of the Conservative party, but also to the great personal ascendancy of [Derby].'[392]

Derby returned to opposition in June 1859 with a united party behind him. Promising young talent, Stanley, Cairns, Carnarvon, Gathorne Hardy, Sotheron-Estcourt, and Northcote, had gained valuable ministerial experience. Moderation had been affirmed as the keynote of official Conservatism. It was no longer possible to dismiss his party as devoid of ability or the tool of reactionary sentiment. But the careful neutrality maintained by Derby in foreign policy had been dramatically subverted in mid-April by Austrian precipitancy. Hastily improvised accusations of pro-Austrian Conservative bias and the lofty cry of greater Italian autonomy brought together leading Peelites, Whigs, Liberals, and radicals, who were sharply divided over parliamentary Reform. On 11 June the Queen sent for Granville and charged him with the formation of a government. Granville's brokership was defeated, however, by Palmerston and Russell's differences. Reluctantly, the following day the Queen sent for Palmerston, who undertook to form an administration with or without Russell.

It was against this backdrop that the end of Derby's second ministry added a final footnote to the personal resentment between Disraeli and Malmesbury. Throughout the previous months Disraeli had drip-fed Derby with suggestions of Malmesbury's inadequacies. The Foreign Secretary, meanwhile, had informed Disraeli on Saturday 2 June that in three days' time a Blue Book would be published conclusively refuting unfair allegations of pro-Austrian bias in Conservative diplomacy. Malmesbury presented the Blue Book to the Lords, but inexplicably Disraeli never produced it in the Commons. The French and Italian correspondence it contained, Malmesbury insisted, would have saved the government. Why Disraeli chose not to present this correspondence to the Commons remains a mystery. At least twelve or fourteen opposition MPs would have voted for the government on Hartington's motion, Malmesbury subsequently reported, if they had read the correspondence before 10 June. This crucial shift of votes would have secured a majority for the ministry. Clarendon affirmed that Disraeli's failure to present the Blue Book lost the Conservatives the division.[393] The Duke of Bedford observed that 'Malmesbury's despatches appear to be liked, and to have raised his reputation.'[394] *The Times* agreed, after scrutinizing the diplomatic correspondence of Derby's government, that 'the charge of endangering English neutrality has been unjustly brought against Lord Malmesbury and the rest of the Tory ministry'.[395] Returning by train to London from Windsor, on Saturday 18 June, after surrendering their seals of office, Malmesbury's colleagues all praised the Blue Book, except Disraeli, 'who never said a word'.[396] Sullen silence was an appropriate conclusion to the hostile official relations between Disraeli and Malmesbury, as Disraeli reserved to himself a loyalty that should have gone to his party.

There was, therefore, an unacknowledged irony when, a few weeks later, Disraeli declared to 300 Conservative peers and MPs, gathered at the Merchant Taylors' Hall, that 'party government and parliamentary government were identical—no party, no parliament'.[397] Without strong parliamentary parties, he pronounced, there could be no barrier against the authority of the Crown or defence against the overbearing ambition of a minister. As Derby and Malmesbury well knew, Disraeli's extolling of party discipline was a slender constraint on his own self-interested behaviour. What was free of irony was Derby's preceding declaration, at the same occasion, that the Conservatives, though defeated, were not disgraced, discouraged, or disheartened.[398] They were returning to opposition, after pursuing moderation in both domestic and foreign policy while in office, united, determined, and resolute. As *The Times* acknowledged, 'the stable organisation of [Derby's] party under such violent changes of opinion and so many disasters is not a little attributable to the steady good faith with which [Derby] has treated his adherents'.[399]

CHAPTER 5

Watching and Waiting: 1859–1866

We ought to adhere, as far as possible, to our policy of making every *obstructive* motion come from the Liberal side of the House.

(Derby to Pakington, 28 May 1860)

... our policy this year as well as last must be the 'masterly inactivity' which was found so successful.

(Derby to Malmesbury, 4 December 1860)

Parties are united by shared animosities as much as by common aspirations. Prior to 1859 Whigs and Liberals displayed an easy contempt for Conservatism and an anxious disparagement of radicalism. In turn, despite their differences, radicals shared an abhorrence of Whig condescension and the pious phrases that supported oligarchic Whig assumptions. During the 1850s the Peelite remnant sustained a self-congratulatory sense of superiority, enshrined in the cult of their dead leader. But, by June 1859, such attitudes no longer offered an effective means of defining a common Liberal purpose. Following the Willis's Rooms meeting radicals accommodated themselves to being in power alongside Whigs; prominent Peelites were forced to step down from their pedestal of high-minded independence; and Whigs recognized that holding office required sharing ministerial authority with others. Long-standing personal rivalries, however, continued to plague Liberal relations. Russell refused the relegation of serving under Granville as prime minister. As a result, Palmerston was asked by the Queen to form an administration which, as Clarendon described it, was 'a great bundle of sticks'.[1] Palmerston recognized that it was necessary 'to construct the government upon a different principle and ... out of a larger range of political parties'.[2] This rich mix of ministerial ingredients appeared to Derby an inherently unstable blend.

Derby resumed opposition in June 1859 with a keen sense of expectation. Disraeli believed that 'the difficulties of Lord Palmerston are so great, that the new ministry, instead of being formed on the boasted broad basis, will be merely a *refacimento* of the old Palmerston clique. That won't last long, and only can subsist by our support.'[3] When the Queen received the outgoing Conservative ministers at Windsor on Saturday 18 June, she too expressed her doubts about the new government being able to survive in office for long.[4] Derby's own contribution to Liberal instability was the rehabilitation of the Conservatives as a party capable of moderate government. During 1858–9 his cabinet supported the admission of practising Jews to parliament, Gladstone's fiscal settlement of 1853 was reinstated by Disraeli's budgets, the property qualification for MPs was abolished, the government of India was reformed, a conciliatory resolution of the church rates issue proposed, and legislative concessions to Catholics passed. In foreign affairs, in which Derby took a close interest, a sober *via media* eased Anglo-American tensions over central America, the Orsini crisis with France was resolved, and the *Cagliari* dispute with the Neapolitan government defused. Increased naval expenditure strengthened national defence and, during May 1859, official sanction was given to the Volunteer Movement. Only unexpected diplomatic events threw a damaging light, in retrospect, on the cabinet's Italian policy, while Russell's tactical ingenuity in April 1859 sabotaged a deliberately moderate parliamentary Reform measure. Yet lofty disdain for Conservatism was no longer a ready means of defining Liberal aims.

In June 1859 Russell insisted upon the Foreign Secretaryship, aware that Italy formed the strongest bond between the new ministers. Desperate to escape isolation, Gladstone accepted the Chancellorship of the Exchequer and crossed over the bridge to Palmerston that the Italian issue offered. The radical Milner Gibson became President of the Poor Law Board. The Peelite Duke of Newcastle and Sidney Herbert became Colonial Secretary and War Secretary respectively. Sir Charles Wood as Indian Secretary and Sir George Cornewall Lewis as Home Secretary represented moderate Liberal opinion. But, as Lord Panmure bluntly informed Palmerston, the circumstances of this new ministry were very different from his last. Palmerston's first government had been 'composed of men well known to each other in the walks of private life, having the same political aspirations, and desiring nothing from friendship as well as duty but to support you and each other'. By contrast, his new cabinet contained 'sections of all different parties ... and where that is the case you start with the seeds of disunion sown, to vegetate at some future hour.'[5] Wood confessed that 'I do not think we shall be very long lived, after that I shall make my bow, under any circumstances, for I am heartily sick of it.'[6] In all this, Malmesbury dryly confirmed, were 'the seeds of future discord'.[7]

As well as differences within the cabinet, disappointed hopes festered around it. Lord Stanley of Alderley made praiseworthy attempts to be magnanimous, the strain of this effort betraying far darker emotions. Lord Grey was furious at being excluded. Aberdeen voiced dislike of the new government's foreign policy and was 'more grumpy than formerly'.[8] Benjamin Hall identified Gladstone and Wood as the two ministers most disliked by Liberal MPs. Granville expressed his annoyance at sitting alongside Elgin and Newcastle in the Lords, rather than the excluded Lansdowne and Clarendon.[9] When, in mid-June, Granville informed the Lords that those whom Palmerston could not bring in to his cabinet had behaved in the handsomest way possible, Clarendon and Stanley of Alderley, sitting below the gangway, 'did *not* laugh—but [Broughton] saw a smirk on Derby's lips'.[10]

At a Conservative gathering in Arlington Street, on Tuesday 21 June, Derby assured his backbenchers that 'it would be easy to get a majority against the present government as large as that which turned him out'.[11] As London sweltered in record high temperatures of 90° in the shade, Derby and Disraeli were honoured at a gala dinner held at the Merchant Taylors' Hall in Threadneedle Street on Saturday 16 July, presided over by the Earl of March and attended by 300 Conservative MPs and peers. Derby, wearing the blue riband of the Garter, was received with prolonged cheering. Declaring himself proud to be the leader of such an enlightened, united, and resolute party, he pronounced the Conservatives to be defeated, but not disgraced; nor were they discouraged or disheartened.[12] His government, he observed, had been praised for its moderation in both domestic and foreign policy. Looking at the composition of Palmerston's new ministry, he believed that, if the Conservatives were to behave as factiously as Liberals and radicals had acted during the previous months, then it would not be difficult to pass a vote of no confidence, similar to the motion which had just ejected them from office. But, unlike the former opposition, he called on his party to rise above partisan pettiness, to maintain the same forbearance and steadfast unity they had displayed while in power, and to watch closely the conduct of Palmerston's motley administration. While rash government measures would be opposed in the Lords, it was in the Commons, he reminded his audience, that Conservative principles must be firmly maintained. To this end, he reiterated Peel's advice to the party in 1837: 'Register,

register, register.' Palmerston's premiership he portrayed as a temporary arrangement presaging future realignment. Indeed, Palmerston's advanced age (he was now 75 years old) forbade the premier a long term of office.

As the close of the session on 13 August approached, Stanley of Alderley noted the significance of ministerial unease. 'All this makes the Tory party stick together so much closer, and if the session had lasted three months the government might have been in trouble.'[13] Derby prepared to resume a 'masterly inactivity' intended to foster cabinet conflict. As Disraeli observed: 'We shall have to keep together a great party, as Peel had in 1835, whose strength will really increase in proportion to their inaction. But a party does not like to be inert; and to combine repose with a high tone of feeling in the troops is difficult.'[14] Nevertheless, vigilant repose was to be combined with a patriotic avoidance of factiousness.

> Then will I so by word and deed contrive
> That they may gain fresh respite from their toil.
>
> (Derby, *The Iliad of Homer*, ii. 85)

Back at Knowsley in August 1859, while engaged in shooting on his estate, Derby received an invitation to a banquet in his honour organized by local Conservatives in Liverpool. Disraeli was also asked to speak and Derby invited both Disraeli and Mary Anne to stay at Knowsley on 28 October, so that they could talk over the language they should use the following day.[15] The dinner that evening, however, was not a success. In his bantering manner Derby mockingly taunted the eccentric Mary Anne in front of the other guests, causing Disraeli deep offence. As a result, Disraeli resolved never to visit Knowsley again.

Derby's address to a loyal Liverpool audience on 29 October provided him with an opportunity to affirm the high tone of his opposition strategy. On leaving office four months earlier, he had been requested by the Queen not to use the power given to him by the nearly balanced state of parties to upset the new government while foreign uncertainties prevailed. His temperate subsequent public statements dutifully complied with this royal request, while leaving his party unfettered on any particular point of policy. The moral and material condition of the country, Derby pronounced at Liverpool, was unprecedentedly prosperous. This was evident in the soundness of national commerce and the prosperity of the working classes.

Moderate Conservative government had ensured the orderly comfort of the country.[16] Only the succession of temporary governments, subject to the caprice of half a dozen votes in the House of Commons, he warned, threatened to unsettle the nation's stability. Nor would it be to the advantage of the Conservative party to return prematurely to office without sufficient strength to maintain itself. Rather, Conservatives should look to the future and a more permanent alignment of parliamentary opinion. He hoped for a quiet settlement of the Reform question, if the government brought forward a moderate measure. This might lead to a reconstruction of party connection strengthening Conservative opinion. In a shorter speech, Disraeli echoed Derby's themes, warning any 'foreign potentate' who saw an opportunity for aggression against England not to mistake 'the character and genius of the English people'.

Derby's analysis was astute. In Lancashire many influential middle-class mill owners feared Bright and radicalism more than they disliked the aristocracy. The contact of Derby's elder son with local industrial communities revealed 'an almost feudal respect' for the Stanley family.[17] The Conservative tendencies of large employers and self-made mill owners, except in church matters, suggested untapped reservoirs of party support, only kept at bay by the mingled timidity and pride of Tory country gentlemen. Economic prosperity and social stability, Derby believed, must lead to the popular advancement of Conservatism. A gathering of more than 6,000 delegates from the Mechanics Institutes at the recently built Manchester Free Trade Hall addressed by Disraeli on the theme of education, following the Liverpool banquet, seemed to affirm the increasing strength of popular Conservative feeling in Lancashire. Private dinners at Abney Hall, home of Sir James Watts, Mayor of Manchester, and Lord Wilton's Heaton Hall, as well as one held at Knowsley, buoyed up local party morale.

Only the European crisis over Italy continued to disrupt a sense of national ease. Following Napoleon's costly success at the Battle of Solferino on 24 June 1859, the French and Austrian emperors hurriedly signed an armistice at Villafranca on 12 July. Driven by force of arms from Lombardy, Austria retained Venetia, while Piedmont-Sardinia found herself abandoned by Napoleon III at the negotiating table. This was precisely the diplomatic outcome Malmesbury had predicted six months earlier. The restoration of the rulers ejected from the central duchies and the formation of an Italian confederacy under the Pope, proposed by the Treaty, were far short of the liberal autonomy envisaged by Cavour. Meanwhile, Napoleon's fear of a conflict with Prussia and his horror at the large amount of French blood spilt at Solferino (which he witnessed at first hand as commander in the field) made a quick, if not decisive, settlement desirable. Yet Piedmont-Sardinia remained as reliant as ever on French support. The Treaty of Villafranca was signed at Zurich on 10 November. British distrust of Napoleon was heightened by these events.

At the Conservatives' Merchant Taylors' Hall dinner in mid-July, Derby welcomed the cessation of fighting, but regarded the state of affairs arising out of the peace as more dangerous than anything which had existed before the war, the conflict having commenced on insufficient grounds and false pretexts.[18] France accepted that very territory, Lombardy, to which it was contended Austria had no right. France then contemptuously flung it into the hands of her ally Piedmont-Sardinia. Tuscany and Modena were restored to their former status, while nothing was done to reform government in the Papal States. This, Derby scathingly observed, was the result for the promised liberty of Italy that emerged from the carnage which had occurred. He praised Napoleon III for swiftly stopping the war, before further loss of life. But the passions of Europe had been excited. Great armaments had been brought together. French military ardour had been aroused. An efficient French army and a powerful navy, beyond that necessary for mere self-defence, had been assembled. Derby earnestly hoped that France wished to maintain peaceful relations with Britain. But, he warned, it was the first duty of the British government to be thoroughly prepared for her own defence; no niggardly parsimony should deprive her of adequate means to protect herself. Given the volatile state of European affairs, Gladstonian retrenchment must not render Britain vulnerable.

During the summer Palmerston, who was anti-Austrian, Russell, who was pro-Italian and suspicious of France, Gladstone, who was enthusiastically pro-Italian, and other cabinet members, who were generally inclined to neutrality, debated the best diplomatic course to adopt, while the Queen and Prince Albert became increasingly fearful that Austrian humiliation would encourage French expansionism. With cabinet ministers divided, Derby's public comments at Liverpool in October were intended to disabuse foreign observers, particularly those in Paris, from believing that governmental change implied confusion over Britain's national interests. The Conservatives, he loyally asserted, remained firmly committed to their patriotic duty.[19] Domestic political dissension was not to be interpreted overseas as a weakening of national resolve.

Derby's statement of loyal opposition was calculated to apply subversive pressure on cabinet unity. He implied that, if Palmerston fell out with his difficult Peelite and radical colleagues, then congenial support awaited him on the Conservative benches. Parliamentary Reform, as well as national finances, remained the test of this strategy. The fig leaf of Italy barely covered the embarrassment of deep Liberal differences over Reform. Russell entered Palmerston's cabinet on the understanding that a government Reform Bill would be proposed in 1860. In November 1859 Palmerston appointed a cabinet committee, chaired by Cornewall Lewis, to draw up a measure. The fashioning of a Reform Bill acceptable to all shades of Liberal and radical opinion, however, was a task guaranteed to tax Cornewall Lewis's resourcefulness. In early November, Clarendon observed that 'Derby knows how to keep his forces together.' In contrast, there was 'no union and consequently no strength in a set of men like the Liberals', who are 'jealous of each other, who recognise no Chief, who have different objects and no principle of cohesion'.[20] Derby prepared for ministerial rifts, while communicating a readiness for loyal compliance in any moderate proposals. He declined to support the renegade Whig Lord Grey in a premature attack on the Address, criticizing the raising of loans for national defence and denouncing extensive Reform.[21] Rather than give cause for the cabinet to rally together, he preferred to await the government's Reform measure and budget, so allowing events to prompt alarmed ministerial moderates to approach him. On Sunday 1 January 1860 Malmesbury reported to Knowsley that Palmerston had 'been beaten several times in his cabinet and was nearly wearied out'. Only the urgings of his wife and friends persuaded the prime minister 'to go on and ... play the whole game'. It was predicted by the government's partisans and foreign ambassadors, Malmesbury related, that the ministry must soon 'break up'.[22]

Derby did not have long to wait for a ministerial overture. In early August 1859 Disraeli advised Jolliffe that it was 'of the utmost importance, that the confidential relations between the two parties should be maintained'.[23] In January 1860 Disraeli informed Derby that a cabinet minister, Charles Villiers, had approached him seeking confidential communications on behalf of Palmerston and Russell over Reform. Derby confessed to being startled at such 'a correspondence with a member of the cabinet on such a subject ... but if the correspondence be sanctioned by the Head of the government and his chief supporter (and rival), I do not see that it is our duty to remonstrate on the part of the rest of the cabinet'.[24] The Duke of Newcastle reassured Derby that the Reform Bill would be a mild measure presenting the Conservatives with no difficulty in supporting it. Over the next fortnight Villiers apprised Derby, through Disraeli, of the progress of cabinet discussion. Villiers sounded out Disraeli about an acceptable 'temperate measure', given that the uniform borough and county franchise proposed by the Conservatives had failed. Derby indicated his preference for an £8 borough franchise, anything less giving an undue preponderance to the lowest class of voters in the towns.[25] Palmerston suggested a £10 county franchise (which might be modified to a £20 franchise if the Lords insisted), a £7 rated value borough franchise, and disfranchisement dealt with in a separate bill. Disraeli responded that a £7 or £6 borough franchise made little difference in Conservative eyes, believing the majority of the cabinet committee preferred an £8 suffrage, which would alienate the radicals. On Wednesday 18 January, Disraeli reported to Derby that the 'moderate party' in the cabinet had gained the upper hand and 'Lord John is checked.'[26] As Derby hoped, Conservative friendship was emphasizing the prime minister's differences with his more radical colleagues. At a dinner at Liverpool Town Hall, on 19 January, Derby expressed his wish to see the Reform issue settled and promised to refrain from factious opposition if the government brought forward a substantial, if moderate, measure.

Alongside Reform, relations with France were also straining cabinet relations. With Russell and Gladstone's blessing, Cobden was in Paris negotiating an Anglo-French Free Trade Treaty. Clarendon privately informed Malmesbury he thought the Treaty 'thoroughly unsound and a great mistake'. But rejecting the Treaty, once negotiations were begun, would be 'a far greater mistake', making an enemy of Napoleon III and delighting his foes.[27] During discussions the French attempted to link ratification of the commercial Treaty with British support for their policy in Italy. Palmerston, meanwhile, was strengthening Britain's defences and increasing military expenditure as a curb on French expansion, while looking for the opportunity to have the unsatisfactory Treaty of Villafranca laid aside, without giving France cause to take offence. The restoration of the central Italian duchies and the creation of a confederacy under the Pope, proposed in the Villafranca Treaty, Palmerston regarded as impractical. The Emperor's deft coupling of Cobden's commercial Treaty with a proposed Anglo-French alliance immediately divided the cabinet. While Palmerston and Russell supported the idea, as a means of controlling Napoleon III, a majority of the cabinet rejected it. Gladstone favoured the proposal under 'the double inducement of his Italo-mania and his Free Trade policy'. Russell, it appeared, was entirely under the control of Palmerston, as the more experienced hand in foreign affairs. Clarendon feared, however, that Palmerston's hatred of Austria amounted to a monomania.[28] Derby was alarmed at the prospect of 'an alliance, *offensive* and *defensive*, with France, and a joint guarantee of the independence of central Italy!'[29] Palmerston's subsequent defeat in cabinet over this proposal he judged 'very damaging' to the prime minister and 'both embarrassing and irritating to the Emperor'. In January 1860 the Cobden–Chevalier Treaty was signed, but an Anglo-French alliance failed to materialize. Continuing fear in Britain of a French invasion, manifested in the Volunteer Movement, sustained popular agitation over the state of foreign relations. This added to ministerial discord and encouraged Conservative hopes of a pending ministerial rupture. Palmerston's characteristic confidence contrasted with Granville's fear of imminent defeat on some vital question.

Derby's response to the Royal Address, when parliament assembled on Tuesday 24 January 1860, maintained pressure on cabinet unity. Derby, Greville noted, 'made a very good and moderate speech', although Derby thought that both Houses seemed 'very flat and inanimate'.[30] Derby congratulated the Lords on the happy domestic condition of the country.[31] Only a little ebullition of Irish feeling marred the prevailing contentment. Public opinion appeared uninterested in Reform. If parliament treated the issue in a dispassionate manner, he advised, then there need be no great dread of a revolutionary measure. He expressed satisfaction with the suppression of the revolt in India and praised Lord Canning for restoring the feudal system in Oudh, a policy which would consolidate British power in the Asian subcontinent. Derby also recommended the deferment of discussion on Lord Grey's motion criticizing the government's actions in China. In June 1859 Britain's newly appointed first British Minister to China, Lord Elgin's younger brother Frederick Bruce, was prevented from reaching Pei-ching to ratify a treaty with the Chinese Emperor. Fire was exchanged between the British naval forces under Admiral Hope and the Taku forts at the mouth of the Pei river. Bruce's mission was forced to withdraw. A large military force, drawn from Britain and India, including some French as well as Russian and American troops, prepared in the New Year to crush Chinese resistance. The situation was unclear, Derby observed. If Britain was at war, then the Chinese attack was justified. But if Britain was at peace with China, then she had no right to resort to the force of arms. Nevertheless, Derby declined to debate these events in detail, contenting himself with a tribute to the devotion to duty and heroic bravery of the Royal Navy. Relations with France and the condition of Italy, on the other hand, drew his direct approbation.

Derby declared that the recently negotiated commercial Treaty with France was not a cause for congratulation. While the advantages it brought to France were immediate, the benefits it promised to Britain were only prospective. The articles admitted to France free of duty were of vital importance to her warlike purposes. The articles admitted to Britain, under the Treaty's reciprocal arrangements, were of a totally different nature. Moreover, with British expenditure on defence increasing and the income tax drawing to an end, it was an inappropriate moment to reduce revenues and consider binding the country to an Anglo-French alliance from which it could not withdraw. Under the commercial Treaty wine duties were to be mitigated, but the duty on hops and malt left untouched. The differing treatment of duties on tea and sugar also revealed a fundamental inconsistency. The ministry's intentions with regard to Italy, furthermore, were clouded in obscurity. Did the ministry favour a European Congress on Italy as proposed by Napoleon III? A clear statement of government policy, he insisted, was required. For himself, he was convinced that, with regard to Italy, any separate treaty with France was unwise. Thus, he sought to snatch away the fig leaf of Italy and expose the embarrassment of cabinet differences over the fate of the peninsula. In reply, Granville pointed out that two years previously Derby had condemned Canning's conduct in Oudh. He characterized Derby's comments on the Anglo-French commercial Treaty as the old opinions on Protection presented in a new guise. Removing artificial obstructions to their commerce benefited both countries, promoted their mutual interests, and strengthened their shared desire for continued peace. Britain was, Granville declared, unfettered by any alliance and free of any pledge or guarantee. Reports regarding the French annexation of Savoy, however, maintained hostile pressure on the government. Derby called Malmesbury up from Heron Court to support Lord Normanby's motion criticizing the annexation.

On Tuesday 7 February, Derby rallied near-unanimous Lords opposition to French annexation of Savoy and Nice. Piedmont-Sardinia was bound by a treaty with Switzerland not to cede Savoy to France, he observed.[32] Moreover, such a step would destroy all confidence in the French Emperor's pronouncements of peace and suggest that Austria had been expelled from Italy for the furtherance of France's selfish ends. There was a great opportunity, he concluded, for Napoleon III to establish a character for peace by declaring he entertained no intention of extending French frontiers. With this warning the debate closed and Normanby agreed to withdraw his motion. The French Ambassador was infuriated, Malmesbury noted, while, for good measure, Derby forwarded for printing in the public press a French petition he received urging the English people to oppose the annexation of Savoy.[33]

Following a well-attended meeting of the Conservative party in mid-February, Derby was 'in great spirits' and seemed ready to resume office. He was encouraged by Gladstone's conversation, during a dinner he attended given by Russell, indicating that the Chancellor of the Exchequer regarded adoption of the French commercial Treaty as a question of confidence for the ministry.[34] Espousing moderation, repudiating any factious purpose, and allowing domestic prosperity to stimulate Conservative sentiment offered reward in doing little. Malmesbury, writing to Derby in early February 1860, endorsed his strategic logic.

> As to our coming into office, I confess I have the strongest repugnance to do so upon our *former* basis, twice tried, and twice with the same result—namely, ten or twelve months of sufferance, then a beating, then a dissolution, and then an ejection. Personally, none of us can desire to play so disagreeable a *rôle* once more with the same play and the same parts, and still less can we wish it for the good of the country. It is, therefore, with great satisfaction I hear you say that we must help to keep these cripples on their legs.[35]

Patiently acting as a patriotic support to the invalid Palmerston promised, in due course, a more lasting prospect of power. On Wednesday 15 February, Derby travelled with Malmesbury to Heron Court to enjoy a few relaxing days of wildfowl shooting.

In the Commons, during February 1860, the Cobden–Chevalier Treaty and Gladstone's budget occupied MPs. Derby encouraged Conservatives to confine their criticisms to the export of coal to France, because it was a munition of war. But Gladstone successfully reasserted his financial mastery over his predecessor. Malmesbury reported to Derby that 'Dizzy ... cannot hold his own.'[36] This quickly rekindled Conservative backbench distrust of Disraeli. Greville was intrigued to observe that 'Derby himself, when he heard how his colleague had been demolished, did not seem to care much about it.'[37] Derby's indifference reflected his renewed wariness of Disraeli's conduct. Just three months earlier he had been caused public embarrassment over Disraeli's confidential communications with William Lindsay during May 1859. An associate of Lindsay, William Miller, Liberal MP for Leith, declared to his constituents in October 1859 that Derby had formally endorsed their understanding with Disraeli of the previous May, promising support for the Conservative ministry against any hostile opposition motion. Derby, who had remained unaware of these discussions, was outraged at the sudden linking of his name with such collusion. He regarded it as a public slur on his integrity and honour. Disraeli was acutely embarrassed by Miller's disclosure. While Derby, in his Liverpool speech of 29 October, dismissed Miller's assertion as totally baseless, Disraeli engaged in disingenuous shuffling.

The episode revived Derby's misgivings about Disraeli's trustworthiness and, following the serious social breach between Derby and Disraeli during the Knowsley visit of October, led him to regard Disraeli's personal humiliation at the hands of Gladstone in February 1860 with a detached unconcern. What mattered to Derby more was reports of Palmerston's disquiet about Gladstone's financial policy. Gladstone's call for retrenchment, the reduction of indirect taxation, and the repeal of the paper duties discomfited the prime minister, who refused to countenance his Chancellor's demand for a reduction in defence expenditure. Derby's warning the previous July against false economy weakening the nation's defences acquired increasing force. 'Lord Derby and his friends', G. M. Dallas noted, 'are tranquilly watching the course of incidents, quite sure that the pear is rapidly ripening, and must fall into their hands before two months elapse.'[38]

Confirmation at the beginning of March that Napoleon III intended to annex Savoy and Nice, without the sanction of other European Powers, brought Derby back to St James's Square. Palmerston was reportedly ill with gout and Russell 'very much out of humour, and on very bad terms with the Emperor'.[39] France's extension of her frontiers, officially announced on 13 March and embodied in a treaty with Piedmont-Sardinia on 24 March, outraged opinion in Britain. The 'concerted villainy' of Napoleon III, with 'the connivance of Cavour', excited 'the most intense disgust and indignation'.[40] Conservative wrath turned on the government for yielding to French intrigue. Derby saw Gladstone's budget, Cobden's Anglo-French commercial Treaty, and French annexation of Savoy as inextricably linked. Conservative criticism 'ought not to be frittered away in separate discussions'.[41] But opposition should be carried 'no further than would enable [him] to record a protest'. An outright rejection of the Treaty, despite the urgings of Lord Grey, was better avoided.

On Thursday 15 March, Derby spoke in the Lords laying out his objections to the government's policy.[42] He believed the eleventh article of the commercial Treaty, regarding the export of coal to France, required an Act of Parliament which was unnecessary to approval of the other terms of the Treaty. But even if the Treaty was judged desirable, the present was an inappropriate time to implement it. The country faced a financial deficit. Although remitting indirect taxation, Gladstone was forced to raise income tax. The supposed benefits of the Treaty were to be achieved by a great sacrifice of revenue at a most unsuitable time, the Treaty being merely a sop thrown to England by Napoleon to convey the impression that their interests were aligned. The government had thereby become culpable in the French acquisition of Savoy, an act engendering mutual suspicion in Europe and prompting a dangerous build-up of armaments.

Having registered his protest, Derby found Grey forcing the debate to a division, against his own wish to avoid a vote. As Derby feared, Grey's belligerence delivered the government a reprieve, ministers securing a majority of thirty votes. Nonetheless, confidence in the government appeared shaken. In response, on Friday 23 March, Russell made a violent speech against Napoleon III to an electrified Commons asserting that French territorial expansion had destroyed any faith in France's protestations of peace. Popular domestic alarm at the possibility of a French invasion, giving further momentum to the Volunteer Movement, intensified. Revelations of secret correspondence between Palmerston and Napoleon III in late March and the exclusion of cabinet colleagues from discussion of Anglo-French relations increased ministerial resentment of Palmerston, Russell, and Gladstone. They were playing, Greville feared, 'into the Emperor Napoleon's hands, who has only to be patient and bide his time, and he will be able to treat all Europe, England included, in any way he pleases'.[43]

Against these European anxieties, Russell's Reform Bill, presented to the Commons on Thursday 1 March, was received with apathy. Russell refused the request of his cabinet colleagues to defer the measure. Profound indifference greeted the bill's proposed £10 county and £6 borough franchises, and a moderate redistribution of twenty-five seats. Moreover, Russell's failure to address the intrusion of urban freehold votes into county constituencies (indeed his scheme threatened to add leaseholders and copyholders to their number) and his dropping of any 'merit franchises', such as he proposed in 1854 and the Conservatives suggested in 1859, rendered the bill unpalatable to the opposition. Derby advised Clarendon 'that if twenty-five or even twenty Liberals would *take a lead* in opposing this bill, the whole Conservative party would support them'.[44] If Russell's bill would be disastrous for the Conservative party electorally, Derby commented to Disraeli, for the Whigs it would bring 'political annihilation'.[45] Derby opened a correspondence with Lord Grey affirming his preference for an identical county and borough £10 franchise. It was, he informed Grey, 'undesirable to lower the borough franchise at all'.[46] The 'merit franchises' proposed in the Conservative bill of 1859 would counteract the effects of a £6 borough suffrage, but if these were impracticable, a high-class lodger franchise would 'neutralise the low constituency introduced by [Russell's] bill'. As the tendency of Gladstone's fiscal policy seemed to be towards the augmentation of direct taxes, Derby observed, there appeared additional ground for the introduction of a superior lodger franchise. 'I think, moreover, that no Reform bill can be looked upon as "complete" which wholly omits to deal with the kindred questions of registration and polling—the evils of both of which the government bill leaves untouched.' Extensive Reform threatened no political party more seriously, he believed, than the moderate Liberals, 'in other words those who are not content blindly to follow a democratic leadership to all its consequences'. From Rose he commissioned a report on the effect of a lowered franchise in various boroughs. Lord Grey, meanwhile, gave notice for a Lords Committee to inquire into the effect of a reduction of the suffrage qualification. Derby anticipated the ministry opposing such a Committee, while proceeding with their own measure.[47] On 12 April he advised Grey that 'the practical question' was how to escape 'the fatal consequences which must result if [Russell's] bill is carried; and carried it will be unless there be some tacit understanding at least between the two sides … as to the mode of getting rid of it, or rendering it comparatively harmless'.[48] Getting rid of Russell's bill was Derby's preferred course, no future government then being under an immediate obligation to propose another Reform measure.

   In the debate on Lord Grey's motion on Thursday 19 April, Derby recounted the course taken by his own government over Reform in 1859.[49] In considering the admission of the working classes to the franchise, his ministry did not think it fit to reduce the £10 borough franchise in order to admit that flood of the working classes which would inundate the rest of the electorate. They had proposed an equalization of the county and borough franchise as the best means of avoiding further agitation. While their 1859 measure had not met with approval in the Commons, nor was it met with a counter-proposition. Rather, it was defeated by an abstract resolution framed with peculiar ingenuity. Yet the Conservative measure would have admitted the best-qualified, the most intelligent, the most enterprising, and least migratory portions of the working classes, together with a large class of educated persons who did not live in £10 houses, but who were well fitted to exercise the franchise for the benefit of the country. By contrast, Russell's Reform measure, which excited no enthusiasm, proceeded on the principle of numbers, a criterion to which Derby strongly objected. This appeared to be the basis for Russell's proposal to give additional MPs to Manchester, Liverpool, Leeds, and

Birmingham. Yet the data upon which these numbers and the effect of a lowered borough franchise were calculated were highly questionable. Estimates of the number of borough voters created by a £6 franchise varied enormously. The critical need for reliable information made Grey's request for a Committee necessary. Derby concluded by declaring Russell's bill the most unsatisfactory, unstatesmanlike, and inconclusive measure ever submitted to parliament. Extending the borough franchise would throw the determination of the taxation of the country into the hands of those who believed that the upper classes were keeping up a large national expenditure for their own benefit. It would give the democratic element a vast preponderance in the constitution. It would, moreover, prepare the way to ever lower qualifications, ending in universal suffrage, which would ultimately sweep away their Lordships' House and the monarchy of the kingdom. The Lords agreed to Grey's motion and a Committee was appointed.

In the Commons, Russell's Reform Bill, bogged down by indifference, encountered successive delays. This was an outcome Palmerston watched with satisfaction. On Monday 23 April, Malmesbury conveyed to Derby information from William Hayter, former Liberal chief whip, that Palmerston wished Russell's Reform Bill to be withdrawn. Palmerston sought from Derby assurances that the Conservatives would not take advantage of the death of the bill, and that, if Russell's resignation and the desertion of Bright and the radicals followed, he could rely on the Conservatives' 'reasonable' support'.[50] Derby's friendly assurances brought him closer to that strategic goal he had envisaged at the opening of the session. Palmerston was becoming increasingly reliant on Derby's support in resisting the demands of his more radical colleagues.

During May, Derby took up firm opposition to Gladstone's proposed repeal of the paper duties, aware that Palmerston also objected to his Chancellor's policy. Again, Derby sought to demonstrate how Conservative aid might rescue the prime minister from his own ministers. While dining with Clarendon, Derby laid out his objections to Gladstone's Paper Duties Bill, clearly having taken considerable efforts to master the details of the issue. Derby, Clarendon noted, 'did not talk rashly and in Rupert vein, but gave a well-considered and well-argued statement of the grounds on which he purposed to proceed'.[51] In the course of impugning the whole financial policy of the government, on Thursday 10 May, Derby declared to the Lords he would do all in his power to ensure the rejection of repeal of the paper duties.[52] An extraordinary private exchange then followed as Lady Palmerston, in conversation with Malmesbury, expressed her hope that Gladstone's measure would be defeated. At Derby's request, Malmesbury assured Lady Palmerston that the Conservatives meant to throw out Gladstone's bill. Lady Palmerston thanked Malmesbury for this information. Malmesbury continued that, if Russell, Gladstone, and Milner Gibson joined the radicals against Palmerston following the defeat of the Reform Bill, then the Conservatives would support the prime minister for the rest of the session.[53] Lady Palmerston was grateful for this offer and denounced Napoleon III as a rogue who had deceived the premier. It was 'a queer state of things indeed when the prime minister', Greville observed, 'desires to see the defeat of a measure so precious to his own Chancellor of the Exchequer'.[54] This remarkable conversation prepared the way for Derby's powerful speech, one week later, on the recklessness of Gladstone's financial policies.[55] Granville confessed that there was nobody on the Liberal side of the Lords 'able to grapple with Derby, Monteagle, Overstone and Grey on such a question'.[56]

Prior to the Lords debate, Derby studied the history of the power of the two Houses, concluding that, although the Lords could not introduce a money bill, there was no restraint on the authority of the Lords to reject or amend one. He then informed the Lords on 21 May that he had no desire to overthrow the ministry. But he delivered an extended condemnation of the government's financial measures.[57] To reduce indirect taxation, in the face of a national deficit, was not the policy of a statesman, he asserted, but the action of an improvident gambler. Gladstone's views on national finances over recent years, he continued, revealed an alarming inconsistency. In 1853 Gladstone had pledged himself to ending income tax in 1860. In 1857 he had supported a Conservative amendment to Cornewall Lewis's budget calling for an adjustment in government income and expenditure allowing the remittance of income tax in 1860. Up to 1858 Gladstone had declared himself solemnly bound to redeem this pledge. But the Chancellor now played into the hands of the Manchester School radicals, who, by rendering taxation odious by the pressure of direct taxes, hoped to prevent the country from going to war under any circumstances. Gladstone, Derby concluded, was pursuing a policy which was both inconsistent and unpatriotic. This bravura performance was received with loud cheering from all parts of the House. The peers' benches and the ladies' gallery were crowded, while the steps of the throne and the strangers' gallery were crammed. Lady Palmerston was seated in the gallery 'openly expressing her wishes that the bill might be rejected by a large majority'.[58] Repeal of the paper duties was soundly defeated in the Lords by eighty-nine votes, a greater defeat than even the pessimistic Granville had anticipated. It prompted a dramatic change in Gladstone's reputation. Three months before, the Chancellor had been hailed as a 'prodigious genius'. By May his budget and commercial Treaty were 'pronounced enormous and dangerous blunders'.[59] Regard for Gladstone, Disraeli confirmed, had 'collapsed more suddenly and completely than anything since Jonah's gourd'.[60] When a mortified Gladstone complained to Palmerston about the Lords' behaviour, the premier tartly replied that the Chancellor's disappointment was nothing to his own at having his likely winner unable to enter the Derby. Certainly Derby had strong reason to assume, as he left London for the Epsom Downs and Derby Day on 23 May, that his satisfaction at Gladstone's defeat was fully shared at Cambridge House.

By June, Malmesbury believed the government to be 'in convulsions'.[61] Russell was threatening to resign over the delays to his Reform Bill. Gladstone was making the same threat unless the ministry censored the Lords for rejecting his repeal of the paper duties. Palmerston drolly observed to Delane that Gladstone's letters of threatened resignation had fed the study fire at Broadlands until the chimney was in flames; while to the Queen, with his mind on the defensive fortifications under construction to deter any possible French invasion, he commented that he would rather lose Gladstone than run the risk of losing Portsmouth or Plymouth.[62] In this critical state of affairs Derby again sent Malmesbury to Lady Palmerston with an assurance of the Conservatives' wholehearted support against the radicals. Malmesbury conveyed a positive promise that the Conservatives would not coalesce with the radicals in or out of office. He met privately with both Palmerston and his wife. The prime minister appeared as anxious as the Conservatives to get rid of Russell's Reform Bill. Although Palmerston seemed reluctant to lose Lord John, he indicated that he 'would be very glad if Gladstone resigned'.[63] Reports of a round robin, signed by a number of Whigs, protesting against Russell's handling of foreign policy, however, rendered Lord John's position no less precarious than that of the Chancellor. Russell informed Granville that, if Gladstone resigned, he would 'take an early opportunity of following him'.[64]

In the face of ministerial collapse Derby insisted that 'we ought to adhere, as far as possible, to our policy of making every *obstructive* motion come from the Liberal side of the House'.[65] Disraeli agreed that 'our tactics are to watch circumstances, and not attempt to create them. The cards will play into our hands if we are quiet.'[66] Taylor, Jolliffe's successor as Commons chief whip, endorsed this line. To this end, in late March and early May, Derby had dissuaded Sotheron-Estcourt from extending the debate on church rates.[67] Pakington was deflected from calling for a

Royal Commission on Reform. Lord Montagu was persuaded by Derby to drop his Sunday Trading Bill.[68] Meanwhile, the evidence of witnesses to the Lords Committee on Reform was suggesting that the improved habits of the working classes in manufacturing districts was effectively widening the suffrage without a lowering of the borough franchise. The 'gradual improvement of the class of houses occupied by the best of the working classes', Derby observed, 'is insensibly operating under the present franchise a larger admission of their class to electoral power'. As one witness declared, 'they are growing to it'.[69]

While Derby attended Ascot week (where his 3-year-old Tom Bowline convincingly won the St James's Palace Stakes by three lengths), Russell, on Monday 11 June, withdrew his Reform Bill. In cabinet only Gladstone favoured going on with it. Listening in the Commons to Russell smothering his offspring, Palmerston looked nervous, Wood and Cornewall Lewis exchanged chuckles of evident delight, while Gladstone busied himself with papers. At the same time, Palmerston defused the clash threatening to erupt with the House of Lords over the rejection of Gladstone's Paper Duties Bill. The prime minister referred the procedural question, of whether the Lords could reject a finance bill approved by the Commons, to a Committee of Privileges. Walpole served as chairman of the Committee, whose members also included Palmerston, George Grey, Cornewall Lewis, and Graham. Derby's worry at Walpole's well-known 'tendency to endeavour to smooth down difficulties by making concessions' was countered by the premier's resistance to radical demands. The Committee rejected the strong language for their report pressed by Bright and supported by Gladstone and Russell.[70] A more anodyne report, that the Lords did possess such power, was presented by Palmerston to the Commons at the beginning of July. In his speech Palmerston implied reservations about his Chancellor's financial policy. It was, Derby commented admiringly, 'the best tight-rope dancing he ever saw'.[71] To general surprise Gladstone, though provoked into making a thinly disguised Commons attack on the prime minister, did not resign. In a private interview with Gladstone, Palmerston declared that, if he did resign, no one would believe that he left the government because he did not want the country defended, that it would be thought that he was running away from the consequences of his budget, and that the only future he would have would be the political ruin of companionship with Bright.[72]

On Saturday 23 June 1860 the Queen reviewed a parade in Hyde Park of 20,000 well-disciplined Volunteers. Derby spoke to a large audience at the Merchant Taylors' Hall that evening. He emphasized the moral to be drawn from the military review by the authorities in France. 'If the bare possibility of an insult to England could in six months raise a force of 130,000 Volunteers, there is no doubt that, were the danger imminent, we should have three times that number.'[73] This captured the groundswell of popular patriotism produced by increasing fear of Napoleonic aggrandizement. As Dallas observed, 'Lord Derby and his wary associates ... do much to consolidate the foundations of their party, and to give it a European position, by seizing as theirs the popular dread of Napoleon's designs.'[74] During July, despite Gladstone's demands for retrenchment, Palmerston successfully secured increased expenditure for defence. In office, prior to June 1859, Derby had increased naval spending and endorsed the fledgling Volunteer Movement, policies carried forward by Palmerston during 1860, supplemented by extensive coastal fortification. Heightened patriotism and enhanced national defence provided another bond between the prime minister and the Conservative leader.

As parliament prorogued in August 1860 Derby had good reason to regard the session with satisfaction. His strategy of assisting Palmerston in subduing his more radical ministerial colleagues, thereby emphasizing the incompatibility of those varied elements comprising Palmerston's government, had achieved some notable success. Russell's Reform Bill proved stillborn. Gladstone's attempt to repeal the duties on paper was defeated, a victory in the course of which Derby successfully asserted the authority of the House of Lords and his own pre-eminence within it. Meanwhile, mounting fear of expansionist French ambition, creating a rising tide of patriotic feeling, had brought Derby and Palmerston alongside each other, both men protecting national defence from Gladstonian frugality. All this eroded Russell's credibility and drove Gladstone into radical company. The government seemed on the point of fracturing. In particular, the 'half-dead, broken-down, tempest-tossed' Gladstone appeared deeply disenchanted with his position.[75]

Derby's broader hope, that restrained reform, economic prosperity, and patriotism might stimulate the Conservative feelings of the country, also appeared closer to being realized. The Conservative essayist William Aytoun endorsed Derby's strategy in the pages of *Blackwood's Magazine*: 'We do not wish to see the present ministry displaced. We are content with the knowledge that the opposition is so strong that the Palmerston cabinet dare not deviate from the path of duty and sound British policy without experiencing a fatal reverse.'[76] The acerbic Tory critic of Disraeli's leadership Lord Robert Cecil penned an article in the July *Quarterly Review* heralding a 'Conservative Reaction'. The radical bubble, Cecil celebrated, was now burst.[77] Stanley noted that even some radical intellectuals were expressing concerns about the enfranchisement of the working classes; 'when philosophers turn Conservative', he observed, 'there is real reaction'.[78] To Disraeli, in October 1860, he reported that the towns were 'full of money—and of Conservative opinion disguised as moderate liberalism'.[79] As Gladstone complained to Graham, 'We live in anti-reforming times. All improvements have to be urged in apologetic, almost supplicatory, tones.'[80]

The anniversary banquet of the Conservative Registration Association, held at Willis's Rooms on 29 June and chaired by the Earl of Shrewsbury, *The Times* reported, demonstrated the 'undiminished union and vitality of the party'. Although neither Derby nor Disraeli attended, many former cabinet members, over seventy Conservative MPs, and 300 party supporters gathered to applaud Manners extolling the shibboleth 'Church and State' as those 'magic words' of the great historic party to which they belonged, a party whose illustrious pedigree reached back to Strafford, Clarendon, Samuel Johnson, and on, through Burke, Pitt, Canning, and Peel, to Derby and Disraeli. General Peel praised Pakington for restoring the Navy to efficiency, while Pakington congratulated the Conservatives for maintaining, since being ejected from office, a united and patriotic opposition. A quick retribution had fallen on that factious combination by which they had been overthrown. Russell's abortive Reform Bill had brought humiliation. After denouncing Malmesbury's diplomacy, Palmerston's government was unable to prevent the seizure of Savoy by France. A rash and improvident budget, proposed by Gladstone, represented an unworthy concession to Bright and the radicals. In that very room a year before, Pakington observed, 'a hollow truce was patched up' between political sections 'having nothing in common but the word "Liberal", which equally applied to all right-minded Englishmen'.[81] In contrast to the deeply divided government could be seen, Pakington concluded, the growing influence of Conservative feeling in the Commons, in the Lords, and in the country. To loud cheers he echoed the celebrated watchword 'Register, register, register'.

    ... and before them plac'd
Ambrosial provender.

    (Derby, *The Iliad of Homer*, ii. 3)

On returning to Knowsley in August 1860, Derby prepared for the marriage of his 24-year-old daughter Lady Emma to the 43-year-old

Hon. Sir Patrick Chetwynd Talbot. The youngest son of the Earl of Shrewsbury, Talbot had served as Derby's private secretary in 1852 and 1858, had commanded the 1st Staffordshire Militia in the Ionian Islands during the Crimean War, and was appointed Serjeant-at-Arms in the Lords in May 1859. Aged just 16, Emma had first met Talbot at Hatfield House in late 1851 and, despite her father's objections, was determined she would marry no one else. Derby doubted the wisdom of the match because of Talbot's lack of financial means. But the pleas of his wife and daughter eventually overcame his misgivings and in October 1860 the marriage took place at Knowsley church, followed by a private luncheon at Knowsley Hall; the newly-weds spending their honeymoon at Blyth Hall, near Ormskirk, home of Derby's brother-in-law Colonel Edward Wilbraham. Derby was rewarded with the arrival of his first grandchild in 1862, Charles Stanley Talbot. As a token of his delight, Derby presented Emma, on the occasion of her birthday that year, with a cheque for £5,000 under her napkin on the breakfast table. Two granddaughters followed in 1864 and 1865. In all, Lady Emma Talbot bore eight children, five of whom Derby lived to see come into the world.

Prior to his daughter's marriage Derby also hosted, in September 1860, a review of the Lancashire Volunteers. The parade was held on the wide expanse of flat ground to the west of Knowsley Hall. Together with a great many police, the Volunteers, including 2,000 artillery men, numbered 13,000. They formed up in battalions in a line that extended for three-quarters of a mile. A crowd of 25,000 local people watched the parade. 'It must have been', Clarendon observed, 'a proud day for Derby as the enthusiasm for him appears to have exceeded that which was expressed for the Queen in Hyde Park.'[82] During the following weeks Derby organized a company of Volunteers from among sixty-three young men living in the immediate neighbourhood. Having formed them as the Knowsley Rifle Volunteers, Derby procured a drill sergeant for the company as well as nominating a captain and lieutenant.[83] In 1862 he accepted a commission as the Honorary Colonel of the 1st Lancashire Rifle Volunteer Corps.

An attack of autumnal gout in early October 1860, however, forced Derby to his bed. Rumours of his ill health excited speculation over a realignment of parties should he retire. Confined to Knowsley Hall, he was too ill to attend the marriage at Knowsley church of his daughter, who was given away at the ceremony by her elder brother, Lord Stanley. It was with difficulty that he attended the ceremony in Liverpool on 18 October marking the formal opening of the Liverpool Museum and Library on William Brown Street, accommodating his father's zoological collection. Designed by the corporation surveyor John Weightman, fronted by a portico supported by Corinthian columns and flanked by bays in a Graeco-Roman style, the new Museum and Library echoed the civic landmark of St George's Hall, on the opposite side of William Brown Street. Following the opening ceremony, Derby promptly returned to his sickbed at Knowsley. As he slowly recovered during the weeks immediately prior to Christmas, he remained committed to the parliamentary strategy which had served the Conservatives so well the previous session. 'I apprehend', he advised Malmesbury on 4 December, 'that our policy this year as well as last must be the "masterly inactivity" which was found so successful.'[84] The Conservatives, he informed Disraeli, should stick to 'keeping the present men in, and resisting all temptations to avail ourselves of a casual majority'.[85]

Italy remained, Derby noted, 'a grand *imbroglio*'. By August 1860 the revolutionary Garibaldi and his Red Shirts had wrested control of Sicily from the King of Naples. Cavour, meanwhile, stirred up revolt in the Papal States and, on 11 September, Piedmontese troops marched into the papal territories under the pretext of restoring order. As King Victor Emmanuel led his Piedmontese army into central Italy, so Garibaldi's troops entered Naples in early September. On 26 October, Garibaldi greeted Victor Emmanuel with the words 'Hail to the King of Italy'. The unification of Italy was achieved, as British diplomacy followed breathlessly behind the rapid succession of events. Russell's hurried dispatches oscillated between admitting the right of Austria to Venetia and approving of Victor Emmanuel's invasion of the Papal States, betraying the Foreign Secretary's malaise at the sudden turn of events. As Naples, Sicily and the Papal States subsequently voted for union under the house of Savoy, only the city of Rome and Venetia remained outside Victor Emmanuel's new kingdom. But Britain's influence on events was marginal. Italy proved more important to Liberal unity than British Liberalism proved to Italian unification.[86]

None of this swayed Derby from his strategy of luring Palmerston away from his more radical colleagues. He remained 'entirely against our *originating* any measure', while avoiding 'shutting the door beforehand against any overtures of our opponents'.[87] Despite the severity of the cold weather at Knowsley during December, his slow recovery from gout continued. He managed to hobble about the house, but still had to be carried down flights of stairs. Over Christmas he urged Malmesbury to renew his confidential communications with Cambridge House:

I should not be afraid of entering on these quasi-negotiations too soon. I believe Disraeli is quite accurate in his estimate of the relations between the government and the Bright and Cobden party—and that the hopes, and the tools, of the latter in the cabinet are the two *quondam* Tories, Gibson and Gladstone! I think that in your communications with Palmerston you cannot be too explicit. He is a gentleman, and will know that you and I are dealing with him *de bonne foi*, and will not seek a 'dodge', if we make any exception to our promise of support. I should, however, be quite ready to assure him that though we might, in debate, object to some of the 'sayings and doings' of the Foreign Office (and chiefly the sayings, or rather writings) we would not countenance on the subject of foreign policy any movement calculated to defeat the government, unless it were the impossible supposition that they should desire us to take an active part in an attack by France and Sardinia on Venetia.[88]

On 26 January 1861 Malmesbury reported that Palmerston was pleased to accept an arrangement similar to the last session, and that the prime minister agreed to their exception to a general support. Palmerston was aware that Bright wanted to substitute his ministry with a Conservative government. Encouraged by Cobden, some sixty radical MPs signed a round robin demanding a reduction in government expenditure on armaments. Bright told the Speaker of the Commons that, 'if he succeeded, a Liberal opposition would soon become a radical one, but that a Conservative opposition never could'.[89] Derby judged Malmesbury's conversation with Palmerston 'very satisfactory'. The arrangement would enable Palmerston to hold his own against the radicals in and out of the cabinet, while a breach between the prime minister and Gladstone, if not Russell, was likely.[90] Malmesbury's confidential negotiations would result in the radicals being 'checkmated in the approaching session'.[91] During January 1861 a fully recovered Derby restrained his backbenchers from hostile moves against the government. Lord Robert Montagu was dissuaded from moving an amendment to the Address on foreign policy.[92] Similarly, Derby prevented Lord Leitrim from moving an amendment to the Address over Lord Carlisle's policy in Ireland, despite his disapproval of Carlisle's actions. Such an amendment, he insisted, would be 'inexpedient'.[93]

Palmerston reported his confidential discussion with Malmesbury to the Queen on Sunday 27 January. If Gladstone were 'to propose a democratic Budget making a great transfer of burthens from indirect to direct taxation, and if, the cabinet refusing its concurrence, Mr. Gladstone were to retire, the Conservative party would give the government substantial support, except in the case of the government wishing to take an active part in war against Austria'.[94] Palmerston understood that this did not mean an abstinence from the usual criticisms in debate. But no step, he assured the Queen, would be taken by the Conservatives to produce a change of government. The premier knew that Bright had approached Disraeli in order to engineer his ejection from office. Bright anticipated the Conservatives then being in office for two years, during which time he would prepare for an extensive Reform Bill and the return of an advanced Liberal government. But, following his conversation with Malmesbury, Palmerston was able to reassure the Queen that the Conservatives had immediately rejected Bright's overture. Palmerston conveyed, through Malmesbury, his appreciation of the Conservatives' 'handsome communication', recognizing 'the honourable and patriotic motives by which it had been prompted'.[95]

Derby's warmer relations with the Queen, in contrast to his chilly encounters with Victoria in the early 1850s, were one benefit of such communication. During 1860 he was invited to dine with the Queen and Prince Albert on three occasions. On Sunday 27 January 1861 Disraeli also visited Windsor and found the Queen and Prince Albert 'very gracious and communicative', although 'greatly distressed and disgusted with public affairs'.[96] The Queen complained of a deficiency of armaments and feared the country was undefended. Disraeli informed Prince Albert that the Conservatives were now a unified opposition of 300 MPs, with no wish for an immediate return to office but anxious to strengthen the hands of the government in a bold national policy. When Prince Albert peevishly countered that the country was now governed by the newspapers and that the Conservatives did not have a newspaper, Disraeli retorted that the whole English press, except *The Times*, was influenced by foreign governments. The Queen then broke in declaring that *The Times* was as corrupt as the rest. As Disraeli reported to his confidant Mrs Brydges Willyams, 'forbearance and patience are clearly our game'.[97] He now anticipated Palmerston's death or retirement to be near, which would inevitably lead to a break-up of the Liberal party.[98]

When the Lancashire Liberal and Liverpool shipowner George Melly visited Knowsley after the New Year he stated that fear of France in the country 'could not be overrated, and that it would lead to the return of a thoroughly Conservative H. of Commons'.[99] The movement of opinion towards the Conservatives was evident in a series of by-elections held in February 1861. At Leicester on 7 February the Conservatives won one of the borough seats, both of which had been held by Reformers since 1837, the successful Conservative William Heygate defeating both his Liberal opponents. In Aberdeenshire, on 13 February, the Conservative William Leslie defeated the Liberal candidate Arthur Gordon, youngest son of the former premier Lord Aberdeen. The Gordon family had held the county seat, largely unchallenged, since 1818. Disraeli 'exulted' in the gain.[100] On 14 February the Conservative Colonel Bathurst became MP for South Wiltshire, following the elevation of the former Peelite Sidney Herbert to the Lords. Finally, on 28 February, the Conservatives won a dramatic victory in the Cork by-election, a county held by the Liberals since 1832. This success was interpreted by Disraeli as a sign of deep Catholic disenchantment with the Liberal party. Following a meeting with Cardinal Wiseman, Earle reported to Disraeli 'a very good feeling towards us' and the Cardinal's comments that they 'were quite right in looking to the R.C.'s for our majority, for they could give it us'.[101] All this reinforced the wisdom of patiently allowing 'masterly inactivity' to deliver power into Conservative hands. Jolliffe calculated Conservative numbers in the Commons, including their by-election gains, to be 307 or 308 MPs.[102] Disraeli, meanwhile, saw the quarrel between the Whigs and the radicals as irreconcilable and, in private conversation with Stanley, renewed discussion of a possible fusion, with Sir George Grey, Cornewall Lewis, and perhaps Clarendon joining Derby.

At the opening of the parliamentary session, on Tuesday 5 February 1861, Derby 'made one of his slashing speeches on the foreign policy of the government'.[103] It demonstrated his recovery from his illness of the autumn, rallied the spirits of his party, and attacked Russell's inconsistency.[104] At one moment, Derby observed, Russell deprecated Sardinian interference in Naples; at another moment he welcomed the collapse of the Bourbon monarchy. But, as agreed with Palmerston, Derby avoided a knockout blow. The government had been duped, he pronounced, by Napoleon's specious promises. The desirable object of Anglo-French friendship could only stand on mutual trust. As it was, confidence had given way to apprehension and uncertainty. France was engaged in a race of military and naval preparation, suggesting a further expansion of French power and territory. How long, under the guise of peace, were preparations for war to continue? With regard to events in Italy, Derby described Garibaldi as an honest politician, but he was supported by a Piedmontese policy which was a flagrant violation of international law. He called for a distinct statement of the government's policy. In reply, Granville asserted that Britain's relations with France were founded not on blind distrust or blind confidence, but on a joint pursuit of those general interests beneficial to Europe. The Lords then agreed the Royal Address without a division.

In the Commons a motion to amend the Address, calling for further parliamentary Reform, moved by the advanced Liberal James White (MP for Brighton), was met with ironical banter from Russell and swiftly defeated by 129 to 46 votes. The radical Trelawny 'never knew a session open more tamely'.[105]

Disraeli sensed in the Conservative public mood a rallying of popular support for the Established Church. While encouraging links with English and Irish Catholics, he saw the defence of the Church of England against militant Nonconformists as a valuable consolidation of Conservative support in the English counties. During the 1860 recess he stepped forward as a stalwart champion of the Anglican Church against the demand for the abolition of church rates. In a speech at Amersham on 4 December 1860 he declared 'the majority against Church Rates, which had sat like an incubus on the Church for twenty years', to have 'virtually disappeared'. He urged the Anglican clergy to petition parliament and to organize church defence associations to crush conclusively the radical campaign.[106] As often before, Derby believed Disraeli had 'gone rather too far in his declarations'.[107] Though agreeing with Disraeli in principle, Derby feared that, by pronouncing 'no compromise' on church rates, Disraeli was throwing away the Conservative advantage gained by their own moderation and the refusal of the other side to listen to any terms. 'I am afraid', Derby confided to Malmesbury, 'that Disraeli's outspoken declaration will lose us this advantage, which will not be counterbalanced by the increased support of the thoroughgoing Churchman.' Derby conveyed his alarm to Disraeli, who responded that since his speech he had been working to counteract any mischief he might have caused.[108] By way of justification, Disraeli explained that he had only taken the step after 'great inquiry and reflection; and I think if I had not taken it our counties would have slipped away'.[109] But Stanley agreed with his father that Disraeli's ideas about church rates were 'very wild, no two of the party agreed as to what should be done'.[110] A pitched battle was then avoided by Palmerston's private agreement, through his son-in-law Lord Shaftesbury, not to make the issue a party question. Like Derby, Palmerston wished to avoid sectarian differences becoming the basis of party distinction.

During February and March 1861 cooperation between Palmerston and the Conservative leadership smothered radical initiatives. On Thursday 14 February, Disraeli seconded Palmerston's loyal vote of thanks to the naval and military forces supporting Lord Elgin, who, after burning down the Chinese Emperor's Summer Palace in Pei-ching, secured a favourable convention in October 1860 ratifying the Treaty of T'ien-chin, allowing foreign merchants and missionaries to travel freely throughout China. The premier then supported the Conservatives in defeating Locke King's bill to reduce the county franchise to £10. Palmerston made 'an opposition speech from the Treasury bench' and 'threw cold water on [the] proposal'.[111] In return, the Conservatives supported the premier's plan to omit naval officers' pay from the remit of a Committee of Inquiry, against the opposition of the advanced Liberals. 'Truly', the radical Trelawny concluded, 'this looks like a reaction towards Conservatism.'[112] During mid-February the Liberal chief whip Henry Brand approached Stanley and confided that there was now a broad agreement between the Whigs and the moderate Conservatives. Brand talked of fusion, so that together they could restrain the radicals. Although Stanley supposed Brand was talking without the authorization of Palmerston, the conversation, he noted, was 'significant'.[113] For his part, Derby took every public opportunity to highlight the divisions disabling the cabinet. In particular, he emphasized the incipient radicalism of Gladstone. To a banquet of Conservative peers and MPs, hosted by the Lord Mayor at the Mansion House on 1 May, he described Gladstone as 'the Coryphaeus and mouthpiece of discredited radicalism'.[114]

As in 1860, it was Gladstone's budget that became the focus of fierce contention. It also proved a watershed. The conclusion of hostilities in China aided the Chancellor in proposing a penny off the income tax and again the repeal of the paper duties. So as to prevent the Lords from selecting particular tax proposals for approval or rejection, Gladstone brought forward his financial measures in one bill. Tellingly, the bitterest discussion of Gladstone's proposals occurred within the cabinet, rather than parliament. Gladstone later recalled that 'the battle in parliament was hard, but was as nothing to the internal fighting'.[115] In January and again in March he threatened to resign. During ministerial discussion the usually poised Palmerston openly lost his temper and informed an astonished Gladstone that he did not consider the budget a critical issue for the government in the Commons, where it was anticipated that the opposition would use every effort to destroy it. Cabinet meetings during early April were acrimonious. Gladstone eventually gained the support of a majority of the cabinet. But Palmerston continued to regard the fate of his Chancellor's budget as not a matter of confidence for the government. The premier caustically observed to Granville, in an echo of Derby's assertion, that it appeared that Bright was 'our real budget maker and chancellor of the exchequer'.[116]

The immediate parliamentary significance of Gladstone's finance measure was that Derby saw it as a violation of his understanding with

Palmerston. It seemed proof of the advanced Liberal ascendancy in the cabinet. Disraeli prolonged debate as long as possible and watched the temper of the Commons. At the same time, the Conservatives endeavoured to substitute a reduction of the duty on tea for repeal of the paper duty. This, Disraeli and Stanley agreed, had the political advantage of being a concession to the poorer, rather than the richer, classes. Derby sent a scribbled note to Palmerston saying, 'Is it to be tea and turn out?', to which the prime minister drolly replied, 'No; paper and stationery.'[117] An opposition motion to reduce the tea duty was defeated in the Commons, and on 30 May repeal of the paper duty was narrowly passed by 296 to 281 votes. Gladstone was jubilant. A number of Conservatives stayed away from the division. Some resented what they believed was an alliance between Disraeli and Irish MPs against the government. Others were absent because they did not wish to see the ministry disturbed, though they wanted it to be kept in check.[118] Derby wrote directly to Newdegate to prevent him from bringing forward a motion hostile to the budget.[119] Malmesbury believed the Conservative dissidents also feared a dissolution. Disraeli withdrew from the House for a number of days as a conspicuous sign of his disgust. The Conservative chief whip, Taylor, talked of treachery. Derby was equally sickened by this backbench revolt. Over twenty Conservatives had stayed away from the division, giving Gladstone his majority of fifteen votes on repeal of the paper duty. Derby had hoped to defeat Gladstone, of whom he spoke in private in very angry terms.[120] The budget, he believed, contravened his pact with Palmerston, repeal of the paper duty being a long-standing radical demand. Palmerston had failed to restrain his Chancellor. But equally, the Conservatives in the Commons failed to defeat Gladstone's populist policies. If Derby's understanding with Palmerston now seemed hollow, the strategy of 'masterly inactivity' began to look dangerously like impotence.

In a speech to the Lords on Friday 7 June 1861 Derby indicated he would not rouse the peers to reject a budget approved by the Commons. He believed repeal of the paper duty would not work the miracles which were prophesied. It would only benefit the editors of penny newspapers. But he would not take responsibility for putting the Lords in conflict with the Commons. Nor would he call on the Lords to divide Gladstone's measure into two bills and send them both back separately to the Commons. Such a course, he advised, would appear merely retaliatory.[121] At a meeting of the Conservative leadership at Lord Salisbury's house in Arlington Street, on Tuesday 17 June, simmering discontent among many Conservatives, especially the Protestant Irish, was acknowledged. Objections to Disraeli personally, as well as his mooted alliance with Catholic Irish MPs, was identified as the main cause of their grievance. Disraeli, however, was unrepentant. 'Ireland is agricultural, aristocratic and religious: therefore Ireland ought to be Tory,' he insisted. But this, Stanley noted, 'does not allow enough for the antipathies of religion and race'.[122] The differences evident at the Arlington Street gathering, crystallizing around suspicion of Disraeli, signalled the fracturing of Conservative unity in the aftermath of Gladstone's budget success. 'Masterly inactivity', while frustrating more ardent Conservative backbenchers, had seemingly failed to deliver its anticipated reward. And, as before, the resentment arising from Derby's opposition strategy found a ready release in mistrust of Disraeli. During a walk with Bulwer Lytton in Hatfield Park on Thursday 1 August, Stanley concurred that a Derby ministry was now neither probable nor desirable.[123]

On 28 June, Derby attended a concert at Buckingham Palace. Yet, despite his abiding love for literature, he found less pleasure in the delights of music; it was words, rather than harmony, that engaged his emotions and fired his imagination. While waiting for his carriage at the end of the evening he was joined by Russell. Derby promptly commented that Lord John had got into bad company. With a grim smile Russell looked back at him and replied, 'I see I have.' Derby then observed that Russell was incorrectly dressed, having on his Levée uniform, instead of the full dress he ought to have worn. Russell admitted that when he arrived the porter had wanted to turn him out. 'Oh, did he?' exclaimed Derby. 'Thou canst not say *I* did it.' This ready Shakespearian quote, from Macbeth's confrontation with the ghost of Banquo, drew much laughter from all those around them, including Lord John himself.[124]

> So, for many years, are we condemn'd
> To wage a fruitless war.
>
> (Derby, *The Iliad of Homer*, i. 51)

Gladstone's 1861 budget success proved a turning point. Dissensions within Palmerston's cabinet abated. Divisions among Conservatives MPs increased. During June, Pakington protested bitterly about Disraeli's failure to consult his colleagues: 'I cannot admit', he complained to Disraeli, 'that we should have neither voice in the course of action to be taken, nor knowledge what the course is upon which you have determined.'[125] Rumours of Disraeli's impending resignation as opposition leader circulated. Meanwhile, Gladstone's transformation into the 'People's William' gathered pace, as the Chancellor's mission of ensuring Free Trade and minimal indirect taxation supported his moral vision of an economically liberated populace growing in self-reliance and civic maturity. Palmerston and Derby's avoidance of suggesting religious differences as the basis of party distinctions highlighted Gladstone's moral zeal, as the Chancellor's religious intensity, evident piety, and personal devotion began to resonate with communities of popular sentiment such as the Nonconformists. If Derby and Palmerston were patently men of the world, Gladstone was equally clearly a man of God.

Other events heightened the sense of significant political change. Russell was now a fading presence. As Clarendon bluntly noted, Russell 'is nobody and sinking fast'.[126] The death of Russell's elder brother, the Duke of Bedford, apathy over Reform, and the passing of the Italian crisis prompted Lord John, in May 1861, to request his elevation to the Lords. At the end of the session, while retaining the Foreign Secretaryship, he entered the Lords as Earl Russell, his relinquishing of the battleground of the Commons a public acknowledgement of his increasing political marginalization. With characteristic jocularity, Derby welcomed Russell to the Lords with the bantering remark, 'What fun we shall have, now you have come!'[127] But Derby's lifelong antagonist, if not quite Banquo's ghost, was no longer a potent political force. Clarendon predicted that Russell would not be successful in the Lords, 'and he will not have the temper for the pokes that Derby will delight in giving him'.[128] Russell's elevation was one indication of shifts in the political landscape. Death amplified the sense of transformation. Lord Aberdeen's demise in December 1860 was followed, in late October 1861, by Graham's death. Aged 69, Graham died at Netherby Hall, weighed down by a feeling of oppressive isolation. Derby's loyal companion of the 1820s and 1830s was now a silent voice. In his own words, Graham had joined the party which reposed without. In 1854 Derby had asked Graham to remove him as an executor from his will. Graham reluctantly agreed, although regarding Derby's appointment as executor as 'the last proof of the confidence and friendship which were the pride and comfort of 20 years of my life'.[129] But by 1854 political differences between the two former colleagues had become too great for Derby to feel such an arrangement was appropriate. With sadness Graham acquiesced. Graham was predeceased by Sidney Herbert, aged a mere 51, on Friday 2 August 1861. The Peelite first Viceroy of India, Lord Canning, died in 1862. On 4 March 1861 the 81-year-old Lansdowne, deaf and infirm, made his last speech in the Lords and Derby's early mentor died at Bowood on 31 January 1863. Derby's last living link with the Whiggism of his youth was now gone. A bleak valedictory sense of a world slipping away descended as, at the end of 1861, Derby began making legal arrangements for his estate in the event of his own death. Then, during the evening of Saturday 14 December 1861, Prince Albert unexpectedly died aged 42, leaving a distraught Queen in anguished mourning.

Following the quiet end of the 1861 session and after presiding at the Wellington College prize day, Derby withdrew to Knowsley. The familiar cyclical pattern of ill health ensued. On 14 September, while visiting the Earl of Ellesmere at Worsley Hall and meeting members of the British Association for the Advancement of Science, the 62-year-old Derby suffered a serious attack of gout, complicated by a bilious infection. After returning immediately to Knowsley, his recovery was slow. It was not until the end of the month that he was able to sit downstairs with the family in the evening. As before, sedentary comfort was provided by classical authors, as he occupied himself with translating works by Homer, Horace, and Catullus. Yet the slowness of his recovery suggested to Stanley that his father's retirement from public life was a possibility.[130] On Sunday 10 November, Derby braced himself for the painful journey to London to attend a meeting of the governors of Wellington College, but afterwards he immediately returned to Knowsley to resume his recuperation. When Stanley delivered a speech in King's Lynn at the end of the month, calling for continued domestic reform in the areas of law, the military, education, and the church rates, his father's response, when Stanley returned to Knowsley, was decidedly cold.[131] The fact that Stanley was, aged 35, unmarried, that he chose to spend much of his time in the company of the married Lady Salisbury, and therefore was still not in a position to produce an heir, remained a continuing source of disquiet between them. Lady Derby expressed her anxiety that they had an 'eldest son who ignores womankind and is a sort of political monk'.[132] That Stanley did not share Derby's passion for the turf, and privately felt unease about the expense of such amusements, exacerbated these tensions. Though their coolness soon thawed, Derby's protracted illness rendered him all the more susceptible to the irritation of what he saw as filial waywardness.

Serious illness rendered Derby for long periods a semi-invalid over the next two years. At the end of December 1861 he met with his lawyers to ensure that his affairs were in order for when Stanley would succeed to the earldom. Slowly recovering during the early part of 1862 from the gout and infections of the previous autumn, once again in October 1862 he collapsed into his sickbed. Gout, which affected his wrists and ankles, was complicated by what Disraeli called a 'paroxysmal affection', bringing on the symptoms of a stroke or fit.[133] Derby remained in fragile health throughout 1863. In the summer of 1864 he suffered another prolonged attack of gout, compounded in November 1864 by an ulcerated sore throat, and for nearly five weeks, he informed Disraeli in early December, 'I have been a prisoner in my room, from which I have not yet emerged.'[134] This prompted him to dwell on the short span of life that might be remaining to him. As before, depression and irritability accompanied prolonged periods of acute pain. When, during the autumn of 1862, Stanley also suffered 'a very disagreeable depression of mind' while at Knowsley, he ascribed it to the wet climate of Lancashire, combined with the prevailing east wind, which came loaded with foul vapours from the industrial towns inland.[135] Prevailing medical orthodoxy ascribed the spread of contagious disease to the presence of noxious vapours, unwholesome exhalation creating a miasma of infection. Certainly the pattern of Derby's ill health and depression increasingly accompanied his prolonged residency at Knowsley. His declining health and extended periods in the dampness of Knowsley formed the private backdrop to his political passivity during 1862 to 1864. Although great efforts were made to keep Derby's ill health secret, rumours of their leader's incapacity inevitably spread gloom among the Conservative rank and file.

Yet, despite his deteriorating health, Derby did not seriously contemplate retirement. Two considerations kept him in the saddle. First, he wished to retire only when the Conservatives had recovered a parliamentary majority. This was the goal to which he had worked consistently since 1846. As the final vindication of his efforts as party leader, he had no wish to step down before it was achieved. Secondly, he saw no fit successor who could preserve Conservative unity. He maintained a working relationship with Disraeli, but it remained, following the social chill that descended on their relations after the Knowsley visit of October 1859, an association lacking cordiality. After May 1861 the contagion of distrust of the 56-year-old Disraeli assumed a renewed intensity, infecting the opposition front bench, as well as sections of the Commons rank and file. In early June, Pakington openly stated his dissatisfaction with Disraeli.[136] Bulwer Lytton displayed 'a singular mixture of feelings towards Disraeli', admiring him, sneering at him, and envying his position.[137] Walpole and Henley remained sources of deep discontent, while the knot of vehement anti-Disraeli backbenchers associated with Ben Bentinck and Lord Robert Cecil assiduously maintained their cutting denigration of the Commons leader. Stanley, the coming man of the 1850s, also failed to command loyalty. He was, many Tory backbenchers suspected, a closet Liberal, who only remained with the party out of filial obligation. Derby himself, when in 1863 Stanley travelled to King's Lynn to give a speech, confessed, 'I am always rather apprehensive as to what he might say on these occasions.'[138] When in July 1862 Stanley spoke in the Commons against giving the police increased powers in dealing with poachers at a time when many in Lancashire were starving, Derby made his anger with his elder son plain.[139] Stanley himself thought Walpole, Pakington, and Malmesbury were 'at best colleagues, not chiefs: Lytton has genius, but neither judgement nor health—and—there is no one else'.[140]

Gladstone's ascendancy, Russell's fading influence, the passing of familiar contemporaries, and the serious deterioration of Derby's health cast a dispiriting pall over political affairs, affirmed by the outbreak of a bloody civil war in the United States. The conflict in America swiftly succeeded Italy at the forefront of foreign affairs. The Southern Confederacy seceded from the Union and in April 1861 Fort Sumter fell to Confederate forces. In July the first Battle of Bull Run led to large-scale mobilization in both the North and the South. Palmerston privately welcomed the war as a brake on American expansionism. Publicly he adopted a strict neutrality. Derby hoped for a prolonged conflict between the Union and the Confederacy, 'that both may be effectually humbled'.[141] There was in this kind of language, Stanley noted, some national feeling, but also a good deal of class jealousy. 'America is the country of equality, and has thus succeeded, in the minds of our upper classes, to the place which France filled in the days of the great revolution.' Malmesbury worried about the North acquiring a powerful army which might be used to invade Canada, 'a country difficult to defend'.[142] Then, in November 1861, a Union vessel stopped a British ship, the *Trent*, and forcibly arrested two Confederate envoys en route to London, James Mason and John Slidell. The War between the States threatened to become an international crisis.

Derby's response to the *Trent* incident mingled intense patriotic anger with sombre regret. A British war with the Union, however just and necessary, would be 'an incalculable misfortune'.[143] Yet a patent violation of international law could not go unpunished. He judged the act deliberately contemplated and ordered by the Northern government. It was unlikely, therefore, that they would offer either an apology or restitution. The withdrawal of the British Ambassador from Washington and the sending home of the US Ambassador to St James's seemed inevitable. But Derby feared that Palmerston would wish to stop there. 'If he does, I must say, it will be a very inadequate retribution for the insult and wrong which has been perpetrated.'[144] The argument of the Union, that ambassadors were contraband of war, that Mason and Slidell were ambassadors, and therefore it was lawful to search neutral vessels for contraband of war, he felt to be specious. Such an argument recognized the belligerent rights of the South, for if Mason and Slidell were just rebels then they were under British protection. In fact, Derby doubted whether they were ambassadors, and therefore there was no diplomatic liability. Moreover, if the North 'wished to pick a quarrel with us they could not have chosen a worse ground than one which ensured to us the sympathy of the whole South'.[145]

Only a robust response, Derby believed, would have any effect in Washington. 'The only mode of dealing with the American "people", who are the government,' he advised Newcastle, 'is to let them know plainly what we mean, and that we will stand no nonsense.'[146] He privately congratulated Granville 'that the government has taken a tone which will satisfy the American "mob" that we are in earnest … they should understand that blustering is not always safe, and (as such are the motives by which they are governed) it will not in the end improve their "personal position" '.[147] The domestic effect of the *Trent* affair, he believed, would be to make Palmerston's political position more secure. Despite the premier being seriously ill and seeming near retirement, the crisis provided a reason for Conservatives not to add to the embarrassment of the government. Moreover, 'a war will help to cover the delinquencies and deficiencies of the Chancellor of the Exchequer'.[148] Meanwhile, Derby enjoyed the premier's new tag of 'Palma Vecchio', ascribed to him by Granville, as 'ben traveto'.[149] An early Renaissance painter from Lombardy, Palma il Vecchio was known for his delicate touch in bringing out the contrast between light and shade. Granville's epithet, Derby acknowledged, was amusingly apt.

In mid-January 1862 President Lincoln backed down and Mason and Slidell were released, resuming their voyage across the Atlantic and arriving in Southampton on 30 January. This prevented the *Trent* crisis from erupting into war between Britain and the Northern States. The continued escalation of the Civil War itself, however, divided domestic British feeling along complex fault lines. Aristocratic opinion felt a natural affinity towards the land-owning classes of the South, although Derby, as well as Palmerston, felt deep moral revulsion for the South's 'peculiar institution' of slavery. Radical leaders felt an attachment to the democracy of the North; although Cobden's enthusiasm was tempered by the Union's espousal of economic Protection. The North's blockade of the South, moreover, interrupted the supply of raw cotton to the factories of the

Midlands, about 80 per cent of Britain's import of raw cotton coming from the Confederacy. As approximately 20 per cent of the British population lived directly or indirectly from the cotton industry, mass unemployment in regions such as Lancashire was unavoidable. At the same time, the collapse of America's mercantile marine created new opportunities for British merchants to expand into vacant markets. The investment of major British finance houses such as Barings and Rothschilds in the economy of the North, moreover, was a countervailing pressure to the interest of the cotton industry in the South. Some British commentators, mindful of Plato's warning that any pure democracy must eventually descend into either despotism or anarchy, believed that the great territorial expansion of the United States since the 1790s had extended government beyond the physical limits of a common sovereignty. Excessive geographical expansion had sapped democratic government of its vigour and, by suppressing the Confederacy's secession by force of arms, the North had plunged towards a coercive despotism. Palmerston maintained a strict neutrality, recognizing the belligerency, but not the independence, of the South.

As the danger of imminent war with the Union receded during January 1862, so Palmerston's serious ill health, prompting his physician to warn of possible paralysis, raised speculation about impending party realignment. Despite his own fragile health, Derby discussed with Malmesbury his doubts about Palmerston's being strong enough to carry on in government.[150] Granville, observing that the elderly premier had taken to wearing a green shade, thought Palmerston resembled a 'retired old *croupier* from Baden'.[151] The ageing Russell was Palmerston's obvious successor. But Derby believed a Russell ministry would be neither strong nor durable. This, in turn, might open the way to a Conservative return to office and encourage fusion with disenchanted Whigs and moderate Liberals. He talked over with Malmesbury a possible future government.[152] Disraeli, however, evinced less apparent eagerness than formerly for a resumption of power. 'He had had enough', he told Stanley, 'of being a minister on sufferance, and did not wish for such a position again.'[153] In any event, the importance of not alienating possible Whig adherents recommended a cautious line, avoiding any precipitous move, and allowing Palmerston's physical collapse and Russell's impetuosity to determine events.

It was, therefore, with a careful patriotic statement on the Address that Derby spoke to the Lords at the opening of the session on Thursday 6 February 1862.[154] In an eloquent tribute to Prince Albert, he affirmed a deep national sense of loss and described the Prince's unremitting attention to the happiness, domestic comfort, and mental and moral welfare of all Her

Majesty's subjects. He then expressed his cordial approval of the neutrality adopted by the government towards America. He doubted the efficiency of the Northern blockade. Some cotton manufacturers had accumulated stocks of raw cotton and a considerable surplus in manufactured goods. This meant distress was localized, although the most acute suffering was felt by workers in Lancashire. Derby praised the forbearance shown by the working classes in manufacturing districts. The time might shortly come, he predicted, when the government should recognize the successful revolt of the Confederacy. Moreover, the delusion that Canada might wish for annexation by the United States could be dismissed for ever. Over the *Trent* affair the Union, he concluded, had committed an injustice from which they had withdrawn only when demands for retribution were backed by force. The speech was carefully calibrated so as to express loyal support for the government, while applying maximum pressure on cabinet unanimity. Through her secretary Sir Charles Phipps the grieving Queen sent her grateful thanks to Derby for his fulsome tribute to her dearly beloved husband.[155] On 1 March, at the request of the Queen, Derby hosted a meeting, attended by Clarendon, the Lord Mayor of London, Sir Charles Eastlake, and the President of the Royal Academy, at St James's Square to consider the appropriate design and location for a national memorial to the late Prince Consort.

During February and March political events hung on the strength of Palmerston's pulse. A convalescent Derby, while attending meetings of the Great Exhibition Commissioners, awaited events, only an education debate on 4 March raising him to his feet in the Lords.[156] Then, in early April, an attack of gout combined with influenza forced him back to his sickbed. On 17 April, accompanied by Lady Derby and Stanley, he travelled back to Knowsley for the Easter recess, the train journey made bearable by his resting in a bed-carriage all the way. On this occasion the warmer spring weather in Lancashire appeared to raise his spirits, as he discussed with Stanley his intention to print some of his translations into English verse of Homer, Horace, and Catullus.[157] Nonetheless, he announced to the family his retirement from the turf. He was now reluctantly resolved to sell off his remaining horses. At the same time, he continued the careful ordering of his affairs, in anticipation of his fragile health forcing him into permanent seclusion at Knowsley.

Meanwhile, Palmerston's 78-year-old pulse, contrary to expectation, began to beat more strongly. Premonitions of ministerial collapse faded. Upon parliament reassembling on 28 April, Disraeli seized on Gladstone's financial policy, subverted by the impact of the war in America and

Treasury miscalculation. As well as serving Disraeli's lingering hope of using radical votes to disturb the government, the move reflected Northcote's increasing influence on Disraeli's thinking. The Devonshire baronet, with Gladstonian conviction, disparaged prevalent fears of French aggression and urged the need for economy.[158] National finances were labouring under a mounting deficit. Revenue from the paper duties had been sacrificed. Income tax was to be continued, while military and defence expenditure was increased. Having abandoned Reform, Disraeli pungently observed, the clearly discomfited Chancellor now forsook retrenchment. With war taxation sapping the strength of the country, Gladstone was financing 'bloated armaments' in time of peace. Such invective, however, only intensified Conservative suspicion of Disraeli's flirtation with the radicals. As proof of his physical recovery Palmerston, on Monday 19 May, gave 'one of his usual joyous and jaunty replies'.[159] Speaking 'with as much agility and briskness as if he had been forty years-old instead of seventy-eight as he is', Palmerston seized on Disraeli's studied harangue and, with cheers following each of his statements, appeared 'to have renewed his youth'.[160] Derby, meanwhile, who put defence above economy, felt deepening doubts about Disraeli's line of attack.

On Wednesday 21 May, Derby sought to moderate Disraeli's rhetoric. He feared raising expectations, especially if they were to lead to a re-sumption of office, which could not be realized without endangering the defences of the country. He reminded Disraeli that, when in office in 1858, they had increased naval expenditure.[161] On Saturday 24 May he called a meeting of twenty leading Conservative MPs at St James's Square to discuss the practical possibility of reducing defence expenditure. Opinion was divided. Some, such as Pakington, were for maintaining spending at the current level. Others, such as Disraeli and Stanley, favoured retrenchment.[162] After three hours of discussion it was eventually agreed not to censure the government for prodigal expenditure. Such a move, Derby anticipated, would only enlist radical votes in support of a Con-servative attack, this unnatural alliance leading to acrimony within their own ranks. But both the radicals and Palmerston raised the stakes. The advanced Liberal James Stansfeld brought forward a Commons motion calling for a reduction in national expenditure, thereby unfurling the radical banner of retrenchment. Palmerston, in response, gave notice of a motion expressing satisfaction at the economies already achieved and stressing the need to ensure national security.

At a large meeting of the Conservative party at the Duke of Marlbor-ough's house, 12 Upper Belgrave Street, on Monday 2 June, attended by

186 MPs, the dilemma in which this placed the opposition was discussed. To support Stansfeld's motion would cast the Conservatives as the allies of a radical manoeuvre to unseat Palmerston. But to support Palmerston would make a mockery of Disraeli's denunciation of Gladstonian prodigality. Derby rescued the party from its predicament by producing a motion pointing to more economy, but emphasizing the need to reduce the burden of those taxes, such as the income tax, avowedly of a temporary and exceptional character.[163] He also indicated to Disraeli that he did not regard the motion, if carried, as requiring the resignation of the government.[164] Derby's resolution was entrusted to Walpole. At the outset of the Commons debate on 3 June, however, Palmerston raised the stakes further by declaring that Walpole's proposed motion would constitute a vote of confidence in the government. As a result, Walpole, seized with panic, declined to bring his motion forward. A mortified Disraeli suddenly found himself engaged in a humiliating retreat. On the eve of Derby Day, Disraeli explained to the Commons, he now found his favourite had bolted. Stansfeld's resolution was subsequently defeated by a large majority. Palmerston's victory was complete. It was, he reported to the Queen, 'a most triumphant night'.[165]

Stanley attributed Walpole's collapse of nerve to a visceral dislike of Disraeli and an expectation that the Whigs might propose him for the Speakership.[166] This was an appointment earnestly desired by Walpole's ambitious wife. Yet, whatever Walpole's motives, the effect of his failure was to destroy any prospect, for the foreseeable future, of another Conservative offensive against the government. Palmerston's grip on power, which weeks before had seemed faltering, was firmly restored. Derby's doubts about Disraeli's economic initiative were vindicated. Fresh bouts of anti-Disraeli feeling erupted among the Conservative backbenchers. A humiliated Disraeli effectively withdrew from the fray, a retreat from Westminster which persisted over the next two years. Out of 188 Commons divisions during the session of 1863 Disraeli voted in only eight. In 1864, of 156 Commons divisions he voted in only seventeen. It was with difficulty that Derby retained Disraeli's engagement in the strategic discussions of the party leadership. In January 1863, with 'our parliamentary campaign ... about to begin', he had to impress upon Disraeli the critical importance of 'a conference on the general state of affairs'.[167] From being a party with a suspect leader, after June 1862 the Conservatives were in danger of becoming a party with no effective Commons leader at all.

Recognizing this danger, Derby actively sought to shore up Disraeli's authority. He reassured his disconsolate Commons leader: 'I will do my best to smooth matters; but I fear it will require time to reunite the party.'[168] He insisted to Sotheron-Estcourt that 'the vast majority of the party recognises Disraeli as their leader, and know perfectly well that they cannot dispense with his services'.[169] But this reflected Derby's earnest hope, rather than reality. He sought to bring Walpole and Henley back onto the opposition front bench and off the backbench seats they had assumed in 1859. 'Walpole is far too honourable to lend himself to any underhand intrigue; but there is a small, but very active, malcontent section who, from dislike of Disraeli, do not hesitate to thwart the policy agreed upon by the party generally to which they profess to belong.' Sitting around Walpole, these malcontents, Derby believed, exploited Walpole's 'good natured weakness' and 'use him as their unconscious tool'.[170] Sotheron-Estcourt was deputed to draw Walpole back into the leadership of the party. But Derby recognized the demoralized state of the Commons party and the impossibility, after the debacle of Walpole's abortive motion, of rallying Conservative MPs behind any new offensive. As he confessed to Whiteside: 'I have too much experience of the difference between strength enough to turn a government out, and strength to keep a government in, to be in a hurry to repeat the experiment of 1852 and 1858.'[171]

On Sunday 15 June, Derby had an interview with the Queen, who repeatedly broke off their conversation to dwell upon Prince Albert's final illness and death. 'She allows nothing to be touched in the room where he died: all remains as it was during his last illness.'[172] She was determined 'to carry into execution all the Prince's plans, employ everyone who he was in the habit of employing, and act generally as though he was still living'. Following their interview, through Clarendon, the Queen conveyed her strong wish to avoid a dissolution or ministerial crisis, because of her mourning for the Prince Consort. On Friday 20 June, Derby assured Clarendon that he saw no difficulty in avoiding giving the government even a pretext for resigning or dissolving during the remainder of the session.[173] Loyal duty and party incapacity became aligned. He could unhesitatingly promise his sovereign what, for other reasons, he knew was a path his party must follow.

I wish my people's safety, not their death.

(Derby, *The Iliad of Homer*, i. 7)

Prior to the collapse of Derby's health in mid-September 1862, civic events in Lancashire affirmed his close ties with the county community.

On Tuesday 2 September he participated in the ceremonies marking the laying of the first stone of the new Town Hall by the Mayor in Preston. The almost feudal regard for Derby existing in the region remained evident. As he processed through the town the crowd 'cheered him vehemently: some carried their welcome so far as to shake hands, slap him on the back, lay hold of his arm, and asked if he remembered them, all of which familiarities he took in excellent part'. It was 'an honest welcome, though a rough one'.[174] The following day, at the Preston agricultural show, Derby chaired a large dinner in a tent, 'which let water in so freely that during heavy showers we had to sit under heavy umbrellas'. Following the dinner he spoke for an hour 'like a farmer' on the 'necessity of manuring, utilising sewage, and so forth'. He 'was very cordially received'.[175] On Thursday 4 September, alongside Preston's Mayor, he reviewed a parade of local tradesmen, who all gave the Earl 'a hearty cheer.'

Derby was forcibly struck by the good humour, despite the persistent rain, shown by Preston's inhabitants. The suffering of the local working classes because of the 'Cotton Famine', manufacturers' stocks now being exhausted, was real. But the 'air of contentment' and enthusiasm to participate in the passing ceremonials deeply impressed him.[176] The loyalty of the Lancashire workers, facing increasing hardship with dignity, endorsed his conviction of the responsibility owed by the rich to the poor. The suffering of Lancashire was a challenge to the Christian duty of private charity, a test which the county's upper classes should neither fail nor ignore. Already, on 2 July 1862, he had chaired in London a meeting to organize a subscription for the relief of distress in Lancashire. His own initial contribution of £1,000 was supplemented by smaller subscriptions from Lord Ellesmere and his uncle Algernon Egerton (Conservative MP for South Lancashire), John Wilson Patten (Conservative MP for North Lancashire), the 3rd Earl of Ducie, and Lord Skelmersdale (Lady Derby's nephew).[177] Following the meeting the Queen also contributed £2,000 to the subscription. The fund rose to £40,000 by August, eventually reaching the sum of £52,000. Wilson Patten agreed to be Honorary Treasurer and Sir James Kay Shuttleworth, former reforming Secretary to the Privy Council Committee on Education, agreed to act as Secretary to the Fund.

While overcoming severe gout, in October and November 1862 Derby threw his limited energies into chairing the Central Relief Fund for Lancashire, which oversaw the activities of 143 local committees collecting clothing and donations. He was supported by Kay Shuttleworth as

Vice-Chairman and John Maclure, a Manchester Tory (who in 1868 would become Chairman of the Manchester Conservative Association), as Secretary. By December, Derby's correspondence was dominated by his efforts to alleviate suffering in the manufacturing districts.[178] The 'distress here is rapidly and fearfully augmenting', he informed Malmesbury, 'and we fully expect that by Christmas there will be over 240,000 paupers in twenty-four unions!' The prospects for the winter, 'especially if it should be a severe one, are fearful; and admirably as the people have behaved hitherto, it is impossible to say what continued and aggravated suffering may lead them to'.[179] The dark spectre of increasing destitution giving way to civil disorder reinforced the moral imperative of Christian charity. Despite persistent pain in his ankles and wrists, on 2 December he spoke to a rally in Manchester Town Hall acknowledging the 'noble manner, a manner beyond all praise, in which this destitution has been borne by the population of this great county'.[180] Chaired by Lord Sefton and attended by major Lancashire landowners, including Lord Wilton, Lord Skelmersdale, Lord Egerton of Tatton, and Sir Robert Gerard, the meeting listened to Derby's graphic description of the disaster, which had turned the county from a 'teeming hive of industry into a stagnant desert of compulsory inaction and idleness'. Out of a local population of 2 million, he declared, there were now over 430,000 persons dependent for their daily subsistence upon parochial relief or charity. They were gathered, he continued, to consider 'the best means of palliating—would to God I could say removing!—a great national calamity'. Such suffering, he affirmed, was a bounden call on Christian charity. Only as a desperate last resort should an appeal be made to the government. Far better, he concluded, that Lancashire should alleviate its distress by its own voluntary efforts. This appeal raised a further £130,000 for the Relief Fund.

Clear principles underlay Derby's organization of the relief for Lancashire, which he outlined to the Executive Committee on 19 January 1863.[181] First, relief must come from private charity, not public funds. The crisis was a challenge to individual Christian conscience, not a call on government finances. To do otherwise, he believed, would deprive the rich of the opportunity granted by Providence to perform their bounden duty and subvert the dignity of workers and their families by rendering them dependants of the State. Private charity was doubly blessed, consecrating both those who gave and those who received. Secondly, Derby believed it was important to distinguish the honest and the industrious from the idle and profligate. It was no less a duty to ensure that charity was given responsibly, or else it merely encouraged the idle further away from diligent self-reliance. Indiscriminate charity was both a waste and a moral temptation to the indolent. No relief should be given to those who had money in savings banks or were paying contributions to sick clubs, but the claims of cottage holders should be judged only on the amount of income received, omitting the value of property from which no yield was returned. Similarly, small shopkeepers threatened with destitution by the distress of their customers could fairly be considered to have a claim upon the Fund. In judging individual cases, he advised, the Relief Committee should err on the side of liberality, rather than too great strictness. By January 1863 almost half a million people within the county were receiving relief of one form or another, exceeding Derby's own forecast. In 1864 the number fell to just over 203,000. The worst of Lancashire's suffering, he reported to parliament on Thursday 4 February 1864, was coming to an end.[182]

Never was Derby's loyal devotion to the interests of Lancashire more tangibly demonstrated than in the face of the Cotton Famine. In total he personally contributed £12,000 to the Fund, on one occasion giving £5,000. This was widely regarded, at the time, as the largest single subscription ever made by an individual Englishman to a public fund for a specific purpose. Disraeli observed that Derby's 'subscription of many thousands was munificent, but his administrative talent in managing the vast sums entrusted to the Central Committee by the nation not less admirable'.[183] John Wilson Patten reported to Sotheron-Estcourt that 'Lord Derby has ... by his character and influence done an immense amount of good which will be long felt. You would be amused to see him sitting in a c[ommitt]ee composed of all creeds and politics, cordially cooperating with men some of whom go even further than Bright.'[184] Derby's conduct 'gained him golden opinions from all parties',[185] his achievement being all the more impressive because of the acute pain that dogged him throughout this period. During 1862-4 over £800,000 of private charity was distributed, under his chairmanship, to the destitute workers of Lancashire. This was an achievement, *The Times* applauded, 'absolutely unparalleled ... in the history of benevolence'.[186]

As well as devoting himself to the suffering of Lancashire, Derby responded decisively to the ravages of chemical manufacture in the county. Since the 1820s the damage caused to the landscape by rapidly expanding alkali manufacture, particularly in St Helens, Widnes, and Runcorn, had blighted large parts of south-east Lancashire. Producing a synthetic soda, essential to the processes of the glass and soap industries and providing a bleaching powder required by the textile industry, the alkali works around Knowsley created large quantities of solid and liquid industrial waste, as

THE GREAT DERBY DAY.

1. Punch, in May 1852,
asks Derby which horse he is
going to back to win, Disraeli
on Free Trade or Protection?

2. Derby as Chancellor of
Oxford University. His appearance,
Sir William Fraser recalled, 'was
magnificent. Dressed in his rich
robes of black satin, with masses of
gold; tall; of exceptionally dignified
presence; no one could look the
Chancellor better than he.'

3. The shy conscientious bachelor Lord Stanley, painted in 1858, whose political sympathies reached beyond partisan loyalties, yet who was, Lady Derby observed, a sort of 'political monk'.

4. A world-weary wistful Disraeli, photographed in the early 1860s, whose fragile Commons leadership was reliant on the grace of Derby's endorsement.

5. Derby's political confidant, sporting companion and Foreign Secretary Lord Malmesbury, whose public reputation obscured his private diligence and sound common sense.

CARTOON, AUGUST, 1874.

THE LONDON SKETCH BOOK.

THE DISRAELI ADMINISTRATION.

EARL OF MALMESBURY.
(Lord Privy Seal.)

6. Lord John Russell, whose liberal rectitude, Derby believed, led to pious posturing and ineffectual gestures.

7. *Left* The dogged and resourceful Lord Palmerston, photographed in 1858. Both a potential ally and a formidable opponent, Derby regarded Palmerston as a political chameleon.

8. *Below* The intensely religious, highly-wrought and often inscrutable William Gladstone. A dangerous politician, Derby observed, who having taken up an idea followed it with a passion, rendering him utterly reckless of consequences.

THE GREAT CHINESE WARRIORS DAH-BEE AND COB-DEN

EARL OF D—RB—Y.   C—BD—N.   P—LM—RST—N.

9. *Above* Derby and Cobden challenge Palmerston over the Arrow affair, Punch cartoon of March 1857.

THE FRANTIC FOOTMAN,

WHO HAS HAD WARNING.

10. Surrounded by the broken remnants of his Reform bill, an angry Derby throws down a dissolution of parliament, Punch cartoon of April 1859.

11. A leonine Derby in the early 1860s, twice premier, benefactor of Lancashire, and the patrician embodiment of mid-Victorian Conservative values.

THE HONEST POTBOY.

12. The landlord Derby instructs his potboy Disraeli to give John Bull a full measure of Reform, while the inspectors Gladstone and Russell watch closely from outside, Punch cartoon 1867.

13. Derby's cabinet, post-March 1867, showing (from left to right) the Earl of Mayo, Lord Stanley (seated), Gathorne Hardy, Sir John Pakington (seated), Benjamin Disraeli, the Duke of Richmond, the Duke of Buckingham (seated), the Duke of Marlborough, Sir Stafford Northcote, Lord Malmesbury, Lord Chelmsford, Spencer Walpole, Lord Derby, Lord John Manners and Henry Corry.

14. The 70-year-old Derby, still the beleaguered champion of the Church of Ireland, as depicted by 'Ape' (Carlo Pelligrini) in Vanity Fair, May 1869.

well as spewing noxious gases into the atmosphere. The devastation to local vegetation—oaks, ashes, poplars, walnuts, and fruit trees being the worst affected—was caused by caustic toxic vapour emitted into the air, which also produced a slaty-blue-coloured soot that settled on nearby houses. In addition, waste dilute hydrochloric acid was allowed to drain into local brooks, rivers, and canals. As a result, *The Times* noted, 'whole tracts of country, once as fertile as the fields of Devonshire, have been swept by deadly blights till they are as barren as the shores of the Dead Sea or the banks of the Great Salt Lake'.[187] In December 1861 Derby's exasperated neighbour Sir Robert Gerard, whose estate lay to the north-east of St Helens, wrote to him declaring that this desperate situation required an urgent legislative remedy.[188] Derby immediately agreed. He proposed the establishment of a Select Committee of the House of Lords to gather evidence of the magnitude of the evil, the inadequacy of present remedies, and the practicality of prevention. Only then, he anticipated, would the opposition of local manufacturers to regulation be overcome.[189] He entrusted his Liverpool solicitor John Stanistreet with the task of collecting evidence from local landowners through their land agents. He also began organizing key witnesses to be called before the Select Committee, the establishment of which he moved in the Lords on 9 May 1862.[190] In his speech he emphasized that this was not a hostile move by Lancashire landowners against local manufacturers. Lancashire's 'prosperity or deterioration depended on the prosperity or depression of the manufacturing interest'. The existing difficulties of the cotton industry in the county demonstrated the critical importance of manufacturing to the local economy. Rather, he sought a consensual remedy to an obvious blight, that was in the interests of all sections of the community.

The work of the Select Committee, dubbed 'Lord Derby's Smell Committee' by *Punch*, proceeded quickly. Chaired by Derby, four landowners with estates in areas where alkali manufacture operated, lords Grey, Ravensworth, Stanley of Alderley, and Egerton, were also appointed to the Committee, and an additional ten Liberal and Conservative peers enlisted. Between 13 May and 18 July 1862 the Committee met ten times and interviewed a total of forty-eight witnesses. These included the scientific expert Lyon Playfair, who had been persuaded to appear by Derby. Playfair testified to the damaging effect of industrial emissions and suggested effective methods of prevention. The Committee also called Widnes alkali manufacturer John Hutchinson, who pledged the support and cooperation of the manufacturers for a reasonable measure. The final report of the

Committee contained two sets of recommendations. First, that the existing Smoke Prevention Act applied to metropolitan areas be extended to the country as a whole, and that alkali manufacturers be required to put their waste gas emissions through a condensation process which would dramatically reduce the release of toxic vapours into the atmosphere. Secondly, to enforce this legislation, it was proposed that an inspectorate, wholly independent of local control, be authorized to visit factories on a regular basis to ensure compliance.[191]

Drawing on the Select Committee report, in April 1863, Lord Stanley of Alderley introduced to the Lords, on behalf of the government, the Alkali Works Regulation Bill. The measure required alkali producers to condense at least 95 per cent of all hydrogen chloride emissions by whatever method they preferred, and appointed inspectors, authorized to prosecute for non-compliance, employed by the Board of Trade. Debate on the bill in the Commons focused on the fact that it instituted, for the first time, an inspection for the protection of property, and not for the safety of workmen. As a result, the bill was amended, the requirements for obtaining a conviction being made more stringent, so as to protect manufacturers against improper interference. Throughout, Derby insisted that it was not an attack on manufacturers by the landowning interest, but a necessary remedy to an environmental hazard that afflicted all sections of society. He was careful to ensure that the deliberations of the Select Committee did not alienate the goodwill of the alkali manufacturers by commenting on the appalling working conditions of employees in the works. That local alkali manufacturers, such as John Hutchinson, proved amenable to some form of control helped to ensure that the measure did not become a divisive issue. The potentially controversial principle contained in the legislation of the state regulation of property was thus avoided by concentration on the pragmatic remedy to a specific evil. Not until 1878 was there serious parliamentary discussion of the propriety of the Alkali Act in a free society.[192] The Alkali Works Regulation Act was passed by parliament in July 1863 and came into effect in January 1864. As a result, it was subsequently estimated that the weekly escape of toxic gas from alkali works of approximately 4,000 tons in 1863 was reduced to 43 tons by the end of 1864. With admirable speed Derby led the successful campaign to control the industrial pollution created by expanding manufacture in Lancashire. This, alongside his relief work for destitute workers, constituted a signal service to his county, an achievement the more notable because of the chronic ill health from which he suffered over these same months.

Infirmity and confinement at Knowsley were made bearable by cloistered hours of patient Greek, Latin, and Italian translation. In 1860 Derby engaged the architect William Burn to extend the north end of the eighteenth-century wing of Knowsley to accommodate his large library, beyond which projected a series of conservatories. Surrounded by his books, an invalid Derby immersed himself in literary study. In 1862 he privately published his *Translations of Poems: Ancient and Modern*, containing translations of the classical Greek poet Anacreon and the Latin verse of Horace and Catullus, renderings of Latin epitaphs by Bishop Lowth and the Marquess of Wellesley, the French poet Charles Millevoye, the Italian verse of Abbe Pietro Matastasio, Vincenzo da Filicaja, and Alessandro Manzoni, and translations of Schiller's poetry from German. During 1863 he also continued to work on Homer's epic *The Iliad*. It was an ambitious undertaking, the standard English edition being that by Alexander Pope published between 1715 and 1720. He did not hope to supplant Pope's polished brilliance on poetic grounds. But he did see value in a more literal translation, conveying something of the spirit, as well as the simplicity, of the great original. 'Pope's Iliad can hardly be said to be Homer's Iliad.'[193] Rather, 'it was a happy adaptation of the Homeric story to the spirit of English poetry'. Derby looked to complete a more precise translation of the ancient epic, particularly as he feared that the appreciation of classical literature was on the decline. Earlier translations had adopted various metres, the ordinary couplet in rhyme, the Spenserian stanza, the trochaic or ballad metre, and even that 'pestilent heresy' the so-called English hexameter, which, Derby pronounced, 'can only be pressed into service by a violation of every rule of prosody'. Only heroic blank verse, he believed, could do justice to the easy flow and majestic simplicity of Homer's original. It could adapt to 'the finished poetry of the numerous similes, in which every touch is nature, and nothing is overcoloured or exaggerated, down to the simple, almost homely, style of some portions of the narrative'. Above all, blank verse did 'full justice to the spirit and freedom of the various speeches, in which the old warriors give utterance, without disguise or restraint, to all their strong and genuine emotions'.

Through his prolonged periods of illness during 1863 and 1864 Derby diligently stuck to his Homeric task. 'Otherwise', Stanley noted, 'the continual and absolute seclusion of his Knowsley life would be depressing.'[194] By October 1864 the undertaking was complete. Dedicated to the Prince of Wales, 'with profound respect and dutiful attachment', it was published in two volumes by John Murray and, as Derby commented, 'left to the impartial decision of such of the public as may honour this work with their perusal'.[195] The public response was favourable. *The Times* applauded the clearness and precision of his translation. The Whiggish *Edinburgh Review* voiced high praise for his accomplishment. Bulwer Lytton observed to Lady Salisbury, 'I have just read Lord Derby's *Homer*. I admire it intensely. In fact it amazed me.'[196] That sternest of Homeric critics Gladstone deemed it 'a very notable production'. With characteristic thoroughness Gladstone read Derby's text alongside I. C. Wright's blank-verse rendition of the *Iliad* of 1859 and Vincenzo Monti's translation into Italian, the *Iliade di Omero* of 1812. For good measure, Gladstone 'did a very little bit of Shield [of Achilles] in blank verse with difficulty'.[197] To the Duchess of Sutherland Gladstone concluded: Derby 'always had in high degree the inborn faculty of a scholar, with this he has an enviable power of expression, and an immense command of the English tongue; add the quality of dash which appears in his version quite as much as in his speeches'. Derby's translation, Gladstone judged, was 'of very high excellence'.[198] The first edition of 1,000 copies sold out in a week. A second edition of 2,000 copies came off the presses in mid-December. A further seven British and five American editions followed. Derby regarded the public praise for his *Iliad* with measured pleasure. 'I never was more astonished in my life', he wrote to Malmesbury, 'than on reading the puff of it in the "Times"!'[199] What his translation lacked in poetic polish was compensated for, he hoped, by its literary precision. As *Fraser's Magazine* concluded in 1868, an authentic simple force, rather than lofty passion, characterized his text.

The dedication of his translation of Homer to the Prince of Wales marked the continued warming of relations between Derby and the court. In early February 1863 Derby, alongside Argyll, Granville, and the Duke of Cambridge, accompanied the Prince as he took his seat in the House of Lords. On 10 March he attended the marriage of the Prince to Princess Alexandra of Denmark at Windsor Castle. The Queen, still in mourning, observed the ceremony in isolation from the gallery in St George's Chapel. Then, on 17 June, presiding as Chancellor of Oxford, Derby conferred an honorary DCL on the Prince of Wales at the Sheldonian Theatre. Over a period of three days the newly married royal couple were lavishly entertained at Christ Church and elsewhere in the University. The following month Derby, alongside Granville and Lieutenant-General Knollys (controller of the Prince's household), was appointed by the Queen as a trustee of the grant of annuity of £40,000 established for the Prince of Wales. In January 1864, as a further indication of her increasing regard for the Conservative leader, the Queen offered Derby the Presidency of the Royal Commission overseeing the late Prince Consort's favourite project of setting up national museums of the sciences and arts in South Kensington, funded by the proceeds of the Great Exhibition. Derby initially declined the invitation, suggesting that Granville, as long-serving chairman of the Commission's finance committee, would be a more appropriate choice. But the Queen insisted and in April 1864 he was elected President of the Royal Commission, a position he held until his death. Under Derby the Commission planned the building of the Royal Albert Hall, designed by Francis Fowke, which was eventually opened in May 1871. He also oversaw the proposal to construct the Albert Memorial, designed by Sir George Gilbert Scott to commemorate the Prince Consort's life and works, which was finally completed in 1876.[200] But he failed to secure the setting-up of a National Gallery in South Kensington, which he proposed as President in May 1866. The Royal Academy scuttled the plan by refusing to move from Burlington House. Nonetheless, Derby's crucial role in fulfilling the reclusive Queen's plans for commemorating 'her dear Albert' firmly cemented his relationship with the monarch.

> Forward he darted, as a swift-wing'd hawk,
> That swoops amid the starlings and the daws.
>
> (Derby, *The Iliad of Homer*, ii. 143)

During 1863 and 1864 foreign policy dominated parliamentary debate. 'The Greek affair, I am afraid,' Derby wrote to Malmesbury from his sickbed in October 1862, 'may be most formidable, and altogether, with the Italian, Greek, Montenegrin, Danish and Polish questions all in a ferment at once, I can hardly imagine a more unpleasant state of foreign affairs.'[201] His scorn for Russell's diplomacy, aggravated by persistent acute pain in his ankles and wrists, was fierce.

> I hardly know in what question Johnny has most mismanaged the Foreign Office. In point of absurdity, I think the cool proposal to the Pope to take refuge in Malta! surpassed them all ... But this is *only* an absurdity and can lead to no practical mischief. But his conduct in the Danish question casts discredit on British policy ... and as to the Greek question, and the intended (but not yet effected) secession of the Ionian Islands, it is hard to point out a single possible blunder which he has not made.[202]

This litany of incompetence revealed, he believed, a chronic weakness for strong rhetoric and a fear of decisive action, rendering Britain a marginal force in European affairs. 'Johnny has made more blunders than I thought possible,' he commented to Disraeli. Caught between fear of French ambition, the growing infirmity of the premier, the naive inexperience of Russell, the credulity of public opinion, and the inflammatory language of the daily press, the experienced diplomat Count Vitzthum (Ambassador for Saxony in London) observed, Palmerston's government was trapped 'in a vortex of embarrassments'.[203] Russell's ineptitude became the target of Derby's derision; a focus for his invective that kept up Conservative morale while avoiding personal attacks on Palmerston. As the European settlement of 1815 was dismantled and the map of Europe redrawn during the 1860s, Russell's liberal pronouncements and diplomatic timidity, Derby maintained, produced a foreign policy comprised of hollow posturing. As Britain's influence diminished, so the Foreign Secretary retreated into a succession of dangerously ineffectual gestures.

Both the endgame of Italian unification and preserving a strict neutrality over the American Civil War continued to create diplomatic problems. News reached London in August 1862 that, in apparent defiance of King Victor Emmanuel, Garibaldi was leading an army of Red Shirts to seize Rome. On 29 August, at Aspromonte, Garibaldi was seriously wounded and taken prisoner by the King's forces. Malmesbury correctly believed, however, that Victor Emmanuel was playing a double game, secretly encouraging Garibaldi, while foiling his military expedition, to prove to Europe that Italy could never secure peace until she controlled Rome and the Pope's temporal power was overthrown. Derby believed Garibaldi would become an 'embarrassing prisoner to the Italian government unless, which in the hands of Italian doctors is most probable, he should die of his wounds'. Clearly the Italian prime minister Rattazzi (Cavour having died in June 1861) had 'made Garibaldi the dupe, and then threw him over'.[204] The fate of Garibaldi remained an awkwardness, until his release and quiet retirement to his farm on Capresa.

During the autumn of 1862 Palmerston's cabinet also grappled with the question of whether to recognize officially the independence of the Southern Confederacy. A parliamentary campaign during the 1862 session to recognize the South, led by the Liberal shipowner William Lindsay, was rejected by Palmerston. But Southern victories during the summer and the possibility of Washington's being occupied by the Confederate army kept the issue an open question. By September 1862 both Palmerston and Russell, urged on by Gladstone, were willing to consider such a diplomatic move, accompanied by a European initiative, favoured by Napoleon III, to mediate between the belligerents. Granville and Cornewall Lewis, however, expressed serious doubts.[205] In October an enthusiastic Russell circulated a memorandum to his cabinet colleagues advocating a diplomatic intervention. But President Lincoln's Emancipation decree brought the slavery issue to the fore, the Confederacy failed to win a conclusive victory at Antietam, and Palmerston stepped back from Russell's proposal. On 22 October, Palmerston informed Russell that the government 'must continue to be lookers-on till the war shall have taken a more decided turn'.[206]

Derby consistently supported Palmerston's policy of recognizing the belligerency, but not the independence, of the Confederacy, 'especially as our "recognition" would do nothing unless accompanied by an active interference, which England would not support, or a mediation, which the North would not accept'.[207] In the Lords on 5 February 1863 he affirmed that recognition of the independence of the South would be neither wise nor even legitimate.[208] Parliamentary debate came to a head in June when, in the Commons, the Liberal Edward Horsman brought forward a motion proposing recognition. An inconclusive rehearsal of the countervailing arguments, however, left any move to future events. When, on 2 July, Derby met about ten Conservative members from each House to consider the question, only Pakington and Sir William Vesey-Fitzgerald (MP for Horsham and Foreign Office Under-Secretary from 1858 to 1859) favoured recognizing the South, the others thinking it premature. Derby spoke strongly in support of the majority.[209] A second meeting of the Conservative leadership on 9 July confirmed the opposition to recognition.[210] The consideration of whether an offer of mediation should be recommended to the government, as proposed by the radical Roebuck, however, proved inconclusive. To leave the matter in the hands of the government might appear an abdication of duty. To support a radical proposal certain of rejection by the Union would be a dangerous act of futility. The North's victory at Vicksburg and General Lee's abandonment of the battlefield at Gettysburg in early July 1863 then suggested a decisive change of military fortunes, with the South forced onto the defensive. This effectively closed any further British consideration of either recognition of the South or diplomatic intervention.

It was events in Greece, Poland, and Denmark, however, that for Derby exposed the true feebleness of Russell's diplomacy. In October 1862 London learnt that the unpopular King Otho of Greece had been deposed. Palmerston had been among those who had pressed for placing the Bavarian King Otho on the Greek throne in 1832. But he recognized that, while 'it seemed at the time the best arrangement', it had proved 'impossible to make a silk purse out of him'.[211] Greek leaders sought a suitable monarchical replacement from the aristocratic families of Europe.

Initially, Queen Victoria's second son, Prince Alfred, was a favoured candidate.[212] Russell's hasty response was to offer to cede the Ionian Islands to Greece as an inducement. When, following a conversation with Cornewall Lewis on 19 December, Stanley informed his father of the Foreign Secretary's intentions, Derby was aghast at Russell's egregious folly. 'It seems to me to combine every possible mistake of precipitating uncertainty, and undue neglect of parliament.'[213] The Ionian Islands were a British protectorate under the terms of an international treaty of 1815. Without consulting parliament Russell now proposed to hand the islands over to Greece. Derby was incensed.

> Whether the cession under any circumstances be defensible or desirable I will not undertake to say; but to promise a country in the very crisis of a revolution that in certain contingencies which cannot be ascertained for years, we will endeavour to induce other powers to relieve us of an European trust (some of those powers being notoriously indisposed to sanction the transfer) and to make this publicly known to our own dependencies, whom we govern with great trouble, and yet whom we must retain according to the government, in default of certain conditions, over the fulfilment of which they have no control, seems to me to be nothing short of infatuation.[214]

Russell, he declared to Normanby, was disregarding all the most important aspects of the issue. The protectorate in the Ionian Islands was a trust confided in Britain by Europe; it is 'not ours to dispose of as we wish'.[215] Moreover, Russell was acting on a sudden resolution without consulting parliament, although the opening of the 1863 session was only a few weeks away. Russell's proposal, therefore, had the appearance of 'a tricky coup d'état'. Russell should have deferred any decision until the Greek revolution was over. In short, 'the Kings whom Greece are offered won't take Greece; Greece does not want the Ionian Islands. The respectable part of the Ionians are aghast at the idea of cession. The Great Powers are divided on a question which need never have been raised; and an important step has been taken, to which the approval of parliament has not, and perhaps will not, be given. A prettier volunteer imbroglio', Derby concluded, 'it would have been difficult to get up!'[216] An alarmed Queen, learning of Derby's anger, talked to the Conservative leader and, as six months earlier, appealed for calm. The ordeal of a parliamentary crisis, she urged, would be beyond her strength.[217] Victoria's entreaty fell on sympathetic ears. Nonetheless, Derby planned to give Russell 'a gallop over the Ionian course'.[218] On 5 February 1863 he advised the Lords that the country must prevent 'an act which is one of the most suicidal and imprudent I ever recollect'.[219] Privately, he described the proposal to cede the Ionian Islands to Greece as 'sheer madness'.[220] But he refrained from pressing the question as a matter of confidence in the government.

Meanwhile, the diplomatic game of pass the Greek crown continued. Queen Victoria blocked consideration of Prince Alfred. Derby concurred that the selection of the Queen's second son would be 'the greatest possible blunder', antagonizing France and Russia, and embroiling the British royal family directly in the complexities of Greek politics.[221] King Ferdinand of Portugal, favoured by Palmerston's cabinet, declined the Greek throne in January 1863. Another candidate favoured by Britain, Prince Nicholas of Nassau, was objected to by Napoleon III. The Duke of d'Aumale, proposed by Napoleon III, was rejected by Palmerston. It was at this point that Lord Stanley's name was mentioned. But Stanley 'never treated it otherwise than as a joke',[222] and Derby did not encourage his son to take the proposal seriously. Palmerston was privately scathing. 'Fancy Lord Stanley King of Greece. Demosthenes *with* his pebbles.'[223] Captivated by the 'infinite romance' of the idea, Disraeli saw it as 'a dazzling adventure for the House of Stanley, but they are not an imaginative race, and, I fancy they will prefer Knowsley to the Parthenon and Lancashire to the Attic plain'.[224] Eventually, Prince William of Baden was elected King of Greece by the Greek Assembly under the name of George the First. Queen Victoria, Palmerston, and Russell supported his candidature and in October 1863 King George of the Hellenes arrived in Athens bringing with him, to Derby's exasperation, the Ionian Islands as a gift from Britain.

Russell's response to the insurrection in Poland against Russian control that erupted in January 1863 intensified Derby's disgust. Russell's expressions of moral indignation, in support of Polish grievances, were translated into feeble action. His diplomatic initiatives were blocked by the continental European powers. Having encouraged the Poles, he then abandoned them to their fate. As a result, the abortive Polish insurrection was prolonged, Russia was alienated, the prospects of future Anglo-French cooperation undermined, and the way prepared for an alteration in the European balance of power that would eventually lead to the unification of Germany. As Disraeli memorably described it, 'the Polish question is a diplomatic Frankenstein created out of cadaverous elements, by the mystic blundering of Lord Russell'.[225] In the Lords, on 13 July 1863, Derby recognized the suffering and gallantry of the Poles, by way of condemning Russell's encouragement of Polish hopes which could not be gratified.[226] During the autumn Russian military rule in Poland was restored.

The Schleswig-Holstein question, which preoccupied European foreign ministries during 1863 and 1864, finally called the diplomatic bluff of British Liberal pretensions. Without a powerful army Britain's self-righteous voice was a distraction other European powers could ignore. The crisis proved a watershed, as Britain withdrew into diplomatic isolation. Under the terms of the 1852 Treaty of London—hosted by Malmesbury and signed by Britain, France, Austria, Russia, Prussia, and Sweden—the duchies of Schleswig and Holstein were governed by Denmark. Over the following years renewed German claims to Holstein grew in intensity. Then, on 24 September 1862, Russell overthrew previous British policy by advising Denmark to cede Holstein to the German Confederation. Despite his infirmity, Derby's alarm was immediate. 'What on earth does [Russell] mean by turning round on Denmark, and taking up all at once the Prussian views about the Duchies? And how can Palmerston stand it, the original author of the Protocol which was the basis of the treaty of 1852?' Yet again, Russell's ill-advised meddling was steering Britain into dangerous waters. 'I think John Russell is getting us into all sorts of complications; and that the state of Europe becomes more and more critical every day.'[227] Malmesbury agreed that Russell's dispatch to Denmark was 'a most extraordinary and offensive one, giving advice upon subjects of internal administration, in which we have no business to meddle'. Russell's 'restless and impotent meddling' had only succeeded in reopening the whole question of Schleswig-Holstein.[228] That, on 30 November, under pressure from Palmerston, Russell recanted his Danish dispatch left matters in even greater confusion.

At the Chapel Royal at Windsor Castle, on 10 March 1863, the Prince of Wales married Princess Alexandra of Denmark. Three weeks later the King of Denmark announced a new constitution for Holstein and brought Schleswig directly under the authority of the Danish legislature. Prussia, meanwhile, increased the pressure on Denmark to cede the duchies. On Friday 15 May, upon Lord Ellenborough's calling for Britain to give its support to Denmark against German encroachment, by force of arms if necessary, the House of Lords held a full-scale debate. Derby strongly supported Ellenborough's pro-Danish line and condemned Russell's reversal of long-standing British policy. Britain's true interests, he declared, lay in protecting Denmark, as a free and constitutional kingdom, from German aggression.[229] The debate closed with Russell's former Under-Secretary the Liberal Lord Wodehouse, encouraged by Clarendon, joining in the condemnation of the Foreign Secretary's 'foolish despatch' of September.[230] In response, a few weeks later, Palmerston slipped into a Commons statement a declaration that 'all reasonable men in Europe' hoped that 'the independence, the integrity, and rights of Denmark' should be maintained.[231]

During the summer of 1863 relations between Denmark and Prussia, whose policy was now being directed by Count Bismarck, deteriorated rapidly. By October war appeared inevitable and Russell's clumsy attempts to champion a diplomatic settlement proved fruitless. Lingering hopes of Anglo-French diplomatic cooperation were dashed when, in November, Russell precipitously rejected Napoleon III's call for a Great Power Congress to settle all European territorial disputes, including Poland, Italy, and Moldo-Wallachia, as well as Schleswig-Holstein.[232] Already strained over Russell's views on Poland, Anglo-French relations became openly antagonistic, further offence being given to the Emperor by the printing of Russell's dispatch rejecting the Congress in the London press, before it was delivered to the French government. In December, Prussian and Austrian troops entered Holstein. Derby, who remained strongly pro-Danish, attributed the confusion that now hung over British policy entirely to Russell's vacillation. Europe faced 'a ruinous war occasioned by the madness not of Kings, but of people; for it is quite clear that both Danes and Germans are driving their respective sovereigns farther than they wish to be driven'.[233] Russell's inept attempts 'to bell the cat' had proved disastrous. A wiser course, he believed, would have been to take a line dependent upon the views of those states with a direct interest in the question. But, by irresponsible interference, Russell had only succeeded in alienating France, Britain's most powerful ally. 'I fear', he wrote to Malmesbury, 'that with the Germans just now passion is too strong for reason.'[234] Only a firm tone, rather than Russell's confused intervention, would prevent war.

The critical state of Britain's foreign relations in January 1864 drew Derby's thoughts to the composition of a future Conservative cabinet. It appeared possible that the government might shortly be forced to resign. Despite a serious recurrence of gout, weakness in his wrists and ankles, and a feeling of general debility, he roused himself for a resumption of office. The 80-year-old Palmerston's precarious health suggested his public career was drawing to an imminent close. The 'sole support of the government' appeared to be Palmerston's genial popularity.[235] But this had become a fragile prop upon which to brace the ministry's standing. Russell's diplomatic interventions had become increasingly distasteful to both his cabinet colleagues and many Liberal backbenchers. Gladstone's Peelite instincts and desire for economy constantly baulked at Russell's diplomatic meddling, while Cobdenite radicals preached non-intervention. Whigs such as Granville, Wood, and Clarendon privately regretted Russell's foreign adventures, while young Liberal peers, such as Lord Wodehouse, openly criticized the Foreign Secretary's interference in European affairs.[236] Increasingly, Palmerstonian bluster grated on Liberal sensibilities. As Disraeli observed in December 1863, 'foreign affairs were now those on which all interest is concentrated, there are no domestic questions'.[237] Clarendon judged Palmerston's position to be acutely precarious: 'Few of the great acrobats die a natural death and I expect that Palmerston one of these days will finish himself off by doing something more than any other man ever attempted. Even Lady Palmerston, who is a sort of Lady Blondin in her way, thinks her husband is taxing his Herculean powers too much.'[238] Derby believed a general election could not be far distant.[239]

Derby addressed a large gathering of Conservative peers and MPs at a dinner at the Mansion House on 1 July 1863. The banquet was hosted by the Lord Mayor, who, in inviting Derby to speak, noted that under Derby's last government crucial improvements to national defence, in particular the Navy, had been secured. Derby's own warmly received speech was a call to prepare for a forthcoming election.[240] He praised, to loud cheers, the firm, patient, self-denying, and patriotic conduct of his party since 1859, when they had been factiously ejected from office. Numerically far superior to any of the sections which made up the so-called Liberal party, he declared, the Conservatives remained not very inferior numerically to all of those sections combined. Nonetheless, they had studiously abstained from throwing the country into confusion. With a party, as with an army, he continued, while the heat of engagement tried their mettle, it was holding their position, while exposed to fire from the enemy, waiting for the moment when victory might be achieved and avoiding defeat by attacking too early, that tested the discipline and courage of the troops. For four years the Conservatives had adopted a patient forbearance, without suffering, he asserted, a material diminution of their spirit as a party. During that same period the advanced Liberals had been satisfied to leave their favourite projects in abeyance. Palmerston's premiership, meanwhile, had proved a success of personal popularity, not of statesmanship. The resilience of the premier's youthful spirits, Derby observed to much laughter, had barely kept pace with the elasticity of his political principles. Palmerston had pluck, he acknowledged. But retaining office by flattering social attentions, as a triumph of personal affability, was a poor substitute for consistent principle and coherent policy. As a result, the country suffered from the greatest misfortune of a weak government, which was reliant on the forbearance and even support of its political adversaries. The current session of parliament had produced no useful legislation and had witnessed repeated ministerial defeats. But this unfortunate state of affairs could not last much longer. Soon, he believed, the Conservatives would reap both for themselves and the country the reward which, if patiently obtained, would be more surely retained than if seized prematurely. Again echoing Peel's cry, Derby concluded with the plea to 'Register, register, register'. His appeal depicted patience as strength. So, he suggested, might 'masterly inactivity' deliver real power, rather than office on sufferance.

As European crises accumulated, ministerial discord and Russell's isolation increased. The Queen differed fundamentally with Russell and Palmerston over the Schleswig-Holstein emergency. Her sympathies were decidedly pro-German and Granville championed her views in cabinet, with Gladstone and Wood, among others, arguing strongly for non-intervention. On 10 December, Derby discussed with Stanley 'the necessity of having a cabinet ready, in case he should be called upon'.[241] Malmesbury would return to the Foreign Office. Derby 'spoke also of Hardwicke as necessary to him personally, as a man on whose fidelity he could rely, and who would follow him whatever he did'. Disraeli at the Exchequer, Pakington at the Admiralty, and Gathorne Hardy at the Home Office would be a reinstatement of former cabinet positions. Stanley was discussed for India or the Colonies, although he indicated little enthusiasm for either post. Yet, the real difficulty, Derby confided to his elder son, would be 'in providing for young rising men, in consequence of the claims of those who have held office before'.[242] The grooming of the 45-year-old Cairns as an eventual replacement for Chelmsford as Lord Chancellor was one solution. Entrusting the Board of Trade to Stafford Northcote was another. The advancement of Sir William Vesey-Fitzgerald to a cabinet post would also gratify a talented aspirant.

Derby, meanwhile, sought to dissolve the tight knot of anti-Disraeli backbenchers gathered around Ben Bentinck and Newdegate, by skimming off their talent and experience. He carefully repaired relations with Henley, with a view to his appointment, because of Henley's declining health, to some undemanding cabinet office such as the Duchy of Lancaster.[243] Derby also considered appointing the acerbic Lord Robert Cecil as Malmesbury's Under-Secretary at the Foreign Office. This would, he calculated, deflect Cecil's trenchant scepticism, by bringing it onto the front bench. During October 1863 Newdegate and Knightley hatched an abortive scheme to replace Disraeli with General Jonathan Peel as Commons leader. In

December they approached the Duke of Marlborough with an invitation to act as their leader in the Lords, a role Marlborough immediately declined.[244] That Newdegate, Knightley, and Bentinck looked upon Cecil as their best hope confirmed the wisdom of bringing him into the Conservative leadership.

In cabinet on Wednesday 27 January 1864, Russell failed to secure agreement to armed assistance for Denmark from Britain in the event of German aggression.[245] This left the government with no clear policy to recommend to parliament. The following day the Queen asked for an interview with Derby. This fuelled speculation about Derby's shortly being requested to form a Conservative administration. Firmly opposed to unilateral intervention by Britain in aid of Denmark, the Queen asked for the Conservative view of the issue. Although pro-Danish personally, Derby noted the opposition of many Conservatives, as well as the court, to British armed involvement on behalf of Denmark.[246] Once again, in response to the Queen's entreaties, he agreed to avoid precipitating a ministerial crisis. For her part, the Queen ensured that the Royal Address touched on the Danish question in only vague terms. Nonetheless, Derby prepared to deliver a comprehensive critique of Russell's foreign policy, stopping short of demanding the cabinet's resignation. As news reached London on 2 February that Prussian troops had marched into Schleswig, he carefully drafted a sweeping condemnation of Russell's diplomatic bungling.[247]

Despite his physical frailty, Derby delivered in the Lords on Thursday 4 February a scathing denunciation of Russell's diplomacy, reminiscent of his indictment of the Don Pacifico affair fourteen years before. Russell's policy, he declared, could be summed up in two homely, but expressive, words: 'meddle and muddle'.[248] In the course of interfering in every European issue Russell had, he averred, engaged in 'lecturing, scolding, blustering and retreating'. As a result, Britain had been humiliated in the eyes of every foreign power. Thanks to Russell, Britain did not have one single friend in Europe, her menaces were disregarded, her magniloquent language ridiculed, and her remonstrances treated with contemptuous indifference. Derby compared Russell unfavourably to Bottom the weaver and Snug the joiner of *A Midsummer Night's Dream*; the Foreign Secretary's roar frightened no one. In painful detail Derby catalogued the course of 'meddle and muddle' pursued by Russell in every important aspect of foreign policy. There was hardly a single question, he declared, on which the government had not thwarted the policy of Napoleon III. The Anglo-French alliance, therefore, had been undermined. The Schleswig-Holstein question 'with a little good judgement, a little good management, and a little good temper ... ought to have been settled without a frightful appeal to arms'. As it was, a European conflict was now imminent, Russell having alienated both contending parties. The same result had been achieved by Russell with regard to the Confederacy and the Union in North America.

Palmerston visited the Lords to hear Derby's speech and listened to the storm of applause that greeted Derby's attack. Vitzthum, who was standing by him, noted that the prime minister 'left the House in evident uneasiness. His game was up.'[249] Derby's slashing condemnation prompted Palmerston to abandon his Foreign Secretary to his critics. Russell was forced to accept that there was no possibility of Britain's single-handedly aiding Denmark militarily. During February, Prussian and Austrian troops overran Schleswig and marched into Jutland. The British government, meanwhile, ordered the Royal Navy to return to British waters and cabinet ministers distanced themselves from Russell's warlike dispatches.[250] The Conservatives, however, resisted the temptation to move a hostile Commons motion. At a meeting called by Derby at St James's Square on Saturday 12 March, Disraeli, Stanley, Lytton, Cecil, Naas, Taylor, Cairns, Peel, Manners, Northcote, and Pakington advised restraint. They feared Conservatives staying away from a hostile vote out of dislike of displacing Palmerston, the divisions within Conservative ranks which a debate might reveal, and the bringing on of a dissolution if an opposition attack succeeded.[251]

The visit to England of the Italian hero Garibaldi in April 1864 increased the tensions within Conservative ranks. Fêted by radicals and lionized by popular delegations, Garibaldi was closely chaperoned by prominent Whigs, particularly the Duke of Sutherland, so as to keep him away from dangerous company, such as the republican Mazzini. When Derby and Malmesbury attended a dinner for Garibaldi at Stafford House on Wednesday 13 April, accompanied by Palmerston, Russell, Gladstone, Argyll, and Shaftesbury, many Conservatives were deeply affronted. Lady Shaftesbury informed Malmesbury, 'in a *méchante* manner', that he and Derby 'had fallen into a trap'.[252] Prior to the dinner, Lord Bath warned Derby that attendance at Stafford House would offend English and Irish Catholics, who 'have in many instances been disposed to support you', and 'deeply wound' his own feelings of attachment to Derby personally.[253] But Derby felt a refusal of Sutherland's private invitation would be a public snub contrary to good manners.[254] Following the Stafford House dinner, on Saturday 16 April, an incensed Bath resigned his position as assistant whip.[255] Garibaldi's subsequent abrupt abandonment of a provincial tour, popularly perceived as the result of pressure from Gladstone and Sutherland, saw the Lion of Caprera quietly slip back to Italy after just three weeks in England. But the embarrassment Garibaldi's presence created for the leading Conservatives was evident. Mindful of the Catholic vote and maintaining his characteristic pose of ironic detachment, Disraeli stood back from the celebrations.[256] That Derby and Malmesbury felt they could not do likewise ruffled Conservative sensibilities at a time when the party's course over the Danish crisis was unclear. Disraeli drew comfort from the thought that Garibaldi's visit had emphasized Gladstone's susceptibility to radical acclaim, evident in the popular celebration of Garibaldi's presence in London. Though the Russells and Cavendishes might accommodate themselves to Gladstone's increasingly populist programme, Disraeli believed that 'the smaller Whigs, Beaumonts, Ramsdens, and perhaps Lansdownes and Fitzwilliams, may detach themselves'.[257] When Clarendon accepted the Chancellorship of the Duchy of Lancaster in Palmerston's cabinet during March, he confessed to Granville that he felt as though he was taking 'an oar in a sinking boat'.[258]

With his hopes of aiding Denmark militarily firmly blocked, during April Russell retreated to calling for a European conference to settle the Schleswig-Holstein conflict. This was accepted with little enthusiasm by the other European powers. The London Conference opened on 25 April and eventually secured a temporary armistice. A permanent solution eluded the Conference, however, which broke up on 25 June. The next day hostilities were resumed. Russell was forced to acknowledge that further diplomatic efforts were hopeless. On 1 August a cowed Denmark agreed to cede Schleswig-Holstein to Austria and Prussia. The ashes of Russell's diplomacy now lay around his feet. The gibe circulated Westminster that 'nature had intended [Russell] for a schoolmaster: accident had made him a cabinet minister'.[259]

The Schleswig-Holstein conflict left Derby perplexed. Conservatives, as well as Liberals, were divided over the issue. He warned Disraeli against being 'rather less guarded than is your wont'.[260] While Derby's personal sympathies were with the Danes, the advice of colleagues and his loyal undertaking to the Queen to avoid a ministerial crisis stayed his hand. To Stanley he confessed the pain it caused him to keep silent on the conduct of ministers. He irritatedly tossed aside Stanley's arguments for non-intervention as 'pig-philosophy'.[261] Nevertheless, when, on Monday 27 June, Russell, in an almost inaudible statement, explained to the Lords that the government were committed to peace and would therefore abandon the Danes, Derby deprecated any further discussion.[262]

The collapse of Derby's health enforced his promise to the Queen to avoid a crisis. In late April 1864 his weakness and loss of appetite caused his London physician Dr Robert Ferguson serious alarm. Derby 'shut himself up, refusing to dine out anywhere, and on only one or two occasions having friends to dine with him'.[263] His spirits were low and Stanley feared that the stimulants prescribed by Ferguson—large quantities of wine and brandy—were a short-term restorative causing long-term harm. In June the familiar suffering of chronic gout returned. He resisted the suggestions of his family that he should visit a German spa. 'He can bear pain better than ennui,' Stanley observed, 'and has not crossed the Channel for forty years.'[264] By early July, Derby's pain was so severe that he deputed Malmesbury to lead the Conservative peers in the forthcoming Schleswig-Holstein debate.

In Derby's absence, Malmesbury discussed with Salisbury, Donough-more, Colville, Hardwicke, Carnarvon, and Chelmsford on 3 July the Conservative response to Russell's statement on Schleswig-Holstein.[265] At a larger meeting of Conservative peers, held in Arlington Street the following day, the majority, including Malmesbury, agreed to proposing a hostile motion, Disraeli to do the same in the Commons. Buccleuch, Stanhope, Winchester, and Bath reluctantly accepted the decision. On 8 July, Malmesbury brought forward a motion criticizing the government's policy, supported by Chelmsford and Carnarvon.[266] The motion confined their attack to the Danish question, avoided the suggestion of a general vote of want of confidence, and refrained from any commitment in terms of future policy. This was a response to Derby's caution, who remained bedridden in severe pain. At 2.30 a.m. the Conservatives secured a majority of nine for Malmesbury's motion, 177 peers voting for it, 168 voting against. Russell's speech was regarded as 'rather feeble', Clarendon remarking privately 'that it was amusing to hear Lord Russell refuting in his speech all his own arguments (in the cabinet) for war'.[267] The same motion brought forward by Disraeli in the Commons, however, was defeated by the government. In the early hours of Saturday 9 July a slim Commons majority of eighteen votes, larger than the prime minister had expected, saved Palmerston's cabinet from a humiliating defeat. At 3 a.m. an ecstatic 80-year-old Palmerston scrambled up the stairs to the Commons gallery to embrace Lady Palmerston.[268] A dispirited Disraeli predicted (with what proved to be remarkable accuracy) that it would be another two years before the Conservatives could expect to return to power.[269]

... for their limbs were faint with toil.

(Derby, *The Iliad of Homer*, ii. 5)

The Commons vote on Schleswig-Holstein in July 1864 crystallized party sentiment. Ten Irish Roman Catholic MPs, who had voted with the Liberals in June 1859, voted with the Conservatives. Twelve radical and Peelite MPs, including Gladstone, who had voted with Disraeli in June 1859, supported Palmerston in July 1864. Fear of Disraeli's alliance with Irish Catholicism prompted a dozen Conservative MPs to absent themselves from the Danish vote. The single most important factor in Palmerston's victory, however, was the solid support given to the government by the radicals. Many radicals in 1861 and 1862 had opposed Palmerston. They spoke of the desirability of a Conservative government, allowing them to gain influence in a Liberal opposition. By 1864 Gladstone's transformation into the 'People's William' was persuading them of the value of Palmerston's Liberal alliance. Palmerston, during debate on Disraeli's motion, portrayed his government's aims as economy and prosperity at home and non-intervention abroad. The binding of radical votes to the Liberal alliance averted ministerial disaster.

Since 1859 Derby had banked his hopes on the incompatibility of those Whig, Liberal, Peelite, and radical elements comprising the Liberal alliance. Disgust for foreign intervention, blustering diplomacy, and extravagant expenditure, as well as indifference to Reform, he calculated, must eventually estrange the radicals from their Whig colleagues. But in July 1864 Peelite cement, in the person of Gladstone, helped to adhere these jarring elements. Palmerston's forsaking of aggressive diplomacy for the more pacific path of non-intervention secured the bond. Diplomatically, Palmerston's conversion was the inescapable acknowledgement of Bismarckian realities. Politically, it was essential to preserving his parliamentary majority. From being the fulfilment of Derby's expectation of Liberal rupture, the Danish crisis of 1864 proved the unexpected resilience of Liberal connection. Party realignment, Derby now acknowledged, would have to await Palmerston's departure from the political scene—an event, given the prime minister's advanced age, which could not be too far distant. 'The Tories', the Liberal Lord Wodehouse observed, 'are wonderfully down in the mouth and politics as dull as ditchwater.'[270]

Palmerston's success in July 1864 forced Derby's thoughts towards the next general election. Gladstone's speaking tour in Lancashire and Palmerston's addresses in Bradford and Bolton during the late summer and autumn suggested that the government were bidding for immediate popularity in anticipation of a dissolution. 'I need say nothing to *you*', he wrote to Disraeli in mid-October, 'of the vital importance of the next election. It will decide the fate of parties, at all events, for *my* time.'[271] By the end of the month, upon information from Lord Stanhope, Derby advised Taylor that the government had no intention of dissolving. This dashed his anticipation of an immediate election, but 'makes an election *next* year a *certainty*'.[272] The political timetable was set. The 1865 session, with a fading prime minister presiding over a dying parliament, would be the prelude to a critical general election, the Danish Commons vote of July 1864 having shown that, in the meantime, any Conservative assault against Palmerston's cabinet was best deferred. During the autumn Derby's ill health persisted. In early September he was unable to walk or shoot on his estate and declined an invitation to Lord Chesterfield's Ashby-de-la-Zouch residence, Bretby Hall. Gout was complicated by an ulcerated sore throat and the family was alarmed when 'the gout would not come out'.[273] For five weeks, until the middle of December, he was confined to his bedroom. News of his grave illness became public when a visit to Knowsley by the Prince of Wales had to be postponed. It was 23 January 1865 before Derby could go shooting on his estate. A week later he succumbed to yet another attack of gout and was forced back to his sickbed. The attack, Malmesbury noted, was 'very serious, and for some hours he was in great danger'.[274] Malmesbury himself was injured in a shooting accident in November and was also laid up in bed through the winter.

Looking to the approaching session, Derby observed that, 'as of old, our strength will be to sit still'. From Knowsley on 30 January, he declared that the Conservatives' strategy 'must be that of "masterly inactivity"'.[275] He made the difficult journey down to London for the opening of parliament, managing a response to the Address on Tuesday 7 February 1865. Though he spoke with great fluency he looked 'very ill'.[276] The Address was bland and his comment brief. His brevity was not just a symptom of fragile health. Disraeli advised against saying too much. The government's assumption that the opposition were bound to give their 'quasi-official opinion on the conduct of every department', Disraeli warned, was 'very injurious to us'. It forced them 'to show our cards the first night of the session, and the government profit accordingly. They see where the breakers are ahead, and what perils they have escaped.'[277] Derby's statement was short. The Message from the Throne, he declared, was that of 'an aged Minister to a moribund Parliament, whose dissolution no event could postpone; so that all its experienced advisers could do was to find it some gentle occupation, and take care that its dying moments were not disturbed by any unnecessary excitement'.[278] He devoted most of his speech to the vulnerability of Canada's border to aggression from the Northern States. The violent subjugation of the Confederacy by the Union, which now appeared to be the certain outcome of the Civil War, was an event 'repugnant to all humane and generous feeling'. Washington was also proposing the termination of the Reciprocity Treaty which secured the neutrality of the American Lakes. All this highlighted the potential peril to Canada, with its 'long frontier, peculiarly open to aggression, being accessible by water as well as by land'. Derby welcomed, therefore, the proposed federation of the Canadian provinces as a counter to American encroachment. It showed the earnest desire of Canadians to maintain the connection with Britain and their determined preference for monarchical over republican institutions. He spoke again on Canadian defence two weeks later, calling on the government to make greater preparations against a real and impending danger.[279]

The strain this effort placed on Derby was immediately apparent. It was evident in his increasing flashes of disproportionate anger. At the end of March, Clarendon had a confidential conversation with Stanley about his father's erratic manner, now a subject of comment among his fellow peers.[280] During committee meetings Derby showed great irritability without apparent cause, indicating his deep annoyance with the proceedings. Stanley interpreted his father's behaviour as betraying the approach of another severe fit of gout. Derby also began to suffer violent shaking in his hands, preventing him from lifting a cup or glass or, at times, from writing. Ferguson attributed this affliction to gout and prescribed a regime of stimulants in the form of further large doses of brandy and wine. Certainly Derby's response was uncompromisingly severe when, during March, the advanced Liberal MP Lewis Dillwyn brought a motion before the Commons effectively calling for the Church of Ireland to be disestablished. Derby's implacable opposition was combined with deep irritation at Disraeli's lack of exertion. Abolition of the Irish Establishment, he insisted, would 'be fatal to our hold on Ireland and an injury to Ireland itself'; it would 'only be a prelude' to an attack on the Church of England; and any slackness on the part of the Conservatives in defending the Irish Church would forfeit Protestant support for the party in Ireland, without gaining compensatory support from Irish Catholics.[281] He hoped, he pointedly observed, that Disraeli would break 'the profound silence' he had adopted during the session so far, particularly as Disraeli had, on previous occasions, stressed church questions as the Conservatives' 'main *cheval de bataille*'. His own caution over raising the Protestant cry as a bulwark of Conservative support intensified his exasperation at Disraeli's inertia, Disraeli having, unwisely from Derby's point of view, presented himself during 1861 and 1862 as the militant champion of the Anglican Church. Dillwyn's motion was defeated. Derby's pointed criticism of Disraeli's apathy, however, proved a further example of that intemperate peevishness others noticed in his demeanour.

In mid-April 1865 Palmerston's health also collapsed. During the previous weeks the premier showed symptoms of failure, not catching the point of questions and unable to keep a succession of points clear in his mind.[282] His physician Dr Drage diagnosed the crisis as the beginning of the end, although the prime minister could live for some months yet. Sustained by Drage's prescription of sago and brandy, Palmerston might see through the dissolution and general election, whereupon Russell would probably succeed him as prime minister with Gladstone as leader of the Commons. Gladstone's future course now loomed large in all calculation. Palmerston observed to his son-in-law Shaftesbury that, 'whenever [Gladstone] gets my place, we shall have strange doings'.[283] Clarendon recalled Aberdeen's warning about Gladstone: 'You must keep that d——d fellow always in office, give him plenty to do, else he is sure to do mischief.'[284] Certainly, Gladstone's own volatile behaviour during the spring of 1865 suggested the imminent danger of mischief, as the Chancellor forged ever stronger links with radical opinion.

In April, Taylor reported that the dissolution of parliament would occur on 15 July 1865 and that his calculations suggested a Conservative gain of twenty-five seats in the ensuing general election.[285] Fear of Russell's impulsiveness and Gladstone's extremism might be counted on to stimulate a Conservative reaction. The difficulty remained Palmerston's benign presence as an amiable restraint on radical change. Derby's awareness of Palmerston's popularity inclined him to discount predictions of significant Conservative electoral gains. Indeed, he doubted the election, while Palmerston survived, bringing any increase of party strength in the Commons. Only after Palmerston's retirement or death could the Conservatives hope to acquire broader support. During June, Palmerston's illness became critical. He seldom attended the Commons and, when he did, it was only to say a few words and then leave. His colleagues appeared anxious to get the general election over as soon as possible. In the meantime, Derby saw little to encourage the opposition. Disraeli continued to withdraw from active leadership, remaining silent on the Address in February, as well as a debate on disestablishment of the Irish Church in March. Only five years

Derby's junior, in private Disraeli was despondent about public affairs. His appetite for the political fray seemed much diminished, in part, perhaps, because his financial situation had significantly improved. Upon the death of his Torquay confidant Mrs Brydges Willyams in late 1863, he had been bequeathed £40,000 from her estate; the allure of an official salary was, as a consequence, lessened. Clarendon's opinion in late April was that Derby 'cannot refuse office if it is thrust upon him, but he is the *party* and he feels the want of good men wherewith to form a stable government—he hates and distrusts Dizzy whom he can't do with or without'.[286] There was, Stanley confirmed, now 'no very cordial feeling' between Disraeli and his father.[287] The chill in their relations, which had descended in 1853, 1856, and 1863, returned.

Derby attended the Lords on Monday 1 May to second a motion expressing sorrow and indignation at the news of President Lincoln's assassination.[288] Six weeks later he spoke briefly to express his hope that the Union would treat the leaders of the defeated Confederacy with leniency.[289] On Monday 26 June he returned to oppose the attempt to amend the parliamentary oath established in 1829, which, opponents argued, discriminated against Catholics by requiring them to pledge not to challenge the existing settlement of property or subvert the Protestant Establishment. The measure was ill-timed, he asserted, coming on the eve of a general election and likely to excite religious animosities.[290] Proponents of the measure, he believed, brought forward imaginary grievances which, by inciting sectarian passions, would only delay the removal of any real disadvantages under which Catholics laboured. The recently elected radical MP for Louth, Tristram Kennedy, who was supported by the influence of the Catholic priesthood, Derby noted, declared that 'the object of this bill was to unmuzzle the senators; and why? Because we are harmless? No. Because we want to bite.' If a man comes to me with a dog with a muzzle on, Derby continued, and says, 'Take the muzzle of this poor creature; he will do us no harm; and, besides, the muzzle is half-rotten and affords no great protection', I will understand him; but if he says, 'This is a most vicious animal, and nothing prevents his pulling you and me to pieces except the muzzle which is put around his nose, and therefore I want to take it off', I am inclined to say, 'I am very much obliged to you, but I had rather keep the muzzle on'. This unfortunate extension of Kennedy's unflattering metaphor gave ready ammunition to Derby's detractors. It was, he later acknowledged, an unlucky reference. His partisan ardour, enemies charged, led him into excessive impropriety. It seemed another expression of that irritability he had exhibited over recent months. Nonetheless, he was resolutely opposed to hasty amendments to the parliamentary oath, removing safeguards for the Established Church, 'at the time when I am approaching the confines of the grave'. He secured a Lords majority against the measure, which left any amendment of the parliamentary oath to be dealt with by a new parliament following the imminent election.

All attention now focused on the constituencies. Derby had already secured the candidacy of his younger son, Freddy Stanley, for Preston. In May 1864 the 23-year-old Freddy married Clarendon's eldest daughter, Lady Constance Villiers, despite Clarendon's personal dislike of Derby. Derby's nephew Lord Skelmersdale had married Clarendon's second daughter, Lady Alice Villiers, in 1860, and was delighted by the announcement. 'I know what a good fellow Freddy is and what a dear girl Constance is'; Lady Alice, he informed his uncle, 'is quite out of her mind with joy and excitement'.[291] As a wedding present Derby gave Freddy and Lady Constance the Witherslack estate in Westmorland, an area of beautiful limestone woodland, as a married residence, and their first child, a son baptized Edward George (later 17th Earl of Derby), was, following a difficult delivery, born in April the following year. Derby was delighted by the arrival of a male grandchild named after him. He had been dreading, Clarendon noted, the title passing 'into the hands of his scamp brother [Henry Stanley] who has a lot of scamp sons'. Clarendon was amused that Lord Stanley, 'that queerest of fishes', who was still a bachelor, referred to the child as the 'heir presumptive'. Lady Constance was looked upon by her parents-in-law 'in the light of a benefactress'.[292] In 1865 Freddy Stanley resigned his commission in the Grenadier Guards and began building Witherslack Hall, set in an extensive park inhabited by deer, and managing the estate. Freddy shared his father's passion for horse racing, was a keen yachtsman, and by providing a male heir eased Derby's deep anxiety about the future of the family title. But Freddy lacked the sharp intelligence and high seriousness of his elder brother, was prone to overweight from an early age, and often exhibited a lethargy that contrasted with Lord Stanley's earnest diligence. Nonetheless, Freddy and Lady Constance provided Derby with an extended family and domestic company which gave him much comfort during his periods of prolonged illness. Visitors were struck by his affectionate devotion to his grandson.

The local Conservative election agent in Preston, Robert Parker, first wrote to Derby in December 1864 requesting the Earl's permission to allow Freddy Stanley to stand at the next election. On 5 January 1865 Derby wrote to Parker agreeing to the request. Lord Stanley, fifteen years Freddy's senior, immediately offered his younger brother advice. Freddy, he suggested, should prepare for speaking in the Commons by reading aloud and avoid committing himself too early to strong party views.[293] On 11 July 1865, in an uncontested election, Freddy was duly elected MP for Preston, his fellow member, the Conservative Sir Thomas Hesketh, retaining the seat he had won in 1862. At Knowsley, on 28 August, Derby hosted a convivial dinner for 300 Preston butchers, who had all voted for his younger son's candidature. He now had the paternal satisfaction of both his sons sitting in the Commons, a pleasing sequel to the celebration of his fortieth wedding anniversary at the end of May.

Far less gratification was to be had, however, from the party's electoral performance elsewhere. As Derby feared, the Conservatives lost, rather than gained, seats, perhaps fifteen in all, leaving them with about 287 MPs. The *Annual Register* recorded that the elections took place 'under circumstances of as little excitement as can perhaps ever be expected to attend the choosing by a great nation of its representative body'. There appeared 'no prominent question or pending controversy upon which voters had to decide'.[294] While the Conservatives held onto their share of English counties and boroughs, seats were lost in Scotland and Wales. Indeed, in Scotland, Derby declared, they had suffered 'an utter rout'. He rejected Disraeli's suggestion that his unlucky reference to 'muzzling' Catholics, during the Catholic oaths debate in the Lords, had lost them votes. Their chief losses, he insisted, had occurred in constituencies where such a cause would have had little effect. In South Lancashire, a stronghold of the Catholic vote, they had 'lost by Conservatives(!) splitting on Gladstone'. Derby cited one example of an 'R.C. lady who would not allow her servants to vote for us, because *I had met Garibaldi* at dinner! and so she assists in returning *Gladstone*!!' A purely Conservative government, he concluded, was 'all but hopeless until, upon Palmerston's death (for he will never resign), Gladstone tries his hand with a radical government and alarms the middle classes'. But such a reaction 'will probably be too late for *my* time; and I see no prospect of any state of affairs which shall again place me at the head of a government'.[295] He attributed the Conservatives' disappointing electoral performance to overconfidence and want of exertion, a charge which stung Disraeli into a defensive response. But Disraeli acknowledged that influence in the Scottish constituencies was slipping away from their proprietors.[296] He defended the 'energy, resource and general efficiency' of Spofforth's efforts as party agent. But Derby entertained increasing doubts about Spofforth's effectiveness, which was unhelpfully combined, he believed, with constant meddling. Malmesbury found the party 'much disheartened'.[297] Some of their best men, Seymour Fitzgerald at Horsham, Sir James Elphinstone at Portsmouth, and Sir John Hay at Wakefield, were defeated. Spofforth admitted to Derby that the election results had been 'disastrous'.[298] Taylor feared they had 'almost demolished the party'.[299]

In early August the 61-year-old Disraeli wrote to Derby declaring his career in the Commons, so far as office was concerned, to have concluded. 'The leadership of hopeless opposition', he pronounced, 'is a gloomy affair.'[300] He felt 'in the decline of life' and offered to step down from the Commons leadership, so as to avail Derby 'of those confidential connections which you have among the Whigs'. Derby would then be able 'to form an anti-revolutionary government on a broad basis'. Derby declined Disraeli's offer. He praised the forlorn Disraeli for the ability, faithfulness, and perseverance with which he had served the party, though he did not deny that the Conservatives appeared mired in a Slough of Despond with little to encourage them.[301] Echoing Disraeli's lamentation, he saw no acceptable alternative Commons leader waiting in the wings, even if a number of moderate Liberals were willing to join them. Nor did he see much chance of such an accession of strength as would enable a Conservative government to secure a firm grasp on power, while remaining true to Conservative principles. All they could do was endeavour to keep the party together, 'so as to be ready to avail ourselves of any contingency which may arise, or any serious breach in our opponents' ranks in the event of Palmerston's death, however little we may expect it even then'. Derby shared his conviction with Stanley that neither he nor Disraeli would hold office again. The most likely prospect was the formation of a new moderate party made up of Whigs and Liberal Conservatives, following an inevitable split between the Whig and radical sections.[302] But this was an outcome, Derby believed, in which he would have little active part to play. 'As I can never hold any office, but the first,' he observed to Disraeli, 'so neither can I be the head of any but a *bona fide* Conservative government.'[303] A serious attack of gout in September forced him back to his sickbed in acute pain. Both Lord Stanley and Freddy Stanley saw their father's incapacity as aggravated by his seclusion at Knowsley. Derby 'lives in almost extreme solitude, allowing no one to walk with him, receiving no guests … and passes most of the day in his room'. He thought 'badly of his own health, and often said among friends that he [did] not think his life worth more than three or four years' purchase'.[304] In the remote and damp fastness of Knowsley he became preoccupied with his own mortality. In correspondence with Stanley he laid out his plans for the family's estates in the event of his death.[305]

Falls a proud ash, conspicuous from afar.

(Derby, *The Iliad of Homer*, ii. 10)

Then, on Wednesday 18 October 1865, two days short of his eighty-first birthday, Palmerston died. In harness to the end, his last intelligible words related to Belgium and the acknowledgement of its independence by France.[306] The political situation was immediately transformed. The Liberal MP Robert Lowe feared that Palmerston had 'left his party without tradition, chart or compass, to drift on a stormy sea on which their only landmark was his personal popularity'.[307] Clarendon dreaded the inevitable ascendancy of Russell and Gladstone, the latter, having the real power, seemingly prepared to do anything for popularity and likely to ally himself with the radicals. 'Dislike and fear of Gladstone', Stanley noted, 'are the strongest feelings in Lords C.'s mind where politics are concerned.'[308] Coming away from Palmerston's funeral service at Westminster Abbey, which neither Derby nor Disraeli attended, Sir Charles Wood was similarly apprehensive: 'Our quiet days are over; no more peace for us.' Disraeli immediately recognized that 'the truce of parties' was ended: 'I foresee tempestuous times, and great vicissitudes in public life.'[309]

As anticipated, with Palmerston gone, the frail 74-year-old Russell assumed the premiership (surrendering the Foreign Office to Clarendon) and Gladstone became Leader of the Commons (alongside his responsibilities at the Exchequer). Both saw this rearrangement as a new beginning, rather than a continuation of the Palmerstonian regime. Upon returning to the Foreign Office, an apprehensive Clarendon privately confessed that he felt as though he had boarded 'a steamer in a gale'.[310] Russell rejected Gladstone's suggestion of having Bright in the cabinet, but the middle-class radicals G. J. Goschen, W. E. Forster, and James Stansfeld were brought into the ministry. Both Russell and Gladstone agreed that a parliamentary Reform Bill must be brought forward. So Palmerston's passing opened up the Pandora's box of Liberal aspirations.

The word 'reconstruction' instantly sprang to Conservative lips. Over the next weeks Derby's spirits lifted. His fatalistic despondency dissipated. Visiting Hughenden at the end of October, Stanley also found Disraeli 'in good health and excellent spirits. It seemed as if the prospect of renewed political life had excited him afresh, and that he had thrown off the lethargy which had been growing upon him for the last year or two.'[311] From 30 October to 3 November the Prince and Princess of Wales, making the visit postponed from the previous autumn, stayed at Knowsley. Enjoying magnificent weather, Derby gave the Prince and his party two very good days' shooting, bagging 1,684 head in all, followed by conversation and smoking until 3 a.m., allowing the host and his family only four or five hours' sleep each night. Both the Prince and Princess 'made themselves exceedingly agreeable, discarding all approach to form, and setting everybody at their ease'.[312] On 31 October, Derby accompanied the Prince and Princess into Liverpool, where, watched by an immense crowd, they reviewed 4,000 Volunteers, the packed route being lined with Union Jacks and the Danish colours. They then boarded the steamer *Woodside* and, followed by a large flotilla of boats, viewed Liverpool, Birkenhead, and Merseyside docks, as well as the Birkenhead and Mersey Iron and Steel Works. They then attended a formal luncheon at the Town Hall hosted by the Mayor, accompanied by the band of the Grenadier Guards playing, among other pieces, a Parade March composed by Derby's daughter Lady Emma Talbot, after which they listened to a gala concert of Handel and Bach performed on the organ at St George's Hall, returning to Knowsley that evening. Though wearied by the royal visit, Derby now looked to the immediate political future with fresh hope. By mid-November he was 'in high spirits', although still declining to take exercise or leave the house.[313] A visit from Malmesbury at the end of November further buoyed up his strength, although Malmesbury felt he 'never saw thro' a glass so darkly as now in regard to politics'. On one side there was a 'numerous and hungry Conservative party'; on the other was a Whig party 'to which office has become second nature'. Between them stood 'two very clever and very ambitious middle-class men, namely Disraeli and Gladstone, who never can act in the same play and who ... never will assist any fusion into which they would respectively be joined'.[314] Derby acknowledged that the fierce rivalry between Disraeli and Gladstone sprang from 'the strong aversion felt by each for the other and for each by the great body of their respective opponents, and not a few of their respective supporters'.[315]

Expectation reanimated Derby's resolve. The cabinet rearrangements, he judged, were 'mere patchwork among themselves'.[316] Just two appointments he saw as significant: the placing of the MP for the City of London and Director of the Bank of England, George Goschen, 'a very clever man, but an advanced Radical', at the Board of Trade, and Chichester Fortescue's succession to the bungling Peel as Chief Secretary for Ireland. The latter appointment suggested a more radical policy might be pursued in Ireland. Indeed, Irish issues, Derby observed to Disraeli, caused him far greater anxiety than Reform. He anticipated the ministry attempting to bribe Irish Catholics with the promise of a Catholic university, probably endowed by the State, and the disestablishment of the Irish Church. This, he believed, would be a reckless course. Characteristically, however, he rejected the suggestion put forward by Taylor and Sir Joseph Napier (former MP for Dublin University) that a large Conservative meeting be held in Dublin, declaring the party's support for the protection of property rights, the maintenance of the Irish Church Establishment, and the preservation of the Union. Derby feared a public meeting would involve a double risk: 'the risk of failure and the risk of confusion'.[317] The meeting might be thinly attended or supported by just one section of the Irish Conservative party, while a free discussion in public of all the controversial issues bearing on Irish politics might create 'a scene of irretrievable confusion'. Derby was pleased that the influential James Whiteside, a forceful legal advocate, Napier's brother-in-law, and MP for Dublin University, endorsed his view of the inexpediency of such a meeting. Better, he agreed with Whiteside, that the party's views on Ireland be expressed in parliament, where 'we shall have to sustain a serious attack and must be prepared … to effect a firm resistance'.[318] He believed the government were alarmed by the disaffection prevailing among the Catholic lower and lower-middle classes in Ireland. Yet, they were also apprehensive of alienating Protestant feeling. The Catholic University proposal, to which they seemed inclined to accede, would destroy the Queen's colleges, their own creation, and bring the two principles of mixed and denominational education into direct antagonism. Yet Derby also declined Whiteside's suggestion that the Conservatives, immediately upon parliament meeting, call for a Committee of Inquiry into the whole conduct of the government of Ireland since 1859. Such a move would merely unite a divided Liberal party, issue an open declaration of war at the very beginning of the parliamentary campaign, repel Whig overtures, and risk an opposition defeat, 'discouraging to our people, and tending to unite the various shades of Liberals'.[319] The issue of parliamentary Reform was more likely to break up Russell's ministry, 'if we do not assist them by any imprudence on our part'.

With regard to parliamentary Reform, Derby believed the government must either shelve the issue or propose a bill satisfying nobody. If Russell brought in a moderate Reform Bill, as the new prime minister reassured Clarendon was his intention, then a breach with Bright and the radicals was inevitable. This, in turn, must lead to centrist fusion. If, on the other hand, Russell introduced an extensive Reform Bill, then the Conservatives would welcome moderate Liberal deserters to their camp. Derby proposed shaping Conservative tactics to the conduct of the ministry. 'Our policy', he advised Malmesbury, Carnarvon, and Pakington, 'must be formed upon theirs. If they quarrel with the radicals, we must do our best to support them, and widen and perpetuate the breach; if they throw themselves into the extreme party, we must offer them a strenuous opposition, relying on the aid of their moderate men to prevent mischief.'[320]

Accordingly, the Conservative by-election candidate Sir John Hay, contesting Palmerston's former Devon constituency of Tiverton, was advised to say nothing that would suggest Conservative policy on Reform, except to refute Bright and espouse Conservative progress.[321] Similarly, Derby advised Pakington, who was preparing to speak at a Conservative rally in Droitwich, to 'do full justice' to Palmerston's adroitness in checking the extreme Liberals, to suggest the imminent danger now that his guiding hand was withdrawn, to refute the charge that the Conservatives opposed all change, but to avoid anything that might be construed as a pledge.[322] In early December, Derby discussed with Taylor the election petitions arising from the previous general election. They agreed not to question 'the return of moderate men' pledged to Palmerston, 'who may not unreasonably be expected to shake themselves free from an allegiance to Lord Russell if … he brings in a comprehensive Reform bill'.[323] Disraeli confirmed the likelihood of Russell's ministry being short-lived, first, because the prime minister and Foreign Secretary's both being in the Lords was a source of weakness, and secondly, 'because all the younger portion of the Liberal party, including those in the ministry, think that, by getting rid of Lord Russell, they will obtain more, and higher, place' under Gladstone.[324] There was a general impression on both sides, Spofforth confirmed, 'that the government will not last long'.[325]

In a bold move, at the beginning of November, Russell, at Gladstone's suggestion, invited Stanley to join his cabinet. Russell recognized that, with both himself and Clarendon in the Lords, his Commons front bench needed strengthening. Derby feigned to treat the possibility 'with entire indifference'.[326] Stanley himself suspected Russell's approach was purely for show, the objections to his accepting the offer being overwhelming. He could not honourably abandon Disraeli, 'nor would it be safe, considering Lord D.'s temperament and his absolute control over estate affairs, to risk a personal rupture with him'.[327] As in 1855, the prospect of a public family rift blocked a political separation. Stanley's rejection of Russell's invitation, at a meeting with the prime minister on 10 November, caused him not a moment of regret. The prime minister only responded by citing the fate of Peel and Canning as examples of the danger of looking to office with liberal ideas and Conservative allies.

By January 1866 Derby's health and frame of mind were greatly improved. Stanley had 'seldom seen [his father] in more equally good spirits'.[328] A singular regime of never leaving the house and taking all his exercise in the form of a game of billiards after luncheon gradually restored Derby's élan. In addition to bringing forward a Reform Bill, he anticipated Russell's cabinet proposing the disestablishment of the Irish Church. He was determined, if they did so, to defend the Church of Ireland to the utmost.[329] Disraeli agreed that the Conservatives must firmly oppose 'considerable changes ... both in Church and State which neither the necessities of the country require, nor its feelings really sanction'.[330] He found Derby 'more keen than ever for power, and prepared to make any sacrifices in order to attain it'.[331]

Derby's revived hopes reflected Russell's mounting difficulties. In a startling Commons statement in May 1864 Gladstone had seemingly endorsed a broad extension of the franchise. In July 1865 he was rejected by his constituency of eighteen years, Oxford University, and returned for the large populous constituency of South Lancashire. This was a move which, it was anticipated, would free Gladstone to follow a more radical path. Bright also emerged refreshed, after the dark days of 1860–1, when the flame of Reform appeared about to flicker and die, forming the Manchester-based National Reform Union in 1864, working alongside the artisan National Reform League. During 1865 Bright gave renewed force to the radical demand for further Reform, portraying 'the people' as the source of true political morality, smothered by Whiggish oligarchy. Laying aside redistribution and the ballot as the touchstone of genuine Reform, Bright advocated an extension of the suffrage as the essence of the popular struggle for freedom. Rather than aligning the vote with property, the Whiggish framework for debate over Reform prior to 1864, both Bright and Gladstone now sought to align the franchise with respectability. The vote was a moral entitlement not a legal dispensation. Against this moral populism Russell had to reconcile Whig caution, an onerous brokership which left the details of the government's Reform Bill undecided during the first weeks of the 1866 session. Russell's attempt to paper over the cracks of cabinet differences on Reform was further complicated by Fenian unrest in Ireland, a cattle plague in England, a revolt against Governor Eyre in Jamaica, and a financial crisis bringing on the collapse of the Overend and Gurney Bank.

Russell's tribulations provided Derby with an easy theme, during debate on the Address on Tuesday 6 February 1866, allowing the Conservative leader to avoid any commitment with regard to Reform.[332] In criticizing

Governor Eyre's conduct in suppressing the Jamaica insurrection, the government had been unjust in the highest degree. Tardiness in responding to the cattle plague compounded complacency with neglect. Dangerous negligence over Fenian treason confused leniency with laxness, while, by meeting parliament without a Reform Bill ready, the ministry seemed unprepared to proceed with what they claimed to be the crucial issue facing the nation. Nonetheless, Derby promised to treat a ministerial Reform Bill with fair debate and honourable opposition, without resort to underhand methods, in pointed contrast to the factious manoeuvring of Russell and his colleagues in 1859. He hoped for a reasonable settlement of this grave question. But if it proved imperfect, inadequate, or dangerous, tending to lead to future agitation, then the Conservatives would oppose it. So Derby defined a stance, rather than a policy, over Reform. He privately urged restraint on Disraeli. The government faced an extreme situation in Ireland and might want to suspend Habeas Corpus. But, although they were in a vulnerable situation, Disraeli should not attack the ministry in a factious way.[333] A loyal defence of the national interest should be the keynote of their opposition strategy.

During February, Derby received reports, conveyed by Wood via Stanley, of cabinet disarray over Reform. Wood, Clarendon, the Duke of Somerset, and Ripon objected to Russell's insistence on proceeding with a Reform Bill. Outside the cabinet Lord Grey, Lord Lichfield, Lord Spencer, and other Whigs echoed their misgivings. But Russell remained determined to push ahead. In order to highlight Liberal divisions, at a meeting on Friday 9 March, Derby 'impressed caution and silence' upon Conservative MPs, his clear, straightforward directive carrying all with him.[334] Liberal differences over Reform were then magnified when, in a heavy and rather dreary speech on Monday 12 March, Gladstone presented to the Commons the government measure for broadening the franchise in England and Wales. While extending the vote to £14 county householders and £7 borough householders, a £10 lodger franchise in the boroughs was proposed, as well as the enfranchisement of those with deposits of at least £50 in saving banks. It was estimated this would add approximately 400,000 voters to the electorate. Under separate redistribution legislation, forty-nine small boroughs were to be disfranchised, and twenty-six new county seats, twenty-two new borough seats, and one MP for London University were to be created. The franchise measure met with either hostility or indifference. There was 'no enthusiasm for it and sound reason against' it, Gathorne Hardy noted from the Conservative benches.[335] Bright, meanwhile, described the bill as 'a fraud of the worst character'.[336]

Some Liberals, resenting Gladstone's overbearing manner and the extent of the changes proposed, voiced their disgust at Gladstone's attempt not to lead, but to drive, the Commons party. That Gladstone openly lost his temper during debate revealed his own mental excitement and apparent lack of self-control. A Conservative friend of Gladstone, Sir William Heathcote (MP for Oxford University), was struck by 'the apparent loss of power of his mind' and Gladstone's inability 'to grasp, or to decide, anything'.[337]

As Liberal unity dissolved, the Conservatives prepared their opposition. While remaining uncommitted on Reform, the Conservatives chose to portray Gladstone as an unacceptable danger to Whig and moderate Liberal opinion. At a Conservative gathering on 16 March, Disraeli launched a bitter attack on Gladstone, 'throwing all the blame for the present agitation' on the Liberal Commons leader.[338] But in March, Derby was again forced to his sickbed with a crippling attack of gout. On Thursday 15 March, Malmesbury succumbed to a severe attack of gout in both knees and feet. At the same time, Lady Derby was gravely ill with congestion of the lungs and, for a while, was thought close to death. During mid-March both Lord and Lady Derby were confined to their respective sickbeds in St James's Square, with Freddy Stanley and Lady Constance in close attendance. At one point a frail Derby was informed that Lady Derby was dying and he sent her a farewell message via his daughter-in-law, who was advised by the doctor that Lady Derby was in too dangerous a condition to receive her husband's parting words.[339] As death appeared to hover over Derby House rumours flew around the clubs of Derby's imminent retirement. Stories which prompted Cairns to consider the Whig Duke of Somerset as a successor encouraged the clique gathered around the disaffected Lord Bath to advocate new leadership, and sent an anxious General Peel round to St James's Square for reassurance. By late March, however, both Derby (as he celebrated his sixty-seventh birthday) and Lady Derby were slowly recovering and the double threat receded. On 26 March they left London for recuperative country air.

On Wednesday 11 April, Derby spoke to the Conservative party at Lord Salisbury's Arlington Street residence. Addressing the gathering seated, as he was not able to stand for long periods, he was 'very well received'.[340] Speculation about a post-Derby leadership fell away. Meanwhile, close secret communications via Disraeli, Stanley, and Carnarvon with dissident Whigs and moderate Liberals were established. While Derby had been incapacitated, Disraeli had busily encouraged private cross-party discussions. The former Peelite Scottish landowner and Liberal MP for

Haddingtonshire, Lord Elcho (eldest son of the Earl of Wemyss), emerged as a key figure. He gave organizational impetus to Whig–Liberal rebellion. Lord Grosvenor, Whig MP for Chester and heir to the vast Westminster estates, was drawn in by Elcho to provide respectability. A hostile amendment prepared by Derby, calling for the postponement of the Franchise Bill until a Redistribution measure was also introduced, was presented to Grosvenor, who was persuaded by Elcho and Stanley to table it in the Commons. Stanley agreed to second the motion. Derby's resolution was skilfully drafted. It accepted the principle of Reform, calling for a final settlement of the question, but declared a comprehensive agreement impossible unless redistribution was considered alongside extension of the franchise. A number of radicals had already given warning in the Commons that a Liberal suffrage bill, unless accompanied by redistribution, would be unacceptable. Derby placed in Grosvenor's hands 'a [bomb]shell' potentially fatal to the ministry's franchise bill, which, nonetheless, preserved for the Conservatives complete freedom of action.[341]

On Thursday 12 April, Grosvenor moved his hostile amendment, seconded by Stanley. Gladstone, as Derby hoped, impatiently responded with a singular lack of restraint. By his incorrigible temper and impatience of contradiction, Elcho observed to Grosvenor, Gladstone showed himself 'unfit ... to lead an assembly of gentlemen'.[342] Gladstone's intemperate defiance defined the ground upon which Conservatives and disenchanted Liberals might come together. Lowe, in particular, gave trenchant expression to the case against extensive Reform. Bright labelled Lowe, Elcho, Grosvenor, and their colleague Edward Horsman the Cave of Adullam, a biblical reference to the refuge found by David in his flight from Saul. When Disraeli clashed with Gladstone over the ministry's sentimental illogicalities, evasive pronouncements, and self-righteous hubris, Gladstone portentously declared, 'you cannot fight against the future. Time is on our side.'[343] On Friday 27 April, after eight intense nights of Commons debate, Grosvenor's motion was defeated by a narrow majority of five votes, 313 MPs supporting Grosvenor and 318 MPs standing by the ministry. The government's majority was far smaller than they had anticipated. Thirty-five Liberals voted against Gladstone and a further six absented themselves from the division. Any pretence of Liberal consensus over Reform was now shattered. But, contrary to the hope of a number of ministers, Russell did not resign. Instead, on Monday 30 April, Gladstone announced that the government would introduce a Redistribution Bill and Franchise bills for Scotland and Ireland to accompany their Franchise Bill for England and Wales. This dogged persistence merely prolonged the

Liberal collapse. Some wavering backbench Liberals were reassured by Gladstone's statement. The Adullamites, however, seized on it as proof that a comprehensive Reform Bill was an impossibility in the remaining weeks of the session. Liberal discord now played directly into the Conservatives' hands.

The events of April to June 1866 confirmed Derby's long-held belief that a broad alliance of non-Conservatives was an inherently unstable alignment. The question remained: what new configuration of parties might follow? In the opposition vote on Grosvenor's motion Derby counted 284 Conservatives and thirty-three Whig secessionists. Collectively this did not comprise a Commons majority, 'but if they all pulled together it would be hard to defeat them'.[344] He doubted the inclination of the Adullamites to join a government under his premiership. Disraeli might also be an obstacle to fusion. Both Delane of *The Times*, having withdrawn his support for Russell, and the Adullamites, in particular Robert Lowe, talked of an alliance under the premiership of Stanley.[345] During May much Whig speculation focused on a possible centrist coalition under Stanley's leadership. Disraeli privately pressed Stanley to accept the premiership if called upon, offering to serve under Stanley if this occurred. But Stanley remained reluctant. As well as paternal loyalty, he doubted his own physical and mental capacity for the task.[346] This did not stop moderate Liberals and anxious Whigs, however, from talking up the arrangement. Derby recognized the difficulty of drawing Whig secessionists under his own leadership.[347] But Disraeli urged him to maintain a combative line, thereby applying increasing pressure on the fragmenting Liberal party. Uncertain about the precise outcome, Derby duly sustained opposition pressure on the ministry. In a confidential conversation, on 29 May, the Queen indicated that she anticipated very soon having to ask him to form an administration. His response emphasized Russell's extremism and his own desire, in accordance with the Queen's wishes, to form a broadly based 'safe and constitutional government'.[348] He had hoped, he explained, to work with Russell to deliver a moderate settlement of Reform. But Russell had miscalculated the current of public opinion and, sensible of the loss of strength to the government from Palmerston's death, had sought to create a factious excitement in his favour, the result of which had been to alienate his truest friends and to reveal the government to be in concert with the extreme radicals and republicans. Derby's analysis confirmed the Queen's deepest concerns, but also reassured her that, when the moment came, he was fully prepared to ensure that a moderate administration, under his leadership, would seek a consensual settlement of Reform.

During May and early June a total of six opposition Commons amendments were moved against the government's Reform legislation. As Conservative hostility intensified, Whig unrest increased. Derby, while attending the wedding of Princess Mary to Prince Francis von Teck at Kew and presiding at the Wellington College speech day, also began organizing opposition in the Lords. Conservative peers, he now anticipated, would be joined by Whig rebels such as lords Grey, Shaftesbury, Fitzwilliam, Lansdowne, Westminster, Harrowby, and Lichfield.[349] He called an anti-Reform meeting of peers at Lansdowne's house in early June, from which emerged another hostile amendment, proposing that the borough franchise qualification be based upon the payment of rates, rather than on residential rental value. The popular Adullamite Lord Dunkellin, MP for Co. Galway and eldest son of the Marquess of Clanricarde, was chosen to move the amendment in the Commons. Dunkellin's motion proved the death knell of Gladstone and Russell's Reform Bill. Caught in a fog of statistical detail, the ministry's response was hesitant and confused, while Conservatives seized the opportunity to decry the handing over of electoral power to the working classes. On Monday 18 June, Dunkellin's amendment was carried by 315 to 304 votes. Loud cheering and the waving of hats erupted on the Conservative benches, while Gladstone sat looking perplexed and disconcerted.[350] The Liberal rebels of Grosvenor's motion were joined by a further fifteen Liberal MPs. Russell never forgave them. After desperate attempts to repair Liberal unity failed, Russell's divided cabinet, amid bitter recrimination, resigned on 26 June.

The Conservative chief whip, Taylor, calculated that forty-two Liberal MPs had voted with the opposition on Dunkellin's motion.[351] Their desertion had been critical. What was yet to be determined was how these Liberal rebels, led by Elcho, Lowe, and Horsman, would respond to the creation of a Conservative ministry. Derby doubted Adullamite cooperation in the formation of a cabinet led by Disraeli and himself. He deliberately did not initiate consultation with the Adullamites, in preparation for an assumption of office. He waited for the Liberal dissidents to approach him and state their terms. The Adullamites eventually indicated their conditions for collaboration: Clarendon must hold the premiership and Stanley become leader in the Commons. 'So much for Adullamite cooperation!' was Derby's terse comment to Disraeli.[352] Disraeli declared such terms inconsistent with the honour of the Conservative party. With Derby by turn despondent and then sanguine, Disraeli urged him not to refuse office if it was offered. 'You *must* take the government: the honour of your house and the necessity of the country alike require it.'[353] When

Clanricarde visited St James's Square on 24 June and advised Derby that
a Conservative government 'might be successful in obtaining considerable
support from the moderate Whigs', Derby remained sceptical of Adullamite support.[354] The Conservative leader, his elder son noted, seemed
'very nervous and uncomfortable'.[355]

Russell's resignation forced matters to a head. In his statement to the
Lords on Tuesday 26 June, announcing his surrender of the premiership, an
embittered Russell angrily accused Derby of reneging on his undertaking
to avoid factiousness. This immediately brought Derby to his feet, in
response to what he characterized as a personal attack. His pledge to avoid
unfair opposition, he insisted, had been scrupulously observed.[356] Nearly
all the important amendments to the Reform Bill, he reminded Russell,
had proceeded from the ministerial side. He then went on to condemn
the government's conduct over Reform as hasty and inconsiderate. The
following morning the Queen's private secretary, General Charles Grey,
called on Derby at St James's Square with a commission to form an
administration. The Queen hoped some Whigs, particularly Clarendon,
could be included in any new cabinet. After consulting Disraeli, Derby
called together the Conservative leadership. With the exception of Lord
Bath, who remained 'more of a "frondeur" than ever',[357] all agreed that
Derby must undertake the government and endeavour to obtain Whig
support. During the afternoon he travelled to Windsor to accept the
Queen's commission. But, as he anticipated, the Liberal dissidents stayed
aloof.[358] Malmesbury had already informed Derby that illness prevented
him from resuming the Foreign Office.[359] Not only ill health, but also
the bitter memory of Disraeli's incessant attempts to undermine his
authority when Foreign Secretary during 1858–9, prompted Malmesbury
to decline returning to the Foreign Office.[360] Disraeli's insistence that
any Conservative Foreign Secretary must sit in the Commons, Stanley
confirmed to his father, 'had a merely personal origin'. It was also
true, Stanley observed, that 'our friend Malmesbury never succeeded
in attaining public confidence: he did not do himself justice in debate, and
justice was not done him'.[361] Derby, therefore, offered the Foreign Office
to Clarendon. But, as he expected, Clarendon declined.[362] Horsman
and Lowe rejected Derby's invitation to join his cabinet, although the
latter promised independent support. Disraeli suggested an approach to
Lord Shaftesbury, which was also declined. Derby was not surprised by
Shaftesbury's refusal, but hoped he was pleased by the offer. Only the
Catholic moderate Liberal Michael Morris (MP for Galway City) was
secured, as Irish Solicitor-General, as an appointment from outside the

party. But the failure to secure a non-Conservative ministerial presence only hardened Derby's resolve. Derby's confidant Sir William Hornby believed him to be 'more disappointed by political failure than he will allow', and therefore he was intent on resuming power.[363] By Friday 29 June, despite earlier comments that he would not accept office unless assured of some support from beyond his own party, Derby was determined to persevere with the Queen's commission. Piqued by Adullamite refusals, he was also urged on by Disraeli's insistence that 'to refuse office is fatal to a party'.[364] 'Nothing can prevent your winning, if you *grasp* the helm', Disraeli pressed him.[365] Elcho visited St James's Square on Sunday 1 July and, in a long conversation, confirmed that Derby could not expect any official support from the Adullamites, who seemed, Derby concluded, in a state of 'complete disorganisation'.[366]

On Monday 2 July 1866 Derby travelled to Windsor to present his cabinet appointments to the Queen. Stanley took responsibility for the Foreign Office, despite the Queen's concern that Derby's elder son would be too inclined to diplomatic non-interference. The Queen had been irritated by Stanley's failure, during 1858–9, to send her all Foreign Office dispatches for review. Stanley's response to this complaint was blunt: 'I will take care that despatches of importance are sent to the Queen, though I doubt her reading them.'[367] Uniquely, the premiership and the Foreign Secretaryship were occupied by father and son, Stanley proving an even more zealous advocate of the Conservative foreign policy of cautious European diplomacy than his father and Malmesbury had been in 1852 and 1858–9. Malmesbury accepted the less arduous post of Lord Privy Seal. Disraeli returned to the Exchequer, Walpole resumed the Home Office, General Peel once again became War Secretary, Lord John Manners accepted his former post of First Commissioner of Works, and Pakington returned to the Admiralty. New blood was provided by Carnarvon's appointment as Colonial Secretary, the Duke of Buckingham's acceptance of the Lord Presidency, Lord Robert Cecil (now Lord Cranborne) becoming Indian Secretary, and Gathorne Hardy's appointment as President of the Poor Law Board. Disraeli also secured a cabinet place for Sir Stafford Northcote as President of the Board of Trade. During 1861 Northcote had delivered a number of widely applauded Commons speeches on taxation, and in 1862 he published his book *Twenty Years of Financial Policy*, criticizing an over-reliance on the income tax and excessive government expenditure. As a strong supporter of Disraeli, he also advocated strict economy in military expenditure. Lord Chelmsford returned as Lord Chancellor, because the more able Cairns could not be spared from the Commons.

As Attorney General, although outside the cabinet, Cairns, alongside Northcote, Gathorne Hardy, and Cranborne on the Commons front bench, represented the rising young talent of the Conservative party. Lord Naas was an obvious capable appointment as Chief Secretary for Ireland, who was brought into the cabinet so as to ensure at least one Irish or Scottish presence at the cabinet table. The Marquess of Abercorn, an Ulster landowner, a prominent Freemason, and married to a daughter of the Duke of Bedford, was appointed Lord Lieutenant of Ireland. Irish difficulties, most pressingly Fenian disturbances and campaigns for Irish Church disestablishment, remained at the forefront of Derby's concerns. In Naas and Abercorn, he believed, he possessed an able Irish executive capable of alleviating Irish tensions. Jolliffe and Bulwer Lytton were not given appointments, but Derby secured peerages for both men, as Lord Hylton and Lord Lytton respectively.

After attending the marriage of the Queen's third daughter, Princess Helena, to Prince Christian of Schleswig-Holstein at St George's Chapel, Windsor, on 5 July, Derby and his new ministers returned to Windsor Castle the following day to receive their seals of office. On Monday 9 July the government met in cabinet for the first time at 10 Downing Street. Derby's third cabinet, Stanley observed, 'though not brilliant, is respectable'.[368] *The Times* agreed, declaring it 'a very tolerable ministry'.[369] Notably, unlike preceding Liberal governments, nearly all the leading ministerial posts were held by members of the Commons. Even the Foreign Office, as well as the Exchequer, the First Lordship of the Admiralty, the Home Office, the War Office, and the India Office, were headed by MPs. The embarrassing paucity of experience of Derby's first cabinet in 1852 was now, fourteen years later, a distant memory. 'History rarely reproduces itself with perfect exactness,' *The Times* observed, 'and though Lord Derby has succeeded to office under circumstances so similar to those of his first and second administrations, it would be rash to conclude that the fate of the third will be that of the predecessors.'

CHAPTER 6

Derby's Third Premiership: 1866–1868

... safe and steady progress, strengthening, rather than subverting, the institutions of the country, and maintaining that balance between the various parts
of our constitutional system—a monarchy limited, an aristocracy tempered,
a House of Commons not altogether democratic—the consequence of which
has been a progressive improvement in our legislation according with the
temper and character of the times.

(Derby to the Lords, 9 July 1866, *Hansard*, 3rd ser., clxxxiv. 744)

The dramatic events of July 1866, placing Derby for a third time in
office as prime minister, appeared a clear, if belated, affirmation
of his long-held belief that the Willis's Rooms alliance of 1859 was
inherently unstable. Dread of Gladstone, division over Reform, and fear of
a dissolution had fragmented the Liberal party. The pungent anti-Reform
arguments of Robert Lowe and the radical exhortations of John Bright
exposed those irreconcilable differences temporarily deferred, not resolved,
by Palmerston's genial presence. In July 1859 Derby portrayed Palmerston's
leadership as a provisional arrangement. Only by factious manoeuvre, in
defiance of the national interest, had Derby been ejected from office: this
was a deep and abiding Conservative grievance. Following Palmerston's
death a sense of flux immediately descended on Westminster. By 1866 a
realignment of party connection appeared at hand.

Reconstruction seemed in the air. But the elements stubbornly refused
to coalesce. The Adullamites demanded Derby's retirement as the price of
adhesion. But Derby refused to offer himself up as a sacrifice to centrist
merger. For twenty years he had laboured to rehabilitate the Conservatives
as a credible party of government. Vigilant repose in opposition and
judicious reform in office had saved the party from languishing as an
atavistic rump of rural protest. By 1866 the incompatibility of Whig
caution and radical enthusiasm suggested his patience was about to receive
its reward. But he had no intention of becoming a humble supplicant for

support. If Adullamites and Whigs would not accept his leadership, then he would steadfastly persevere on his own. His view was quite clear: 'He would never hold a subordinate place. He would never be a minister on sufferance again.'[1] Government by coalition, he declared, in the wake of Adullamite demands, implied a sacrifice of individual principles for the purpose of obtaining extended political strength, and there was always something repugnant to the feelings of Englishmen in any sacrifice of principle for the sake of political power. Despite his declining health, even at the age of 67, he had no intention of stepping aside to allow others to seize his prize. Yet 'few governments', *The Times* observed, 'have succeeded to a more arduous position or have entered upon office at a more critical time'.[2]

Thou hear what seems to me the wisest course.

(Derby, *The Iliad of Homer*, ii. 39)

Immediately upon becoming prime minister for a third time Derby affirmed, in the Lords on Monday 9 July 1866, the moderate aims of Conservative government. Malmesbury noticed that he looked 'very pale and nervous' when he rose to speak, still evidently enfeebled by illness. Nevertheless, the new premier's speech was 'good, and in some parts very eloquent'.[3] As in 1828, he believed that stubborn Toryism must yield to the increasing liberality of the age. As in his 'Knowsley Creed' of 1834, the energies of the nation should be channelled towards progress with propriety. As in 1858, constant progress required measured change, with improvement of the old system meeting the altered demands of society. 'Safe and steady progress', he informed parliament in July 1866, 'strengthening, rather than subverting, the institutions of the country', must secure improvement though a legislative response to the temper and character of the times.[4] Domestic improvement was to be complemented by a foreign policy preserving peace and avoiding needless interference with the internal affairs of other nations. Conservative government was neither bellicose nor blustering, neither reactionary nor reckless.

In July 1866 moderation might be safely defined by posthumous praise of Palmerston's sagacity and by forceful repudiation of Russell's rashness. Derby reminded the Lords of how the Conservatives, after 1859, had assisted Palmerston in restraining his more extreme supporters. The clamour of popular passions was to be controlled. The diplomatic dangers created by Russell's ill-judged foreign policy were to be avoided. Vexatious meddling, when diplomatic menace was not followed by decisive action, was to be resisted. Rather, the Conservative ministry would seek to keep on good terms with neighbouring nations and not entangle Britain in separate alliances. The ambitions of the Second French Empire, the Italian Risorgimento, the defeats inflicted on Austria, the rise of Prussian militarism, the Schleswig-Holstein crisis, and the diminished influence of Russia, presented a dramatically altered European scene. Nonetheless, Derby's foreign policy remained the same as he had pursued in 1852 and 1858–9. Careful reform at home and the preservation of peace abroad were the watchwords of his ministry.

The new prime minister welcomed the cessation of the Civil War in the United States. The return of peace, he hoped, would allow harmonious relations to be restored between Britain and the great Republic. He praised the steadfast loyalty of their Canadian subjects in resisting the recent Fenian insurrection. He gratefully acknowledged the decisive measures adopted by the United States in regard to the absurd and mischievous conspiracy inspired by Irish republicanism. Priority would be given to the amendment of the Poor Law, while it was possible that a renewal of the Habeas Corpus Suspension Act in Ireland, to suppress violation of the law from whatever quarter it might proceed, would be sought. On the pressing issue of parliamentary Reform, the government would seek a safe and lasting settlement, acceptable to the parliamentary majority. His cabinet, he affirmed, were entirely free and unpledged on this critical question. He did not deny that there were practical anomalies in the existing representative system, which it was desirable to redress. There were persons currently excluded from the franchise who had a fair claim to be admitted to it. Recognizing these legitimate claims, not surrendering to radical agitation for extensive change, and securing a lasting settlement broadly supported by parliament were his aims. Judicious conciliation, responsible reform, and preservation of the public peace were the keynotes of Conservative policy. His statement, he reported to the Queen, 'was very favourably received in a very full House'.[5] It evinced, *The Times* noted approvingly, a wise and prudent reserve.[6]

Little remained of the 1866 session. The imminent respite of the recess offered the cabinet an opportunity to ease into their ministerial seats. Popular protest over Reform, however, denied the Home Secretary, Spencer Walpole, immediate comfort. On Friday 29 June 10,000 people marched from Trafalgar Square to outside the Carlton Club, where their jeering vented their frustration at the defeat of Gladstone's Reform Bill.

The Reform League Committee, headed by Edmond Beales, then held a 'monster meeting' in Hyde Park on Monday 23 July. A nervous Walpole, as advised by Derby, instructed the police to close the Park to protesters. Then, when Beales and other Committee members led a column of approximately 20,000 marchers up to the closed Park gates, jostling and confusion broke out. Amid the scuffling the park railings were pushed over, protesters scrambled into the Park, and the police weighed in with truncheons to expel them. In the subsequent fighting 200 people were injured and a policeman later died of his wounds. Not until the following morning, with the support of a regiment of Life Guards, did the police clear the Park. Walpole was shocked by these events. Derby and most of Walpole's cabinet colleagues, however, saw little real threat in the incident. 'There was more mischief than malice in the affair,' Stanley concluded, 'and more of mere larking than either.'[7] Despite 'a good deal of wanton aimless mischief, destroying trees, shrubs, etc.', the Foreign Secretary believed 'the effect on the respectable classes' of the fracas was 'rather good than otherwise—as it shows what a mass of ruffianism we are living over: though it is fair to say that there appears to have been no malice in the proceedings, only love of destruction, noise and fighting'.[8] Some windows at 23 St James's Square were broken by stones thrown later in the evening of 23 July, but Derby, like his elder son, regarded the disorder with patrician calm. In the Lords, on Tuesday 24 July, Derby censured the leaders of the protest for bringing tens of thousands of people together in Hyde Park in defiance of police orders. Many in the crowd, he observed, were young men and boys with little serious interest in the demonstration, but who saw it as an opportunity to cause mischief.[9] The radical leaders claimed a right to free assembly to debate openly the Reform question. But calm discussion was impossible in such circumstances, Derby asserted, and merely provided a pretence for the real intention of overawing parliament with a demonstration of physical force. The rights of the Crown over the parks had never been disputed and there should be no doubt that the object of closing the gates was to avoid a collision between the crowds and the police. From the opposition benches Granville agreed that in such large gatherings deliberation was impossible. He assured the government of Liberal cooperation in the maintenance of public peace. Granville's statement indicated that popular protest would not receive Whig support. Equally importantly, unlike 1830–2, there was little sign that the Whig or Liberal gentry in the country were prepared to identify themselves with radical agitation.

On Thursday 26 July, as isolated groups of young 'roughs' in Hyde Park 'passed the day in pelting carriages and people', the cabinet met to consider what should be done in the light of the Reform League's intention to hold another mass meeting in the Park on Monday 30 July.[10] The previous day an indecisive Walpole had reportedly broken down when confronted by a deputation from the Reform League led by Beales. Derby thought that Walpole's conduct threatened to turn the issue into a 'fiasco'.[11] The cabinet quickly resolved to refuse access to Hyde Park for another meeting and offered the League Primrose Hill as an alternative venue away from the West End.[12] Radical MPs in the Commons that evening accepted the cabinet's proposal as they preferred to be seen as moderating, rather than being driven by, popular protest. In the Lords, Derby stifled Shaftesbury's attempt to discuss the right of public access to the Royal Parks.[13] Derby's imperturbability during cabinet meetings, on Friday 27 and Saturday 28 July, maintained ministerial calm, while Walpole's seeming weakness, his manner a mixture of pathos and solemnity, only rendered him a ludicrous figure in the eyes of his colleagues. 'It has not been the mob that has frightened me', Manners wrote to his brother, 'so much as the indecision of some who have to maintain the peace and order of the metropolis.'[14] During the following weeks rumours in the press, surreptitiously encouraged by Disraeli, predicted that Walpole would soon be replaced at the Home Office by Gathorne Hardy.

For a brief moment, while order was being restored in Hyde Park, Disraeli saw the opportunity to steal a march on Reform. To Derby, on Sunday 29 July, he proposed immediately picking up on Gladstone's rejected measure and promptly bringing forward a bill of their own, proposing a £6 rating franchise for the boroughs, a £20 rating franchise for the counties, and the creation of constituencies for the northern boroughs, disfranchisement of any kind being avoided. This would pre-empt radical agitation during the recess, 'cut the ground entirely from under Gladstone', and 'smash the Bath Cabal'—those diehard anti-Disraeli Tories looking to Lord Bath for leadership.[15] With Reform resolved, Disraeli suggested, the way would then be set fair for the government in the 1867 session. Derby, however, rejected a sudden rush at Reform. Securing a lasting settlement, he believed, required a calmer, more considered response. Moreover, holding back would allow divisions between the radicals, Liberals, and Whigs to deepen. That Granville and radical MPs distanced themselves from the more extreme elements associated with the Hyde Park riot confirmed that no broad unity of progressive purpose was likely to emerge over the coming months. Indeed, delay would allow a reaction against radical agitation to gather momentum. In conversation over dinner, a noticeably friendly Lord Enfield assured Stanley that twenty-five Whigs, not Adullamites, wished to help the government settle the Reform question.[16] Disraeli's enthusiasm for Reform very quickly cooled. After July a more typical circumspection replaced his momentary eagerness. In the Lords, on Friday 3 August, Derby denounced Russell's 'uncalled-for attack' on the government's handling of the Hyde Park disturbances. The ministry, he insisted, were simply restoring order and, so as to provide greater safety for the public enjoying legitimate recreation in Hyde Park, better lighting would be installed on the main thoroughfares and footpaths.[17] Prior to parliament being prorogued on Friday 10 August, the cabinet quietly attended to more mundane departmental business.

Peel, as Secretary for War, and Pakington, as First Lord of the Admiralty, pushed hard for increased naval expenditure; Pakington's vanity, Stanley judged, made him 'anxious to distinguish himself personally by another reconstruction of the Navy'.[18] Derby favoured Pakington's plan. But Pakington's 'extravagance' was firmly checked by Disraeli and other cabinet colleagues. At the Colonial Office, Carnarvon oversaw the process of Canadian confederation. A delegation from the Canadian provinces arrived in London in November and over the following weeks Carnarvon negotiated the details of a bill uniting Canada, New Brunswick, and Nova Scotia. In the process, the names 'the kingdom of Canada' and 'Viceroyalty' were rejected in favour of Dominion, although Derby thought the term 'rather absurd'.[19] Northcote, at the Board of Trade, 'brought forward a variety of propositions, useful, but not very interesting, nor well understood by most'.[20]

At the Foreign Office, Stanley, in friendly communication with Clarendon, confronted the diplomatic consequences of the decisive Prussian victory over the Austrians at Sadowa on 3 July. 'Bismarck', Stanley acknowledged, 'is master of the situation: and no man is less likely to use his power with moderation.'[21] Napoleon III's attempts to arbitrate signalled the failure of French diplomatic support for Austria and their hope that a prolonged war would enfeeble both German powers. By mid-July the terms of a peace treaty were agreed by the belligerents, which formed the text of the Peace of Prague signed on 23 August. Throughout Stanley conscientiously abstained from interference. Empty gestures were avoided. 'Armed intervention on our part', Stanley confirmed on 13 July, 'would be absurd.'[22] As the Continental powers nervously adjusted to the emergence of Prussia as a powerful and unpredictable neighbour, Stanley observed that 'England is simply a spectator of events.'[23] In the Lords, Derby upheld this policy of strict non-intervention. On Friday 20 July he declined to be drawn by Lord Stratford de Redcliffe into a wide-ranging discussion on the general state of European affairs. 'Nothing could be more inconsistent with our public duty', he declared, 'than that we should take an active part on either one side or the other in the present conflict.'[24] In a veiled reference to Russell's diplomacy, he observed that Britain must avoid any temptation to threaten or menace. Again, on Monday 23 July, in response to Clanricarde, he declared that Britain was not going to take an active part in diplomatic negotiations. 'We have not been asked for advice and we have not offered any,' he concluded. 'We have simply stood aloof.'[25]

So Britain stood by impassively as the Prussian victory at Sadowa produced a profound shift in the European balance of power. Not only was Austria defeated, not only was the foundation for Prussia's subsequent unification of the German states firmly laid, but French diplomatic influence was decisively checked and Napoleon III's dynastic ambition to be the arbiter of Europe was shattered. The Austro-Prussian War also threw up a specific diplomatic problem which, because it involved the personal interests of the Queen, took up a considerable amount of Derby's time during August and September 1866. The King of Hanover, George V, wishing to curb the rise of Prussia, declared his support for Austria in June 1866. Five days before the Battle of Sadowa, on 28 June at Langensalza, a Prussian army routed the Hanoverian forces. During the following weeks it became clear that Prussia, as reported by the British Ambassador in Berlin, Lord Augustus Loftus, intended to depose the King, confiscate his property, and annex Hanover. But the King was Victoria's cousin and Hanover the birthplace of her family.

On 30 July the Queen indicated to Derby that it would hardly be becoming if no interest was expressed by the British government in the King of Hanover's fate.[26] Yet it was a further complication that Victoria thought the King, 'though he is my cousin', to be 'a very foolish man'.[27] Derby informed the Queen on 31 July, following consultation with Stanley at the Foreign Office, that Lord Loftus would advise the Prussian government of the 'deep pain the utter ruin' of King George V would cause Her Majesty.[28] But any further action would run counter to Conservative policy, entangling Britain in Bismarckian policy. Nonetheless, continued royal pressure came to bear on Derby from the Queen's cousin the Duke of Cambridge, who suggested that the prime minister was acting as an apologist for Prussia's actions. The Duke was next in the Hanoverian line of succession to King George V and his son. Derby firmly denied the charge. He acknowledged that Prussia's treatment of Hanover was exceptionally harsh. But this was in large part, he stated, the consequence of the King's own decisions, who 'has not played his cards judiciously'.[29] The King had rejected neutrality, so making himself an enemy of Prussia, without the power to resist Prussian annexation. He had given Prussia the pretext for the confiscation of which he was now the victim. The King of Hanover's future income and place of residence, he recognized, comprised 'a delicate question'.[30] But the Queen, because of her personal dislike for her Hanoverian cousin, did not favour offering him asylum in England, the course both Derby and the Prussian government thought best. Therefore, Derby concluded, all that could be done was to rely on Bismarck's assurances that he would grant the deposed monarch an 'income equal to that of the wealthiest of English Dukes' and allow him to take up a private existence, while retaining his English title of Duke of Cumberland. The issue remained a minor sub-plot in the main European drama of an emergent Prussian ascendancy. But the Queen's family interests required Derby to devote considerable time to the issue, without any tangible effect on the final outcome, during the summer and early autumn of 1866.

On Monday 6 August, Derby made his last major contribution to the 1866 parliamentary session by recommending the continuation of the suspension of Habeas Corpus in Ireland.[31] Fenian disturbances rendered the force of ordinary law inadequate. In particular, the subversive actions of self-expatriated Irishmen from America maintained a threat of treasonable conspiracy. The continued suspension of Habeas Corpus in Ireland was subsequently agreed. Following the prorogation of parliament, both Derby and Lady Derby appeared 'in good health and spirits'.[32] At a grand ministerial dinner at the Mansion House on Wednesday 1 August, Derby was 'heartily received'.[33] In their final cabinet meeting before the summer recess, on 10 August, he gave each of his 'colleagues their "holiday task" to prepare for November', keeping consideration of parliamentary Reform to himself.[34] Ministers then dispersed. With official business winding down, in consultation with Carnarvon as High Steward of Oxford University, Derby then appointed the medieval historian the Revd William Stubbs as Regius Professor of Modern History at Oxford. Stubbs's conservative politics and his reputation as a strong Churchman, in contrast to the reforming opinions of his predecessor, Goldwin Smith, recommended his appointment over the rival candidates E. A. Freeman and J. A. Froude. On Thursday 23 August, Derby and Lady Emma left London for Knowsley. When Stanley visited his father a week later, a buoyant Derby shared with him papers relating to national finances showing the economy was flourishing, notwithstanding the commercial panic of earlier in the year. No imminent suffering, Derby believed, was anticipated among the labouring classes.[35] This was a comfort with regard to Reform, suggesting that the popular demand for enfranchisement would not be driven to excess by economic hardship. That, at the end of August, Bright launched a campaign of outdoor meetings, over 150,000 gathering in Birmingham on 27 August, also provided encouragement, by rendering tangible the radical threat that existed if respectable men did not support a lasting moderate settlement. Subsequent meetings addressed by Bright in Manchester during September and in Glasgow in October, it was anticipated, must increase Whig alarm and further discomfit Gladstone. Stanley privately concurred that Bright's 'eloquent, violent' speeches 'have frightened employers (who are rapidly becoming conservative) and excited some, but not a great degree of political feeling among the masses'. Among parliamentarians only the radical MP W. E. Forster, who nonetheless differed with Bright on numerous points, openly supported him; 'no person of importance has joined Bright. Many say he is doing his cause more harm than good.'[36] Now, Derby decided, was a favourable moment for the Conservative cabinet to move on Reform and offer parliament a permanent conciliatory settlement.[37]

It was Derby who now pressed forward government discussion of Reform. Disraeli's fleeting earlier enthusiasm had quickly dissipated, once the possibility of swift action in late July had passed. During August he urged administrative reform of the Admiralty as a greater concern. When, in early September, Longmans invited Disraeli to publish a collection of his speeches on parliamentary Reform he acquiesced with reluctance. His secretary, the faithful Montagu Corry, was charged with editing the volume, Disraeli's concern being the inclusion of his brief statement in 1852 that, in any future change, the claims of the working classes ought to be considered.[38] In September, Derby informed Disraeli that 'there is a genuine demand *now*, however it may have been excited, but in favour of the acceptance of a moderate and conservative measure'.[39] The precise form such a measure might take was yet to be decided. But Derby recognized that circumstances were creating a favourable opening for a decisive move in the approaching session. We 'shall have to deal with the question of Reform', he insisted.[40]

On Sunday 16 September Derby encouraged Disraeli to consider how best to proceed, proposing a set of resolutions as the basis of a future bill. 'We *need* not make the adoption of any of the resolutions a vital question; while, if we should be beaten on some great leading principle, we should have a definite issue on which to go to the country.'[41] Resolutions approved by the Commons might then be submitted to an all-party Royal Commission of Inquiry, perhaps under the chairmanship of Lord Grey, which could frame legislation for parliament. This was how the Conservative ministry had secured a settlement of the contentious issue of Indian government in 1858, legislation emerging from a cross-bench consensus on broad principles agreed in the form of resolutions. A similar procedure might obtain as an equally satisfactory outcome over Reform. It would also avoid any moderate proposal emerging from ministerial discussions with the Adullamites, which would afford the Adullamites the opportunity of claiming that they were determining government policy. Derby enclosed a sketch of a Reform Bill drawn up by R. Dudley Baxter, a Conservative statistician and party draftsman, aimed to secure moderate Liberal support by a £6 rating borough franchise, a £14 occupation county franchise, the removal of some borough freehold votes from the counties, the extension of the boundaries of large boroughs, and the establishment of educational franchises. But Derby remained open to alternative proposals. His immediate concern was the process, rather than the detailed substance, of their measure.

On Wednesday 19 September, Derby left Knowsley to attend the Queen at Balmoral. Five days later Disraeli wrote to him cautioning against the introduction of a Reform Bill. It would divide the party and unite the opposition, Disraeli warned.[42] But at Balmoral, Derby found the Queen was anxious to secure a lasting settlement of the question, so as to quiet further popular agitation. He took the opportunity to impress upon the Queen the factious behaviour of Gladstone and the Liberals, in contrast to the patriotic conduct of the Conservative government. On Thursday 27 September, Derby again wrote to Disraeli from Scotland, firmly declaring that 'we cannot escape doing something'.[43] The Queen was worried and wished to see the question settled, while Derby restated that 'the violence of Bright's language is … in our favour'. Once again he proposed proceeding by resolutions, which would 'afford many advantages'. The sense of the Commons might be taken on each resolution separately and 'defeat on one or two might not be fatal'. But again Disraeli sought to defer legislation by suggesting the government establish a Commission for Boundaries.

Derby's reply from Knowsley on Tuesday 9 October was patiently insistent: 'I come myself more and more to the conclusion that in some shape or other we must deal with it, and that immediately.'[44] With careful deliberation he explained the merits of proceeding by resolution. It would enable them to put an end to the accusation that they were the opponents of all Reform; this would be an advantage in any subsequent appeal to the country. Yet, by bringing forward resolutions, the government would reduce the likelihood of an election, the prospect of a dissolution being postponed being welcomed by the Commons in general. Resolutions would be less of a commitment for the government than the main provisions of a bill, while any opposition to the resolutions would be seen as a factious attempt to obstruct legislation. Finally, approval of their resolutions would pledge the Commons to general principles, leaving the government 'in a much better position for hereafter discussing details'. Any subsequent opposition would bring the radicals into conflict with the moderate Liberals, so widening the breach between them. The success of their resolutions, Derby concluded, 'would place us on velvet'. At the same time, he rejected Disraeli's suggestion of appointing a separate Commission to review constituency boundaries, a subject on which their colleagues were 'scattered about in all directions', and he reaffirmed the Queen's earnest wish to see the Reform issue 'settled by *us*'. He intended, he advised Disraeli, to call a cabinet meeting on 1 November to discuss the question. Disraeli's diffidence was decisively pushed aside by Derby's resolve.

The same day, Derby drafted a list of Reform resolutions. They stated the desirability of lowering the franchise qualification in both counties and boroughs; qualifications to be defined in terms of the rateable value of property; under any redistribution of seats no borough was to be disfranchised entirely, but up to fifty small boroughs currently returning two members should be reduced to one MP; in order to estimate the importance of different constituencies, the combined ratio of population to registered voters should be considered; additional seats should be given to populous counties and large towns; the boundaries of smaller boroughs returning one member might be extended to embrace neighbouring unrepresented towns; and, finally, following acceptance of the resolutions by parliament, a Royal Commission should gather updated statistical data, revise constituency boundaries, and propose possible franchise qualifications, such as would lay the ground for well-considered legislation in the next session of parliament.[45] Unaware that Derby's thinking on Reform was so well developed, Disraeli reluctantly agreed to discuss with the premier possible resolutions: 'They must, however,' he warned, 'be distinct enough for us to fall back upon, as a clear policy, for the country, in case we are forced to appeal to it, which Heaven forfend!'[46]

In London, at the beginning of November, Derby kept initial cabinet discussion of Reform at a general level, avoiding detail. This, he calculated, would avoid immediately alarming more cautious ministers such as Peel and Cranborne, their consternation, in turn, exciting the diehard Tories associated with Lord Bath. The government faced, he suggested to the cabinet, three alternatives. They might do nothing, bring in a bill, or initiate an inquiry preparatory to a bill. All agreed that the first course was impossible; a majority favoured the last option.[47] With the necessity of action on Reform seemingly accepted, and procedure by Royal Commission, following parliament's approval of general resolutions, apparently favoured by ministers, Derby brought forward his draft Reform resolutions. Discussion with Disraeli had altered his initial resolutions of early October in detail, but not in substance, and they now numbered thirteen.

At a cabinet meeting on Thursday 8 November, Derby forced through acceptance of his resolutions. They affirmed that the electorate ought to be increased; that the increase should be effected by reducing the property qualification in both boroughs and counties, as well as by other sorts of franchise; that the occupation franchise in both boroughs and counties should be based upon the principle of rating; that, while some representation of the labouring classes should be granted, no one class or interest should possess a predominating power; that the distribution of seats should be revised; that, while not disfranchising any existing borough, places possessing sufficient population and property should be enfranchised; that the number of electors in any borough should be greater than an as yet unspecified minimum; that a Royal Commission inquiring into existing constituency boundaries, as a basis for redrawing the boundaries, should reflect expanding urban populations; that the Commission should also review the electoral registers; that electors should be given the option of voting by polling paper; and that additional polling places in larger constituencies should be established.[48] The revised resolutions contained no detailed commitment. This suited Derby's purposes. It would allow the specific terms of any scheme to be shaped by Conservative concerns and opposition responses. Yet, crucially, they committed his cabinet to doing something and seeking the basis of a lasting settlement. To this extent he secured agreement and so far preserved cabinet unity, despite Disraeli's reluctance and the misgivings of Cranborne and Peel.

By 25 November the cabinet had provisionally agreed to proceed by resolution, preparatory to the appointment of a Commission. As to deciding the details of any government scheme that might emerge from these general resolutions, a Royal Commission, possibly chaired by Lord Grey and including some radicals as well as moderate Liberals and Conservatives, Derby believed, would be a safe avenue. Lord Grey's book on parliamentary Reform, published in 1858, had shown his firm adherence to the principles of 'parliamentary government' and his commitment to safeguarding the autonomy of parliament against a popular electorate. Derby believed that Grey, therefore, would be a safe pair of Whig hands to which to entrust the detailed consideration of franchise extension. In 1858 Derby had shepherded his cabinet towards a moderate Reform measure by way of a cabinet committee. In 1866 he led ministers towards a comprehensive settlement by way of general resolutions he had drafted himself, elaborated by a Commission. Both were a means of securing the same strategic purpose: to allow, with minimum cabinet division, a consensus to develop, against the background of radical agitation, embracing Conservatives, Whigs, and moderate Liberals agreed upon the necessity of a moderate settlement. 'The late government thought they had a sufficient majority, and they found their mistake. We know we have not,' he warned Pakington.[49]

Yet the devil was always going to lie in the details. The precise extent of any enlargement of the franchise still lacked clear definition. As, during November and early December, the cabinet discussed Derby's resolutions, the need for some clear, defensible demarcation, prescribing the eligibility to vote, became increasingly pressing. What combination of rated residential qualification, merit franchises linked to profession or personal savings, or other criteria should confer the entitlement to vote? Where, on the slippery slope to democracy, could a distinct line be drawn defining the respectable adult male population? Disraeli, meanwhile, persisted in dragging his feet. In mid-November he suggested that the discussion of the government's Reform resolutions might be deferred until well after the beginning of the forthcoming session. His continuing hesitancy irritated Derby. When Disraeli suggested that the cabinet might swiftly complete their preparations for the approaching session by 21 November, Derby could not imagine from what source he derived such a happy delusion. Ministers had yet to discuss 'very difficult Irish questions', such as reform of the landlord and tenant law, a Catholic university, and national education, Derby pointedly observed, while further discussion of Reform was necessary.[50] Disraeli, in turn, questioned the justification for a Commission, unless its brief was sufficient to merit such a procedure. The resolutions as presently drafted, he feared, would alienate MPs representing small boroughs (their constituency boundaries being extended to recognize expanding urban populations), while the current vague brief was an inadequate justification for the resort to a Commission.[51] In response, Derby acknowledged that 'the difficulties of finding sufficient reason for a reference to a Commission are very great; but they *must* be found'.[52] He remained insistent that the government's attempt to settle Reform must proceed. It was, he assured Disraeli, 'our only hope of escaping shipwreck'.

By early December, Derby believed he had found a clear, safe, and defensible principle of demarcation for extending the borough franchise. Over dinner with Stanley, at St James's Square on Tuesday 4 December, he floated 'the idea of household suffrage, with a plurality of votes: but a Commission to be appointed in the first instance, to ascertain what the effect would be'.[53] In cabinet on 8 November, Carnarvon had tentatively mentioned such an option, but was quickly overruled by his colleagues. Derby, however, now took up the rated residential household borough suffrage, mitigated by plural voting, as the defining principle of a substantial, responsible, and permanent Reform settlement. Plural voting had been included by John Stuart Mill in his *Thoughts on Parliamentary Reform*, published in 1859, as well as being advocated by a number of Conservative writers as a means of counteracting large numbers of working-class voters.

On Thursday 6 December, Derby left St James's Square for Knowsley, with the principle of the rated residential household borough suffrage, hedged by plural votes, fermenting in his mind. Hosting a visit to Knowsley by the newly-wed Prince Christian of Schleswig-Holstein and Princess Helena on 10 December, with a distinguished party including the Prince of Saxe-Weimar, drew Derby into four days of extensive shooting on the estate. But, after giving consideration to how best to extricate themselves 'from the Reform dilemma', he wrote to Disraeli from Knowsley on 22 December.[54] He emphasized two conclusions. First, they must have a Commission, given greater powers than merely inquiry. 'We must have … a Commission for our *Buffer*.' Secondly, of all possible hares to start, he did not know of a better one than an extension of the borough franchise 'to household suffrage *coupled with plurality of voting*'. The key to the government's position, he argued, 'is the substantiality of the Commission'. Not only providing updated statistics, but also examining borough constituency boundaries, would give the Commission genuine work to do. By taking a minimum population of 7,000 as their criterion for granting a single member to a borough, there would be, he calculated, thirty boroughs whose boundaries would need to be extended, but not to any great extent. This, he believed, would avert the danger, to which Disraeli alluded, of alienating those MPs directly affected. Moreover, the Commission could investigate the effect of a £10 lodger franchise, ascertaining 'what *class* of voters it would introduce'; examine a possible savings bank franchise; look at the issue of bribery and polling papers; and consider the rated household borough suffrage coupled with plurality of voting. As well as substantiating the Commission's brief, Derby concluded, this would provide the opportunity for 'feeling the pulse of parliament and the country' on all these questions, showing 'how many doubtful points there are to be cleared up before parliament commits itself to so great and irrevocable a change', while, at the same time, not binding the government to the adoption of any specific proposal.

Proceeding by way of a Commission, examining resolutions proposed by the government, and looking to extend the borough franchise to a household suffrage, safeguarded by plural voting, now became central to Derby's thinking. By giving voters of £10 and upwards two votes and voters of £20 and upwards three votes, they 'might with safety go as low as household suffrage for single votes'.[55] The household borough suffrage had first been advocated by the radical Hume and taken up by Bright in 1858. Accompanied by plural voting, Derby now saw it as the logical stopping point in any lowering of the borough franchise, offering the prospect of finality. That statistics subsequently produced by Baxter suggested that the household suffrage would create a smaller number of additional voters than many feared was reassuring. Lord Nelson, former chief whip in the Lords, confirmed that conjoining the household suffrage with plural voting would enable the Conservatives 'to go far enough to *stop*, instead of stopping short, as the previous bill did, to invite further agitation on the subject'.[56] On 27 December, Derby agreed revised Reform resolutions with Disraeli, which were 'judiciously conceived' and gave 'no ground for complaint that enough work is not provided for the Commission'.[57] In response to Disraeli's wavering over plural voting, Derby informed him that 'you will have to allude to it in your introductory [Commons] speech as a subject deserving consideration'. Baxter's statistics were conclusive, he stated to Disraeli on the eve of the session, 'that without plurality of voting we cannot propose household suffrage, which would give the working classes a majority nearly 2:1. Even Gladstone repudiates the idea of giving them *any* majority.'[58] On Boxing Day, Disraeli disingenuously wrote to Cranborne that he had 'throughout been against legislation, and continue[d] so'.[59] But, despite Disraeli's lassitude, Derby firmly prescribed the process, resolutions submitted to a Commission, and the defensible principle, the household borough suffrage safeguarded by plural voting, by which a moderate and lasting Conservative settlement of Reform might be achieved.

The Queen remained an important ally in securing the settlement Derby envisaged. The promise of permanence might be strengthened by the appeal to patriotic duty. The vehemence of Bright's Reform speeches in Manchester and Glasgow, as the spokesman for the brittle alliance between working men and middle-class Reformers, had alarmed Gladstone and was already opening up a division between the radicals and moderate Liberals. Proceeding by resolutions, expressing broad principles, and then a Royal Commission, considering the effect of possible changes in the electoral body and boundaries, Derby reassured the Queen on 10 January, would allow a final settlement of Reform to be secured. It would enable the government to feel 'the pulse of the House of Commons' and ascertain 'how far a community of opinion might be relied upon between the moderate sections of both sides, to the exclusion of the extreme Democratic party'.[60] On 12 January the Queen approved the household borough suffrage as 'the course dictated by commonsense, and which all who are sincerely desirous of seeing the question settled, and who do not use it as a mere weapon of party warfare, are bound to support'.[61] To Disraeli, Derby reported that, regarding the court, 'we are not only on velvet, but we may look at it at present as *Partisan*; and we can have their intervention when, and as, we choose'.[62]

Derby's immediate difficulty, however, remained keeping his cabinet together. Manners, like Disraeli, continued to question the necessity for legislation on Reform. Northcote voiced deep reservations, but reluctantly conceded that Derby's plan of proceeding by way of resolutions was the best of a bad lot. Cranborne and Carnarvon, meanwhile, were receptive to Disraeli's subversive intimations that he shared their anxieties about attempting any legislation. Naas preferred keeping the franchise question out of the Commission's deliberations, restricting its brief to the enlargement of the borough boundaries. As Derby's thinking became more firmly grounded, cabinet discussion remained fractious and unsettled. Only on Thursday 10 January did the cabinet finally agree to introduce the revised resolutions to parliament, with the promise of an all-party Commission, if they were acceptable to the Commons.[63] During late January, Derby succumbed to a brief attack of gout, which prolonged cabinet havering. Only on Tuesday 29 January did ministers agree to include mention of Reform in the forthcoming Queen's Speech, although reference was kept vague in order to keep the opposition guessing as to whether the government intended to proceed by a bill or by resolutions.[64] Derby decided that a confidential copy of the Queen's Speech should not be sent to the Adullamites prior to parliament meeting, an act which would inflate the Adullamites' sense of their own importance and suggest a recognition of the group as a distinct party.[65] Better to let them remain an irritant within Liberal counsel. Ministers, meanwhile, continued to receive reports of the aversion to Gladstone felt by the Whigs, while accounts of Gladstone's table talk in Italy suggested he might take a conservative line once back in England. When parliament met on Tuesday 5 February, Stanley found it 'singular' that no explanation was demanded of the government by the opposition of how Reform was to be dealt with.[66] Not until Saturday 9 February did the cabinet eventually agree to the final form of the resolutions to be put to the Commons.

The success of Derby's coaxing of ministers over the recess was evident in the fact that the resolutions finally agreed by the cabinet in early February were essentially those he had drafted the previous November. Moreover, despite persistent ministerial unease, only Peel threatened to resign at mention of a possible household suffrage in the draft resolutions considered by the cabinet on Thursday 7 February. Peel's eyes, Disraeli observed, lit up with insanity at mention of the phrase, although Peel had no definite understanding of the proposal.[67] After two days' consultation Peel was eventually persuaded not to resign by the replacement of the words 'household suffrage' with reference to enlargement of the borough franchise on an extensive basis. Thus Derby preserved cabinet unity over a set of resolutions capable of meaning, if not now specifying, a household borough suffrage. Shaftesbury wrote to Derby that 'a measure of Reform is indispensable. But you can, I am sure, construct one, extensive, safe and satisfactory.'[68] A further 'crumb of comfort' was offered by conversation with Delane in early February. During late January *The Times* printed a series of articles pressing for a settlement of the Reform question. Delane is 'cordially with us', Derby subsequently reported to Disraeli, 'and will do all in his power to carry us through. He listened most attentively to the whole of our programme and pronounced oracularly, "I think it will do." '[69] It appeared that *The Times*, as well as the court, were now behind them.

Acknowledging their King ...

(Derby, *The Iliad of Homer*, ii. 2)

Derby commanded his cabinet. During the recess of 1866 he focused ministerial minds on Reform. He prescribed the process by which Reform might be resolved and he pushed forward the principle by which a permanent settlement might be achieved. Around Derby's direction other cabinet members pursued their own agendas. But none challenged his overall authority and other government business accommodated itself to the priority of Reform.

At the Exchequer, Disraeli enforced a policy of rigid economy. This required keeping a tight rein on Pakington's naval estimates. Derby was supportive of Pakington's plans, but was forcefully informed by Stanley that they would encounter strong opposition, both in the cabinet and in the Commons.[70] In cabinet, on 22 January 1867, both Pakington and Peel were required to reduce their proposed expenditure. Unexpectedly, Cranborne joined with Disraeli and Stanley in pressing for economy.[71] On 2 February, Disraeli pleaded that the 'Admiralty is beyond the control of the Chancellor of the Exchequer, or any other subordinate minister. It is the prime minister that can alone deal with that department.'[72] Again pressure was put on Pakington to reduce his estimates further in cabinet later that day. The City's slow recovery from the banking crisis of May, a bad harvest threatening to reduce revenue from the malt tax, and anxiety over the financial stability of some railway companies fuelled Disraeli's push for retrenchment. As a result, Disraeli approached his 1867 budget with the prospect of an estimated surplus. As in the 1850s, he looked to claim a reputation for fiscal probity and sound budgets as a direct riposte to Gladstone's financial mastery.

At the Foreign Office, Stanley, guided by Derby officially and Clarendon informally, maintained his policy of strict non-intervention. In response to the Austro-Prussian War of 1866 he informed the Commons that 'there never was a great European war in which the direct national interests of England were less concerned'.[73] When a revolt against the Turks broke out in Crete during the summer of 1866, creating a Franco-Austrian diplomatic alliance on one side and a Russo-Prussian alignment on the other, Stanley kept Britain apart from the crisis. At the same time, he resisted Bismarck's attempts to draw Britain into an anti-French alignment of Powers over the Grand Duchy of Luxembourg. 'There was never a time', he declared to General Charles Grey, the Queen's private secretary, 'when the English public was more thoroughly bent on incurring no fresh responsibilities for Continental objects.'[74]

Retrenchment at home and neutrality abroad helped to mitigate the blow to the ministry when, in October 1866, the dour yet able Cairns, for reasons of health, resigned the Attorney Generalship. The departure of this trusted orator was a significant jolt to the government, particularly to Disraeli, who confessed that, in debate, Cairns 'was my right arm'.[75] Derby agreed that it was 'a very heavy loss'.[76] From the opposition Lowe privately concurred that Cairns was 'the man who has most thoroughly studied the Reform question and whose opinions would have had most weight' among the Conservatives.[77] When another capable ministerial Irishman Lord Naas indicated dissatisfaction with his position as Chief Secretary for Ireland during late September, Disraeli begged Derby to dissuade Naas from resigning. The liberal Naas was frustrated by the stubbornness of Irish landlords who, he claimed, had undermined his efforts in the Tipperary by-election. But Derby successfully prevailed on Naas to remain in post. With the regrettable exception of Cairns, therefore, government disruption was avoided during the recess, despite the unsettling anxieties excited by Reform.

Up to the meeting of parliament in early February 1867 Derby's mastery over his ministers defined a process and presented a principle promising resolution of the Reform question, without precipitating resignations from the cabinet. Peel was persuaded to stay. Domestic retrenchment and diplomatic non-intervention bolstered the government's position, avoiding giving the opposition ready cause for complaint. But the situation remained delicate and the poise of the cabinet was precarious. The difficulties posed by the Reform question were immense. 'The Asian mystery was never more insoluble,' *The Times* declared.[78] When, after 9 February, the government found itself pitched into turbulent parliamentary debate, the fragile unanimity of the cabinet quickly came under even greater pressure.

> As, when the dust lies deepest on the roads,
> Before the boisterous winds the storm drives fast,
> And high at once the whirling clouds are toss'd,
> So was the fight confus'd.
>
> (Derby, *The Iliad of Homer*, ii. 18)

The next tempestuous three weeks proved one of the most intense political periods of Derby's career. Preserving cabinet unity, keeping Conservative backbenchers together, retaining the confidence of the Queen, exploiting opposition differences, and courting moderate opinion stretched the 67-year-old Derby's energy and skill to their limits. Unsurprisingly, in early March 1867 his health broke down. In the meantime, the pressure of rapidly shifting ministerial, parliamentary, and popular feeling bore down on him, as he steered the cabinet through the storm. As Disraeli nonchalantly observed to the premier on 24 March: 'It is very trying, and no doubt we shall, both of us, always remember 1867.'[79]

Radical leaders maintained their public agitation, intimating that greater violence would surely follow any dismissal of their demands. Derby was both unimpressed and unperturbed, however, by such pronouncements. A Reform demonstration in London in early December he judged a 'fiasco', the number of protesters threatened not materializing.[80] Another London demonstration, held on the morning of Monday 11 February 1867, was also deemed a failure. The weather was fine, and notice had been given weeks in advance. But only 20,000 gathered, although five or six times that number had been anticipated. The crowd appeared in good humour, there was little excitement, and few if any accidents.[81] Observing the procession from the Travellers' Club, the Liberal Lord Kimberley thought it 'a flat affair'.[82] All this reassured Conservative ministers that the time was now ripe for a calmly considered, comprehensive, and moderate Reform settlement. Certainly there was no sense of the cabinet being panicked into taking radical steps by furious popular agitation. On the contrary, ministers believed that the quiet mass of responsible extra-parliamentary opinion wished for a measured solution to a question which had, for too long, disrupted public debate. What remained less clear was how compliant the Commons might prove in securing such a settlement. The Liberal Commons chief whip, Henry Brand, confessed that the opposition were at 'sixes and sevens', while the Liberal MP for Sutherland, Sir David Dundas, complained to Lord Halifax that there seemed to be 'no leaders, no plan, no union, no sympathy' among the opposition.[83]

The opening of parliamentary debate on 5 February, however, did have an immediate and significant effect on Derby's thinking, prompting him to reconsider his carefully prepared procedural strategy on Reform. It was clear, he observed to Disraeli, that the opposition, though much divided, were 'very hot on Reform *without delay*'. Russell's asperity in the Lords, where he reviewed past abortive attempts to pass a Reform Bill, he reported to the Queen, did 'not augur well for an amicable settlement of the question'.[84] Given the impatient mood of the opposition, he now began to think it inadvisable to announce, at the very commencement of the session, that their Reform resolutions would be referred to a Royal Commission. Such a declaration, he feared, would expose the government to the charge of 'seeking to dally with the question, and finding an excuse for doing nothing at present'.[85] He did not give up hope of resorting to a Commission in due course. He anticipated that Commons discussion of their resolutions might raise so many questions as eventually to render a

Commission necessary. But his intention of announcing such a procedure, prior to debate on their resolutions, was revised by the opposition's clear desire that something of legislative substance must be proposed by the ministry sooner rather than later. Any perceived reluctance to press ahead with a Reform Bill would give righteous cause to Commons hostility. Opposition impatience might require their Reform resolutions to be promptly followed by a bill. In cabinet on 6 February majority agreement was reached on the precise wording of their resolutions. Derby now awaited the Commons response, persuaded that an immediate commitment to a Commission was best deferred. So might the resolutions 'lay down broad principles of action, without at the same time pledging the government to the specific mode of carrying them out'.[86]

At 4.30 p.m. on Monday 11 February, Disraeli described, but did not present, the government's Reform resolutions to the Commons. It was a hesitant, lacklustre, and disappointing performance. Malmesbury found Disraeli's speech, which lasted two and a quarter hours, 'too long and ambiguous'.[87] Stanley thought it 'unequal, heavy in parts, and [it] did not seem to bear as closely as one might wish on the point to be proved—viz. the necessity of proceeding otherwise than by a bill'.[88] The hostile Kimberley judged the speech 'dull, empty and pompous'.[89] It was a plea on the text of mutual concession and common consent. Reform should no longer, Disraeli declared, be the contested ground of bitter party conflict. Rather, a lasting settlement should be secured through disinterested cooperation. The resolutions would propose a reduction of the county and borough franchise; any new suffrage to be determined on the basis of the payment of rates; and a settlement attending to redistribution, boundaries, and bribery. Agreement to these general principles, he maintained, would allow a mutually acceptable, but yet to be specified, measure to be drawn up. Disraeli concluded that debate on the resolutions would be resumed on 25 February. In reply Gladstone was equivocal, apparently keeping open the option of opposing or supporting any government measure, while declaring the proposed resolutions unclear and ambiguous. His urging that the question must be brought to a quick legislative conclusion, however, put further pressure on the government to move without delay towards a bill. Derby's hope of acquiring time, during which to feel the pulse of the Commons, appeared increasingly forlorn. The House, Stanley noted, seemed undecided. Much 'will turn on the votes of "the Cave": which is itself supposed to be divided. If they agree, they can turn us out: but they are at present very far from being agreed'.[90]

What was immediately clear was that the description of the government's resolutions failed to separate Liberals and radicals. Derby's hope of a consensus of moderate opinion quickly emerging from discussion of their resolutions, excluding the extreme Democratic party, was dashed. He suddenly called an emergency cabinet meeting at ten o'clock that evening, as reports arrived of an abortive Fenian raid on Chester Castle. This signalled the incursion of revolutionary Irish republicanism onto the British mainland and, when those ministers able to attend quickly gathered at the Home Office, it was agreed to hold 500 soldiers from the Guards regiments in readiness.[91] Parliamentary attention, however, remained focused on Reform. In particular, the opposition's demand that the ministry must soon present a Reform Bill, as opposed to general resolutions, acquired increasing force. On Tuesday 12 February the Liberal leadership met at Gladstone's house in Carlton Gardens. No clear line emerged from their discussion. Russell urged immediate action to eject the Conservatives from office. But Gladstone counselled delay, reserving the option of moving a vote of censure on 25 February, if ministers refused to state in more detail what they meant to do about Reform. Clarendon hoped the government 'may remain in, as it will do the Whigs good to remain out in the cold'.[92] If the opposition's precise intentions remained opaque, it was, nonetheless, evident that Disraeli's resolutions had not, as the cabinet hoped, promptly estranged the Liberals from their radical colleagues.

Disraeli remained sanguine. But others now began to doubt the efficacy of proceeding with the resolutions. If they did not separate the Liberals from Bright and his fellow radicals, then the prospect of an acrimonious bipartisan confrontation seemed likely. This disturbing possibility deeply alarmed the Queen. On Wednesday 13 February she wrote to Derby anxiously reminding him that the resolutions were intended to be the means of avoiding a party contest.[93] Her hope that Reform could be settled by mutual concession had persuaded her to support Derby's plan to proceed by resolution. But it now seemed that they would not secure common agreement. The following day Derby acknowledged that the impression produced by Disraeli's announcement of their resolutions had been 'the reverse of favourable', increasing 'the feeling of disappointment which undoubtedly prevailed'.[94] His own hope that 'the leaders of the "Liberal" party' would 'enter into any such arrangements' as he envisaged 'for a settlement of the question, irrespective of personal considerations' he recognized was now unlikely. Yet, it remained the case that '"Liberal" counsels are hopelessly divided ... Ld. Russell desires to regain the head of the party and is more acrimonious than any of his colleagues. Mr Gladstone seems to be the recognised leader of the opposition; and *he* seriously in doubt as to the course to be pursued.'[95] Derby reluctantly accepted that the government should now present parliament with a sketch of the bill they would introduce, if their resolutions were passed. This would stake out the ground on which the support of moderate Liberals and Whigs might be gained. Moreover, it would prevent Gladstone from seizing the initiative by introducing detailed proposals of his own. Having relinquished any initial reference to a Commission, Derby now found himself forced to modify his position on their resolutions, a sketch of a proposed bill now seeming necessary.

As a result, in response to an arranged question from Lord Robert Montagu on Thursday 14 February, Disraeli suggested to the Commons that the government might bring forward a Reform Bill sooner rather than later. Yet this immediately confronted the cabinet with the difficulty of drawing up a measure which was acceptable to all ministers, including Stanley and Northcote as well as Peel and Cranborne. But cabinet agreement was not to be reached on the basis of the household suffrage. Could the requirements of cabinet unity and Commons expectation be reconciled? This critical question haunted subsequent ministerial discussion. The following day Disraeli drew up a bill abandoning giving double votes to borough electors above the £10 level, but based on Baxter's parochial voting framework supplemented by merit savings and taxation franchises.[96] Yet when, later on Friday 15 February, Disraeli sounded out Cranborne on this scheme, Cranborne firmly rejected the rated household suffrage so uncertainly protected and, in response, insisted on a £5 rated borough franchise. Having ascertained what the glowering Cranborne would accept, Disraeli immediately drew up an alternative plan based on Cranborne's stated preference. Household suffrage, as the basis for a permanent settlement, was laid aside. What the new plan offered was a possible basis for preserving cabinet unity.

At 1 p.m. on Saturday 16 February the cabinet met. Significantly, no ministers objected to Disraeli's having committed them to declaring their hand on Reform. The idea of a Commission was quietly abandoned. But, when Disraeli brought forward his plan for a £5 rated borough franchise, with additional votes for those with £50 in savings, an educational franchise, and another founded on direct taxation, immediate objections were voiced. Disraeli estimated that his merit franchises would give an additional 680,000 borough votes to property, offsetting the additional 360,000 borough votes created by lowering the franchise. But Stanley, Northcote, and Pakington opposed the plan as certain to be rejected by the Commons.[97] If plural voting was to be accepted, they argued, no single person should be given more than two votes. At the same time, Peel fiercely objected to any plans which lowered the borough suffrage at all, whatever checks or counterpoises might be devised. No argument had any effect on him and again he expressed his intention to resign, rather than agree to the proposed scheme.[98] Cranborne accepted the plan, although he thought the Commons would not agree to it. The cabinet meeting finally concluded at 3 p.m. with all, except Peel, endorsing Disraeli's plan with varying degrees of enthusiasm. To this extent cabinet unity was preserved, but at the high cost of abandoning the household borough suffrage safeguarded by plural voting. That evening Lady Derby hosted a party at Downing Street which Gladstone attended. Securing the support of the Queen and closely monitoring the reaction of the Commons opposition was now critical.

On Sunday 17 February, Derby dispatched Disraeli to Osborne to consult the Queen. Disraeli assured her that Derby would not quit office until Reform was settled. In the meantime, the government hoped the Queen would continue to aid the cabinet in the face of Peel's threatened resignation. To Disraeli's relief, Victoria was wholly cooperative and offered to talk to Peel.[99] Such an approach, Derby hoped, might yet dissuade Peel from leaving the cabinet. This royal intervention worked. Following the Queen's urgent appeal for loyal support at this critical moment, Peel dutifully informed Derby on the morning of Tuesday 19 February that he would stand by any Reform Bill Derby brought forward. 'I have this instant seen Peel,' Derby immediately reported to Disraeli. 'He *consents* and *remains!*'[100]

With the Queen behind him and Peel brought back in line, Derby's attention shifted towards the Commons opposition. On Monday 18 February, Gladstone promised in the Commons his cooperation over Reform, if the government dropped their resolutions and proceeded with a bill which offered the prospect of an effectual settlement. What parliament and the country desired, Gladstone suggested, was a lasting legislative solution. In order to secure a settlement he would support a Conservative measure, if it was sufficiently progressive. At the same time, Derby had a private conversation with Lord Grosvenor as a representative of the Adullamite Cave. On Sunday 17 February the Cave had met to agree that no standing point between the current borough franchise and household suffrage was tenable. If the borough franchise was lowered, as clearly it must be, then stopping short of household suffrage would only constitute a short-lived compromise and further Reform agitation ensue. The democratic tendencies of the household suffrage might be mitigated, however, by cumulative, rather than plural, voting. Grosvenor conveyed this view to Derby. On 19 February, Derby advised Grosvenor that, while they agreed with each other on the necessity of the household suffrage as a basis for a permanent settlement, plural voting, rather than cumulative voting, was preferable.[101]

These exchanges persuaded Derby that the government must immediately revert to the rated household suffrage. Only on this ground would support from the Adullamites be secured and a public opening created for Gladstonian cooperation. It promised finality. It delivered a clear substantial enfranchisement in the boroughs, sufficient to commit Gladstone to his public avowal of collaboration. It also provided a principle sufficiently distinct from the proposals contained in the 1866 bill to justify ejecting Russell from office. With a now compliant Peel brought back on board by the Queen, the imminent danger of cabinet secessions appeared to have passed. The £5 rated borough franchise was promptly abandoned in cabinet on Tuesday 19 February as Derby, supported by Disraeli, again forcefully pressed the case for household suffrage. This element, at least, of his Reform plan of the recess might now be rescued. In response to the cabinet discussion of the preceding Saturday, it was also proposed that plural votes be limited to two.[102] Derby informed ministers that the Queen believed that the security of her throne was dependent upon the settlement of Reform, if possible, by the present government.[103] Patriotic duty was added to the inducements to proceed with legislation delivering the household suffrage coupled with modified plurality. Peel withdrew his objections and the cabinet acquiesced. Disraeli was asked to estimate figures to show the effect in the boroughs of such a reduction, so that a final discussion of their bill could form the agenda for the meeting of cabinet on Saturday 23 February. Gathorne Hardy recorded in his journal that 'all was smooth, the nodus had been untied by no mean hand'.[104] Derby's central principle of extending the borough vote to householders, while containing its democratic tendencies with a plurality of votes, was restored. A slight attack of gout on 22 February did not weaken his determination to proceed with a lasting settlement of Reform on this basis.

Montagu Corry and Baxter worked hard preparing statistics for Disraeli.[105] But the result of their calculations was disturbing. Determining eligibility for the vote based upon personal savings proved complicated and difficult. Likewise, the effect of a vote based on direct taxation proved impossible to calculate with any precision. Indeed, the absence of reliable statistical information made the impact of any of the electoral changes recommended in cabinet on 19 February largely a matter of guesswork.

Even estimating the number of those paying rates in each borough constituency was problematic.[106] In the absence of precise statistics, what remained was the force of the phrase household suffrage in suggesting a basis for finality.

Over the next few days ministers continued to receive reports that the Whigs were frightened and disposed to be moderate, and that Gladstone especially was anxious to demonstrate he was not in thrall to Bright. In truth, Kimberley noted, the Liberals were in 'great perplexity' over Reform.[107] This reinforced Derby's sense that the household borough suffrage cry would now provide both finality and the opportunity for moderate Liberals and Whigs to cooperate with the government in the national interest. When the cabinet met at 3 p.m. on Saturday 23 February, Derby swiftly pushed through the household suffrage proposal, allied with plural voting based on property. A bribery bill was 'scrambled over' and a redistribution bill mentioned.[108] This would prevent either the 'Cave' or Gladstone from seizing the initiative and, it was hoped, carry them along with the government. Derby allowed little time for discussion. At the opening of the meeting he announced he had another pressing engagement and the cabinet meeting must be brief. He was committed to catching the 6.15 p.m. train to Windsor to have an audience with the Queen. While Cranborne voiced some reservations, the rest of the cabinet quickly assented.[109] The previous day Cranborne had begun to study the statistics, which troubled him.[110] But, either because the discussion moved too quickly, or because he was biding his time, he did not express any objection. Following the meeting a relieved Derby reported to the Queen that evening that the cabinet were unanimously in support of the measure.

But cabinet agreement, secured in haste on Saturday, quickly began to unravel when, the following day, Cranborne, breaking his sabbath observance, analysed the statistics more thoroughly. During Sunday 24 February he became deeply alarmed at the changes to which the cabinet had consented. During the evening he visited Carnarvon to share his unease. Both promptly agreed that the household suffrage would bring about 'a complete revolution' in the boroughs.[111] Cranborne indicated he must now resign, but Carnarvon persuaded him to request another cabinet meeting so that they could air their concerns. After a rushed dinner, late that evening Carnarvon roused Peel from his bed to inform him of their views. In response, Peel declared that he would also quit the cabinet if both Cranborne and Carnarvon resigned. Meanwhile, Cranborne wrote a letter to Derby demanding a cabinet meeting the next day and indicating that the commitment to the household suffrage required his resignation.

On Monday 25 February, Disraeli was committed to sketching out a possible government Reform Bill in the Commons as part of the debate on their resolutions. At 2.30 that afternoon Derby had arranged for a meeting of Conservative MPs at Downing Street to ensure united party support during the debate. But over his breakfast at 6.45 that morning he opened Cranborne's letter.[112] It was followed fifteen minutes later by a similar communication from Carnarvon.[113] Derby was both astonished and infuriated. He believed he could handle Peel and that Carnarvon, by himself, might be prevailed upon. But the cynical and prickly Cranborne was a different kettle of fish; his obduracy would give Peel and Carnarvon the courage to leave the front bench. An angry Derby immediately sent a note to Disraeli at Grosvenor Gate, who was still in bed. 'The enclosed, just received, is utter ruin,' Derby wrote: 'What on earth are we to do?'[114] A second note from Derby then arrived at Grosvenor Gate informing Disraeli that a report from Baxter confirmed Cranborne's calculations.[115] Disraeli's reaction was terse. 'This is stabbing in the back! ... It seems like treachery.'[116] The cabinet was quickly summoned to meet at St James's Square at 12.30 p.m. It was, Derby informed the Queen, a gathering of 'a most unpleasant character'.[117]

A tight-lipped Derby opened the cabinet meeting with strong expressions of his deep dismay at the turn of events. He was clearly very angry.[118] Disraeli was as white as a sheet. Walpole sat silently in the corner of the room. Cranborne arrived late and Carnarvon had initially to face the full brunt of Derby's fury alone. Naas also arrived late and could not make out what was being discussed so heatedly, assuming it must be the suspension of the Habeas Corpus Act. Prolonged discussion did not placate any of the contending parties. By 2 p.m. vehement disagreement still prevailed. Carnarvon's suggestion of a household suffrage in large boroughs and a £6 rating franchise in smaller ones was angrily dismissed while, to the exasperation of his colleagues, Pakington proposed that perhaps they should resign. Tempers were not cooled by Cranborne's admission that he had shared his misgivings with individuals outside the government, such as Elcho. The beginning of the Conservative meeting in Downing Street was now fast approaching. Ministers were committed to presenting a bill. It was at this point that Stanley, as a desperate expedient, proposed a £6 rating franchise for the boroughs without any dual voting and a £20 rating franchise for the counties. A majority of those ministers present, including Buckingham, Chelmsford, Gathorne Hardy, Pakington, Northcote, and Manners, disliked this hasty compromise. But Pakington observed that they now had only ten minutes left to make up their minds. With time

rapidly running out, at Derby and Disraeli's prompting, it was reluctantly accepted. This £6 rating plan subsequently became tagged the 'Ten
Minutes Bill'.

Derby immediately left for Downing Street, where he addressed the
assembled Conservative MPs. His ill temper was not improved when the
£6 rating proposal was received with little enthusiasm, while household
suffrage, which he candidly admitted favouring, was evidently preferred
by the backbenchers.[119] Nonetheless, Conservative MPs acquiesced to the
compromise scheme as the price of preserving cabinet unity. At 4.30
p.m. Disraeli spoke to a packed Commons, taking up discussion of the
government's resolutions as the occasion to describe a possible bill based
upon the £6 rating borough franchise. Various merit franchises were
mentioned, but the principle of plurality, adopted in the resolutions, was
given up. Unsurprisingly in the circumstances, it was a confused and
hollow performance. The Reform proposal Disraeli briefly sketched out,
which the government might introduce once their resolutions were passed,
bore a close resemblance to the Liberal bill rejected by the Commons in
1866. When Disraeli sat down, after speaking for an hour, Lowe, Bright,
and Gladstone immediately launched into the government. Apart from
Walpole, not a single Conservative MP spoke in support of the proposal.
Under the force of the opposition's ferocious attack Disraeli half-withdrew
some of the resolutions and offered to resume discussion of the others in
three days' time. It was a dispiriting performance.

The next morning's cabinet meeting was blighted by deep despondency
and simmering irritation.[120] Derby retained his hope of securing Whig
support or using the influence of the Queen to tame Gladstone. Royal intervention, he hoped, might possibly persuade Cranborne to accept a more
extensive measure, although he suspected that the sardonic Cranborne was
not 'a man to be swayed by the Queen's opinion'.[121] In cabinet the dissidents
said very little. Derby, supported by Disraeli and Pakington, urged that
their resolutions be withdrawn and a Reform Bill brought forward. Although absent from the cabinet meeting, Stanley concurred that 'there was
in fact no alternative'.[122] That afternoon 290 opposition MPs attended a
meeting called by Gladstone. Withdrawal of the government's resolutions
was to be demanded. It was also agreed to support a Conservative bill, but
in doing so to seek to extend it. Patriotic duty and party advantage might
be thus combined. It was anticipated that any alterations proposed by the
Liberals would be rejected by the government. Once again, Disraeli acted
quickly to deny Gladstone the initiative. As Stanley confirmed: 'What
must be done is best done without the appearance of compulsion'.[123] In the

Commons that evening Disraeli withdrew the government's resolutions, effectively forestalling Gladstone, who had come to the House with the intention of demanding the same.

By Wednesday 27 February persistent ministerial disagreements left Derby in very low spirits. Amending their intentions on Reform had not placated Cranborne, Carnarvon, and Peel. The hastily devised 'Ten Minutes Bill' had not appeased any section of the opposition. At the same time, Conservative backbenchers had indicated their preference for the borough household suffrage, suitably hedged, as a basis for securing a permanent settlement. Reports of the feeling at the Carlton Club, conveyed to Derby by his private secretary, George Barrington, indicated a general regret that the larger plan promised by the rated residential household suffrage had, at the last minute, been abandoned by the cabinet. Conservative MPs favoured the household suffrage, safeguarded by plural voting, for a number of reasons. It offered finality and a defensible bulwark against democracy. It provided a powerful resonant cry in the event of facing the electorate. It would be a Conservative settlement sufficiently distinct from the Liberal bill of 1866 to justify having ejected Russell and Gladstone from office. But most importantly, it would allow the Conservatives to resolve authoritatively for a generation an issue upon which the Liberals claimed a monopoly of wisdom. Not only would it secure a permanent settlement, but, above all, it would be a solution delivered by the Conservative party.

As a dispirited Derby travelled to his audience with the Queen at Windsor on Wednesday 27 February the thought revived of once again reverting to the household suffrage. If ministerial resignations were unavoidable, better they occurred on this ground than on any other.[124] The Queen was surprised by his low spirits. She again affirmed her support for a settlement and offered encouragement. Disraeli also urged Derby not to overemphasize the difficulties of forsaking the unpopular £6 rating plan for the household suffrage. Walpole, Disraeli informed Derby, agreed, 'if certain persons left, and you reorganised your ministry, that it would not be looked upon as changing our front, but that, with a frank and obvious explanation, it would do us good and strengthen us in the country'.[125] Stanley too believed that 'there was only one thing to be done, and that was to recur to our original position'.[126] Cranborne, Carnarvon, and Peel, as was evident from conversations at the Carlton Club, Disraeli confirmed, 'have completely misapprehended the feeling and spirit of the party'.[127] During the course of Wednesday 27 February, Derby's spirits improved. The next day about 150 Conservative backbenchers, under the chairmanship of Sir Matthew Ridley, met at the Carlton Club, the over-whelming majority expressing themselves in favour of household suffrage, protected by three years' residence and the personal payment of rates. Only a small minority, led by Beresford-Hope, James Lowther, and Cavendish Bentinck, supported the £6 rating franchise. That evening Disraeli wrote to Derby: 'All I hear and observe more and more convinces me that the bold line is the safer one, and, moreover, that it will be successful'.[128] Ridley gave a personal report of the Carlton Club meeting to Derby, which the premier regarded as 'a strong argument for meeting our fate on the bolder line'.[129]

By Thursday 28 February, Derby's resolve and optimism had revived. He now determined to push ahead on the basis of a suitably safeguarded rated residential household suffrage, reassured that the Queen and the party would support him. Further encouragement was provided by the news that the Adullamites still preferred the household suffrage and plurality. Reports that Gladstone had committed himself to a £5 rating borough franchise also buoyed up Derby's spirits. The Conservative advocacy of household suffrage would decisively undercut Gladstone. If, in these circumstances, the Liberals overthrew their measure, Disraeli observed to Derby, 'you could dissolve with honour and a prospect of success, and meet parliament, at any rate, with a powerful party'.[130] Derby prepared to give the Conservative back benches what they now thirsted for: bold and decisive leadership. He instructed Baxter immediately to draw up a household rating bill.[131]

Firmly to stand and cheer your comrades on.
(Derby, *The Iliad of Homer*, ii. 4)

On Friday 1 March, Derby took up a firm and distinctive Conservative policy, no longer seeking to accommodate isolated cabinet dissidents or solicitously courting Adullamite and Whig endorsement. If the hope of a Conservative measure being accepted by the Commons remained uncertain, at least the ministry would have a clear policy with which to appeal to the country. He wrote to Cranborne, Carnarvon, and Peel stating his intention to revert to the household borough suffrage. They had only abandoned it five days earlier because of 'great and sudden pressure', he informed Cranborne, 'and my own opinion is very strong that it is our only chance of safety'. The cabinet must retrace its steps or face 'disaster', he wrote to Carnarvon; while to Peel, Derby warned that only the rated residential household suffrage could save the ministry from being cut to pieces by Gladstone and falling ignomoniously.[132] From Heron Court, where he was attending his sick wife, Malmesbury applauded Derby's revived resolve.

I always preferred household suffrage (properly counterpoised) to any half-way resting place, and I believe the whole country is of that opinion. If it is yours also, as it seemed to me when I last met you in cabinet, I would urge you to act upon it. The loss of three able and honourable men is a great one, but far greater would be the loss of reputation which a vacillating and subservient policy would inevitably bring upon us personally, and upon our party. No colleagues can be worth that sacrifice.

Malmesbury concluded that 'the *only* course that can serve our credit before the country is for your master-mind to determine what is the best bill'.[133] Northcote declared to Derby the wish of the great majority of the cabinet to 'stand by you to the utmost of our power'.[134] Walpole stated he was now ready 'to stand by Lord Derby through thick and thin'.[135] A dissolution, following the rejection by the Commons of a Conservative measure, still seemed likely. But, armed with a renewed commitment to household suffrage, Derby faced such a prospect with less apprehension than before.

At the meeting of the cabinet at 3 p.m. on Saturday 2 March, Derby, 'in an agitated but firm voice', announced that the ministry must proceed with a borough household suffrage bill with plural voting.[136] The awkward subsequent discussion lasted for a grim two hours. Colleagues, particularly Northcote and Manners, tried hard to dissuade Cranborne, Carnarvon, and Peel from resigning. Carnarvon and Peel wavered, looking to Cranborne for their cue, but Cranborne remained implacable. As each member of the cabinet was asked individually if they accepted Derby's recommended course of action, Cranborne refused to assent. Resignation was now unavoidable. The cabinet meeting ended. As Cranborne silently left the room, Derby sighed, closed his red dispatch box, and murmured: 'The Tory party is ruined!'[137] 'Poor Tory party,' added Disraeli ironically.[138] A dogged resolve, rather than any sense of triumph, characterized Derby's mood. When later he encountered Lady Cranborne he enquired grimly, 'Is Robert still doing his sums?'[139]

The following day, Sunday 3 March, Disraeli secured the promotion of three of his adherents, following the departure of Cranborne, Carnarvon, and Peel. While the Duke of Buckingham succeeded Carnarvon as

Colonial Secretary, Pakington took over Peel's position at the War Office, and Northcote replaced Cranborne as Secretary for India; the Duke of Richmond, the Duke of Marlborough, and Henry Corry (father of Disraeli's secretary Montagu Corry) were brought into the cabinet. In the Lords, on Monday 4 March, Derby explained the circumstances of the ministerial changes.[140] Differences had arisen over the detail, he stated, not the fundamental principle of necessary Reform. All were agreed that the political nation should be enlarged. The question was how many of those currently excluded from the vote should be enfranchised and, more particularly, how to prevent the electoral body from being swamped by any one class. It was this issue which had prompted the three resignations from his cabinet. In resolving this question he looked to take the Commons into his counsel. Carnarvon's subsequent explanation of his decision to resign, Derby felt, went into more detail than necessary. In the Commons, Disraeli made a very short speech announcing the ministerial resignations and committing the government to introducing a Reform Bill in a fortnight's time. Gladstone's response, Stanley noted, contained a good deal of his customary vehemence, 'showing as it were an undercurrent of bitterness'.[141] Gladstone was cheered by the radicals, but received with silence by the Liberal benches behind him. A hostile opposition motion, Disraeli believed, was imminent. Only fear of a dissolution might inhibit them.

Disraeli spoke at greater length to the Commons on Tuesday 5 March.[142] He acknowledged that the 'Ten Minutes Bill' had not given satisfaction to any party. Therefore, Derby had advised a reversion to their original plan of Reform in order to secure a settlement. 'What was [Derby's] first opinion early in the autumn is his last opinion, and is one upon which he is prepared to act,' Disraeli informed the Commons. Both Disraeli's language, though vague, and Cranborne's response, which was openly critical, suggested that household suffrage would be the basis of the scheme to which the cabinet were reverting. The state of the party and the Reform question, Stanley believed, was 'now more critical than it has been at any former time'.[143] Despite there being no excitement for Reform among the great mass of people, he felt the educated classes were both preoccupied with and apprehensive about it. The radical press, of course, was screaming the loudest. *The Times* had disapproved of the cabinet's resolutions and the 'Ten Minutes Bill', but was anxious for a settlement, if possible delivered by the present ministry. Conservative MPs were divided, 'but not disinclined to action'. Stanley's own conviction, therefore, was that 'after two failures we ought to stake everything on this last trick and refuse to accept modification of the plan, except on points of detail'. On grounds of consistency they could not propose a real transfer of power to the working class. Nor could the cabinet give any credence to the accusation that they were ready to concede in office what they had rejected when in opposition. The only option open to them was to stick to household suffrage, despite the possibility of its rejection in the Commons, and at least possess a clear and defensible policy when forced to face the country following a dissolution. Stanley's views mirrored Derby's determination. Firm resolve, even in the event of parliamentary defeat, would furnish the Conservatives with a credible cry before the electorate. Stanley's own contribution to Commons debate on 5 March was a pledge that the government would stand or fall by their forthcoming measure. But he repudiated the notion that they 'were outbidding the Whigs in a race for popularity'.[144] Rather, the household suffrage, suitably protected, provided a clear principle upon which the ministry would stake its position and authority.

On Thursday 7 March, Derby held a drafting meeting with Disraeli and Gathorne Hardy at St James's Square. Their commitment to household suffrage was now agreed. But Disraeli began to express doubts about the prospect of carrying the dual voting proposals intended to offset the lowered borough suffrage.[145] Stanley agreed that this aspect of their proposed plan was unlikely to be accepted by the Commons. In cabinet on Saturday 9 March, Disraeli pressed for the abandonment of dual voting, recommending the government stand or fall on the borough household suffrage pure and simple.[146] While all the other members of the cabinet opposed Disraeli's suggestion, Derby wavered a good deal. During their discussion Derby passed a note to Disraeli: 'If we do not take care, we shall have another break-up. Duality will defeat us—abandonment of it will destroy us'.[147] In conversation with Stanley the following day, Derby stated his commitment to remaining in power at whatever cost and expressed his willingness to make the largest concessions with that object in view.[148] But Lord Buckingham called on him at St James's Square on Sunday 10 March to declare that, without the dual vote, he did not see how he could support their proposed bill.[149] In addition, Peel also indicated that the abandonment of dual voting would force him to oppose the bill on its second reading. Derby's anxieties were revived, as was evident in his report of Peel's view to Disraeli: 'It is indeed a regular debacle on all sides!'[150] Disraeli doubted the possibility of getting their bill through the Commons, but clung to household suffrage as the cabinet's life jacket in shooting the subsequent electoral rapids.

It was at this point that an exhausted Derby, on Monday 11 March, fell ill. The unrelenting exertion and political contention of the previous three weeks left him chronically fatigued. Gathorne Hardy believed that 'the mortification and annoyance had a permanent effect on him'.[151] Certainly, after March 1867 Derby never again enjoyed good health, only managing to rally himself for critical occasions and then relapsing into incapacity. Nonetheless, in cabinet meetings on Tuesday 12 March and Thursday 14 March a revised Reform plan was agreed.[152] It was decided to enfranchise all male borough residents who had personally paid poor rates and resided in the constituency for a minimum of two years. Derby reduced the residency requirement from three years to two years when Baxter's statistics suggested difficulties in determining eligibility on that basis. In order to placate Buckingham, Walpole, and Hardy, he also insisted on giving a second vote to those who paid both rates and direct taxes, although he accepted privately that such a system of dual voting should not be regarded as a critical issue by the government.[153] A rateable definition of the household suffrage, determined by personal payment, now comprised the essential core of their measure. It provided a clear demarcation of respectability. Baxter's drafting of the bill, however, was deemed unsatisfactory and the Home Office legal expert Henry Thring was quickly brought in to draw up the legislation more competently. Derby deemed Thring 'a safe man, a good draftsman and a fair politician'.[154] An indignant Baxter resigned in protest.

Derby rallied himself on Friday 15 March to address a large Conservative meeting in Downing Street.[155] Ensuring unified support for their Reform Bill was now crucial. In a highly unusual step he described the cabinet's plan to his backbenchers, three days before it was presented to the Commons. In all, 195 Conservative MPs attended and a further forty-three sent notes affirming their loyalty. Derby declared the borough household suffrage, defined by the personal payment of rates, with a two-year residency requirement, consistent with the principles of the constitution, and a means by which the Conservative government could deliver a lasting settlement. The dual vote would also be proposed, but the ministry were not, he added, wedded to it. Additional votes would be given to those paying at least 20s. in direct taxation, possessing £50 or more in funds or saving banks, and with certain educational qualifications. The county occupation franchise was to be reduced from £50 to a £15 rating qualification, and redistribution confined to fifteen seats. The party responded enthusiastically to Derby's announcement. Cranborne, Peel, and Carnarvon remained silent and the full isolation of their position became apparent.[156] As often before, Derby's decisive leadership was received by Conservative MPs with enthusiastic endorsement. The vacillation of the previous weeks dissipated.

Over the following weeks, having finally successfully brought his cabinet and party behind the household borough suffrage, an ailing Derby offered encouragement from the sidelines of Commons debate. Denied direct participation, he cheered on as the Commons leadership, primarily Disraeli, played out their Reform strategy, although a severe attack of gout at the end of March emphasized his remoteness from events.[157] Inevitably, on 18 March, when Disraeli introduced the Conservative Reform Bill to a packed Commons, control gradually slipped from Derby's grasp. Prior to March 1867 the Conservatives' handling of Reform reflected Derby's priorities and strategic views. Thereafter, it quickly became subject to Disraeli's tactical dexterity. On the eve of Disraeli's presentation of their bill to the Commons, Derby reassured the Queen that Disraeli would attempt to keep the measure separate from personal political considerations and conveyed his belief that they would receive the aid of 'no inconsiderable portion of the "Liberals" '.[158]

In presenting the government's Reform Bill on Monday 18 March, Disraeli spoke well, although some detected in his manner the anticipation of eventual defeat.[159] The household borough suffrage, he declared, would strengthen the character of the Commons by establishing it on a broad popular basis, while the requirement that rates were paid personally would guarantee that the vote was given only to those of proven regularity of life and general trustworthiness of conduct. Gladstone immediately fiercely attacked what he saw as the extensive inconsistencies in the measure. The principle of the double vote was widely condemned. Gladstone pronounced it a 'gigantic engine of fraud'.[160] But Gladstone's vehemence unsettled many Liberal backbenchers. On Wednesday 20 March the cabinet decided to make no concessions or changes on the second reading, while reserving the option of accepting amendments in committee.[161] Nonetheless, on Saturday 23 March the cabinet agreed to abandon dual voting.[162] The following day Buckingham wrote to Derby to confirm that, despite his misgivings, he would not resign, but would support the bill when it came up to the Lords.[163] On Monday 25 March, Gladstone again attacked the bill. Gathorne Hardy with great effect defended it. Derby considered the debate 'excellent', Gathorne Hardy successfully placing himself in the front rank as a debater.[164] Derby urged Disraeli to close the debate on Tuesday 26 March with a short, pithy statement hitting the keynote, namely, that the government wished to consult the opinion of the Commons, but refused to submit to the dictation of Gladstone as '*one assumed* leader of a party'. He advised Disraeli to point out to the Commons that the year before Sir Robert Peel had declared 'that there was no safe standing-point short of household suffrage!' Delane, Derby heard from Talbot, remarked that 'Gladstone has done [the government] more good than all [their] cabinets together'.[165] Disraeli's subsequent Commons performance proved a great success, in particular his demonstration that some of the provisions Gladstone denounced most vehemently had been included in earlier Reform bills, for example in 1854, which Gladstone had supported. The second reading passed without a division. Gathorne Hardy judged it 'a brilliant speech'.[166] Derby was delighted.

> I cannot let the day pass over without offering you my cordial congratulations on your splendid achievement of last night. I hear from all quarters that it was the finest speech you ever made; and you seem to have carried the House bodily with you. In fact, you have won our game for us; and in writing to the Queen this morning to announce your "triumphant success", I told H.M. that I now, for the first time, entertained a sanguine hope of carrying a bill through in the course of the present session.[167]

Stanley confirmed that Disraeli's speech had secured 'a complete change in the position of the Reform question and the ministry'. Gladstone was in a state of great excitement, apparently wishing to oppose everything, while the Liberal party was too much divided to give him effective support.[168] Derby observed to General Grey: 'I must own I distrust [Gladstone] more than any other public man I know, for when he has taken up an idea, he follows it up with a passion which makes him utterly reckless of consequences'.[169]

On Saturday 29 March, Derby celebrated his sixty-eighth birthday in a mood of new-found optimism. But the following day he swiftly succumbed to another debilitating attack of gout, as the stress of the previous weeks overcame him. He was absent from cabinet meetings during early April, and on 16 April left St James's Square to recuperate. With Lady Emma he retreated to a rented villa in Roehampton, 'a pleasant old-fashioned house' down Putney Lane 'with large grounds well shaded with trees, and a good large garden'.[170] They were joined by their son Freddy and a pregnant Lady Constance, as well as their 2-year-old grandson Edward. In brief escapes from the Foreign Office, Stanley also visited them to enjoy some relaxation away from the hotbed of Westminster and Whitehall.

With Derby resting in the garden at Roehampton, command of the party passed over to Disraeli. On 7 May the Queen was advised by her private secretary that 'Mr Disraeli is evidently the directing mind of the ministry, and ... he is the person to whom any representation can now be most effectively made'.[171] Having led the party into the battle over Reform, Derby relinquished command to his resourceful lieutenant.

During April and May, Disraeli's 'directing mind' drove Reform forward through committee, destroying the unity of Gladstone's Liberal party. An attempt by Gladstone to substitute a £5 value franchise in the boroughs for the rating household suffrage dramatically failed as, on 12 April, fifty-two Liberal and radical MPs rebelled against him. The Commons dispersed for Easter with the opposition in disarray and the Conservatives consolidated behind Disraeli's leadership. When debate resumed after the recess Gladstone declined to play a conspicuous part. Disraeli, meanwhile, pressed onward, compliantly accepting successive amendments that stripped the household borough suffrage of its restrictions. Success had now become an end in itself, any settlement of Reform having become desirable, as long as it was delivered by the Conservative ministry. The two-year residential qualification was reduced to one year; a £10 lodger franchise in the boroughs was accepted; the county suffrage was extended from a £15 to a £12 annual rental qualification; while those owning land worth £5 or more were also given the county vote. The most startling concession, however, was the acceptance of the advanced Liberal Grosvenor Hodgkinson's amendment, on 17 May, which, by abolishing the compounding of rates, removed the largest single obstacle to small urban tenants receiving the vote. That Derby was not consulted on Hodgkinson's amendment was a measure of how far removed he now was from rapidly moving events. Yet neither did he complain to Disraeli of the concessions accepted during April and May. Although remote from events, he remained prepared to countenance such submission in order to ensure that his party retained control of the Reform settlement.

During May, Derby managed to attend a Royal Academy dinner, where he and Disraeli both spoke. At a Conservative gathering at St James's Square during the evening of Monday 6 May, Derby soothed the jangled nerves of backbenchers unsettled by Disraeli's concessions. Once again Derby's firm reassurances quickly restored confidence;[172] although, as he observed to the Queen, the Commons is 'so capricious, that it is hardly possible to anticipate from day to day what may take place'.[173] He also oversaw the long-anticipated replacement of the discredited Walpole by Gathorne Hardy at the Home Office. Walpole 'is in a state of mind which

I can hardly describe', Derby reported to the Queen on 8 May, although the former Home Secretary agreed to remain in the cabinet without office.[174] On Wednesday 15 May he discussed a boundary commission with Disraeli.[175] Redrawing the constituencies offered an opportunity to mitigate the effect of a borough household suffrage stripped of safeguards. Although still not fully recovered, Derby was in good spirits, relaxing over games of chess with his elder son during the evenings. On Wednesday 22 May he attended the Derby on Epsom Downs. On the occasion of the Queen's birthday on Saturday 25 May he hosted a large party at St James's Square, which, owing to the number attending, proved 'a frightful squeeze'.[176] But at the end of June a serious recurrence of gout was accompanied by rheumatism, and the prospect of his resuming active command of the Conservative cabinet faded from view. When Gathorne Hardy visited Derby's bedside at St James's Square on Saturday 29 June he found the prime minister much preoccupied with the 'troublesome John Brown', her highland gillie, whose inappropriate intimacy with the Queen, he feared, threatened to bring scandal on the monarch.[177]

The problem of the Queen's petulant behaviour became acute in 1867. Since the death of the Prince Consort in 1861, Victoria had remained a secluded bereaved widow, displaying intense irritation at any requirement for public appearances and constantly complaining of the unbearable demands placed on her. The Queen's long-suffering private secretary, General Charles Grey, bore the brunt of her emotional outbursts, sharing his difficulties in confidential correspondence with Derby as prime minister. Criticism of the Queen's neglect of public duty, while allegedly hoarding her Civil List income, appeared in the radical press. These journalistic attacks increased during 1866, when a public dowry was voted by parliament for Princess Helena, on her marriage, and an annuity granted to Prince Alfred, on his coming of age. *The Times*, in more moderate tones, complained that the Queen's widowed seclusion was unbalancing the constitution. In November 1866, despite Grey and Derby's concerns and her stubborn reluctance to appear in public on more formal occasions, the Queen insisted on travelling to Wolverhampton to unveil a statue of 'her beloved Albert'. Derby feared, 'Wolverhampton being a very radical town', that a Fenian attempt on her life might be attempted or that 'some "roughs" may endeavour to get up a political demonstration'.[178] He also worried that a royal visit to Wolverhampton would offend the civic dignitaries of Manchester and Liverpool, far larger towns, which were not similarly honoured. But the Queen's behaviour became increasingly difficult to manage.

In January 1867, with great reluctance and complaining of the trying exertion it imposed on her, Victoria eventually agreed to open parliament in person. Given the importance of the impending debate on parliamentary Reform, Derby was delighted that the Queen agreed. He reassured her that it would 'produce a great beneficial effect'.[179] But the occasion did not go smoothly. Even before parliament met, the Queen was outraged by mild criticism of her public remoteness in the *Daily Telegraph*. With her intentions '*misunderstood* and *misrepresented*', she raged to a disheartened Grey, 'the *ingratitude* of the Public is disgraceful'.[180] Then, when travelling to Westminster to deliver the Royal Address on 5 February, she heard some hissing and groaning among the crowd. Again she railed to Grey and Derby about public ingratitude.[181] Derby attempted to soothe the Queen by pointing out that the hostile noises emitted by part of the crowd, which 'included a large number of the lowest class of the population', was on her going to, rather than returning from, the House of Lords to deliver the Royal Address, when those assembled were, as yet, unaware of the government's intentions with regard to parliamentary Reform. He comforted her that 'the Speech has been universally approved'.[182]

By June, Grey was writing to Derby from Balmoral of his growing anxiety at the Queen's 'unwillingness to submit to anything which could damage, in the smallest degree, the daily routine of her life'.[183] The nature of Victoria's relationship with John Brown was now also a subject of critical public speculation, anti-monarchical publications suggesting not only that was he an unsavoury influence, but that he was also the Queen's lover. The embarrassment of Brown's status became entwined in the delicate negotiations in which both Derby and Grey found themselves engaged, during July, over the ceremonies marking the state visit of Abdul Aziz, the Sultan of Turkey, and his numerous entourage. With Victoria declining to attend public events required by protocol and refusing to discuss engagements she found disagreeable, a despairing Grey, on 4 July, wrote in secret from Windsor Castle to Derby: 'We are come to a crisis as regards the Queen'.[184] When Victoria indicated that she would not accompany the Sultan to a military review in Hyde Park, but proposed that the Prince of Wales represent her instead, a desperate Grey urged Derby to use his influence on the monarch. Her response was reluctantly to agree, but to insist that John Brown attend in her carriage, an arrangement that both Derby and Grey concurred would only dangerously inflame popular feeling. The bedridden Derby was advised of rumoured plans 'to hoot John Brown at the approaching review, if he appears with the Queen'.[185] He immediately suggested to Grey that Brown might 'have some ailment' which would prevent his attending the Queen that day.[186] Lord Alfred Paget, a member of the royal household, meanwhile, complained to Stanley of Brown's hold over the monarch. 'The Queen unluckily parades this man about London behind her carriage, in his Highland dress, so that every street boy knows him.' Paget believed the rumours of their being lovers were unfounded, 'but says plainly that [Brown] has great influence, that she consults him about everything, has him in her room at all hours, etc.'.[187] When, finally agreeing to stay at Windsor to receive the Sultan, the Queen asked her physician Dr Jenner to send Derby a report confirming the precariousness of her health, Jenner stating that Victoria was suffering from 'so much weakness of nerves, and liability to excitement, that any great departure from her usual way of life, or more than ordinary agitation, might produce insanity'.[188] She was already suffering from bouts of nervous vomiting. Both Derby and Grey were 'thoroughly alarmed'. On 6 July the cabinet formally discussed the state of the Queen's health and it was decided to postpone the Hyde Park review.[189]

By the autumn the highly wrought Victoria was preoccupied with the threat of Fenian assassination. She refused to leave Osborne, fearing her presence on the mainland would expose her to attempts against her life. Derby privately believed 'the danger is all but imaginary', but agreed with Gathorne Hardy that 'where the Queen is concerned we must guard against possibilities as well as probabilities'. In order to avoid obvious signs of additional precaution, it was decided to post plain-clothes policemen, rather than soldiers, around the Queen and to restrict her movement in the grounds of Osborne. Rather than feeling reassured, however, Victoria took to complaining that she had become 'almost a state prisoner'.[190] During the exhausting summer of 1867, while suffering himself from very poor health, Derby found much of his time and attention devoted to managing a temperamentally volatile Queen and supporting, as best he could, an exasperated Grey. Yet, in addition, leading his government's Reform Bill through the Lords remained an unavoidable responsibility.

On Monday 15 July the Conservative Reform Bill passed its third reading in the Commons. Derby wrote to Cairns two days earlier appealing for his help in seeing the bill through the Lords: 'I will stand in need of all the assistance I can obtain'.[191] Cairns had given Disraeli much advice during Commons debate and no other members of the Lords, not excepting the cabinet, Derby believed, had so intimate a knowledge of the details of the measure. The Queen hoped amendments might be introduced by the Lords averting a great increase in democratic power.[192] Derby, however, was not hopeful. Although there were one or two provisions inserted by the Commons which he would have preferred omitted, such as Hodgkinson's amendment, he regarded the overall measure as satisfactory.[193] Forcing restrictive amendments through the Lords, he feared, ran the risk of rejection by the Commons and the consequent loss of the bill. When, on Thursday 18 July, Lord Grey, following the bill's first reading in the Upper House two days earlier, brought forward a motion rejecting the current form of the measure and calling for amendment in committee, Derby sent out a strong whip against it.[194] Rumours that the Lords opposition were plotting with Carnarvon to throw out the bill caused him serious concern. Carnarvon supported Grey's resolution.

As a consequence a frail Derby called a meeting of leading Conservative peers at St James's Square on Friday 19 July to demand party unity in support of the measure. Rejection of the bill, he declared, would prompt his resignation. This, he warned, would replicate the Conservative schism of 1846 and leave the party in the political wilderness.[195] He reviewed the recent history of the Reform issue. The events of 1859 had shown the necessity for a reduction of the borough franchise. The Liberal measure of 1866, sabotaged by Gladstone's imperiousness, had stopped short of a permanent settlement, only offering a stepping stone to further demands. Since assuming office his main objective had been 'to act so as to place the Tory party permanently in power and not to place them in a position to be beaten as soon as they had served the purpose of the opposition'.[196] The bill they were now considering, he maintained, was the most conservative measure possible, based on an intelligible principle, and unanimously supported by the Commons. The adoption of Grey's resolution, he predicted, would kill the bill and therefore bring about the downfall of the Conservative government. Despite Carnarvon and Rutland's expressing misgivings, the great majority of those present agreed to vote against Grey's resolution. The success of Lord Grey's motion, Derby commented to General Grey, would be the equivalent to the rejection of the bill, while Carnarvon remained 'very bitter against his late colleagues and very personal in his attacks'.[197]

In the garden at Roehampton, on Sunday 21 July, Derby carefully prepared his speech for the following evening, opening the second Lords reading of the Reform Bill. His nervous exhaustion was revealed by his momentary confusion over the number of seats available for redistribution, Disraeli the next morning clarifying the situation.[198] An embarrassed Derby immediately confessed: 'I am very nervous about what I have to do tonight, though Grey appears to have collapsed'.[199] On Monday 22 July he delivered one more, possibly his last, major parliamentary statement.[200] He began with reminiscence, recalling the electoral system of his youth, forty years before, prior to the 1832 Reform Act. He described the great struggle to secure Reform during 1831–2, in which he had played a prominent part. Since then, Russell had reopened the Reform question and made another measure inevitable, despite earlier protestations of finality. This being the case, Derby stated candidly his motives for introducing a comprehensive measure:

> I do not intend for a third time to be made a mere stop-gap until it would suit the convenience of the Liberal party to forget their dissensions and bring forward a measure which would oust us from office and replace them there: and I determined that I would take such a course as would convert, if possible, an existing minority into a practical majority. As our political opponents had failed in carrying a measure, the carrying of which was of vital importance to the interests of the country, and the postponement of which, added to the public inconvenience and embarrassment year after year, and the agitation for which was standing in the way of every measure of practical improvement and practical legislation, I felt it to be my duty to undertake this difficult task—a task which, as I thought, it was all but impossible to fulfil; and despite of any taunts of inconsistency, despite of any opposition to endeavour towards the close of my political career to settle one great and important question of vital importance to the interests of the country.[201]

In describing the government's measure he asserted that, once the £10 borough franchise was abandoned, only household suffrage, accompanied by residence and rate-paying requirements, provided the basis for a lasting settlement. The permanently established ratepayer defined the intelligent honest voter. At the same time, enfranchising some large towns would remove urban votes from the counties and lowering the franchise would transfer many freehold votes from county to borough constituencies. This resolved his long-standing concern over the intrusion of urban freehold votes into county constituencies. These provisions would mitigate the effect of enlarging the electorate. Thus the bill comprised a large, extensive, and Conservative settlement. As debate continued, opposition collapsed, Grey withdrew his resolution, and the Reform Bill successfully passed its second Lords reading.

This exertion immediately forced Derby back to his sickbed. Weak prior to his speech on 22 July, the effort left him dangerously exhausted, as the ravages of gout and rheumatism returned. Unable to use his right arm, he was forced to dictate his correspondence from his sickbed to his private secretary, Barrington (MP for Eye), Lady Derby, and Freddy Stanley.[202]

Medication, containing small amounts of opium and wine, eased his acute discomfort. Nonetheless, his caustic wit survived. One story was reported of a wine merchant attempting to sell Derby his sherry as a cure for gout, a proposition to which he replied: 'I have tasted your sherry and prefer the gout'.[203] Yet family and friends had no doubt that the vexatious Reform debate was the principal cause of Derby's prolonged illness during the remainder of the year. Freddy Stanley believed his father 'was not half-cured when he went down to his place in the House. It was, however, a worthy occasion for that amount of risk'.[204]

Malmesbury, supported by the Lord Chancellor, Chelmsford, saw the Reform Bill through its committee stage in the Lords, although Gathorne Hardy recognized that 'Lord Derby's absence from the House is a real misfortune'.[205] In compliance with Derby's orders, Malmesbury resisted further amendments to the measure. Nevertheless, Cairns, from the Conservative benches, managed to alter the measure significantly in its final form. Cairns proposed that electors in three-member constituencies should have a maximum of two votes. This would allow minorities in the large cities, who possessed 'the greatest amount of property and intelligence', to gain representation.[206] Russell led the Whigs in support of the amendment, which passed by 142 to 51 votes. A number of other amendments, intended to restrict the popular vote, were defeated. When Lord Grey proposed the redistribution of an additional twenty-three seats, Derby rose from his sickbed on 1 August to oppose the amendment.[207] Grey's motion was rejected by twelve votes. During the third Lords reading of the bill on 6 August a very frail Derby again struggled to parliament to deliver a concluding ministerial statement. Russell taunted him by reminding the House that in 1830 a fickle popular electorate in Preston had rejected the then young Stanley in favour of the radical 'Orator' Hunt.[208] But Derby refused to be drawn by Russell's gibes. He had 'the greatest confidence in the sound sense of my fellow-countrymen' and that the extended franchise they had approved would 'be the means of placing the institutions of the country on a firmer basis', increasing the loyalty and contentment of a great portion of Her Majesty's subjects.[209] With these high sentiments he brought down the curtain on the dramatic course of English Reform in 1867. But as he sat down, the *Guardian* observed, he looked 'pale, feeble, and very tired, the expression of his features more than ever seeming to say that he had had enough of it'.[210]

It was in his speech of 6 August that Derby famously described the Reform Bill as 'a leap in the dark'. This was a phrase with rich historic resonance. Supposedly Thomas Hobbes's last words, as he approached death, were that he now faced his 'last voyage, a great leap in the dark'. Shortly after, the playwright John Vanbrugh gave the words an ironic twist in *The Provoked Wife* when, on the threshold of marriage, his character Heartfree declared he was 'in for Hobbes's voyage, a great leap in the dark'. In 1860 Palmerston described Russell's Reform Bill as 'taking a leap in the dark'. Gladstone's 1866 Reform Bill was described by a number of MPs, notably Horsman, as an invitation to 'take a leap in the dark'. Derby was fond of the phrase and had used it himself, in very different circumstances, prior to 1867. Writing to Disraeli in November 1854, he privately described the Aberdeen coalition's response to the Crimean conflict as a succession of leaps in the dark.[211] In June 1867 Clarendon, writing to Lady Salisbury, described the Conservative Reform Bill as a 'leap in the dark'.[212] Derby used the familiar phrase in early August to acknowledge that the Conservative bill inevitably comprised an act of faith. But it was no more or less an experiment, in that sense, than the Liberal Reform bills, which had been described similarly, of 1860 and 1866. It was a vault, he believed, destined to deliver constitutional stability for a generation. It was a settlement, moreover, secured by a Conservative government. In another favoured contemporary phrase, the Conservatives had 'dished the Whigs'. Derby, an apprentice to Bowood Whiggism in the 1820s, had successfully circumvented the nominal Whigs of the 1860s and refuted their claim to a monopoly of progressive wisdom.

In retrospect, the dramatic events of 1866–7 were given differing in- terpretative glosses. Extensive Reform was delivered either by popular agitation (the radical myth), by effective opposition (the Liberal myth), or by generous design (the Conservative myth). The Conservative version of events drew on crucial elements of Derby's thinking: first, that the intractabilities of Reform must scatter those Liberal sections provisionally brought together under Palmerston's leadership in 1859; secondly, that, by exploiting Liberal disarray, the Conservatives might deliver a comprehen- sive Reform settlement; thirdly, that a far-reaching settlement, promising stability for the foreseeable future, would disprove Liberal claims to an exclusive possession of progressive wisdom; fourthly, that the rated resi- dential borough household suffrage defined a distinct and defensible de- marcation of urban political intelligence; finally, Derby recognized that the distribution of the electorate was as important as the extent of the vote, involving in particular the insulation of county constituencies from urban voters.

Between March and July 1867 Disraeli relinquished the franchise safe- guards hedging the borough household suffrage; a subsequent boundary commission, however, offered the opportunity to ensure that an enlarged electorate was contained within a Conservative redrawing of the constituencies. But it was Disraeli, not the ill and rapidly ageing Derby, who received the accolades of posterity. In the following months Disraeli claimed he had 'educated' the Conservative party. But, in truth, it was Derby who, at the close of his long career, had carefully shepherded the Conservatives towards a far-reaching settlement of Reform. It was left to Gathorne Hardy to confide to his diary the hopes and anxieties of prominent Conservatives, accommodating themselves to the unfamiliar terrain into which Derby had led them. 'What an unknown world we are to enter, but I believe more safely, or at least as safely, and more permanently than a £5 franchise would enable us to do. If the gentry take their part they will be adopted as leaders. If we are left to the demagogues, God help us!'[213]

The public honour to his valour due.

(Derby, *The Iliad of Homer*, ii. 24)

Putting a brave face on what they had done, Conservatives honoured Derby for his resolute leadership. 'I have, very much *contre cœur*', he wearily informed Disraeli from Knowsley in mid-August, 'accepted an invitation, sometime in October, to a Conservative "Banquet" in Manchester!! and I am threatened with another in Liverpool.'[214] Not only modesty, but deteriorating health, sapped his enthusiasm for such celebratory occasions. On 10 September he warned Disraeli that the 'time cannot be far distant when I must seek for restoration to health in absolute withdrawal from public service'.[215] Freddy Stanley noted that, although the gout was slowly abating, his father remained 'entirely disabled'.[216] Ten days later Lady Derby wrote that 'that restless woman' the Queen of Holland had 'invaded' England and intended to visit them at Knowsley on 28 September.[217] On 26 September, Lady Derby advised Disraeli that her husband was so weak and in such dreadful pain that he could not even talk. It was, Lady Derby confided, 'the worst fit of gout he has had for a very long time'.[218] Nonetheless, the royal visit to Knowsley took place and the Dutch Queen was shocked by Derby's frail condition. The prime minister was 'carried up and down stairs, not from *pain*, but from *weakness*, and it was positive *exertion* to lead me from the drawing room to the dining room. At dinner his colour would get ghastly white, like a corpse … he seemed like a candle burning out. His feverish eyes, his ghastly paleness, were at times quite frightful.'[219]

By early October, Derby was sufficiently recovered to travel to London, where he attended a cabinet meeting and hosted a Conservative dinner. 'The attendance was very large', Malmesbury noted, 'and Lord Derby's reception enthusiastic.'[220] From London, Derby journeyed to Manchester to attend the grand banquet organized in his honour and held in the Free Trade Hall. On the evening of Thursday 17 October, 800 local notables attended the gala occasion, with 1,200 sitting in the gallery looking on. Accompanied by Lady Derby, Lord Stanley (as Foreign Secretary), Lord Malmesbury (Lord Privy Seal), Lord Wilton, Lord Naas (formerly Chief Secretary for Ireland and recently elevated to the Lords as 6th Earl of Mayo), Lord John Manners (Commissioner of Works), Sir John Pakington (Secretary of the War Office), Sir Charles Adderley (Under-Secretary for the Colonies), and John Wilson Patten (recently appointed Chancellor of the Duchy of Lancaster), Derby was received with rapturous acclaim. The Conservative MP for South-East Lancashire the Hon. Algernon Egerton, uncle of the Earl of Ellesmere and a younger son of Derby's close Eton and Christ Church friend Lord Leveson-Gower, presided, and a mood of enthusiastic celebration infused the event. Partisan loyalty and local pride fuelled the rousing tribute Derby received. When confirming arrangements with Derby for the banquet, Egerton had indicated that the working classes in Manchester wished to hold a mass meeting, earlier in the day, expressing their gratitude for Derby's work on their behalf during the Cotton Famine. But Derby had suggested that it would be more appropriate if a working man's address was presented to him immediately prior to the dinner.[221]

In toasting Derby at the end of the banquet, Egerton praised his leadership, particularly since the Conservatives were factiously displaced from office in 1859. Egerton also paid homage to Derby's efforts on behalf of the working classes of Lancashire during the Cotton Famine. Derby's subsequent hour-long speech, despite a certain feebleness in his voice, proved a skilful working of his audience's loyal enthusiasm. After acknowledging Disraeli's accomplished Commons leadership during the recent Reform debate, which had secured a triumphant success in the face of disastrous failure, Derby elaborated three main themes.[222] First, he described how his admiration for the intelligence, fortitude, and dignity demonstrated by the working classes during the suffering of the Cotton Famine had shown him they were deserving of the vote. Their reasonableness, sound sense, and lack of social prejudice had convinced him that the working classes could be entrusted with the electoral representation which his government had now put in their hands. Secondly, to the great amusement of his audience, he offered repeated sarcastic references to the 'great "united" Liberal party', whose bitter disunity had subverted all efforts to translate their high-minded talk of Reform into effective legislation. In 1859 'the great "united" Liberal party (loud laughter)' had factiously opposed the Conservative Reform Bill. 'Under the soporiferous reign of Lord Palmerston the question of Reform was allowed to sleep.' In 1866 the Liberal government's Reform Bill had been opposed, not by the Conservatives, but by 'the supporters of the government and the "united" Liberal party. (Cheers and laughter)'. This had required the Conservatives, despite the fierce opposition of Gladstone, to secure 'a well-considered, safe and liberal measure of Reform'. Finally, Derby explained how the necessity of Reform had led him to the personal conviction that 'boldness was safety', with an extended franchise to be based on some sound and intelligent principle. No basis for a new franchise, he declared, could be safer than the occupation of premises and compliance with the fiscal liabilities of that occupation. It embodied a sure definition of respectability.

The whole course of his political and private life, Derby concluded, had shown him to be a friend of the working classes, or those who might, he suggested, be better described as the wage-paid classes. Those men who depended upon daily, weekly, or monthly wages, Derby pronounced, had shown themselves to be loyal and sound. It was a source of profound consolation that, in the midst of the sufferings of the Cotton Famine, the middle, the higher, and the lower classes had all combined in one fellowship of feeling. Although many wage earners were not Anglicans, they had renounced hostility to the Established Church, and instead espoused a deep attachment to the institutions of the country. Wage earners, he proposed, had shown themselves to be responsible, loyal, and virtuous. By recognizing and rewarding these qualities, his government had strengthened that mutual respect and essential trust which cemented the nation's loyalty to its institutions.

Derby's eloquent Manchester homage to the decency and respectability of the working classes and the electoral reward gratefully bestowed by the Conservatives on them proved his last major public address. Opponents raised an eyebrow of wry surprise at Derby's striking presentation of himself as a champion of the working man. Those with long memories recalled his denunciations of popular electoral politics of nearly forty years earlier. In its editorial *The Times* alluded to such. But in October 1867 Derby sketched out that entity which later generations of Conservatives fashioned into 'Tory

Democracy'. He evoked a hierarchical view of British society as a ranked and stable order, a seamless web of integrated, subtly differentiated, status. He reinforced the view that the welfare of each section of society consisted in the prosperity, happiness, and harmony of the whole. In the early 1850s Malmesbury suggested that the urban labourers were more Conservative and less radically inclined than many £5 householders.[223] In the industrial communities of Lancashire, Stanley found 'an almost feudal respect for our family'.[224] The warmth of the popular welcome given to Derby when he visited Preston in 1862 apparently affirmed such feeling. Respect for the virtuous working man, Derby believed by 1867, would consolidate a Conservative sense of organic community. So might the confrontation between 'the people' and an aristocratic elite, depicted by populist radicalism, be repudiated. To his Free Trade Hall audience he acknowledged that his graphic, if hardly original, description of the 1867 Reform Act as 'a leap in the dark' had been considered by some as imprudent. Undoubtedly, he admitted, it was impossible to predict with absolute certainty how the extended franchise would be exercised by new voters. Yet, he was firmly convinced that 'boldness was safety', when the virtuous qualities of responsible wage earners had been so clearly shown during their sufferings of the early 1860s.[225] If the Conservatives did not reward such behaviour, then the danger existed of radicals and demagogues misleading working men into believing that only they represented the wage earner's interests. It was the Conservatives, Derby forcefully declared, who were committed to preserving that cordial union between labour and capital, that harmony between the employers of labour and the employed, which was threatened by radical agitation and divisive Liberal rhetoric.

Strikingly, in subsequent weeks it was Derby, rather than Disraeli, who approved the efforts of the energetic young barrister Henry Raikes in organizing the National Union of Conservative and Constitutional Associations, providing an umbrella for the local Conservative associations and clubs enlisting working-class votes to the party cause. Disraeli disliked the class separation implied in Raikes's activities and the alarm among middle-class opinion they might cause. But for Derby, with his first-hand experience of popular Conservative loyalty in Lancashire, such efforts promised to consolidate that cordial union of feeling between wage earners, employers, and landowners which he believed the 1867 Reform Act had established. When Disraeli learnt of the London and Westminster Conservative Association's plan to hold a grand banquet of Conservative working men at the Crystal Palace in Sydenham to celebrate the government's Reform Act, he expressed considerable reservations. The response of Gerard Noel, assistant Conservative whip in the Commons, who was helping to distribute circulars to MPs and peers soliciting support for the National Union, however, was blunt. The circulars, he declared, 'had been seen and approved by Lord Derby or I should not have sent them out'.[226]

Derby closed his Manchester Free Trade Hall address with a spirited rebuttal of rumours that he was about to retire. He fully intended, he asserted, to continue in office and public life. Privately, however, Derby immediately reported to Disraeli that, although the Manchester dinner had been 'a very great success (and the crowd outside were just as enthusiastic as those within)', he was 'paying the penalty in a renewed attack of gout'.[227] His physical frailty was evident when, a week later, he laid the foundation stone for the New Southern Hospital in Liverpool, attended by the Mayor of Liverpool, the Bishop of Chester, the two MPs for Liverpool who were both Conservatives, Thomas Horsfall and Samuel Graves, the Conservative MP for South Lancashire, Charles Turner, and the Conservative MP for Birkenhead, John Laird. An obviously fatigued Derby publicly acknowledged he was not capable of much exertion. The following day he informed Disraeli: 'I had a triumphant reception at Liverpool yesterday, but was very far from being up to the mark'.[228] When Clarendon visited Knowsley to see his daughter Lady Constance, who had just delivered a second son, he found Derby looking 'ragged and weak', but 'in high good humour and spirits, talking freely about foreign affairs', though remaining 'silent about Reform'. Derby seemed relieved that he did not have to attend the grand banquet at Edinburgh being given to Disraeli, who was to receive the freedom of the city and an honorary doctorate from the University. When Clarendon observed that at Edinburgh Disraeli was 'to be made all sorts of things' and asked 'whether among them he wanted to be made a Christian', for 'altho there was abundant evidence of his circumcision, there was none of his baptism', Derby, Clarendon observed, laughed a good deal.[229] But, by early November, Derby was again bedridden at Knowsley with severe gout. His weak state, Gathorne Hardy noted, had become 'a very serious matter'.[230]

On 29 October, Disraeli, who had not accompanied Derby to Manchester twelve days earlier, delivered at Edinburgh his own memorable eulogium on Conservative Reform. Derby greatly regretted Disraeli's absence at Manchester and had urged him to attend. Not to join him, he advised Disraeli, would create not just 'great disappointment', but also 'great dissatisfaction'. Disraeli, however, replied that ill health prevented him from attending.[231] Much of Disraeli's Edinburgh address elaborated themes Derby had already presented at Manchester: the right and obligation of the Conservatives to settle a vexed question which a divided Liberal party had proved unable to resolve; the necessity for a comprehensive Reform settlement founded upon an intelligible principle; and the requirement that such a principle be in harmony with the manners and customs of the English people.[232] Most strikingly, however, Disraeli claimed for himself the accolade of having led the Conservative party to a triumphant recognition of the necessity for far-reaching Reform. He, Disraeli asserted, had prepared the mind of the country and educated the Conservative party for the necessity of comprehensive Reform, a process in which Derby and his colleagues had acquiesced. In an audacious performance Disraeli, not for the first time, gathered to himself the acclaim rightfully belonging to Derby. Unsurprisingly, visitors to Knowsley found Derby scathingly dismissive of Disraeli's Edinburgh performance. In 1858 it was Derby, not a distracted Disraeli, who pressed the Conservative leadership towards a Reform measure. In September 1866 it was Derby, not a reluctant Disraeli, who directed ministerial minds towards a comprehensive solution of Reform. In December 1866 it was Derby, not a hesitant Disraeli, who championed the urban household suffrage as an intelligible principle, suitably safeguarded, upon which to secure a permanent settlement. Both in 1858 and in 1866 Disraeli, as Chancellor of the Exchequer, had preferred national finance as the question upon which to stake Conservative credibility as a governing party. Moreover, in November 1867 it was Derby, not Disraeli, who approved of efforts to celebrate popular Conservative feeling at the Crystal Palace. That passages in Disraeli's Edinburgh address directly echoed elements of the 'Knowsley Creed' of 1834 and Derby's prime ministerial statements of March 1858 and July 1866 compounded the effrontery. 'In a progressive country change is constant,' Disraeli informed his Scottish audience, 'and the great question is, not whether you should resist change which is inevitable, but whether that change should be carried out in deference to the manners, the customs, the laws, the traditions of the people ... '.[233] This was Derby's sentiment masquerading as Disraeli's insight. In truth, it was Derby, not Disraeli, who 'educated' the Conservative party. Yet such an attribution did not serve Disraeli's own purposes in October 1867. Nor was it to suit the needs of future Conservatives anxious to manufacture a Beaconsfield legacy as an endorsement of their own aims. Nonetheless, it was upon Derby's achievement that Disraeli prepared to stand as the architect of popular Conservatism.

But he, their chief, was lying rack'd with pain.

(Derby, *The Iliad of Homer*, i. 72)

Derby's inexorable physical decline made Disraeli's audacity possible. By November 1867 Derby was a fading presence and Disraeli the effective head of the Conservative ministry, although Disraeli was also incapacitated by serious illness during the autumn, which left the direction of much cabinet discussion to Northcote and Stanley. Meanwhile, the seizure of British subjects by King Theodore of Abyssinia and the cabinet's decision to send Indian troops to secure their release, as well as a Fenian outrage in Manchester resulting in the death of a policeman, rendered a meeting of parliament unavoidable. Derby deeply regretted the necessity for parliament to meet. He feared that it would prove difficult to confine debate to the Abyssinia crisis. But Disraeli, Stanley, and Walpole were convinced it was an 'unpleasant necessity'. Derby hoped it would be possible to avoid a prolonged session, parliament meeting in late November and adjourning by the first week of December. In the event, parliament gathered on 19 November and sat until 7 December.[234] On Saturday 2 November, with great difficulty, Derby travelled down to London, and was immediately laid up at St James's Square with a renewed attack of gout. By Wednesday 13 November he was partially recovered. A week later he took his seat in the Lords. Opposite him sat the ill 75-year-old Russell, suffering from fainting fits, and the two old warriors once again wearily took up their rhetorical cudgels.

In response to the Fenian threat Derby privately advised Disraeli to resist the temptation of meddling in Ireland.[235] But reports of further Fenian plots and rumours of the existence of an assassination committee in Dublin intensified ministerial anxiety. At a cabinet meeting on Thursday 7 November, from which Derby was absent, an inconclusive discussion took place. Subsequently, Disraeli proposed that Habeas Corpus be suspended in areas of England, but Derby feared a public reaction against such a dramatic step. While a firm response to the Fenian threat might strengthen the government politically, he disliked 'an indiscriminate proscription of the Irish Roman Catholics'.[236] The attempt by Irish Republicans to free Fenian prisoners from Clerkenwell jail in early December caused twelve deaths and many injuries. In mid-December the cabinet received intelligence of assassination plots against Derby, Stanley, and Gathorne Hardy, as well as the Queen. Police protection was posted outside 23 St James's

Square. But Derby remained opposed to taking extreme measures. Disraeli saw political advantage in a Fenian panic, which would, he anticipated, make the government's work in the 1868 session easier and divert attention from other party issues such as Irish Church disestablishment. But Derby consistently checked Disraeli's proposals for strong repressive measures. Immediate advantage, he insisted, would quickly give way to long-term difficulties. Following the Clerkenwell incident, he believed, 'we shall rather have to moderate, than to stimulate, the anti-*Irish*, rather than the anti-*Fenian*, feeling which is likely to arise'.[237] Nor, he judged, were the public sufficiently alarmed as 'to tolerate the suspension of Habeas Corpus in England'. The government 'must trust to the operation of the ordinary law'.[238] Stanley agreed with his father that an extreme course would be 'a doubtful and dangerous policy'.[239]

Parliament endorsed the sending of a British military expedition from India to Abyssinia and on 7 December the short emergency session was adjourned. On Tuesday 10 December, Derby and Lady Emma left for Knowsley, only to return to St James's Square a week later for a cabinet discussion of the Fenian threat. Ministers agreed on Thursday 19 December to strengthen the Metropolitan Police, increase the number of detectives, and take any other precautionary measures that might be necessary.[240] Yet, Derby remained opposed to any panic overreaction. The following day he returned to Knowsley. By Christmas the Fenian scare appeared to be abating in the public mind, although a robbery of arms at Cork and an attack on a Martello tower near Queenstown showed 'there are plenty of desperate adventurers ready to risk their lives for a chance of making mischief'.[241]

On New Year's Day 1868 Disraeli sent Derby a congratulatory note: 'It is the first time that you have been premier for three consecutive years—66–67 and 68! I hope a good omen.'[242] But the view of political affairs from Knowsley was not bright. Derby saw more to worry than reassure him in both foreign and domestic policy. Diplomatic relations with the United States were strained. Napoleon III was once again embroiled in Italian affairs, with French troops back in the Papal States, safeguarding the Pope from the Italian government's desire to annex Rome. The ascendancy of Prussia, meanwhile, was eroding the French Emperor's diplomatic influence and shattering his dynastic vision of being the arbiter of Europe. Derby believed that the ailing Napoleon III had 'lost much of the nerve and decision which had formerly carried him through; and his prestige in France is diminished accordingly'.[243] The British Admiralty were seriously concerned about the greater number of ironclads in the French navy than those commissioned for the Royal Navy, and was pressing for increased expenditure. But Derby disliked the look of the Exchequer's finances, falling revenues from Customs and Excise preventing any increase of expenditure. Moreover, he was averse to Disraeli and the Duke of Marlborough's proposal to establish a Ministry of Education. Nor was he won over by Disraeli's suggestion that Walpole might be made a Minister of Education. Walpole, the premier responded, 'was originally estimated too high, and his undeniable failure has probably had the effect of unduly lowering him in public opinion'.[244] Nearer to home, Derby was greatly concerned at the heightened sectarian tensions between Catholics and Protestants in Lancashire following the Fenian disturbances.[245] Only the prospect of victory in Abyssinia, if the British forces under Sir Robert Napier resolutely pushed forward to Magdala, promised good news. 'If we could meet parliament with tidings of success!!'

Derby's worsening health aggravated his gloomy political prognostications. Following a visit by Prince Christian and Princess Helena to Knowsley in early January, he suffered a predictable collapse. On 12 January gout broke out in his right hand and foot. Through Barrington, Disraeli was regularly updated on Derby's condition, the premier's plan to return to London on 20 January to prepare for the approaching session being postponed. On 19 January, Barrington reported that Derby was finally pretty free from pain, but remained bedridden. The invalid premier, no longer receiving doses of laudanum, was 'quite clear in his head' and attending to routine business 'without mental friction'.[246] But by 22 January he was 'sluggish and disinclined to do anything' as a result of the administration of opium.[247] Disraeli was advised to make his own decisions regarding cabinet business.[248] Four days later a despondent Derby declared himself to be 'everything that a prime minister ought not to be', still bedridden, unable to use his right hand with any comfort, and incapable of writing.[249] In his absence, Disraeli chaired heated cabinet discussions on education, parliamentary Reform for Scotland, and amendments to the 1858 India Act. But this was clearly a provisional arrangement, which could not be sustained indefinitely. On 6 February, Derby informed General Charles Grey that, in the not too distant future, he must resign the premiership.[250] Isolated and incapacitated at Knowsley, extremely weak and with no appetite, he remained too ill to attend the opening of parliament on 13 February. The Queen, however, urged him to remain in office, Disraeli badly needing his authority during the coming session.[251] In response, he dutifully set aside thoughts of immediate resignation.

'Parliament sitting, and I still lying here, like a useless log!', Derby lamented to Disraeli on 13 February. 'You may imagine how much this annoys me.'[252] His doctors, he advised, could give no indication of when he might be able to travel to London. For the past year his health had been broken, his doctors patching him up for particular occasions. He now suffered from symptoms which required constant vigilance and the danger of a complete collapse was very real. But, if his colleagues were able to overlook his inefficiency, he had promised the Queen he would attempt to continue. But another chronic attack of gout on Sunday 16 February abruptly hastened events. The distressing suicide of a Knowsley servant three days earlier, who in a fit of depression cut his throat, added a melodramatic domestic backdrop to Derby's decline. In the early hours of Monday 17 February, Stanley received a telegram in London summoning him to Knowsley. Bringing a doctor from London with him, Stanley arrived to find his father, although still gravely ill, past the immediate crisis. But Derby now recognized that he must retire from official life. During the morning of Tuesday 18 February he informed Stanley that his doctors advised that only complete rest would enable him to recover. He must resign from office: 'it was for him a matter of life and death'.[253] Believing 'him to be right, and that a longer continuance in office will probably kill him', Stanley did not try to dissuade his father. Lady Emma shared with her son that Derby had 'constantly been oppressed with the sense of business left undone, and of responsibility for measures in advising which he had no share'. At his father's request, Stanley immediately wrote to Disraeli preparing him for the unavoidable announcement.

On Wednesday 19 February, Derby wrote to Disraeli, informing him of 'the absolute necessity of my resigning my present office'.[254] Only 'absolute repose of mind and body', his doctors insisted, would enable him to regain 'a moderate degree of health'. He hoped Disraeli would accept the premiership, which, in all probability, the Queen would ask him to undertake. Indeed, Disraeli was already preparing his succession. Six days earlier, on 13 February, through a mutual acquaintance, the society physician Dr Frederick Quin, Disraeli sounded out Granville about becoming leader of the Lords under his premiership.[255] Such a merger would block Malmesbury's natural claim and signal a significant realignment of party connection, encouraging Whig and moderate Liberal MPs to give the new Conservative government their support in the aftermath of the Reform debates. At the same time Disraeli began giving thought to a package of legislative reforms, including concurrent endowment for the Anglican, Catholic, and Presbyterian churches in Ireland, the setting up of a Catholic university in Dublin, and the establishing of separate ministries of Health and Education, which would provide a progressive policy upon which Whigs and Conservatives might combine. Disraeli did not share these plans, however, with Derby. Rather, he carefully maintained towards his departing invalid chief a pose of dutiful loyalty. On receiving Derby's letter of 19 February, the following day Disraeli replied that his long-held expectation had been that he would retire from public life alongside Derby, but affirmed that he would undertake the premiership if the Queen asked him to do so.[256]

On receiving Disraeli's communication, Derby wrote of his intention to resign to the Queen at Osborne, adding that only Disraeli 'could command the cordial support, *en masse*, of his present colleagues'.[257] Derby wished, however, to be allowed to surrender his office to the Queen in person, also indicating that he hoped the Queen would signal her gratitude for his services by approving five or six names he wished to recommend for the peerage. He had already made judicious use of his powers of patronage during his premiership. As Disraeli observed, 'You have done very well for your friends: 3 Garters, 4 Bishoprics, 8 Lord Lieutenancies, and almost the whole Bench in the three kingdoms.'[258] The Queen's brief reply to Derby expressed her hope that he would remain in the cabinet without office, but made no mention of the proposed peerages. Derby was irritated by the letter, 'which was curt and totally without expressions of sympathy or regret'.[259] It suggested that the Queen was already thinking of the attractions of a Disraeli premiership, foreshadowing their more collusive relationship of the 1870s. Derby telegraphed Stanley an allusive text to be shared with Disraeli: 'Do nothing formal till you hear. A few days indispensable to me.'[260]

On 25 February Derby wrote again to the Queen regretting that his health prevented him from remaining in the cabinet and again requesting the honour of the peerage for 'some few gentlemen whose political support has been of the greatest value to the government'.[261] Despite having refused a similar request from Russell in 1866, the Queen reluctantly agreed to the creations. The wealthy and loyal Derbyite MPs Sir John Trollope, Sir John Walsh, Sir Brook Bridges, and Sir William Stirling-Maxwell were elevated to the Lords. Derby then immediately sent his formal resignation to the Queen, being too ill to do so in person. On 25 February, Disraeli, whom Stanley found in a 'very anxious and agitated' frame of mind, travelled down to Osborne to kiss the Queen's hand.[262] Granville had still not responded to his indirect soundings. Not until 26 February, after consulting with Gladstone, did Granville, via Quin, convey his regret at not being able to accept Disraeli's invitation.[263] Disraeli was clearly not going to be able to construct his administration on the broad basis which he had hoped.

Release from the burdens of office had an immediate beneficial effect on Derby's health. When Stanley visited his father at Knowsley a week later he found him 'wonderfully recovered, his spirits excellent, voice clear and strong, but he is still very weak in the limbs'.[264] Derby talked 'of the Queen's way of writing to him, about which he was at first very sore', but which he now recognized as part of her nature. 'She is civil to persons in power under her, whose good will contributes to her comfort (and not always to them): but sees no reason for wasting civility on those who can no longer be of use to her.'[265] Both Derby's sons resented what they saw as the Queen's selfish, not to say callous, behaviour towards their father during his prolonged chronic illness. For her own self-absorbed reasons, they believed, she had deferred his resignation from office and so protracted his suffering. The tone of her communications, moreover, conveyed scant sympathy for his distress. By contrast, the social niceties were meticulously observed by Disraeli. On 27 February, Disraeli informed Derby that he would 'always consider myself your deputy. Your wishes will always be commands to me, and commands that will be heartily obeyed.' He hoped Derby would never 'permit any sentiment of estrangement to arise between us, but to extend to me for ever that complete confidence which has so long subsisted between us; which has been the pride and honour of my life'.[266] In less indulgent, if equally elegant, prose Derby responded in a similar spirit the following day that there was 'no danger of any sentiment of estrangement arising between us, who for more than twenty years have worked together with unreserved and unbroken confidence'.[267] This delicacy of feeling glossed over what had, in truth, been an often difficult and strained relationship, dogged by suspicion and mistrust. But fulsome expressions of loyal devotion at the appropriate occasion were, as Queen Victoria later learnt to appreciate, a ready part of Disraeli's repertoire.

CHAPTER 7

Recession and Reputation: 1868–1869

I have nothing left but to go away.

(Derby's words to Cairns on departing the Lords for the last time)

After February 1868 Derby became the 'guardian angel' of the Conservative government, a venerated, if somewhat spectral, presence hovering over Disraeli's shoulder. The Conservative leadership anxiously adjusted themselves to the new order. Derby's old confidant Malmesbury, despite Disraeli's personal hostility, became Conservative leader in the Lords, the earlier indirect sounding out of Granville for the position having come to naught. Disraeli's second choice, the Duke of Marlborough, declined the post, saying it must go to Malmesbury. The ineffectual Chelmsford was ejected from the Lord Chancellorship, nursing a grievance which he aired to all willing to listen. Cairns replaced him. The relatively obscure George Ward Hunt, regarded as sensible though dull, took over the Chancellorship of the Exchequer from Disraeli. Northcote's strong claims to the Exchequer, as the acknowledged financial expert of the party, were ignored and he remained at the India Office. Invitations extended by Disraeli to Cranborne, Carnarvon, and Peel to rejoin the cabinet were sharply rejected.

By late March, as he celebrated his sixty-ninth birthday, Derby's strength was sufficiently recovered for him to travel down to St James's Square. Yet, though cheerful, he was 'still very weak and unable to move about'.[1] He confided to General Grey that he was not able to move from one room to another without difficulty and was obliged to be carried downstairs.[2] On 3 April the Queen visited him. The meeting soothed Derby's irritation over the Queen's curt communications of the previous weeks and provided them with an opportunity to share their concerns over the Irish issues confronting the cabinet. These constituted, Derby warned Disraeli, 'your greatest danger'.[3] Britain's relations with Ireland had dominated Derby's career. During his final year of public life Ireland, once again, was a preoccupation. In a pre-sessional speech at Bristol, Stanley, surrounded by other Conservative ministers, declared the condition of Ireland to be 'the question of the hour'.[4] But, whereas Derby had immense authority on Irish matters, having defended Whig reforms during the early 1830s against young Tories such as Gladstone, his departure opened up opportunities for Liberal initiatives which Disraeli's lack of command on Irish affairs could not contain. As soon as Derby's resignation was announced, indeed, Gladstone began to consider 'the personnel of our party with a view to contingencies', i.e. Liberal ministerial appointments following the defeat of the Conservative government.[5] Gathorne Hardy noted in his diary: 'I foresee storms and doubt if the ship will not founder.'[6]

During March 1868 the Irish land question, Lord Mayo's plan for a Catholic college in Dublin, and the status of the Church of Ireland were on the cabinet's agenda. They formed part of the ambitious legislative programme, including establishing separate ministries of Health and Education, which Disraeli busily constructed during his first exhilarating days as premier. But, as more cautious minds and practical requirements bore down on him, his plans, like a bloom in the desert sands, quickly faded. Derby had already written to Mayo from Knowsley discouraging him from pursuing his proposal to charter a Catholic college. Mayo believed it would preserve Protestant education at Trinity College and protect the Anglican Establishment. But Derby feared that Catholic promises of support were not to be relied on and Protestant opinion in Ireland too easily disaffected for such a move to be wise.[7] In early March ministers agreed not to oppose the repeal of the Ecclesiastical Titles Act, the legislation which had caused Russell self-inflicted agonies in 1851. They agreed to a new Devon Commission to investigate the Irish land issue. At the same time, the cabinet, 'approached with great caution'[8] the Irish Church question, by considering the concurrent endowment of the Anglican, Catholic, and Presbyterian churches in Ireland. Both Disraeli and Stanley strongly favoured the plan. Concurrent endowment might provide a constructive response to Liberal attack on the Irish Church Establishment and float a policy upon which Whigs, such as Granville and Clarendon, might be brought on board. But more cautious ministerial colleagues held back. As a result, Stanley's distaste for the religious bigotry of partisan Toryism intensified, an abiding contempt which affirmed his aversion to ever becoming Conservative party leader. Again, Derby's shade, from the remoteness of Knowsley, exerted restraint. Ministers agreed not to pledge themselves to legislation until the new parliament. While endeavouring to commit themselves as little as possible, they looked 'to tide over the present session', leaving church matters to be dealt with in due course. This was a decision with which Derby heartily concurred. It was hardly necessary for him to remind Disraeli that he had always entertained a very strong objection to the alienation of the property of the Church of Ireland or of any other corporation. 'It seems to be generally assumed that this principle is no longer tenable; but the moment you depart from it, you will find yourself involved in inextricable difficulty.'[9] Since Russell's succession to the premiership in 1865, Derby had anticipated the Liberals bringing forward the cry of Irish disestablishment, a proposal which should be firmly opposed. The cabinet must, he advised, 'abstain from making any proposition whatever'. The opposition might attempt to carry an abstract resolution, condemnatory of the Irish Church Establishment, 'but if called upon to say how they propose to deal with it, they will be found at hopeless variance among themselves'. In familiar language, he advised Disraeli that 'your safety is to sit still, and, instead of showing your hand, to compel your adversaries to exhibit theirs, with all their discrepancies and contradictions'.[10]

But Disraeli's political position was too weak to maintain such a Derbyite pose, particularly as Gladstone and other leading Liberals recognized, as Argyll candidly admitted, that Irish disestablishment offered the only way of 'getting Dizzy out of office'.[11] Inextricable difficulties immediately ensued. On 16 March, Gladstone, with notable vehemence, announced to the Commons that the Anglican Establishment in Ireland should be swept away as grossly unrepresentative of the Irish people's religious beliefs. This cry immediately galvanized those disparate sections of the Liberal party scattered by parliamentary Reform. Gladstone's proposal, Disraeli observed to Cairns, 'has come upon us like a thief in the night', threatening to rob them of their Reform triumph. On 23 March, Gladstone produced three resolutions calling for the Irish Church's disestablishment, its gradual disendowment, and the placing of the Crown's interest in the church temporalities at the disposal of parliament. When Derby arrived at St James's Square on 24 March, Disraeli quickly conferred with his old chief. Disraeli proposed an amendment, to be moved by Stanley, acknowledging that 'considerable modifications' to the Irish Church's temporalities might be expedient, but deferring any decision until after the next general election. Predictably, Derby objected to the phrase 'considerable modifications', but conceded that his views were probably not those of the majority.[12] He also, accurately as it proved, doubted Stanley's determination in facing down Gladstone's assault. When, in the

Commons on 27 March, Stanley responded mildly to Gladstone's rousing cry by coolly reiterating the government's intention to reserve any decision for a new parliament, it sounded, an appalled Gathorne Hardy confessed, like 'the cry of a whipped hound!'[13] It was left to Gathorne Hardy, whose ecclesiastical views were much closer to Derby's own convictions than the more latitudinarian inclinations of his elder son, to offer spirited objections to Gladstone's resolutions. Derby applauded Gathorne Hardy's defence of the Church of Ireland. But on Friday 3 April, Gladstone secured majorities on two divisions arising from his resolutions. The opposition, Gathorne Hardy observed, 'has tasted blood'.[14]

When the Queen visited Derby at St James's Square on 3 April they agreed to persuade Disraeli not to resign. Victoria dreaded Gladstone taking office. Derby communicated this to Disraeli. The cabinet agreed to remain. But their vulnerability was all too painfully apparent. Although thinking it right that they decided not to resign, an apprehensive Pakington recognized the government's 'position is become very difficult, and I suspect Mayo and Hunt are right that we shall be exposed to vexatious opposition and defeat on all sorts of questions, in the hope of driving us out'.[15] Likewise, Gathorne Hardy anticipated the Liberal opposition 'will bully and endeavour to control us, so as to place us in minorities constantly'.[16] By early April the loss to the authority of the government from Derby's resignation was evident in the growing sense that Disraeli's cabinet was not up to withstanding the Gladstonian offensive. The passage of the government's Scottish and Irish Reform bills and the proceedings of the Boundaries Commission seemed in jeopardy.

Derby offered ministers constant, invariably cautious, advice on parliamentary tactics. His return to the fray in the Lords also provided much-needed help to Malmesbury. Following the Easter recess, on 23 April, for the first time since December, Derby addressed the House. He spoke against Gladstone's proposal to abolish compulsory church rates in favour of voluntary assessments. Condemning the proposal as tending to put the Established Church on the same footing as other churches, at Disraeli's request, he held off calling for a division.[17] Subsequent extensive alterations to the bill were pressed by the evangelical Orangeman Cairns, backed by the Low Church bishops. Although the abolition of compulsory church rates survived this extensive redrafting, the measure was far different from the legislation Gladstone had originally proposed. Nonetheless, Gladstone accepted the modified measure as the best settlement possible, and the long-running struggle over church rates came to a close. A week later, on 27 April, Derby asked for clarification as to whether Gladstone's

Irish Church resolutions would be referred to the Lords. Refraining from direct comment on the merits of the resolutions, he warned that their approval by the Commons would pit the Lords and Commons against each other and stir up bitter religious animosities.[18] He pointed out, moreover, that over the last two years Russell appeared to have changed his mind four times over the issue of Irish Church disestablishment. Russell tamely responded that a bill would eventually be brought before parliament.

With Derby's encouragement, by early May, Disraeli was resolved, despite the reservations of some cabinet colleagues, to brazen out Liberal attacks and to wait to call a dissolution once preparations for the new franchise and revised constituencies were in place. This effectively deferred a general election, he anticipated, until November. A crushing British victory in Abyssinia, the release of British captives, the seizure of Magdala, and the suicide of King Theodore, in late April, gave the government a much-needed boost and an opportunity for Disraeli to describe, in purple prose, the flag of St George flying triumphant in the mountains of Rasselas. Over the same weeks Stanley characteristically resisted being drawn into bilateral diplomatic negotiations with Russia intended to produce a joint declaration of policy with regard to Persia; such a course, he insisted, would do more harm than good. The ministry's broader legislative package of Reform, meanwhile, was guided through Westminster. Their Redistribution Bill for England and Wales reflected those preoccupations that had shaped ministerial thinking about the suffrage; namely, that small Conservative boroughs should be preserved and the county constituencies insulated from the expanding suburbs. Following fierce criticism of their first Redistribution Bill, in June 1867 Disraeli introduced a revised scheme which gave nineteen seats to new boroughs, twenty-five additional seats to the counties, and one MP to London University. A Liberal amendment added an extra member to the three northern cities with more than 250,000 in population. A Commission, packed with Conservatives, then attended to redrawing constituency boundaries, ensuring that not only adjoining suburbs were incorporated into urban boroughs, but also nearby villages likely to become suburbs. Presented to parliament in March 1868, the Commission's report, however, was referred to a Commons Select Committee, chaired by Walpole, which during May reduced the number of urban county freehold votes transferred to neighbouring boroughs. Under intense pressure of time, dictated by the calendar for voter registration, the Select Committee's revised proposals were subsequently rushed through both Houses. The Scottish Reform Bill, brought forward by Disraeli in May 1867, introduced the same suffrage qualifications as proposed for England

and Wales, without the lodger franchise. But bitter arguments over redistribution dragged down the bill and in February 1868 Disraeli reintroduced the bill with slightly altered redistribution proposals, Scotland acquiring seven additional seats drawn from small English boroughs. An Irish Reform Bill, creating a small increase in the electorate by reducing the borough suffrage qualification from £8 to £4 while maintaining the 1850 county franchise of £12, was stripped of its redistribution clauses. By the summer of 1868 redistribution for England and Wales, Scottish Reform, and Irish Reform had passed into statute.[19] Bills transferring the consideration of election petitions from the Commons to judicial committees, banning public executions, and authorizing the purchase of all telegraph lines by the government were also passed. The ministry's Education Bill, however, was jettisoned. At the end of May, Derby congratulated Disraeli 'on being master of the position for the remainder of the session, which I presume you will close as soon as you can'.[20]

In sweltering summer heat it was the Lords discussion of the Irish Church in late June that roused the Upper House to impassioned debate. Ministers in the Commons had been forced to accept a bill introduced by Gladstone suspending Irish ecclesiastical appointments. Derby assured Disraeli that the Lords would dispose of it as soon as possible.[21] Once again, on 25 June, Derby stepped forward as the champion of the Church of Ireland, citing the motto *Nullum tempus occurrit Ecclesiae*. It was, the hostile Kimberley observed, 'a regular Church and State party speech'.[22] Referring to the confiscation of monastic lands by Henry VIII and praising William of Orange, whom Derby described as 'the Deliverer', he drew his extended historical narrative through to the coronation oath of Queen Victoria.[23] It was a speech rooted in his reading in the library at Bowood under the tutelage of Lansdowne of nearly fifty years before. Its central precept was the sacrosanct nature of property, enshrined in the legally designated rights bestowed by parliament. Disestablishment of the Irish Church, he insisted, was far too important to be decided upon by a dying parliament. The Lords should throw out Gladstone's measure, even if, as he acknowledged, this was not a popular course. 'I have never yet', he concluded, 'courted popularity for the sake of popularity.' Furious debate ensued. Kimberley thought Derby's reference to the coronation oath 'most improper'.[24] Carnarvon made a bitter attack on the government from which he had just resigned. Russell, declaring that earlier generations of Derby's family had sought to place the Catholic Mary Queen of Scots on the English throne, denounced Derby's arguments. Effective support from Cranborne, who had recently succeeded to the title of Lord Salisbury, and the pugnacious Cairns, however, secured the defeat of Gladstone's measure by a majority of ninety-five votes. Derby delivered the rejection of the bill he had promised Disraeli.

As parliament prepared to prorogue on 31 July, Derby left London for Knowsley. Immediately prior to leaving, he and Lady Derby celebrated their elder son's forty-second birthday, although a recurrence of Stanley's kidney complaint had been brought on by exhaustion and long hours at the Foreign Office. After a very hot and dusty journey to Lancashire, Derby reported to Stanley that 'the old place is looking well ... notwithstanding the heat and drought, the latter of which is beginning to be very serious'.[25] On 8 August he greeted 2,000 members of the Liverpool Conservative Working Men's Association, who gathered for a picnic in the grounds. The rural routine of the recess was resumed, cheered by the news that Disraeli intended to offer Freddy Stanley the Civil Lordship of the Admiralty. Derby had enquired after the post on behalf of his younger son, who was 'a little nettled' that his father had done so without consulting him.[26] Disraeli thought Freddy's tenure of office might last longer than some imagined. But as new electoral registers were prepared for a general election in November, Derby believed Disraeli's optimism was misplaced. 'Stanley's language as to the results of the elections', he informed Disraeli in August, 'is absolute despondency—he hardly seems to think the battle worth fighting.'[27] Derby was also deeply disturbed by Stanley's language about the Irish Church. At the close of the session a dispirited and ill Stanley dissuaded Disraeli from making the strong statement in support of the Irish Church that the prime minister had proposed. Derby feared that his elder son was not to be relied upon; Stanley's scepticism about religion, as well as his despondency, rendered him too susceptible to some sort of compromise. During the recess Derby urged Disraeli to use 'to the utmost your personal influence' on his heir. 'I am sure [Stanley] would be very unwilling to do something which at such a moment should break up the Conservative party. But, knowing as I do what his feelings are, with regard to the Irish Church, I cannot but be apprehensive.'[28] Disraeli subsequently appealed to Stanley not to 'stab me in the back'.[29]

That Derby's reserved elder son was still, aged 42, unmarried and not in a position to produce an heir, continued to strain their relationship. Stanley's long-standing friendship with Mary, Lady Salisbury, and his frequent sojourns to Hatfield House were a poor substitute, in Derby's eyes, for a formal courtship. Derby's comfort, as he entered his last days, was that Freddy and Lady Constance proved prodigiously fruitful; sons born in 1865 and 1867 were followed by six further sons and two daughters born prior to 1878. Derby delighted in the company of his grandchildren. Charles Chetwynd-Talbot, his daughter's eldest son born in 1862, was an especial favourite. Freddy Stanley's eldest son, Edward Stanley (future 17th Earl of Derby), born in 1865, fondly remembered playing with his grandfather at Knowsley with small cork sailing boats in the gutter outside the Old Hall door. 'By blocking one end and turning on the tap we got a stream. They were cork boats with coloured paper sails. I can just remember my grandfather's excitement over it.'[30]

While enjoying the company of his family during the recess, as the extraordinary heat and drought of the summer continued, Derby was consulted closely by Disraeli on church appointments. Derby's views remained a consistent expression of his moderate evangelicalism, his concern at the seductive errors of High ritualism, and his wish to maintain the Anglican Establishment as a broad inclusive Church, avoiding extremes. His preferences in church appointments had been apparent while prime minister. In August 1866 he appointed the Revd Samuel Butcher, a former professor of divinity at Trinity College, Dublin, a staunch defender of the Irish establishment, but known for his moderation and avoidance of extreme partisanship, to the Irish bishopric of Meath. He recommended the Revd Hawson, Principal of the Liverpool Collegiate Institution (the first of the major Victorian public schools, founded in 1839), for the Deanery of Chester, because Hawson's 'religious views incline to what is called "Broad Church"; but he is a sound theologian, and well known for several works, including the Life and Epistles of St. Paul'.[31] Likewise, when asking for advice from his brother-in-law the Revd Frank Hopwood about suitable candidates for the deanery of Exeter, he described his wish to appoint an individual 'moderate in his religious and political views—as respects the former, inclining to the Low, rather than the High Church'.[32] In October 1867 he supported the Revd Charles Vaughan's appointment as Vicar of Doncaster. A protégé of Thomas Arnold at Rugby and a distinguished undergraduate at Trinity, Cambridge, Vaughan had been a successful Headmaster at Harrow from 1844 to 1859. Most importantly, however, 'Vaughan's opinions incline rather to the Low, than the High Church party.'[33] Derby had 'as strong an objection to the Ritualist clergy as Her Majesty', he reassured the Queen, and 'she need not apprehend any submission of the names of any of them for preferment',[34] although he believed that many clergy had been mistakenly stigmatized as High Church, 'who are no more so than I am myself', and so were blocked as well-qualified candidates for high office within the Church. Scholarly clergy of moderate

Broad Church views, inclining to Low Church sympathies, embodied his ideal of ecclesiastical preferment.

On these grounds, in March 1867, Derby rejected the proposal, supported by Cairns, of the fiery evangelical Liverpool preacher and Canon of Chester the Revd Hugh McNeile to the deanery of Hereford. He recognized that McNeile's appointment would gratify the Evangelical party, but he feared that McNeile 'represents opinion so extreme, that I should not feel justified in preferring him to 20 other candidates who are already on my list'.[35] In 1868 Disraeli, encouraged by Spofforth, believed that ritualism was so unpopular in the country that he appointed the anti-papist McNeile to the deanery of Ripon. Derby considered Disraeli's appointment a 'rather hazardous bid for the extreme Low Church'.[36] While gaining the support of Orange Toryism in Lancashire, it deeply alarmed moderate Anglicans, exactly that body of support upon which Disraeli would have to rely in resisting Gladstone's assault on the Irish Establishment. Without mentioning his earlier rejection of McNeile's preferment to the deanery of Hereford, Derby simply observed to Disraeli: 'I don't think *I* should have ventured on it.'[37] It was important, Derby advised the prime minister, to dispense patronage to all parties within the Anglican Church, although Disraeli confessed that political anxieties about the Irish Church and theological divisions within the Anglican Church made clerical appointments 'critical and complicated'.[38] Disraeli's subsequent appointment of the urbane and witty Revd William Magee, a moderate evangelical who abhorred fanatical excess and was a staunch defender of the Establishment both in Ireland and in England, to the bishopric of Peterborough repaired some of the damage caused by McNeile's preferment and followed Derby's advice not to restrict church patronage to one party. The experienced Derby comforted the new premier that general satisfaction, in the vexed matter of ecclesiastical appointments, was hardly to be hoped for; Disraeli should be gratified if his preferments did not produce general discontent.[39]

In October 1868 the Archbishop of Canterbury, Charles Longley, who had inaugurated the first Lambeth Conference a year earlier, died. The Queen favoured the liberal Broad Churchman Archibald Tait, Bishop of London, for the Anglican primacy. But the Edinburgh-born Tait, who since 1856 had been his immediate neighbour at 22 St James's Square, Derby believed would be neither a popular nor a judicious choice. In the early 1850s he had clashed with Tait over Oxford University reform. He objected to Tait's toleration of ritualism within the London diocese. He harboured, he acknowledged to Disraeli, a personal dislike and distrust of

Tait, who he also suspected might compromise on the principle of the Irish Establishment. But the 'range of choices [was] limited'.[40] Derby regarded the Bishop of Gloucester, the Revd Charles Ellicott, as 'a learned man, and I believe a sound Churchman'.[41] But the Bishop inclined to the High Church party, did not possess much strength of character, and was afflicted with a foolish voice and manner, which made him appear weaker than he was. Personally, Derby favoured the Bishop of Rochester, the Revd Thomas Claughton, but Disraeli yielded to the Queen's preference for Tait. That Disraeli then passed over the unctuous High Church Samuel Wilberforce, Bishop of Oxford, for the see of London vacated by Tait gained Disraeli a prominent enemy within the Anglican Church. The reputable, but duller, John Jackson, Bishop of Lincoln, was subsequently appointed Bishop of London. Such ecclesiastical patronage mattered as clearly one question was to dominate the coming election, Gladstone's call for the disestablishment of the Church of Ireland. It would prove, Disraeli anticipated, 'a great Protestant struggle'.[42]

Prior to the general election in November 1868, Disraeli was surprisingly optimistic, anticipating a large Conservative majority. Derby doubted such a prospect. 'I hope you are right, but I own I am unable to see from whence a majority is to be obtained,' he cautioned the prime minister.[43] Increasingly critical of Spofforth, Derby was disconcerted by the number of constituencies which were not to be contested. Too many seats, he feared, were being abandoned without a struggle.[44] *The Times* calculated that there were fully 120 more seats uncontested by the Conservatives than by the Liberals.[45] Derby focused his own influence and financial resources on the redrawn Lancashire constituencies. His efforts were amply rewarded. He hoped eighteen of the thirty-three county and borough seats within Lancashire would be secured for the Conservatives. In fact they won twenty-two seats. Most spectacularly, in the new constituency of South-West Lancashire, Gladstone was defeated. Both Conservative candidates, the barrister Richard Cross, born in Preston, and the Liverpool merchant Charles Turner, gained more votes than the Liberal leader. Gladstone's election speeches, Derby observed, had done him more harm than good. The intensity of Gladstone's stumping, at one point making six speeches in three days, Derby thought to be beneath his position and an indication of a conscious sense of weakness.[46] On the hustings Gladstone's deep dismay was obvious to those watching the polling on 21 November, as was an offensive remark made by the defeated candidate to the High Sheriff. The next day Gladstone was obliged to send a written apology.[47] Derby judged this victory for Lancashire Toryism a fitting response to 'the balderdash and braggadocio in which Gladstone had been indulging on his stumping tour'.[48] Gladstone retreated to the safe Liberal seat of Greenwich. The two Conservative candidates in South-East Lancashire, Algernon Egerton, who had presided over the Free Trade Hall banquet for Derby in October 1867, and the Manchester merchant John Henry, beat both Liberal candidates, one of whom was Sir Robert Peel's second son, Frederick Peel. In North Lancashire, Freddy Stanley was returned top of the poll, along with the Conservative John Wilson Patten, recently appointed Lord Mayo's successor as Chief Secretary for Ireland. The sitting Liberal member, the Marquess of Hartington (son of the Duke of Devonshire), was soundly defeated. Personally Derby was on good terms with Hartington who, he believed, had only undertaken the contested election because he was 'driven on by his party'. Yet, Derby had not forgotten that Hartington 'was the chosen instrument for my ejection from office in '59'.[49] It was, therefore, a gratifying Stanley family victory over 'Grand Whiggery'. Freddy Stanley's electoral expenses came to a sizeable £17,000, to which Derby willingly contributed £10,000. Likewise, in North-East Lancashire both Conservative candidates, the firm Anglican Churchman James Holt and the Burnley-born John Starkie, defeated their Liberal rivals. Two of the three Liverpool seats were won by the Conservatives, Samuel Graves, a Liverpool shipowner and former Mayor, and Viscount Sandon, eldest son of the Earl of Harrowby, defeating Liberal candidates. In Preston both seats were won by Conservatives, as were both seats in Bolton, both seats in Salford, and the seats for Ashton under Lyne, Stalybridge, and Clitheroe. William Hornby, comptroller of the Knowsley estate and Derby's close companion, with his fellow Conservative candidate the elderly Joseph Feilden, defeated both Liberal challengers in Blackburn. Only in Burnley, Bury, Manchester, Oldham, Rochdale, Warrington, and Wigan were Liberal candidates successfully elected, although Derby believed that 'sheer mismanagement' had lost them the Wigan seat and that Warrington had been gained by the Liberals through the 'rascality' of the polling clerk.[50] This was a striking vindication of Derby's faith in the Conservatism of newly enfranchised Lancashire voters, justifying the warm tribute he had paid them at Manchester twelve months before.

But victories in Lancashire were the one bright spot for the Conservatives in an otherwise devastatingly dark electoral picture. Disraeli's Commons majority emphatically failed to materialize. Even Derby's more modest expectations were disappointed. By the end of November it was clear that the Liberals had secured a crushing Commons majority of nearly

100 MPs. In England overall Conservative successes in the counties were erased by losses in the boroughs. Derby approved of Disraeli's decision to dismiss Spofforth as the party's election manager. 'I believe he was honest ... but he was anything but judicious in the choice of candidates, and disposed to meddle when he had better have left things alone.'[51] It was the worst Conservative electoral performance since 1835. A stunned Disraeli prepared to resign immediately, without meeting parliament. This was a constitutional innovation against which Derby cautioned him. Better, he urged, the cabinet indicate in the Queen's Speech that a reform, rather than the disestablishment, of the Church of Ireland would be brought forward. This would allow the Conservative government to go down defending the Irish Church.[52] But on 28 November ministers, with only one dissenting voice, agreed to resign without a struggle. By 3 December, Gladstone was prime minister, fired with a mission to pacify Ireland by disestablishing the Church of Ireland. 'The Almighty seems to sustain and spare me for some purpose of His own,' Gladstone recorded in his diary.[53] That beleaguered institution, to which the 69-year-old Derby had devoted so much of his public life, now confronted an inexorable Gladstonian sense of righteous destiny, backed by an overwhelming Commons majority.

> ... and with winged words
> Thus to a phantom form he gave command.
>
> (Derby, *The Iliad of Homer*, i. 34)

In politics moments of fulfilment are elusive, failure and a feeling of business left undone the haunting emotions to which elderly statesmen commonly succumb. The demise of the Church of Ireland became directly aligned with the close of Derby's political life, marking a painful end to a distinguished career. A cruel sense of the world moving irresistibly on and a slackening grasp on events denied the comfort of consummate achievement. Gladstone's wish to redress what he saw as the historic injustices visited upon a long-suffering Ireland compounded Derby's disillusion. As he approached his seventieth birthday in March 1869, an increasingly frail Derby witnessed the dismantling of that institution to which he had dedicated so much of his political career. His first major Commons speech, as a young Whig in 1824, had been a forthright defence of the Irish Church's property. As a resolute Irish Chief Secretary in the early 1830s he had reformed the Church of Ireland in order to preserve

its privileged status. Thereafter, the central importance of the Anglican
Established Church to the survival of the Union was a consistent thread in
Derby's thinking on Irish affairs. His firm defence of the Church of Ireland,
however, never hardened into Protestant bigotry. He distanced himself
from the visceral anti-Catholicism of Conservatives such as Newdegate
and Beresford. He favoured civil and religious liberty for the Catholic
laity. But Catholic civil and religious liberty could never be a concession to
the political and institutional pretensions of the papacy and ultramontane
priesthood. The Church of Ireland's status was an integral part of the
Union between Britain and Ireland. Abandon the Irish Church and the
Union would be dangerously weakened. Sacrifice the Church of Ireland's
property and the legal underpinnings of civil society would be loosened.
Yet this was precisely what Gladstone, with a providential sense of
transcendent mission, now proposed.

Bedridden through most of the winter, being carried up- and downstairs
at Knowsley, Derby anticipated the 1869 session with deep apprehension.
He reluctantly approved of Malmesbury's handing over the Conservative
leadership in the Lords to Cairns. He now also accepted that Disraeli
had acted wisely in resigning office before meeting parliament. The party
seemed to applaud what they deemed 'a dignified and honest course'.[54]
Struggling down to London for the opening of parliament on 13 February
1869 Derby attended the Lords as often as his weak condition allowed. Over
the winter he discussed with Lady Derby spending the month of March
in Cannes, where the warm sunshine of the French Riviera might ease his
suffering. But the imminence of the Irish Church disestablishment debate
and his continuing weakness, his strength being insufficient to undertake
such a long journey, forced them to abandon their plans.

On 1 March, Gladstone introduced to the Commons, in a speech of three
hours, his sweeping Irish Church Bill proposing both the disestablishment
and the disendowment of the Church. For good measure it abolished the
right of Church of Ireland bishops to sit in the House of Lords after January
1871. It was, Gathorne Hardy observed, a measure 'of pains, penalties and
confiscation'.[55] Malmesbury considered it 'a complete act of spoliation, and
far beyond what was expected'.[56] To Gathorne Hardy, Derby immediately
laid out what he believed to be a legal flaw in Gladstone's legislation.[57]
Gladstone called for the Act relating to the Established Church of Ireland
to be abolished. But no such Act existed, Derby insisted. The Act of Union
recognized a pre-existing established and endowed Church, stating that
this established Church was to be indissolubly united, for all time to come,
with the Church of England. If this was the Act to which Gladstone

referred, then its abolition merely revived the Irish Church's previous established independent status prior to 1800. But, if Gladstone meant to go back to the time of the Reformation, Derby understood the decision of parliament at that time was confined to requiring that all clergy, on pain of forfeiture, should conform to the doctrine and discipline of the Reformed Church. Abolition of this Act would revive the former rights of the Church of Rome, which was not, he archly observed, what was intended. This ingenious legalistic argument provided Gathorne Hardy with ammunition, but could not stem a seemingly irresistible movement of Commons support for disestablishment. Disraeli moved the rejection of the bill on its second Commons reading, but he acted with little resolve, Gathorne Hardy providing Conservative opposition with backbone. By the end of March the second Commons reading had been secured by the Liberal government with a crushing majority of 118 votes. On 31 May the Irish Church Bill passed its third Commons reading by 361 to 247 votes and the measure was sent up to the Lords.

Given the commanding Liberal majority in the Commons, the real battle over Irish disestablishment was clearly going to occur in the Lords. The questions which now raised Derby to his feet in the Upper House were precisely those issues which had always been important to him, the status of the peerage, parliamentary procedure, and the Irish Church. On Thursday 4 March he supported the second reading of Lord Salisbury's bill to reform the proceedings of parliament, so as to avoid the Lords' having to consider in haste a large number of bills sent up from the Commons at the very end of the session. Salisbury's measure encountered exactly the same opposition as his own proposal of 1848. The following Monday, 8 March, Derby urged the government to consult the former Commons Speaker Lord Eversley (Charles Shaw-Lefevre) so as to arrive at an acceptable resolution of the problem. But a solution once again eluded the legislature. A week later Derby spoke very briefly during debate of the Habitual Criminals Bill, but even such limited effort took its toll. In mid-March he travelled down to Tunbridge Wells for a few days' recuperation, away from the strains of Westminster.

When Malmesbury called on his old friend at St James's Square on 20 April, he found Derby still suffering from the exertion of attending the Upper House. Nonetheless, on Tuesday 27 April, Derby supported Cairns in allowing the second reading of Russell's Life Peerage Bill to pass.[58] Their lordships understood that only two life peers were to be created each year and that the total number would be limited to twenty-eight. Derby gave a detailed account of the Wensleydale debates of 1856 and the unsuccessful attempt to reach a compromise on the question. Then the issue had centred on the power, left in long abeyance, of the royal prerogative to create, without the sanction of the House, an indefinite number of life peers in order to strengthen the appellate jurisdiction of the Lords. Though the current measure required careful examination, he supported the bill as recognizing the sanction of the Lords as necessary to the creation of life peerages confined strictly within the limits of proved or probable necessity.[59] Russell's legislation, he believed, rested on a different basis from that proposed in 1856. The earlier legislation sought to assert a long-neglected prerogative. Russell's bill, by contrast, called for the conferral of such a prerogative, acknowledged to be non-existent, limited by clear restrictions. On these grounds, he did not oppose it.[60]

But compromise over life peerages did not temper Derby's intransigent opposition to Irish disestablishment. Debate on Irish disestablishment was prefigured on Thursday 13 May, when Russell pressed for an explanation from the government regarding the response to increasing crime in Ireland and reform of the law relating to Irish land tenure. On behalf of the Liberal ministry, Granville fobbed Russell off by referring to his frequent absences from the House and the fact that he had already addressed the current state of Ireland three times that session. Derby, having returned from two weeks of rest at Tunbridge Wells the day before, immediately rose to his feet to assert that Russell was fully justified in raising the question.[61] Derby reminded the House that for the past forty-five years he had directly managed his Ballykisteen estate, which was situated in an area recently disturbed by the worst civil disorder. Every year he laid out a considerable sum on improvements and for several years he had received no return from the estate. But the recent actions of the government, he stated, had encouraged even law-abiding tenants to defy their landlords. The release of Fenian prisoners had discredited legal authority, and ministerial talk of land reform had encouraged many tenants to believe that a radical redistribution of land in Ireland was imminent. In particular, Derby attacked recent statements by Bright regarding land reform which had, albeit unintentionally, excited the Irish peasantry to illegal resistance against their landlords. This irresponsible behaviour by a minister of the Crown, he declared, had created a very real threat to life and property. An ill-tempered wrangle with Kimberley immediately ensued, during which the young Liberal former Lord Lieutenant of Ireland accused Derby of gross misrepresentation. Although Kimberley privately acknowledged that Bright's statements had been 'imprudent', he believed Derby's attack was 'a most unseemly exhibition of malignant party hatred'.[62]

During June, Cairns, encouraged by Disraeli, sought a compromise over Irish Church disestablishment by way of Lords amendments to Gladstone's sweeping measure. As Derby feared, the newly appointed Archibald Tait, as Archbishop of Canterbury, supported these moves. But, when a group of Conservative peers met at Lambeth Palace to discuss how best to proceed, Derby refused to attend. There was 'no consideration on earth', he declared to Cairns, that would induce him to compromise on such an issue. 'I am afraid that my presence would in no degree tend to the harmony of the meeting.' The main principle of the measure was 'founded on the gravest injustice, and violent disregard of the rights of property'.[63] A good number of Conservative peers agreed with him. At a Carlton Club gathering on 1 June opinion was divided, but a majority were for throwing the bill out. This threatened a double schism, a split between the Conservative leadership in the Lords, headed by Cairns, and the backbenchers rallying around Derby, compounding a collision between the two Houses, should the bill approved by the Commons be rejected by the Lords.

Disraeli, the Queen, Cairns, and Archbishop Tait sought to defuse the imminent crisis. But Derby steadfastly refused to compromise. He could not sacrifice his personal honour and character, he informed the Queen, by abstaining from opposition to the measure. 'Every amendment proposed in the Commons tending to mitigate the severity of the Enactment has been summarily and even contemptuously rejected by Mr Gladstone, and the majority which blindly follows him.' The Liberal government, he pronounced, were employing 'the language of menace and coercion'.[64] On 7 June he assured a delegation from the National Conservative Association that he would do all he could to throw out the bill. Derby attended a small meeting of Conservative peers at Marlborough House at which it was agreed to oppose the second reading of the Irish Church Bill. He fiercely denounced, in writing to Cairns, the view encouraged by the Liberal government that any amendment passed by the Lords would be tantamount to a rejection of the bill. 'This is thrusting it down our throats with a vengeance, and under such circumstances I decline to swallow.'[65]

When, on Thursday 17 June, Derby rose to speak on the Irish Church Bill the galleries were packed. But the performance revealed his sadly diminished abilities. His voice, a distressed Malmesbury observed, 'was feeble, he looked pale and ill, and his manner had lost its energy'.[66] The hostile Kimberley thought he resembled 'an old toothless lion'.[67] While giving his speech Derby felt at times, he subsequently confessed to his elder son, unable to continue.[68] Altogether, Kimberley concluded, 'it was a very painful exhibition'.[69] It was a fading shadow of that forceful oratory with which, in earlier years, Derby had thrilled, amused, and provoked his listeners. The simple passion of his conviction, however, shone through as he gave vivid power to his outrage by quoting from his favourite modern author, Sir Walter Scott. Reciting the haunting words of the frenzied gipsy woman from *Guy Mannering*, dispossessed by the Laird of Ellangowen, he declaimed: 'Ride your ways, Laird of Ellangowen! Ride your ways, Godfrey Bertram! This day have ye quenched seven smoking hearths—see if the fire in your ain parlour burn the blither for that. Ye have riven the thack off seven cottar houses—look if your ain roof-tree stand the faster.' So, with sorrow and resentment, might the Protestants of Ireland look to the government from whom they deserved protection and declare: 'Go your way, ye ministers of England. Ye have this day, in so far as in you lay, quenched the light of spiritual truth in 1,500 parishes. See if your own Church stand the faster for that.'[70] Thus was the loyalty of Irish Protestants, who had shed their blood at the Battle of the Boyne in defence of their freedom and religious belief, repaid with oppression. Nowhere in the world in which the Roman Catholic religion was dominant, he pronounced, was the principle of religious equality tolerated. Despoiling the Anglican Irish Church would inevitably erode those cherished liberties granted by parliament. Responding to fierce accusations of misrepresentation interjected by Clarendon, he concluded with a poignant peroration:

> My Lords, I am now an old man; and like many of your Lordships, I have already passed the three score years and ten. My official life is entirely closed; my political life is nearly so; and, in the course of nature, my natural life cannot now be long. That natural life commenced with the bloody suppression of a formidable rebellion in Ireland, which immediately preceded the Union between the two countries. And may God grant that its close may not witness a renewal of the one and the dissolution of the other! I do not pretend, my Lords, to be able to penetrate the veil which hides from mortal vision the events of the future; whatever may be the issue of this great controversy—whatever may be the result of your Lordships' present deliberations—I say, for my own part, even if it should be for the last time I now have the honour of addressing you, that it will be to my dying day a satisfaction to me that I should have been enabled to lift my voice against the adoption of a measure of which, I believe, the political folly is only equalled by its moral injustice.

These valedictory words concluded the last major speech Derby delivered to parliament. His Westminster career of forty-seven years closed with the dire warning that defence of the Established Church was essential to the preservation of parliamentary freedoms.

In the division on the second Lords reading of the Irish Church Bill 143 Conservative peers joined Derby in opposing the measure. But thirty-two Conservatives followed Cairns into the government lobby. About sixty Conservative peers were absent. As a result, the measure passed by a majority of thirty-three votes. During the subsequent fraught committee stage, Cairns consulted with Granville so as to secure amendments rendering the bill acceptable to both Houses. On Thursday 1 July, Derby briefly joined in debate over the most controversial clauses.[71] Some thirty-five Lords amendments to the bill were eventually accepted by the Commons. Derby's opposition remained implacable, however, as he joined fifty-five other Conservative peers in signing a protest asserting that the right of parliament to confiscate the Irish Church's property was doubtful. He spoke briefly to the Lords for a last time on Monday 12 July, when giving notice of the petition.[72] But Cairns's cross-bench negotiations eventually bore fruit when, on 22 July, the Irish Church Bill passed its third Lords reading. As an angry and frail Derby passed by Cairns, he tersely remarked: 'I have nothing left but to go away.'[73]

> Griev'd at his baffled hopes and broken spear.
>
> (Derby, *The Iliad of Homer*, ii. 10)

For the last time, in late July 1869, Derby left 23 St James's Square for Knowsley. His health deteriorated further and his prognostications for Ireland darkened. Disestablishment of the Irish Church, he brooded, would lead to the break-up of the Union. When Stanley visited Knowsley in early September his father was preoccupied with selling off his Tipperary estate. Ballykisteen had been his first married home, a tangible expression of his lifelong involvement in Irish affairs. He had always taken great personal pride in his careful management of the estate and in the harmonious relations he had formerly maintained with his tenants. But now was the time, he apprehended, to sever the family's links with 'John Bull's other island'. He was deeply disappointed by the recent hostility demonstrated by his Irish tenantry, despite half the rental of his estate having been spent, for many years, on improvements. Reports of the enmity of tenants in Tipperary, 'the peasantry full of vague hopes which perhaps they can hardly define to themselves', and the increasing hostility of Catholic priests to strangers and Protestants, confirmed his deep despondency.[74] Liberal irresponsibility and Irish ingratitude made remaining an English landlord in Ireland an unpalatable prospect. On 6 September, Derby wrote to Jasper Bolton requesting a full account of the current condition of the estate.[75] Stanley suggested investing the proceeds from Ballykisteen in the purchase of additional land in North Lancashire. This would provide an estate for Freddy Stanley and consolidate the family's influence in the county.

But, before he could oversee the selling-off of his Irish estate, Derby's health dramatically worsened. At the end of August he was afflicted by digestive pains, the result, his doctors advised, of gout which refused to come out.[76] The accounts of Derby, Malmesbury noted on 14 September, 'are bad and I am very unhappy. I got a sad letter from Freddy Stanley, but he does not seem to have quite given up all hope.'[77] Two days later Stanley informed Disraeli that he could not 'report very well of my father: he has become more of an invalid in his habits, goes out but little, and is seldom quite free from gout in some form: but he has on the other hand no severe attacks and his spirits continue good. He thinks badly of the political future, but speaks of it without excitement or annoyance.'[78] Bringing his affairs into order at the beginning of October, Derby established Freddy Stanley with his growing family as the tenant for life of his Witherslack estate, near Kendal in Westmoreland, leaving his other estates to be managed by his elder son on his inheritance. But, by 6 October, Derby was 'suffering a good deal'.[79] His son-in-law and former private secretary Colonel Talbot advised Malmesbury that there was no hope and that the Earl was 'gradually sinking'.[80]

On Monday 11 October, Derby's local physician Dr Gorst prescribed a strong dose of opium to relieve his patient's pain, but this precipitated a collapse from which Derby never rallied. Lord Stanley was immediately summoned back from London. Arriving at Knowsley just after eight o'clock that evening, he found his father in a state of partial consciousness and relapsing into a stupor. Derby's other local physician, Dr Miller, advised Stanley that the case was hopeless as his father was extremely weak and refusing all nourishment. Lady Derby insisted on remaining at her husband's bedside, where she was joined by both her sons. At 11 p.m. Miller judged the end was near. Lady Derby, Lord Stanley, Freddy Stanley, and their sister Emma each took their leave of Derby by 'kissing his forehead, as he lay breathing, but insensible'. A 'more painful and touching scene I never went through', Stanley recorded, 'and I trust I never may again'.[81] But Derby survived the night and during the following day appeared slightly better, managing to drink some milk. Premature reports of his passing, meanwhile, spread round London, as the Earl hung between life and death.

By Wednesday 13 October Derby was regaining consciousness for short periods, evidently recognizing the family members gathered around his bed and unsuccessfully trying to speak. Following another disturbed night, at 6 a.m. on Thursday morning Miller emptied Derby's bladder by means of a catheter, after which the Earl seemed to sleep more easily. That afternoon his 4-year-old grandson Eddy Stanley was brought to his bedside. Upon the young boy saying ' "he was sorry for grandpa", Lord D. answered quickly, and as it seemed with a touch of the old humour, "Grandpa is very sorry for himself" '.[82] But, by Friday 15 October, Derby's symptoms had worsened. As well as passing blood, indicating ulcerations in his intestines, he lapsed into bouts of incoherent rambling. When Lord Stanley asked him how he was feeling, Derby replied: 'Bored to the utmost power of extinction.' Evidently reminiscing of his racing days, at one point he whispered, 'with horse flesh like that … ', but the rest of his sentence was lost.[83] An exhausted and distressed Lady Derby, meanwhile, refused to leave him and could hardly be persuaded to lie down, so a sofa was placed by the Earl's bedside that she might remain constantly by him. For a further seven days of anguish and uncertainty the family watched over him, Lady Derby only breaking her vigil to join her sons and daughter for prayers in the chapel. Occasional violent muscular movements in his face suggested that Derby was now suffering severe pain. His rambling became more acute. 'Once the words "my government" and "Gladstone" were caught.'[84] But more often, he seemed to be imagining himself talking to his beloved grandchildren. Lord Stanley 'heard him say quite distinctly, "No, no, young gentlemen" and I think he added "that won't do" '. Meanwhile, Lady Derby sat, 'with her eyes fixed on his, and a look on her face', Stanley observed, 'which I had not seen since she was 20 years younger: I cannot describe it'. Still unable to take food, Derby's periods of unconsciousness were now interrupted by 'spasms and convulsive struggles, with distortion of the face, very painful to witness'.[85] Lady Derby, from grief and exhaustion, sat weeping bitterly by his bed. Then, on Friday 22 October, the convulsions abruptly ceased. Stanley noted that his father's face 'lost its habitual expression of late years, that of a man sinking into old age, and … returned to what I remember it 8, 10 or 12 years ago'.[86] Stanley and Freddy watched over their father during that night. Though scarcely moving, and breathing heavily, he appeared free of pain. At 6.55 a.m., on Saturday 23 October, his breathing suddenly stopped, without the slightest struggle, his face 'perfectly calm, like that of a man in deep sleep'.[87] Derby had finally passed peacefully away. 'In him', Malmesbury recorded, 'I lose my greatest friend, and the country a most brilliant and accomplished statesman.'[88]

At Derby's request, his funeral involved only the immediate family; it was held at St Mary's Church in Knowsley on Friday 29 October. Derby's predecessors since 1592, including his father and grandfather, had been buried in the family vault at Ormskirk. But Derby had overseen the building of the red sandstone Gothic revival parish church in Knowsley, endowed by his father in 1839, and closely superintended the construction of a family vault for himself and his heirs. During his lifetime and again in the final weeks he instructed his family that no great public display should accompany his interment, which should be attended only by his family and the staff and tenants of the Knowsley estate. His request was strictly observed. An enquiry whether a representative of the Queen might attend was politely declined, as were similar requests from local corporations. Derby's clear wish 'was to be buried among his own people; to rest, after death, among those by whom he was best known and appreciated, and to avoid everything like pomp and parade'.[89] At just after midday on Friday 29 October the hearse, drawn by six horses and preceded by a servant, carrying Derby's coronet on a velvet cushion, travelled the mile from Knowsley Hall through the park and then the final half-mile to the church. Eight mourning coaches followed, carrying Derby's two sons, his younger brother the Hon. Henry Stanley, his brothers-in-law Colonel Samuel Long and the Revd Frank Hopwood, Lady Derby's brother William Wilbraham and her nephew Lord Skelmersdale, Lord Wilton, Sir William Hornby, comptroller of the estate, as well as Derby's local physicians, Dr Gorst and Dr Miller, and the Knowsley land agent, George Hale. Following the coaches walked about seventy servants, members of the household and estate workers, wearing black scarves and hatbands. Hundreds of local residents lined the route to pay their last respects. At precisely one o'clock the cortège reached St Mary's Church, where they were met by the incumbent, the Revd William Feilden. Inside the church the coffin was placed on trestles and Derby's cap and coronet laid on the lid. As the moment came to lower the coffin into the vault Lord Stanley (now the 15th Earl of Derby), who had hitherto maintained a dignified composure, broke down in unconcealed grief.

Wise in council, foremost in the fight.

(Derby, *The Iliad of Homer*, i. 48)

Public tributes immediately followed Derby's death. On Monday 25 October *The Times* printed an extended obituary memorializing 'a most

wonderful man ... born to command'.⁹⁰ The notice warmly recognized
Derby's personal qualities, but was cool about his political achievements,
particularly as Conservative leader. As a debater, in his best days, it
commented, he had been more than a match for any adversary. The fame
of his battles with Daniel O'Connell in the Commons was still vivid,
while more recent speeches in the Lords had 'stamped him as the first
of our orators'. What the obituary emphasized in Derby's nature was his
strong fighting instinct. He was never cowed by unfavourable odds. Each
of his three premierships had struggled with Commons minorities. His
love of *The Iliad* lay in the din of battle which pervades it, his critically
acclaimed translation giving graphic force to Homer's epic of heroic
bravery. His devotion to the turf was one more expression of his love of
contest. It was these fighting qualities, combined with the brilliancy of
his manner, which had secured the loyalty of his followers. He was, *The
Times* judged,

> a splendid specimen of an Englishman, and whether he was engaged in
> furious debate with demagogues, or in lowly conversation on religion with
> little children, or in parley with jockeys, while training Toxophilite, or
> rendering Homer into verse, or in a stately Latin discourse as the Chancellor
> of his university, or in joyous talk in a drawing-room among ladies, whom he
> delighted to chaff, or in caring for the needs of Lancashire operatives—there
> was a force and fire about him that acted like a spell.

He was, the obituary acknowledged, one of the most remarkable and irresistible men of the age. Privately beloved, publicly admired, extraordinarily
clever, a great orator, he had proved the most brilliant, though not the
most successful, parliamentary leader of the last half-century. Two things
were clear, *The Times* concluded disparagingly, about his Conservative
leadership. Never was the leader of a great party so implicitly trusted and
never was a leader so wanting in a declared policy. He was, in short, a
popular leader without political ideas.

Liberal journalism predictably amplified this criticism. Derby's change
of party, his alleged shifts of opinion, his supposed unstatesmanlike
behaviour, and his lack of appropriate *gravitas* marred his talents, denying
him any lasting achievement. Like Homer's hero Achilles, born of a god
and a mortal, his bravery too easily became recklessness and his courage too
often displayed itself as arrogance. Equally predictably, the Conservative
press lamented the irreplaceable loss of an illustrious embodiment of
aristocracy, land, and Church. His intellectual powers and mastery of
oratory were formidable. As a young Tory MP, entering parliament in

1832, William Gladstone was dazzled by Derby's gifts: 'When I heard Stanley in the House of Commons, I thought him the very cleverest man I had ever seen—he seemed quicker than thought itself.'[91] Talented, capable, and undaunted, after 1846 Derby vigorously personified the society Conservatives saw threatened by urban demagogues, freethinkers, and the apostles of precipitous change. As the *Illustrated Times* observed in 1860, he was 'the first patrician in England'.[92] His impeccable credentials, as a landed aristocrat with country habits and debating skill, invested him with a natural authority that brought him genuine popularity. He was not burdened with the commercial origins of Sir Robert Peel, or the metropolitan literary background of Benjamin Disraeli. Instead, the broad acres of the Knowsley estate, the inheritance of a distinguished title going back to 1485, the patronage of numerous Anglican livings, and his passion for field and turf, as well as his forceful public eloquence and mordant private wit, represented the Conservative rank and file as they liked to see themselves.

Derby's cheerful, often teasing, social manner, his evident delight in the boisterous company of racing men at Newmarket or among his tenants at Knowsley, his conscientious devotion to the interests of Lancashire, his lightly worn scholarship, his accomplishments as a powerful parliamentary orator, and his dignity as premier and Chancellor of Oxford University embodied an English aristocratic ideal at the heart of mid-Victorian Conservative sensibilities. In 1861 the *Illustrated London News* noted that he was 'nearly adored by all his party'.[93] As a former Conservative MP wrote to Jolliffe in November 1859, 'what has kept the party together is the influence and most successful leadership of Lord Derby'.[94] Strong affection cemented party loyalty. He combined, Kebbel observed, the high rank, spotless character, and great wealth of Lord Rockingham with the intellectual force, fervid eloquence, and happy wit of Charles James Fox.[95] Throughout the 1850s and 1860s the Conservatives were the most unified body of parliamentary votes during a period of shifting, often fractured, Peelite, Whig, Liberal, and radical alignment. Granville conceded in June 1859 that 'the close attendance of [Derby's] supporters both in and out of office was very remarkable'. This was owing 'not merely to a stricter system of discipline, which is characteristic of the Conservative party', but also to 'the great personal ascendancy' of Lord Derby.[96]

As prime minister Derby exercised an unchallenged authority over his cabinets. Few other Victorian premiers, perhaps only Peel and for certain periods Gladstone, maintained as firm a control of their governments.

There were no ministerial loose cannons, such as Palmerston under Russell, in Derby's administrations. On occasion, Disraeli might challenge Derby's command. But his Chancellor's attempts to press forward a financial coup or interfere in foreign policy were always decisively checked. Ministers never doubted that it was Derby who directed their policies and legislation. The Reform bills of 1859 and 1867 bore the stamp of his endorsement. He maintained a close oversight of foreign policy. Only after March 1867, when rapidly moving events in the Commons swept along the Conservatives' Reform Bill, did the grip of the ageing 68-year-old Derby slacken. Until then, he was as prime minister first among unequals. This was not merely the function of a poverty of talent or a meagreness of ambition among his ministerial front bench. Lack of ability is not a necessary check on aspiration. More importantly, Derby possessed an intellectual ability, an administrative resourcefulness, and a weight of official experience which invested him with a natural authority. When, in November 1852, he drew up in one sitting without erasures the detailed memorandum laying out his government's response to the establishment of the Second Empire in France, he displayed that formidable competence and mastery of detail which affirmed his ascendancy within his cabinet. Similarly, in November 1858 it was Derby who drafted the report of his cabinet committee on Reform, which laid out the basis of what he believed to be a lasting settlement of a long-disputed issue.

Few Conservative leaders have retired at moments of their own choosing. Many have been pushed; few have jumped. Most recently, Edward Heath, Margaret Thatcher, John Major, William Hague, and Iain Duncan Smith, like their predecessor Arthur Balfour, have stepped down nursing a bitter sense of betrayal. Few have enjoyed sustained and largely unquestioned support. Derby, like Baldwin, is a member of this very select group, despite leading the party for twenty-two years. Not only did he head a party for longer than any other politician in modern British politics, he did so without challenge by a serious rival and without the threat of a substantial desertion of support. Although a number of MPs and peers quietly moved over to the Conservatives after 1846, notably seventy Peelite MPs who had split from the party over Corn Law repeal, hardly any Conservatives permanently revoked the party whip between 1846 and 1869. Frequently, mistrust of Disraeli served as a safety valve for the frustration prompted by Derby's policies. The vast bulk of Conservatives found it easier to distrust Disraeli than be disloyal to Derby. Most Conservative leaders, moreover, have come to harbour a private contempt for those under their command. Peel's disdain for the Conservative back benches was apparent before and obvious after the party schism of 1846. Disraeli retained a lifelong sense that the Tory squires were undeserving of his genius. But Derby never succumbed to a private scorn for his supporters, despite the inevitable aggravations of the political fray. Leadership remained a solemn obligation born of public duty and mutual trust.

The posthumous criticism of opponents focused on two aspects of Derby's career: first, a purported weakness of temperament, evident in his inappropriate levity, the suggestion that he saw politics as merely a diverting game—a failing which betrayed his fundamental lack of earnestness; secondly, the indictment that he possessed no political ideas—his was a career devoid of consistent doctrine. For pious Liberals and self-righteous radicals these were grievous defects, a comforting proof of their retrospective belief that, between Peel and Disraeli, the Conservative party was doctrinally impotent. From 1846 and 1869, they suggested, the Conservatives had languished in the political wilderness. That both accusations were hostile misrepresentations did not prevent them from becoming a staple part of subsequent historical literature. Posterity took its cue from such denigration. Thirty years after his death, the venerable *Dictionary of National Biography* memorialized the judgement that Derby 'was not a statesman of profoundly settled convictions or of widely constructive views. He was a man rather of intense vitality than of great intellect.'[97]

Posterity's dismissal of Derby demands revision. The first allegation confuses manner with motivation. For Derby, raised in the Foxite milieu of his grandfather's household, an air of patrician detachment was the natural appurtenance of aristocratic birth. A formal public pose of lofty indifference to personal advancement complemented his conviction that political office was a duty required by his devotion to the national interest. Power was not a prize to be striven for with obvious earnestness. Rather, a light nonchalance was the defining tone of aristocratic behaviour. A language of patriotic detachment from narrow partisan purpose was the public face of a private commitment to party advantage. When in opposition it was important to eschew factiousness and to be seen to be giving the Queen's government 'a fair trial'. The aristocratic statesman should appear unafraid of office, while not seeming eager to seize it. As Derby advised Pakington in November 1865, it was necessary in speeches to 'disclaim any factious opposition or desire to embarrass ministers'.[98] But such language was not, as it has been usually understood, a symptom of Derby's private belief 'that office was scarcely a prize to be sought and the apprehension that in office the Conservatives had little that was distinctive to offer the nation'.[99] Rather, such public expressions of patriotic detachment served to enhance statesmanlike claims to office. 'By this disinterested kind of language', Derby observed in 1849, 'I am much more likely to secure a young man than if I showed eagerness to get his vote.'[100] Political rhetoric serves to persuade, not explain.

Behind such conventional aristocratic language lay genuine dedication. Derby was not a dilettante. His strong sense of public duty was sincere. Public expressions of high-minded disinterest cloaked his earnest commitment, just as his carefully penned memorandums on administrative aspects of government revealed his private seriousness. When ejected from office in December 1852, for example, his determination survived. 'The game is lost', he confessed to his elder son, 'but I think it ought to be played and I will play it out to the last.'[101] In 1849 he pressed the point on a sullen Disraeli, who was contemplating withdrawing from public life: 'He who has put his hand to the parliamentary plough cannot draw back.'[102] Depression and gout, especially when closeted in the damp autumnal fastness of Knowsley, often left him fatigued and despondent. Toxic environmental pollution from neighbouring alkali works added to the detrimental effect of residence during the recess at the family estate. By the late 1840s a familiar cyclical pattern of shifting moods, resolute energy during the exhilaration of the parliamentary session and the racing season giving way during the recess to depressed spirits aggravated by disabling gout, came to mark out the year. Yet a seasonal susceptibility to weary gloom never prompted him to abandon what he saw as his public duty. Observers in social and sporting situations, witnessing Derby's enthusiastic immersion in the diversions of the moment at Newmarket or Epsom, were often affronted by his casual behaviour. Banter and teasing wit characterized his ebullient social manner when engaged in pleasure and relaxation. Yet, as Malmesbury witnessed on many occasions, with equal commitment he could immediately turn to political matters and shut all else out of his mind. Derby was very fond of the expression 'One thing at a time'. That his affability was rarely translated into easy familiarity shielded his private seriousness from others. Derby's intimates were few. He remained a man of many acquaintances but few close friends.

If hostile critics confused style for substance in the man, it was equally misleading to suggest that Derby was a frivolous politician without ideas. The enduring foundations of his public doctrine were firmly laid in youth. The high ideals and low pursuits of Foxite Whiggery, inherited from his grandfather, shaped his political views, while the earnest evangelicalism of his mother formed his religious faith. Here lay the core of his private convictions regarding personal responsibility and public obligation. 'A more perfect liturgy was never devised' than that contained in the Anglican Book of Common Prayer, he informed the Lords in 1858.[103] It was 'a work of the utmost importance and of the greatest beauty'. A bounden duty and service to God, the earnest repentance of sins, and charity towards your neighbour were the personal responsibilities he carefully elaborated in his writings on the parables and Christ's miracles. Maternal evangelical instruction gave him a strong sense of the Christian duty to serve others, a moral obligation to be taken all the more seriously because of the privilege into which he had been born. As a husband and father Derby's domestic life was a model of propriety and affection. Derby and Lady Derby's correspondence with their young children reveals those affectionate attachments which comprised their warm and loving home, extended in the 1860s by Derby's delight in the company of his grandchildren.

Marital fidelity and Derby's devotion to his family, which included unfailing financial support for his dissolute younger brother, also extended to care for those who served him and charity for the innocent victims of unforeseen hardship. Upon succeeding to the title in 1851 he paid £300 each year to his local physician Dr Gorst to provide free medical care for the residents on the Knowsley estate. In 1856 he set up an insurance society for those living in the village of Knowsley. At a rural fete, which he hosted at Knowsley in September 1859 for the young children of the Prescot schools, sack races, football, other games, and a brass band concert were organized, during which, the *Liverpool Courier* reported, 'Derby was quite "at home"—never was he seen happier than in the midst of these little children.'[104] In his will he left the equivalent of two months' wages for every year of service to each of the Knowsley Hall servants. The genuine affection with which he was regarded by his tenants and estates workers was strikingly evident to visitors. The recreational rituals which accompanied his passion for battue shooting on the Knowsley estate, bringing together tenants, workers acting as beaters, and other local residents as observers, affirmed a tangible shared sense of immediate community. During the severe suffering of the Cotton Famine he famously organized and generously contributed to private charity for impoverished local cotton operatives and their families. As with the Irish famine in the 1840s, his moderate evangelicalism prescribed private charity, not public finance, as the cure for Lancastrian suffering in the face of Providential chastisement. His generous beneficence towards the needy of his London parish of St James's, Piccadilly, and his anonymous contribution of £4,000 towards the building of an additional church within the parish were also gratefully remembered. The incumbent of St James's, the Revd Kempe, recalled that Derby's address, when laying the foundation stone of the church, was clearly animated by a deep Christian spirit.[105] As a young man Derby had feared lapsing into an idle and selfish life, a temptation he successfully avoided by his commitment to public life and private benevolence. The privileges of aristocratic status, he well understood, entailed important social and moral obligations.

Derby's sense of public duty, shaped by his Whig upbringing and maternal evangelicalism, complemented a secure belief in his own aristocratic status and hereditary authority. An assured self-confidence, noted in the Eton schoolboy, fleshed out the manner of the mature politician. Resolute public self-belief and sure self-regard, which exhibited few symptoms of self-doubt, reinforced perceptions of his brusque arrogance, offhand disdain, and overbearing aloofness. Only in private, most notably during the early months of 1846, were painful personal doubts about his course of action revealed. Throughout his life, despite his famed fondness for pricking the dignity of others, he was acutely sensitive to slurs on his own honour. This strong sense of his own social standing, in turn, enforced an expectation of deference from others, a subservience most naturally found in the congenial company of his tenants and estate workers at Knowsley. But it was an expectation that often brought him into conflict with senior public servants, who regarded their own expertise and status due greater consideration. At the Colonial Office, James Stephen and Henry Taylor never forgave Derby for his disregard of their advice in 1833, a perceived arrogance pithily, if obliquely, condemned by Taylor in his 1836 essay *The Statesman*. Likewise, the long-serving Clerk to the Privy Council Charles Greville found Derby's casual aristocratic hauteur, which contrasted with his informality at Newmarket and Goodwood, deeply offensive. When Derby became prime minister Greville, a grandson of the Duke of Portland, initially chose not to attend Privy Council meetings himself, sending a colleague instead, such was the strong dislike he felt for the premier. On this being pointed out to Derby, the prime minister breezily replied: 'Is that the case? I had not observed it: when I order coals to be put on the fire, I do not notice whether it is John or Thomas who does it.'[106] Such a lofty assumption of dutiful subservience was a trait that often antagonized men sensitive to their own status.

Derby's patrician manner, his sharp intelligence, his rhetorical brilliance, his cutting humour, and his boisterous informality effectively cloaked the deeper recesses of his private motivation. They formed a formidable carapace, covering that ultimately unknowable and complex amalgam, common to dedicated politicians, of pure duty, raw ambition, principled belief, and the need to dominate lesser men, which constitutes the private stimulus to public conduct. It is an inner region into which the biographer treads warily, inferring from fragments of evidence and patterns of behaviour. In Derby's own case, duty, pride, ambition, self-belief, and principle converged on his private conviction that, as a prominent member of the nation's ruling landed elite, his talents must be devoted to the country's interest, just as in scriptural terms he was taught by his mother that of those to whom much was given much would be expected. Duty and ambition merged in the service of those principles he believed necessary to the stability, prosperity, and progress of the nation. They were at the heart of that discrepancy, between self-perception and the judgement of others, which characterized so much of his social interaction. Where opponents saw an arrogant disregard, an inappropriate levity, an overbearing bullying, a cynical opportunism, and a lack of earnestness, Derby held close to his commitment to public service as an aristocratic duty, realized through the imperfect, yet necessary, means of virtuous party association in parliament.

The young Derby's Bowood apprenticeship, under the 3rd Marquess of Lansdowne, strengthened those Whig principles held sacrosanct in the Knowsley household of his childhood. Progress, he learnt, was the defining attribute of modern civilization. Intellectual, moral, and social advancement was the hallmark of the contemporary age. His 'Knowsley Creed' of 1834 gave eloquent expression to the responsibility this placed on the nation's leadership.

> His will be a glorious destiny who knows how to direct and turn into the proper channels the energies of the people, and to conduct with propriety, at this period, the government of this great nation; but if he shall imagine himself capable of stemming and abruptly resisting its force onwards, he will be swept along with the torrent.[107]

For the nation's leaders, true wisdom lay in discerning genuine improvement from mere change, distinguishing real progress from dangerous novelty. In turn, protecting the foundations of civilized society, while accommodating improvement, was the mark of enlightened and responsible leadership. His commitment to what he saw as the necessary conditions for genuine progress was consistent. The essential prerequisites of civil order were the legally endorsed rights of property, parliamentary liberties upheld by the rule of law, and obedience to those scriptural truths safeguarded by the Anglican Church. Public virtue and the moral welfare of the people

stood on these foundations. Disregard for these requirements differentiated reckless change from genuine improvement. Unlike the promiscuous
Disraeli in the 1850s, Derby held firmly to the fundamental truth that implacable hostility to radicalism was a defining element of Conservatism. As
Burke warned, it was a fallacy to believe that those who complained loudest
for the public good were most anxious for its welfare. Equally, resisting
narrow-minded Ultra Tory boorishness he saw as essential to establishing
the Conservatives as credible custodians of the national interest. These
convictions informed his thinking throughout his career. They shaped his
distaste for unreasoning reaction and contempt for reckless radicalism.
They were the basis upon which in 1824 he opposed the confiscation
of the Irish Church's legally designated property. They determined his
staunch opposition in 1834 to Irish appropriation. Thirty-five years later, in
1869, they underpinned his absolute resistance to the disestablishment and
disendowment of the Church of Ireland. As Chief Secretary for Ireland,
between 1830 and 1833, he upheld the rule of law as the only basis upon
which responsible reforms might be safely introduced to Ireland. In doing
so he safeguarded what he saw as the necessary conditions for civilized
progress, maintaining the delicate balance between inherited blessings
and legitimate aspirations. The advance of a dynamic society required
continual and careful adjustment of existing relations, so that the stable
equilibrium of progressive social interests might be preserved.

Derby saw ensuring the stability of a progressive society, founded
upon civil order, parliamentary liberties, and scriptural authority, as the
particular responsibility of his own class as an enlightened aristocracy.
Vivid memories of the violent excesses of the French Revolution and
subsequent political upheavals in France in 1799, 1830, and 1848, as well as
the divisive demands of domestic English and Irish radicalism, underscored
the importance of diligent and disinterested aristocratic service as a public
trust. Upon the British aristocracy lay a historic duty to improve national
institutions for the benefit of society as a whole. Their main public
responsibility was to govern in the interest of all. Their highest calling
was to govern the nation's affairs. Aristocratic privilege imposed a duty
to safeguard the mutual dependence of all classes, Derby declared to an
appreciative audience of agriculturalists in Liverpool in October 1835, and
all classes should 'be convinced of the great truth, that in the concord and
welfare of each class consist the prosperity, the glory, and the happiness
of the whole'.[108] So the natural interdependence of diverse social interests
should be preserved and the intricate weave of the national community
protected.

Derby preferred to portray Britain as a hierarchy of ranked and stable, if also dynamic, social order; a seamless web of integrated, subtly differentiated, status, in which the contentment of each section of society ensured the harmony of the whole nation. On occasion he evoked Adam Smith's depiction of British society as comprising three constituent 'orders', those who lived on rents, those who lived by profit, and those who exchanged their labour for wages. What he consistently repudiated was the populist depiction of 'the people' combating the entrenched selfish and privileged interests of a governing clique. This was a refutation of radical accusations that aristocratic power merely offered a socially exclusive political elite the benefits of private profit and personal gain. Disinterested governance, Derby insisted, was the essential public duty of an aristocracy which had inherited a historical responsibility to direct the nation's affairs. If there was little that was original or distinctive in such views for one of a Whiggish upbringing, these beliefs were especially significant in Derby's case for two reasons: first, they clearly refute the commonly made charge that he was devoid of political ideas; secondly, these beliefs informed his thinking as Conservative leader after 1846. In short, the policies of mid-Victorian Conservatism were shaped by Derby's Whiggish principles.

Derby's fundamental objection to Free Trade, immediately after 1846, was that it threatened to rend the social, political, and colonial fabric of the nation. He saw Protectionism as a broad inclusive system which safeguarded Britain's historic territorial constitution, warding off the narrow sectional demands of populist democracy. Free Trade was a dangerous political and divisive social experiment, not merely an ill-advised economic doctrine. The delicate equilibrium of the national economy, as domestic producers and colonial traders were exposed to unfettered foreign competition, was endangered by the special pleading of urban radicals. Moreover, import tariffs not only protected domestic producers, but also safeguarded Britain's colonial commercial relations. As he advised the Commons in 1843, reform of the Corn Laws was not a narrow fiscal issue. More importantly, it was an imperial question. If, through Free Trade, the reciprocal commercial relations enjoyed by Britain and her colonies were abandoned, then British national influence would be diminished and the nation sink into the condition of a second-rate power. Ultimately, Free Trade risked an elemental collision between estranged sections of British society, precipitating a dangerous slide towards unrestrained democracy. The populist rhetoric of the Anti-Corn Law League suggested that the legitimate aspirations of 'the people' were being suppressed by a self-interested aristocratic elite, a dangerous and divisive denial of those bonds of mutual benefit binding society together as a cohesive whole. Urban Free Trade radicals in Westminster argued that MPs were the instructed delegates of particular social interests, rather than guardians of the nation, discerning the broad national interest through the calm deliberation of parliament as a sovereign assembly.

By 1851, like Disraeli, Derby saw fiscal reform as the practical alternative to import tariffs as a mechanism for maintaining the stability of national interests, given the dominance of Free Trade opinion in parliament. The delicate equilibrium between urban consumers, industrial manufacturers, and agricultural producers might be restored by adjustments to taxation, reinstating harmonious social relations. Similarly, in 1859 and 1867 Derby saw parliamentary Reform as a means of binding emergent wealth, intelligence, and respectability to the historical establishments of the political nation, particularly the institution of parliament. Extending the franchise to responsible adult males able to exercise a judgement on the genuine interests of the nation would bring respectable taxpayers within the pale of the constitution. So might the entitlements of a stable progressive society be advanced, while the status of the aristocracy and the authority of the Established Church were preserved.

From his Bowood education Derby also learnt of the importance of party to parliamentary sovereignty. One of his celebrated bon mots was that the definition of an independent MP was a politician who could not be depended on. As he urged one wayward Conservative backbencher in 1849, 'Don't go against your party unless your conviction is very strong indeed: if there is any doubt in your mind give them the benefit of it; hear what they have to say with an inclination to think them right.'[109] By virtuous men combining in Westminster, fractious evil in society might be checked. An arbitrary prerogative and an unruly populace were the dangers to be resisted. Without cohesive, yet fluid, parties in parliament either the monarch or the populace would rule. It was within Westminster that the nation's government was chosen, the national interest defined, public debate informed, and wise law enacted. Parliament was sovereign. As the 3rd Earl Grey summarized it in 1858, 'our whole system of Parliamentary Government rests ... upon the Ministers of the Crown possessing such authority in parliament as to enable them generally to direct its proceedings'.[110] Therefore, parliamentary parties should be cohesive enough to fulfil the needs of stable ministerial existence without a demeaning reliance on the prerogative. In 1835 a Whig ministry and in 1841 a Conservative government assumed power against the personal wishes of the monarch. Yet, parties should be fluid enough to avoid rendering the choice of government wholly dependent upon the verdict of a general election. Between 1832 and 1868 every parliament during its lifetime removed one, sometimes two, governments from power, changes of ministry not normally being directly aligned with general elections. Eight of the nine governments formed between 1835 and 1868 came to an end as the consequence of a defeat in the House of Commons, the one exception being Palmerston's second ministry, which ended with the premier's death in October 1865. This did not signal party confusion or chaos as is sometimes suggested. Rather, it marked the workings of cohesive, yet fluid, parliamentary parties preserving the autonomy of the Commons, as prescribed by their essential constitutional function, within the context of parliamentary government.

This remained Derby's view of the nature of parliamentary party throughout his life. Voluntary association, not unconditional obedience, held parties together, drawing on family connection, tradition, friendship, and partisan feeling, as well as shared ideas. As he described it in 1854, parliamentary parties were made up of those 'who are in the habit of acting together'.[111] They were associations born of voluntary affiliation. From this understanding sprang important considerations. Mutual trust was essential to party integrity. He believed that party leaders must at times follow, as well as command, their parliamentary rank and file. Consent, not coercion, cemented party attachments. Party policy, he believed, should be that to which the party generally agreed. Party leaders should direct and guide, but not dictate. He always addressed his parliamentary supporters as 'his friends', rather than as enlisted subordinates. Allegiance was solicitously sought, not curtly demanded. As his elder son noted in his journal, 'a party could not be disciplined like a regiment'.[112] Peel's grave crime in 1846, Derby maintained, was the contemptuous disregard Peel showed for his party's sensibilities; hence, when confronted with the decision to suspend the Corn Laws in December 1845, his parting words to Peel's cabinet: 'We cannot do this as gentlemen.'[113] Peel's great error, he advised Lord George Bentinck, 'has always been disregarding the opinion of his party, whenever it did not exactly square with his own; and I am confident that no man these days can hope to lead a party who cannot make up his mind sometimes to follow it'.[114] By arrogantly ignoring the strong convictions of his parliamentary party and conspicuously praising the populist views of radicals such as Cobden in 1846, Peel mistook, Derby declared, 'the brawling torrent of agitation for the still deep current of public opinion'.[115]

This understanding rendered party cohesion crucially dependent upon personal loyalty to the party leader. Derby's own popularity was vital to

Conservative unity after 1846. Repeatedly his personal appeals for party solidarity, when it was threatened by faction or disaffection, were received with enthusiastic acclaim. When in office the party remained firmly united, even when individual ministers, such as Walpole and Henley in 1859 and Cranborne, Carnarvon, and Peel in 1867, resigned from the cabinet. Party solidarity even survived the unexpected contortions of the fast-moving Reform debate during April and May 1867; this was Derby's gift to the dexterous Disraeli. As much as representing particular political principles, Derby's authority rested on his personification of an ideal of public virtue. His commitment to party fidelity, his statesmanlike expressions of public disinterest, his affirmation of the cohesive interdependence of varied social interests, his assertion of the desirability of judicious progress, his advocacy of agricultural improvement under the stewardship of conscientious landlords, and his personal probity embodied an exemplar of aristocratic service which sustained his authority on moral, as well as ideological, grounds. Backbench Conservatives offered Derby their unswerving loyalty. In return, he recognized that effective leadership required shepherding, not driving, his parliamentary support. Proof of his success lay in the fact that the Conservatives, throughout the 1850s and 1860s, were the largest unified body of Commons votes, in contrast to the divisions constantly disrupting Whig, Liberal, and radical party connection. As Palmerston noted in December 1855, acutely aware of the differences fracturing his own side of the Commons, 'when it comes to a division' the Conservatives 'will go together into the same lobby like sheep through a gap'.[116]

Shepherding party support in the Lords after 1846 required much of Derby's tact and skill. The Corn Law crisis destroyed the Conservative majority in the Lords enjoyed by Wellington. In May 1846 ninety-one Conservative peers supported Peel, while 146 Conservative peers followed Derby in opposing Corn Law repeal. Derby's difficulties were increased by the fact that the ecclesiastical Lords (twenty-six archbishops and bishops from the Church of England and four from the Church of Ireland) were often reluctant to follow his lead. In 1850 he estimated that about forty Peelite lay peers held the balance of power.[117] But, by 1858, he had rebuilt a Conservative majority in the Upper House. His effective control of the election of the sixteen Scottish and twenty-eight Irish representative peers, as well as the gradual return of numerous Peelite peers to the Conservative fold, slowly strengthened his hand. One disgruntled Liberal Irish peer complained that the representative peers 'were made in Lord Derby's drawing-room'. Granville protested in 1867 that Derby 'has a power almost superior to the Queen's prerogative of making peers, by practically having the selection of Scotch and Irish representative peers'.[118] The three large-scale Lords votes after 1859, over the Paper Duties Bill in May 1860, the Danish censure motion in July 1864, and the Roman Catholic Oath Bill in June 1865, all resulted in opposition victories over the government. But Derby was careful never to push this power to a point of crisis between the Lords and the Commons. Over the Wensleydale peerage in 1856, the Jewish Disabilities Bill in 1858, and the Paper Duties bill in 1860, he sought compromise, rather than forcing a destructive collision between the two Houses. He recognized that ultimate constitutional sovereignty lay in the Commons. It was in the Commons, not the Lords, that governments were made and unmade. He believed that the Commons was the best *originator* and the Lords the best *reviser* of legislation.[119] But that the British aristocracy was not a closed caste, as in France prior to 1789, legitimized its role in reviewing and improving hasty or overly partisan legislation. This ensured that the mid-Victorian House of Lords was neither merely a compliant or ceremonial attachment to a powerful Commons, nor a reactionary impediment to enlightened progress. Rather, as the most influential politician in the Lords, Derby pursued a constructive engagement with the Commons, as an endorsement of the natural influence of the aristocracy as historical trustees of the national interest.

Between 1846 and 1868 the Conservative party was led by an aristocrat schooled in the beliefs of Bowood Whiggism. As the storm clouds of Reform gathered over Westminster in October 1866, the Queen's secretary, General Charles Grey, applauded Derby's adherence to the Whig principles of his youth, beliefs which underlay Derby's advocacy of Conservative progress, as distinct from those nominal Whigs who had succumbed to radical pressure. 'I have no personal predilection for any party,' Grey observed to Derby. 'My interest in party politics ceased when my father left office in 1834.' But, he continued, 'I still believe in Whig doctrine and principles as I was taught them forty years ago and if I was to choose the side of the House on which I find them best represented, it might very probably be yours.'[120] The policy of moderate reform safeguarding responsible progress, which Derby resolutely upheld when premier after 1846, was the product of his own education. The Conservatives should not attempt to stem the irresistible flow of progress, but safely channel the current so as to preserve the nation's prosperity and stability. He privately referred, more than once, to the conviction which had been forced upon him early in public life, 'that real political power was not to be had in England: at best you could only a little advance or retard the progress of an inevitable movement'. Thus, 'an English minister had more responsibility, more labour, and less authority, than the ruler of any people on earth'.[121] In this sense, the 1867 Reform Act was the last great Whig measure of the nineteenth century. Respectable adult males, defined in terms of their property status, were brought within the political nation. As a minister in Lord Grey's government in 1832, Derby had been a powerful advocate of the English Reform Bill. Ten years later, as a Conservative cabinet member under Peel, he defended the 1832 Reform Act on the principle that 'the vote was not an inherent right, but a privilege to be granted to such a class of the community as from their intelligence, station and education might be capable of exercising that privilege wisely and usefully for the benefit of the whole nation'.[122] In 1867 this informed his advocacy of further parliamentary Reform as a lasting settlement of the nation's constitutional affairs. So the advancement of wealth and intelligence was to be reconciled with the safeguarding of the historic institution of parliament as the nation's sovereign assembly.

It was Derby, not Disraeli, who 'educated' the mid-Victorian Conservative party. It was Derby who ensured that the party, after 1846, did not lapse into an atavistic rump of rural protest. He saved it from becoming mired in regretful nostalgia. After 1850 he supported fiscal reform as a replacement for the reimposition of import tariffs, while restraining popular Protectionist ardour and postponing the formal abandonment of Protection until the general election of July 1852. So he skilfully discarded a lost parliamentary cause, while not alienating his Commons rank and file. He avoided inflaming sectarian differences as the basis of party distinctions. The visceral anti-Catholicism of Tory backbenchers was held in check. He pursued a cautious placatory foreign policy. Russell's blustering, Palmerston's bravado, and radical moralizing were rejected, as he sought to work with the Continental Powers of Russia, Austria, Prussia, and France. So might peace be preserved within the framework of the Concert of Europe. He discouraged aggressive colonial expansion. Trade, not territory, he believed, underpinned Britain's international pre-eminence, protected by the shield of her naval supremacy. Commerce secured Britain's position as a world power, not additional colonial possessions involving extra expense and unnecessary political entanglements. Gradually, but surely, this rehabilitated the Conservatives as a party of moderate government delivering safe progress.

So Derby's Whiggish convictions as Conservative leader, when in office, shaped the broad pattern of mid-Victorian politics. Unlike much of continental Europe, Britain did not possess an embittered party of strong reactionary sentiment. Instead, Victorian politics became a contest between major parties which, albeit to differing degrees, acknowledged the benefits of sustained progress. Compared to continental European politics, where the polarities of monarchy, republicanism, militarism, and socialism stretched political conflict across a far broader ideological spectrum, the mainstream of Victorian politics in Britain, reflected in the social homogeneity of the party leaderships, appeared remarkable for its consensus, defining far narrower parameters of debate. Aristocrats such as Derby, Malmesbury, Palmerston, Russell, Clarendon, Granville, and Hartington, alongside middle-class recruits such as Disraeli and Gladstone, disputed the precise nature of enlightened reform. But none contested the fundamental reality of progressive advancement. Clashes occurred over the pace, not the ultimate desirability, of constructive change. As *The Times* observed in 1851, as Derby slowly weaned the Conservative party from Protectionism: 'No party can now disclaim resolutions of progress; the question is scarcely one of route—only of speed.'[123]

Prior to the 1820s the term 'reform' had been associated with the violent revolutionary excesses of France after 1789. By the 1830s young Whigs, such as Derby, aided by their reading of Burke, had adapted the term, associating it with prudent pragmatic adjustment, rather than dangerous radical change. Whiggish reform promised moral, economic, and political improvement, rather than reckless innovation. By the 1850s Derby was accommodating the Conservative party to careful reform, so helping to establish a shared wish for responsible improvement—meaning the judicious adjustment of a dynamic civil society to economic and social progress—as the inclusive defining characteristic of mid-Victorian political culture. This 'tacit unanimity', Lord Robert Cecil observed in 1858 with characteristic acerbity, 'laid aside the ingenious network of first principles which the industry of three centuries of theorists had woven'.[124] Derby's belief in sustained progress, his reconciliation of the Conservative party to continued improvement, and his commitment to responsible reform played a crucial part in shaping the broadly liberal character of the mid-Victorian State.

In opposition Derby steadily pursued a strategy of 'masterly inactivity' as the complement to moderate progressivism when in office. Opposition quiescence was a shrewd course for a united minority party facing a fractious majority in the Commons. It was not, as Liberal critics claimed, an involuntary confession of doctrinal bankruptcy. Rather, it was a conscious strategy intended to cleave Derby's opponents along the natural grain of Peelite, Whig, Liberal, and radical differences. By refraining from initiatives, providing his opponents with a ready sense of collective purpose, Derby anticipated that divisions among non-Conservatives would inevitably be brought to the fore. It was no accident that in 1851, 1852, 1855, 1858, and 1866 Whig–Liberal governments or coalitions were forced out of office by internal disputes. Radical initiatives in 1855 and 1858 ejected Whigs and Liberals from power. It was a radical attack in March 1857 that prompted Palmerston to call a general election. In 1851, 1852, and 1866 the revolt of moderate Liberals ended Russell's premierships. On each occasion the Conservatives happily reaped the harvest of their opponents' discord. Powerful strains were placed on Conservative unity by opposition quiescence. In 1853, 1856, and 1863 Conservative morale collapsed, as doing little allowed internal suspicion and acrimony to fester. Yet, after each period of opposition malaise, Derby's vigorous reassertion of his own authority galvanized the Conservatives' collective will, enabling them to exploit their opponents' disarray.

The purpose of 'killing with kindness' while in opposition, or as Derby termed it in 1853 and 1860 'armed neutrality', was to encourage centrist realignment. Political parties in Britain recover power by reclaiming the middle ground. Surrender to doctrinaire extremists, whatever the temptations of consolidating core support, condemns them to impotent exclusion. Guided by his centrist instincts, Derby recognized this necessity. While aware of the need to shepherd, not drive or defy, his parliamentary support, he also saw the need to draw together moderate opinion within Westminster. So was doctrinaire Protectionism tempered, bigoted anti-Catholicism checked, and dogmatic objection to parliamentary Reform curbed. Regaining power required leadership that, while respecting back-bench sensibilities, allowed the party to assimilate moderate opinion. 'Masterly inactivity' in opposition, combined with moderate progressivism when in office, enabled Derby to reclaim the middle ground, to rein in his extreme supporters, and to encourage centrist realignment.

Between 1846 and 1851 Derby hoped to reunite Peelites and Conservatives. A total of seventy, mostly backbench, Peelite MPs eventually returned to the Conservative fold. This included a large number of back-bench Peelites, fifty-nine MPs in all, who rejoined the Conservatives after December 1852, once Protectionism had been abandoned. Yet a minority of leading Peelites, Peel himself, Herbert, Cardwell, and particularly Graham, proved irreconcilable. By 1851 Derby concluded that rapprochement with these leading Peelites was impossible. Despite his agreement with Derby over foreign policy, Aberdeen's flirtations during 1850 and 1851 lacked serious strategic purpose, given Graham's hostility to Conservative reunion. This left a distressed Gladstone isolated and mistrusted. A minority of thirty-two Peelite MPs, mostly former prominent office holders under Peel, eventually joined the Liberals by 1859. Yet the great majority of backbench Peelites, it is important to remember, did not travel the high road to Victorian Liberalism, but rather chose quietly to rejoin the Conservatives under Derby.

The ultimate party allegiance of those surviving 'Dilly' MPs of the 1830s, who were still in parliament during the 1850s, affirmed this trend. By 1846 there were sixteen former Dilly MPs in the Commons; fourteen were Conservatives and two were Liberals. Of the Conservatives, eleven voted with Peel on Corn Law repeal and three became Protectionists. But after 1850 six former Dilly Peelites rejoined the Conservatives under Derby: William Copeland, Thomas Greene, John Johnstone, Sir John Johnstone, Sir James Tennent, and Thomas Whitmore. Only two of their number did not return to the Conservatives: Graham, who aligned himself with Russell, and George Harcourt, who became a Palmerstonian Liberal. The three remaining former Dilly Peelites were no longer in the Commons after 1850. Our conventional perspective of mid-Victorian politics emphasizes the transition from Peelite Conservatism to Gladstonian Liberalism as the salient route through the complex landscape of the 1850s and 1860s. But the weight of historical scholarship privileging Gladstone's often idiosyncratic course cannot stand proxy for the passage of other MPs. The twisting trail that finally led to Gladstonian Liberalism after 1868 was a path the great majority of Peelites elected not to take. For most, by the end of the 1850s, the comfort of Derby's moderate Conservatism provided a far more welcoming destination.

After 1851 Derby increasingly looked to merger with those moderate Liberals and Whigs unsettled by their radical associates. He entertained the prospect of a natural alliance between Whigs and Conservatives. Such 'real Conservatives', as he described them, shared a commitment to those conditions necessary to safe progress, threatened by divisive radicalism, Russellite rectitude, and Peelite populism. The future merger of landed Whigs and moderate Conservatives, first proposed by Derby in 1848, came to underlie his long-term expectation of party realignment as an alliance based upon the protection of property, the defence of parliamentary sovereignty, and the safeguarding of Protestant scriptural authority. This elusive prospect hovered before his eyes throughout the 1850s and 1860s. It assumed the form, in 1860, of a covert 'truce of parties' established with Palmerston, to protect the premier from his more radical colleagues. As a result, in 50 per cent of whipped Commons divisions in 1860, Conservatives and moderate Liberals combined against a minority of radical votes. Only a bare 5 per cent of whipped divisions followed a straight two-party vote, with Conservatives facing off against the Liberals.[125] This was Derby's contribution to mid-Victorian equipoise.

In 1866, as parliamentary Reform scattered Whigs, Liberals, and radicals, centrist fusion seemed on the cards. But his resignation as Conservative leader, which the Adullamites audaciously demanded as the price of merger, was a sacrifice Derby refused to countenance. The moment passed. In 1868 Gladstone brought together the broken shards of a Liberal party shattered by Reform with the emotive cry of Irish disestablishment. Not until 1886, in a crisis precipitated by Gladstone's Home Rule crusade, did the reconfiguration of parties long anticipated by Derby eventually occur. The migration of landed Liberal Unionists under Lord Hartington over to the Conservative party, consolidated during the 1890s, finally realized that party realignment foreseen by Derby thirty years before. As a result, the Conservatives became the most successful party in modern British politics. For the next 100 years the Conservative and Unionist party, either alone or in coalition, formed the natural party of government.

How does the rehabilitation of Derby alter our broader view of Victorian politics, a perspective from which he has been conventionally airbrushed out? It is changed in significant ways. Most strikingly, it reveals a Conservative tradition of governance subsequently overlain by later celebrations of Disraeli, Churchill, and Thatcher. Derby subscribed to the core principles of Conservative thinking during the nineteenth and twentieth centuries. He believed that there existed limits to human rationality, defined by the reality of a higher Providential wisdom. This was the basis for his quip that, while Palmerston belonged to the pre-moral, he belonged to the pre-scientific school. The aspirations of man were subject to the superior purposes of God. He was deeply sceptical of speculative theory, especially when divorced from historical experience. He held a deep attachment to established customs and institutions, which informed his aversion to sudden and violent change. He saw society as a natural organic whole, not as a mere aggregate of individual experience, but as a rich seamless weave of varied complementary interests, in which the community comprised far more than merely the sum of discrete social concerns. Yet, while remaining faithful to these shared presuppositions, successive generations of Conservatives have defined their particular policies and specific aims in a variety of ways. In the 1870s Disraeli abandoned Derby's placatory foreign policy and aversion to colonial expansion by taking up a robust patriotic and imperialist rhetoric celebrating British civilization as the ornament and honour of the world; while, a century later, Margaret Thatcher stretched Conservative belief in the organic nature of society to its limits by her forceful advocacy of free market economics. In their different ways, both Disraeli and Thatcher became powerful symbols of distinctive strands in Conservative thinking.

Neglect of Derby, however, has obscured an alternative Conservative tradition of governance which, nonetheless, remains an important part of the party's history. This was a quieter, more pious tradition, whose echoes were later to resonate in the conciliatory and consensual rhetoric of Stanley Baldwin, another astute, popular, and long-serving, though easily disregarded, Conservative leader. In a period of significant change, Baldwin's emollient public language also defined the political middle ground by appealing across social distinctions with a vision of ordered freedom embedded in the professed English native genius for stable progress. In a speech at the Royal Albert Hall in 1924 Baldwin added the term 'One Nation' Conservatism to the party lexicon. Just as Derby's depiction, during the 1850s and 1860s, of a stable society of interdependent interests sought to soothe the bitter political and religious antagonisms of the 1830s and 1840s, so Baldwin's language, during the inter-war years, sought to apply a salve to the clash between capital and labour.

Through Baldwin a Derbyite tradition of Conservative governance was passed on to post-war frontbenchers such as R. A. B. Butler, an 'appeaser' in the 1930s, whose brand of caring Conservatism informed the Industrial Charter of 1947 and the consensual Butskellism of the 1950s. Prior to becoming party leader and prime minister in 1957, Harold Macmillan, author of the Knowsleyite-entitled publication *The Middle Way* in 1938, held up the alliance between Liberal Unionists and Conservatives of 1886 as a model for a party looking to reject socialism but embrace progress. Yet Macmillan's resignation as premier in 1963 heralded a significant shift away from the patrician, progressive, and socially conciliatory Conservatism embodied by Derby a century earlier. The election of Edward Heath as Conservative leader in 1965 marked the trend, affirmed by the emergence of Margaret Thatcher as his successor in 1975. By the early 1980s notions of pragmatic consensus proved an inadequate bulwark for ministerial 'wets', such as Jim Prior, William Whitelaw, Peter Walker, Christopher Soames, Mark Carlisle, and Ian Gilmour, against the vigorous astringency of Thatcherism. So a venerable Derbyite tradition of moderate gentlemanly Conservatism succumbed to monetarist theory and radical-rightist reform. Just as mid-Victorian Liberals and radicals contemptuously caricatured

Derbyite Conservatism as vacillating weakness, so Thatcherites scornfully dismissed their centrist colleagues as feeble and spineless.

For Derby, like Baldwin, Macmillan, and Butler, authentic Conservatism possessed an innate wariness of strident jingoism, an allergic sensitivity to divisive ideology, and an overriding sense that, above all, the nation wished to be at ease with measured progress. A cautious scepticism pointed to the illusory nature of rational panaceas for society's ills. History and human nature revealed the practical limits of political agency and warned of the unforeseen consequences of utopian aspirations. The presence of a higher Providential purpose, the limits of human understanding, the flawed intricacy of human nature, the subtle complexity of social needs, the impact of contingency on rational design, and the weight of historical experience on perception of the future encouraged humility in the exercise of political power. It shaped a pragmatic tradition of Conservative governance committed to what was possible. Doctrinaire inflexibility, in defiance of pragmatic moderation, was a recipe for disillusion and disappointment. The sovereignty of parliament, the rule of law, and the essential scriptural truths of Christianity were the guides to responsible statesmanship. This, Derby believed, was what the respectable members of the political nation, cognizant of both their duties and their privileges, desired.

The intelligent, amiable, horse-loving Conservatism of Derby, shaped by subtle scepticism rather than coarse prejudice, enjoyed its dynastic afterglow in the person of his great-grandson Oliver Stanley, the second son of Freddy's heir, Eddy Stanley (17th Earl of Derby). After Edwardian Eton, Oxford, and military service in the First World War (winning the Military Cross and the Croix de Guerre), as a cabinet minister under Ramsay MacDonald, Stanley Baldwin, Neville Chamberlain, and Winston Churchill, Oliver Stanley, possessed of his great-grandfather's sharp intellect and speaking skills, was touted as a future prime minister. In the 1920s he was part of the youthful, pious, and progressive Conservative backbench ginger group, which also included Macmillan, dubbed the YMCA. Only a nervous collapse in 1935 temporarily halted his charmed rise. His premature death in 1950, however, abruptly ended the family presence in front-line Conservative politics. Yet through Derby, Baldwin, Macmillan, Butler, and Oliver Stanley a tradition of Conservative governance was sustained that sought responsible progress combined with judicious reform, reconciling the inherited blessings of the nation's venerated past with the emergent demands of dynamic social interests.

In upholding this tradition, despite his combative debating style, Derby ultimately sought, whenever possible, consensual conciliation, rather than adversarial conflict, as the desirable basis for resolving political differences. When *The Times* alighted on the exhilaration of contest as an obvious key to his temperament, that facet of his personality most immediately apparent to others, it glossed over a deeper disposition for reconciliation. This was a discrepancy between manner and motive which led some to think he engaged in politics as a frivolous diversion, that his involvement in political dispute lacked seriousness. In truth, a wish to resolve, not aggravate, public antagonisms more often shaped his fundamental purposes. It underlay his lifelong allegiance to what he saw as the political centre, as encapsulated in the Knowsley Creed. It sustained his aversion for radical or reactionary extremism. It informed his repudiation of that populist radical rhetoric which portrayed 'the people' in conflict with the aristocracy. When, for example, remedying the chemical blight of industrial pollution in the immediate vicinity of Knowsley, he assiduously worked with, rather than against, the owners of alkali works in St Helens and Widnes to improve the Lancashire environment. A bitter confrontation between landowners and industrialists within his local community was a danger to be strenuously avoided. By turning to fiscal reform in 1850–1, he hoped to mediate the conflict between outraged Protectionists and recent converts to Free Trade, in order to prevent a collision between rural and urban communities deeply divided over import tariffs. By seeking a defensible extension of the suffrage in 1867, he hoped to secure a lasting settlement of parliamentary Reform, when radical agitation threatened to pit boroughs against counties and urban voters against rural electorates. Over the Wensleydale peerage in 1856, the Jewish disabilities and the church rates questions in 1858, as well as the crisis over paper duties in 1860, he staved off a constitutional confrontation between the Commons and the Lords by seeking compromise, preserving the dignity of both Houses. Likewise, in foreign policy he sought to work with the Continental Powers, within the framework of the Concert of Europe, rather than needlessly provoking quarrels with France, Prussia, Russia, and Austria by meddlesome diplomatic intervention. Negotiated compromise between moderate men, he believed, was preferable to disruptive conflict, whose uncertain outcomes and divisive legacies were deeply damaging.

All this was the benign perspective, from the Knowsley estate, of an aristocratic Lancashire magnate secure in his status and authority, with an annual income of approximately £110,000. Of all Britain's prime ministers only Lord Rosebery, after his marriage to a Rothschild, enjoyed a larger personal income. The temperamental contrast with men who had to make their own way in the world was striking. Disraeli, for example, impelled by a sense of Byronic destiny and battling what he saw as the hostility of a turbulent world, was forced to achieve prominence by subversion and attack. Conflict was Disraeli's *métier*. He sought to savage, not to soothe. 'My life has been passed in constant combat,' he observed with characteristic self-dramatization in 1858.[126] Early social notoriety was secured by his scandalous novels, with which he hoped to corrupt public taste. Political eminence was achieved by his devastating sarcasm, targeted at the integrity of Peel. As Derby reminded Queen Victoria in 1851, self-made men often had to say and do things that those whose place in the world was secure did not. For Derby authority and responsibility were not rare prizes to be fiercely fought for, but inherited duties to be diligently assumed. They comprised a historic trusteeship. Conciliation and compromise were not symptoms of weakness or failure. Rather, they were the natural expression of an instinctive commitment to stable progress and social harmony, in which the judicious resolution of differences, not antagonistic struggle, lay at the heart of responsible politics. Derby's patrician beliefs proved an important aspect of the survival of aristocratic authority and influence during the mid-Victorian period.

Appreciation of Derby's Bowood apprenticeship helps to delineate those varied strands of Whiggism comprising the opposition of the 1820s. Family tradition, aristocratic status, intellectual interest, and literary taste, shaped by a classical education providing a broadness of view necessary to enlightened statesmanship, affirmed the young Derby's Whig allegiance. The supremacy of parliament, safeguarded by virtuous party connection and mediating popular demands through the deliberation of Westminster, protecting a stable hierarchical society, legal liberties, and property rights, underpinned his public doctrine. But from Lansdowne the young Derby also acquired a familiarity with political economy. Lansdowne Whigs, as distinct from the habitués of Holland House, courted liberal Tories and provided a progressive leaven in Canning's coalition ministry of 1827. Derby's maternal evangelicalism reinforced his belief in the importance of individual diligence and exertion in the cause of economic and moral self-improvement, establishing points of sympathy with liberal Tory ministers such as Huskisson. Thus Derby supported Canning's careful liberalization of the Corn Laws by the introduction of a sliding scale of import duty. But, like Canning and Huskisson, the young Derby also retained a belief in the desirability of import tariffs, suitably amended, as a means of regulating the domestic economy, ensuring the balanced integration of social interests, and protecting the maritime prosperity of Britain's colonial relations. When Peel proposed the abandonment of corn duties in 1846 it was to the authority of Canning and Huskisson that Derby appealed. After Canning's premature death, which dashed the prospects of a merger between liberal Tories and moderate Whigs, Derby, formerly Lansdowne's protégé, looked, in 1828, to become Canning's self-appointed political executor. Catholic emancipation, moderate parliamentary Reform, and modification of the Corn Laws defined his centrist agenda. Peel's conversion to Catholic Emancipation in 1829 and Wellington's obstruction of Reform in 1830, however, disrupted such hopes.

As an influential member of Lord Grey's reforming ministry Derby proved a powerful advocate for the judicious extension of the parliamentary suffrage. He devised a national scheme of education for Ireland providing common religious instruction for Protestant and Catholic children and pushed through the abolition of slavery within the British Empire. All this was consistent with his Bowood education and Canning's legacy. But the youthful Derby's commitment to the rule of law and the sanctity of property, evident in his various coercive measures for Ireland, exposed serious strains within early nineteenth-century Whiggism, which came increasingly to the fore once parliamentary Reform had been secured in 1832. Derby became estranged from more advanced cabinet colleagues, such as Russell and Althorp, as violent public disorder, populist radical agitation, and vehement sectarian attack on the Established Church in Ireland stripped his Whiggism down to its prescriptive essentials.

After 1833 Irish Church reform, church rates, and relief for Dissenters exposed those differences among Whigs and Reformers formerly masked by parliamentary Reform. These disagreements gave substance to Derby's 'visions of the helm'. The latitudinarian anticlericalism of Russell, Duncannon, and Morpeth collided with Derby's commitment to the Church Establishment. Derby and Graham's moderate evangelicalism distanced them from Russell's Liberal Anglicanism and his interventionist centralizing instincts over social and economic issues. Yet, in 1835, Russell successfully took up Irish appropriation, which had previously divided Whigs and Reformers in 1833 and 1834, to rally a unified opposition, while dampening down radical initiatives. This, as Russell anticipated, forced Derby and Graham towards Peel's Conservatives.

Restoring Derby's pivotal role in the climactic events of 1834–6 illuminates Peel and Russell's actions in critical ways. Derby hoped to hold the ring against Ultra Tory and radical extremes and resurrect the Canningite project. His ambition was the crucial context for Peel and Russell's calculations. It was around Derby that Peel and Russell manoeuvred. Peel, in his Tamworth Manifesto, and Russell, in the Lichfield House Compact, sought to forestall Derby's triumph as the champion of moderate progress. The attraction of Derby's centrist gospel, the Knowsley Creed, enunciated at Glasgow in December 1834, was endorsed by William IV, lords Grey and Melbourne, former Canningites such as Lord George Bentinck, and liberal Conservatives. Yet, by March 1835, Peel's pre-emptive Manifesto and Russell's tactical skill had decisively undercut Derby's prospects. Peel and Russell avoided becoming hostages to their extreme supporters, so eroding the Knowsleyite centre ground. Denied any distinctive standing, Derby was forced to choose sides. Thereafter, his benign hierarchical conception of society was assailed by the populist rhetoric employed by the Chartists and the Anti-Corn Law League, depicting a fundamental conflict between 'the people' and a privileged elite. When, in 1846, Derby saw Peel's dangerous susceptibility to populism leading him towards Corn Law repeal, he feared an impending forlorn struggle between aristocracy and democracy, threatening to subvert Britain's parliamentary constitution.

Moreover, the political polarization of the late 1830s and 1840s mirrored escalating religious contention. Just as Derby's Knowsley Creed defined the political middle ground, appealing to moderate men and seeking to marginalize extreme radical and Tory partisans, so it advocated a Broad Church Anglicanism, spurning Tractarian ritualism and extreme evangelicalism. He saw a *via media* rooted in the Anglican liturgy. 'The wisdom of the Church of England', as described in the preface of the Book of Common Prayer, lay in keeping the mean between extremes and of avoiding 'too much stiffness in refusing, and … too much easiness in admitting any variation from it'. But the 1830s saw the moderate Anglican community beset by powerful antagonistic religious parties. Sectarian dispute permeated political asperities. In 1835 Graham observed that the infusion of religious enmity into political differences had created a caustic compound that 'has never failed to produce the bitterest potion'.[127] So Derby's moderate Anglicanism, as a facet of his political centrism, became a victim of those centrifugal forces pulling apart religious consensus. Recalling the vehemence of parliamentary politics after 1835, one MP remembered it as a period of 'inveterate squabbling', bringing a 'moral winter of hatred, malice, and all uncharitableness … among political parties'.[128] This acrimonious atmosphere smothered Stanley's centrism, his frustrated hopes bearing the seed of subsequent dejection.

By 1837 a humbled Derby was accommodating himself to a subordinate role within Peelite Conservatism. Russellite Whigs, he declared, had forsaken their historic commitment to political moderation, under the subversive pressure of Irish and English radicalism. The Whigs, he contended, kept their name while abandoning their principles. He, on the other hand, had kept his principles and was indifferent to the name. In the face of demoralizing defeat he clutched the comforting blanket of his integrity ever closer. But his failure should not obscure the genuine fluidity of party connection prevailing within Westminster during late 1834 and early 1835. Nor did Derby forget the painful lesson of that failure. Never again would he look to assume power until the divisions of his opponents were clearly affirmed. Never again would he allow the alluring prospect of power to entice him into a premature bid for office. 'It is a bungling fisherman who strikes at the first nibble,' he commented in 1851. 'I shall wait until my fish has gorged his bait, and then I am sure to land him.'[129]

Derby's failure within Westminster in 1835, as his 'visions of the helm' evaporated, was decisively affirmed electorally, as constituency politics, prompted by the mechanics of voter registration introduced by the 1832 Reform Act, became increasingly partisan. Conservative and Reform associations in the constituencies brought a new partisan edge to local party voting in 1835 and 1837, as electoral lists became fiercely contested. This highlighted the vulnerability of the Derby Dilly as a purely Westminster phenomenon. The Dilly remained a parliamentary cadre without an organizational presence in the constituencies. Reflecting his Bowood education, Derby saw party as a desirable feature of parliamentary politics, representing the virtuous association of like-thinking peers and MPs. But he regarded constituency politics as primarily a function of legitimate local influence, responsibly exercised by prominent property owners within their community. In June 1835 he publicly opposed the formation of the North Lancashire Conservative Association, not because he disagreed with the Association's political views, but because the formation of such bodies must inevitably intensify partisan feeling and deeply divide local communities. Conservative constituency activism would merely stimulate more extreme radical activity. He maintained a consistent interest in patronage matters as Conservative leader, particularly in cases where it affected the local electoral fortunes of Conservative candidates. What, throughout his life, he disparaged was the efforts of extra-parliamentary organizations to determine debate in Westminster.

Derby saw parliament as a sovereign assembly. He firmly resisted the claims of the Anti-Corn Law League, the Chartists, Protestant associations, or Protectionist societies to dictate the deliberations of parliament. As he commented to the Duke of Newcastle in April 1849: 'I look on principle with great jealousy at the formation of clubs and associations of any sort, for the purposes of checking and influencing the executive government.'¹³⁰ It was within Westminster, he insisted, that the authentic national interest was defined. Parliament, in particular the Commons, chose the government. It was the approval of the Commons that kept ministers in office. Elections, on the other hand, were the expression of traditional local allegiances. As he reminded the Commons in February 1841, 'it was known that when any man attempted to estimate the probable result of a county election, it was ascertained by calculating the number of great landed proprietors in the county, and weighing the number of occupiers under them'. It 'was a matter of pride and satisfaction to the landlords of England that their tenants usually felt a desire to comply with their landlords' wishes', although he 'condemned the exorbitant or undue exercise of the power'.¹³¹ Again, this was the perspective of a Lancashire magnate, whose landed status exercised an almost feudal authority within his county. It was a perspective, however, which condemned Dilly MPs to rejection en masse in the general election of 1837, as they found themselves exposed to the marshalled hostility of local Conservative and Reform associations.

As Colonial Secretary between 1841 and 1845, Derby sought to strengthen Britain's economic ties with her existing overseas possessions and to resist further territorial expansion. He saw preferential tariffs as crucial to the safeguarding of harmonious colonial relations. The adjustment of Canadian corn duties was a necessary enhancement of the reciprocal commercial advantages enjoyed by Britain and her colonies. Yet over enlargement he was repeatedly forced to give way to local political, strategic, religious, and commercial pressures, often intensified by indigenous resistance along the contested frontiers of colonial control in China, India, and South Africa. His dislike of the additional expense and diplomatic difficulties accompanying territorial expansion could not stem the local impetus to extending colonial boundaries. Loyal support for Britain's representatives overseas required his reluctant acquiescence. The acquisition of Hong Kong and Natal occurred despite the intentions of the Colonial Office. He referred to the colonies and spoke of the Empire. What he never invoked was imperialism as an active spirit of expansion, giving a beneficial momentum to colonial enlargement.

For Derby and most of his contemporaries during the 1840s, imperialism was an exotic, negative, un-English, Continental term evoking the vainglorious ambitions of Napoleon Bonaparte or the autocratic repression of Russia. During the 1850s imperialism became associated with the militaristic, decadent, and ostentatious ambitions of Napoleon III and despotic, aggressive Russian expansionism. Not until the 1870s, under the inspiration of Disraeli, did imperialism begin to acquire a more favourable, less alien, flavour, describing the moral obligation of British civilization towards conquered, less advanced peoples around the world. For Derby, in the 1840s, the colonies comprised an overseas network of increasingly federated, mutually sustaining possessions free of slavery, supporting Britain's commercial pre-eminence, behind the shield of her naval supremacy, based upon trade not territory. This was a conception of empire, though secured by conquest and force of arms, seen as compatible with the prosperity and domestic liberties of British parliamentary government. So Derby's period as Colonial Secretary from 1841 to 1845 revealed those ambiguities of meaning and aspiration existing at the heart of the mid-Victorian Empire.

It is intriguing to speculate how the party politics of the 1840s and 1850s would have been changed if Derby had remained in the Commons after 1845. Undoubtedly, as Gladstone later observed, they would have been significantly different. Derby's presence as an MP, directly engaged in Commons debate, would have substantially altered the dynamics of Conservative relations, given the paucity of effective talent and the surfeit of aggrieved sentiment suffusing Protectionist ranks. As it was, prompted by his personal sense of marginalization, he migrated to the Lords on the eve of the Corn Law crisis and found himself observing the Conservative schism at one remove from the cockpit of Commons acrimony. As he struggled with the obligations of party loyalty, his wish to guide, rather than drive, backbench feeling, and his objections to Peel's high-handedness, an anguished Derby sought to preserve Conservative unity during the early months of 1846. He preferred careful modification, rather than the abrupt abandonment of non-colonial import tariffs. Yet the vehemence of the schism in the Commons exposed the painful contradictions of measured dissent in the cause of party loyalty. It was with reluctance that he became the leader of the Conservative majority enraged by Peel's renunciation of Protection.

That, as Conservative leader and later as prime minister, Derby directed his party colleagues from the Upper House complicated the often fraught issue of the Commons leadership. Both Bentinck and Disraeli after 1846 strained at the imposition of Derby's authority from the Lords. As Jolliffe remarked in 1857, when the party leader sits in the Lords command of the Commons is inevitably contentious. While premier in the Lords from 1852 to 1855, Aberdeen was dogged by the Commons rivalry between Palmerston and Russell. Likewise, throughout the 1850s and 1860s, deep-rooted backbench distrust of Disraeli constantly disturbed Conservative unity.

Dissuading Disraeli from seeking unacceptable parliamentary allies, and on other occasions bolstering Disraeli's precarious authority, demanded much of Derby's tact. Yet, Derby's aloofness from the Commons also shielded his own authority from those natural frustrations and simmering resentments aroused by his opposition strategy of vigilant inactivity. Disraeli's unpopularity often served as a convenient lightning rod for flashes of backbench anger, insulating Derby from dangerous discharges of discontent.

That, from 1846 to 1868, the Conservatives were led by a landed aristocrat schooled in moderate Whiggism is crucial to understanding both the successes and the failures of the mid-Victorian party. Derby ensured they did not become the beleaguered refuge of rural reaction, recoiling from the brashness of the modern age. He rehabilitated the parliamentary party as credible custodians of measured progress. So the Knowsley Creed was effectively played out in the altered circumstances of the 1850s and 1860s. By judicious change, improving the existing system, domestic institutions might be adapted to those modified purposes required by continuing progress. This was close to fulfilling Disraeli's epigram that 'sound Conservative government' consisted of 'Tory men and Whig measures'. As, following the demise of Chartism in 1848, the acceptance of Free Trade as a fiscal orthodoxy, and the easing of social tensions by economic prosperity, the gradual domestication of radical demands within Westminster took hold, so the divisive populist antagonisms of the 1830s and 1840s abated. This gave Derby's advocacy of moderate Conservative progress renewed cogency. His abolition of the property qualification for MPs (a Chartist cry of the 1840s), his argument for prudent parliamentary Reform, and his evoking of a cohesive social order affirming the mutual reliance of respectable social interests presented Conservative principles aligned with what he saw as the nation's defining aspirations. Sectarian animosities were tempered, as he resisted establishing religious differences as the basis of party distinctions.

As, by the early 1850s, religious asperities softened, so Derby's advocacy of scriptural consensus acquired new force. His belief in Broad Church Anglicanism, after the bitter dissensions of the 1830s and 1840s, came to mirror the less fraught religious temper of the 1850s and early 1860s. While defending the rule of law and the Established Church, he supported the extension of civil liberties to non-Anglicans. He never regretted his vote for Catholic Emancipation in 1829. His objections to Catholic ultramontanism were to the institutional pretensions of Rome, not to the inherent disloyalty of the Queen's Catholic subjects. After 1846 this distinguished his views from the harsh Protestant bigotry of Ultra Tories such as Charles Newdegate and William Beresford. In November 1850 he passively watched Russell's self-inflicted agonies over the papal aggression issue. A year later he advised Conservatives to 'avoid irritating language to the Roman Catholic *laity* and abuse of their religion', while denouncing 'the political power of the priesthood'.[132] As premier in 1858 he oversaw the removal of Jewish political disabilities and supported a compromise settlement of the long-contested church rates question. In an age of religious revival he saw personal faith as too important to be prominent in defining political feeling. This was a view shared by Palmerston. What mattered was that personal faith was consistent with obedience to scriptural truth, the rule of law, and recognition of the authority of parliament. Derby's fear in old age, after 1865, was that inflamed religious passions were again inciting civil disorder and subverting that legal authority and the dominion of parliament which sustained the equilibrium of national stability. In Ireland the toxic blend of ultramontane Catholicism and radical nationalism was undermining the Union. His strong distaste for the moral fervour of Gladstone's impassioned populist campaigns, all 'balderdash and braggadocio',[133] sprang from his profound consternation at religious ardour infusing political feeling.

Derby also committed the mid-Victorian Conservative party to a cautious placatory foreign policy, which rejected Palmerstonian bluster and ineffectual Russellite posturing. This was not, as caricatured by Liberal opponents, weak vacillation. Rather, it was a deliberate shunning of that Liberal 'meddle and muddle' which involved Britain in destabilizing Continental quarrels. Britain's real strength, he maintained, lay in her global maritime Empire outside Europe, not as a diplomatic bit player in the vexatious disputes of the Continental Powers. Britain was a great naval power; her relatively limited military strength was a constraint on her Continental influence. Conciliatory negotiation, not aggressive sabre-rattling, was seen by Derby and his foreign secretaries (his elder son Lord Stanley and the much-maligned Malmesbury) as the only responsible means of ensuring European peace and preserving cordial diplomatic relations with the Continental Great Powers. In 1852 he maintained friendly relations with the emergent French Second Empire, while also working with Russia to deter, through diplomatic means, suspected French intentions of annexing Belgium. Likewise, in 1859 he supported Malmesbury's attempt, via Cowley's mission to Vienna, to defuse the Continental crisis over Italy.

If, in his early years, Derby's domestic politics were defined by Canning's agenda, in his later years, as Conservative prime minister, his foreign policy sustained the aspirations of Castlereagh. Provocative unilateral intervention by Britain, as opposed to negotiated settlement, should be avoided. Derby's foreign policy, refraining from meddlesome interference in the internal affairs of other European powers and informed by an awareness of Britain's limited military power, upheld these aims. As his disciple in diplomacy, Malmesbury damningly pronounced to the Lords in June 1863, of the Palmerstonian dictum *Civis Romanus sum*, that 'of all the foolish misapplications of a dead language of a semi-barbarous country to a living and civilised nation, I never heard of a worse'. There was not, Malmesbury insisted, the slightest parallel between ancient Rome and their own time, when British subjects took a legitimate pride, not in wielding an overbearing power, but in belonging to 'a nation in the vanguard of civilization ... founded on respect for municipal and international law'.[134] This was a Conservative foreign policy sustained by Derby's elder son as Foreign Secretary during the 1860s and 1870s. It was premised on the rational wish of civilized men to reach reasonable diplomatic solutions avoiding conflict. Labelled 'appeasement', it ultimately suffered an ignominious fate under Neville Chamberlain in the dark days of 1938, when confronted by the totalitarian cynicism of German Nazism.

Within Westminster, Derby effectively restored the Conservatives as a credible party of government. Yet, in the country, Conservative constituency organization foundered. During the late 1840s Protectionist associations and Protestant societies rushed in to fill the void. Disraeli showed little interest in electoral organization. Bentinck dismissed the revision of voter registration lists as 'old women's work'.[135] Beresford's embarrassing mismanagement courted electoral disaster. Derby's views, meanwhile, were shaped by his belief in the legitimate influence of local landed elites, the world graphically described by Anthony Trollope in his Palliser novels, where the Duke of Omnium's interest in his 'pocket borough' of Silverbridge is loyally maintained by Mr Spurgeon and Mr Sprout. Derby supported the efforts of Jolliffe and Rose to resuscitate constituency organization after 1853, a revival of local partisan loyalties that was not without success. In July 1859 and July 1863 he echoed Peel's famous exhortation to the party faithful: 'Register, register, register'. But equally, Derby's views rendered him hostile to independent populist bodies claiming to represent an authentic public opinion, distinct from the judgement of deferential local communities and Westminster. The brawling torrent of agitation should not be mistaken for the still, deep current of genuine national opinion. While he restored the Conservatives as a credible governing parliamentary party, it was left to his successors to extend that achievement through the revival of Conservatism as a dynamic organizational force in the country.

Derby was, Gladstone observed, too much of a parliamentary politician to seek the 'strength of public opinion'.[136] For Derby, public opinion was embedded in the historic relations of traditional local communities. Certainly he expended little effort in cultivating the press, despite the expansion of political journalism in the 1850s. A few weeks before his death, he gave a characteristic response to Colville's suggestion that leading Conservatives raise a subscription to purchase *The Globe*. 'I cannot conceal from you that, in my opinion,' he replied, 'even in a political sense, there is no more unsatisfactory mode of spending money than the purchase of a second class newspaper.'[137] He 'has never been able to realise the sudden growth and power of the political press', Malmesbury noted, 'for which he has no partiality, which feeling is reciprocated by its members'.[138] This too encouraged the neglect of posterity. Unexceptionally, prior to 1844, Derby did not engage in extra-parliamentary speaking, his addresses outside Westminster being confined to hustings speeches. The signal exception, in political terms, was his landmark address at Glasgow University in December 1834. But even this was a formal event occasioned by his election as Lord Rector. It was the extraordinary political circumstances of late 1834 that invested it with singular significance.

After his elevation to the Lords, as custom decreed, Derby did not undertake popular political speaking. He possessed, his elder son noted, 'a strong dislike to being made the object of public curiosity'.[139] Only civic occasions in Lancashire, as required by his position as the leading local landowner, saw him address popular audiences. It was the conventional settings of royal visits, museum openings, agricultural shows, and Conservative party banquets that saw him speak directly to the local community. 'The whole life of English politics', Bagehot stated in his description of the constitution, 'is the action and reaction between the ministry and the parliament.'[140] This accurately traced the boundaries of Derby's political world.

Yet Derby's achievement is genuinely significant, even if it has been much misunderstood and unduly neglected. Prolonged opposition and brief minority government has suggested to historians that, under Derby after 1846, the Conservatives were an ineffectual force headed by an indifferent leader. Organizational decay, intellectual stagnation, and political failure, it has been proposed, characterized his leadership. But to what extent were the party's undoubted difficulties Derby's fault? In truth, after 1846 any Conservative leader would have faced formidable obstacles. Prominent politicians, as Karl Marx observed, are condemned to shaping events in circumstances not of their own choosing. Alleged shortcomings, imposed by larger adverse forces, should not be ascribed primarily to Derby's personal failure. The disastrous schism of 1846, which confined the Conservatives to parliamentary opposition for much of the next twenty-eight years, was a bitter split that he deeply regretted and which he earnestly sought to repair. Until the early 1850s the gospel of Free Trade firmly held leading Peelites, Whigs, Liberals, and radicals together as an anti-Conservative bloc in Westminster. Conservative backbench fervency required Derby publicly to uphold the cry against Free Trade until, in 1852, Protection was electorally dismissed as a lost cause. The relative economic prosperity of the 1850s and early 1860s denied the Conservatives a ready role as the champions of a threatened social order. Parliamentary Reform, unlike the early 1830s, did not prompt violent clashes between belligerent social interests. Softened religious asperities dulled the edge of Conservative pleas for the staunch defence of a beleaguered Anglican Church. Not until 1868, under the charismatic Gladstone, did the Liberal party emerge as a powerful parliamentary force demanding far-reaching, morally charged, meritocratic change. Prior to 1868 parliamentary Liberalism was largely led by landed Whigs under the benign trusteeship of the elderly, socially conservative, Palmerston. During the 1850s and 1860s the urban coarse-grained radicalism of the 1830s and 1840s acquired a sleeker gloss. As personified by young politicians such as George Goschen, Charles Dilke, and George Trevelyan, and as expounded by influential thinkers such as John Stuart Mill, radicalism became respectable. These were developments Derby could neither control nor defy. Only in foreign affairs were there ready opportunities to establish a distinctive Conservative policy, as an antidote to Liberal interference and radical moralizing, openings which Derby effectively exploited.

Yet, if under the grip of hostile factors the Conservatives did not dominate British politics after 1846, they did survive. To what extent was the party's survival Derby's personal achievement? Here his leadership was crucial. The continuing prestige of landed wealth and aristocratic influence assisted him. But it was his containment of rural reaction, his tempering of sectarian animosity, his patient exploitation of opponents' differences, and his sustained pursuit of responsible moderation while in office that preserved the Conservative party, despite a scarcity of young talent, as a significant presence within Westminster. He played a weak hand with skill and forbearance. Peel has been hailed, notably by Norman Gash, as the founder of the Conservative party, a somewhat ironic tribute to a man who did not believe in parliamentary party as the source of executive authority. In 1846 Peel split the newly fledged party he had brought into power in 1841. Derby, who did believe in the essential constitutional status of parties in parliament, ensured the survival of the young Conservative party traumatized by the acrimonious schism of 1846. He nursed the tormented agricultural rump of the late 1840s through to the vigorous adolescence of 1867 and early maturity of the 1870s. He bequeathed his successors a credible parliamentary party capable of moderate government, rescuing the Conservatives from blinkered reaction and rural nostalgia. In the Burkean sense of reforming in order to preserve, he left a party reconciled to progress. This was a priceless legacy. It made the political dominance of the Conservative party, in the decades after his death, possible. The 1867 Reform Act proved a fitting capstone to his career, the success of 1867 being as much Derby's long-term triumph as an ingenious improvisation conjured up by Disraeli's dexterity. Just as he had been a prominent advocate of the 1832 Reform Act, so Derby was the commanding ministerial presence that launched the second Reform Act forty-five years later. This stands alongside his achievements as the first British statesman to become prime minister three times and the longest-serving party leader in modern British politics.

Yet it was a novel constitutional setting into which political parties rapidly moved after 1867. In the sardonic words of Robert Lowe, MPs became supplicants for popular favour. With politicians drawn out from their parliamentary seclusion, so national parties, recruiting a mass membership and enjoying central bureaucratic organization, began to appeal directly to a partisan electorate. The historian J. A. Froude dryly observed in 1874 that it was becoming assumed that the nation was wiser than its leaders.[141] After 1867 changes of government became aligned with electoral judgement. By the 1890s the notion of the electoral mandate was providing cabinets with the authority to govern. Programmatic politics began to emerge. Gladstone's moral crusades, Disraeli's 'jingoism', the renewed prominence of religious issues, militant Nonconformity, organized labour, and a cheap daily press were transforming the nature of national politics. Government control of parliamentary procedure tightened and the independent judgement of Westminster was subjected to executive and electoral constraint. The Conservative peer Lord Selborne bleakly observed in 1912: 'There is no more a House of Commons than a House of Lords. There is nothing but the cabinet, subject to a continuous but slight check of the Crown, and the violent but occasional check of the electors.'[142] In the celebratory rhetoric of the Birmingham radical Joseph Chamberlain, following the 1884 Reform Act, 'now we have a government of the people by the people'.[143] The elderly Gladstone's depiction of 'the masses' locked in struggle with 'the classes' revived the populist radical portrayal of a contest between 'the people' and the peerage, a struggle that assumed the complexion of an ideological conflict between capital and labour. An increasing focus on the structural causes of social inequality suggested a more interventionist role for central government, marking a fundamental departure from Derby's view of social hardship as a call on individual Christian charity. His benign social vision of a seamless web of integrated interests, with Westminster as the authoritative arbiter of the national interest, was swept away by the harsher class-based rhetoric of national political parties.

Derby, therefore, was the last British prime minister to uphold the axioms of Victorian 'parliamentary government': the view of Westminster as a sovereign deliberative assembly, where parliamentary parties defined an authoritative national interest, distinct from the preferences of the prerogative or the clamour of the populace. The Commons, it could be credibly claimed in the mid-1860s, was 'the only real depository of all political power'.[144] Bagehot believed 'it was impossible to overrate the importance of the English parliament'. It stood as 'the most efficient instrument for expressing the practical opinion of cultivated men the world has ever seen'.[145] For Derby, the authority and autonomy of Westminster were fundamental to the beneficial workings of the British political system. It was the benevolent product of Britain's unique past, safeguarding the historic blessings of ordered freedom and judicious progress. It restrained the undue influence of the Crown and checked the disruptive forces of democratic populism. It invested governments with executive authority. It was central to those close social relations constituting the community of leading men. Around the party dynamics of Westminster the intimate world of St James's and the Pall Mall clubs, entertainments given by aristocratic hostesses, and social gatherings at country estates during the recess comprised, as Trollope observed, a 'single special set that dominates all other sets in our English world'.[146] This was the comfortable world Derby entered as a young aristocratic Whig MP in 1822. For the next forty-seven years it framed his political aspirations, reinforcing his social views and sustaining his political beliefs. But it did not survive his passing. Both Derby's immediate successors as prime minister, Gladstone and Disraeli, surrendered the autonomy of parliament to a notion of popular sovereignty expressed through the mass partisanship of national political parties. 'The change since 1865', Bagehot observed of the constitution seven years later, 'is a change not in one point, but in a thousand points; it is a change not of particular details but of pervading spirit.' So Derby, following Peel, Aberdeen, Palmerston, and Russell, proved the last of those Bagehot called 'the pre-'32 statesmen' to hold power.[147] As the political world became more extensive, more complex, more diverse, and as the electoral platform supplanted parliament, Derby quickly appeared an illustrious anachronism, the gifted aristocratic adornment of a past political age.

Notes

CHAPTER I. DERBY'S FIRST PREMIERSHIP: 1852

1. Benjamin Disraeli, *Lord George Bentinck* (1852), 10.
2. *The Times*, 13 Dec. 1851, 6.
3. Derby to Eglinton, 29 Nov. 1851, Derby MSS, 182/1.
4. Derby to Disraeli, 26 Oct. 1851, Hughenden MSS, B/XX/S/39.
5. Lord Malmesbury, *Memoirs of an Ex-Minister*, 2 vols (1885), i. 288.
6. Ibid. 289.
7. Disraeli to Manners, 13 Jan. 1852, cited in W. F. Monypenny and G. E. Buckle, *The Life of Benjamin Disraeli, Earl of Beaconsfield*, 6 vols (1910–20), iii. 313.
8. Derby to Disraeli, 18 Jan. 1852, cited in Monypenny and Buckle, *Disraeli*, iii. 316–17. The Latin quotation is from Horace's *Epistles*, which warns against the misguided imitation of a foolish example.
9. Derby to Croker, 22 Sept. 1851, Derby MSS, 182/1, cited in L. J. Jennings (ed.), *The Croker Papers*, 3 vols (1884), iii. 241.
10. Ibid.
11. Ibid.
12. Derby to Disraeli, 26 Oct. 1851, Hughenden MSS, B/XX/S/39.
13. Derby to Eglinton, 29 Nov. 1851, Derby MSS, 182/1.
14. Ibid.
15. Derby to Disraeli, 26 Oct. 1851, Hughenden MSS, B/XX/S/39.
16. Ibid.
17. Derby to Walpole, 13 Dec. 1851, Derby MSS, 179/1.
18. Derby to Disraeli, 5 Feb. 1852, Hughenden MSS, B/XX/S/44.
19. Malmesbury, *Memoirs*, i. 287.
20. *The Times*, 8 Dec. 1851, 5.
21. Derby to Disraeli, 11 Dec. 1851, Hughenden MSS, B/XX/S/41.
22. Derby to Hope, 15 Dec. 1851, Derby MSS, 179/1.
23. Malmesbury to Disraeli, 6 Jan. 1852, Hughenden MSS, B/XX/Hs/12.
24. H. C. F. Bell, *Lord Palmerston*, 2 vols (1936), ii. 52.
25. Truro to Russell, Jan. 1852, Russell MSS, PRO 30/22/10/A, fo. 80, cited in David Brown, *Palmerston and the Politics of Foreign Policy, 1846–1855* (Manchester, 2002), 135.

26. Parkes to Ellice, 26 Dec. 1852, Ellice MSS, E38, cited in J. Prest, *Lord John Russell* (1972), 337.

27. Disraeli to Derby, 4 Jan. 1852, Derby MSS, 145/2.

28. Derby to Malmesbury, 7 Jan. 1852, cited in Malmesbury, *Memoirs*, i. 298.

29. Derby to Disraeli, 7 Jan. 1852, Hughenden MSS, B/XX/S/42.

30. Derby to Stanley, 4 Jan. 1852, Derby MSS, 920DER(15), 'Letters from Parents'.

31. Derby to Beresford, 8 Jan. 1852, Derby MSS, 179/1.

32. Derby to Croker, 22 Dec. 1851, cited in Jennings (ed.), *Croker Papers*, iii. 250.

33. Ibid. 251.

34. Ibid. 252.

35. Disraeli to Sarah Disraeli, 7 Dec. 1851, cited in *Benjamin Disraeli's Letters*, v: *1848–1851*, ed. M. G. Wiebe, J. B. Conacher, J. P. Matthews, and Mary S. Millar (Toronto, 1993), 493.

36. Disraeli to Rose, 13 Jan. 1852, cited in *Benjamin Disraeli's Letters*, vi: *1852–1856*, ed. M. G. Wiebe, Mary S. Millar, and Ann P. Robson (Toronto, 1997), 14.

37. Disraeli to Sarah Disraeli, 26 Jan. 1852, cited in Disraeli, *Letters*, vi. 17.

38. *The Times*, 3 Feb. 1852, 5.

39. Derby to Disraeli, 8 Feb. 1852, Hughenden MSS, B/XX/S/45.

40. Malmesbury, *Memoirs*, i. 301.

41. Ibid.

42. Derby to Disraeli, 15 Feb. 1852, Hughenden MSS, B/XX/S/47.

43. Bell, *Palmerston*, ii. 58.

44. Ibid.

45. Malmesbury, *Memoirs*, i. 304.

46. Prince Albert, memorandum, 22 Feb. 1852, cited in Queen Victoria, *The Letters of Queen Victoria, 1st Series*, ed. A. C. Benson and Viscount Esher, 3 vols (1907), ii. 447–8.

47. Disraeli to Derby, 20 Feb. 1852, Derby MSS, 145/2, cited in Disraeli, *Letters*, vi. 21.

48. Derby to Disraeli, 21 Feb. 1852, Hughenden MSS, B/XX/S/48.

49. Beresford to Derby, 21 Feb. 1852, Derby MSS, 149/3.

50. Disraeli, memorandum, n.d., Hughenden MSS, A/X/A/25, cited in Benjamin Disraeli, *Disraeli's Reminiscences*, ed. Helen Swartz and Marvin Swartz (1975), 51.

51. Ibid.

52. Palmerston to Temple, 30 Apr. 1852, cited in E. Ashley, *The Life and Correspondence of Henry John Temple, Viscount Palmerston*, 2 vols (1879), i. 336–41.

53. Disraeli, memorandum, n.d., Hughenden MSS, A/X/A/25, cited in Disraeli, *Reminiscences*, 52.

54. Malmesbury, *Memoirs*, ii. 305.

55. See C. Whibley, *Lord John Manners and his Friends*, 2 vols (Edinburgh, 1925), ii. 47.

56. Disraeli, memorandum, n.d., Hughenden MSS, A/X/A/25, cited in Disraeli, *Reminiscences*, 53.

57. Malmesbury, *Memoirs*, i. 312.

58. G. E. B. Saintsbury, *The Earl of Derby* (1892), 74.

59. Disraeli to Sarah Disraeli, [14 May 1852], cited in Disraeli, *Letters*, vi. 60.

60. See Monypenny and Buckle, *Disraeli*, iii. 346.

61. Queen Victoria to the King of the Belgians, 24 Feb. 1852, cited in Queen Victoria, *Letters*, ed. Benson and Esher, ii. 450.

62. See Lady Frances Balfour, *The Life of George, Fourth Earl of Aberdeen*, 2 vols (1923), ii. 161.

63. *The Economist*, 28 Feb. 1852, 273.

64. *The Guardian*, 25 Feb. 1852.

65. *The Times*, 25 Feb. 1852, 5.

66. Queen Victoria to the King of the Belgians, 23 Mar. 1852, cited in Queen Victoria, *Letters*, ed. Benson and Esher, ii. 467.

67. Derby to Croker, 11 Mar. 1852, cited in Jennings (ed.), *Croker Papers*, iii. 258.

68. Malmesbury, *Memoirs*, i. 312.

69. Prest, *Russell*, 350.

70. Duke of Argyll, *George Douglas, 8th Duke of Argyll: Autobiography and Memoirs*, ed. Dowager Duchess of Argyll, 2 vols (1906), i. 361.

71. Derby to Disraeli, [27 Feb. 1852], Hughenden MSS, B/XX/S/105.

72. M. S. Hardcastle, *A Life of Lord Campbell*, 2 vols (1881), ii. 303.

73. Derby, 27 Feb. 1852, *Hansard Parliamentary Debates*, 3rd ser. (1830–91), cxix. 889.

74. Hardcastle, *Life of Lord Campbell*, ii. 373.

75. Derby to Disraeli, 18 Jan. 1852, Hughenden MSS, B/XX/S/43.

76. Derby, 27 Feb. 1852, *Hansard*, 3rd ser., cxix. 906.

77. Disraeli to the Queen, 15 Mar. 1852, cited in Queen Victoria, *Letters*, ed. Benson and Esher, ii. 462.

78. Derby to Disraeli, 15 Mar. 1852, Hughenden MSS, B/XX/S/52.

79. Ibid.

80. Derby to Disraeli, [18 Mar. 1852], Hughenden MSS, B/XX/S/106.

81. Disraeli to Sarah Disraeli, 17 Mar. 1852, cited in Disraeli, *Letters*, vi. 40.

82. Derby to Disraeli, [18 Mar. 1852], Hughenden MSS, B/XX/S/106.

83. Derby to Disraeli, [18 Mar. 1852], Hughenden MSS, B/XX/S/109.

84. Derby to Disraeli, [18 Mar. 1852], Hughenden MSS, B/XX/S/106.

85. Derby, 16 Mar. 1852, *Hansard*, 3rd ser., cxix. 1133–9.

86. Derby, 18 Mar. 1852, *Hansard*, 3rd ser., cxix. 1129, 1237.

87. Derby, 19 Mar. 1852, *Hansard*, 3rd ser., cxix. 1273–80.

88. Prince Albert, memorandum, 22 Mar. 1852, cited in Queen Victoria, *Letters*, ed. Benson and Esher, ii. 465.

89. Disraeli to Sarah Disraeli, 17 Mar. 1852, cited in Disraeli, *Letters*, vi. 39.

90. Derby, 25 Mar. 1852, *Hansard*, 3rd ser., cxx. 55–6.

91. Derby, 26 Mar. 1852, *Hansard*, 3rd ser., cxx. 172–3.

92. Derby, 29 Mar. 1852, *Hansard*, 3rd ser., cxx. 258–63.

93. Derby, 30 Mar. 1852, *Hansard*, 3rd ser., cxx. 345–6, 347–8.

94. See A. H. Gordon, Baron Stanmore, *Sidney Herbert, Lord Herbert of Lea: A Memoir*, 2 vols (1906), i. 154.

95. C. C. F. Greville, *A Journal of the Reigns of King George IV, King William IV, and Queen Victoria*, ed. H. Reeve, 8 vols (1888), vi. 459.

96. Prince Albert, memorandum, 2 May 1852, cited in Disraeli, *Letters*, vi. 52.

97. Derby, 2 Apr. 1852, *Hansard*, 3rd ser., cxx. 654–9.

98. Derby, 20 Apr. 1852, *Hansard*, 3rd ser., cxx. 879–82.

99. Derby, 29 Apr. 1852, *Hansard*, 3rd ser., cxx. 1300–9.

100. *Illustrated London News*, 1 May 1852, 334.

101. Greville, *Journal*, vi. 462.

102. Queen Victoria to the King of the Belgians, 30 Mar. 1852, cited in Queen Victoria, *Letters*, ed. Benson and Esher, ii. 467.

103. Manners to Disraeli, 26 Jan. 1852, cited in Disraeli, *Letters*, vi. 8.

104. Prince Albert, memorandum, 22 Mar. 1852, cited in Queen Victoria, *Letters*, ed. Benson and Esher, ii. 466.

105. Sir Algernon West, *Recollections, 1832 to 1886*, 2 vols (1899), i. 64.

106. *The Times*, 27 Feb. 1852, 4.

107. Derby to Disraeli, 30 Apr. 1852, Hughenden MSS, B/XX/S/54.

108. *The Times*, 1 May 1852, 5.

109. Derby to Disraeli, 30 Apr. 1852, Hughenden MSS, B/XX/S/54.

110. Malmesbury, *Memoirs*, i. 332.

111. Greville, *Journal*, vi. 459.

112. Prince Albert, memorandum, 2 May 1852, cited in Disraeli, *Letters*, vi. 55.

113. Greville, *Journal*, vi. 463.

114. Stanley, diary, June 1852, cited in 15th Earl of Derby, *Disraeli, Derby and the Conservative Party: The Political Journals of Lord Stanley, 1849–1869*, ed. J. Vincent (Hassocks, 1978), 70.

115. *Illustrated London News*, 8 May 1852.

116. Derby, 3 May 1852, *Hansard*, 3rd ser., cxxi. 94–6.

117. Derby, 3 May 1852, *Hansard*, 3rd ser., cxxi. 97–9.

118. Derby, 4 May 1852, *Hansard*, 3rd ser., cxxi. 193–7.

119. Derby, 10 May 1852, *Hansard*, 3rd ser., cxxi. 428–9.

120. Derby to Gladstone, 9 May 1852, and Gladstone to Derby, 10 May 1852, Gladstone MSS, 44140.

121. Derby to Disraeli, 11 May 1852, Hughenden MSS, B/XX/S/56.

122. Greville, *Journal*, vi. 462.

123. Eglinton to Derby, 12 May 1852, Derby MSS, 148/2.

124. Disraeli to Queen Victoria, 28 May 1852, cited in Disraeli, *Letters*, vi. 63.

125. Greville, *Journal*, vi. 463.

126. Ibid. 465.

127. Disraeli to Sarah Disraeli, 14 May 1852, cited in Disraeli, *Letters*, vi. 59.

128. Derby, 18 May 1852, *Hansard*, 3rd ser., cxxi. 985–8.

129. Derby, 21 May 1852, *Hansard*, 3rd ser., cxxi. 879–80.

130. Derby, 24 May 1852, *Hansard*, 3rd ser., cxxi. 985–8.

131. Derby, 27 May 1852, *Hansard*, 3rd ser., cxxi. 1186–92.

132. Derby, 7 June 1852, *Hansard*, 3rd ser., cxxii. 80–94.

133. Derby, 10 June 1852, *Hansard*, 3rd ser., cxxii. 382–3.

134. Disraeli to Queen Victoria, 21 June 1852, cited in Queen Victoria, *Letters*, ed. Benson and Esher, ii. 474.

135. Greville, *Journal*, vi. 456.

136. Derby, 25 June 1852, *Hansard*, 3rd ser., cxxii. 1287–8.

137. Queen Victoria, memorandum, 26 Feb. 1852, cited in Queen Victoria, *Letters*, ed. Benson and Esher, ii. 453.

138. Derby to Malmesbury, 15 Mar. 1852, Malmesbury MSS, 9M73/451.

139. Aberdeen to Princess Lieven, 3 Mar. 1852, Aberdeen MSS, 43055, fo. 258

140. Stanley, diary, 1856, cited in Derby, *Disraeli, Derby and the Conservative Party*, 351.

141. Derby, 21 June 1852, *Hansard*, 3rd ser., cxxii. 1057.

142. Malmesbury, *Memoirs*, i. 340.

143. Derby, 27 Apr. 1852, *Hansard*, 3rd ser., cxx. 1196–1200.

144. Derby, 24 June 1852, *Hansard*, 3rd ser., cxxii. 1258–9.

145. Derby, 30 June 1852, *Hansard*, 3rd ser., cxxii. 1409.

146. *The Economist*, 10 July 1852, 756.

147. Queen Victoria to the King of the Belgians, 17 Mar. 1852, cited in Queen Victoria, *Letters*, ed. Benson and Esher, ii. 464.

148. Greville, *Journal*, vi. 462.

149. Derby to Disraeli, 3 June 1852, Hughenden MSS, B/XX/S/62.

150. Disraeli's address to the Electors of Buckinghamshire, 6 June 1852, cited in Disraeli, *Letters*, vi. 73.

151. *Edinburgh Review* (Oct. 1852), 536.

152. Ibid.

153. *Fraser's Magazine* (July 1852), 113.

154. Greville, *Journal*, vi. 464.

155. Stanley to Disraeli, 19 July 1982, Hughenden MSS, B/XX/S/554.

156. Lennox to Disraeli, 7 Aug. 1852, Hughenden MSS, B/XX/Lx/8.

157. Stanley, diary, 2 Aug. 1852, cited in Derby, *Disraeli, Derby and the Conservative Party*, 78–9.

158. Eglinton to Derby, 4 Aug. 1852, Derby MSS, 148/2.

159. *Morning Post*, 6 Aug. 1852.

160. Beresford to Derby, 5 Nov. 1852, Derby MSS, 149/3.

161. Stanley, diary, 28 July 1852, cited in Derby, *Disraeli, Derby and the Conservative Party*, 76–7.

162. Stanley to Disraeli, 19 July 1852, Hughenden MSS, B/XX/S/554.

163. Stanley, diary, 12 July 1852, cited in Derby, *Disraeli, Derby and the Conservative Party*, 75.

164. Stanley to Disraeli, 19 July 1852, Hughenden MSS, B/XX/S/554.

165. Stanley, diary, 28 July 1852, cited in Derby, *Disraeli, Derby and the Conservative Party*, 77.

166. Ibid. 78.

167. Disraeli to Derby, 5 Sept. 1852, Derby MSS, 145/2.

168. For a discussion of press analysis of the 1852 election, see J. B. Conacher, *The Peelites and the Party System, 1846–1852* (Newton Abbot, 1972), 115–18.

169. Disraeli to Lennox, 7 Aug. 1852, cited in Disraeli, *Letters*, vi. 102.

170. Disraeli to Stanley, 18 July 1852, cited in Disraeli, *Letters*, vi. 95.

171. Derby to Malmesbury, 17 Oct. 1852, Malmesbury MSS, 9M73/451.

172. Greville, *Journal*, vi. 467.

173. Ibid. 472.

174. Malmesbury to Disraeli, 24 Sept. 1852, Hughenden MSS, B/SS/Hs/27.

175. Clarendon to Lansdowne, 3 Sept. 1852, Lansdowne MSS, (3) 32.

176. Clarendon to Cornewall Lewis, 12 Aug. 1852, cited in Sir Herbert Maxwell, *The Life and Letters of the Fourth Earl of Clarendon*, 2 vols (1913), i. 346.

177. St. Leonards to Croker, 28 June 1852, Croker MSS, XVIII-F.

178. Disraeli to Derby, 13 Aug. 1852, Derby MSS, 145/2.

179. Disraeli to Derby, 1 Aug. 1852, Derby MSS, 145/2.

180. Croker to Derby, 11 Aug. 1852, cited in Jennings (ed.), *Croker Papers*, iii. 258.

181. Greville, *Journal*, vi. 481.

182. Malmesbury, *Memoirs*, i. 345.

183. Disraeli to Malmesbury, 13 Aug. 1852, cited in Malmesbury, *Memoirs*, i. 343.

184. Disraeli to Stanley, 11 Aug. 1852, cited in Disraeli, *Letters*, vi. 111.

185. Stanley to Disraeli, 9 Aug. 1852, Hughenden MSS, B/XX/S/560.

186. Disraeli to Derby, 13 Aug. 1852, Derby MSS, 145/2.

187. Malmesbury to Disraeli, 12 Aug. 1852, Hughenden MSS, B/XX/Hs/21.

188. Disraeli to Malmesbury, 13 Aug. 1852, cited in Disraeli, *Letters*, vi. 112.

189. Derby to Disraeli, 12 Sept. 1852, Hughenden MSS, B/XX/S/72.

190. Queen Victoria to the King of the Belgians, 17 Sept. 1852, cited in Queen Victoria, *Letters*, ed. Benson and Esher, ii. 478.

191. Prince Albert, memorandum, 17 Sept. 1852, cited in Queen Victoria, *Letters*, ed. Benson and Esher, ii. 476.

192. Derby to Malmesbury, 3 Oct. 1852, cited in Malmesbury, *Memoirs*, i. 353–4.

193. Ibid. 359.

194. Ibid. 363.

195. Derby, 19 Nov. 1852, *Hansard*, 3rd ser., cxxii. 240.

196. Stanley, diary, 8 Dec. 1852, cited in Derby, *Disraeli, Derby and the Conservative Party*, 88.

197. Derby to Disraeli, n.d. [20 Nov. 1852?], Hughenden MSS, B/XX/S/102.

198. Derby to Queen Victoria, 21 Nov. 1852, Derby MSS, 181/2.
199. Derby, 11 Nov. 1852, *Hansard*, 3rd ser., cxxiii. 52–5.
200. Greville, *Journal*, vii. 8.
201. Disraeli to Derby, 19 Nov. 1852, Derby MSS, 145/2.
202. Ibid.
203. Palmerston, 25 Nov. 1852, *Hansard*, 3rd ser., cxxiii. 454.
204. Greville to Clarendon, 21 Oct. 1852, cited in Maxwell, *Clarendon*, i. 350.
205. Cornewall Lewis to Graham, 8 Sept. 1852, Graham MSS, 112.
206. Prince Albert, memorandum, 28 Nov. 1852, cited in Queen Victoria, *Letters*, ed. Benson and Esher, ii. 491.
207. Prince Albert, memorandum, 25 Nov. 1852, cited in Disraeli, *Letters*, vi. 188.
208. Prince Albert to Derby, 26 Nov. 1852, cited in Monypenny and Buckle, *Disraeli*, iii. 423.
209. Prince Albert, memorandum, 25 Nov. 1852, cited in Disraeli, *Letters*, vi. 88.
210. Gladstone, memorandum, 27 Nov. 1852, Gladstone MSS, 44778, fo. 48.
211. Prince Albert, memorandum, 28 Nov. 1852, cited in Queen Victoria, *Letters*, ed. Benson and Esher, ii. 491.
212. Malmesbury, diary, 28 Nov. 1852, Malmesbury MSS, 9M73/79.
213. Derby, 22 Nov. 1852, *Hansard*, 3rd ser., cxxiii. 273–6.
214. Wodehouse, 22 Nov. 1852, *Hansard*, 3rd ser., cxxiii. 290–3.
215. In his journal Wodehouse noted: 'I never saw Derby so angry. I of course had to withdraw the expression which was decidedly unparliamentary, but I retain my opinion unchanged that nothing could be more mean than to drive Peel out of office on the question of Protection, to keep up an opposition for five years on the grounds that Protection was essential to the prosperity of agriculture, to take all possible advantage of the Protection cry at the hustings and then quietly to kick away the ladder by which he had mounted to the leadership of the Tory party' (A. Hawkins and J. Powell (eds), *The Journal of John Wodehouse, First Earl of Kimberley for 1862–1902*, Camden Society, 5th ser., 9 (Cambridge, 1997), 46).
216. Derby, 6 Dec. 1852, *Hansard*, 3rd ser., cxxiii. 942–53.
217. Malmesbury, 6 Dec. 1852, *Hansard*, 3rd ser., cxxiii. 971.
218. Disraeli to Derby, 30 Nov. 1852, Derby MSS, 145/2.
219. Derby to Disraeli, 30 Nov. 1852, Hughenden MSS, B/XX/S/81.
220. Disraeli to Derby, 30 Nov. 1852, Derby MSS, 145/2.
221. Derby to Queen Victoria, 3 Dec. 1852, cited in Queen Victoria, *Letters*, ed. Benson and Esher, ii. 493.
222. Disraeli, 3 Dec. 1852, *Hansard*, 3rd ser., cxxiii. 836–907.
223. Derby to Queen Victoria, 3 Dec. 1852, cited in Queen Victoria, *Letters*, ed. Benson and Esher, ii. 493.
224. Derby to Disraeli, 4 Dec. 1852, Hughenden MSS, B/XX/S/100.
225. Queen Victoria to Disraeli, 5 Dec. 1852, cited in Monypenny and Buckle, *Disraeli*, iii. 434.

226. Greville, *Journal*, vii. 14.

227. Wood, 10 Dec. 1852, *Hansard*, 3rd ser., cxxiii. 1292–1311; Disraeli, 16 Dec. 1852, *Hansard*, 3rd ser., cxxiii. 1653; Disraeli, 10 Dec. 1852, *Hansard*, 3rd ser., cxxiii. 1238–41.

228. See R. Blake, *Disraeli* (1966), 339; John Morley, *The Life of William Ewart Gladstone*, 3 vols (1903), i. 438–40; G. O. Trevelyan, *The Life and Letters of Lord Macaulay*, 2 vols (1876), ii. 277; Bulwer Lytton, 10 Dec. 1852, *Hansard*, 3rd ser., cxxiii. 1231.

229. Derby, 14 Dec. 1852, *Hansard*, 3rd ser., cxxiii. 1420.

230. Bright, diary, 15 Dec. 1852, cited in John Bright, *The Diaries of John Bright*, ed. R. A. J. Walling (1930), 130.

231. Malmesbury, diary, 24 Dec. 1852, Malmesbury MSS, 9M73/79.

232. Malmesbury, diary, 15 Dec. 1852, Malmesbury MSS, 9M73/79.

233. Derby to Disraeli, 15 Dec. 1852, Hughenden MSS, B/XX/S/83.

234. Disraeli, 16 Dec. 1852, *Hansard*, 3rd ser., cxxiii. 1629–66.

235. Londonderry to Disraeli, 21 Dec. 1852, Hughenden MSS, B/XX/V/88.

236. Gladstone, 16 Dec. 1852, *Hansard*, 3rd ser., cxxiii. 1666–93.

237. Stanley, diary, 16 Dec. 1852, cited in Derby, *Disraeli, Derby and the Conservative Party*, 89.

238. Monypenny and Buckle, *Disraeli*, iii. 448.

239. Ibid.

240. Mabel, Countess of Airlie, *Lady Palmerston and her Times*, 2 vols (1922), ii. 311.

241. Malmesbury, diary, 17 Dec. 1852, Malmesbury MSS, 9M73/79.

242. Prince Albert, memorandum, 18 Dec. 1852, cited in Queen Victoria, *Letters*, ed. Benson and Esher, ii. 500–2.

243. Stanley, diary, 17 Dec. 1852, cited in Derby, *Disraeli, Derby and the Conservative Party*, 90.

244. Ibid. 91.

245. Derby, 20 Dec. 1852, *Hansard*, 3rd ser., cxxiii. 1698–1705.

246. *The Times*, 21 Dec. 1852, 4.

247. *The Times*, 23 Dec. 1852, 5.

248. Croker to Hardwicke, 31 Dec. 1852, cited in Jennings (ed.), *Croker Papers*, iii. 261–2.

CHAPTER 2. 'KILLING WITH KINDNESS': 1853–1855

1. T . E. Kebbel, *Lord Beaconsfield and Other Tory Memories* (1907), 92.

2. C. S. Parker, *Life and Letters of Sir James Graham, Second Baronet of Netherby*, 2 vols (1907), ii. 198.

3. Shaftesbury, diary, 30 Dec. 1852, Broadlands MSS, SHA/PD/6.

4. Malmesbury, diary, 26 Dec. 1852, Malmesbury MSS, 9M73/79.

5. Greville, *Journal*, vii. 17.

6. Ibid. 24.

7. Argyll, *Autobiography and Memoirs*, i. 389.

8. Greville, *Journal*, vii. 24.

9. Malmesbury, diary, 24 Dec. 1852, Malmesbury MSS, 9M73/79.

10. Disraeli to Londonderry, 31 Dec. 1852, cited in Derby, *Disraeli's Letters*, vi. 203.

11. Greville, *Journal*, vii. 17.

12. Stanley, diary, 20 Dec. 1852, cited in Derby, *Disraeli, Derby and the Conservative Party*, 92.

13. Ibid. 94.

14. Derby to Liddell, 4 Jan. 1852, Derby MSS, 182/1.

15. Aberdeen, 27 Dec. 1852, *Hansard*, 3rd ser., cxxiii. 1721–7.

16. Derby, 27 Dec. 1852, *Hansard*, 3rd ser., cxxiii. 1727–41.

17. Malmesbury to Disraeli, 3 Feb. 1853, Hughenden MSS, B/XX/Hs/30.

18. Derby to Disraeli, 30 Jan. 1853, Hughenden MSS, B/XX/S/111.

19. Sir Walter Scott, Appendix to *Rob Roy* (1817).

20. Stanley, diary, 1851, cited in Derby, *Disraeli, Derby and the Conservative Party*, 31.

21. Disraeli to Stanley, 26 Jan. 1853, cited in Disraeli, *Letters*, vi. 208.

22. *The Times*, 13 May 1853, 5.

23. Stanley, diary, 9 Feb. 1853, cited in Derby, *Disraeli, Derby and the Conservative Party*, 96.

24. Greville, *Journal*, vii. 44.

25. Stanley, diary, 5 Apr. 1853, cited in Derby, *Disraeli, Derby and the Conservative Party*, 104.

26. Greville, *Journal*, vi. 424.

27. Derby to Disraeli, n.d., Hughenden MSS, B/XX/S/101.

28. Stanley, diary, 14 Jan. 1853, cited in Derby, *Disraeli, Derby and the Conservative Party*, 95.

29. Ibid. 99.

30. Stanley to Disraeli, 28 Jan. 1853, Hughenden MSS, B/XX/S/588.

31. Stanley, diary, 4 Apr. 1853, cited in Derby, *Disraeli, Derby and the Conservative Party*, 104.

32. Ibid. 96.

33. Lonsdale to Disraeli, 26 Mar. 1853, Hughenden MSS, B/XX/L/272.

34. Stanley, diary, 16 Apr. 1853, cited in Derby, *Disraeli, Derby and the Conservative Party*, 106.

35. Ibid. 96.

36. Malmesbury to Disraeli, 3 Feb. 1853, Hughenden MSS, B/XX/Hs/30.

37. Stanley, diary, 14 Mar. 1853, cited in Derby, *Disraeli, Derby and the Conservative Party*, 103.

38. Monypenny and Buckle, *Disraeli*, iii. 495–7.

39. Stanley, diary, 24 Mar. 1853, cited in Derby, *Disraeli, Derby and the Conservative Party*, 104.

40. Disraeli to Mary Anne Disraeli, 12 Dec. 1853, Hughenden MSS, A/1/A/277, cited in Disraeli, *Letters*, vi. 293.

41. Malmesbury, *Memoirs*, i. 414.

42. Stanley, diary, 17 Feb. 1853, cited in Derby, *Disraeli, Derby and the Conservative Party*, 99.

43. Disraeli to Malmesbury, 24 Jan. 1853, cited in Malmesbury, *Memoirs*, i. 382.

44. Stanley, diary, 24 Mar. 1853, cited in Derby, *Disraeli, Derby and the Conservative Party*, 104.

45. Malmesbury, *Memoirs*, i. 398.

46. Stanley, diary, 16 Apr. 1853, cited in Derby, *Disraeli, Derby and the Conservative Party*, 106.

47. Ibid. 106.

48. Greville, *Journal*, vii. 61-2.

49. Derby, 25 Apr. 1853, *Hansard*, 3rd ser., cxxvi. 381-401.

50. See J. B. Conacher, *The Aberdeen Coalition, 1852-1855: A Study in Mid-Nineteenth Century Party Politics* (Cambridge, 1968), 101.

51. Greville, *Journal*, vii. 61. The line 'That one may smile, and smile, and be a villain' is from *Hamlet*, I. v. 105.

52. Derby, 10 May 1853, *Hansard*, 3rd ser., cxxvii. 45-55.

53. Conacher, *Aberdeen Coalition*, 75.

54. Derby, 27 May 1853, *Hansard*, 3rd ser., cxxvii. 673-84.

55. Derby, 22 June 1853, *Hansard*, 3rd ser., cxxvii. 482-9.

56. Derby, 22 June 1853, *Hansard*, 3rd ser., cxxix. 592-612.

57. Greville, *Journal*, vii. 78.

58. See Conacher, *Aberdeen Coalition*, 84-6.

59. Bright, *Diaries*, 145-7.

60. Stanley, 23 June 1853, *Hansard*, 3rd ser., cxxvii. 1169-94.

61. Derby to Disraeli, 27 Mar. 1853, Hughenden MSS, B/XX/S/115.

62. Derby to Disraeli, 20 June 1853, Hughenden MSS, B/XX/S/118.

63. Cornewall Lewis to Graham, 4 Jan. 1853, Graham MSS, 124.

64. Cornewall Lewis to Graham, 23 Aug. 1853, Graham MSS, 124.

65. Stanley, diary, 30 June 1853, cited in Derby, *Disraeli, Derby and the Conservative Party*, 108.

66. Ibid. 109.

67. Derby to Disraeli, 20 June 1853, Hughenden MSS, B/XX/S/118.

68. Disraeli to Herries, 11 Aug. 1853, Hughenden MSS, B/11/34, cited in Disraeli, *Letters*, vi. 248.

69. Disraeli to Londonderry, 26 Sept. 1853, cited in Disraeli, *Letters*, vi. 260.

70. Jolliffe to Derby, 18 Aug. 1853, Derby MSS, 158/10.

71. Derby to Disraeli, 14 Nov. 1853, Derby MSS, 182/1.

72. Malmesbury to Derby, 8 Sept. [1853], Derby MSS, 144/1.

73. Sir William Fraser, *Disraeli and his Day* (1891), 347.
74. Malmesbury, *Memoirs*, i. 404.
75. Fraser, *Disraeli and his Day*, 348.
76. *The Times*, 30 May 1853, 4.
77. Derby to Disraeli, 27 Apr. 1853, Hughenden MSS, B/XX/S/117.
78. Fraser, *Disraeli and his Day*, 348.
79. Ibid. 354.
80. Gladstone, diary, 8 June 1853, cited in *The Gladstone Diaries*, ed. H. C. G. Matthew and M. R. D. Foot, 14 vols (Oxford, 1968–94), iv. 533.
81. Conacher, *Aberdeen Coalition*, 153.
82. Derby to Malmesbury, 22 May 1853, cited in Malmesbury, *Memoirs*, i. 400.
83. Malmesbury, *Memoirs*, i. 401.
84. Malmesbury, 14 Aug. 1853, *Hansard*, 3rd ser., cxxix. 1605–24.
85. Malmesbury, *Memoirs*, i. 405.
86. Derby to Malmesbury, 24 Sept. 1853, Derby MSS, 182/2.
87. Graham to Clarendon, 16 Aug. 1853, Clarendon MSS, C.4.
88. Malmesbury to Derby, 8 Sept. 1853, Derby MSS, 144/1.
89. Greville, *Journal*, vii. 83.
90. *The Times*, 10 Oct. 1853, 5.
91. Aberdeen to Queen Victoria, 10 Nov. 1853, cited in Conacher, *Aberdeen Coalition*, 211.
92. Malmesbury to Disraeli, 15 Oct. 1853, Hughenden MSS, B/XX/Hs/35.
93. Disraeli to Derby, 28 Oct. 1853, Derby MSS, 145/3.
94. Derby to Disraeli, 14 Nov. 1853, Hughenden MSS, B/XX/S/121.
95. Stanley to Disraeli, 28 Nov. 1853, Hughenden MSS, B/XX/S/601.
96. Disraeli to Derby, 2 Dec. 1853, Derby MSS, 145/3.
97. Pakington to Disraeli, 16 Dec. 1853, Hughenden MSS, B/XX/P/11.
98. Malmesbury, *Memoirs*, i. 414.
99. Derby to Walpole, 16 Dec. 1853, Derby MSS, 182/2.
100. Disraeli to Derby, 13 Dec. 1853, Derby MSS, 145/3.
101. Derby to Disraeli, 18 Dec. 1853, Hughenden MSS, B/XX/S/123.
102. Derby to Malmesbury, 18 Dec. 1853, cited in Malmesbury, *Memoirs*, i. 416.
103. Malmesbury to Derby, [Dec. 1853?], Derby MSS, 144/1.
104. Malmesbury to Derby, 21 Dec. 1853, Derby MSS, 144/1.
105. Conacher, *Aberdeen Coalition*, 219.
106. Bell, *Palmerston*, ii. 97.
107. Graham to Russell, 11 Dec. 1853, Russell MSS, PRO 30/22/11/B.
108. Stanley, diary, 22 Dec. 1853, cited in Derby, *Disraeli, Derby and the Conservative Party*, 114.
109. Malmesbury, *Memoirs*, i. 420.
110. Stanley, diary, 31 Dec. 1853, cited in Derby, *Disraeli, Derby and the Conservative Party*, 115.
111. Disraeli to Derby, n.d. [24 Dec. 1853?], Derby MSS, 145/3.

112. Malmesbury, *Memoirs*, i. 421.
113. Stanley, diary, 25 Jan. 1854, cited in Derby, *Disraeli, Derby and the Conservative Party*, 117.
114. Disraeli to Derby, 19 Dec. 1853, Derby MSS, 145/3.
115. Derby to Jolliffe, 6 Jan. 1854, Hylton MSS, 18/1.
116. Jolliffe to Derby, 3 Jan. 1854, Derby MSS, 158/10.
117. Malmesbury to Disraeli, 17 Jan. 1854, Hughenden MSS, B/XX/Hs/40.
118. Malmesbury to Disraeli, 21 Jan. 1854, Hughenden MSS, B/VI/44.
119. Stanley, diary, 31 Jan. 1854, cited in Derby, *Disraeli, Derby and the Conservative Party*, 118.
120. Ibid.
121. Stanley, diary, 25 Jan. 1854, cited in Derby, *Disraeli, Derby and the Conservative Party*, 117.
122. Ibid. 118.
123. Greville, *Journal*, vii. 133.
124. Derby, 31 Jan. 1854, *Hansard*, 3rd ser., cxxx. 65–86.
125. Grey, 31 Jan. 1854, *Hansard*, 3rd ser., cxxx. 19–35.
126. Aberdeen, 31 Jan. 1854, *Hansard*, 3rd ser., cxxx. 86–94.
127. Derby to Malmesbury, 11 Feb. 1854, Derby MSS, 182/2.
128. Derby, 14 Feb. 1854, *Hansard*, 3rd ser., cxxx. 627–44. On 17 March, Derby again attacked the diplomatic bungling of the government and the honour of Delane when *The Times* announced Britain's ultimatum, preceding the declaration of war, prior to it being received in St Petersburg by the Tsar (Derby, 17 Mar. 1854, *Hansard*, 3rd ser., cxxi. 881). In a leading article the following morning Delane spiritedly defended his conduct.
129. Malmesbury, *Memoirs*, i. 425.
130. Stanley, diary, 20 Feb. 1854, cited in Derby, *Disraeli, Derby and the Conservative Party*, 120.
131. Ibid.
132. Ibid. 122.
133. Disraeli to Lennox, 27 Feb. 1854, cited in Disraeli, *Letters*, vi. 324–5.
134. Stanley, diary, 23 Feb. 1854, cited in Derby, *Disraeli, Derby and the Conservative Party*, 121.
135. Ibid. 125–6.
136. Ibid. 120.
137. Ibid. 121.
138. Malmesbury to Disraeli, 1 Mar. 1854, Hughenden MSS, B/XX/Hs/42.
139. Wood to Russell, 28 Feb. 1854, Russell MSS, PRO 30/22/11/C.
140. Disraeli to Blackwood, 8 Mar. 1854, cited in Disraeli, *Letters*, vi. 327.
141. Graham to Russell, 4 Apr. 1854, cited in Conacher, *Aberdeen Coalition*, 304.
142. Russell to Aberdeen, 6 Apr. 1854, cited in Conacher, *Aberdeen Coalition*, 305.
143. Stanley, diary, 11 Apr. 1854, cited in Derby, *Disraeli, Derby and the Conservative Party*, 124.

144. Greville, *Journal*, vii. 150.

145. Stanley, diary, 10 Apr. 1854, cited in Derby, *Disraeli, Derby and the Conservative Party*, 124.

146. Derby, 31 Mar. 1854, *Hansard*, 3rd ser., cxxxii. 153–74.

147. Disraeli, 15 May 1854, *Hansard*, 3rd ser., cxxxiii. 585–93.

148. Greville, *Journal*, vii. 154.

149. Malmesbury, *Memoirs*, i. 434.

150. Derby to Disraeli, 14 Nov. 1853, Derby MSS, 182/1.

151. *The Press*, 24 Dec. 1853, cited in Disraeli, *Letters*, vi. 302.

152. See Disraeli, *Letters*, vi. 367.

153. Disraeli to Robinson, 16 Sept. 1854, Hughenden MSS, B/11/40a.

154. Stanley to Disraeli, 24 Oct. 1854, Hughenden MSS, B/XX/S/612.

155. Derby to Disraeli, 14 Nov. 1853, Derby MSS, 182/1.

156. See Conacher, *Aberdeen Coalition*, 336.

157. Russell, 17 Mar. 1854, *Hansard*, 3rd ser., cxxxi. 892–911.

158. Derby, 6 July 1854, *Hansard*, 3rd ser., cxxxiv. 1212–40.

159. C. E. Mallet, *A History of the University of Oxford*, 3 vols (1937), iii. 32. See Conacher, *Aberdeen Coalition*, 343–4.

160. *The Times*, 11 Aug. 1854, 6.

161. Disraeli to Lady Londonderry, 7 Aug. 1854, cited in Disraeli, *Letters*, vi. 355.

162. Derby to Malmesbury, 2 Oct. 1854, cited in Malmesbury, *Memoirs*, i. 439.

163. Ibid.

164. Malmesbury to Disraeli, 26 Nov. 1854, Hughenden MSS, B/XX/Hs/46.

165. Derby to Malmesbury, 2 Oct. 1854, cited in Malmesbury, *Memoirs*, i. 439.

166. Derby to Disraeli, 3 Dec. 1854, Hughenden MSS, B/XX/S/128.

167. Malmesbury, *Memoirs*, i. 446.

168. Derby to Disraeli, 3 Dec. 1854, Hughenden MSS, B/XX/S/128.

169. Disraeli to Lennox, 2 Dec. 1854, cited in Disraeli, *Letters*, vi. 384.

170. Derby, 12 Dec. 1854, *Hansard*, 3rd ser., cxxxvi. 10–36.

171. Greville, *Journal*, vii. 210.

172. Disraeli to Pemberton Milnes, 23 Dec. 1854, cited in Disraeli, *Letters*, vi. 387.

173. *The Times*, 19 Dec. 1854, 5.

174. Bright, 22 Dec. 1854, *Hansard*, 3rd ser., cxxxvi. 893.

175. Greville, *Journal*, vii. 221.

176. Derby to Eglinton, 9 Jan. 1855, Derby MSS, 183/1.

177. Disraeli to Jolliffe, 9 Jan. 1855, cited in Disraeli, *Letters*, vi. 395.

178. Derby to Jolliffe, 14 Jan. 1855, Derby MSS, 183/1.

179. Jolliffe to Derby, 16 Jan. 1855, Derby MSS, 158/10.

180. Jolliffe to Disraeli, [Jan. 1855], Hughenden MSS, B/XX/J/16.

181. Malmesbury to Derby, 19 Jan. 1855, Derby MSS, 144/1.

182. Ibid.

183. Derby to Disraeli, 23 Jan. 1855, Hughenden MSS, B/XX/S/121.

184. Stanley, diary, 22–30 Jan. 1855, cited in Derby, *Disraeli, Derby and the Conservative Party*, 127.

185. Disraeli to Jolliffe, 25 Jan. 1855, Hylton MSS, DD/HY/C2165, cited in Disraeli, *Letters*, vi. 401.
186. Stanley, diary, 22–30 Jan. 1855, cited in Derby, *Disraeli, Derby and the Conservative Party*, 128.
187. Ibid.
188. Jolliffe, memorandum, [Jan. 1855], Hylton MSS, DD/HY/18/8, fos. 107–8.
189. Disraeli, 29 Jan. 1855, *Hansard*, 3rd ser., cxxxvi. 1216.
190. Stanley, diary, 22–30 Jan. 1855, cited in Derby, *Disraeli, Derby and the Conservative Party*, 129.
191. Palmerston to Queen Victoria, 30 Jan. 1855, cited in Queen Victoria, *Letters*, ed. Benson and Esher, iii. 100.
192. Greville, *Journal*, vii. 236.
193. Stanley, diary, 30 Jan. 1855, cited in Derby, *Disraeli, Derby and the Conservative Party*, 130.
194. Queen Victoria, memorandum, 31 Jan. 1855, cited in Queen Victoria, *Letters*, ed. Benson and Esher, iii. 102.
195. Ibid. 104.
196. Ibid. 102.
197. Ibid. 104.
198. Greville, *Journal*, vii. 236.
199. Ibid. 237.
200. Stanley, diary, 31 Jan. 1855, cited in Derby, *Disraeli, Derby and the Conservative Party*, 131.
201. Gladstone to Derby, 31 Jan. 1855, Derby MSS, 135/9.
202. Stanley, diary, 31 Jan. 1855, cited in Derby, *Disraeli, Derby and the Conservative Party*, 131. See also Derby to Queen Victoria, 31 Jan. 1855, cited in Queen Victoria, *Letters*, ed. Benson and Esher, iii. 104–5.
203. Prince Albert, memorandum, 1 Feb. 1855, cited in Queen Victoria, *Letters*, ed. Benson and Esher, iii. 106–7.
204. Stanley, diary, 1 Feb. 1855, cited in Derby, *Disraeli, Derby and the Conservative Party*, 131.
205. Stanley to Disraeli, 31 Jan. 1855, Hughenden MSS, B/XX/S/617.
206. Stanley, diary, 1 Feb. 1855, cited in Derby, *Disraeli, Derby and the Conservative Party*, 132.
207. Derby to Ellenborough, 3 Feb. 1855, Derby MSS, 183/1.
208. Derby, 1 Feb. 1855, *Hansard*, 3rd ser., cxxxvi. 1256–60.
209. Queen Victoria, memorandum, 3 Feb. 1855, cited in Queen Victoria, *Letters*, ed. Benson and Esher, iii. 117.
210. Ibid. 118.
211. Pakington to Jolliffe, 5 Feb. 1855, Hylton MSS, DD/HY/24/IX/109.
212. Queen Victoria to Palmerston, 4 Feb. 1855, cited in Queen Victoria, *Letters*, ed. Benson and Esher, iii. 122.
213. Malmesbury, *Memoirs*, ii. 12.

214. Ibid. 8.

215. Greville, *Memoirs*, vii. 242.

216. Lennox to Disraeli, 12 Feb. 1855, Hughenden MSS, B/XX/Lx/58.

217. Stanley, diary, 6 Feb. 1855, cited in Derby, *Disraeli, Derby and the Conservative Party*, 133.

218. Pakington to Disraeli, 9 Feb. 1855, Hughenden MSS, B/XX/P/21.

219. Malmesbury to Derby, [Feb. 1855?], Derby MSS, 144/1.

220. Lennox to Disraeli, 12 Feb. 1855, Hughenden MSS, B/XX/Lx/58.

221. J. Morley, *The Life of Richard Cobden*, 2 vols (1879), ii. 170.

222. Malmesbury, *Memoirs*, ii. 9.

223. Derby, 8 Feb. 1855, *Hansard*, 3rd ser., cxxxvi. 1332–50.

224. Malmesbury, *Memoirs*, ii. 8.

225. Hamilton to Jolliffe, n.d., Hylton MSS, DD/HY/24/9.

226. Disraeli to Mary Anne Disraeli, 20 Feb. 1855, cited in Disraeli, *Letters*, vi. 406. Although Disraeli continued: 'It met everything except the chief point—namely, that we did not accept office because we were afraid and incompetent.'

227. Malmesbury, *Memoirs*, ii. 10.

228. Taylor to Jolliffe, n.d., Hylton MSS, DD/HY/24/9.

229. Hamilton to Disraeli, [Feb. 1855], Hughenden MSS, B/XX/H/44.

230. Malmesbury, *Memoirs*, ii. 10.

231. Ibid.

232. Disraeli to Lady Londonderry, 25 Feb. 1855, and Disraeli to Sarah Brydges Willyams, 25 Feb. 1855, cited in Disraeli, *Letters*, vi. 407, 409.

233. Greville, *Journal*, vii. 247.

CHAPTER 3. WAR AND PEACE: 1855–1858

1. Greville, *Journal*, vii. 253.

2. Ibid.

3. Malmesbury to Derby, [Feb. 1855], Derby MSS, 144/1.

4. Derby to Ellenborough, 3 Feb. 1855, Derby MSS, 183/1.

5. Greville, *Journal*, vii. 254.

6. Malmesbury, *Memoirs*, ii. 22.

7. Ibid. 23.

8. Ellenborough to Disraeli, 21 May 1855, Hughenden MSS, B/XX/E/148.

9. Derby to Ellenborough, 30 May 1855, Derby MSS, 183/1.

10. Disraeli to Lennox, 8 June 1855, cited in Disraeli, *Letters*, vi. 425.

11. Greville, *Journal*, vii. 264.

12. Malmesbury, *Memoirs*, ii. 300.

13. Ibid.

14. Derby to Disraeli, 16 July 1855, Hughenden MSS, B/XX/S/137.

15. *The Times*, 6 Oct. 1855, 6.

16. Derby to Disraeli, 11 July 1855, Hughenden MSS, B/XX/S/136.

17. Russell to Minto, 22 July 1855, Minto MSS, 11775, fo. 102.

18. Stanley, memorandum, Nov. 1855, cited in Derby, *Disraeli, Derby and the Conservative Party*, 134.

19. Monypenny and Buckle, *Disraeli*, iv. 18.

20. Lennox to Disraeli, 10 Oct. 1855, Hughenden MSS, B/XX/Lx/63.

21. Stanley, memorandum, Nov. 1855, cited in Derby, *Disraeli, Derby and the Conservative Party*, 135.

22. Derby to Jolliffe, 19 Oct. 1855, Hylton MSS, DD/HY/18/1.

23. Jolliffe to Derby, 23 Oct. 1855, Derby MSS, 158/10.

24. Derby to Disraeli, 25 Oct. 1855, Hughenden MSS, B/XX/S/138.

25. Malmesbury to Derby, 25 Nov. 1855, Derby MSS, 144/1.

26. Disraeli to Lennox, 1 Nov. 1855, cited in Disraeli, *Letters*, vi. 444.

27. Disraeli to Derby, 7 Nov. 1855, Derby MSS, 145/3.

28. Taylor to Jolliffe, 14 Oct. 1855, Hylton MSS, DD/HY/24.

29. Greville, *Journal*, vii. 194.

30. Lennox to Disraeli, 10 Oct. 1855, Hughenden MSS, B/XX/Lx/63.

31. Disraeli to Pakington, 5 Jan. 1855, Hampton MSS, 3835; Derby, *Disraeli, Derby and the Conservative Party*, 143–5.

32. *The Times*, 22 Aug. 1855, 6. From Gordon Castle, where he was visiting the Duke of Richmond, Derby congratulated Stanley on the success of the event. 'I was glad to receive from all quarters reports of the complete success of your gathering at Knowsley, where everything seems to have gone off to a wish; and I hear that your speech was very well received.' He offered to make Knowsley available for similar events in the future. Derby to Stanley, 26 Aug. 1855, Derby MSS, 920DER(15), 'Letters from Parents'.

33. W. D. Jones, *Lord Derby and Victorian Conservatism* (Oxford, 1956), 214.

34. Stanley, diary, 31 Oct. 1855, cited in Derby, *Disraeli, Derby and the Conservative Party*, 139.

35. See Derby, *Disraeli, Derby and the Conservative Party*, 362.

36. Derby to Jolliffe, 6 Nov. 1855, Hylton MSS, DD/HY/18/1.

37. Stanley, diary, 31 Oct. 1855, cited in Derby, *Disraeli, Derby and the Conservative Party*, 140.

38. Derby to Jolliffe, 20 Nov. 1855, Hylton MSS, DD/HY/18/1.

39. Disraeli to Jolliffe, 7 Nov. 1855, Hylton MSS, DD/HY/35, cited in Disraeli, *Letters*, vi. 449.

40. Derby to Stanley, 5 Jan. 1856, Derby MSS, 920DER(15), 'Letters from Parents'.

41. Palmerston to Clarendon, 23 Jan. 1856, Clarendon MSS, C.49.

42. Derby, 31 Jan. 1856, *Hansard*, 3rd ser., cxl. 17–39.

43. *The Times*, 11 Oct. 1855, 4.

44. Derby to Malmesbury, 19 Jan. 1856, cited in Malmesbury, *Memoirs*, ii. 41.

45. Derby, 7 Feb. 1856, *Hansard*, 3rd ser., cxl. 364–74.

46. Greville, *Journal*, viii. 16.

47. Derby, 22 Feb. 1856, *Hansard*, 3rd ser., cxl. 1149.

48. Malmesbury, *Memoirs*, ii. 43.

49. See Lord E. Fitzmaurice, *The Life of Granville George Leveson-Gower, Second Earl Granville*, 2 vols (1905), i. 158, 167–8.

50. See Olive Anderson, 'The Wensleydale Peerage Case and the Position of the House of Lords in the Mid-Nineteenth Century', *English Historical Review*, 82 (1967), 486–502.

51. Holland to Brougham, 14 July [1856], Brougham MSS, 16295.

52. Derby, 31 Jan. 1856, *Hansard*, 3rd ser., cxl. 18.

53. Derby, 5 May 1856, *Hansard*, 3rd ser., cxli. 2002.

54. Derby to Malmesbury, 25 Aug. 1856, Derby MSS, 183/2, cited in Malmesbury, *Memoirs*, ii. 50.

55. Derby to Malmesbury, 15 Dec. 1856, Derby MSS, 183/2, cited in Malmesbury, *Memoirs*, ii. 54.

56. Ibid.

57. Disraeli to Malmesbury, 30 Nov. 1855, cited in Disraeli, *Letters*, vi. 455. See also Malmesbury, *Memoirs*, ii. 37.

58. Jolliffe to Disraeli, 1 May [1856], Hughenden MSS, B/XX/J/35.

59. See A. Lang, *Sir Stafford Northcote, First Earl of Iddesleigh*, 2 vols (1890), i. 89–90.

60. Ibid.

61. See Andrew Roberts, *Salisbury: Victorian Titan* (1999), 68–9.

62. Malmesbury, *Memoirs*, ii. 46.

63. Holland to Brougham, 12 Dec. 1856, Brougham MSS, 16301.

64. Holland to Brougham, 19 Sept. 1856, Brougham MSS, 16298.

65. Miles to Jolliffe, [Sept. 1856], Hylton MSS, DD/HY/24/9, fo. 98.

66. Greville, *Journal*, viii. 41.

67. Malmesbury to Derby, 7 Dec. 1856, Derby MSS, 144/1.

68. Derby to Warren, 23 Nov. 1856, Derby MSS, 183/2.

69. Malmesbury, *Memoirs*, ii. 45.

70. Ibid. 46.

71. Malmesbury to Derby, 7 Dec. 1856, Derby MSS, 144/1.

72. Taylor to Jolliffe, 12 Nov. 1856, Hylton MSS, DD/HY/24.

73. Pakington to Jolliffe, 11 Nov. 1856, Hylton MSS, DD/HY/18/11.

74. Malmesbury to Derby, 7 Dec. 1856, Derby MSS, 144/1.

75. Derby to Malmesbury, 15 Dec. 1856, Derby MSS, 183/2.

76. Jolliffe to Disraeli, 27 Dec. 1856, Hughenden MSS, B/XX/J/40.

77. Derby to Jolliffe, 11 Jan. 1857, Hylton MSS, DD/HY18/2.

78. Jolliffe to Derby, 3 Jan. 1857, Derby MSS, 158/10.

79. Malmesbury to Jolliffe, 13 Jan. 1857, Hylton MSS, DD/HY/24/19.

80. Derby to Dalhousie, 27 Dec. 1856, Derby MSS, 183/2.

81. Malmesbury to Derby, 7 Dec. 1856, Derby MSS, 144/1.

82. Lennox to Derby, 7 Jan. 1857, Hughenden MSS, B/XX/Lx/83.

83. Stanley to Disraeli, 27 Jan. 1857, Hughenden MSS, B/XX/S/626.

84. Stanley, diary, 2 Feb. 1857, cited in Derby, *Disraeli, Derby and the Conservative Party*, 148.

85. Pakington to Disraeli, 23 and 26 Jan. 1857, Hughenden MSS, B/XX/P/23–4.

86. Gladstone to Aberdeen, 13 Oct. 1856, Aberdeen MSS, 43071, fo. 321; Gladstone, memorandum, n.d., Gladstone MSS, 44685, fo. 235.

87. Elwin to Gladstone, 28 Oct. 1856, Gladstone MSS, 44152.

88. Gladstone to Aberdeen, 2 Dec. 1856, Gladstone MSS, 44089.

89. Derby to Gladstone, 25 Jan. 1857, Gladstone MSS, 44140, fo. 205.

90. Derby to Jolliffe, 11 Jan. 1857, Hylton MSS, DD/HY/18/2.

91. Jolliffe to Disraeli, 29 Jan. 1857, Hughenden MSS, B/XX/J/43.

92. Malmesbury, *Memoirs*, ii. 57.

93. Hayward to Gladstone, 17 Dec. 1856, cited in A Hayward, *A Selection from the Correspondence of Abraham Hayward Q.C.*, ed. H. C. Carlisle, 2 vols (1886), i. 301.

94. Aberdeen to Graham, 31 Jan. 1857, Graham MSS, 131.

95. Graham to Aberdeen, 20 Dec. 1856, Aberdeen MSS, 43192.

96. Clarendon to his wife, 2 Feb. 1857, cited in Maxwell, *Clarendon*, ii. 138; Broughton, diary, 7 June 1857, Broughton MSS, 43760, fo. 119.

97. Clarendon to his wife, 2 Feb. 1857, cited in Maxwell, *Clarendon*, ii. 138.

98. Hamilton to Jolliffe, 17 Dec. [1856], Hylton MSS, DD/HY/24/10.

99. Stanley, diary, 2 Feb. 1857, cited in Derby, *Disraeli, Derby and the Conservative Party*, 148.

100. Disraeli to Derby, 28 Jan. 1857, Derby MSS, 145/3.

101. Jolliffe to Disraeli, 29 Jan. 1857, Hughenden MSS, B/XX/J/43.

102. Greville, *Memoirs*, viii. 85.

103. Malmesbury, *Memoirs*, ii. 58.

104. Grey, diary, 9 Feb. 1857, Grey MSS, C3/19.

105. Malmesbury, *Memoirs*, ii. 59.

106. Gladstone, memorandum, [4 Feb. 1857], Gladstone MSS, 44747, fo. 2, cited in Gladstone, *Diaries*, v. 193–4.

107. Malmesbury, *Memoirs*, ii. 59.

108. Disraeli to Derby, 4 Feb. 1857, Derby MSS, 145/3.

109. Derby to Disraeli, 4 Feb. 1857, Hughenden MSS, B/XX/S/144.

110. Derby to Gladstone, 11 Feb. 1857, Gladstone MSS, 44140, fo. 214.

111. Ibid.

112. Gladstone, memorandum, 14 Feb. 1857, Gladstone MSS, 44747, fo. 8, cited in Gladstone, *Diaries*, v. 197–8.

113. Frewen to Jolliffe, 15 Feb. 1857, Hylton MSS, DD/HY/18/5.

114. Derby to Bentinck, 20 Feb. 1857, Derby MSS, 183/2; Bentinck to Derby, 28 Feb. 1857, Derby MSS, 111/B.

115. Argyll, *Autobiography and Memoirs*, ii. 73.
116. Derby to Disraeli, 11 Feb. 1857, Hughenden MSS, B/XX/S/146.
117. Malmesbury, *Memoirs*, ii. 61.
118. Gladstone, diary, 24 Feb. 1857, cited in Gladstone, *Diaries*, v. 201.
119. Derby, 24 Feb. 1857, *Hansard*, 3rd ser., cxliv. 1155–94.
120. Greville, *Journal*, viii. 93.
121. *The Times*, 2 Mar. 1857, 8.
122. R. Lowe, 'The Past Session and the New Parliament', *Edinburgh Review*, 105 (Apr. 1857), 562.
123. Greville, *Journal*, viii. 93; Palmerston to Clarendon, 27 Feb. 1857, Clarendon MSS, C.69, fo. 154.
124. Malmesbury, *Memoirs*, ii. 62.
125. *The Times*, 2 Mar. 1857, 8.
126. *The Times*, 3 Mar. 1857, 9.
127. Milner Gibson, 3 Mar. 1857, *Hansard*, 3rd ser., cxliv. 1745–52.
128. Disraeli, 3 Mar. 1857, *Hansard*, 3rd ser., cxliv. 1834–40.
129. Jolliffe to Derby, 4 Mar. 1857, Derby MSS, 158/10. Derby replied that the manner in which Jolliffe had ensured that the party 'were brought to the post' reflected 'the very highest credit on [Jolliffe's] good management' (Derby to Jolliffe, 4 Mar. 1857, Hylton MSS, DD/HY/18/2).
130. *The Times*, 5 Mar. 1857, 12.
131. Argyll, *Autobiography and Memoirs*, ii. 70.
132. Ibid.
133. Clarendon to Howard de Walden, 7 Mar. 1857, Clarendon MSS, C.541.
134. Derby, 16 Mar. 1857, *Hansard*, 3rd ser., cxliv. 2334.
135. Disraeli to Mrs Brydges Willyams, 23 Mar. 1857, cited in *Benjamin Disraeli's Letters*, vii: *1857–1859*, ed. M. G. Wiebe, Mary S. Millar, Ann P. Robson, and Ellen Hawman (Toronto, 2004), 30.
136. George Meredith, *Beauchamp's Career*, World's Classics (Oxford, 1988), 254.
137. *The Times*, 3 Apr. 1857, 7.
138. See Philip Salmon, *Electoral Reform at Work: Local Politics and National Parties, 1832–1841* (Woodbridge, 2002).
139. Bentinck to Stanley, n.d., Derby MSS, 149/1
140. Eglinton to Jolliffe, 20 Mar. 1857, Hylton MSS, DD/HY18/8.
141. Rose to Jolliffe, Mar. 1855, cited in R. Stewart, *The Foundation of the Conservative Party, 1830–1867* (1978), 329.
142. Derby to Sondes, 14 Mar. 1857, Derby MSS, 183/2.
143. *The Times*, 20 Mar. 1857, 7.
144. Granville to Canning, 8 Apr. 1857, Granville MSS, PRO 30/39/21/2, fo. 11.
145. Clark to the Dean of Bristol, [Apr. 1857?], Russell MSS, PRO 30/22/13/C, fo. 19.
146. Derby to Disraeli, 24 Apr. 1857, Hughenden MSS, B/XX/S/148.
147. Disraeli to Derby, 21 Apr. 1857, Derby MSS, 145/3, cited in Disraeli, *Letters*, vii. 41.

148. Derby to Disraeli, 24 Apr. 1857, Hughenden MSS, B/XX/S/148.

149. Derby to Malmesbury, 30 Apr. 1857, Derby MSS, 183/2.

150. Disraeli to Mrs Brydges Willyams, 13 Apr. 1857, cited in Disraeli, *Letters*, vii. 37.

151. Jolliffe to Derby, 16 Apr. 1857, Derby MSS, 158/10.

152. Pakington to Derby, 11 Mar. 1857, Derby MSS, 141/9. It is significant that Pakington gave his allegiance to Derby not Disraeli.

153. Taylor, memorandum, [Apr. 1857], Hylton MSS, DD/HY/24/11, fos. 43−4.

154. Disraeli to Mrs Brydges Willyams, 13 Apr. 1857, cited in Disraeli, *Letters*, vii. 37.

155. Herbert to Aberdeen, 12 Apr. 1857, Aberdeen MSS, 43197, fo. 153.

156. Graham to Herbert, 15 Apr. 1857, cited in Gordon, *Herbert*, ii. 95−6.

157. *The Times*, 3 Apr. 1857, 7.

158. Graham to Cobden, 26 Apr. 1857, Cobden MSS, 43669.

159. Malmesbury to Derby, 1 May 1857, Derby MSS, 144/1.

160. Hamilton to Disraeli, 25 Apr. 1857, Hughenden MSS, B/XX/H/62.

161. Jolliffe to Derby, 13 Apr. 1857, Derby MSS, 158/10.

162. Malmesbury to Derby, 13 Apr. 1857, Derby MSS, 144/1.

163. Derby to Manners, 31 Mar. 1857, Derby MSS, 183/2.

164. Malmesbury, *Memoirs*, ii. 69.

165. Malmesbury to Derby, 1 May 1857, Derby MSS, 144/1.

166. Malmesbury, *Memoirs*, ii. 72.

167. Ibid. 79.

168. Derby to Disraeli, 12 May 1857, Hughenden MSS, B/XX/S/149.

169. Malmesbury to Derby, 8 May 1857, Derby MSS, 144/1.

170. Derby to Disraeli, 12 May 1857, Hughenden MSS, B/XX/S/149.

171. Graham to Aberdeen, [Aug. 1857?], Aberdeen MSS, 43192.

172. Graham to Aberdeen, 23 Sept. 1857, Aberdeen MSS, 43192.

173. Disraeli to Pakington, 6 Oct. 1857, Hampton MSS, 3835/7, cited in Disraeli, *Letters*, vii. 78.

174. Granville to Canning, 24 Oct. 1857, Granville MSS, PRO 30/29/21/2, fo. 41.

175. Disraeli to Lennox, 4 Jan. 1858, cited in Disraeli, *Letters*, vii. 112.

176. Dallas to Cass, 20 Oct. 1857, cited in G. M. Dallas, *Letters from London, 1856−1860*, ed. J. Dallas, 2 vols (1870), i. 217.

177. Lennox to Disraeli, 19 Nov. 1857, Hughenden MSS, B/XX/Lx/94.

178. Derby to Disraeli, 15 Nov. 1857, Hughenden MSS, B/XX/S/150.

179. Disraeli to Lennox, 7 Nov. 1857, cited in Disraeli, *Letters*, vii. 90.

180. Disraeli to Derby, 18 Nov. 1857, Derby MSS, 145/3, cited in Disraeli, *Letters*, vii. 95.

181. Derby to Hamilton, 20 Sept. 1857, Derby MSS, 183/2.

182. Derby to Disraeli, 15 Nov. 1857, Hughenden MSS, B/XX/S/150.

183. Jolliffe to Derby, 24 Nov. 1857, Derby MSS, 158/10.

184. Derby to Jolliffe, 25 Nov. 1857, Hylton MSS, DD/HY/18/2.

185. Derby to Disraeli, 2 Dec. 1857, Hughenden MSS, B/XX/S/156a.

186. Malmesbury, *Memoirs*, ii. 90.

187. Derby, 3 Dec. 1857, *Hansard*, 3rd ser., cxlviii. 24–55.

188. Ibid.

189. Bessborough to Granville, 8 Dec. [1857], Granville MSS, PRO 30/29/23/10.

190. Granville to Canning, 23 Dec. 1857, Granville MSS, PRO 30/29/21/2.

191. Graham to Cardwell, 13 Dec. 1857, Cardwell MSS, PRO 30/48/8/47.

192. Greville, *Journal*, vii. 147.

193. Herbert to Graham, 17 Jan. 1858, Graham MSS, 133. In Gordon, *Herbert*, ii. 105, this comment is transcribed as Lansdowne asking Palmerston if he was 'out of his mind'.

194. Parkes to Ellice, 29 Dec. 1857, Ellice MSS, 15042, fo. 97.

195. Grey, diary, 4 Feb. 1855, Grey MSS, C3/18A.

196. Disraeli to Lady Londonderry, 7 Jan. 1858, cited in Disraeli, *Letters*, vii. 113. It was also suggested that the appointment was a reward for Clanricarde's exertions in getting his eldest son, Lord Dunkellin, into the Commons as a supporter of the ministry.

197. Parkes to Ellice, 30 Jan. 1858, Ellice MSS, 15043, fo. 108.

198. Clarendon to Palmerston, 30 Jan. 1858, Broadlands MSS, GC/CL/1146.

199. George Grey to Clarendon, 1 Feb. 1858, Clarendon MSS, C.82, fo. 154.

200. Russell to George Grey, 2 Feb. 1858, Russell MSS, PRO 30/22/13/E.

201. Palmerston to Clarendon, 4 Feb. 1858, Clarendon MSS, C.82, fo. 76.

202. Greville, *Journal*, vii. 162–3.

203. Roebuck, 5 Feb. 1858, *Hansard*, 3rd ser., cxlviii. 762–6.

204. Derby to Warren, 12 Feb. 1858, Derby MSS, 184/1.

205. Russell, 9 Feb. 1858, *Hansard*, 3rd ser., cxlviii. 1035–49.

206. Disraeli, 9 Feb. 1858, *Hansard*, 3rd ser., cxlviii. 1053–63.

207. Greville, *Journal*, viii. 165.

208. Malmesbury, *Memoirs*, ii. 95.

209. Palmerston, diary, 18 Feb. 1858, Broadlands MSS, D/18.

210. Greville, *Journal*, viii. 165.

211. Palmerston to the Queen, 19 Feb. 1858, cited in Queen Victoria, *Letters*, ed. Benson and Esher, iii. 336.

212. Derby to Disraeli, 16 Feb. 1858, Hughenden MSS, B/XX/S/204.

213. Grey, diary, 20 Feb. 1858, Grey MSS, C3/20.

214. Knatchbull-Hugessen diary, 19 Feb. 1858, Brabourne MSS, F. 29.

215. Derby to Disraeli, 16 Feb. 1858, Hughenden MSS, B/XX/S/204.

216. Granville to Canning, 24 Feb. 1858, Granville MSS, PRO 30/29/21/2.

217. Derby to Clarendon, 20 Feb. 1858, Derby MSS, 184/1.

218. Derby to Disraeli, 16 Feb. 1858, Hughenden MSS, B/XX/S/204.

219. Derby to Palmerston, 22 Feb. 1858, Broadlands MSS, GC/DE/66.

220. Palmerston to Queen Victoria, 19 Feb. 1858, cited in Queen Victoria, *Letters*, ed. Benson and Esher, iii. 337.

221. W. White, *The Inner Life of the House of Commons*, ed. J. McCarthy, 2 vols (1897), i. 43.
222. Malmesbury, *Memoirs*, ii. 96.
223. Bright to Cobden, 20 Feb. 1858, Cobden MSS, 43384.
224. Grey, diary, 20 Feb. 1858, Grey MSS, C3/20.
225. Stanley, diary, 20 Feb. 1858, cited in Derby, *Disraeli, Derby and the Conservative Party*, 154.
226. Airlie, *Lady Palmerston and her Times*, ii. 169–70.
227. Greville, *Journal*, viii. 168.
228. Prince Albert, memorandum, 21 Feb. 1858, cited in Queen Victoria, *Letters*, ed. Benson and Esher, iii. 337.
229. Stanley, diary, 20 Feb. 1858, cited in Derby, *Disraeli, Derby and the Conservative Party*, 154.
230. Malmesbury, *Memoirs*, ii. 95.

CHAPTER 4. DERBY'S SECOND PREMIERSHIP: 1858–1859

1. Prince Albert, memorandum, 21 Feb. 1858, cited in Queen Victoria, *Letters*, ed. Benson and Esher, iii. 339.
2. Stanley, diary, 20 Feb. 1858, cited in Derby, *Disraeli, Derby and the Conservative Party*, 154.
3. Prince Albert, memorandum, 21 Feb. 1858, cited in Queen Victoria, *Letters*, ed. Benson and Esher, iii. 340.
4. Queen Victoria to Derby, 21 Feb. 1858, cited in Queen Victoria, *Letters*, ed. Benson and Esher, iii. 340.
5. Derby to Queen Victoria, 21 Feb. 1858, cited in Queen Victoria, *Letters*, ed. Benson and Esher, iii. 341.
6. Stanley, diary, 21 Feb. 1858, cited in Derby, *Disraeli, Derby and the Conservative Party*, 155–6.
7. Derby to Northumberland, 22 Feb. 1858, Derby MSS, 184/1.
8. Derby to Disraeli, 21 Feb. 1858, Hughenden MSS, B/XX/S/159.
9. Grey, diary, 21 Feb. 1858, Grey MSS, C3/20.
10. Broughton, diary, 6 Mar. 1858, Broughton MSS, 43761, fo. 46.
11. Gladstone to Derby, 21 Feb. 1858, Gladstone MSS, 44140, fo. 236.
12. Galway to Jolliffe, [24 Feb. 1858?], Hylton MSS, DD/SY/24/B, fo. 47.
13. Grey diary, 22 Feb. 1858, Grey MSS, C3/20.
14. Disraeli to Delane, 22 Feb. 1858, cited in Disraeli, *Letters*, vii. 122.
15. Disraeli to Derby, 22 Feb. 1858, Derby MSS, 146/1, cited in Disraeli, *Letters*, vii. 124.
16. Walpole to Derby, 23 Feb. 1858, Derby MSS, 153/2.
17. Knatchbull-Hugessen diary, 12 Mar. 1858, Brabourne MSS, F. 29.
18. Derby to Disraeli, 25 Feb. 1858, Hughenden MSS, B/XX/S/161.

19. *The Times*, 23 Feb. 1858, 5.
20. Disraeli to Delane, [25 Feb. 1858], cited in Disraeli, *Letters*, vii. 130.
21. Malmesbury, *Memoirs*, ii. 107.
22. Greville, *Journal*, viii. 176.
23. White, *Inner Life of the House of Commons*, i. 49.
24. Disraeli to Delane, 22 Feb. 1858, cited in Disraeli, *Letters*, vii. 123.
25. Derby, 1 Mar. 1858, *Hansard*, 3rd ser., cxlix. 22–44.
26. Palmerston, diary, 1 Mar. 1858, Broadlands MSS, D/18.
27. *The Times*, 2 Mar. 1858, 6.
28. *The Times*, 8 Mar. 1858, 4.
29. *The Times*, 4 Mar. 1858, 4.
30. *The Times*, 6 Mar. 1858, 5.
31. *The Times*, 5 Mar. 1858, 5.
32. Disraeli, 15 Mar. 1858, *Hansard*, 3rd ser., cxlix. 198.
33. Malmesbury, *Memoirs*, ii. 104.
34. Ibid.
35. Disraeli to Queen Victoria, 12 Mar. 1858, cited in Disraeli, *Letters*, vii. 141.
36. Disraeli to Queen Victoria, 15 Mar. 1858, cited in Disraeli, *Letters*, vii. 144.
37. Disraeli to Mrs Brydges Willyams, 16 Mar. 1858, cited in Disraeli, *Letters*, vii. 145.
38. Malmesbury, *Memoirs*, ii. 123.
39. Broughton, diary, 18 Mar. 1858, Broughton MSS, 43761, fo. 54.
40. Greville, *Journal*, viii. 177.
41. Dallas to Cass, 26 Mar. 1858, cited in Dallas, *Letters from London*, ii. 7.
42. Disraeli to Derby, [18 Mar. 1858], Derby MSS, 146/1.
43. Dallas to Cass, 26 Mar. 1858, cited in Dallas, *Letters from London*, ii. 7.
44. Carnarvon, memorandum, [Mar. 1858?], cited in Sir Arthur Hardinge, *The Life of H. E. M. Herbert, Fourth Earl of Carnarvon, 1831–1890*, 3 vols (1925), i. 115.
45. Disraeli, 26 Mar. 1858, *Hansard*, 3rd ser., cxlix. 818–33.
46. Roebuck, 26 Mar. 1858, *Hansard*, 3rd ser., cxlix. 842–3.
47. Bright, 26 Mar. 1858, *Hansard*, 3rd ser., cxlix. 843–5.
48. Bright to Cobden, 31 Mar. 1858, Bright MSS, 43384, fo. 121.
49. Broughton diary, 27 Mar. 1858, Broughton MSS, 43761, fo. 57.
50. Gathorne Hardy, diary, 28 Mar. 1858, Cranbrook MSS, T501/291, fo. 123.
51. *The Times*, 25 Mar. 1858, 8.
52. Earle to Disraeli, 28 Mar. 1858, Hughenden MSS, B/XX/E/34a.
53. Bulwer Lytton to Derby, 30 Mar. 1858, Hughenden MSS, B/XX/S/166a.
54. Ellenborough to Derby, 29 Mar. 1858, Ellenborough MSS, PRO 30/12/19, fo. 1891.
55. *The Times*, 7 Apr. 1858, 6.
56. Clarendon to Palmerston, 9 Apr. 1858, Broadlands MSS, GC/CL 1162. Greville noted that Derby's 'striking speech at the Mansion House' indicated

that he did not mean to resign, 'and that the government will not go out, unless they are positively turned out' (Greville, *Journal*, viii. 188).

57. Disraeli to Derby, 2 Apr. 1858, Derby MSS, 146/1.

58. Derby to Disraeli, 7 Apr. 1858, Hughenden MSS, B/XX/S/169.

59. Disraeli, 12 Apr. 1858, *Hansard*, 3rd ser., cxlix. 857, 861; Russell, 12 Apr. 1858, *Hansard*, 3rd ser., cxlix. 858–61.

60. Wood, 12 Apr. 1858, *Hansard*, 3rd ser., cxlix. 864–6.

61. Disraeli, 12 Apr. 1858, *Hansard*, 3rd ser., cxlix. 873.

62. Disraeli to Queen Victoria, 12 Apr. 1858, cited in Disraeli, *Letters*, vii. 165.

63. Palmerston, 12 Apr. 1858, *Hansard*, 3rd ser., cxlix. 1674.

64. Disraeli to Pakington, 3 Apr. 1858, Hampton MSS, 3835/7, cited in Disraeli, *Letters*, vii. 157.

65. Ibid. See also Walpole, memorandum, 8 Apr. 1858, Walpole MSS, 77B.

66. Henley to Derby, 7 Apr. 1858, Derby MSS, 156/14.

67. Locke King, 22 Apr. 1858, *Hansard*, 3rd ser., cxlix. 1543–4; Walpole, 6 May 1858, *Hansard*, 3rd ser., cl. 226–7.

68. *The Times*, 3 June 1858, 9.

69. Ibid.

70. Sir Stafford Northcote, *Twenty Years of Financial Policy: A Summary of the Chief Financial Measures Passed between 1842 and 1861, with a Table of Budgets* (1862), 339.

71. Earle to Disraeli, 15 July 1858, Hughenden MSS, B/XX/E/39.

72. Disraeli, 19 Apr. 1858, *Hansard*, 3rd ser., cxlix. 1286.

73. Greville, *Journal*, viii. 190.

74. Derby to Disraeli, 20 Apr. 1858, Hughenden MSS, B/XX/S/170.

75. Manners to Derby, 21 Apr. 1858, Derby MSS, 161/7.

76. Cornewall Lewis to Clarendon, 11 Apr. [1858], Clarendon MSS, C.531.

77. Dallas to Cass, 23 Apr. 1858, cited in Dallas, *Letters from London*, ii. 14. See also Grey, diary, 13 May 1858, Grey MSS, C3/21.

78. Derby to Disraeli, 20 Apr. 1858, Hughenden MSS, B/XX/S/170.

79. Broughton, diary, 15 Apr. 1858, Broughton MSS, 43761, fo. 64.

80. Derby to Disraeli, 30 Apr. 1858, Hughenden MSS, B/XX/S/171.

81. Disraeli to Queen Victoria, 30 Apr. 1858, cited in Disraeli, *Letters*, vii. 178.

82. Ellice to Panmure, [19 Apr. 1858?], Dalhousie MSS, GD 45/14/644.

83. Ellenborough to Derby, 13 May 1858, Derby MSS, 137/7.

84. Granville to Canning, 10 May 1858, Granville MSS, PRO 30/29/21/2, fo. 118.

85. Fraser, *Disraeli and his Day*, 253.

86. Broughton, diary, 10 May 1858, Broughton MSS, 43761, fo. 22.

87. Fraser, *Disraeli and his Day*, 260.

88. Ellenborough, 10 May 1858, *Hansard*, 3rd ser., cl. 324.

89. *The Times*, 12 May 1858, 8.

90. Prince Albert, memorandum, 11 May 1858, cited in Queen Victoria, *Letters*, ed. Benson and Esher, iii. 359. The constitutional propriety of Derby's

request was uncertain; both the Queen and Prince Albert had serious doubts.

91. Phipp, memorandum, [15 May 1858?], cited in Queen Victoria, *Letters*, ed. Benson and Esher, iii. 363–4.
92. Prince Albert, memorandum, 16 May 1858, cited in Queen Victoria, *Letters*, ed. Benson and Esher, iii. 367.
93. Ibid.
94. Cairns, 14 May 1858, *Hansard*, 3rd ser., cl. 693–711.
95. White, *Inner Life of the House of Commons*, i. 73.
96. Derby to Jolliffe, 20 May 1858, Derby MSS, 184/1.
97. Derby to Queen Victoria, 21 May 1858, Derby MSS, 184/1.
98. Greville, *Journal*, viii. 201.
99. Derby in his speech at Slough, *The Times*, 27 May 1858, 5.
100. Disraeli to Mrs Brydges Willyams, 22 May 1858, cited in Disraeli, *Letters*, vii. 191.
101. Monypenny and Buckle, *Disraeli*, iv. 152.
102. Fraser, *Disraeli and his Day*, 257.
103. Gathorne Hardy, diary, 24 May 1858, Cranbrook MSS, T501/291, fo. 142.
104. Derby to Queen Victoria, 23 May 1858, Derby MSS, 184/1.
105. Graham to Aberdeen, 28 May 1858, Aberdeen MSS, 43192, fo. 218.
106. Dallas to Cass, 25 May 1858, cited in Dallas, *Letters from London*, ii. 25.
107. Carnarvon, memorandum, 1858, cited in Hardinge, *Carnarvon*, i. 115.
108. *The Times*, 20 May 1858, 8.
109. Lyndhurst to Brougham, 23 July [1858], Brougham MSS, 13317.
110. Trelawny, diary, 29 July 1858, cited in Sir John Trelawny, *The Parliamentary Diaries of Sir John Trelawny, 1858–1865*, ed. T. Jenkins, Camden Society, 4th ser., 40 (1990), 62.
111. *The Times*, 31 May 1858, 8.
112. Graham to Gladstone, 25 May 1858, Gladstone MSS, 44164, fo. 165.
113. Graham to Aberdeen, 25 May 1858, Aberdeen MSS, 43192, fo. 218.
114. Disraeli to Gladstone, 25 May 1858, Gladstone MSS, 44389, fo. 225.
115. Derby to Disraeli, 27 May 1858, Hughenden MSS, B/XX/S/175.
116. Graham to Aberdeen, 28 May 1858, Aberdeen MSS, 43192, fo. 218, cited in Parker, *Graham*, ii. 352–3.
117. Disraeli to Derby, [17 June 1858], Derby MSS, 146/1; Russell, 17 June 1858, *Hansard*, 3rd ser., cl. 2241.
118. Greville, *Journal*, viii. 216.
119. Derby, 22 Apr. 1858, *Hansard*, 3rd ser., cxlix. 1479–80.
120. Ellesmere to Derby, 18 May 1858, Derby MSS, 111.
121. Lucan, 31 May 1858, *Hansard*, 3rd ser., cl. 1156–68.
122. Derby to Lyndhurst, 13 June 1858, Derby MSS, 184/1.
123. Derby, memorandum, 9 June 1858, Salisbury MSS.
124. G. I. T. Machin, *Politics and the Churches in Great Britain, 1832 to 1868* (Oxford, 1977), 272.

125. Disraeli to Queen Victoria, 18 June 1858, cited in Disraeli, *Letters*, vii. 208.
126. *The Times*, 3 Aug. 1858, 6.
127. Disraeli to Mrs Brydges Willyams, 26 July 1858, cited in Disraeli, *Letters*, vii. 222.
128. Ibid. 223.
129. Dallas to Cass, 13 Aug. 1858, cited in Dallas, *Letters from London*, ii. 44. Prince Albert described the Derby government as a 'Tory ministry, with a Radical programme, carrying out Republican measures, with a Conservative majority against a Liberal opposition' (Bell, *Palmerston*, ii. 191).
130. Hardcastle, *Campbell*, ii. 430.
131. *The Times*, 28 June 1858, 6.
132. *The Times*, 2 July 1858, 8.
133. *The Times*, 20 Sept. 1858, 7.
134. Malmesbury, *Memoirs*, ii. 140.
135. Ibid. 142.
136. Clarendon to Palmerston, 25 Nov. 1858, Broadlands MSS, GC/CL 1177.
137. Disraeli to Londonderry, 27 Nov. 1858, cited in Disraeli, *Letters*, vii. 282.
138. Ibid.
139. Argyll to George Grey, 21 Oct. 1858, cited in Argyll, *Autobiography and Memoirs*, ii. 124.
140. *The Times*, 21 Sept. 1858, 9.
141. Russell to Granville, 27 Aug. 1858, Granville MSS, PRO 30/29/19/23, fo. 43.
142. Broughton diary, 6 July 1858, Broughton MSS, 43761, fo. 104.
143. Herbert to Graham, 10 Jan. 1859, cited in Stanmore, *Herbert*, ii. 165.
144. Graham to Ellice, 7 Jan. 1859, Ellice MSS, 15109, fo. 46.
145. Villiers to Bright, 8 Dec. 1858, Bright MSS, 43389, fo. 244.
146. Palmerston to Granville, 30 Aug. 1858, Granville MSS, PRO 30/29/18/6, fo. 64, cited in Bell, *Palmerston*, ii. 191.
147. Derby to Disraeli, 4 Oct. 1858, Hughenden MSS, B/XX/S/181.
148. Clarendon to Palmerston, 25 Nov. 1858, Broadlands MSS, GC/CL 1177.
149. Parkes to Ellice, Jr., 1 Jan. 1859, Ellice MSS, 15043, fo. 96.
150. Clarendon to Cornewall Lewis, 21 Sept. 1858, Clarendon MSS, C.533.
151. Clarendon to Duchess of Manchester, 25 Dec. 1858, cited in A. L. Kennedy (ed.), *'Dear Duchess': Social and Political Letters to the Duchess of Manchester, 1858–1869* (1956), 37.
152. Rose to Disraeli, 11 Aug. 1858, Hughenden MSS, R/1/B/43a.
153. Disraeli to Derby, 26 Aug. 1858, Derby MSS, 146/1.
154. Derby to Jolliffe, 3 Aug. 1858, Hylton MSS, DD/HY/18/2, fo. 32.
155. Stanley to Disraeli, 12 Aug. 1858, Hughenden MSS, B/XX/S/640.
156. Derby to Disraeli, 25 Aug. 1858, Hughenden MSS, B/XX/S/180.
157. Disraeli to Derby, 26 Aug. 1858, Derby MSS, 146/1.
158. Gathorne Hardy diary, 6 Sept. 1858, Cranbrook MSS, T501/290, fo. 175.
159. Pakington to Derby, 6 Oct. 1858, Derby MSS, 141/10.

160. Pakington to Disraeli, 8 Oct. 1858, Hughenden MSS, B/XX/P/33.
161. Greville, *Journal*, viii. 213.
162. Bedford to Brougham, 19 Oct. 1858, Brougham MSS, 30407.
163. Stanley of Alderley to Granville, 23 Oct. 1858, Granville MSS, PRO 30/29/19/23, fo. 25.
164. Holland to Brougham, 24 Sept. 1858, Brougham MSS, 16328.
165. Graham to Russell, 27 Nov. 1858, Russell MSS, PRO 30/22/13/F, fo. 171.
166. Jolliffe to Disraeli, 27 Oct. 1858, Hughenden MSS, B/XX/J/60.
167. Derby to Stanley, 26 Oct. 1858, Derby MSS, 920DER(15), 47/2. For Stanley's report of the offer to Derby, see Stanley to Derby, 25 Oct. 1858, Derby MSS, 105/5.
168. *The Times*, 25 Nov. 1858, 7.
169. *The Times*, 3 Jan. 1859, 9.
170. *The Times*, 25 Nov. 1858, 7.
171. Graham to Aberdeen, 14 Aug. 1858, Aberdeen MSS, 43192, fo. 226.
172. Aberdeen to Gladstone, 8 Oct. 1858, Gladstone MSS, 44089, fo. 275, cited in Morley, *Gladstone*, i. 596.
173. Gladstone to Aberdeen, 30 Oct. 1858, Aberdeen MSS, 43071, fo. 393, cited in Morley, *Gladstone*, i. 595–7.
174. Graham to Aberdeen, 3 Nov. 1858, Aberdeen MSS, 43192, fo. 258.
175. Cardwell to Gordon, 4 Nov. 1858, cited in A. H. Gordon, Baron Stanmore, *Gordon Diary with Extracts from the Correspondence of Lord Aberdeen* (privately printed by Lord Stanmore), British Library, B.P.12 (10–12), 399.
176. Hayward to Cornewall Lewis, 11 Nov. 1858, Harpton Court MSS, C/1490.
177. *The Times*, 9 Nov. 1858, 6. The French general Desaix snatched victory for Napoleon Bonaparte from the jaws of defeat at the Battle of Marengo in June 1800 by arriving at a critical moment with reinforcements, Bonaparte's victory driving Austria out of Italy. Privately Gladstone described Reform as 'an unattractive subject' over which he could not see his way to 'being right and also practicable' (Gladstone to Aberdeen, 20 Sept. 1858, Aberdeen MSS, 43071; Gladstone to Newcastle, 31 Sept. 1858, Gladstone MSS, 44551).
178. Disraeli to Malmesbury, 29 Sept. 1858, Malmesbury MSS, 9M73/22/119.
179. Sotheron-Estcourt, diary, 20 Oct. 1858, Sotheron-Estcourt MSS, F.408.
180. Malmesbury, *Memoirs*, ii. 142.
181. Manners to Granby, [Nov.?] 1858, cited in Whibley, *Manners and his Friends*, ii. 109.
182. Walpole to Derby, 8 Nov. 1858, Derby MSS, 153/2.
183. Derby, memorandum, 21 Nov. 1858, Derby MSS, 47.
184. Derby, memorandum, [21 Nov. 1858?], Hughenden MSS, B/XX/S/191.
185. Pakington to Derby, 23 Nov. 1858, Derby MSS, 141/10.
186. Pakington to Disraeli, 29 Nov. 1858, Hughenden MSS, B/XX/P/35.
187. Jolliffe to Disraeli, 29 Nov. 1858, Hughenden MSS, B/XX/J/63.
188. Derby to Queen Victoria, 1 Dec. 1858, Derby MSS, 186/1.

189. Malmesbury to Disraeli, 26 Dec. 1858, Hughenden MSS, B/XX/Hs/76. See also Disraeli to Derby, 1 Jan. 1859, Derby MSS, 146/1.
190. Derby to Malmesbury, 28 Dec. 1858, Malmesbury MSS, 9M73/20/45.
191. Derby to Disraeli, 21 Dec. 1858, Hughenden MSS, B/XX/S/188.
192. Henley to Derby, 27 Dec. 1858, Derby MSS, 156/4. See also Derby to Disraeli, 30 Dec. 1858, Hughenden MSS, B/XX/S/193.
193. Pakington to Derby, 30 Dec. 1858, Derby MSS, 141/10.
194. Derby to Disraeli, 2 Jan. 1859, Hughenden MSS, B/XX/S/205.
195. F. C. Fortescue, '... and Mr Fortescue': A Selection from the Diaries of Chichester Fortescue, Lord Carlingford, ed. O. W. Hewett (1958), 82.
196. Bulwer Lytton to Derby, 16 Dec. 1858, Derby MSS, 162/1.
197. Derby to Bulwer Lytton, 19 Dec. 1858, Hughenden MSS, B/XX/S/187.
198. Disraeli to Derby, 27 Dec. 1858, Derby MSS, 146/1.
199. Disraeli to Derby, 20 Dec. 1858, Derby MSS, 146/1.
200. Ibid.
201. Derby to Disraeli, 25 Dec. 1858, Hughenden MSS, B/XX/S/189.
202. Henley to Derby, 24 Dec. 1858, Derby MSS, 156/14.
203. Derby to Disraeli, 25 Dec. 1858, Hughenden MSS, B/XX/S/189.
204. Disraeli to Derby, 27 Dec. 1858, Derby MSS, 146/1.
205. Ibid.
206. Disraeli to Derby, 1 Jan. 1859 Derby MSS, 146/1.
207. Disraeli to Malmesbury, 29 Sept. 1858, Malmesbury MSS, 9M73/22/19, cited in Disraeli, Letters, vii. 250.
208. Disraeli to Derby, 26 Oct. 1858, Derby MSS, 146/1. See also Derby to Pakington, 25 Oct. 1858, Hampton MSS, 3835/11(iii).
209. Disraeli to Mrs Brydges Willyams, 11 Oct. 1858, cited in Disraeli, Letters, vii. 260.
210. Derby to Walpole (copy), 6 Jan. 1859, Hughenden MSS, B/XX/S/207a.
211. Derby to Disraeli, 14 Jan. 1859, Hughenden MSS, B/XX/S/211.
212. Stanley to Derby, 13 Jan. 1859, Derby MSS, 105/5.
213. Derby to Stanley, 14 Jan. 1859, Derby MSS, 187/1.
214. Walpole to Derby, 27 Jan. 1859, Derby MSS, 153/2; Henley to Derby, 28 Jan. 1859, Derby MSS, 156/14.
215. Walpole to Derby, 28 Jan. 1859, Derby MSS, 153/2.
216. Rose, memorandum, 24 Jan. 1859, Derby MSS, 48/3.
217. Malmesbury, Memoirs, ii. 129.
218. Derby to Malmesbury, 16 Aug. 1858, Malmesbury MSS, 9M73/20/15.
219. Malmesbury to Derby, 21 Aug. 1858, Derby MSS, 144/2.
220. Malmesbury to Derby, 2 Jan. 1859, Derby MSS, 144/2.
221. Malmesbury to Derby, 28 Dec. 1858, Derby MSS, 144/2.
222. Derby to Malmesbury, 5 Jan. 1859, Malmesbury MSS, 9M73/20/48.
223. Malmesbury to Hudson, 13 Jan. 1859, Malmesbury MSS, 9M73/54.
224. Derby to Malmesbury, 5 and 6 Jan. 1859, Malmesbury MSS, 9M73/20/48, 49.

225. Derby, 3 Feb. 1859, *Hansard*, 3rd ser., clii. 34–49.
226. Aberdeen to Gordon, 8 Feb. 1859, Aberdeen MSS, 43226, fo. 353.
227. Cowley to Palmerston, 25 Jan. 1859, cited in H. R. Wellesley, *The Paris Embassy during the Second Empire*, ed. F. A. Wellesley (1928), 174.
228. *The Times*, 4 Feb. 1859, 9.
229. Palmerston, 25 Feb. 1859, *Hansard*, 3rd ser., clii. 869–78.
230. Disraeli, 25 Feb. 1859, *Hansard*, 3rd ser., clii. 878–81.
231. Russell, 25 Feb. 1859, *Hansard*, 3rd ser., clii. 881–2.
232. Cairns, 11 Feb. 1859, *Hansard*, 3rd ser., clii. 277–304.
233. Walpole, 21 Feb. 1859, *Hansard*, 3rd ser., clii. 610–29.
234. Jolliffe to Disraeli, 22 Feb. 1859, Hughenden MSS, B/XX/J/70.
235. *The Times*, 19 Feb. 1859, 9.
236. Herbert to Gladstone, 7 Feb. 1859, Gladstone MSS, 44211, fo. 32.
237. Argyll to Aberdeen, 7 Feb. 1859, Aberdeen MSS, 43199, fo. 163.
238. *The Times*, 5 Feb. 1859, 8.
239. Derby, memorandum, 7 Feb. 1859, Derby MSS, 47/3.
240. Ibid. By excluding redistribution from their bill, Derby continued, 'we shall to a certain extent disappoint public *expectation*: but I question whether we shall not conciliate public and still more private *support*'.
241. See Derby MSS, 47/3, for Derby's correspondence with Disraeli, Bulwer Lytton, Walpole, Salisbury, Peel, and Hardwicke on 7 Feb. 1859. See also Disraeli to Derby, 8 Feb. 1859, Derby MSS, 146/1.
242. Derby to Disraeli, 8 Feb. 1859, Derby MSS, 47/3.
243. Stanley to Disraeli, 9 Feb. 1859, Hughenden MSS, B/XX/S/676.
244. Derby to Queen Victoria, 13 Feb. 1859, Derby MSS, 186/2.
245. Supplemental Paper No. I: 'Considerations on the Proposed Extension of the Franchise to the Working Classes' [1859], Hylton MSS, DD/HY/24/15.
246. Derby to Queen Victoria, 15 Feb. 1859, Derby MSS, 187/1.
247. Derby to Queen Victoria, 13 Feb. 1859, Derby MSS, 186/2.
248. Derby, memorandum, 16 Feb. 1859, Derby MSS, 47/3.
249. Clarendon to Duchess of Manchester, 14 Feb. 1859, cited in Kennedy (ed.), *'Dear Duchess'*, 39.
250. Derby to Disraeli, 8 Feb. 1859, Derby MSS, 186/2.
251. Pakington to Derby, 15 Feb. 1859, Derby MSS, 141/10.
252. Derby to Disraeli, 25 Feb. 1859, Hughenden MSS, B/XX/S/214. Financial considerations were critical for Lord Chandos because of the bankruptcy of his father, the Duke of Buckingham. See Blake, *Disraeli*, 400.
253. Earle to Disraeli, 20 Feb. 1859, Hughenden MSS, B/XX/E/150; Disraeli to Derby, 20 Dec. 1858, Derby MSS, 146/1.
254. Disraeli to Derby, 23 Feb. 1859, Derby MSS, 146/1.
255. Ibid.
256. Derby to Disraeli, 25 Feb. 1859, Hughenden MSS, B/XX/S/214.
257. Jolliffe, memorandum, 21 Feb. 1859, Hylton MSS, DD/HY/18/8, fo. 2; Earle to Disraeli, [11 Feb. 1859?], Hughenden MSS, B/XX/E/147.

258. Derby to Pakington, 27 Feb. 1859, Hampton MSS, 3835/11(iii).
259. Henley to Walpole, [Feb. 1859?], Walpole MSS, 5991. See also Derby to Disraeli, 28 Feb. 1859, Hughenden MSS, B/XX/S/248. Derby's 1858–9 cabinet proved prone to leaks. When, in August 1858, *The Times* printed details of the confidential details of the financial arrangements surrounding the conferment of a baronetcy on Sir John Lawrence, future Viceroy of India, Stanley complained to his father: 'I wish I knew who of our colleagues go about chatting and gossiping in mixed companies. It is not the first time secrets have leaked, and it ought to be stopped' (Stanley to Derby, 11 Aug. 1858, Derby MSS, 105/5).
260. Disraeli to Derby, 1 Mar. 1859, Derby MSS, 146/1.
261. Earle to Disraeli, [27 Feb. 1859?], Hughenden MSS, B/XX/E/156.
262. *The Times*, 28 Feb. 1859, 8.
263. Gathorne Hardy, diary, 2 Mar. 1859, Cranbrook MSS, T501/291, fo. 236.
264. Derby to Disraeli, 28 Feb. 1859, Hughenden MSS, B/XX/S/248.
265. Disraeli, 28 Feb. 1859, *Hansard*, 3rd ser., clii. 966–1005.
266. Granville to Canning, 3 Mar. 1859, Granville MSS, PRO 30/29/21/3, fo. 13.
267. Gathorne Hardy, diary, 2 Mar. 1859, Cranbrook MSS, T501/291.
268. Fortescue, diary, 28 Feb. 1859, Carlingford MSS, DD/SH 358.
269. Ellice to Panmure, 2 Mar. 1859, Dalhousie MSS, GD 45/14/644.
270. Argyll to Russell, 8 Mar. 1859, Russell MSS, PRO 30/22/13/G, fo. 155.
271. *The Times*, 1 Mar. 1859, 8.
272. *Morning Herald*, 1 Mar. 1859, 5.
273. *Morning Chronicle*, 1 Mar. 1859, 5.
274. *The Globe*, 1 Mar. 1859, 2.
275. Hayward to Lady Holland, 4 Mar. 1859, Holland House MSS.
276. ? to Disraeli, 3 Mar. 1859, Hughenden MSS, B/XVIII/C/28.
277. Clarendon to Duchess of Manchester, 12 Mar. 1859, cited in Kennedy (ed.), *'Dear Duchess'*, 43.
278. Ellice to Panmure, 4 Mar. 1859, Dalhousie MSS, GD 45/14/644.
279. Greville, *Journal*, viii. 227.
280. *The Times*, 1 Mar. 1859, 8.
281. Malmesbury, *Memoirs*, ii. 158.
282. Dallas to Cass, 4 Mar. 1859, cited in Dallas, *Letters from London*, ii. 95.
283. *The Times*, 2 Mar. 1859, 9.
284. Derby to Disraeli, 4 Mar. 1859, Hughenden MSS, B/XX/S/216.
285. Newdegate to Derby, 9 Mar. 1859, Newdegate MSS, B.6641.
286. Derby to Newdegate, 10 Mar. 1859, Newdegate MSS, B.6642.
287. Sotheron-Estcourt, diary, 10 Mar. 1859, Sotheron-Estcourt MSS, C.409.
288. Newdegate to his mother, 13 Mar. 1859, Newdegate MSS, B.3279.
289. Malmesbury, diary, 19 Mar. 1859, Malmesbury MSS, 9M73/79.
290. Derby to Disraeli, 16 Mar. 1859, Derby MSS, 186/2.
291. Granville to Canning, 3 Mar. 1859, Granville MSS, PRO 30/29/21/3, fo. 33.

292. *The Times*, 11 Mar. 1859, 8.

293. *The Times*, 12 Mar. 1859, 9.

294. Grey to Elcho, 12 Mar. 1859, *The Times*, 15 Mar. 1859, 9.

295. Derby to Queen Victoria, 20 Mar. 1859, Derby MSS, 187/2.

296. Clarendon to Lady Salisbury, 17 Mar. 1866, cited in Maxwell, *Clarendon*, ii. 310.

297. Derby to Disraeli, 20 Mar. 1859, Hughenden MSS, B/XX/S/246.

298. Derby to Campden, 23 Mar. 1859, Derby MSS, 187/2.

299. Derby to Queen Victoria, 23 Mar. 1859, Derby MSS, 187/2.

300. Bulwer Lytton, 22 Mar. 1859, *Hansard*, 3rd ser., cliii. 542–59.

301. Disraeli to Queen Victoria, 22 Mar. 1859, cited in Disraeli, *Letters*, vii. 347.

302. Grey, diary, 4 Apr. 1859, Grey MSS, C3/21.

303. Graham, 28 Mar. 1859, *Hansard*, 3rd ser., cliii. 970–85.

304. Palmerston, 25 Mar. 1859, *Hansard*, 3rd ser., cliii. 873–85; Dallas to Cass, 25 Mar. 1859, cited in Dallas, *Letters from London*, ii. 104.

305. Granville to Duchess of Manchester, 28 Mar. 1859, cited in Kennedy (ed.), *'Dear Duchess'*, 48.

306. *The Times*, 28 Mar. 1859, 8.

307. Derby to Queen Victoria, 23 Mar. 1859, Derby MSS, 187/2.

308. *The Times*, 23 Mar. 1859, 9.

309. Derby to Eglinton, 31 Mar. 1859, Derby MSS, 187/2.

310. Disraeli, 31 Mar. 1859, *Hansard*, 3rd ser., cliii. 1230–57.

311. *The Times*, 1 Apr. 1859, 9.

312. Derby to Queen Victoria, 1 Apr. 1859, Derby MSS, 187/2.

313. Malmesbury, diary, 1 Apr. 1859, Malmesbury MSS, 9M73/79.

314. Queen Victoria to the Prince of Wales, 1 Apr. 1859, cited in Prest, *Russell*, 383.

315. *The Times*, 2 Apr. 1859, 8.

316. Derby, 4 Apr. 1859, *Hansard*, 3rd ser., cliii. 1267–91.

317. Broughton, diary, 13 Apr. 1859, Broughton MSS, 43761, fo. 165.

318. Wellesley, *The Paris Embassy during the Second Empire*, 179.

319. Malmesbury, diary, 14 Apr. 1859, Malmesbury MSS, 9M73/79.

320. Malmesbury, 18 Apr. 1859, *Hansard*, 3rd ser., cliii. 1830–9.

321. Derby, 18 Apr. 1859, *Hansard*, 3rd ser., cliii. 1849–57.

322. Malmesbury, *Memoirs*, ii. 170.

323. Derby to Queen Victoria, 19 Apr. 1859, Derby MSS, 186/2.

324. Malmesbury, *Memoirs*, ii. 173.

325. *The Times*, 16 Apr. 1859, 5.

326. Palmerston to Clarendon, 17 Apr. 1859, Clarendon MSS, C.524.

327. Malmesbury, diary, 19 Apr. 1859, Malmesbury MSS, 9M73/79.

328. Malmesbury, diary, 24 Apr. 1859, Malmesbury MSS, 9M73/79.

329. Aberdeen to Graham, 26 Apr. 1859, cited in Gordon, *Diary with Extracts from the Correspondence of Lord Aberdeen*, B.P.12 (12A), 107.

330. Palmerston to Clarendon, 24 Apr. 1859, Clarendon MSS, C.524.

331. Palmerston to Granville, 22 Apr. 1859, Granville MSS, PRO 30/29/19/24, fo. 1.
332. Russell at the Shaftesbury Hall, cited in *The Times*, 25 Apr. 1859, 12, and at the Albion Hall, cited in *The Times*, 30 Apr. 1859, 5.
333. *The Times*, 26 Apr. 1859, 5.
334. Derby to Malmesbury, 26 Apr. 1859, Malmesbury MSS, 9M73/20/51.
335. R. J. Lucas, *Lord Glenesk and the 'Morning Post'* (1910), 181–2.
336. Aberdeen to Graham, 26 May 1859, cited in Gordon, *Diary with Extracts from the Correspondence of Lord Aberdeen*, B.P.12 (12A), 109; Parker, *Graham*, ii. 380.
337. Derby to Queen Victoria, 21 Apr. 1859, cited in Queen Victoria, *Letters*, ed. Benson and Esher, iii. 418.
338. Malmesbury to Derby, 27 Apr. 1859, Derby MSS, 144/2.
339. Derby to Pakington, 26 Apr. 1859, Hampton MSS, 3835/11(iii).
340. Derby to Malmesbury, 26 Apr. 1859, Malmesbury MSS, 9M73/20/51.
341. Ellice to Panmure, 26 Apr. 1859, Dalhousie MSS, GD45/13/644.
342. *The Times*, 30 Apr. 1859, 9.
343. Newcastle to Hayward, 24 Apr. 1859, Newcastle MSS, Nec 12, 379.
344. Derby to Jolliffe, 25 Apr. 1859, Hylton MSS, DD/HY/18/3, fo. 1; Derby to Disraeli, n.d. [Apr. 1859?], Hughenden MSS, B/XX/S/239.
345. Derby to Queen Victoria, 2 May 1859, Derby MSS, 188/1.
346. Jolliffe, memorandum, [May 1859?], Hylton MSS, DD/HY/24/1.
347. *The Times*, 21 May 1859, 8.
348. Derby to Lambert, 27 May 1859, Derby MSS, 188/1.
349. Derby to Eglinton, 9 May 1859, Derby MSS, 188/1.
350. Derby to Eglinton, 18 May 1859, Derby MSS, 188/1.
351. Beresford to Newdegate, 21 May 1859, Newdegate MSS, B.6279.
352. Disraeli to Palmerston, 3 May 1859, Broadlands MSS, GC/D1/140/1, cited in Disraeli, *Letters*, vii. 370.
353. Graham to Aberdeen, 9 May 1859, Graham MSS, 135.
354. Ellice to Panmure, 8 May 1859, Dalhousie MSS, GD45/14/644.
355. Disraeli to Palmerston, 3 May 1859, Broadlands MSS, GC/D1/140/1, cited in Disraeli, *Letters*, vii. 370.
356. Palmerston to Disraeli, 3 May 1859, Hughenden MSS, B/XX/P/84.
357. Malmesbury, diary, 12 May 1859, Malmesbury MSS, 9M73/79.
358. Disraeli to Derby, 8 May 1859, Derby MSS, 145/6.
359. Ibid.
360. Derby to Disraeli, 8 May 1859, Hughenden MSS, B/XX/S/242.
361. Gladstone to Derby, 19 May 1859, Hughenden MSS, B/XX/S/244. Derby immediately forwarded Gladstone's letter onto Disraeli. On 22 May, Mrs Gladstone assumed her husband would join Derby rather than Palmerston. Wood, diary, 22 May 1859, Hickleton MSS, A8/D.
362. Ibid.

363. Gladstone to Heathcote, 16 June 1859, Gladstone MSS, 44209, fo. 38, cited in Morley, *Gladstone*, i. 627–8.
364. Derby to Disraeli, 8 May 1859, Hughenden MSS, B/XX/S/242.
365. *The Times*, 24 May 1859, 6.
366. Earle to Disraeli, [June 1859?], Hughenden MSS, B/XX/E/172.
367. *The Times*, 31 May 1859, 10.
368. *The Times*, 2 June 1859, 8.
369. Earle to Disraeli, [June 1859?], Hughenden MSS, B/XX/E/172.
370. Disraeli to Derby, 2 June 1859, Derby MSS, 145/6.
371. Derby to Queen Victoria, [2 June 1859?], Derby MSS, 188/1, cited in Queen Victoria, *Letters*, ed. Benson and Esher, iii. 430.
372. Malmesbury, diary, 5 June 1859, Malmesbury MSS, 9M73/79.
373. Trelawny, diary, 6 June 1859, cited in Trelawny, *Diaries*, 81.
374. Greville, *Journal*, viii. 250.
375. *Saturday Review*, 11 June 1859, 710.
376. Graham, 9 June 1859, *Hansard*, 3rd ser., cliv. 262–77.
377. *The Times*, 11 June 1859, 9.
378. Pakington to Disraeli, 6 June 1859, Hughenden MSS, B/XX/P/54.
379. Derby to Jolliffe, [11 June 1859?], Hylton MSS, DD/HY/18/4.
380. Derby to Queen Victoria, 8 June 1859, Derby MSS, 186/2.
381. Derby to Queen Victoria, 9 June 1859, Derby MSS, 188/1.
382. Derby to Queen Victoria, 10 June 1859, Derby MSS, 186/2.
383. Disraeli to Derby, 10 June 1859, Derby MSS, 145/6.
384. Clarendon to Palmerston, 5 June 1859, Broadlands MSS, GC/CL/1195.
385. Granville to Canning, 10 June 1859, Granville MSS, PRO 30/29/23/1, fo. 95.
386. Trelawny diary, 10 June 1859, cited in Trelawny, *Diaries*, 84.
387. Malmesbury, *Memoirs*, ii. 188.
388. Ibid. 189.
389. Queen Victoria, diary, 11 June 1859, cited in B. Connell (ed.), *Regina v. Palmerston: The Correspondence between Queen Victoria and her Foreign and Prime Minister, 1837–1865* (1962), 255.
390. *The Times*, 15 June 1859, 8.
391. Malmesbury to Disraeli, 6 July 1858, Hughenden MSS, B/XX/Hs/67.
392. Granville to Palmerston, 18 June 1859, Broadlands MSS, GC/GR/1863.
393. Malmesbury, *Memoirs*, ii. 190.
394. Bedford to Clarendon, 20 June 1859, Clarendon MSS, C.561.
395. *The Times*, 15 June 1859, 8.
396. Malmesbury, *Memoirs*, ii. 189–90. Kebbel noted that Disraeli was acutely sensitive when questioned later about the episode, Disraeli merely replying sharply (and inaccurately): 'Why, how could I produce [the Blue Books] when they were not printed?' (Kebbel, *Lord Beaconsfield and Other Memories*, 18).
397. *The Times*, 18 July 1859, 6.

398. Ibid.
399. *The Times*, 22 June 1859, 8.

CHAPTER 5. WATCHING AND WAITING: 1859–1866

1. Fitzmaurice, *Granville*, i. 487.
2. Palmerston to Bruce, 26 Nov. 1860, cited in E. D. Steele, *Palmerston and Liberalism, 1855–1865* (Cambridge, 1991), 94.
3. Disraeli to Mrs Brydges Willyams, 16 June 1859, cited in Disraeli, *Letters*, vii. 398.
4. Malmesbury, diary, 18 June 1859, Malmesbury MSS, 9M73/79.
5. Panmure to Palmerston, 15 June 1859, Broadlands MSS, GC/PA/170.
6. Wood to Panmure, 16 June 1859, Dalhousie MSS, GD45/14/689.
7. Malmesbury, *Memoirs*, ii. 191.
8. Granville to Canning, 10 Aug. 1859, Granville MSS, PRO 30/29/31/1.
9. Granville to Canning, 27 June 1859, Granville MSS, PRO 30/29/31/1, cited in Fitzmaurice, *Granville*, i. 345.
10. Broughton, diary, 30 June 1859, Broughton MSS, 43762, fo. 22.
11. Broughton, diary, 21 June 1859, Broughton MSS, 43762, fo. 14.
12. *The Times*, 18 July 1859, 6.
13. Stanley of Alderley to Panmure, 30 July 1859, Dalhousie MSS, GD45/14/655.
14. Disraeli to ?, n.d. [June 1859?], cited in Disraeli, *Letters*, vii. 404.
15. Derby to Disraeli, 6 Sept. 1859, Hughenden MSS, B/XX/S/234. It does seem likely that a serious social breach occurred between Disraeli and Derby during the visit. In his memoirs Sir Henry Drummond Wolff records that Disraeli and his wife were 'invited to stay at the country-house of one of the greatest of Conservative magnates, who was fond of banter. The master of the house passed the first evening in what is called chaffing Mrs Disraeli, for the amusement of his guests, but much to her distress. An eye-witness told me that Mr Disraeli sat perfectly still, and apparently without emotion; but the next day he made the use of some pretext to leave the house, and never returned, though frequently invited, and though he was working in the closest and most continuous manner with the politician in question' (Sir Henry Drummond Wolff, *Rambling Recollections*, 2 vols (1908), ii. 132). The host's behaviour matches Derby's manner on similar occasions and Disraeli, who always resented any disrespect shown to his wife, never again visited Knowsley after October 1859. Mary Anne Disraeli, who was given to absurd remarks, would have offered Derby an easy target for mockery as she could never remember who came first, the classical Greeks or the Romans. Derby's behaviour on this occasion may also have been affected by the embarrassment he felt at revelations of Disraeli's collusion with William Lindsay during the Reform debates of the previous May; collusion

publicly revealed by the Liberal MP William Miller to his constituents on 14 October.

16. *The Times*, 31 Oct. 1859, 6.
17. Stanley, diary, 22 Nov. 1853, cited in Derby, *Disraeli, Derby and the Conservative Party*, 112.
18. *The Times*, 18 July 1859, 6.
19. *The Times*, 31 Oct. 1859, 4.
20. Clarendon to Duchess of Manchester, 6 Nov. 1859, cited in Kennedy (ed.), '*Dear Duchess*', 79.
21. Malmesbury, *Memoirs*, ii. 212.
22. Malmesbury to Derby, 1 Jan. 1860, Derby MSS, 144/2a.
23. Disraeli to Jolliffe, 5 Aug. 1859, Hylton MSS, DD/HY/C/2165.
24. Derby to Disraeli, 19 Jan. 1860, Hughenden MSS, B/XX/S/262.
25. Disraeli to Derby, 8 Jan. 1860, Derby MSS, 146/1; Derby to Disraeli, 19 Jan. 1860, Hughenden MSS, B/XX/S/262.
26. Disraeli to Derby, 18 Jan. 1860, Derby MSS, 146/1.
27. Clarendon to Malmesbury, 8 Feb. 1860, cited in Malmesbury, *Memoirs*, ii. 216.
28. Greville, *Journal*, viii. 277.
29. Derby to Malmesbury, 15 Jan. 1860, cited in Malmesbury, *Memoirs*, ii. 213.
30. Greville, *Journal*, viii. 293; Derby to Disraeli, 26 Jan. 1860, Hughenden MSS, B/XX/S/263.
31. Derby, 24 Jan. 1860, *Hansard*, 3rd ser., clvi. 44–64.
32. Derby, 7 Feb. 1860, *Hansard*, 3rd ser., clvi. 599–605.
33. Malmesbury, *Memoirs*, ii. 216.
34. Ibid. Derby to Disraeli, 2 Feb. 1860, Hughenden MSS, B/XX/S/265.
35. Malmesbury to Derby, 6 Feb. 1860, Derby MSS, 144/2a, cited in Malmesbury, *Memoirs*, ii. 215.
36. Malmesbury to Derby, 6 Mar. 1860, Derby MSS, 144/2a.
37. Greville, *Journal*, viii. 298.
38. Dallas to Cass, 10 Feb. 1860, cited in Dallas, *Letters from London*, ii. 323.
39. Derby to Malmesbury, 5 Mar. 1860, Derby MSS, 186/2, cited in Malmesbury, *Memoirs*, ii. 219.
40. Greville, *Journal*, viii. 302.
41. Derby to Malmesbury, 5 Mar. 1860, Derby MSS, 186/2, cited in Malmesbury, *Memoirs*, ii. 220.
42. Derby, 15 Mar. 1860, *Hansard*, 3rd ser., clviii. 616–34.
43. Greville, *Journal*, viii. 305.
44. Ibid. 305.
45. Derby to Disraeli, 13 Mar. 1860, Hughenden MSS, B/XX/S/268.
46. Derby to Grey, 30 Mar. 1860, Derby MSS, 188/2.
47. Derby to Rose, 30 Mar. 1860, Derby MSS, 188/2.
48. Derby to Grey, 12 Apr. 1860, Derby MSS, 188/2.

49. Derby, 19 Apr. 1860, *Hansard*, 3rd ser., clvii. 1951–65.

50. Malmesbury to Derby, 23 Apr. 1860, Derby MSS, 144/2a.

51. Greville, *Journal*, viii. 315.

52. Derby, 10 May 1860, *Hansard*, 3rd ser., clviii. 1002–5.

53. Malmesbury to Derby, 13 May 1860, Derby MSS, 144/2a.

54. Greville, *Journal*, viii. 316.

55. Derby, 21 May 1860, *Hansard*, 3rd ser., clvii. 1525–44.

56. Greville, *Journal*, viii. 316.

57. Derby, 21 May 1860, *Hansard*, 3rd ser., clvii. 1525–44.

58. Greville, *Journal*, viii. 317.

59. Ibid. 315.

60. Disraeli to Mrs Brydges Willyams, 14 May 1860, cited in Monypenny and Buckle, *Disraeli*, iv. 278.

61. Malmesbury, *Memoirs*, ii. 228.

62. See Bell, *Palmerston*, ii. 262.

63. Malmesbury, *Memoirs*, ii. 229.

64. Prest, *Russell*, 390.

65. Derby to Pakington, 28 May 1860, Derby MSS, 188/2.

66. Disraeli to Derby, 27 May 1860, Derby MSS, 146/1.

67. Derby to Sotheron-Estcourt, 23 Mar. 1860, Derby MSS, 188/2; Derby to Sotheron-Estcourt, 2 May 1860, Derby MSS, 188/2.

68. Derby to Montagu, 30 June 1860, Derby MSS, 188/2.

69. Derby to Grey, 4 June 1860, Derby MSS, 188/2.

70. Derby to Disraeli, 27 June 1860, Hughenden MSS, B/XX/S/274; Cornwall Lewis, diary, 25 June 1860, Harpton Court MSS, 3574.

71. Malmesbury, *Memoirs*, ii. 231.

72. Palmerston, diary, 5 June 1860, Broadlands MSS, D.20.

73. Malmesbury, *Memoirs*, ii. 230.

74. Dallas to Cass, 6 Mar. 1860, cited in Dallas, *Letters from London*, ii. 328.

75. Greville, *Journal*, viii. 321.

76. W. Aytoun, 'The Anglo-Gallican Budget', *Blackwood's Magazine*, 87 (1860), 381.

77. Lord Robert Cecil, 'The Conservative Reaction', *Quarterly Review*, 108 (July 1860), 265–302.

78. Stanley to Disraeli, 6 Apr. 1860, Hughenden MSS, B/XX/S/701.

79. Stanley to Disraeli, 13 Oct. 1860, Hughenden MSS, B/XX/S/702.

80. Gladstone to Graham, 27 Nov. 1860, cited in Morley, *Gladstone*, ii. 37.

81. *The Times*, 30 June 1860, 12.

82. Clarendon to Duchess of Manchester, 20 Sept. 1860, cited in Kennedy (ed.), '*Dear Duchess*', 115. *The Times* observed: 'When it is remembered that the force assembled at Knowsley represented only a county parade, its strength will appear astonishing' (*The Times*, 4 Sept. 1860, 6).

83. Derby to Sefton, 25 Jan. 1861, Derby MSS, 188/2.

84. Derby to Malmesbury, 4 Dec. 1860, Derby MSS, 188/2, cited in Malmesbury, *Memoirs*, ii. 242.

85. Derby to Disraeli, 12 Dec. 1860, Hughenden MSS, B/XX/S/277.

86. T. A. Jenkins, *The Liberal Ascendancy, 1830–1886* (1994), 90.

87. Derby to Malmesbury, 25 Dec. 1860, Derby MSS, 188/2.

88. Ibid.

89. Malmesbury to Derby, 26 Jan. 1861, Derby MSS, 144/26.

90. Derby to Malmesbury, 27 Jan. 1861, Derby MSS, 188/2.

91. Derby to Disraeli, 27 Jan. 1861, Hughenden MSS, B/XX/S/280.

92. Derby to Montague, 22 Jan. 1861, Derby MSS, 188/2.

93. Derby to Leitrim, 29 Jan. 1861, Derby MSS, 188/2.

94. Palmerston to Queen Victoria, 27 Jan. 1861, cited in Queen Victoria, *Letters*, ed. Benson and Esher, iii. 547–8.

95. Ibid.

96. Disraeli to Derby, 28 Jan. 1861, Derby MSS, 146/1.

97. Disraeli to Mrs Brydges Willyams, 9 Feb. 1861, cited in Monypenny and Buckle, *Disraeli*, iv. 295.

98. Stanley, diary, 29 Jan. 1861, cited in Derby, *Disraeli, Derby and the Conservative Party*, 165.

99. Ibid. 164.

100. Ibid. 167.

101. Earle to Disraeli, 26 Apr. 1861, Hughenden MSS, B/XX/E/219.

102. Stanley, diary, 11 Feb. 1861, cited in Derby, *Disraeli, Derby and the Conservative Party*, 166.

103. Malmesbury, *Memoirs*, ii. 247.

104. Derby, 5 Feb. 1861, *Hansard*, 3rd ser., clxi. 14–33.

105. Trelawny, diary, 15 Feb. 1861, cited in Trelawny, *Diaries*, 151.

106. Monypenny and Buckle, *Disraeli*, iv. 357.

107. Derby to Malmesbury, 25 Dec. 1860, Derby MSS, 188/2.

108. Derby to Disraeli, 12 Dec. 1860, Hughenden MSS, B/XX/S/277.

109. Disraeli to Derby, 28 Jan. 1861, Derby MSS, 146/1.

110. Stanley, diary, 4 Feb. 1861, cited in Derby, *Disraeli, Derby and the Conservative Party*, 166.

111. Trelawny, diary, 19 Feb. 1861, cited in Trelawny, *Diaries*, 151.

112. Trelawny, diary, 13 Mar. 1861, cited in Trelawny, *Diaries*, 162.

113. Stanley, diary, 17 Feb. 1861, cited in Derby, *Disraeli, Derby and the Conservative Party*, 167.

114. *The Times*, 2 May 1861, 9. A Coryphaeus was the main speaker of the chorus in Greek drama and therefore, figuratively, the leader of a group.

115. Gladstone, memorandum, 1 Sept. 1897, Gladstone MSS, 44791, fo. 130.

116. Palmerston to Granville, 15 Apr. 1851, cited in Bell, *Palmerston*, ii. 283.

117. West, *Recollections*, i. 279.
118. Stanley, diary, 31 May 1861, cited in Derby, *Disraeli, Derby and the Conservative Party*, 171. See also Disraeli to Heathcote, 27 May 1861, cited in Monypenny and Buckle, *Disraeli*, iv. 298–9.
119. Derby to Newdegate, 23 May 1861, Derby MSS, 188/2.
120. Stanley, diary, 31 May 1861, cited in Derby, *Disraeli, Derby and the Conservative Party*, 171.
121. Derby, 7 June 1861, *Hansard*, 3rd ser., clxiii. 710–27.
122. Stanley, diary, 17 June 1861, cited in Derby, *Disraeli, Derby and the Conservative Party*, 173.
123. Stanley, diary, 1 Aug. 1861, cited in Derby, *Disraeli, Derby and the Conservative Party*, 174.
124. Malmesbury, *Memoirs*, ii. 255. Macbeth says: 'Thou canst not say I did it: never shake | Thy gory locks at me' (*Macbeth*, III. iv. 50).
125. Pakington to Disraeli, 8 June 1861, Hughenden MSS, B/XX/P/64.
126. Clarendon to Cornewall Lewis, 10 Oct. 1860, cited in Maxwell, *Clarendon*, ii. 228.
127. Georgiana Peel, *Recollections of Lady Georgiana Peel*, ed. Ethel Peel (1920), 172.
128. Clarendon to Cornewall Lewis, 10 Oct. 1860, cited in Maxwell, *Clarendon*, ii. 228.
129. Graham to Derby, 12 May 1854, Graham MSS, 119.
130. Stanley, diary, 18 Oct. 1861, cited in Derby, *Disraeli, Derby and the Conservative Party*, 177.
131. Stanley, diary, 26 Nov. 1861, cited in Derby, *Disraeli, Derby and the Conservative Party*, 178.
132. Clarendon to Duchess of Manchester, 7 Aug. 1860, cited in Kennedy (ed.), *'Dear Duchess'*, 112.
133. Disraeli to Mary Anne Disraeli, 26 Jan. 1863, Hughenden MSS, A/1/A/313.
134. Derby to Disraeli, 15 Oct. 1864, Hughenden MSS, B/XX/S/325; Derby to Disraeli, 10 Dec. 1864, Hughenden MSS, B/XX/S/327.
135. Stanley, diary, 21 Sept. 1862, cited in Derby, *Disraeli, Derby and the Conservative Party*, 192.
136. Pakington to Disraeli, 8 June 1861, Hughenden MSS, B/XX/P/64.
137. Stanley, diary, 14 Oct. 1861, cited in Derby, *Disraeli, Derby and the Conservative Party*, 177.
138. Derby to Disraeli, 19 Nov. 1863, Hughenden MSS, B/XX/S/317.
139. Stanley, diary, 23 July 1862, cited in Derby, *Disraeli, Derby and the Conservative Party*, 190. In July 1861 four of Derby's gamekeepers had been violently assaulted and seriously injured when trying to apprehend a large group of poachers on the Knowsley estate. See *The Times*, 8 July 1861, 11.
140. Stanley, diary, 30 Nov. 1861, cited in Derby, *Disraeli, Derby and the Conservative Party*, 179.

141. Stanley, diary, 1 Dec. 1861, cited in Derby, *Disraeli, Derby and the Conservative Party*, 179.

142. Malmesbury, *Memoirs*, ii. 261.

143. Derby to Lyndhurst, 8 Dec. 1861, Derby MSS, 189/1.

144. Derby to Normanby, 1 Dec. 1861, Derby MSS, 189/1.

145. Ibid.

146. Derby to Newcastle, 5 Jan. 1862, Derby MSS, 189/1.

147. Derby to Granville, 3 Jan. 1862, Derby MSS, 189/1.

148. Derby to Lyndhurst, 8 Dec. 1861, Derby MSS, 189/1.

149. Derby to Granville, 3 Jan. 1862, Derby MSS, 189/1.

150. Malmesbury, *Memoirs*, ii. 267.

151. Fitzmaurice, *Granville*, i. 407.

152. Malmesbury, *Memoirs*, ii. 267.

153. Stanley, diary, 23 Jan. 1862, cited in Derby, *Disraeli, Derby and the Conservative Party*, 182.

154. Derby, 6 Feb. 1862, *Hansard*, 3rd ser., clxv. 26–39.

155. Derby to Disraeli, [8 Feb. 1862], Hughenden MSS, B/XX/S/294.

156. Derby, 4 Mar. 1862, *Hansard*, 3rd ser., cxlv. 1013–18.

157. Stanley, diary, 17 Apr. 1862, cited in Derby, *Disraeli, Derby and the Conservative Party*, 184.

158. Northcote to Disraeli, 19 and 25 Apr. 1862, Iddesleigh MSS, 50015.

159. Trelawny, diary, 19 May 1862, cited in Trelawny, *Diaries*, 204.

160. White, *The Inner Life of the House of Commons*, i. 173.

161. Derby to Disraeli, 21 May 1862, Hughenden MSS, B/XX/S/298.

162. Stanley, diary, 24 May 1862, cited in Derby, *Disraeli, Derby and the Conservative Party*, 185.

163. Stanley, diary, 2 June 1862, cited in Derby, *Disraeli, Derby and the Conservative Party*, 186.

164. Derby to Disraeli, 7 June 1862, Hughenden MSS, B/XX/S/300.

165. Palmerston to Queen Victoria, 3 June 1862, cited in Bell, *Palmerston*, ii. 325.

166. Stanley, diary, 3 June 1862, cited in Derby, *Disraeli, Derby and the Conservative Party*, 187.

167. Derby to Disraeli, 29 Jan. 1863, Hughenden MSS, B/XX/S/311.

168. Derby to Disraeli, 17 June 1862, Hughenden MSS, B/XX/S/300.

169. Derby to Sotheron-Estcourt, 20 June 1862, Derby MSS, 189/1.

170. Ibid.

171. Derby to Whiteside, 8 June 1862, Derby MSS, 189/1.

172. Stanley, diary, 16 June 1862, cited in Derby, *Disraeli, Derby and the Conservative Party*, 188.

173. Derby to Clarendon, 20 June 1862, Derby MSS, 189/1.

174. Stanley, diary, 2 Sept. 1862, cited in Derby, *Disraeli, Derby and the Conservative Party*, 190.

175. Ibid.

176. Derby to Malmesbury, 4 Sept. 1862, Derby MSS, 189/1.
177. See W. O. Henderson, *The Lancashire Cotton Famine 1861–1865* (Manchester, 1934), 79–80.
178. For Derby's correspondence regarding the cotton famine, mainly with John Maclure and Sir James Kay-Shuttleworth, see Derby MSS, 114.
179. Derby to Malmesbury, 31 Oct. 1862, cited in Malmesbury, *Memoirs*, ii. 285.
180. *The Times*, 3 Dec. 1862, 5. In its editorial *The Times* stated that 'the crisis has been met in a manner which is worthy of our character as a great Christian nation' (*The Times*, 3 Dec. 1862, 9).
181. *The Times*, 22 Jan. 1863, 10, and Henderson, *The Lancashire Cotton Famine*, 85.
182. Derby, 4 Feb. 1864, *Hansard*, 3rd ser., clxxiii. 22.
183. Disraeli to Mrs Brydges Willyams, 7 Feb. 1863, cited in Monypenny and Buckle, *Disraeli*, iv. 332.
184. Patten to Sotheron-Estcourt, 7 Feb. 1863, Sotheron-Estcourt MSS, D1571/F.367.
185. Disraeli to Mrs Brydges Willyams, 7 Feb. 1863, cited in Monypenny and Buckle, *Disraeli*, iv. 332.
186. *The Times*, 8 July 1863, 8.
187. *The Times*, 12 May 1862, 8.
188. Gerard to Derby, 2 Dec. 1861, Derby MSS, 107/7.
189. Derby to Gerard, 9 Dec. 1861, Derby MSS, 189/1.
190. Derby, 9 May 1862, *Hansard*, 3rd ser., clxvi. 1453–6.
191. A. E. Dingle, '"The Monster Nuisance of All": Landowners, Alkali Manufacturers, and Air Pollution', *Economic History Review*, 35/4 (1982), 529–48.
192. Ibid. 547.
193. Derby, *The Iliad of Homer*, i. vi.
194. Stanley, diary, 2 Sept. 1864, cited in Derby, *Disraeli, Derby and the Conservative Party*, 224.
195. Derby, *The Iliad of Homer*, vol. i, p. ix.
196. Bulwer Lytton to Lady Salisbury, 11 Jan. 1865, cited in Lady Burghclere (ed.), *A Great Lady's Friendships: Letters to Mary, Marchioness of Salisbury, Countess Derby, 1862–1890* (1933), 61.
197. Gladstone, diary, 14 Dec. 1864, cited in Gladstone, *Diaries*, vi. 319.
198. Gladstone to Duchess of Sutherland, 28 Dec. 1864, cited in Morley, *Gladstone*, ii. 193.
199. Derby to Malmesbury, 9 Dec. 1864, cited in Malmesbury, *Memoirs*, ii. 332.
200. For Derby's extensive correspondence during this period with the Prince of Wales and the Queen's private secretary, General Charles Grey, about the Commission's planning of the Royal Albert Hall and the Albert Memorial, see Derby MSS, 102/1, 103/6.
201. Derby to Malmesbury, 31 Oct. 1862, cited in Malmesbury, *Memoirs*, ii. 285.
202. Derby to Normanby, 20 Jan. 1863, Derby MSS, 189/2.
203. Derby to Disraeli, 29 Jan. 1863, Hughenden MSS, B/XX/S/311; Bell, *Palmerston*, ii. 345.

204. Derby to Malmesbury, 4 Sept. 1862, Derby MSS, 189/1.

205. Granville to Russell, 30 Sept. 1862, Russell MSS, PRO 30/22/25, cited in Fitzmaurice, *Granville*, i. 442–4.

206. Palmerston to Russell, 22 Oct. 1862, Russell MSS, PRO 30/22/14/D.

207. Derby to Malmesbury, 4 Sept. 1862, Derby MSS, 189/1.

208. Derby, 5 Feb. 1863, *Hansard*, 3rd ser., clxix. 21–41.

209. Stanley, diary, 2 July 1863, cited in Derby, *Disraeli, Derby and the Conservative Party*, 199.

210. Stanley, diary, 9 July 1863, cited in Derby, *Disraeli, Derby and the Conservative Party*, 199.

211. Palmerston to Russell, 26 Oct. 1862, Russell MSS, PRO 30/22/14/D.

212. Palmerston to Russell, 6 Nov. 1862, Russell MSS, PRO 30/22/14/D.

213. Derby to Stanhope, 11 Jan. 1863, Derby MSS, 189/2.

214. Ibid.

215. Derby to Normanby, 20 Jan. 1863, Derby MSS, 189/2.

216. Ibid.

217. Clarendon to Palmerston, 1 Jan. 1863, Broadlands MSS, GC/CL/1208.

218. Clarendon to Cowley, 24 Jan. 1863, cited in David Krein, *The Last Palmerston Government* (Ames, Ia., 1978), 86.

219. Derby, 5 Feb. 1863, *Hansard*, 3rd ser., clxix. 21–41.

220. Derby to Normanby, 9 Apr. 1863, Derby MSS, 189/2.

221. Derby to Malmesbury, 25 Nov. 1862, cited in Malmesbury, *Memoirs*, ii. 287.

222. Stanley, diary, 19 Dec. 1862, cited in Derby, *Disraeli, Derby and the Conservative Party*, 193.

223. Palmerston to Russell, 25 Nov. 1862, Russell MSS, PRO 30/22/14/D.

224. Disraeli to Mrs Brydges Willyams, 9 Dec. 1862, cited in Monypenny and Buckle, *Disraeli*, iv. 331.

225. Disraeli to Mrs Brydges Willyams, 17 Oct. 1863, cited in Monypenny and Buckle, *Disraeli*, iv. 339.

226. Derby, 13 July 1863, *Hansard*, 3rd ser., clxii. 641–8.

227. Derby to Malmesbury, 31 Oct. 1862, cited in Malmesbury, *Memoirs*, ii. 285.

228. Malmesbury, *Memoirs*, ii. 286.

229. Derby, 15 May 1863, *Hansard*, 3rd ser., clxx. 1755–62.

230. Kimberley diary, 15 May 1863, cited in Kimberley, *Journal*, 96.

231. Palmerston, 23 July 1863, *Hansard*, 3rd ser., clxxii. 1252.

232. Russell to Cowley, 25 Nov. 1863, cited in S. Walpole, *The Life of Lord John Russell*, 2 vols (1889), ii. 382.

233. Derby to Stanhope, 22 Dec. 1863, Derby MSS, 189/2.

234. Derby to Malmesbury, 10 Jan. 1864, cited in Malmesbury, *Memoirs*, ii. 310.

235. Derby to Normanby, 9 Apr. 1863, Derby MSS, 189/2.

236. See Wood to Russell, 3 Dec. 1863, Russell MSS, PRO 30/22/14/9.

237. Stanley, diary, 1 Dec. 1863, cited in Derby, *Disraeli, Derby and the Conservative Party*, 203.

238. Clarendon to Cowley, 28 Mar. 1863, cited in Wellesley, *The Paris Embassy during the Second Empire*, 251.

239. Derby to Lady Londonderry, 5 Aug. 1863, Derby MSS, 189/2.

240. *The Times*, 2 July 1863, 11.

241. Stanley, diary, 10 Dec. 1863, cited in Derby, *Disraeli, Derby and the Conservative Party*, 203.

242. Ibid.

243. Derby to Henley, 27 Nov. 1863, Derby MSS, 189/2.

244. Stanley, diary, 18 Dec. 1863, cited in Derby, *Disraeli, Derby and the Conservative Party*, 204.

245. Russell, memorandum, 27 Jan. 1864, Russell MSS, PRO 30/22/27.

246. Derby to Disraeli, 29 Jan. 1864, Hughenden MSS, B/XX/S/321.

247. Malmesbury, *Memoirs*, ii. 313.

248. Derby, 4 Feb. 1864, *Hansard*, 3rd ser., clxxiii. 22–41.

249. Bell, *Palmerston*, ii. 377.

250. Palmerston to Russell, 13 Feb. 1864, Russell MSS, PRO 30/22/15/A.

251. Stanley, diary, 12 Mar. 1864, cited in Derby, *Disraeli, Derby and the Conservative Party*, 211.

252. Malmesbury, *Memoirs*, ii. 320.

253. Bath to Derby, 12 Apr. 1864, Derby MSS, 164/11.

254. Derby to Bath, 13 Apr. 1864, Derby MSS, 189/2.

255. Bath to Derby, 16 Apr. 1864, Derby MSS, 164/11.

256. Stanley found Disraeli 'in his most paradoxical mood, talking of Garibaldi, denying that he ever won a battle, asserting that his Neapolitan success was due wholly to bribery'. Fifteen years before, Stanley had found this sort of conversation captivating, but by 1864 his reaction was very different. 'Amusing at first, but his cynical affectation is apt to grow tedious' (Stanley, diary, 10 Apr. 1864, cited in Derby, *Disraeli, Derby and the Conservative Party*, 213).

257. Disraeli to Derby, 13 May 1864, Derby MSS, 146/1.

258. Clarendon to Granville, 22 Mar. 1864, cited in Maxwell, *Clarendon*, ii. 287.

259. Trelawny, diary, 9 July 1863, cited in Trelawny, *Diaries*, 300.

260. Derby to Disraeli, 12 May 1864, Hughenden MSS, B/XX/S/322.

261. Stanley, diary, 3 June 1864, cited in Derby, *Disraeli, Derby and the Conservative Party*, 217.

262. Russell, 27 June 1864, *Hansard*, 3rd ser., clxxvi. 322; Derby, 27 June 1864, *Hansard*, 3rd ser., clxxvi. 324–31.

263. Stanley, diary, 22 Apr. 1864, cited in Derby, *Disraeli, Derby and the Conservative Party*, 214.

264. Stanley, diary, 3 July 1864, cited in Derby, *Disraeli, Derby and the Conservative Party*, 221.

265. Malmesbury, *Memoirs*, ii. 327.

266. Malmesbury, 8 July 1864, *Hansard*, 3rd ser., clxxvi. 1076–94.

267. Kimberley, *Journal*, 140.

268. Monypenny and Buckle, *Disraeli*, iv. 405.

269. Stanley, diary, 21 July 1864, cited in Derby, *Disraeli, Derby and the Conservative Party*, 222.

270. Kimberley, *Journal*, 141.

271. Derby to Disraeli, 15 Oct. 1864, Hughenden MSS, B/XX/S/325.

272. Derby to Taylor, 27 Oct. 1864, Derby MSS, 190/1.

273. Lennox to Disraeli, 11 Nov. 1864, Hughenden MSS, B/XX/LX/202.

274. Malmesbury, *Memoirs*, ii. 334.

275. Derby to Disraeli, 10 Dec. 1864, Hughenden MSS, B/XX/S/327; Derby to Disraeli, 30 Jan. 1865, Hughenden MSS, B/XX/S/331.

276. Ibid.

277. Disraeli to Derby, 12 Dec. 1864, Derby MSS, 146/1.

278. Derby, 7 Feb. 1865, *Hansard*, 3rd ser., clxxvii. 21–30.

279. Derby, 20 Feb. 1865, *Hansard*, 3rd ser., clxxvii. 425–30.

280. Stanley, diary, 31 Mar. 1865, cited in Derby, *Disraeli, Derby and the Conservative Party*, 230.

281. Derby to Disraeli, 10 Mar. 1865, Hughenden MSS, B/XX/S/332.

282. Bell, *Palmerston*, ii. 386.

283. E. Hodder, *The Life and Work of the Seventh Earl of Shaftesbury*, 3 vols (1886), iii. 187.

284. Stanley, diary, 22 Mar. 1865, cited in Derby, *Disraeli, Derby and the Conservative Party*, 230.

285. Malmesbury, *Memoirs*, ii. 336.

286. Clarendon to Duchess of Manchester, 26 Apr. 1865, cited in Kennedy (ed.), *'Dear Duchess'*, 236.

287. Stanley, diary, 11 Feb. 1865, cited in Derby, *Disraeli, Derby and the Conservative Party*, 227.

288. Derby, 1 May 1865, *Hansard*, 3rd ser., clxxviii. 1223–6. In an editorial the following day *The Times* upbraided Derby for pronouncing that the conduct of the South, if it had authorized Lincoln's assassination, would have been 'worse than a crime, that is, a blunder'. Such cynicism, the paper declared, might not be inappropriate in after-dinner conversation among friends, but deserved the gravest reprehension when stated at such a solemn and momentous public occasion. *The Times*, 2 May 1865, 11.

289. Derby, 12 June 1865, *Hansard*, 3rd ser., clxxx. 1–4.

290. Derby, 26 June 1865, *Hansard*, 3rd ser., clxxx. 772–92.

291. Skelmersdale to Derby, 5 May 1864, Derby MSS, 106/7.

292. Clarendon to Duchess of Manchester, 13 Apr. 1865, cited in Kennedy (ed.), *'Dear Duchess'*, 230.

293. Stanley, diary, 22 Jan. 1865, cited in Derby, *Disraeli, Derby and the Conservative Party*, 226.

294. *Annual Register* (1865), 153. With 'the state of political feeling, and the general quiet, almost apathy, which prevail', *The Times* anticipated 'that

the Liberal party will improve its position' during the elections (*The Times*, 14 June 1865, 11).

295.   Derby to Disraeli, 24 July 1865, Hughenden MSS, B/XX/S/334; Derby to Disraeli, 4 Aug. 1865, Hughenden MSS, B/XX/S/335. A letter from Derby was printed in *The Times* on 7 July in which he expressed his regret at any offence caused to Catholic voters by his statement on the parliamentary oath on 26 June (*The Times*, 7 July 1865, 6).

296.   Disraeli to Derby, 28 July 1865, Derby MSS, 146/1.

297.   Malmesbury, *Memoirs*, ii. 340.

298.   Spofforth to Derby, 2 Aug. 1865, Derby MSS, 104.

299.   Hardy, diary, 25 Sept. 1865, cited in Maurice Cowling, *1867: Disraeli, Gladstone and Revolution: The Passing of the Second Reform Act* (Cambridge, 1967), 80.

300.   Disraeli to Derby, 6 Aug. 1865, Derby MSS, 146/1.

301.   Derby to Disraeli, 12 Aug. 1865, Hughenden MSS, B/XX/S/336.

302.   Stanley, diary, 12 Aug. 1865, cited in Derby, *Disraeli, Derby and the Conservative Party*, 234, where the entry is misdated as 2 Aug. 1865.

303.   Derby to Disraeli, 12 Aug. 1865, Hughenden MSS, B/XX/S/336.

304.   Stanley, diary, 17 Sept. 1865, cited in Derby, *Disraeli, Derby and the Conservative Party*, 235.

305.   Derby to Stanley, 2 Feb. 1865, Derby MSS, 920DER(15), 'Letters from Parents'.

306.   Stanley, diary, 19 Nov. 1865, cited in Derby, *Disraeli, Derby and the Conservative Party*, 241.

307.   A. Martin, *The Life and Letters of the Rt. Hon. Robert Lowe, Viscount Sherbrooke*, 2 vols (1893), ii. 243.

308.   Stanley, diary, 18 July 1865, cited in Derby, *Disraeli, Derby and the Conservative Party*, 233.

309.   West, *Recollections*, i. 306.

310.   Wellesley, *The Paris Embassy during the Second Empire*, 287.

311.   Stanley, diary, 26 Oct. 1865, cited in Derby, *Disraeli, Derby and the Conservative Party*, 237.

312.   Derby to Malmesbury, 6 Nov. 1865, Derby MSS, 190/1.

313.   Stanley, diary, 21 Nov. 1865, cited in Derby, *Disraeli, Derby and the Conservative Party*, 241.

314.   Malmesbury to Derby, 8 Nov. 1865, Derby MSS, 144/2.

315.   Derby to Pakington, 10 Nov. 1865, Derby MSS, 190/1.

316.   Derby to Disraeli, 21 Nov. 1865, Hughenden MSS, B/XX/S/337.

317.   Derby to Taylor, 14 Dec. 1865, Derby MSS, 190/2.

318.   Derby to Whiteside, 28 Dec. 1865, Derby MSS, 190/2.

319.   Derby to Whiteside, 19 Jan. 1866, Derby MSS, 190/2.

320.   Derby to Carnarvon, 7 Nov. 1865, Derby MSS, 190/1.

321.   Spofforth to Disraeli, 5 Jan. 1866, Hughenden MSS, B/XXI/S/405.

322. Derby to Pakington, 10 Nov. 1865, Derby MSS, 190/1.
323. Taylor to Derby, 6 Dec. 1865, Derby MSS, 113; Spofforth to Disraeli, 9 Dec. 1865, Hughenden MSS, B/XXI/S/403.
324. Disraeli to Derby, 24 Nov. 1865, Derby MSS, 146/1.
325. Spofforth to Disraeli, 30 Oct. 1865, Hughenden MSS, B/XXI/S/401.
326. Stanley, diary, 3 Nov. 1865, cited in Derby, *Disraeli, Derby and the Conservative Party*, 239.
327. Ibid.
328. Stanley, diary, 10 Jan. 1866, cited in Derby, *Disraeli, Derby and the Conservative Party*, 244.
329. Derby to Disraeli, 21 Nov. 1865, Hughenden MSS, B/XX/S/337.
330. Disraeli to Derby, 24 Nov. 1865, Derby MSS, 146/1.
331. Stanley, diary, 1 Mar. 1866, cited in Derby, *Disraeli, Derby and the Conservative Party*, 247.
332. Derby, 6 Feb. 1866, *Hansard*, 3rd ser., clxxxi. 87–101.
333. Derby to Disraeli, n.d. [6 Feb. 1866?], Hughenden MSS, B/XX/S/390.
334. A. E. Gathorne Hardy, *The Diary of Gathorne Hardy, Later Lord Cranbrook, 1866–1892*, ed. Nancy Johnson (Oxford, 1981), 5.
335. Ibid. 6.
336. G. M. Trevelyan, *The Life of John Bright* (1913), 354.
337. Northcote, diary, 16 Mar. 1866, Iddesleigh MSS, 50063A.
338. Ibid.
339. Malmesbury, *Memoirs*, ii. 350.
340. Stanley, diary, 11 Apr. 1866, cited in Derby, *Disraeli, Derby and the Conservative Party*, 249.
341. Gathorne Hardy, *Diary*, 7.
342. Elcho to Grosvenor, n.d. [1866], Wemyss MSS, cited in Cowling, *1867*, 101.
343. Gladstone, 27 Apr. 1866, *Hansard*, 3rd ser., clxxxiii. 152.
344. Stanley, diary, 28 Apr. 1866, cited in Derby, *Disraeli, Derby and the Conservative Party*, 249.
345. Stanley, diary, 29 Apr. 1866, cited in Derby, *Disraeli, Derby and the Conservative Party*, 250.
346. Ibid.
347. Derby to Malmesbury, 22 Apr. 1866, cited in Malmesbury, *Memoirs*, ii. 351–2.
348. Derby to Queen Victoria, 30 May 1866, Derby MSS, 190/2.
349. Derby to Disraeli, 10 June 1866, Hughenden MSS, B/XX/S/345.
350. Stanley, diary, 18 June 1866, cited in Derby, *Disraeli, Derby and the Conservative Party*, 253.
351. Monypenny and Buckle, *Disraeli*, iv. 439.
352. Derby to Disraeli, [22 June 1866?], Hughenden MSS, B/XX/S/346
353. Disraeli to Derby, 23 June 1866, Derby MSS, 146/2.
354. Derby to Disraeli, 24 June 1866, Derby MSS, 190/2.

355. Stanley, diary, 25 June 1866, cited in Derby, *Disraeli, Derby and the Conservative Party*, 255.

356. Derby, 26 June 1866, *Hansard*, 3rd ser., clxxxiv. 660–6.

357. Taylor to Disraeli, [27 June 1866?], Hughenden MSS, B/XX/T/70. At the meeting Bath declared that 'a pure Derbyite government' could not last and he urged Derby to hand over the task to Stanley, who would be able to secure a merger with the Whigs. The anti-Disraeli faction, Lord Cadogan, Sir Rainald Knightley, Baillie Cochrane, Cavendish Bentinck, and Beresford Hope, associated themselves with Bath's dissent. Northcote, diary, 28 June 1866, Iddesleigh MSS, 50063A.

358. See Derby, memorandum, 30 June 1866, Hughenden MSS, B/XX/S/349, for the abortive negotiations with the Adullamites conducted through Lord Lansdowne and Lord Grosvenor. On 30 June, Derby suggested to Clanricarde that he might offer William Gregory the Admiralty and Dunkellin the Irish Lordship of the Treasury. But this was a paltry offering, far short of the cabinet presence to which the Adullamites aspired, and one he knew would be refused. Derby to Clanricarde, 30 June 1866, Derby MSS, 191/1.

359. Malmesbury to Derby, 20 Apr. 1866, Derby MSS, 144/2.

360. Malmesbury, diary, 1866, Malmesbury MSS, 9M73/79.

361. Stanley to Derby, 27 Apr. 1866, Derby MSS, 105/7.

362. In his letter to Clarendon, Derby emphasized the Queen's wish for moderate men to come together and her anxiety that the thread of British diplomacy not be broken (Derby to Clarendon, 28 June 1866, Derby MSS, 190/2). Clarendon's rejection of Derby's invitation caused the Queen some irritation. Through General Grey she observed that Clarendon acknowledged that there was no difference with Derby over foreign policy and expressed her annoyance that being 'bound to a particular party, or other association of public men (for party implies some difference of principle) should prevent men acting together where union in government would be for the evident advantage of the country' (General Grey to Derby, 29 June 1866, Derby MSS, 103/6).

363. Stanley, diary, 30 Mar. 1866, cited in Derby, *Disraeli, Derby and the Conservative Party*, 248.

364. Stanley, diary, 29 June 1866, cited in Derby, *Disraeli, Derby and the Conservative Party*, 256.

365. Disraeli to Derby, 25 June 1866, Derby MSS, 146/2.

366. Derby to Disraeli, [1 July 1866?], Hughenden MSS, B/XX/S/397.

367. Stanley to Derby, 11 Aug. 1858, Derby MSS, 105/5.

368. Stanley, diary, 3 July 1866, cited in Derby, *Disraeli, Derby and the Conservative Party*, 257.

369. *The Times*, 5 July 1866, 8.

CHAPTER 6. DERBY'S THIRD PREMIERSHIP: 1866–1868

1. Gathorne Hardy, *Diary*, 11.
2. *The Times*, 7 July 1866, 8.
3. Malmesbury, *Memoirs*, ii. 360–1.
4. Derby, 9 July 1866, *Hansard*, 3rd ser., clxxxiv. 726–44.
5. Derby to the Queen, 10 July 1866, Derby MSS, 191/1.
6. *The Times*, 10 July 1866, 8.
7. Stanley, diary, 24 July 1866, cited in Derby, *Disraeli, Derby and the Conservative Party*, 261.
8. Stanley, diary, 25 July 1866, cited in Derby, *Disraeli, Derby and the Conservative Party*, 261.
9. Derby, 24 July 1866, *Hansard*, 3rd ser., clxxxiv. 1370–4.
10. Malmesbury, *Memoirs*, ii. 362.
11. Derby to Disraeli, 26 July 1866, Hughenden MSS, B/XX/S/357.
12. See Derby to Queen Victoria, 26 July 1866, Derby MSS, 191/1. Derby instructed troops to be brought up from Aldershot and the 14th Lancers to be held in readiness at Hounslow in case Reform protesters, in defiance of their leadership, attempted to hold another demonstration in Hyde Park (Derby to General Grey, 27 July 1866, Derby MSS, 191/1).
13. Derby, 27 July 1866, *Hansard*, 3rd ser., clxxxiv. 1590–1.
14. Manners to his brother, 28 July 1866, cited in Cowling, *1867*, 25.
15. Disraeli to Derby, 29 July 1866, Derby MSS, 146/2.
16. Stanley, diary, 4 July 1866, cited in Derby, *Disraeli, Derby and the Conservative Party*, 258.
17. Derby, 3 Aug. 1866, *Hansard*, 3rd ser., clxxxiv. 1987–90. The previous day Derby wrote to Russell asking him not to bring on a Lords discussion on political meetings in the royal parks, a request which Russell ignored (Derby to Russell, 2 Aug. 1866, Derby MSS, 191/1).
18. Stanley, diary, 23 July 1866, cited in Derby, *Disraeli, Derby and the Conservative Party*, 261.
19. Derby to Carnarvon, 7 Feb. 1867, cited in G. Martin, *Britain and the Origins of Canadian Federation* (1995), 282.
20. Stanley, diary, 15 Nov. 1866, cited in Derby, *Disraeli, Derby and the Conservative Party*, 275.
21. Stanley, diary, 13 July 1866, cited in Derby, *Disraeli, Derby and the Conservative Party*, 259.
22. Ibid.
23. Stanley, diary, 30 July 1866, cited in Derby, *Disraeli, Derby and the Conservative Party*, 262.
24. Derby, 20 July 1866, *Hansard*, 3rd ser., clxxxiv. 1155.
25. Derby, 23 July 1866, *Hansard*, 3rd ser., clxxxiv. 1270–4.
26. General Grey to Derby, 30 July 1866, Derby MSS, 103/6.

27. Stanley, diary, 14 Aug. 1866, cited in Derby, *Disraeli, Derby and the Conservative Party*, 265.

28. Derby to Queen Victoria, 31 July 1866, Derby MSS, 191/2.

29. Derby to Duke of Cambridge, 31 Aug. 1866, Derby MSS, 190/2.

30. Derby to Queen Victoria, 5 Aug. 1866, Derby MSS, 190/2.

31. Derby, 6 Aug. 1866, *Hansard*, 3rd ser., clxxxiv. 2074–7.

32. Stanley, diary, 29 Aug. 1866, cited in Derby, *Disraeli, Derby and the Conservative Party*, 268.

33. Gathorne Hardy, *Diary*, 21.

34. Derby to Cranborne, 11 Aug. 1866, Derby MSS, 191/1.

35. Stanley, diary, 29 Aug. 1866, cited in Derby, *Disraeli, Derby and the Conservative Party*, 268.

36. Stanley, diary, 1 Nov. 1866, cited in Derby, *Disraeli, Derby and the Conservative Party*, 269.

37. Derby to Disraeli, 16 Sept. 1866, Hughenden MSS, B/XX/S/364.

38. Monypenny and Buckle, *Disraeli*, iv. 464.

39. Derby to Disraeli, 27 Sept. 1866, Hughenden MSS, B/XX/S/366.

40. Derby to Disraeli, 16 Sept. 1866, Hughenden MSS, B/XX/S/364.

41. Ibid.

42. Disraeli to Derby, 24 Sept. 1866, Derby MSS, 146/2.

43. Derby to Disraeli, 27 Sept. 1866, Hughenden MSS, B/XX/S/366.

44. Derby to Disraeli, 9 Oct. 1866, Hughenden MSS, B/XX/S/367.

45. Derby, memorandum, 9 Oct. 1866, Derby MSS, 191/2.

46. Disraeli to Derby, 12 Oct. 1866, Derby MSS, 146/2.

47. Stanley, diary, 1 Nov. 1866, cited in Derby, *Disraeli, Derby and the Conservative Party*, 272. Derby reported to the Queen that it was the unanimous opinion of the cabinet that, despite the difficulties surrounding the question, it could not be ignored and must be resolutely grappled with. The manner in which Reform would be handled and the course adopted, he assured the Queen, would allow ample time for the exercise of any influence which she might exert 'towards the settlement of the question, *after* a proposal may have been submitted to parliament, and when, consequently, there can be no ground for a charge of collusion between the heads of rival parties' (Derby to Queen Victoria, 1 Nov. 1866, Derby MSS, 192/1).

48. Derby, memorandum, 8 Nov. 1866, Hughenden MSS, B/XX/S/374.

49. Derby to Pakington, 4 Dec. 1866, Derby MSS, 193/1. Lord Grey, seemingly independently, arrived at a proposal for how to handle the process of a Reform Bill very similar to Derby's own. Throughout the following months Derby's communication with Lord Grey's brother General Grey was close and confidential; Derby and General Grey clearly had a high regard for each other and believed that they shared the same principles and views. General Grey to Derby, 28 Oct. 1866, Derby MSS, 103/6.

50. Derby to Disraeli, 19 Nov. 1866, Hughenden MSS, B/XX/S/375.

51. Disraeli to Derby, 18 Nov. 1866, Derby MSS, 146/2.

52. Derby to Disraeli, 19 Nov. 1866, Hughenden MSS, B/XX/S/375.

53. Stanley, diary, 4 Dec. 1866, cited in Derby, *Disraeli, Derby and the Conservative Party*, 277.

54. Derby to Disraeli, 22 Dec. 1866, Hughenden MSS, B/XX/S/380.

55. Derby to Disraeli, [Dec. 1866?], Hughenden MSS, B/XX/S/383.

56. Nelson to Derby, 17 Nov. 1866, Derby MSS, 150/16.

57. Derby to Disraeli, 27 Dec. 1866, Hughenden MSS, B/XX/S/381.

58. Derby to Disraeli, 2 Feb. 1867, Hughenden MSS, B/XX/S/405.

59. Disraeli to Cranborne, 26 Dec. 1866, cited in Monypenny and Buckle, *Disraeli*, iv. 463.

60. Derby to Queen Victoria, 10 Jan. 1867, Derby MSS, 192/1.

61. Monypenny and Buckle, *Disraeli*, iv. 487.

62. Derby to Disraeli, n.d., Hughenden MSS, B/XX/S/468.

63. Stanley, diary, 10 Jan. 1867, cited in Derby, *Disraeli, Derby and the Conservative Party*, 284.

64. Derby to General Grey, 7 Feb. 1867, Derby MSS, 193/1; Stanley, diary, 29 Jan. 1867, cited in Derby, *Disraeli, Derby and the Conservative Party*, 287.

65. Derby to Disraeli, 2 Feb. 1867, Hughenden MSS, B/XX/S/405.

66. Stanley, diary, 5 Feb. 1867, cited in Derby, *Disraeli, Derby and the Conservative Party*, 287.

67. Disraeli to Derby, [7 Feb. 1867?], Derby MSS, 146/3.

68. Shaftesbury to Derby, 19 Oct. 1866, Derby MSS, 113.

69. Derby to Disraeli, [Feb. 1867?], Hughenden MSS, B/XX/S/414.

70. Stanley, diary, 17 Jan. 1867, cited in Derby, *Disraeli, Derby and the Conservative Party*, 285. For Derby's personal sympathy for Pakington's proposals, see Derby to Pakington, 15 Sept. 1866, Derby MSS, 191/2.

71. Stanley, diary, 22 Jan. 1867, cited in Derby, *Disraeli, Derby and the Conservative Party*, 285–6.

72. Disraeli to Derby, 2 Feb. 1867, Derby MSS, 146/3.

73. Stanley, 20 July 1866, *Hansard*, 3rd ser., clxxxiv. 1256.

74. Stanley to General Grey, 27 Apr. 1867, cited in Queen Victoria, *The Letters of Queen Victoria, 1862–1878, 2nd Series*, ed. G. E. Buckle, 3 vols (1926), i. 423.

75. Disraeli to Northcote, 14 Oct. 1866, cited in Monypenny and Buckle, *Disraeli*, iv. 479.

76. Derby to Disraeli, 10 Oct. 1866, Hughenden MSS, B/XX/S/ 368.

77. Lowe to Lady Salisbury, 15 Oct. 1866, cited in Burghclere (ed.), *A Great Lady's Friendships*, 90–1.

78. *The Times*, 5 Feb. 1867, 8.

79. Disraeli to Derby, 24 Mar. 1867, Derby MSS, 146/3.

80. Derby to Disraeli, 3 Dec. 1866, Hughenden MSS, B/XX/S/379.

81. Stanley, diary, 11 Feb. 1867, cited in Derby, *Disraeli, Derby and the Conservative Party*, 288.

82. Kimberley, *Journal*, 196.

83. Brand to Halifax, 29 Jan. 1867, and Dundas to Halifax, 2 Feb. 1867, cited
     in Maxwell, *Clarendon*, ii. 329–30; Derby to Queen Victoria, 6 Feb. 1867,
     Derby MSS, 192/1.

84. Derby to Disraeli, [6 Feb. 1867], Hughenden MSS, B/XX/S/408.

85. Derby to General Grey, 7 Feb. 1867, Derby MSS, 192/1.

86. Derby to General Grey, 6 Feb. 1867, Derby MSS, 192/1.

87. Malmesbury, *Memoirs*, ii. 365.

88. Stanley, diary, 11 Feb. 1867, cited in Derby, *Disraeli, Derby and the Conser-
     vative Party*, 288.

89. Kimberley, *Journal*, 197.

90. Stanley, diary, 11 Feb. 1867, cited in Derby, *Disraeli, Derby and the Conser-
     vative Party*, 288.

91. Ibid.

92. Clarendon to Mrs Villiers, 8 Feb. 1867, cited in Maxwell, *Clarendon*, ii. 332.

93. Queen Victoria to Derby, 13 Feb. 1867, cited in Monypenny and Buckle,
     Disraeli, iv. 494.

94. Derby to Queen Victoria, 14 Feb. 1867, Derby MSS, 192/1.

95. Derby to the Queen, 14 Feb. 1867, Derby MSS, 192/1.

96. Lady Gwendolyn Cecil, *The Life of Robert, Marquis of Salisbury*, 4 vols
     (1921–32), i. 229–30.

97. Stanley, diary, 16 Feb. 1867, cited in Derby, *Disraeli, Derby and the Conser-
     vative Party*, 289.

98. Ibid.; Malmesbury, *Memoirs*, ii. 365.

99. Queen Victoria to Peel, 17 Feb. 1867, Derby MSS, 103/7; Disraeli, memoran-
     dum, [17 Feb. 1867?], cited in Monypenny and Buckle, *Disraeli*, iv. 495–6.
     Although General Grey thought that 'Peel's resignation on this question
     might help you rather than otherwise—for it would be a practical answer to
     those on the other side, who should think your proposal too Conservative'
     (General Grey to Derby, 18 Feb. 1867, Derby MSS, 103/7).

100. Derby to Disraeli, [19 Feb. 1867?], Hughenden MSS, B/XX/S/460.

101. Grosvenor to Derby, 17 Feb. 1867, Derby MSS, 52/6; Derby to Grosvenor,
     19 Feb. 1867, Derby MSS, 192/2.

102. Stanley, diary, 19 Feb. 1867, cited in Derby, *Disraeli, Derby and the Conser-
     vative Party*, 290.

103. Hardinge, *Carnarvon*, i. 345.

104. A. E. Gathorne Hardy, *Gathorne Hardy, 1st Earl of Cranbrook: A Memoir*, 2
     vols (1910), i. 199.

105. Corry to Disraeli, 22 Feb. 1867, Hughenden MSS, B/XI/J/4.

106. See F. B. Smith, *The Making of the Second Reform Bill* (Cambridge, 1966),
     151–3.

107. Kimberley, *Journal*, 197.

108. Hardinge, *Carnarvon*, i. 345–6.

109. Stanley, diary, 23 Feb. 1867, cited in Derby, *Disraeli, Derby and the Conservative Party*, 290.

110. Cranborne to Carnarvon, 22 Feb. 1867, cited in Hardinge, *Carnarvon*, i. 346.

111. Carnarvon, memorandum, 24 Feb. 1867, cited in Hardinge, *Carnarvon*, i. 347.

112. Cranborne to Derby, [24 Feb. 1867], cited in Monypenny and Buckle, *Disraeli*, iv. 499–500.

113. Carnarvon to Derby, 25 Feb. 1867, Derby MSS, 163/5.

114. Derby to Disraeli, [25 Feb. 1867], Hughenden MSS, B/XX/S/410.

115. Derby to Disraeli, [25 Feb. 1867], Hughenden MSS, B/XX/S/466.

116. Disraeli to Derby, 25 Feb. 1867, cited in Monypenny and Buckle, *Disraeli*, iv. 500.

117. Derby to Queen Victoria, 25 Feb. 1867, Derby MSS, 192/1.

118. Carnarvon, journal, 25 Feb. 1867, cited in Hardinge, *Carnarvon*, i. 348.

119. Derby to Queen Victoria, 25 Feb. 1867, Derby MSS, 192/1.

120. Carnarvon, journal, 26 Feb. 1867, cited in Hardinge, *Carnarvon*, i. 349.

121. Derby to Disraeli, 26 Feb. 1867, Hughenden MSS, B/XX/S/411.

122. Stanley, diary, 26 Feb. 1867, cited in Derby, *Disraeli, Derby and the Conservative Party*, 291.

123. Stanley to Disraeli, 26 Feb. 1867, Hughenden MSS, B/XX/S/766; Stanley, diary, 27 Feb. 1867, cited in Derby, *Disraeli, Derby and the Conservative Party*, 291–2.

124. Derby to Disraeli, 26 Feb. 1867, Hughenden MSS, B/XX/S/411; Stanley, diary, 27 Feb. 1867, cited in Derby, *Disraeli, Derby and the Conservative Party*, 291.

125. Disraeli to Derby, 26 Feb. 1867, Derby MSS, 146/3.

126. Disraeli to Derby, [27 Feb. 1867], Derby MSS, 146/3.

127. Disraeli to Derby, 26 Feb. 1867, Derby MSS, 146/3.

128. Disraeli to Derby, [27 Feb. 1867], Derby MSS, 146/3; Manners to Malmesbury, 28 Feb. 1867, cited in Malmesbury, *Memoirs*, ii. 368.

129. Derby to Disraeli, 28 Feb. 1867, Hughenden MSS, B/XX/S/412.

130. Disraeli to Derby, [27 Feb. 1867], Derby MSS, 146/3.

131. Baxter to Derby, 28 Feb. 1867, Hughenden MSS, B/XI/J/74.

132. Derby to Cranborne, 1 Mar. 1867, Derby MSS, 193/1.

133. Malmesbury to Derby, 1 Mar. 1867, Derby MSS, 144.

134. Northcote to Derby, 2 Mar. 1867, Derby MSS, 162/8.

135. Walpole to Malmesbury, 2 Mar. 1867, cited in Cowling, *1867*, 180.

136. Manners, journal, 2 Mar. 1867, cited in Whibley, *Manners and his Friends*, ii. 125.

137. Ibid. 126.

138. Carnarvon, memorandum, 2 Mar. 1867, cited in Hardinge, *Carnarvon*, i. 350.

139. Cecil, *Salisbury*, i. 236–7.

140. Derby, 4 Mar. 1867, *Hansard*, 3rd ser., clxxxv. 1284–9.

141. Stanley, diary, 4 Mar. 1867, cited in Derby, *Disraeli, Derby and the Conservative Party*, 293.

142. Disraeli, 5 Mar. 1867, *Hansard*, 3rd ser., clxxxv. 1339–45.

143. Stanley, diary, 5 Mar. 1867, cited in Derby, *Disraeli, Derby and the Conservative Party*, 293.

144. Ibid.

145. Stanley, diary, 7 Mar. 1867, cited in Derby, *Disraeli, Derby and the Conservative Party*, 293.

146. Stanley, diary, 9 Mar. 1867, cited in Derby, *Disraeli, Derby and the Conservative Party*, 294.

147. Derby to Disraeli, [9 Mar. 1867], Hughenden MSS, B/XX/S/419.

148. Stanley, diary, 10 Mar. 1867, cited in Derby, *Disraeli, Derby and the Conservative Party*, 294.

149. Derby to Disraeli, 10 Mar. 1867, Hughenden MSS, B/XX/S/420.

150. Ibid.

151. Gathorne Hardy, *Cranbrook*, i. 202.

152. Stanley, diary, 12 and 14 Mar. 1867, cited in Derby, *Disraeli, Derby and the Conservative Party*, 294.

153. Disraeli to General Grey, 15 Mar. 1867, cited in Queen Victoria, *Letters*, ed. Buckle, i. 408.

154. Derby to Disraeli, 14 Mar. 1867, Hughenden MSS, B/XX/S/421.

155. Derby to Disraeli, [12 Mar. 1867?], Hughenden MSS, B/XX/S/420.

156. Monypenny and Buckle, *Disraeli*, iv. 519.

157. Malmesbury, *Memoirs*, ii. 369.

158. Derby to Queen Victoria, 17 Mar. 1867, Derby MSS, 192/1.

159. Disraeli, 18 Mar. 1867, *Hansard*, 3rd ser., clxxxvi. 6–25.

160. Gladstone, 18 Mar. 1867, *Hansard*, 3rd ser., clxxxvi. 26–46.

161. Stanley, diary, 20 Mar. 1867, cited in Derby, *Disraeli, Derby and the Conservative Party*, 295.

162. Malmesbury, *Memoirs*, ii. 368.

163. Buckingham to Derby, 24 Mar. 1867, Derby MSS, 111/B.

164. Derby to Disraeli, [26 Mar. 1867], Hughenden MSS, B/XX/S/425.

165. Ibid.

166. Gathorne Hardy, *Diary*, 35.

167. Derby to Disraeli, 27 Mar. 1867, Hughenden MSS, B/XX/S/426.

168. Stanley, diary, 27 Mar. 1867, cited in Derby, *Disraeli, Derby and the Conservative Party*, 296.

169. Derby to General Grey, 27 Apr. 1867, Derby MSS, 193/2.

170. Stanley, diary, 18 Apr. 1867, cited in Derby, *Disraeli, Derby and the Conservative Party*, 302.

171. General Grey to Queen Victoria, 7 May 1867, cited in Queen Victoria, *Letters*, ed. Buckle, i. 425.

172. Gathorne Hardy, *Diary*, 38.

173. Derby to Queen Victoria, 7 May 1867, Derby MSS, 194/1.
174. Derby to General Grey, 8 May 1867, Derby MSS, 194/1.
175. Derby to Disraeli, 15 May 1867, Hughenden MSS, B/XX/S/430.
176. Gathorne Hardy, *Diary*, 41.
177. Gathorne Hardy, *Diary*, 43.
178. Derby to General Grey, 20 Nov. 1866, Derby MSS, 192/1.
179. Derby to Queen Victoria, 13 Jan. 1867, Derby MSS, 192/1.
180. Queen Victoria to General Grey, 28 Jan. 1867, Derby MSS, 103/7.
181. General Grey to Derby, 5 Feb. 1867, Derby MSS, 103/7.
182. Derby to General Grey, 6 Feb. 1867, Derby MSS, 192/1.
183. General Grey to Derby, 5 June 1867, Derby MSS, 103/7.
184. General Grey to Derby, 4 July 1867, Derby MSS, 103/7.
185. Stanley, diary, 29 June 1867, cited in Derby, *Disraeli, Derby and the Conservative Party*, 312.
186. Derby to General Grey, 27 June 1867, Derby MSS, 194/1.
187. Stanley, diary, 30 June 1867, cited in Derby, *Disraeli, Derby and the Conservative Party*, 313.
188. Stanley, diary, 5 July 1867, cited in Derby, *Disraeli, Derby and the Conservative Party*, 313.
189. Derby to General Grey, 25 Oct. 1867, Derby MSS, 194/1.
190. Derby to General Grey, 23 Dec. 1867, Derby MSS, 195/1.
191. Derby to Cairns, 15 July 1867, Derby MSS, 192/2.
192. Queen Victoria to Derby, 25 June 1867, cited in Queen Victoria, *Letters*, ed. Buckle, i. 434.
193. Derby to Queen Victoria, 26 June 1867, Derby MSS, 194/1.
194. Derby to Disraeli, 18 July 1867, Hughenden MSS, B/XX/S/438.
195. Ibid.
196. Disraeli's notes of Derby's speech to the Conservative peers, 19 July 1867, Hughenden MSS, B/XI/J/217.
197. Derby to General Grey, 20 and 23 July 1867, Derby MSS, 194/1.
198. Derby to Disraeli, [21 July 1867], Hughenden MSS, B/XX/S/439.
199. Derby to Disraeli, 22 July 1867, Hughenden MSS, B/XX/S/440.
200. Derby, 22 July 1867, *Hansard*, 3rd ser., clxxxviii. 1782–1803.
201. Ibid. 1782–3.
202. Barrington to General Grey, 24 July 1867, Derby MSS, 193/2; Barrington to Disraeli, 8 Aug. 1867, Hughenden MSS, B/XX/S/444.
203. Sir Algernon West, *The Private Diaries of the Rt. Hon. Algernon West*, ed. H. Hutchinson (1922), 202.
204. Freddy Stanley to Disraeli, 13 Sept. 1867, Hughenden MSS, B/XX/S/447.
205. Gathorne Hardy, *Diary*, 46.
206. Cairns, 30 July 1867, *Hansard*, 3rd ser., clxxxix. 433–41.
207. Derby, 1 Aug. 1867, *Hansard*, 3rd ser., clxxxix. 526–39.
208. Russell, 6 Aug. 1867, *Hansard*, 3rd ser., clxxxix. 942.

209. Derby, 6 Aug. 1867, *Hansard*, 3rd ser., clxxxix. 952.
210. *The Guardian*, 8 Aug. 1867.
211. Derby to Disraeli, 28 Nov. 1854, Hughenden MSS, B/XX/S/127.
212. Clarendon to Lady Salisbury, 19 June 1867, cited in Maxwell, *Clarendon*, ii. 333.
213. Gathorne Hardy diary, 9 Aug. 1867, cited in Gathorne Hardy, *Cranbrook*, i. 212.
214. Derby to Disraeli, 19 Aug. 1867, Hughenden MSS, B/XX/S/445.
215. Derby to Disraeli, 10 Sept. 1867, Hughenden MSS, B/XX/S/446.
216. Freddy Stanley to Disraeli, 13 Sept. 1867, Hughenden MSS, B/XX/S/447.
217. Lady Derby to Disraeli, 20 Sept. 1867, Hughenden MSS, B/XX/S/448.
218. Lady Derby to Disraeli, 26 Sept. 1867, Hughenden MSS, B/XX/S/524.
219. Burghclere (ed.), *A Great Lady's Friendships*, 173–4.
220. Malmesbury, *Memoirs*, ii. 374.
221. Derby to Egerton, 28 Aug. 1867, Derby MSS, 194/2.
222. *The Times*, 18 Oct. 1867, 10.
223. Stanley to Disraeli, 28 Jan. 1853, Hughenden MSS, B/XX/S/588.
224. Stanley, diary, 22 Nov. 1853, cited in Derby, *Disraeli, Derby and the Conservative Party*, 112.
225. *The Times*, 18 Oct. 1867, 10.
226. Noel to Corry, 7 Nov. 1867, Hughenden MSS, B/IX/D/32c.
227. Derby to Disraeli, 20 Oct. 1867, Hughenden MSS, B/XX/S/453.
228. Derby to Disraeli, 24 Oct. 1867, Hughenden MSS, B/XX/S/454.
229. Clarendon to Lady Salisbury, 31 Oct. 1867, cited in Maxwell, *Clarendon*, ii. 338.
230. Gathorne Hardy, *Diary*, 53.
231. Derby to Disraeli, 6 Oct. 1867, Hughenden MSS, B/XX/S/451. Given that Disraeli's ill health did not prevent him from making the journey to Edinburgh later in the month, two other factors may have prompted his refusal to attend the Manchester celebration. First, he thereby avoided appearing in public in a necessarily subordinate role to Derby. Secondly, following the social breach between Disraeli and Derby that occurred during the visit of October 1859 and Disraeli's resolve never to stay at Knowsley again, not attending the Manchester banquet avoided the sojourn at Knowsley that good manners would have required.
232. Monypenny and Buckle, *Disraeli*, iv. 555–8.
233. Ibid. 557.
234. Derby to Disraeli, 28 Sept. and 8 Oct. 1867, Hughenden MSS, B/XX/S/449, 452.
235. Derby to Disraeli, 6 Oct. 1867, Hughenden MSS, B/XX/S/451.
236. Ibid.
237. Derby to Disraeli, 15 Dec. 1867, Hughenden MSS, B/XX/S/456.
238. Derby to Disraeli, 17 Dec. 1867, Hughenden MSS, B/XX/S/457.

239. Stanley, diary, 19 Dec. 1867, cited in Derby, *Disraeli, Derby and the Conservative Party*, 325.

240. Ibid.

241. Stanley, diary, 31 Dec. 1867, cited in Derby, *Disraeli, Derby and the Conservative Party*, 326.

242. Disraeli to Derby, 1 Jan. 1868, Derby MSS, 146/4.

243. Derby to Disraeli, 3 Jan. 1868, Hughenden MSS, B/XX/S/470.

244. Derby to Disraeli, 11 Jan. 1868, Hughenden MSS, B/XX/S/471.

245. Derby to Disraeli, 3 Jan. 1868, Hughenden MSS, B/XX/S/470.

246. Barrington to Disraeli, 19 Jan. 1868, Hughenden MSS, B/XX/S/474.

247. Barrington to Disraeli, 22 Jan. 1868, Hughenden MSS, B/XX/S/475.

248. Barrington to Disraeli, 17 Jan. 1868, Hughenden MSS, B/XX/S/473.

249. Barrington to Disraeli, 26 Jan. 1868, Hughenden MSS, B/XX/S/476.

250. Derby to General Grey, 6 Feb. 1868, Derby MSS, 195/1.

251. General Grey to Derby, 8 Feb. 1868, Derby MSS, 103/8.

252. Derby to Disraeli, 13 Feb. 1868, Derby MSS, 195/1.

253. Stanley, diary, 18 Feb. 1868, cited in Derby, *Disraeli, Derby and the Conservative Party*, 329.

254. Derby to Disraeli, 19 Feb. 1868, Derby MSS, 195/1.

255. Granville to Gladstone, 13 Feb. 1868, cited in Fitzmaurice, *Granville*, i. 519–20.

256. Disraeli to Derby, 20 Feb. 1868, Derby MSS, 146/4. Stanley wrote to his father the same day: 'I presume you will speedily recommend [Disraeli] to the Queen; that would make her course more simple. Else we may have projects of fusion, which at another time might answer, but are now impossible, and the discussion of which would only waste time and complicate matters' (Stanley to Derby, 20 Feb. 1868, Derby MSS, 105/9).

257. Derby to Queen Victoria, 21 Feb. 1868, Derby MSS, 195/1.

258. Disraeli to Derby, 1 Jan. 1868, Derby MSS, 146/4.

259. Stanley, diary, 27 Feb. 1868, cited in Derby, *Disraeli, Derby and the Conservative Party*, 331.

260. Derby to Stanley, 24 Feb. 1868, Derby MSS, 195/1.

261. Derby to Queen Victoria, 25 Feb. 1868, Derby MSS, 195/1.

262. Stanley to Derby, 24 Feb. 1868, Derby MSS, 105/9.

263. Granville to Quin, 26 Feb. 1868, cited in Fitzmaurice, *Granville*, i. 520.

264. Stanley, diary, 1 Mar. 1868, cited in Derby, *Disraeli, Derby and the Conservative Party*, 331.

265. Ibid. The Prince of Wales, however, wrote immediately to Derby of his 'deep regret' at his resignation; 'altho' you have assigned the "tiller of the vessel" to other hands', the Prince hoped that Derby 'will yet be able occasionally to assist in steering the vessel through the inevitable "shoals and quicksands"' (Prince of Wales to Derby, 1 Mar. 1868, Derby MSS, 102/2). General Grey also wrote that he was unable to express 'how great I think the calamity to

the Queen and the country of your retirement' (General Grey to Derby, 22 Feb. 1868, Derby MSS, 103/8).

266. Disraeli to Derby, 27 Feb. 1868, Derby MSS, 146/4.
267. Derby to Disraeli, 28 Feb. 1868, Derby MSS, 195/1.

CHAPTER 7. RECESSION AND REPUTATION: 1868–1869

1.   Gathorne Hardy, *Diary*, 67.
2.   Derby to General Grey, 28 Mar. 1868, Derby MSS, 197/1.
3.   Derby to Disraeli, 3 Mar. 1868, Hughenden MSS, B/XX/S/483.
4.   *Annual Register* (1868), 2.
5.   Gladstone, diary, 28 Feb. 1868, cited in Gladstone, *Diaries*, vi. 579.
6.   Gathorne Hardy, *Diary*, 65.
7.   Derby to Mayo, 1 Jan. 1868, Derby MSS, 195/1.
8.   Stanley, journal, 2 Mar. 1868, cited in Derby, *Disraeli, Derby and the Conservative Party*, 331.
9.   Derby to Disraeli, 3 Mar. 1868, Hughenden MSS, B/XX/S/483.
10. Ibid.
11. J. P. Parry, *Democracy and Religion: Gladstone and the Liberal Party, 1867–1875* (Cambridge, 1986), 269.
12. Derby to Disraeli, 25 Mar. 1868, Hughenden MSS, B/XX/S/485; Derby to Disraeli, 21 Mar. 1868, Hughenden MSS, B/XX/S/484.
13. Gathorne Hardy, *Cranbrook*, i. 265–6.
14. Gathorne Hardy, *Diary*, 68.
15. Pakington to Northcote, 6 Apr. 1868, Iddesleigh MSS, 50022, fo. 269.
16. Gathorne Hardy, *Diary*, 68.
17. Derby, 23 Apr. 1868, *Hansard*, 3rd ser., cxc. 1124–7.
18. Derby, 27 Apr. 1868, *Hansard*, 3rd ser., cxc. 1425–35.
19. See Smith, *The Making of the Second Reform Bill*, 214–28.
20. Derby to Disraeli, 29 May 1868, Hughenden MSS, B/XX/S/493.
21. Ibid.
22. Kimberley, *Journal*, 221.
23. Derby, 25 June 1868, *Hansard*, 3rd ser., cxcii. 2092–2114.
24. Kimberley, *Journal*, 221.
25. Derby to Stanley, 22 July 1868, Derby MSS, 920DER(15), 'Letters from Parents'.
26. Derby to Disraeli, 15 July 1868, Hughenden MSS, B/XX/S/495; Stanley, journal, 1 Aug. 1868, cited in Derby, *Disraeli, Derby and the Conservative Party*, 335.
27. Derby to Disraeli, 2 Aug. 1868, Hughenden MSS, B/XX/S/498.
28. Derby to Disraeli, 29 Oct. 1868, Hughenden MSS, B/XX/S/502.
29. Disraeli to Stanley, 10 Nov. 1868, cited in Monypenny and Buckle, *Disraeli*, vi. 91.

30. 15th Earl of Derby, *The Later Derby Diaries: Home Rule, Liberal Unionism, and Aristocratic Life in Late Victorian England*, ed. J. Vincent (Bristol, 1981), 136.

31. Derby to Queen Victoria, 25 May 1867, Derby MSS, 194/1.

32. Derby to Hopwood, 10 Oct. 1867, Derby MSS, 194/1.

33. Derby to Queen Victoria, 14 Oct. 1867, Derby MSS, 194/1.

34. Derby to General Grey, 19 Oct. 1867, Derby MSS, 194/1.

35. Derby to Cairns, 16 Mar. 1867, Derby MSS, 193/2.

36. Derby to Disraeli, 14 Sept. 1868, Hughenden MSS, B/XX/S/499.

37. Ibid.

38. Disraeli to Derby, 18 Sept. 1868, Derby MSS, 146/4.

39. Derby to Disraeli, 3 Nov. 1868, Hughenden MSS, B/XX/S/503.

40. Ibid. See also Derby to Disraeli, 14 Nov. 1868, Hughenden MSS, B/XX/S/504.

41. Derby to Disraeli, 3 Nov. 1868, Hughenden MSS, B/XX/S/503.

42. Disraeli to Queen Victoria, 21 Aug. 1868, cited in Blake, *Disraeli*, 508.

43. Derby to Disraeli, 29 Oct. 1868, Hughenden MSS, B/XX/S/502.

44. Derby to Disraeli, 3 Nov. 1868, Hughenden MSS, B/XX/S/503.

45. *The Times*, 2 Nov. 1868, 7.

46. Derby to Disraeli, 14 Nov. 1868, Hughenden MSS, B/XX/S/504.

47. Stanley, journal, 29 Dec. 1868, cited in Derby, *Disraeli, Derby and the Conservative Party*, 338.

48. Derby to Disraeli, 22 Nov. 1868, Hughenden MSS, B/XX/S/505.

49. Derby to Townley Parker, 26 Dec. 1867, Derby MSS, 195/1.

50. Derby to Disraeli, 22 Nov. 1868, Hughenden MSS, B/XX/S/505.

51. Derby to Disraeli, 2 Aug. 1868, Hughenden MSS, B/XX/S/498.

52. Derby to Disraeli, 28 Nov. 1868, Hughenden MSS, B/XX/S/506. See also, Derby to Stanley, 27 Nov. 1868, Derby MSS, 197/1; Stanley to Derby, 28 Nov. 1868, Derby MSS, 105/9.

53. Gladstone, diary, 29 Dec. 1868, cited in Gladstone, *Diaries*, vi. 654.

54. Malmesbury, *Memoirs*, ii. 390.

55. Gathorne Hardy, *Diary*, 90.

56. Malmesbury, *Memoirs*, ii. 391.

57. Derby to Gathorne Hardy, 28 Feb. 1869, Derby MSS, 197/2.

58. In September 1866 Stanley recommended to Derby the creation of life peerages and urged it as a measure that might safely be advocated by the Conservative government. It would reinvigorate and so help to preserve, Stanley argued, the status of the House of Lords. Stanley, memorandum, 'The Creation of Life Peerages', 14 Sept. 1866, Derby MSS, 105/7.

59. Derby, 27 Apr. 1869, *Hansard*, 3rd ser., cxcv. 1648–62.

60. Derby to Cairns, 26 Apr. 1869, Derby MSS, 197/2.

61. Derby, 13 May 1869, *Hansard*, 3rd ser., cxcvi. 718–24.

62. Kimberley, *Journal*, 235.

63. Derby to Cairns, 4 May 1869, Derby MSS, 197/2.
64. Derby to Queen Victoria, 9 June 1869, Derby MSS, 197/2.
65. Derby to Cairns, 6 June 1869, Derby MSS, 197/2.
66. Malmesbury, *Memoirs*, ii. 401.
67. Kimberley, *Journal*, 236.
68. Stanley, journal, 18 June 1869, Derby MSS, 920DER(15).
69. Kimberley, *Journal*, 236.
70. Derby, 17 June 1869, *Hansard*, 3rd ser., cxcvii. 18–41. The quotation from Scott comes from *Guy Mannering*, ch. 8.
71. Derby, 1 July 1869, *Hansard*, 3rd ser., cxcvii. 891, 923, 924.
72. Derby, 12 July 1869, *Hansard*, 3rd ser., cxcvii. 1614.
73. Granville to Queen Victoria, 22 July 1869, cited in Queen Victoria, *Letters*, ed. Buckle, i. 621. Stanley noted in his journal: 'Lord D. I fear is annoyed, thinking that the battle ought to have been fought out to the end. But with what result?' (Stanley, journal, 22 July 1869, Derby MSS, 920DER(15)).
74. Stanley, journal, 24 Feb. 1869, Derby MSS, 920DER(15).
75. Derby to Bolton, 6 Sept. 1869, Derby MSS, 197/2.
76. Stanley, journal, 31 Aug. 1869, Derby MSS, 920DER(15).
77. Malmesbury, *Memoirs*, ii. 411.
78. Stanley to Disraeli, 16 Sept. 1869, Hughenden MSS, B/XX/S/851.
79. Stanley, journal, 6 Oct. 1869, Derby MSS, 920DER(15).
80. Malmesbury, *Memoirs*, ii. 411.
81. Stanley, journal, 11 Oct. 1869, Derby MSS, 920DER(15).
82. Stanley, journal, 14 Oct. 1869, Derby MSS, 920DER(15).
83. Stanley, journal, 15 Oct. 1869, Derby MSS, 920DER(15).
84. Stanley, journal, 18 Oct. 1869, Derby MSS, 920DER(15).
85. Stanley, journal, 20 Oct. 1869, Derby MSS, 920DER(15).
86. Stanley, journal, 22 Oct. 1869, Derby MSS, 920DER(15).
87. Stanley, journal, 23 Oct. 1869, Derby MSS, 920DER(15).
88. Malmesbury, *Memoirs*, ii. 412. The new Earl of Derby wrote to Disraeli on 27 October thanking him for his expression of sympathy: 'You have lost a true friend and colleague: I, a father, to whom I looked up with affection and reverence such as I can never feel again for any human being' (Derby to Disraeli, 27 Oct. 1869, Hughenden MSS, B/XX/S/852).
89. *The Times*, 30 Oct. 1869, 9.
90. *The Times*, 25 Oct. 1869, 7.
91. Gladstone, memorandum, 9 Oct. 1832, Gladstone MSS, 44777, fo. 16.
92. *Illustrated Times*, 9 June 1860.
93. *Illustrated London News*, 15 June 1861.
94. ? to Jolliffe, 22 Nov. 1859, Hylton MSS, DD/HY/24/107.
95. T. E. Kebbel, *A History of Toryism* (1886), 316.
96. Granville to Palmerston, 18 June 1859, Broadlands MSS, GC/GR/1863.

97.   J.A.H., 'Edward Stanley, 14th Earl of Derby', *Dictionary of National Biography*, 22 vols (1908–9).

98.   Derby to Pakington, 10 Nov. 1865, Derby MSS, 190/1.

99.   Stewart, *The Foundation of the Conservative Party*, 223.

100. Stanley, journal, 14 Apr. 1849, cited in Derby, *Disraeli, Derby and the Conservative Party*, 4.

101. Stanley, journal, 28 Dec. 1852, cited in Derby, *Disraeli, Derby and the Conservative Party*, 94.

102. Derby to Disraeli, 6 Jan. 1849, Hughenden MSS, B/XX/S/3. Derby's advice was an echo of Luke 9: 2: 'No man having put his hand to the plough, and looking back, is fit for the Kingdom of God.'

103. Derby, 6 May 1858, *Hansard*, 3rd ser., cl. 161.

104. *Liverpool Courier*, cited in *The Times*, 30 Sept. 1859, 8.

105. *The Times*, 1 Nov. 1869, 5.

106. Fraser, *Disraeli and his Day*, 231.

107. *The Times*, 22 Dec. 1834, 3.

108. *The Times*, 19 Oct. 1835, 3.

109. Stanley, journal, 14 Apr. 1849, cited in Derby, *Disraeli, Derby and the Conservative Party*, 4.

110. Henry, 3rd Earl Grey, *Parliamentary Government Considered with Reference to a Reform of Parliament* (1858), 90.

111. Derby to Blandford, 26 Jan. 1854, Derby MSS, 182/2.

112. Stanley, journal, 14 Mar. 1853, cited in Derby, *Disraeli, Derby and the Conservative Party*, 103.

113. Lord Broughton, *Recollections of a Long Life by Lord Broughton*, ed. Lady Dorchester, 6 vols (1909), vi. 229.

114. Stanley to Bentinck, 27 Oct. 1847, Derby MSS, 177/2.

115. I.W.W., *'Sans Changer', the Real Basis of 'the Morality of Public Men': A Snowball for 'an Englishman'* (1853), 15.

116. Palmerston to Temple, 24 Dec. 1855, Broadlands MSS, GC/TE364.

117. Stanley to Exeter, 13 Apr. 1850, Derby MSS, 178/2.

118. E. A. Smith, *The House of Lords in British Politics and Society, 1815–1911* (1992), 79.

119. Stanley to Shaw-Lefevre, 29 Mar. 1848, Derby MSS, 178/1.

120. General Grey to Derby, 28 Oct. 1866, Derby MSS, 103/6.

121. Stanley, journal, 24 Mar. 1853, cited in Derby, *Disraeli, Derby and the Conservative Party*, 104.

122. Stanley, 21 Apr. 1842, *Hansard*, 3rd ser., lxii. 973.

123. *The Times*, 5 Mar. 1851, 4.

124. Lord Robert Cecil, *The Theories of Parliamentary Reform*, Oxford Essays (1858), 52–79.

125. Hugh Berrington, 'Partisanship and Dissidence in the Nineteenth Century House of Commons', *Parliamentary Affairs*, 21/4 (1968), 344.

126. Disraeli to Mrs Brydges Willyams, 16 June 1858, cited in Monypenny and Buckle, *Disraeli*, vi. 165.

127. Graham to Rooke, 27 July 1835, cited in Ward, *Graham*, 152.

128. J. O'Connell, *Recollections and Experiences during a Parliamentary Career from 1833 to 1848*, 2 vols (1849), i. 120.

129. Stanley, journal, 22 Feb. 1851, cited in Derby, *Disraeli, Derby and the Conservative Party*, 44.

130. Stanley to Newcastle, 4 Apr. 1849, Derby MSS, 178/1.

131. Stanley, 22 Feb. 1841, *Hansard*, 3rd ser., lvi. 809.

132. Derby to Eglinton, 29 Nov. 1851, Derby MSS, 182/1.

133. Derby to Disraeli, 22 Nov. 1868, Hughenden MSS, B/XX/S/505.

134. Malmesbury, 19 June 1863, *Hansard*, 3rd ser., clxxi. 1132.

135. Bentinck to Stanley, n.d., Derby MSS, 149/1.

136. Gladstone, memorandum, 6 Mar. 1857, Gladstone MSS, 44655, fo. 62, cited in Gladstone, *Diaries*, vi. 203.

137. Derby to Colville, 12 Sept. 1869, Derby MSS, 197/2. An interesting exception to this general attitude was in February 1858, when Jolliffe skilfully managed to secure Derby's agreement to a secret loan to the proprietor of two Conservative daily papers, the *Morning Herald* and *The Standard*. Jolliffe was aware of the singular nature of this success. Rose to Disraeli, 19 Feb. 1858, Hughenden MSS, B/XX/R/8.

138. Malmesbury, *Memoirs*, ii. 73.

139. Stanley, journal, 26 Feb. 1851, cited in Derby, *Disraeli, Derby and the Conservative Party*, 48.

140. Walter Bagehot, *The English Constitution*, ed. P. Smith (Cambridge, 2001), 95.

141. J. A. Froude, *Party Politics*, in *Short Studies on Great Subjects*, 3 vols (1894), iii. 437.

142. Selborne to Palmer, 10 Jan. 1912, cited in Earl of Selborne, *The Crisis of British Unionism: The Domestic Papers of the Second Earl of Selborne, 1885–1922*, ed. D. George Boyce (1987), 79.

143. John Robertson, *Chamberlain: A Study* (1905), 26.

144. James FitzJames Stephen, *Horae Sabbaticae*, 2 vols (1892), ii. 201.

145. Walter Bagehot, 'The Non-Legislative Functions of Parliament', *The Economist*, 18 Aug. 1860, cited in Bagehot, *The Collected Works of Walter Bagehot*, ed. N. St John Stevas, 15 vols (1965–86), vi. 43.

146. Anthony Trollope, *Phineas Redux* (1874).

147. Walter Bagehot, 'Introduction to the Second Edition, 1872', cited in Bagehot, *The English Constitution*, 194–5.

Bibliography

This biography draws primarily on the extensive papers of the 14th Earl of Derby held at the Liverpool Record Office. After emerging from Knowsley in the 1960s, the papers were loaned to Lord Blake at the Queen's College, Oxford. But the Derby biography Blake hoped to write was never produced and in 1984 the papers were deposited in the Liverpool Record Office as 920DER(14), where detailed cataloguing was undertaken by the archivist Mrs Naomi Evetts. This work has been continued by her successor, Ms Ruth Hobbins. As well as family, estate, and business letters, the archive contains a large collection of official papers, royal correspondence, general and major political correspondence, and an invaluable set of letter-books for the period from 1828 to 1869, boxes 165–98. Quotations from the 14th Earl's outgoing correspondence, with archival reference to the Derby MSS, come from the copies in these letter-books. Derby manuscripts consulted by the author when in private hands were deposited by him at the Liverpool Record Office in 2004, where they are being catalogued. The papers of the 13th Earl of Derby (920DER(13)) and the papers and journals of the 15th Earl of Derby (920DER(15)), also held at the Liverpool Record Office, provided additional important evidence.

MANUSCRIPT COLLECTIONS

ABERDEEN MSS: Correspondence of the 4th Earl of Aberdeen, British Library.

BRABOURNE MSS: Diaries, papers, and correspondence of Sir Edward Knatchbull-Hugessen, 1st Lord Brabourne, Kent County Archives, Maidstone.

BRAND MSS: Papers and correspondence of H. B. Brand, House of Lords Record Office.

BRIGHT MSS: Correspondence of John Bright, British Library.

BROADLANDS MSS: Diary, papers, and correspondence of Viscount Palmerston, Southampton University Library.

BROUGHAM MSS: Correspondence of Lord Brougham, University College London.

BROUGHTON MSS: Diaries and correspondence of J. C. Hobhouse, Lord Broughton, British Library.

CAIRNS MSS: Papers and correspondence of Sir Hugh McCalmont Cairns, National Archives.

CANNING MSS: Papers and correspondence of Charles, Earl Canning, Leeds District Archives.

CARDWELL MSS: Correspondence of Edward Cardwell, National Archives.

CARLINGFORD MSS: Diary and correspondence of S. Chichester-Fortescue, 1st Lord Carlingford, part of the Strachie collection, Somerset County Record Office, Taunton.

CARNARVON MSS: Papers and correspondence of the 4th Earl of Carnarvon, National Archives.

CLANRICARDE MSS: Papers and correspondence of the Marquess of Clanricarde and correspondence of Lord Dunkellin, Leeds District Archives.

CLARENDON MSS: Papers and correspondence of the 4th Earl Clarendon, Bodleian Library, Oxford.

COBDEN MSS: Correspondence of Richard Cobden, British Library.

COWLEY MSS: Correspondence of H. R. C. Wellesley, 1st Earl Cowley, National Archives.

CRANBROOK MSS: Diaries and correspondence of Gathorne Hardy, Lord Cranbrook, East Suffolk Record Office, Ipswich.

CROKER MSS: Papers of John Wilson Croker, British Library.

DALHOUSIE MSS: Papers and correspondence of Lord Pamure, later 11th Earl of Dalhousie, Scottish Record Office, Edinburgh.

DENISON MSS: Diaries and correspondence of J. E. Denison, University of Nottingham Library.

ELLENBOROUGH MSS: Papers and correspondence of Lord Ellenborough, National Archives.

ELLICE MSS: Correspondence of Edward Ellice Senior and papers and correspondence of Edward Ellice Junior, National Library of Scotland, Edinburgh.

GLADSTONE MSS: Papers and correspondence of W. E. Gladstone, British Library.

GRAHAM MSS: Correspondence of Sir James Graham, seen on microfilm in the Bodleian Library, Oxford.

GRANVILLE MSS: Papers and correspondence of the 2nd Earl Granville, National Archives.

GREY MSS: Diaries, papers, and correspondence of the 3rd Earl Grey, Department of Palaeography and Diplomatic, University of Durham.

HAMPTON MSS: Papers and correspondence of Sir John Pakington, Worcestershire County Record Office, Worcester.

HARDWICKE MSS: Correspondence of Charles Yorke, 4th Earl of Hardwicke, British Library.

HARPTON COURT MSS: Papers and correspondence of Sir George Cornewall Lewis, National Library of Wales, Aberystwyth.

HICKLETON MSS: Diaries and correspondence of Sir Charles Wood, 1st Lord Halifax, consulted at the Borthwick Institute, York.

HUGHENDEN MSS: Papers and correspondence of Benjamin Disraeli, Earl of Beaconsfield, Bodleian Library, Oxford.

HYLTON MSS: Papers and correspondence of Sir William Jolliffe, 1st Lord Hylton, Somerset County Record Office, Taunton.

IDDESLEIGH MSS: Papers and correspondence of Sir Stafford Northcote, British Library.

KNIGHTLEY MSS: Diaries of Lady Louisa Knightley, Northamptonshire County Record Office, Northampton.

LANSDOWNE MSS: Correspondence of the 3rd Marquess of Lansdowne, British Library.

LYTTON MSS: Papers and correspondence of Sir Edward Bulwer Lytton, 1st Lord Lytton, Hertfordshire County Record Office, Hertford.

MALMESBURY MSS: Diaries, papers, and correspondence of James FitzHarris, 3rd Earl of Malmesbury, Hampshire County Record Office, Winchester.

MINTO MSS: Correspondence of the 2nd Earl of Minto and correspondence of Lord Melgund, National Library of Scotland, Edinburgh.

NEWCASTLE MSS: Papers and correspondence of Henry Pelham Clinton, 5th Duke of Newcastle, University of Nottingham Library.

NEWDEGATE MSS: Correspondence of C. N. Newdegate and diaries of his mother, M. Newdegate, Warwickshire County Record Office, Warwick.

PARKES MSS: Correspondence of J. Parkes, University College London.

REDESDALE MSS: Correspondence of J. T. Freeman-Mitford, 2nd Lord Redesdale, Gloucestershire County Record Office, Gloucester.

RUSSELL MSS: Papers and correspondence of Lord John Russell, National Archives.

SALISBURY MSS: Correspondence of Lord Robert Cecil, 3rd Marquis of Salisbury, and papers and correspondence of the 2nd Marquis of Salisbury, Hatfield House, Hertfordshire.

SELBORNE MSS: Papers and correspondence of Roundell Palmer, 1st Lord Selborne, Lambeth Palace Library.

SHAFTESBURY MSS: Diaries and correspondence of the 7th Earl Shaftesbury, part of the Broadlands collection, Southampton University Library.

SOTHERON-ESTCOURT MSS: Diary, papers, and correspondence of T. H. S. Sotheron-Estcourt, Gloucestershire County Record Office, Gloucester.

WALPOLE MSS: Papers and correspondence of S. H. Walpole, in the possession of Mr D. C. L. Holland CB.

WARD HUNT MSS: Papers and correspondence of G. Ward Hunt, Northamptonshire County Record Office, Northampton.

WEMYSS MSS: Correspondence of Lord Elcho, seen on microfilm at the National Register of Archives (Scotland), Edinburgh.

WESTBURY MSS: Correspondence and fragments of a journal of Sir Richard Bethell, 1st Lord Westbury, Bodleian Library, Oxford.

CONTEMPORARY PAMPHLETS AND PUBLICATIONS

AYTOUN, W., 'The Anglo-Gallican Budget', *Blackwood's Magazine*, 87 (1860), 381–96.

BAGEHOT, WALTER, *The Collected Works of Walter Bagehot*, ed. N. St John Stevas, 15 vols (1965–86).

—— *Historical Essays*, ed. N. St John Stevas (1971).

—— *The English Constitution*, ed. P. Smith (Cambridge, 2001).

BRIGHT, J., *Speeches on the Public Affairs of the Last Twenty Years*, ed., J. E. Thorold Rogers, 2 vols (1869).

CECIL, LORD ROBERT, *The Theories of Parliamentary Reform*, Oxford Essays (1858).

—— 'The Conservative Reaction', *Quarterly Review*, 108 (July 1860), 265–302.

COBDEN, R., *The Political Writings of Richard Cobden*, 2 vols (1867).

—— *The Speeches of Richard Cobden on Questions of Public Policy*, ed. J. Bright and J. E. Thorold Rogers, 2 vols (1870).

COX, HOMERSHAM, *Whig and Tory Administration during the Last Thirteen Years* (1868).

DISRAELI BENJAMIN, *Lord George Bentinck* (1852).

—— *Parliamentary Reform: A Series of Speeches on that Subject Delivered in the House of Commons by the Rt. Hon. B. Disraeli, 1848–1866*, ed. M. Corry (1867).

—— *Disraeli's Reminiscences*, ed. Helen Swartz and Marvin Swartz (1975).

DRUMMOND WOLFF, SIR HENRY, *Rambling Recollections*, 2 vols (1908).

GREY, HENRY, 3RD EARL, *Parliamentary Government Considered with Reference to a Reform of Parliament* (1858).

I.W.W., *'Sans Changer', the Real Basis of 'the Morality of Public Men': A Snowball for 'an Englishman'* (1853).

LOWE, ROBERT, 'The Past Session and the New Parliament', *Edinburgh Review*, 105 (Apr. 1857), 555–78.

MEREDITH, GEORGE, *Beauchamp's Career*, World's Classics (Oxford, 1988).

NORTHCOTE, S. H., *Twenty Years of Financial Policy: A Summary of the Chief Financial Measures Passed between 1842 and 1861, with a Table of Budgets* (1862).

ROCHESTER, MARK, *The Derby Ministry* (1858).

BIOGRAPHIES, DIARIES, AND MEMOIRS CONTAINING
CORRESPONDENCE

The place of publication is London, unless otherwise stated.

ACLAND, SIR THOMAS, *The Memoirs and Letters of the Rt. Hon. Sir Thomas Acland*, ed. A. H. D. Acland (1902).

ACTON, JOHN EDWARD DALBERG, *The Correspondence of Lord Acton and Richard Simpson*, ed. J. Althoz, D. McElrath and J. C. Holland, 3 vols (Cambridge, 1971–3).

AIRLIE, MABEL, COUNTESS OF, *Lady Palmerston and her Times*, 2 vols (1922).

ARGYLL, DUKE OF, *George Douglas, 8th Duke of Argyll: Autobiography and Memoirs*, ed. the Dowager Duchess of Argyll, 2 vols (1906).

ASHLEY, E., *The Life and Correspondence of Henry John Temple, Viscount Palmerston*, 2 vols (1879).

AWDRY, F., *A Country Gentleman of the Nineteenth Century: Being a Short Memoir of the Rt. Hon. Sir William Heathcote, Bart. of Hursley, 1801–1881* (1906).

BALFOUR, LADY FRANCES, *The Life of George, Fourth Earl of Aberdeen, K.G., K.T.*, 2 vols (1923).

BARING, F. T., LORD NORTHBROOK, *Journals and Correspondence of Francis Thornhill Baring, Lord Northbrook*, ed. Thomas George, Earl of Northbrook, 2 vols (Winchester, 1905).

BARRINGTON, E. I., *The Life and Works of Walter Bagehot*, 10 vols (1915).

—— *The Servant of All: Pages from the Family, Social and Political Life of my Father James Wilson*, 2 vols (1927).

BRIGHT, J., *The Public Letters of the Rt. Hon. John Bright*, ed. H. J. Leech (1885).

—— *The Diaries of John Bright*, ed. R. A. J. Walling (1930).

BROUGHTON, LORD, *Recollections of a Long Life by Lord Broughton*, ed. Lady Dorchester, 6 vols (1909).

BRUCE, H. A., *Letters of Rt. Hon. H. A. Bruce, Lord Aberdare of Duffryn*, 2 vols (Oxford, 1902).

BULWER, BARON DALLING, *The Life of Henry John Temple, Viscount Palmerston, with Selections from his Diaries and Correspondence*, 5 vols (1870–4).

BURGHCLERE, LADY (ed.), *A Great Lady's Friendships: Letters to Mary, Marchioness of Salisbury, Countess Derby, 1862–1890* (1933).

CAMPBELL, LORD, *The Lives of Lord Lyndhurst and Lord Brougham* (1869).

CECIL, LADY GWENDOLYN, *The Life of Robert, Marquis of Salisbury*, 4 vols (1921–32).

CONNELL, B. (ed.), *Regina v. Palmerston: The Correspondence between Queen Victoria and her Foreign and Prime Minister, 1837–1865* (1962).

CREIGHTON, M., *A Memoir of Sir George Grey* (1884).

CUNNINGHAM, SIR HENRY, *Earl Canning* (Oxford, 1891).

DALHOUSIE, MARQUESS OF, *The Private Letters of the Marquess of Dalhousie*, ed. J. G. A. Baird (1910).

DALLAS, G. M., *Letters from London, 1856–1860*, ed. J. Dallas, 2 vols (1870).

—— *The Diary of G. M. Dallas*, ed. S. Dallas (Philadelphia, 1892).

DASENT, A. I., *John Thadeus Delane, Editor of 'The Times'*, 2 vols (1908).

DENISON, J. E., VISCOUNT OSSINGTON, *Notes from my Journal when Speaker of the House of Commons* (1899).

DERBY, 15th EARL OF, *Speeches and Addresses of Edward Henry, XVth Earl of Derby*, ed. Sir Thomas Sanderson and E. S. Roscoe, 2 vols (1894).

—— *Disraeli, Derby and the Conservative Party: The Political Journals of Lord Stanley, 1849–1869*, ed. J. Vincent (Hassocks, 1978).

—— *The Later Derby Diaries: Home Rule, Liberal Unionism, and Aristocratic Life in Late Victorian England*, ed. J. Vincent (Bristol, 1981).

DERBY, *The Diaries of Edward Henry Stanley, 15th Earl of Derby, 1869–1878,* Camden Society, 5th ser., 4, ed. J. Vincent (1994).

——— *The Diaries of Edward Henry Stanley, 15th Earl of Derby, between 1878 and 1893: A Selection,* ed. J. Vincent (Oxford, 2003).

DISRAELI, B., *Letters from Benjamin Disraeli to Francis Anne, Marchioness of Londonderry 1837–61,* ed. Marchioness of Londonderry (1938).

——— *Benjamin Disraeli Letters,* ed. J. A. W. Gunn *et al.,* 7 vols to date (Toronto, 1982–2004).

DUNCOMBE, T. H., *The Life and Correspondence of T. S. Duncombe,* 2 vols (1868).

ELCHO, LORD, *Memories 1818–1912 by the Earl of March and Wemyss* (privately printed, 1912).

ELGIN, LORD, *The Letters and Journals of Lord Elgin,* ed. T. Walrond (1872).

ESCOTT, T. H. S., *Edward Bulwer, First Baron Lytton of Knebworth: A Social, Personal and Political Monograph* (1910).

FITZMAURICE, LORD E., *The Life of Granville George Leveson-Gower, Second Earl Granville, K.G.,* 2 vols (1905).

FORTESCUE, F. C., '...*and Mr. Fortescue': A Selection from the Diaries from 1851 to 1862 of Chichester Fortescue, Lord Carlingford, K.P.,* ed. O. W. Hewett (1958).

FRASER, SIR WILLIAM, *Disraeli and his Day* (1891).

GATHORNE HARDY, A. E., *Gathorne Hardy, 1st Earl of Cranbrook: A Memoir,* 2 vols (1910).

——— *The Diary of Gathorne Hardy, Later Lord Cranbrook, 1866–1892,* ed. Nancy Johnson (Oxford, 1981).

GLADSTONE, W. E., *The Gladstone Diaries,* ed. H. C. G. Matthew and M. R. D. Foot, 14 vols (Oxford, 1968–94).

——— *The Prime Minister's Papers: W. E. Gladstone,* i: *Autobiographica,* ii: *Autobiographical Memoranda,* ed. J. Brooke and M. Sorenson (1971).

GLEIG, G. R., *The Life of Arthur Duke of Wellington* (1864).

GORDON, A. H., BARON STANMORE, *Gordon Diary with Extracts from the Correspondence of Lord Aberdeen* (privately printed by Lord Stanmore, British Library, B.P.12 (10–12A)).

——— *The Earl of Aberdeen* (1893).

——— *Sidney Herbert, Lord Herbert of Lea: A Memoir,* 2 vols (1906).

GRANT DUFF, SIR MOUNTSTUART ELPHINSTONE, *Notes from a Diary, 1851–1872* (1897).

GREVILLE, C. C. F., *A Journal of the Reigns of King George IV, King William IV and Queen Victoria,* ed. H. Reeve, 8 vols (1888).

——— *The Letters of Charles Greville and Henry Reeve,* ed. Revd A. H. Johnson (1924).

HARDCASTLE, M. S., *A Life of John, Lord Campbell,* 2 vols (1881).

HARDINGE, SIR Arthur, *Life of H. E. M. Herbert, Fourth Earl of Carnarvon, 1831–1890,* 3 vols (1925).

HAYWARD, A., *Lady Palmerston: A Biographical Sketch* (1872).

_____ *Lord Lansdowne: A Biographical Sketch* (1872).

_____ *A Selection from the Correspondence of Abraham Hayward Q.C.*, ed. H. C. Carlisle (1886).

HODDER, E., *The Life and Work of the Seventh Earl of Shaftesbury*, 3 vols (1886).

HUNTER, W., *The Life of the Earl of Mayo*, 2 vols (Oxford, 1875).

JENNINGS, L. J. (ed.), *The Croker Papers*, 3 vols (1884).

KEBBEL, T. E., *English Statesmen since 1815* (1868).

_____ *A History of Toryism* (1886).

_____ *The Earl of Derby* (1893).

_____ *Lord Beaconsfield and Other Tory Memories* (1907).

KENNEDY, A. L. (ed.), *'My Dear Duchess': Social and Political Letters to the Duchess of Manchester, 1858–1869* (1956).

KIMBERLEY, EARL OF, *The Journal of John Wodehouse, Earl of Kimberley for 1862–1902*, Camden Society, 5th ser., 9, ed. A. Hawkins and J. Powell (Cambridge, 1997).

LANG, A., *Sir Stafford Northcote, First Earl of Iddesleigh*, 2 vols (1890).

LEWIS, SIR GEORGE, *Letters of the Rt. Hon. Sir George Cornewall Lewis to Various Friends*, ed. G. F. Lewis (1870).

LIDDON, H., *The Life of Edward Bouverie Pusey*, 3 vols (1893).

MACCARTHY, D., and RUSSELL, A. (eds), *Lady John Russell: A Memoir with Selections from her Diaries and Correspondence* (1910).

MALMESBURY, LORD, *Memoirs of an Ex-Minister*, 2 vols (1885).

MARTIN, A. P., *The Life and Letters of the Rt. Hon. Robert Lowe, Viscount Sherbrooke*, 2 vols (1893).

MARTIN, T., *A Life of Lord Lyndhurst* (1883).

MARTINEAU, J., *The Life of Henry Pelham, Fifth Duke of Newcastle* (1908).

MAXWELL, SIR HERBERT, *The Life and Letters of George William Frederick, the Fourth Earl of Clarendon*, 2 vols (1913).

MONYPENNY, W. F., and BUCKLE, G. E., *The Life of Benjamin Disraeli, Earl of Beaconsfield*, 6 vols (1910–20).

MORLEY, JOHN, *The Life of Richard Cobden*, 2 vols (1879).

_____ *The Life of William Ewart Gladstone*, 3 vols (1903).

NASH, T. A., *The Life of Lord Westbury* (1888).

O'CONNELL, J., *Recollections and Experiences during a Parliamentary Career from 1833 to 1848*, 2 vols (1849).

PALMERSTON, LADY, *The Letters of Lady Palmerston*, ed. T. Lever (1957).

PALMERSTON, VISCOUNT, *The Letters of the Third Viscount Palmerston to Laurence and Elizabeth Sullivan, 1804–1863*, ed. K. Bourne (1979).

PANMURE, LORD, *Panmure Papers*, ed. Sir George Douglas and Sir George Ramsay, 2 vols (1908).

PARKER, C. S., *Life and Letters of Sir James Graham, Second Baronet of Netherby*, 2 vols (1907).

PEEL, GEORGIANA, *Recollections of Lady Georgiana Peel*, ed. Ethel Peel (1920).

REEVE, H., *The Memoirs of Henry Reeve*, ed. J. K. Laughton, 2 vols (1898).

REID, S., *The Life and Letters of Lord Durham*, 2 vols (1906).

RUSSELL, LORD J., *Recollections and Suggestions, 1813–1873* (1875).

____ *The Later Correspondence of Lord Russell*, ed. G. P. Gooch, 2 vols (1925).

SAINTSBURY, G. E. B., *The Earl of Derby* (1892).

SELBORNE, EARL OF, *The Crisis of British Unionism: The Domestic Papers of the Second Earl of Selborne, 1885–1922*, ed. D. George Boyce (1987).

SELWYN, GEORGE, *George Selwyn: His Letters and his Life*, ed. E. S. Roscoe and H. Clerque (1900).

SIMPSON, M. C. M. (*née* SENIOR), *Many Memories of Many People* (1898).

SOMERSET, DUKE OF, *The Letters, Remains and Memoirs of the 12th Duke of Somerset*, ed. W. H. Mallock and Lady Gwendolen Ramsden (1893).

TRELAWNY, SIR JOHN, *The Parliamentary Diaries of Sir John Trelawny, 1858–1865*, Camden Society, 4th ser., 40, ed. T. A. Jenkins (1990).

TREVELYAN, G. O., *The Life and Letters of Lord Macaulay*, 2 vols (1876).

VICTORIA, QUEEN, *The Letters of Queen Victoria, 1st Series*, ed. A. C. Benson and Viscount Esher, 3 vols (1907).

____ *The Letters of Queen Victoria, 2nd Series*, ed. G. E. Buckle, 3 vols (1926–8).

VITZTHUM, COUNT, *St. Petersburg and London in the Years 1852 to 1865: Reminiscences of Count Charles Frederick Vitzthum von Eckstaedt*, ed. H. Reeve, trans. E. F. Taylor, 2 vols (1887).

WALPOLE, S., *The Life of Lord John Russell*, 2 vols (1889).

WELLESLEY, H. R., *The Paris Embassy during the Second Empire*, ed. F. A. Wellesley (1928).

WEST, SIR ALGERNON, *Recollections, 1832 to 1886*, 2 vols (1899).

____ *The Private Diaries of the Rt. Hon. Algernon West*, ed. H. Hutchinson (1922).

WHIBLEY, C., *Lord John Manners and his Friends*, 2 vols (Edinburgh, 1925).

WHITE, W., *The Inner Life of the House of Commons*, ed. J. McCarthy, 2 vols (1897).

SECONDARY SOURCES

ANDERSON, O., *A Liberal State at War: English Politics and Economics during the Crimean War* (1974).

APPLEMAN, P., MADDEN, W. A., and WOLFF, M. (eds), *1859: Entering an Age of Crisis* (Bloomington, Ind., 1959).

ARNSTEIN, W. L., *Protestant versus Catholic in Mid-Victorian England: Mr. Newdegate and the Nuns* (Columbia, Mo., 1982).

AUERBACH, J., *The Great Exhibition of 1851: A Nation on Display* (New Haven, 1999).

BAGLEY, J. J., *The Earls of Derby, 1485–1985* (1985).

BEALES, D. E. D., *England and Italy, 1859–60* (1961).

BEBBINGTON, D. W., *Evangelicalism in Modern Britain: A History from the 1730s to the 1980s* (1989).

BELL, H. C. F., *Lord Palmerston*, 2 vols (1936).

BENTLEY, MICHAEL, *Politics without Democracy: 1815–1914* (1984).

BLAKE, R., *Disraeli* (1966).

——— *The Conservative Party from Peel to Thatcher* (1985).

BOURNE, K., *The Foreign Policy of Victorian England: 1830–1902* (1970).

BROCK, M., and CURTHOYS, M. (eds), *The History of Oxford University*, vi (Oxford, 1997).

BROWN, DAVID, *Palmerston and the Politics of Foreign Policy, 1846–1855* (Manchester, 2002).

BROWN, S. J., *The National Churches of England, Ireland and Scotland, 1801–1846* (Oxford, 2001).

BURROW, J. W., *Whigs and Liberals: Continuity and Change in English Political Thought* (Oxford, 1988).

BUTLER, LORD (ed.), *The Conservatives: A History from their Origins to 1965* (1977).

BUTLER, P., *Gladstone: Church, State and Tractarianism* (Oxford, 1982).

CHADWICK, O., *The Victorian Church*, pt 1: *1829–1860* (1967).

CHAMBERLAIN, M. E., *Lord Aberdeen: A Political Biography* (1983).

COLEMAN, B., *Conservatism and the Conservative Party in Nineteenth-Century Britain* (1988).

CONACHER, J. B., *The Aberdeen Coalition, 1852–1855: A Study in Mid-Nineteenth Century Party Politics* (Cambridge, 1968).

——— *The Peelites and the Party System, 1846–1852* (Newton Abbot, 1972).

——— *Britain and the Crimea, 1855–56: Problems of War and Peace* (1987).

COWLING, M., *1867: Disraeli, Gladstone and Revolution: The Passing of the Second Reform Act* (Cambridge, 1967).

COX, GARY W., *The Efficient Secret: The Cabinet and the Development of Political Parties in Victorian England* (Cambridge, 1987).

CROSBY, T. L., *English Farmers and the Politics of Protection 1815–1852* (Hassocks, 1977).

DAVIS, R. W., *Political Change and Continuity, 1760–1885: A Buckinghamshire Study* (Newton Abbot, 1972).

DENHOLM, A., *Lord Ripon 1827–1909: A Political Biography* (1982).

ELDRIDGE, C. C., *Victorian Imperialism* (1978).

ELLENS, J. P., *Religious Routes to Gladstonian Liberalism: The Church Rate Conflict in England and Wales, 1832–1868* (University Park, Pa., 1994).

ERICKSON, A. B., *The Public Career of Sir James Graham* (1952).

FINLAYSON, G. B. A. M., *The Seventh Earl of Shaftesbury 1801–1885* (1981).

FOSTER, R., *Modern Ireland 1600–1972* (1988).

FROUDE, J. A., *Short Studies on Great Subjects*, 3 vols (1894).

GAMBLES, A., *Protection and Politics: Conservative Economic Discourse, 1815–1852* (Woodbridge, 1999).

GASH, N., *Sir Robert Peel: The Life of Sir Robert Peel after 1830* (1972).

——— *Aristocracy and People: Britain, 1815–1865* (1979).

GILAM, A., *The Emancipation of the Jews in England* (New York, 1982).

HARRISON, BRIAN, *Peaceable Kingdom: Stability and Change in Modern Britain* (Oxford, 1982).

HAWKINS, ANGUS, *Parliament, Party and the Art of Politics in Britain, 1855–59* (1987).

—— *British Party Politics, 1852–1886* (1998).

HEARNSHAW, F. J. C., *Conservatism in England: An Analytical, Historical and Political Survey* (1933).

HENDERSON, W. O., *The Lancashire Cotton Famine 1861–1865* (Manchester, 1934).

HILTON, B., *The Age of Atonement: The Influence of Evangelicalism on Social and Economic Thought 1785–1865* (Oxford, 1988).

HOPPEN, K. T., *Elections, Politics and Society in Ireland 1832–1885* (Oxford, 1984).

—— *Ireland since 1800: Conflict and Conformity* (1989).

—— *The Mid-Victorian Generation, 1846–1886* (Oxford, 1998).

HOWARD, C., *Britain and the 'Casus Belli', 1822–1902: A Study of Britain's International Position from Canning to Salisbury* (1974).

HUGESSEN, H. KNATCHBULL, *A Kentish Family* (1960).

IMLAH, ALBERT H., *Lord Ellenborough: A Biography of Edward Law, Earl of Ellenborough, Governor-General of India* (Cambridge, Mass., 1939).

IREMONGER, LUCILLE, *Lord Aberdeen: A Biography of the Fourth Earl of Aberdeen, K.G., K.T., Prime Minister, 1852–1855* (1978).

JAGGER, PETER J. (ed.), *Gladstone, Politics and Religion* (1985).

JENKINS, BRIAN, *Henry Goulburn 1784–1856: A Political Biography* (Liverpool, 1996).

JENKINS, T. A., *The Liberal Ascendancy, 1830–1886* (1994).

—— *Disraeli and Victorian Conservatism* (1996).

—— *Parliament, Party and Politics in Victorian Britain* (Manchester, 1996).

JONES, W. D., *Lord Derby and Victorian Conservatism* (Oxford, 1956).

—— *'Prosperity' Robinson: The Life of Viscount Goderich, 1782–1859* (1967).

—— *The American Problem in British Diplomacy 1841–1861* (1974).

—— and ERICKSON, A. B., *The Peelites, 1846–1857* (Columbus, Ia., 1973).

KINZER, BRUCE L. (ed.), *The Ballot Question in Nineteenth-Century English Politics* (New York, 1982).

—— (ed.), *The Gladstonian Turn of Mind* (Toronto, 1985).

KREIN, DAVID F., *The Last Palmerston Government: Foreign Policy, Domestic Politics, and the Genesis of 'Splendid Isolation'* (Ames, Ia., 1978).

LEMAY, G. H. L., *The Victorian Constitution: Conventions, Usages and Contingencies* (1979).

LUCAS, R., *Lord Glenesk and the 'Morning Post'* (1910).

McDOWELL, R. B., *British Conservatism, 1832–1914* (1959).

MACHIN, G. I. T., *Politics and the Churches in Great Britain, 1832 to 1868* (Oxford, 1977).

McINTIRE, C. T., *England against the Papacy, 1858–1861: Tories, Liberals, and the Overthrow of Papal Temporal Power during the Italian Risorgimento* (Cambridge, 1983).

McLEAN, I., *Rational Choice in British Politics* (Oxford, 2001).

MALLET, C. E., *A History of the University of Oxford*, 3 vols (1937).

MARTIN, B. K., *The Triumph of Palmerston* (1924).

MARTIN, G., *Britain and the Origins of Canadian Federation* (1995).

MATSUMOTO-BEST, SAHO, *Britain and the Papacy in the Age of Revolution, 1846–1851* (Woodbridge, 2003).

MATTHEW, H. C. G., *Gladstone, 1809–1874* (Oxford, 1986).

—— *Gladstone, 1875–1898* (Oxford, 1995).

MOORE, R. J., *Sir Charles Wood's Indian Policy* (Manchester, 1966).

MUNSELL, F. DARRELL, *The Unfortunate Duke: Henry Pelham, Fifth Duke of Newcastle, 1811–1864* (Columbia, Mo., 1985).

PARRY, J. P., *Democracy and Religion: Gladstone and the Liberal Party, 1867–1875* (Cambridge, 1986).

—— *The Rise and Fall of Liberal Government in Victorian Britain* (New Haven, 1993).

POLLARD, W., *The Stanleys of Knowsley* (1868).

PORTER, A. (ed.), *The Oxford History of the British Empire: The Nineteenth Century* (Oxford, 1999).

PORTER, BERNARD, *The Refugee Question in Mid-Victorian Politics* (Cambridge, 1979).

PREST, J., *Lord John Russell* (1972).

—— *Politics in the Age of Cobden* (1977).

RICHMOND, CHARLES, and SMITH, PAUL (eds), *The Self-Fashioning of Disraeli, 1818–1851* (Cambridge, 1998).

ROBERTS, ANDREW, *Salisbury: Victorian Titan* (1999).

ROBERTSON, JOHN, *Chamberlain: A Study* (1905).

ROBSON, R. (ed.), *Ideas and Institutions of Victorian Britain* (1967).

RÖDDER, ANDREAS, *Die radikale Herausforderung. Die politische Kultur der englischen Konservativen zwischen ländlicher Tradition und industrieller Moderne, 1846–1868* (Munich, 2002).

RUSSELL, G. W. E., *Sixty Years of an Empire, 1837–1897* (1897).

SALBSTEIN, M. C. N., *The Emancipation of the Jews in Britain: The Question of the Admission of the Jews to Parliament 1828–1860* (1982).

SALMON, PHILIP, *Electoral Reform at Work: Local Politics and National Parties, 1832–1841* (Woodbridge, 2002).

SANDISFORD, K. A. P., *Great Britain and the Schleswig Holstein Question* (Toronto, 1975).

SCHERER, P., *Lord John Russell: A Biography* (1999).

SEARLE, G. R., *Entrepreneurial Politics in Mid-Victorian Britain* (Oxford, 1993).

SHANNON, RICHARD, *Gladstone, 1809–1865* (1982).

—— *The Age of Disraeli, 1868–1881* (1992).

—— *Gladstone, 1865–1898* (1999).

SMITH, E. A., *The House of Lords in British Politics and Society, 1815–1911* (1992).

SMITH, F. B., *The Making of the Second Reform Bill* (Cambridge, 1966).

SMITH, P., *Disraelian Conservatism and Social Reform* (1967).
___ *Disraeli: A Brief Life* (Cambridge, 1996).
SOUTHGATE, D., *'The Most English Minister...': The Policies and Politics of Palmerston* (1966).
___ (ed.), *The Conservative Leadership 1832–1932* (1974).
STEELE, E. D., *Palmerston and Liberalism, 1855–1865* (Cambridge, 1991).
STEPHEN, JAMES FITZJAMES, *Horae Sabbaticae*, 2 vols (1892).
STEWART, ROBERT, *The Foundation of the Conservative Party, 1830–1867* (1978).
___ *Henry Brougham: His Public Career 1778–1868* (1985).
TAYLOR, A. J. P., *The Struggle for Mastery in Europe: 1848–1918* (Oxford, 1954).
TAYLOR, M., *The Decline of British Radicalism, 1847–1860* (Oxford, 1995).
TREVELYAN, G. M., *The Life of John Bright* (1913).
VAUGHAN, W. E., *Landlords and Tenants in Mid-Victorian Ireland* (Oxford, 1994).
VINCENT, J., *The Formation of the Liberal Party, 1857–1868* (1966).
___ *Disraeli* (Oxford, 1990).
WALKER, BRIAN M. (ed.), *Parliamentary Election Results in Ireland, 1801–1922* (Dublin, 1978).
WARD, J. T., *Sir James Graham* (1967).
WHYTE, J. H., *The Independent Irish Party, 1850–1859* (Oxford, 1958).
WINTER, J., *Robert Lowe* (Toronto, 1976).
WOLFFE, J., *The Protestant Crusade in Great Britain, 1829–1860* (Oxford, 1991).

ARTICLES

ALDRICH, R., 'Sir John Pakington and the Newcastle Commission', *History of Education*, 8/1 (1979), 21–31.
ANDERSON, OLIVE, 'Cabinet Government and the Crimean War', *English Historical Review*, 79 (1964), 548–51.
___ 'The Janus Face of Mid-Nineteenth Century English Radicalism: The Administrative Reform Association of 1855', *Victorian Studies*, 8/3 (1965), 231–42.
___ 'The Wensleydale Peerage Case and the Position of the House of Lords in the Mid-Nineteenth Century', *English Historical Review*, 82 (1967), 486–502.
BEALES, D. E. D., 'Parliamentary Politics and the "Independent" Member 1810–1860', in R. Robson (ed.), *Ideas and Institutions of Victorian Britain* (1967), 1–19.
BELL, H. C. F., 'Palmerston and Parliamentary Representation', *Journal of Modern History*, 4 (1932), 186–213.
BERRINGTON, HUGH, 'Partisanship and Dissidence in the Nineteenth Century House of Commons', *Parliamentary Affairs*, 21/4 (1968), 338–74.
BOURNE, K., 'Lord Palmerston's "Ginger Beer" Triumph, 1 July 1856', in K. Bourne and D. C. Watt (eds), *Studies in International History: Essays Presented to W. Norton Medlicott* (1967), 145–71.

BYLSMA, J. R., 'Party Structure in the 1852–1857 House of Commons: A Scalogram Analysis', *Journal of Interdisciplinary History*, 7/4 (1977), 375–93.

CLARK, E. A. G., 'Sir Stafford Northcote's "Omnibus": The Genesis of the Industrial Schools Act, 1857', *Journal of Educational and Administrative History*, 14/1 (1982), 27–45.

CROMWELL, VALERIE, 'The Administrative Background to the Presentation to Parliament of Parliamentary Papers on Foreign Affairs in the Mid-Nineteenth Century', *Journal of the Society of Archivists*, 2 (1963), 302–15.

——— 'Mapping the Political World of 1861: A Multidimensional Analysis of House of Commons Division Lists', *Legislative Studies Quarterly*, 7/2 (1982), 281–98.

DINGLE, A. E. ' "The Monster Nuisance of All": Landowners, Alkali Manufacturers, and Air Pollution, 1828–1864', *Economic History Review*, 35/4 (1982), 529–48.

EDSALL, N. C., 'A Failed National Movement: The Parliamentary and Financial Reform Association, 1848–54', *Bulletin of the Institute of Historical Research*, 49 (1976), 108–31.

ELDRIDGE, C. C., 'The Myth of Mid-Victorian "Separatism": The Cession of the Bay Islands and the Ionian Islands in the Early 1860s', *Victorian Studies*, 12/3 (1969), 331–46.

ERICKSON, ARVEL B., 'Edward T. Cardwell: Peelite', *Transactions of the American Philosophical Society*, 49/2 (1959), 5–103.

FOSTER, D., 'The Politics of Uncontested Elections: North Lancashire 1832–1865', *Northern History*, 13 (1977), 232–47.

GALLAGHER, THOMAS F., 'The Second Reform Movement, 1848–1867', *Albion*, 12 (1980), 147–63.

GHOSH, P. R., 'Disraelian Conservatism: A Financial Approach', *English Historical Review*, 99 (1984), 268–96.

GUROWICH, P. M., 'The Continuation of War by Other Means: Party and Politics, 1855–1865', *Historical Journal*, 27/3 (1984), 603–31.

HARRISON, BRIAN, 'The Sunday Trading Riots of 1855', *Historical Journal*, 8/2 (1965), 219–45.

HAWKINS, ANGUS, 'A Forgotten Crisis: Gladstone and the Politics of Finance during the 1850s', *Victorian Studies*, 26/3 (1983), 287–310.

——— 'British Parliamentary Party Alignment and the Indian Issue, 1857–1858', *Journal of British Studies*, 23/2 (1984), 79–105.

——— 'Lord Derby and Victorian Conservatism: A Reappraisal', *Parliamentary History*, 6 (1987), 280–301.

——— ' "Parliamentary Government" and Victorian Political Parties c.1830–c.1880', *English Historical Review*, 104 (1989), 630–69.

——— 'Lord Derby', in R. W. Davis (ed.), *Lords of Parliament, Studies, 1714–1914*, (Stanford, 1995).

HAWKINS, ANGUS, '"A Host in Himself": Lord Derby and Aristocratic Leadership', in R. W. Davis (ed.), *Leaders in the Lords: Government Management and Party Organisation in the Upper Chamber, 1765–1902* (Edinburgh, 2003).

HEARDER, H., 'Napoleon III's Threat to Break Off Diplomatic Relations with England during the Crisis over the Orsini Attempt in 1858', *English Historical Review*, 72 (1957), 474–81.

——— 'Queen Victoria and Foreign Policy: Royal Intervention in the Italian Question, 1859–1860', in K. Bourne and D. C. Watt (eds), *Studies in International History: Essays Presented to W. Norton Medlicott* (1967), 172–88.

HENDERSON, G. B., 'Ralph Anstruther Earle', *English Historical Review*, 58 (1943), 172–89.

HOPPEN, K. T., 'Tories, Catholics, and the General Election of 1859', *Historical Journal*, 13/1 (1970), 48–67.

——— 'The Franchise and Electoral Politics in England and Ireland, 1832–1885', *History*, 70 (1985), 202–17.

JONES, J. R., 'The Conservatives and Gladstone in 1855', *English Historical Review*, 77 (1962), 95–8.

KINZER, BRUCE L., 'The Failure of "Pressure from Without": Richard Cobden, the Ballot Society, and the Coming of the Ballot Act in England', *Canadian Journal of History*, 13/3 (1978), 339–422.

KNOX, BRUCE, 'British Policy and the Ionian Islands 1847–1864: Nationalism and Imperial Administration', *English Historical Review*, 99 (1984), 503–29.

KREIN, DAVID F., 'War and Reform: Russell, Palmerston and the Struggle for Power in the Aberdeen Cabinet, 1853–4', *Maryland Historian*, 7/2 (1976), 67–84.

LLOYD, TREVOR, 'Uncontested Seats in British General Elections, 1852–1910', *Historical Journal*, 8/2 (1965), 260–5.

McCORD, N., 'Cobden and Bright in Politics, 1846–1857', in R. Robson (ed.), *Ideas and Institutions of Victorian Britain* (1967), 87–114.

McGOWEN, R. E., and ARNSTEIN, W. L., 'The Mid-Victorians and the Two Party System', *Albion*, 11/3 (1979), 242–58.

MATTHEW, H. C. G., 'Disraeli, Gladstone and the Politics of Mid-Victorian Budgets', *Historical Journal*, 22/3 (1979), 615–43.

MOORE, D. C., 'The Matter of the Missing Contests: Towards a Theory of the Mid-Nineteenth Century British Political System', *Albion*, 6/2 (1974), 93–119.

PREST, J., 'Gladstone and Russell', *Transactions of the Royal Historical Society*, 5th ser., 16 (1966), 43–64.

RAMM, AGATHA, 'Gladstone's Religion', *Historical Journal*, 28/2 (1985), 327–40.

ROPER, JON, 'Party and Democracy in Nineteenth-Century Britain', *Parliaments, Estates and Representation*, 3/1 (1983), 22–33.

SACK, J. J., 'The Memory of Burke and Pitt: English Conservatism Confronts its Past, 1806–1829', *Historical Journal*, 30 (1987), 623–40.

SAUNDERS, R., 'Lord John Russell and Parliamentary Reform, 1848–67', *English Historical Review*, 120 (2005), 1289–1315.

SIMPSON, F. A., 'England and the Italian War of 1859', *Historical Journal*, 5 (1962), III–21.

STUART, C. H., 'The Formation of the Coalition Cabinet of 1852', *Transactions of the Royal Historical Society*, 5th ser., 4 (1954), 45–68.

——— 'The Prince Consort and Ministerial Politics, 1856–9', in H. R. Trevor Roper (ed.), *Essays in British History Presented to Sir Keith Feiling* (1964), 247–70.

VINCENT, J., 'The Parliamentary Dimension of the Crimean War', *Transactions of the Royal Historical Society*, 31 (1981), 31–49.

WASSON, E. A., 'The Spirit of Reform, 1832 and 1867', *Albion*, 12 (1980), 164–74.

WHYTE, J. H., 'The Influence of the Catholic Clergy on Elections in Mid-Nineteenth Century Ireland', *English Historical Review*, 75 (1960), 239–59.

WINTER, J., 'The Cave of Adullam and Parliamentary Reform', *English Historical Review*, 81 (1966), 38–55.

ZIMMERMAN, K., 'Liberal Speech, Palmerstonian Delay and the Passage of the Second Reform Act', *English Historical Review*, 118 (2003), 1176–1207.

UNPUBLISHED THESES CONSULTED

BYLSMA, J. R., 'Political Issues and Party Unity in the House of Commons, 1852–1857: A Scalogram Analysis', Ph.D. thesis, University of Iowa, 1968.

CHAPMAN, J. K., 'The Career of Arthur Hamilton Gordon 1st Lord Stanmore', Ph.D. thesis, University of London, 1954.

GLYNN, J. K., 'The Private Member of Parliament 1833–1868', Ph.D. thesis, University of London, 1949.

GUROWICH, P. M., 'Party and Independence in the Early and Mid-Victorian House of Commons', Ph.D. thesis, University of Cambridge, 1986.

HEARDER, H., 'The Foreign Policy of Lord Malmesbury, 1858–9', Ph.D. thesis, University of London, 1954.

HICKS, G., 'The Politics of Conservative Foreign Policy: The Derby Governments of 1852 and 1858–9', Ph.D. thesis, University of East Anglia, 2004.

McCRACKEN, D. E., 'The Conservatives in "Power": The Minority Governments of 1852, 1858–9 and 1866–8', Ph.D. thesis, University of Virginia, 1981.

MAJOR, W. E., 'The Public Life of the Third Earl of Malmesbury', Ph.D. thesis, University of Georgia, 1980.

SAUNDERS, R., 'The Parliamentary Reform Debate in Britain, 1848–1867', D.Phil. thesis, University of Oxford, 2004.

SNYDER, C. W., 'Liberty and Morality: A Political Biography of Edward Bulwer Lytton', Ph.D. thesis, University of Virginia, 1979.

WATT, R. G., 'Parties and Politics in Mid-Victorian Britain, 1857 to 1859: A Study in Quantification', Ph.D. thesis, University of Minnesota, 1975.

Index